I0822072

Charlottetown

A History

Peter E. Rider

2009

ISBN 978-0-920434-37-6

Advisory Editor: Boyde Beck

Copy Editor: Laurie Brinklow

Design and Layout: TechnoMedia, Charlottetown

Printed by: Transcontinental
Printed in Canada.

Prince Edward Island Museum and Heritage Foundation
Beaconsfield
2 Kent Street
Charlottetown, Prince Edward Island
Canada, C1A 1M6

Canadian Museum of Civilization Corporation
100 Laurier Street
Gatineau, Quebec
Canada, K1A 0M8

Library and Archives Canada Cataloguing in Publication

Rider, Peter E., 1944-
Charlottetown : a history / Peter E. Rider.

Includes bibliographical references and index.
ISBN 978-0-920434-37-6

1. Charlottetown (P.E.I.)--History. I. Title.

FC2646.4.R54 2009 971.7'5 C2009-902500-0

For My Family:

Jane, Katie, Edward

Contents

Acknowledgements

Many people contributed to this volume, and without their help it could not, and would not, have been written. Although credit for whatever merits the book may have must be shared, blame for mistakes, omissions and misinterpretations lie with the author alone.

For years, the Public Archives and Records Office of Prince Edward Island was a summer home where I was welcomed with friendship and support. I owe a tremendous debt of gratitude to Nicolas de Jong, Harry Holman, Marilyn Bell, Kevin MacDonald, Charlotte Stewart, Jill MacMicken-Wilson, John Boylan, Jannah Toms, Pam Wheatley and their colleagues for all that they have done on my behalf.

Situated as I am in Ottawa, with limited time and funds for travel and research, reliance on others in Charlottetown as research assistants was absolutely necessary. Fortunately, in the early 1980s, the federal government made money available for university students to gain work experience in their chosen subject specialties through the Career-Oriented Summer Employment Program. With the help of Douglas Baldwin, then a member of the UPEI History Department, teams of researchers were hired during the summers of 1981, '82 and '83 to investigate records on the history of Charlottetown. Some of the students worked for a single summer, while others returned for two or three. Their work provided the core of the information utilized in the book, and it proved to be gratifyingly complete. My sincere thanks go to Dale Briggs, Harry Holman, Michael James, Stirling Keizer, Greg Marquis, Valerie Moore, Boyde Beck, and Helen Gill.

Assistance with the research did not stop there. Others helped in specific ways. Deirdre Kessler investigated the R.G. Dun and Company papers held at the Baker Library at Harvard University and transcribed entries for Charlottetown businessmen and their businesses. Lisa Grant plugged gaps in the information on the city's governance between 1878 and 1885. Jannah McCarville (Toms) reviewed the minutes of the Board of Trade for the years 1887-1920 and charted the topics of discussion to reveal the organization's major concerns. Ryan Shackleton surveyed the minutes of Charlottetown City Council between 1946 and 1977 and summarized the proceedings as they touched upon themes pursued in this study. Christine Gordon (Manley) prepared a report on taxes and tax reform in Charlottetown between 1880 and 1980, as well as a chronology of events between 1985 and 2005. Marc MacDonald studied planning, land use and civic amalgamation in the period 1985-2005 and wrote a careful analysis of his findings. Dirk Druet traced the development of Brighton and Victoria Park between 1918 and 1945 and assembled supplementary information on Brighton. Jill McRae undertook various research tasks to provide information that was missing for the period 1985-2005 and to verify or correct specific details in the balance of the manuscript. I would like to express my appreciation to each of them for their work.

Various members of the staff at city hall were generous with both their help and time. Pam Leard went out of her way to facilitate my access to recent city records and to guide me to other sources of information. Joe Coady made time for two lengthy interviews that dealt with Sherwood prior to amalgamation, the amalgamation process itself, and insight into the administration of the enlarged city. Information on other communities that entered the city at amalgamation was provided by Sharon Becker, Nancy Coughlin and Betty Pryor.

The community at large offered similar support. Ed MacDonald of UPEI has been the best of colleagues, generously sharing his research, insights and remarkable sensitivity to Island ways. The late Irene Rogers was both a supporter and helpful informant about Charlottetown's built heritage. Catherine Hennessey has been generous with her hospitality, interest and historical knowledge. Harry Holman was always willing to share his deep understanding of the historical records and his interpretations of them. Michael Arnold provided insights into recent developments in business and the economy. Charles Scott, Sr., of Ottawa, provided an insider's view of the early days of the Confederation Centre and the role of Frank MacKinnon in its creation. Anna MacDonald helped with the Centre's contemporary activities. Harvey MacKinnon and Kathy Hambly of the Greater Charlottetown Area Chamber of Commerce facilitated my research with information and guidance concerning the business community. Calum Beck generously shared his research findings about the religious affiliations of the city's mayors, and Ernie Morello provided important facts concerning CADC projects.

Significant contributions have been made along the way by others who shared their knowledge of Charlottetown. Many were people who I contacted out of the blue to solicit specific pieces of information. Without exception, my enquiries were received courteously and helpfully. Responses have saved the book from many factual errors and added important details. Although these acts of kindness are too numerous to list individually, I hope this collective recognition will convey my gratitude for each of them.

An earlier draft of the manuscript was reviewed by Ed MacDonald, Boyde Beck, John Taylor of Carleton University and Donald Davis of the University of Ottawa. Their questions, critical comments, corrections and suggestions improved the work in many ways, and I would like to express my deep appreciation for their generous investment of so much time and effort. Boyde, of course, has been involved with the project almost as long as the author, and beyond all his other contributions, he has edited the final manuscript for publication and assembled the illustrations. I am very grateful for his tact, wise counsel and especially the numerous improvements that have resulted from his labours. I would also like to thank Laurie Brinklow who as copy editor brought linguistic and factual precision to the text.

This work could not have been completed without the backing of the management of the Canadian Museum of Civilization. I am indebted to Fred Thorpe, who approved the project, and his successors Dan Gallacher and David Morrison, who continued to support it. At various times, Michael Carroll and Chris Laing also provided crucial resources. In the production phase, the late Deborah Brownrigg, Rosemary Nugent and Mark O'Neill ensured that the manuscript, once written, would see the light of day. I wish to thank them for their efforts on its behalf. I also appreciate the willingness of Museums and Heritage Prince Edward Island, and its Executive Director, David Keenlyside, to publish the book.

Last, but far from least, I would like to thank my family, Jane, Katie and Edward, to whom this book is dedicated. My summer research visits became their summer vacations, and together we learned about Charlottetown and developed an affection for it.

Preface

Some readers, particularly those whose interest in cities is confined to major centres, may wonder why an extended history would be written about a relatively small place like Charlottetown. Couldn't a brief account cover all that needs to be said about it? Charlottetonians, on the other hand, might ask why a volume on their home town has not appeared before now, and likely few of them would question the merits of examining the city's past in detail. People are like that — interested in what directly involves them. Because 43 per cent of Canadians live in the six metropolitan areas with a population exceeding one million, it is easy to assume that size matters when it comes to the study of urban history. And, of course, to a degree, it does. The means by which our large cities face the massive challenges of providing employment, physical and social services and a vibrant cultural life for their citizens, while, at the same time, protecting the environment and broad public interest and controlling costs, are important to all Canadians. The problem today is that, in important respects, our large cities no longer seem to work as they should. In response, people are beginning to consider the merits of smaller communities where the issues seem less intractable. Yet, the lack of size also has its problems. They are rooted in realities that may differ from those associated with major centres, but they can be persistent and debilitating. Mastering the challenges of smallness, or failing in the struggle, is a distinct story, and one that deserves to be told.

The impetus to undertake this study of Charlottetown was, however, practical. Newly arrived at the History Division of the National Museum of Man in 1978, the author inherited a number of responsibilities from his predecessor. One involved the management of publications intended for the History of Canadian Cities Series. This project had been started several years previously by one of the museum's historians who had moved on but had remained deeply involved as General Editor. The tasks that stayed with the History Division were to deal with a plethora of authors, work with the co-publisher of the series and offer comments and advice about manuscripts as they were submitted. An understanding of what was entailed in the writing of the books was clearly desirable, and as luck would have it, one city in Atlantic Canada had not been assigned. Charlottetown, the capital and principal place of Prince Edward Island, was not only an important subject for investigation, but it was a community in which the author had lived briefly while teaching at the University of Prince Edward Island.

A commitment to do the book was soon made, and the work begun. The task seemed easy enough. It involved writing an urban biography that would be heavily illustrated and run to a length of some 200 pages. Each volume in the series was to adhere to a prescribed format, following themes that were acknowledged as the main ones of the genre. With each book organized in this fashion, comparison among cities would be possible, and when the series was completed, a synthesis resulting in the over-arching history of the Canadian city could be produced.

Alas, it was not to be. Although a significant number of volumes appeared, including those on Vancouver, Calgary, Regina, Winnipeg, Ottawa, Hamilton and Toronto (two), many authors got bogged down at the research stage. Cities with short histories, or those that had already been the subject of extensive historical investigation, or preferably both, were easier to cover than those with lengthy pasts that had been more or less neglected. When in 1982 the National Museum of Man received the go-ahead to construct a massive new building, the future of projects not related to that objective was put in doubt. With its budgetary resources and personnel required elsewhere, the museum ended its sponsorship of the History of Canadian Cities Series. Some additional publications connected with the series appeared in other ways. Volumes on Quebec City and Kitchener, which more or less conformed to the thematic outline, were issued by other publishers, and lengthy tomes on Kingston and Montreal eventually appeared. Not one of the six books planned for cities in Atlantic Canada materialized, although three distinguished scholars collaborated to write a history of Halifax to coincide with the commemoration in 1999 of the 250th anniversary of the city's founding.

The book on Charlottetown was ensnared by these circumstances. Research began during the summer of 1979 and continued the following summer. The time that could be spent in Charlottetown was limited, and progress was slow. At the rate research was proceeding, 20 years would be required to cover the volumes of material available. Fortunately, a federal government program to assist university students to gain practical work experience in their chosen disciplines made the enlistment of research assistants possible in the summers of 1981, '82 and '83. A collaborative arrangement with Professor Douglas Baldwin of UPEI resulted in teams of six young historians being assigned to investigate various aspects of Charlottetown's history. Vast quantities of new information were discovered and recorded in notes, photocopies and reports. Then the project was put on hold. In subsequent years, short periods of time became available for further research and writing, but completion of the manuscript that was originally intended was not possible. Ironically, 20 years on, arrangements were made to recommence work on it.

Because the original research was organized to follow the guidelines of the History of Canadian Cities Series, and to reinforce the possibilities of comparative analysis offered by this format, the structure of the present work follows what had been planned at the beginning. While this approach interrupts the narrative flow of the text somewhat, the benefits justify the loss, and there is the added advantage of allowing a reader with specific interests to follow them from chapter to chapter without dealing with the balance of the text. The original intention was to focus the work on the years following incorporation of the city in 1855 when the presence of municipal records could sustain a detailed urban history. This focus has been retained. Unknown at the time when the bulk of the research was done, it reached almost to the point where the Prince Edward Island Comprehensive Development Plan ended. A clear break like this provided a suitable end to the intensive coverage of the city's evolution. To introduce the themes and to tie them up at the conclusion, two briefer chapters have been added, one covering the period before incorporation and another running to 2005, the 150th anniversary of incorporation.

The formula for the History of Canadian Cities Series envisioned reasonably brief texts. They were intended to summarize large amounts of information available in other ways, either as publications or other accessible scholarly communications. In 1979, Irene Rogers' splendid book, *Charlottetown: The Life in Its Buildings*, was yet to appear, and most of the very useful articles on the city in *The Island Magazine* were still to be published. A history of Charlottetown, if it were to be written, would have to be based upon findings from primary sources. Since then, a lot of good information became available on the city, but the importance of archival material for the most part remained. Adherence to the original limitations on size for the present study would have required the research to be assessed and the results summarized in a most abbreviated fashion. The details that sustained the overview would have remained hidden and, thus, unavailable for the consideration and use by others. Instead, this work is longer than it was initially expected to be. To accommodate the practicalities of publishing today, the footnotes — some 1,800 of them — citing the origin of the information have been omitted. Brief essays on sources for each chapter have been provided instead. For anyone especially anxious to locate a precise reference, copies of the final manuscript received by the publisher will be available in the Archives of the Canadian Museum of Civilization, and, one hopes, in the Prince Edward Island Public Archives and Records Office. CMC's Archives will also have the notes, reports and other evidence assembled for the project.

The various urban biographical themes and sub-themes traced in the book are easily identifiable from chapter to chapter. In addition to them, three others consistently assert themselves in the pages that follow. One has to do with Charlottetown's position as a city on an island in a region that, in the 20th century, was somewhat outside the mainstream of economic and political power in Canada. This relative isolation had profound implications economically and psychologically. Construction of the Confederation Bridge partly reduced the effects of the city's island location, but the region's distance from the industrial heartland of Ontario and Quebec and the resource-rich West remained. The ongoing consequences of geography will become apparent as the 21st century unfolds. They may not all be ill.

Charlottetown is also a provincial capital, and, in addition to that, by far the most important place in the province. Capital cities have their own set of issues arising from the benefits and challenges of hosting an authority and its attendant bureaucracy that draw their legitimacy from a wider constituency. Despite the old aphorism that "the town could only flourish if the country were prosperous," the interests of the capital and province were not always synonymous, and the relations between their governments, cordial. Today, when the balance of dependency may well be reversing, fundamental questions surrounding political representation and municipal financing persist.

The matter of abundance, or its obverse, scarcity, may underlie some of the inter-jurisdictional tensions, and is a theme that appears discreetly throughout Charlottetown's history. Only in the 19th century did an awareness appear in western civilization that wealth could be increased generally. Until then, the perception existed that one prospered at the other's loss. In some places, this confidence in economic expansion was embraced, but Islanders responded tentatively to it. The implications of this mindset for urban-rural relations are obvious. Even within the city, apprehensions about the security of prosperity prompted a cautious approach to civic administration. This was an ongoing trait of municipal affairs. Where once critics might have castigated this attitude as uninspired timidity, today's fiscal conservatives would praise it as responsible prudence. In any case, Charlottetown did not lack for visionaries and entrepreneurs, but they had to make their way in a community in which caution was often seen as a virtue.

The events that are recorded and explained in this account have not been filtered by preconceived views of right or wrong. They did not constitute an inevitable flow of history to the realities of today. Charlottetonians responded to their circumstances in the ways that they thought best, sometimes with unintended consequences. Frequently their fate was determined by forces beyond their control. It would be neither fair nor accurate to test the actions of previous generations of citizens against the standards of today. Yet, at present, the story seems to be turning out well.

By 2005, times were as prosperous as any since incorporation. Many past problems and shortcomings have been addressed, and a diverse economic base has been created. Challenges remain, of course, and they may prove to be arduous, but the future prognosis is encouraging. Modern communications technology, the return of traditional urbanism, and an impending energy scarcity that favours compact communities with ready access to food supplies and other necessities are influences that are likely to weigh in the city's favour. Moreover, creative approaches to economic and social development adopted in recent decades are now bearing fruit. If all the elements that are now in place can be kept there, Charlottetonians have every right to be optimistic — cautiously optimistic.

CHAPTER 1

Origins

1720-1854

A vessel approaching Charlottetown harbour today slides out of the choppy waves of the Northumberland Strait into the relative calm of Hillsborough Bay, past Governors Island and through the narrow channel between Rocky Point and Keppoch. Before it lies a spacious basin, the confluence of three rivers, the principal of which, the Hillsborough, virtually bisects Prince Edward Island. The shoreline is low and capped with moist grasslands and patches of woodland. Wave action has undermined the bluffs, causing sharp indentations where the dark red soil and crumbly rock have slumped onto the narrow beaches. The water is cold because the scouring action of the tides has prevented the build-up of shallows. The land rises gently from the water's edge, reaching a height of 32 metres 1½ kilometres inland before flowing onwards through softly undulating countryside to the warm sandy beaches on the Island's north shore. The site is not dramatic, but it is beautiful and manicured, combining the vastness of the sea and the neatness and order of well-managed farms. It is a setting unique in all of Canada and unsurpassed in its evocation of peace and stability.

The climate at times, but not invariably, matches this gentleness. Ample rainfall ensures vernal lushness, and cool on-shore breezes moderate much of the summer heat. Bright clear days give autumn scenery a visual crispness that contrasts with the mellow haze of late summer. Winters, however, can be harsh, with violent snowstorms and a stabbing coldness that can linger well into spring if northerly winds push gulf ice into the strait. The climate is moderate with average daily temperatures of 18 °C in July and -7 °C in January, an average annual precipitation of 113 cm and a yearly total of 1,803 hours of sunshine.

Unlike today's tourists, it was not the weather and the scenery that drew the first newcomers to the area, but the search for food. As the glaciers retreated at the end of the last ice age, the freshly exposed landscape developed into rich grasslands that attracted grazing animals such as caribou. Early aboriginal people (now called Paleo-Indians) followed in pursuit of game and are known to have been present on Prince Edward Island around 10,600 years ago. As the land became forested, other natives, the Shellfish People, appeared about 3,500 years ago and harvested marine life, birds and small animals. Approximately 2,000 years ago an Algonquian people, the Mi'kmaq, occupied much of the Maritimes and established a presence on Prince

Edward Island, which they called "Abahquit," meaning "lying parallel with the land."[1] They found a well-forested landscape rich in wildlife and fruit-bearing shrubs. Marine life abounded in the rivers and surrounding sea. The Mi'kmaq led a nomadic existence, setting up substantial camps at the western end of the Island and on the north shore in summer but breaking into smaller groups and seeking more sheltered locales in winter. The ease of access to the interior offered by Charlottetown's three rivers ensured that passersby frequented the area.

Mi'kmaq activity in the river basin increased during the 18th century when the French, in an attempt to secure them as allies, passed out free gunpowder and other gifts. Following the arrival of the English, parties of Mi'kmaq often camped near Charlottetown harbour. Early in the 19th century, natives supplied fish, fowl and vegetables to the community's inhabitants, and later the Mi'kmaq became an important supplier of firewood. As settlement progressed, these services were less in demand, and although they earned some income through the sale of baskets and other handicrafts, impoverishment was widespread. Concern for their welfare prompted a brief attempt to encourage agriculture on a piece of land traditionally used as an encampment on the east side of the harbour, and in 1862 a society for their assistance was formed in Charlottetown. Their condition remained, however, one of penury for most of that century.

THE FRENCH REGIME, 1719-58

The first Europeans to appear in the Charlottetown area were French. Their presence, however, was sporadic, and, for the most part, they let larger strategic concerns determine administration of a small, secluded island, and made no real effort to settle or administer what they called "Île Saint-Jean." It was the domain of fishermen who came during the summer and congregated on the northern shores. Following the Treaty of Utrecht in 1713, which cost France her Acadian territories in modern-day Nova Scotia, French colonial initiatives centred on Île Royale (Cape Breton). Île Saint-Jean, however, was identified as a potential source of agricultural products, and plans were formulated to make it more secure. In 1719 the French government granted the Comte de Saint-Pierre the exclusive right to settle the Island and exploit its fishery and other resources. To this end, in the same year, pilots from Louisbourg found a good location for an administrative centre within a deep bay on the south side of the Island where three rivers merged before entering the bay through a short inlet. From the harbour thus formed, the rivers provided convenient routes inland, by boat in summer and ice in winter. The site offered safe anchorage for large ships and was close to Acadian homesteads in nearby British territories. Acadians, though reluctant to leave their homes, would find the place easily accessible if they chose to move.

In 1720 the Sieur de Gotteville de Belile was commissioned by a company formed by de Saint-Pierre to establish a settlement. De Gotteville led an expedition from

---

1 The modern spelling of the name is "Abegweit."

Rochefort comprising three ships and 300 people, reaching their destination in August. About two-thirds of the immigrants moved on to the north shore, the majority to St. Peter's Bay. Those who remained began the laborious task of establishing a settlement. On the western side of the harbour, just inside its entrance, they built a small group of buildings at a site they called Port-la-Joye. Initially, attempts to establish a viable community there seemed doomed to frustration. De Saint-Pierre's company was heavily in debt, and, by 1724, without adequate financial and material support, most of the colonists from France quit the area. Two years later Île Saint-Jean came directly under the administration of royal officials at Louisbourg, and a small detachment was sent to re-establish a post at Port-la-Joye. The community grew slowly until 1745 when troops from New England, recently victorious at Louisbourg, attacked and destroyed it. Occupied by the British until 1748, the colony was restored to France by the Treaty of Aix-la-Chapelle and, in 1749 a detachment under Denis de Bonaventure constructed a new settlement at Port-la-Joye. This, too, fell to the British after their second conquest of Louisbourg in 1758.

Under French rule the population of Port-la-Joye remained small. Various accounts have provided data on its civilian population, showing uniformly low totals. Denys de La Ronde, an army officer from Louisbourg, recorded the population of Port-la-Joye in 1721 as comprising 16 French and 4 Acadian families, a total of 100 people. This was roughly one-quarter of the permanent European population of the Island at the time. One of the Acadians was Michel Haché-Gallant, who with his wife Anne Cormier had 12 children and occupied land adjacent to the fort fronting on the North-East (Hillsborough) River. Later censuses reported 63 in 1728, 81 in 1740, 39 in 1751 and 71 in 1753. By way of comparison, the population of Annapolis Royal in 1737 was 1,406; that of Pisiquid near present-day Windsor, NS, was 1,623 and Minas, the Grand Pré village area, was 2,113. Although the original de Gotteville colonists were European French, by 1728 almost all the inhabitants of Port-la-Joye had migrated from Acadia, and the Acadian roots of the population remained dominant thereafter. Most Acadians, though, resisted French entreaties to leave their mainland homes, and the main influx of Acadians to Île Saint-Jean came after their deportation from Nova Scotia in 1755.

This inset from a 1734 map shows Port-la-Joye and the proposed fortifications. A fleet of Mi'kmaq canoes can be seen approaching in the lower right hand corner. Port-la-Joye was a meeting place for the annual distribution of gifts from the King of France to the Mi'kmaq people.

Throughout the French regime, the tiny settlement at the mouth of the harbour remained physically unimposing. The original few log houses and small fort overlooking the harbour were soon joined by a little church, St-Jean l'Evangéliste. Many of the remaining buildings, habitually in disrepair, were official or semi-official in nature. They included residences for the detachment commander, surgeon, store man and chaplain; a barracks; storehouses; a stone powder magazine; and later stables, a bakery, a jail and forges. A stone-lined well was completed in 1739. Buildings were placed according to the dictates of the landscape and user convenience rather than any plan. Although an impressive design for a brick and stone fort was drafted in 1751 by an army engineer, Colonel Franquet, it was never built.

Besides a garrison of varying size, Port-la-Joye was a farming settlement that, in times of plenty (there were also years of crop failures and plagues of mice) realized abundant yields of wheat, oats, rye, barley and peas. The military and civil authorities were, nevertheless, essential props for the economy, providing supplies and services to the community. In 1721 three small ships were built to exploit the fishery and trade with Europe and the West Indies, although the fishing was located on the other side of the Island and trade remained rudimentary.

The people who lived at Port-la-Joye were unpretentious. Besides the garrison, there were a few tradesmen, farmers and a priest. The civilians were independent and able to survive on their own resources. One observer called them lazy; others considered them industrious enough to provide the necessities of life while not being embarrassed by ambition. By all accounts, they were an unsophisticated, pragmatic people whose simple lifestyle and alleged responsiveness to clerical and civil authority made them greatly admired by later chroniclers. They were also vulnerable. With the fall of Louisbourg in 1758, outlying communities were virtually defenceless. The British naval commander, Admiral Edward Boscawen, gave Colonel Andrew Rollo the task of clearing all of the French off Île Saint-Jean. On August 7, 1758, just 38 years to the month after the French founded Port-la-Joye, Rollo's troops began to round up the populace. Once the colonists were embarked, their homes and other buildings were abandoned to their fate.

BRITISH SETTLEMENT

The Early Years, 1759-1800

Lord Rollo relocated the defence works to their present site, renamed them Fort Amherst and began strengthening them in case the French attempted to retake the colony. The mapping of newly acquired territories was a strategy by which the British confirmed their ownership and promoted their imperial ambitions, so plans were made to have the Island surveyed after France ceded the territory permanently in the 1763 Treaty of Paris. Samuel Holland, Surveyor General of the Northern District of North America, began this task in 1764. The need to regulate the gulf fishery and to support possible settlement made the establishment of a local administrative centre clearly desirable. Holland identified a suitable location for a townsite across the harbour from Fort Amherst. It occupied a fairly level, gently rising stretch of land comprising 7,300 acres to be divided among town lots, pasture lots, a common and road allowances. Among its chief advantages were the ease of access to overland routes to Halifax via Tatamagouche on the adjacent mainland and some expectations that it might stimulate the economy of the south coast of the Island, which was removed from the north-shore fishery. It was also well-situated to be connected by road to other parts of the colony. A weakness was the number of shifts of sail needed for a vessel to enter and leave the harbour, but this was overridden by the positives of the place. Holland's superiors in London accepted both his recommendations for the site, and that it be named after Charlotte Sophia, the wife of King George III.

Charles Morris, Chief Surveyor of Nova Scotia, was responsible for drafting the initial town plan in 1769, but Thomas Wright, under instructions from Governor Walter Patterson, actually completed it. The design was similar to others laid out by the British along the Atlantic coast, following the model for Halifax, which George Montagu Dunk, the Earl of Halifax and former President of the Board of Trade, ordered should have a "regular" layout of streets and buildings. This reflected current English town planning. The Georgian mindset was one of mankind attempting to impose harmony and order on the disorder of nature. Towns, like society itself, were intended to be structured, rational, controlled and self-sufficient in the face of the wilderness.

Beyond the townsite lay a belt of farmland, the royalty, meant for pasturage. Charlottetown's design provided for substantial town lots and fields in the royalty because the townsmen were expected to grow their own food until rural settlement increased. In addition, the plan prevented strip development along the river fronts and encouraged low-density land use. In fact, in the early years, there were enough unoccupied city lots to allow settlers to pasture their cows within the town. As a result, the pasture lots in the royalty were merged into farms.

Although St. John's Island, renamed Prince Edward Island in 1798, was initially administered as part of Nova Scotia, it was made a separate colony in 1769. Much of the Island at this time was still tree-covered, and a description of it, as viewed from the sea, likened the low, even cliffs of red sandstone surmounted by thick woods running to water's edge as having "a striking resemblance to a Mahogany Cloths [*sic*] Brush." Even so, by 1769 Charlottetown was beginning to emerge from the trees and red soil. Development was at first exceedingly slow, and some early officials suffered from cold and hunger due to inadequate housing and food supply. At this time, there were only two houses and, perhaps, a few log huts. Growth was gradual, with the opening of a store in the late 1760s, for example, and the construction of some hostelries soon after. A visitor in 1774 reported 15 dwellings. A small jail was built on Pownal Square,[2] and a courthouse on the western corner of Queen and King Streets.

2 Pownal Square was informally called Gaol Square for obvious reasons. In 1912 it was renamed Connaught Square in honour of Governor General HRH Arthur, Duke of Connaught.

Charles Morris, 1769

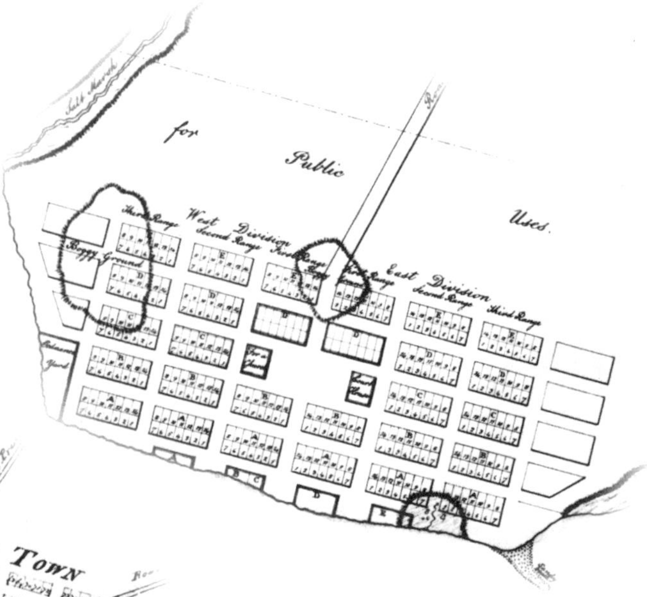

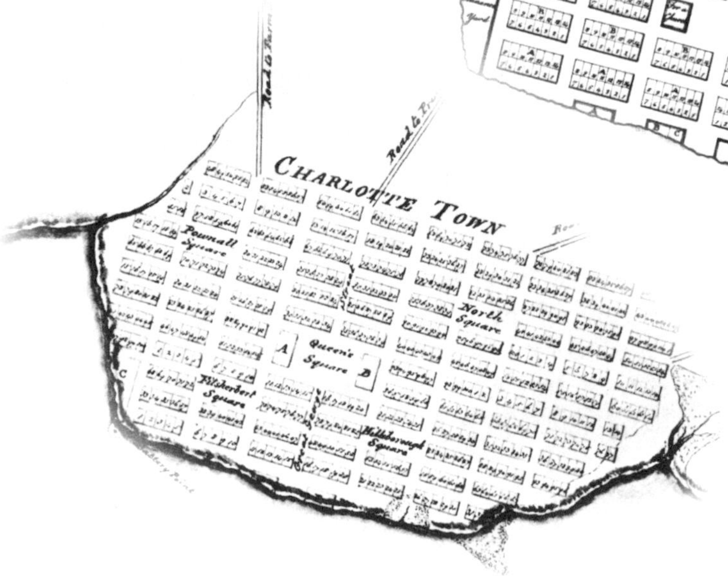

Thomas Wright, 1771

Detail, Bird's Eye Map, 1878

Settlers acquainted with "new towns" in London, Edinburgh, and Bath would have recognized Charlottetown's grid pattern of streets, with a main central square for important public buildings and smaller open green spaces in each of the four quadrants of the grid. Streets running north from the waterfront were 100 feet (30.5 metres) wide to guard against fires, and eventually the cross streets were assigned a width of 40 feet (12.2 metres). Five hundred town lots measuring 84 feet (25.6 metres) by 160 feet (48.8 metres) were plotted, as was an adjacent Common for future expansion. Lots were set aside for an ordnance yard on the waterfront, a house with gardens for the Lieutenant Governor, a cemetery, a court house and a parsonage. There was some concern about the quality of the drinking water because the elevation of the land was so slight, but the location was otherwise regarded as "pleasant."

In 1769 Charles Morris laid out Charlottetown with 6 streets between the Royalty and the waterfront. In 1771 Thomas Wright revised the grid to accommodate 13. As the 1878 Bird's Eye map shows, the final layout was something in between. The 1878 map shows not only how the downtown grid was filling in, but also how the Royalty related to the city proper.

Ashby's 1798 map, based on Samuel Holland's survey, illustrates why Holland recommended the Charlottetown site as the colonial capital. The North, West and Hillsborough Rivers allowed access far into the interior of the colony. The harbour offered similar access to the mainland.

Sometimes, buildings served a number of purposes. When Peter Stewart arrived to assume his duties as Chief Justice, he found that the accommodations temporarily assigned to him had previously been used as a church, a military jail, a meeting place for the colonial assembly, and a courthouse. Needless to say, he found it "quite ruinous."[3] Early docking facilities were equally inadequate. Two early wharves were destroyed by ice and storms, but, in 1772 a more substantial dock, extending 110 yards into the Hillsborough River, was built at the foot of Queen Street and named after the crew of the naval vessel that completed the work, HMS *Tartar*.

As time passed, more improvements occurred. In 1787 a printing shop began to publish government records and some news. Barracks to house the garrison were built around 1778 on the eastern side of Queen and King Streets. Various tradesmen began to open the establishments necessary in a frontier settlement: tailors, joiners, block makers, shoemakers, blacksmiths and others. The first post office only opened in 1802 in Benjamin Chappell's house on Water Street, just west of Prince Street. The by-now inadequate Tartar's Wharf was replaced with an improved facility at the foot of Queen Street, and in 1802 a new courthouse and legislature were built on Queen Square, joining an Anglican church that had been built on the west side of the square in 1801.

Military Affairs

Given that Britain was in an almost constant state of war in Charlottetown's early years, military concerns had a high profile. This was especially so following an assault by rebel American privateers in November 1775, during which homes were plundered and the colony's administrator, Phillips Callbeck, and surveyor, Thomas Wright, were kidnapped. In response the colony built an unimposing defensive work at the point where the Hillsborough and North Rivers meet – a battery named after Governor Walter Patterson, although the name was later changed to George's Battery. In 1800 and 1801, new barracks suitable for two companies were erected on ordnance land behind the Battery. Facing each other across a parade square, the single-storey, colonnaded barracks – "painted white" and "respectable" in appearance – were described as "remarkably well built and commodious." Unfortunately, this was not always to be the case. Nearby were storehouses, a hospital and guard house, and the entire establishment was surrounded by a high picket fence. After 1794, a second defensive position, Kent (later renamed Prince Edward's) Battery, was built at Fanningbank to cover the original defensive work, which, for its part, was repaired. There was also a defensive position at the foot of Great George Street. Named initially after Tartar's Wharf, it was renamed after Prince Edward when some improvements were made to it in 1798. In 1802 it was removed entirely. Completing the defences was a battery at York Point (then called Battery Point) and a blockhouse on the southwest shore of the harbour mouth.

---

3 This may have been the early courthouse which is known to have also been used for church services.

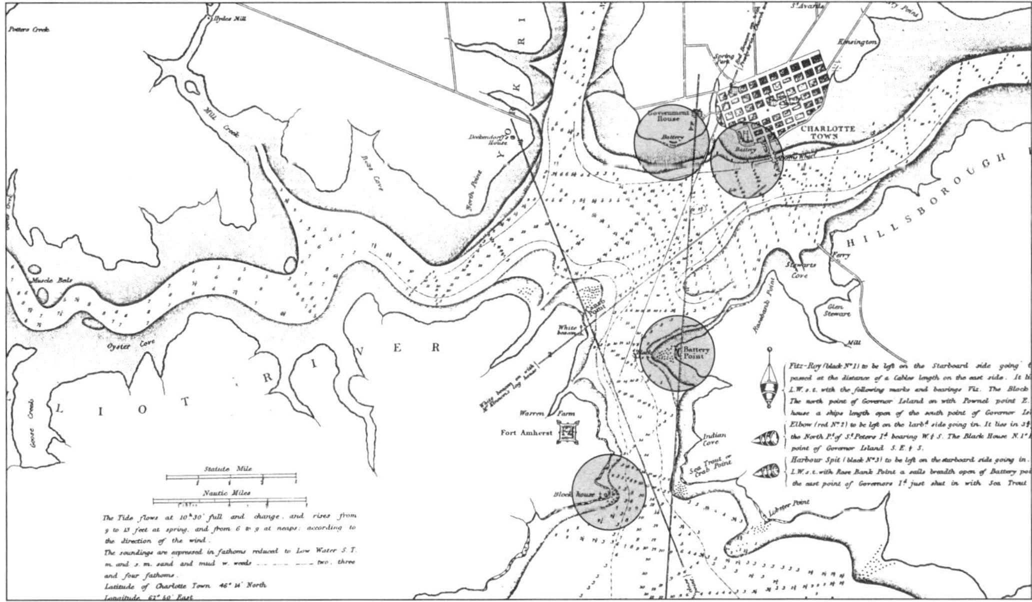

Chart of Hillsborough Bay and the Harbour of Charlotte Town, 1839 (detail), by George Wright and George Peacock. The highlighted areas show the approximate ranges of the four batteries that overlooked the harbour at this time.

In addition to these installations, the community was expected to help defend itself, and the militia became an important part of community life. Following the American Revolution, the garrison shrank to a handful of regular troops, but, with the commencement of hostilities between Great Britain and France in 1793, two companies of local militia were assigned to protect the capital. Having served "perfectly unmolested" until the cessation of hostilities in Europe in 1802, the force was about to be disbanded when a quick resumption of the conflict with France brought about an equally abrupt reversal of these plans. The militia became an ongoing feature of life in this small outpost of empire.

Militia obligations were honoured more in the capital than in the rural areas of the colony. The colonial militia units were expected to muster from time to time in order to drill and attain some rough semblance of military readiness. In 1812, besides 89 regular British soldiers and 10 gunners, the garrison in Charlottetown consisted of 133 active volunteers.[4] These militiamen comprised two companies of infantry and a company of cavalry. They provided their own uniforms and were generally credited with putting on a fine appearance when on parade. They drilled twice a week, in addition to the monthly muster of the Queens County militia held in Charlottetown. The

4 Charlottetown fell within the general ambit of the British military establishment in Halifax. Detachments of troops were sent to Charlottetown in times of insecurity, such as the Napoleonic Wars and the War of 1812-14. At other times they were withdrawn. British regulars returned to Charlottetown in 1830 and stayed until the eve of incorporation.

frequency of county musters diminished as time passed, eventually becoming an annual occasion. Even that was abolished in 1851, after which point in time militia companies were made up of volunteers only. The militia was used by the civil authority to quell disturbances, such as in April 1843 when it was deployed to East Point during unrest by tenant farmers. Alternatively, it could assume garrison duties when the regular forces were sent elsewhere. This occurred in 1847 when the regular troops were dispatched to Belfast to deal with an election riot. Use of the urban militia to maintain order in rural areas created another sensitive issue that separated the town from countryside.

Justice

The town was not so small a place as to exclude deep-seated animosities. Two of its leading citizens and bitter political enemies, John Stewart and John MacDonald, confronted each other with swords drawn in the street one winter day in 1797. Fortunately, the altercation did not end in bloodshed. Crime was not a serious problem, but offences occurred, and justice occasionally was deflected by community attitudes. On one occasion, a woman sentenced to death for robbery was released because no one would perform the execution. Capital crimes included treason, murder, rape, assault, arson, theft and sodomy. Though a death sentence was required in such cases, it was not always exacted, as the case of Jupiter Wise shows. Wise, a black servant of a Captain Burns, was charged with burglary and assault with a deadly weapon. He escaped hanging by pleading benefit of clergy and was sentenced to be transported to the West Indies.[5] Other death sentences were often commuted after petitions for clemency were presented to the Lieutenant Governor.

Capital cases were heard before the colonial Supreme Court. More routine justice was administered by Justices of the Peace, and tasks like the licensing of taverns were handled by a Grand Jury nominated by the colonial Supreme Court. A Board of Wardens, responsible to the Governor-in-Council, made by-laws and imposed fines. Punishments could be severe by today's standards. Sentences might include time standing in the pillory or flogging. In 1842 Christopher Lawson was sentenced to three months in jail, six months hard labour and 39 lashes for three counts of larceny. Lawson was lucky. A generation earlier, Donald McIntyre was sentenced to three sets of 36 lashes, administered over a three-week period, for his petty larceny conviction. A Board of Magistrates could enact police ordinances, and designate part-time citizen constables to enforce penalties. If required, the Board could also call for the aid of the militia or the regular military. Although the fines they imposed helped defray costs and provide remuneration for these part-time officials, lethargy and a hesitancy to offend neighbours and acquaintances resulted in a reluctance to serve. Nominees faced fines if they refused duties, and, in the case of constables, an 1843 act of the legislature compelled them to perform their functions.

---

5 Historically, clerics were exempted from trial in a civil court. Pleading benefit of clergy was an accepted manoeuvre that allowed a person sentenced to death to claim to be a member of the clergy and be given a lighter sentence.

Leisure and Society

Leisure time was filled with home-grown activities. These involved riding, hunting, fishing and sailing in the spring, summer and fall, and hunting and cariole racing in winter. During warm weather, families picnicked along the river banks, while gatherings moved indoors during the winter, at which time parties were typically held every second week. Evening get-togethers often featured suppers, followed by rubbers of whist, round games and, not infrequently, "impromptu" dances. Others engaged in more basic pursuits. A visiting clergyman found in 1791 that Charlottetown was "wicked enough for a larger town. Swearing and drunkenness abounded." Had he come in 1797, he might have been more impressed to learn of the formation that year of the colony's first fraternal society, the Freemasons. The town's various faith groups generated a number of organizations to occupy free time and provide an outlet for religious and social opinions. In 1825 the Benevolent Irish Society was born to cater to the sons of Ireland, both Protestants and Roman Catholics. Another organization linked to Ireland, the Loyal Orange Lodge, appeared in 1849 with the opening of the Boyne Lodge. Despite its roots, it attracted mainly English and Scots Protestants who feared the increasing presence of Irish Roman Catholics and their political assertiveness.

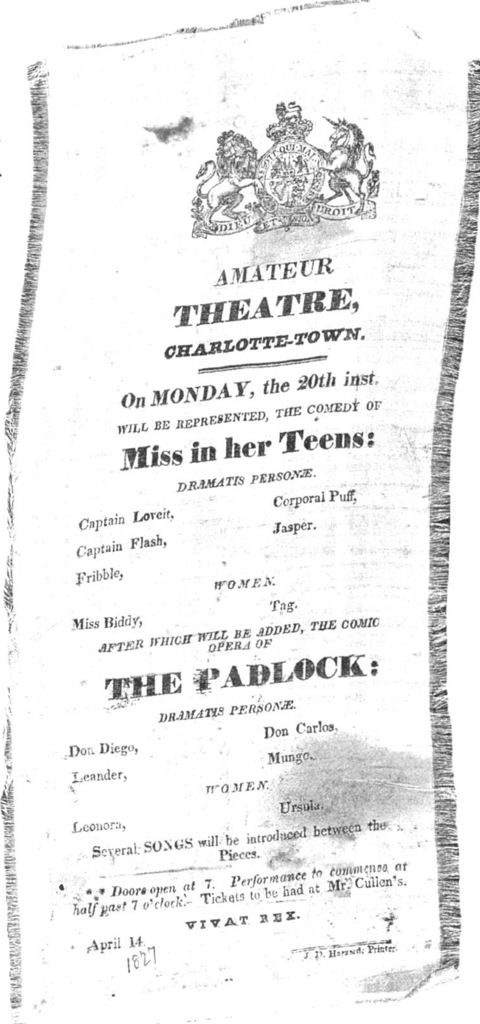

DIEU ET MON DROIT

AMATEUR
THEATRE,
CHARLOTTE-TOWN.

On MONDAY, the 20th inst.
WILL BE REPRESENTED, THE COMEDY OF
Miss in her Teens:

DRAMATIS PERSONÆ.

Captain Loveit, Corporal Puff,
Captain Flash, Jasper.
Fribble,

WOMEN.

Miss Biddy, Tag.

AFTER WHICH WILL BE ADDED, THE COMIC OPERA OF
THE PADLOCK:

DRAMATIS PERSONÆ.

Don Diego, Don Carlos,
Leander, Mungo.

WOMEN.

Leonora, Ursula.

Several SONGS will be introduced between the Pieces.

*** Doors open at 7. Performance to commence at half past 7 o'clock. Tickets to be had at Mr. Cullen's.

VIVAT REX.

April 14.
1827

J. D. Haszard, Printer.

Theatre program, printed on silk, 1827.

As the town grew, entertainment got more elaborate. An amateur theatrical company flourished around 1818, and a cricket club was founded in 1849. In 1829 a touring company of equestrian performers from the United States came to town. This was the first recorded show of its kind in Charlottetown, but far from the last. Just the next year, for instance, Madame Foriosa came to perform. Her reportedly exuberant audience was treated to a program of pantomime, fireworks, a tightrope walk and the fandango danced blindfolded. By the time the city was incorporated, it was already hosting annual "industrial exhibitions," organized by the Royal Agricultural Society, at which "a complete agricultural panorama" of the Island was exhibited. These gala autumn events, held on Queen Square, were very popular. Refreshments of beer, cakes, apples and plums were offered by any vendor with "a semblance of a tent, even four posts – covered with patchwork quilts, old sails or something." Use of Queen Square by the community was common. W. B. Wellner described with pleasure an occasion in July 1853, when "Ross, the great singing man" asked his pupils to assemble at the top of the Colonial Building one night. "The evening was calm," he remembered, "the singing good, and it vibrated through the town very musically, of course it created quite a sensation." Quiet pleasures were supported on the eve of incorporation by a literary society and "a very good" subscription library.

Charlottetonians had their weaknesses as well as their virtues. One description in 1837 gives a somewhat unflattering image of the citizenry as having a lazy, indolent appearance generally. Small as it was, the town had its levels of society and various human conditions, all of which were assessed and disciplined by contemporary standards of moral deportment. Lapses in behaviour came within the purview of the civil authority, but also the clergy. Some pursued their duties with more fervour than others. Father Alexander Thomas Fitzgerald, a Dominican friar who served in St. Dunstan's parish between 1822 and 1830, was one of the stricter kind. Soon after his arrival from Newfoundland, Fitzgerald forced an errant member of his flock to crawl on his knees through the streets from his hut to the chapel and there to explain his "disobedience." Another was flogged out of town. Some Irish Catholics, having fled Fitzgerald in Newfoundland, promptly "decamped." At the gentler end of the spectrum, by the 1850s Charlottetown could also boast of a number of benevolent, Bible and missionary societies dedicated to the performance of good works. There was much for them to do, if a commentary of C. D. Rankin, an enumerator for the 1848 census, is accurate:

> *I have seen many families in extreme destitution of the means of subsistence, living in places resembling Pig Styes more than the dwellings of human beings; the squalid misery of many residing in the back streets, lanes, and alleys, and the infirmity of the air they inhale, must prove very injurious to the health of the community in general.*

Historical memory is cobbled together from the evidence left by our forebears, and that, for the most part, is heavily influenced by the secure, the educated and the well-placed members of society. We know less of the poor: their way of life, their social habits, their hopes and fates. When we catch a glimpse of them, it is often as objects of social discipline or charity. Their absence on the historical page, however, should not be construed as non-existence because any place, including Charlottetown, had its poor, and their presence was an integral part of a town's life.

Social welfare depended heavily upon families or voluntary associations, and, when absolutely necessary, the colonial assembly provided modest sums for this purpose. In some cases, such measures were insufficient. The asylum at Brighton was intended to cover the needs of the mentally ill as well as "imbecile paupers" and the destitute sane. It was accordingly intended to operate as a combined mental institution and workhouse in which the labour of the poor would help defray the costs of caring for the insane. Unfortunately, many of the destitute sane were incapacitated elderly men who were unable to perform the work expected of them. The asylum never functioned as planned.

For the first 40 years, most public services were located in private homes and businesses. The first post office, for instance, was located in 1802 in postmaster Benjamin Chappell's home. (This sketch by C.B. Chappell dates from the late 1800s, but the building was still standing in the 1930s. The fish-shaped weather vane is probably exaggerated.)

Despite its blemishes, Charlottetown's society in the early 19th century was generally reported to have been superior to that usually found in British towns six times its size. A significant number of settlers of independent income had been attracted because of its role as a capital and a centre of administration of the surrounding estates. Officers from the garrison added a dash of cosmopolitanism, and an expanding merchant community contributed the rectitude of the Victorian middle class. As the port of entry for most of the immigrants who came to Prince Edward Island, the town was the final destination for some, a number of whom simply lacked the means to go further. For the most part, society consisted of ordinary people performing unexceptional, but essential, tasks and leading uneventful lives. By mid-century, Charlottetown was above all else a farming community overlain with a veneer of folk who thought they were the better sort of people.

Urban Landscape

Following the construction of St. Paul's Church, no further work was undertaken on Queen Square until a new Legislature and Courthouse was begun in 1811. Designed by John Plaw and completed in 1814, the practical, solid-looking structure was located near Queen Street. A modest market house was erected in 1813 at the centre of the square – a deviation from the original plan for the space that envisaged a largely open area with public buildings on the eastern and western edges. A more substantial market house was built in 1823. The earlier building was hauled to the wharf to serve as a fish market. The new facility, also designed by John Plaw, featured 16 sides surrounded by a protective verandah, topped by a cupola. Although it was a polygon in shape, it came to be known as "round market house." The colonial government paid for its construction, but Charlottetonians were expected to keep it in repair.

The Colony's increasing population and prosperity was reflected in the capital's public buildings. For years, St. Paul's Anglican was the only ecclesiastical building in town, but in 1813 the Methodists opened a chapel on Richmond Street, followed in 1815 by a Roman Catholic chapel on lower Great George. The Presbyterians erected their kirk at the corner of Fitzroy and Pownal Streets in 1831. A new St. Paul's was built in 1836 on the eastern side of Queen Square. It was larger and more imposing than the one it replaced, although still of wood construction. Near the foot of Prince Street, the Methodists in 1847 opened a more spacious chapel designed by C. B. Chappell, while in 1843 the Catholics began construction of a new cathedral that was claimed to be the largest building on Prince Edward Island. Baptists, who had been gathering in homes and meeting rooms, purchased a lot at the corner of Euston and Prince Streets in 1843, and began construction of a substantial church, which opened in

In 1811 the colony commissioned John Plaw to design a Courthouse and Legistature, which was completed in 1814. A modest market house had been erected on Queen Square in 1813, but its successor, the "Round Market" designed by Plaw and opened in 1824, served until the 1860s.

In the 1830s the colony built a jailhouse on Pownal Square. The building was promptly nicknamed "Harvie's Brig" after the long-serving jailer, Nicholas Harvie.

1845. Eight years later, it was moved to a new site on Great George Street between Dorchester and King.

The colonial government commissioned some key projects. Work on a new jail began in 1830. Situated in Pownal Square, it eventually became familiarly known as "Harvie's Brig" after Nicholas Harvie, the long-serving jailer. It opened on the last day of 1831 and was described as "a roomy, commodious and well ventilated building well adapted for the purpose of which it was built." In 1834 a stately Government House in the Georgian style was erected at Fanningbank on a rise of land near Prince Edward's Battery (popularily but inaccurately called "Fort Edward"). This was followed by the construction between 1833 and 1835 of Central Academy, a two-storey edifice, also in the Georgian style, near the corner of Weymouth and Grafton Streets.[6] In 1842 the market house was relocated to the northwest corner of Queen Square to make way for a new Colonial Building. Begun in 1843 and opened in 1847, this stone neoclassical building was designed by a local builder, Isaac Smith, and completed by Islanders using materials that, with the exception of the exterior stone from Nova Scotia, originated on the Island. Impressive in design and fabrication, the three-storey legislature and courthouse, now called Province House, was built in an era of economic and demographic expansion and reflected the buoyancy and optimism of the times. The old Plaw courthouse was relegated to serving as a flour and meal market. As work was proceeding with the new Colonial Building, another significant project was under way – a "lunatic asylum" also designed by Isaac Smith. Begun in 1845, the solid brick building, set in the Common at Brighton, opened in 1847.

Although business growth was uneven, it resulted in a solid but unimposing townscape. Writing in 1899, A. Irwin described Charlottetown as it appeared in "The Olden Times," before 1840. Buildings were fairly close together along Water Street near the foot of Queen Street and for a short distance up Queen Street, but otherwise "houses and other buildings that dotted the town site were very few and far between." Commercial buildings were almost uniformly built of wood, despite the availability from the 1820s of domestically produced bricks. An 1820 report described "several tolerable taverns and public houses." A number of them were found along Water Street, including the Queen's Head Hotel that opened in 1829 at the corner of Pownal Street, and the Victoria Hotel that began operations in the early 1840s near Queen Street. The leading hostelry, however, was the Wellington Hotel on Great George Street. Between 1820 and 1850, it was a focus for political and social events in the young community.

Though the early commercial hub was at the corner of Queen and Water Streets – James Peake had his store on the corner, for instance – development began to edge up Queen Street. In 1843 Daniel Brennan opened a building at the corner of Sydney and Queen. It was brick, erected at a time when such buildings were landmarks on the urban landscape. Commercial development also took place adjacent to Queen Square and its market, particularly along the sunny side of Grafton Street.

6 The building was completed in 1835 after considerable delay and cost overrun.

Builder/architect Isaac Smith designed and built what many consider two of the Island's architectural gems: Government House (aka "Fanningbank") in 1834 and the Colonial Building, which was commenced in 1843 and opened in 1847.

With respect to residential development, a visitor in 1803 reported 72 houses – "all of Wood," and although many of them were "mere Block Houses," several [were] handsome, roomy and convenient." Three years later, another account noted that the town contained 70 houses spread over "a considerable surface." In 1820 there were barely 300 houses in Charlottetown. Reports describe a town without opulence in which houses intermingled with commercial establishments and workshops. An anonymous observer noted in 1818 that the houses were all of wood painted to resemble stone and had "a handsome appearance." Districts that gathered together various social classes had not yet appeared, although the western outskirts, a low-lying, marshy area known as "The Bog," was home to poor Blacks and other marginalized citizens. Even so, an 1839 visitor noted Charlottetown was totally without the mean and dirty habitations along the waterfront often found in European towns. The private homes were unpretentious and, if painted at all, white or straw-coloured. A few houses were brick, and many had gardens. The overall effect, in his view, was "extremely agreeable."

One of the finer earlier residences, Holland Grove, dated from the years after 1815 and stood upon the height of land lying in the block bounded by modern-day University Avenue, Fitzroy, Prince and Euston Streets. It had prominent, Palladian windows and was later remembered as "large and quaint looking – with an observatory on the top." Another residence of note was owned by the widow and a daughter of former Lt. Governor Edmund Fanning. Located between Great George, Richmond, Prince and Sydney Streets, the house, its lavender-coloured barn and extensive gardens and orchards were an adornment to the capital until the house was destroyed by fire in 1847. By this time, other impressive homes had begun to appear. James Peake, a leading merchant, built his sturdy, brick residence in 1835-36 on Water Street. The design featured a spacious central hall and a scotch dormer. Across Prince Street from Holland Grove, T. H. Haviland, an important politician, landowner and agent, built "Fairholm," a massive, hipped-roof, stone residence that boasted a conservatory. The aptly named "Frogmore" was built by Dr. Charles Poole on Rochford Street, near Government Pond, in 1841. Featuring double drawing rooms, four bedrooms and servants' quarters, the house was surrounded by extensive gardens and offered a view across the harbour and beyond to the Northumberland Strait. Not all of the new homes were as imposing as these, but the prosperity of an established elite of merchants, landowners, land agents and professionals was having a significant impact on Charlottetown's built environment. Construction of houses, modest and elaborate alike, was occurring throughout the town, along Water Street and the streets running off it, particularly Great George Street, and in the newer northeastern and northwestern districts.

The overall physical environment, though, was rudimentary with dimly lit streets that were dusty in summer and muddy in spring and fall. They could, in the best of times, strike a visitor as "broad and cheerful," but grumpy locals often thought otherwise. Despite the complaints, John Lawson claimed in 1851 that outside the centre of town every individual lot in the common and royalty was served by good roads. Maintenance of both roads and wells was supported by local assessments. Until 1853, though, responsibility for lighting and maintaining oil-burning street lamps lay with the citizens who resided nearest them.

Economic Growth and Civic Development

By the early 19th century, Charlottetown had assumed well-defined economic roles as a market town, an administrative centre and communications hub. These remained the foundation for the local economy throughout the century. As more and more of the surrounding countryside was brought into agricultural production, the capital reaped the benefits of serving it.

The growing importance of Charlottetown as a market town began to obscure its role as the centre of colonial administration. The latter, however, remained important. Officers occupied a number of substantial houses adjacent to the garrison grounds. Though rarely more than 50 in number, the men of the garrison itself required provisions, recreational and social services. Maintenance of the barracks and fortifications also gave tradesmen and labourers intermittent work. For well-connected merchants and professionals, government appointments provided extra income. A significant number of office-holders and other well-established Charlottetonians also derived income as rural landowners or the agents of landowners.

Some administrative functions associated with the capital provoked resentment beyond its confines. This was particularly true of the collection of quit rents from tenant farmers who were liable to be summoned to town to settle their arrears. Government officials were resented at times. One governor was chastised by a public assembly for not having ventured more than 18 miles into the countryside in a ten-year period, and this distance only once. There was also the suspicion of nepotism in the selection of office-holders to the benefit of a small group of insiders resident in the town.

The economy went through cycles of expansion and recession, but in good times shipbuilding and the timber trade brought prosperity to the community. Other primary products, such as grains and wool, were processed in various mills that sprang

The Victoria Hotel, on Water Street near the corner of Queen, began operations in the 1840s. It burned down in 1860.

up along nearby streams. Most manufactured items, however, had to be imported. In 1822 Walter Johnstone reported the absence of a bookbinder, cutler, nailer, hatter, roper, dyer and cloth dresser. Conditions changed somewhat by 1839, although the town still offered "very fair prospects to joiners, masons, saddlers, brick-makers and tanners," as well as "wheelwrights, blacksmiths, shoemakers, tailors – [and] artisans of any kind who find employment in – English towns." A departure from the usual trades and craft production occurred in 1844 when, not one, but two tobacco factories opened. Subsequently, increased economic diversification was represented by the opening of the Phoenix Foundry on Water Street by George Birnie to manufacture stoves and tools. Although the business did not last a long time – it was offered for sale in 1850 – it was an indication of a growing complexity in the city's manufacturing sector.

The harbour was one of Charlottetown's most striking features – both physically and economically. While the wharf facilities left something to be desired, the harbour itself was commodious and safe, busy with merchant ships, fishing boats, coastal packets and harbour craft. Royal Navy vessels were frequent visitors, and Charlottetown was headquarters for the Navy's hydrographical survey for the Gulf of St. Lawrence. At one time, sealing vessels deposited their sculps at a rendering facility in the area later called the Kensington Range. The brigantine *Hillsborough*, launched in 1810, was the earliest vessel recorded as being built at Charlottetown, and construction continued sporadically thereafter. Ritchie and Morice built the ship *Hayden* in 1825, but it was not until 1843, when John Pippy built the *Kingaloch*, a 178-ton brig, that shipyards came to dominate the waterfront. Other shipyards operating on the waterfront in the 1840s and 1850s included those owned by James Peake, Andrew and James Duncan, William Heard, William McGill and William White. The greatest concentration of such establishments lay along the shoreline between Great George and Hillsborough Streets.

Although shipbuilding was an important element in the local economy, trade was greater. As it was the site of the colony's customs house, much of the outbound timber and agricultural products and most of the inbound consumer goods passed through Charlottetown. On balance, more goods were received than shipped from the port. In 1853, for instance, imports amounted to £148,209 and exports, £49,003.[7] Laws governing accurate measures, fair prices and export of scarce commodities underscored the town's central role in Island commerce. Its leading merchants became some of the wealthiest men in the colony, often financing others in an economy otherwise based on barter because of a scarcity of banks and specie. Just before incorporation, the need for commercial banking was addressed by the opening of a branch of the Westmorland Bank of New Brunswick, although by then efforts were under way to create a locally owned bank. The town's shops were reported in 1836 as being "full of new, imported goods" for which the prices were "frightfully high." The basic necessities of "humble" life, however, were considerably cheaper than in England. One observer

7 Island-built sailing vessels, many of which were sold overseas, added to the total value of exports and were not reflected in this figure.

noted that this, coupled with the higher wages of tradesmen and artisans, allowed for a relatively comfortable life for people of modest means. The weekly market offered a range of farm produce, meat and even livestock for sale. The Mi'kmaq supplied the townsfolk with fish, wild geese, duck and partridge and, in winter, firewood. By 1851, market days were twice a week, Wednesdays and Saturdays, providing "a sufficiency of what are termed by good housewives the substantials of life."

As the colony's principal entrepôt, communication ties were critical to the town's prosperity. The development of steam-driven ships opened a new era in marine transportation, and Charlottetonians wanted to be part of it. In March 1830, leading merchants and community leaders petitioned the Legislative Assembly to offer a grant to companies operating steamships between Quebec City and Halifax to make Charlottetown a port of call. This was the first of many such pleas over the next century. Later that year, the *Richard Smith*, a steamer owned by the Pictou Mines Company, entered the port, followed in September of the next year by the famous *Royal William*, which stopped at Charlottetown during her maiden voyage between Quebec and Halifax. Meanwhile, in May 1832, the steamer *Pocahontas* was commissioned as the mail packet between Charlottetown and Pictou. By 1842, Charlottetown claimed a steamship line of its own, and by the mid-1850s the Pictou mail packet was sailing twice weekly. In winter, though, when ice blocked the Northumberland Strait, the mail (and the occasional hardy passenger) was carried by iceboats, an arduous means of travel dating back to 1788. For local travel, the rivers served as communications links for boats in the open seasons and for sleighs in winter. A ferry link across the Hillsborough River to the south shore was inaugurated early,[8] and in 1838 a small steamer, the *Emo*, entered service there.

Travel by land had its own challenges. Two principal roads led out of the capital: the St. Peter's Road heading eastward to distant settlements in Kings County, and the Prince Town or Malpeque Road running westward into Prince County. In 1839 settlement was reported to have run 14 miles (22.5 kilometres) along the St. Peter's Road and 9-10 miles (14.5-16.1 kilometres) along the Prince Town Road before the bush closed in. Branching off of these roads were others leading to Covehead and Rustico, and, starting in Southport, the Georgetown Road ran to the capital of Kings County. Travel over any of them could be difficult, especially in wet weather and during the spring and fall. In 1839 a new stage coach began twice-a-week service between the capital and Georgetown.

Public services

In 1780 a small school opened in the St. John's Coffee House, and in 1804 citizens decided at a public meeting to hire a schoolmaster, using the income from a fund established by former Governor Walter Patterson to pay the salary. The classes

8 At one point, the ferry was a so-called "team boat," powered by horses turning a windlass that propelled the paddles. The service was operated by T. B. Tremain.

Thomas Heath Haviland (Senior) built Fairholm in 1839 and lived there until 1855. This engraving is from Meacham's 1880 Atlas.

were held in the old courthouse on Queen Street. A number of privately operated elementary schools appeared in the early 19th century, to be followed in 1821 by the National School, a public school and the first to occupy a specially built schoolhouse.[9] The schoolmaster's salary of £10 from the colonial treasury was to be supplemented by fees from the pupils. Although the school was expected to confer some advanced level of education, it is doubtful this goal was attained in a meaningful fashion. In 1829 Central Academy was founded to teach the classics, science and "the higher branches of mathematics." Some years were required to raise the money and build the school, but the academy was finally opened in January 1836. Eventually, an array of schools emerged in the community, including public, private and religious institutions. One of the more notable was the "Bog School," founded in 1848 to provide education for poorer children residing in the area. In 1852 the Free Education Act established a split jurisdiction with respect to education. Under it, the colonial government paid teachers' salaries and local ratepayers maintained the schools. In Charlottetown, the parents or guardians of the pupils were required to pay 2½ shillings quarterly for books,

9 The school was built on Kent Street between Weymouth and Cumberland Streets, and the building was subsequently converted into the Normal School.

rent and repairs to schools. Adult self-improvement was encouraged by the formation of a Mechanics' Institute in 1839, largely at the instigation of Charles Young, who delivered the inaugural lecture. This group may not have continued uninterrupted operations – early attempts to found similar institutes in Halifax in 1832 and Bytown (Ottawa) in 1847 were short-lived – but in 1855 the Legislative Assembly passed a bill to establish a Mechanics' Institute in Charlottetown.

The overall monitoring of public health in Charlottetown was the responsibility of an appointed Board of Health. Health care itself was provided by the family with the intervention of medical practitioners if their services could be afforded or were provided *pro bono*. The earliest doctors to serve in Charlottetown were associated with the garrison, but, by the end of the 18th century, private practitioners had taken up residence. They included Dr. Benjamin de St. Croix and a Dr. MacDonald.[10] Dr. John Mackieson arrived in 1821 to begin a long and distinguished career that only ended with his death in 1885. During that period, he served as medical superintendent of the lunatic asylum and the port health officer. Dr. William Hobkirk emigrated from London, England, in 1838 and also practised until his death in 1888. He, too, was the port health and quarantine officer.

The significance of the port as a factor in public health is obvious, given the stale, cramped conditions on the ocean-going vessels of the day. Passengers with illnesses could be on board for days before their symptoms presented themselves, and by then many others could have been infected. Standard practice was to have arriving vessels remain in quarantine for a number of days before passengers were landed, just to avoid the possibility of the spread of disease to the townsfolk. Even then, mistakes were made. In the case of the *Lady Constable*, bearing famine Irish from Ulster in 1847, the vessel was allowed to dock without being quarantined. Unfortunately, some 50 of the passengers were suffering from typhus, and, as the vessel disgorged its sick and dying, panic hit the streets. The ill were confined to a temporary quarantine hospital, where 12 died, and were then transferred to the new lunatic asylum, where another 11 succumbed.

Proper drinking water and waste disposal are critical aspects of public health in any community. Lord Selkirk, when he visited Charlottetown in 1803, commented in his diary that "the water – is from Pumps and I never tasted finer." A number of pumps were placed in convenient locations such as Queen Square. In periods of drought, citizens had recourse to the natural spring found in the Common at Spring Park, which lay north of the town by the Prince Town (Malpeque) Road. Problems arose with the passage of time. Open cesspools or drywells, often the source of bad odours and pollutants, tainted nearby wells. A prescient John Lawson, though, noted in 1851 that the lay of the land and the presence of nearby rivers would allow the inhabitants "at some future day" to construct sewers that would drain the town "completely."

10 Dr. de St. Croix died in Charlottetown in 1848.

George Hubbard's watercolour of Queen Square, 1849. Note the public pump in the foreground.

Fire was the mortal enemy of a wooden city, and its containment was a matter of general interest. Until 1827, fires were fought on an *ad hoc* basis, but in that year the colonial legislature authorized the formation of a fire engine company. After 1830, residents were obliged by law to keep a two-gallon leather bucket hanging at the ready in each house. Eventually, firefighting was managed by 18 fire wardens, two for each of 9 wards, who were given extensive powers to draft assistants and enter property when combatting blazes, as well as the authority to ensure fire hazards were removed. Fire services were provided by volunteers, with positions of command reflecting prominent social status. Despite the ever-present danger, citizens tended to do without fire insurance, an indication, perhaps, that the danger of a major conflagration remained low in a community spread out over a large area.

The Road to Incorporation

For the first 90 years of its existence, Charlottetown was governed through the Colonial Legislature. Civic politics reflected the town's central role in Island life. The issues were the overriding colonial problems of the day: struggles over land tenure and debates over the role of the governor and his advisors. Sectarian disputes were a particular threat in a community so evenly divided between Protestants and Roman Catholics, although the two groups lived and worked together and generally tried to foster a tolerant atmosphere. When local questions arose, they concerned regulation of trade, control of animals running loose and other apparently mundane matters.

In a community that grew its own food, restraint of a neighbour's greedy hog was an item of some importance.

The growth in population meant that some administrative approaches that worked when the community was small became less practical. Towards the mid-19th century, Charlottetonians were increasingly frustrated by slow, haphazard justice, polluted wells, unkempt streets and squares, poor ferry services and other annoyances. While direct rule by the colony's government had its problems, it had one decided merit: it was cheap. Merchants and wealthy property-owners were not burdened by substantial taxes and were well-placed to protect their interests within the existing structure of government. Incorporation would permit the local Council to borrow money against the property tax base for local improvements. This was seen as a threat to personal finances as well as an opportunity for civic advancement.[11]

Two basic weaknesses appeared in the town's governance by the 1850s. One was the need for the colonial government to attend to municipal concerns. Local matters were regulated by orders of the Governor in Council or by acts of the Legislative Assembly. The legislature dealt with Charlottetown's business when requested by the colonial executive or petitioned by individual members, government officials, influential citizens or the press. Unfortunately, it often failed to assign high priority to these matters. Quite naturally, rural members were more concerned with the views of their constituents than the well-being of Charlottetonians, particularly when the expenditure of general revenues was involved. Given the preponderance of rural members of the legislature, when urban issues were addressed, they were generally resolved in ways that suited rural voters.

The reliance placed upon volunteers for the provision of essential services was a second weakness, particularly when people selected to fill important duties sought to avoid their responsibilities. Underpinning the reliance on volunteer services was the belief that all citizens should labour for the community or pay financial penalties.

Two events, however, propelled the question of incorporation to the fore. Firstly, the granting of responsible government in 1851 increased Islanders' interest in direct political involvement. Then in 1853 London decided to remove the garrison – soldiers who represented the true guarantee of law and order in Charlottetown. Their departure in 1854 made the question of police protection urgent. It was not a coincidence, therefore, that the colonial legislature considered incorporation in 1853 and again in 1854. Creating the City of Charlottetown in 1855 was an expedient way to address these new circumstances.

The prospect of the new municipality excited no one and worried more than a few. Some property-owners feared that municipal taxes would be high, a result perhaps of wasteful expenditures incurred on behalf of tenants. Liberals were alarmed that the Conservatives, who were powerful in Charlottetown, would dominate city councils and use them for partisan political purposes. Ironically, the incorporation

11 The good burghers of Charlottetown were far from unique in their concerns about taxation. In March 1834, a bill in the Newfoundland legislature to establish a town council and police force for St. John's was defeated by local merchants fearing higher taxes.

bill, introduced by a Liberal government, received its strongest support from Tories. Many rural Liberals were basically uninterested in the issue, and even Conservatives reflected considerable ambivalence. Ultimately, both sides agreed to tolerate the measure, and it passed. *Haszard's Gazette*, edited by the soon-to-be-appointed City Recorder, regarded the first election as "a memorable day" and expected increased prosperity to accrue from municipal incorporation. Other journals showed more restraint, merely hoping that some improvements in the level of services might result.

The provisions under the Act of Incorporation mirrored these circumstances. City expenditures were limited to a maximum of £1,000; borrowing could not exceed £5,000. These limits could be broken only under exceptional conditions and after approval by the Legislature.

Five wards were established, each returning two members to the Common Council.[12] Male British subjects over 21 were granted the franchise if they had resided in the city for the previous year, and in the ward in which they intended to vote for the previous two months. They had to own or rent property of a certain value, and their taxes could not be in arrears.[13] The property qualifications were not unduly onerous; an elector had to own real estate with an annual value of £5 within his constituency or be a tenant paying an annual rent of £5. The bar was higher for persons aspiring to be mayor or Councillor. The mayor was required to own £500 worth of real estate in the city; Councillors had to own property valued at £200 or be a tenant with a total annual rent of £40.[14] One particular article of incorporation was to have a significant impact on the new city's future political life: the newly elected Councillors were to draw lots at the last meeting before the first Tuesday in August 1856 to determine five of their number, one from each ward, to "go out of office" prior to elections scheduled for the second Tuesday of that month. Annually thereafter, the mayor and the five Councillors who had served the longest without re-election had to face the polls. That set in motion a system in which Council was composed of five newly elected members and five continuing members. Shifts in public opinion which influenced an election might thus be frustrated by the obstruction of sitting Councillors whose views might differ from the current trend. Council would convene on a quarterly basis, and each session could not last longer than three days. Special meetings of Council could be called by the mayor, or by three Councillors or more, as required.

---

12 Ward boundaries followed major east-west streets. Ward One lay south of Dorchester Street, Ward Two included the blocks between Dorchester and Richmond Streets, and Ward Three ran from Richmond to Grafton Street. Ward Four lay between Grafton and Fitzroy Streets, and Ward Five included everything north of Fitzroy Street, including Charlottetown Common.

13 The generous franchise requirements were in place as early as 1806 when John Stewart reported that all Protestant housekeepers and proprietors could vote or run for office.

14 In 1871, £1 was equivalent to $4.87. In 1870, £5 would buy a cow or eight gallons of wine. Requirements for the franchise varied throughout British North America. In Ottawa voters had to be freeholders of property valued at £36 or leaseholders paying £6. In Saint John all freemen and freeholders could vote until 1855 when a colonial franchise required voters to be assessed for £25, or own property worth £100 or have an income of £100. More was typically required of office-holders. In Ottawa they had to own property valued at £300. Charlottetown's requirements seem to have reflected the norms of the day.

Property values and hence taxes were established annually by a city assessor. A City Marshall was appointed and, under him, a full-time constable for each ward. Other appointments included a recorder (clerk), treasurer, harbour master, wharfingers, pound keeper and a surveyor of roads and bridges. City Council was to be composed of a mayor and two Councillors from each of five wards elected annually in August. Their jurisdiction included commerce, shipping, animal control, sanitary and health standards, poor relief and public morality. The mayor, recorder and one Councillor were empowered to sit as a court for cases involving fines of up to £10 or imprisonment to 30 days.

There was a curious lack of enthusiasm marking the commencement of Charlottetown's existence as a city. There was none of the bravado later associated with the creation of cities on the western frontier. This was partly due to the passage of 90 years of history before incorporation. Granting of a city charter represented an administrative adjustment rather than a heroic beginning. By 1855, Charlottetonians had developed a community ethos; it was one that made few allowances for extravagant expectations. Despite their recent prosperity, they had confronted the limitations imposed by geography on their potential for growth and prosperity. They understood their city was on the periphery of North America's economic mainstream and drew upon a bountiful but restricted hinterland. Optimism was muted by an apprehension of scarcity, made real periodically by the cyclical economic down-turns experienced since the opening of the century.

During most of the following decades, this sense of scarcity was to be gradually but tentatively displaced by a belief in some abundance. There was still an absence of unbounded confidence, expansionary drive, the entrepreneurial assumption of risks and the extravagant demands for civic services found in the newer towns of Ontario and the West. Even the purposeful determination to be masters in their own house displayed by the Halifax local elite when that city was incorporated in 1841 was missing.[15] Civic government was expected to be frugal, and senior governments, particularly the federal after Confederation, were summoned to redress the imbalance that geography and economics had imposed upon the Island capital. Whenever Charlottetonians achieved a sense of communal well-being, it was manifested by a contentment born of a slim hand well-played. Nobody swaggered. Civic misfortunes prompted similarly restrained responses. In such cases, affairs were seen as badly managed, and leadership was regarded as wanting. Self-criticism flowed freely, but there was little despair. At the very least Charlottetown would remain a capital and the county seat of a prosperous farming area. If the citizenry missed the exuberance of boosters, they also lacked the fear of failure that must lurk in the hearts of pioneers.

15 Enthusiasm for local government soon dissipated in the Nova Scotian capital, as it, too, came to grips with the implications that limited taxing powers had for the pace with which municipal improvements could be made.

CHAPTER 2

Struggle

1855-79

The decision to incorporate Charlottetown as a city was a major step in the evolution of governance on Prince Edward Island. It recognized that the affairs of the compact colony could no longer be adequately managed solely by the colonial government with the assistance of three lean county administrations. In creating the city, the government shed important and costly responsibilities but refrained from providing its new creation with adequate fiscal resources. With a mandate bigger than its means, Charlottetown's civic administration was dogged for years by financial problems. Indeed, disputes over money became an ongoing feature of the relationship between the city and the senior level of government.

The root of the problem lay in the distrust felt by the rural majority of Islanders for the city and its residents. Hardworking, economically vulnerable farmers resented the life of ease apparently enjoyed by the merchants and office-holders of the capital. Many believed wealth to be finite; that one man's gain came at the expense of another. The perceived prosperity of the money-lenders and land agents was regarded with jealousy. If there was to be a city, rural politicians were determined it would have minimal impact on the colonial exchequer. Property-owners within the city were equally adamant that real property taxes be kept absolutely as low as possible. At the same time, farmers wanted the city to serve their needs as a market centre and an entrepôt for their exports, and Charlottetown's burghers demanded the improvements that typified cities in the mid-Victorian age. Ultimately, both sides were obliged to realize that urban progress had to be paid for.

POPULATION GROWTH AND ETHNIC RELATIONSHIPS

During its early years, the axiom that Charlottetown flourishes as the Island prospers seems to have been borne out by population growth. The town had a population of 416 in 1798, 2,063 in 1827, 3,896 in 1841 and 6,513 in 1855. Throughout, Charlottetonians represented a steady eight to nine per cent of Prince Edward Islanders. The 1840s and 50s, the Island's "golden age," were a time of particularly rapid expansion. By the time of incorporation, Charlottetown was the 13th largest city in British North America, slightly bigger than St. Catharines, Canada West, and a bit smaller than Cobourg, Canada West, and Trois Rivières, Canada East. In 1873, when the Island entered Confederation, the city's 8,807 people made it the 11th city in size in the new dominion, a position maintained in the census of 1881, when its population of 11,485 was smaller than that of Kingston, Ontario, but considerably greater than the next largest community, Guelph, Ontario, and three other provincial capitals, Victoria, Winnipeg and Fredericton.[1] The city's population growth mirrored that of mid-century Prince Edward Island's and, in addition, benefitted somewhat from migration from the countryside. After this time, while the proportion of Islanders who lived in Charlottetown grew and the city's population expanded accordingly, the overall decline in the province's population resulted in Charlottetown slipping in the order of Canadian cities.[2]

Prior to the 19th century, most of the population were English or Irish in origin, with a smattering of Acadians, and, after the arrival of the Loyalists in 1782, people of Dutch and German origin. A few colonial officials owned black slaves, and, with the arrival of the Loyalists, free blacks, as well as more slaves, were added to the population. The majority were adherents of the Church of England, ministered to by the Rector of Charlotte Parish, Rev. Theophilus DesBrisay. Although over a third of the colony's population was Roman Catholic, very few lived in town at this time. In 1799 Father J-L-J de Calonne, a French émigré, arrived as their priest, but he was gone by 1804. Neither group appears to have been especially devout. DesBrisay performed his duties for years in homes or taverns, despite an attempt by Bishop John Inglis in 1789 to pressure local Anglicans into erecting a church.

The ethnic composition of the community evolved with the influx of immigrants. Nineteenth-century immigration included Scots and, most notably, Irish Roman Catholics. At the same time, natural increase became a significant demographic factor. By 1855, 59.1 per cent of the inhabitants were born in Prince Edward Island, and this percentage grew to 77.5 per cent in 1881. Of the others in 1855, 15.3 per cent were from Ireland, 9.5 per cent from England, 4.0 per cent from Scotland and 11.1 per cent from the rest of British North America. In 1881 those numbers were 4.7 per cent Ireland, 4.1 per cent England, 1.9 per cent Scotland and 10 per cent Canada and Newfoundland. A smattering of people came from other places, and, among the Island-born, there were numbers of Acadians. Among this population in 1855, the census for Charlottetown and the royalty listed 2,669 Roman Catholics, 1,539 Anglicans, 1,202 Methodists, 931 Presbyterians and 168 Baptists. By 1871 there were 3,328 Roman Catholics, 1,602 Presbyterians, 1,507 Anglicans, 1,791 Methodists, 272 Bible Christians and 256 Baptists. The large number of Roman Catholics bore witness to the significance of people with Irish origins, who constituted 40 per cent of the city's population. Incorporation, of course, had little impact on the population structure, which was remarkably homogeneous, based squarely as it was upon the Island's essentially British stock. Charlottetown exhibited little of the ethnic diversity that was beginning to creep into other Canadian centres.

---

1 St. John's, Newfoundland, was also larger, making Charlottetown 12th in British North America.

2 In 1855, 9.1 per cent of Prince Edward Island's population lived in Charlottetown; in 1881, the number had grown to 10.5 per cent.

The ongoing presence of the small Black community was an interesting exception to this demographic uniformity. It remained concentrated in the low-lying marshy area on the western outskirts known as "The Bog," but was entering a period of decline after 1855. Most were Island-born, like their white counterparts, and were largely descendants of slaves brought to Prince Edward Island in the aftermath of the American Revolution. The census of 1881 identified 84 residents of Charlottetown as being "African" in origin, but only 7 were born outside the province. Four were from Nova Scotia, one from each of Barbados and Bermuda, and one from an uncertain location. Outmigration and intermarriage with the dominant population were gradually reducing their numbers.

The gender balance in Charlottetown differed markedly from the Island's overall population. In 1855 there were 102 males to every 100 females on the Island, but in the city and royalty the ratio was 94 to 100. This imbalance grew. In 1881 the ratio was 101 to 100 for the province, but 90 to 100 in Charlottetown and the royalty – 88 to 100 in the city itself. Part of the explanation for this situation may be the migration of women to the city to seek employment as domestics or in other suitable occupations, but part may lie in another set of statistics. The relative size of various age groups in the city was reasonably balanced between males and females throughout the period 1855-81 with two notable exceptions. There was a substantial imbalance of males and females for those aged 15 to 20 in 1855, and for those aged 21 to 44 in 1855, 1861 and 1871. The relatively low numbers of men suggest outmigration of single males in this period, a portent, perhaps, of future economic stagnation.

A final population trend emerged after 1855 in what was to become a significant factor in the city's evolution. At the time of incorporation, approximately 8 per cent of those living within Charlottetown and the royalty lived in the latter. By 1861 over 9 per cent lived in the royalty. This grew to 10.6 per cent in 1871 and declined somewhat to just under 10 per cent in 1881. Suburban development, however, was clearly a feature of urban life which would be increasingly important in the years ahead.

POLITICAL LIFE

The first civic election was held on August 7, 1855. As specified in the Act of Incorporation, once the poll was declared open by the returning officer, voters presented themselves and stated their choices for mayor and councillor. A voter could name any qualified citizen, and his choice was entered into the poll book. Entry of a name was effectively the nomination, although candidates were customarily canvassed by their friends and supporters before election day to indicate their willingness or not to let their name stand. Occasionally, persons received votes without their knowledge or wish to serve in office, and the practice of having a nomination day prior to the vote was eventually adopted. Electors could have their eligibility challenged by onlookers, in which case the returning officer would question the potential voter about his qualifications and perhaps require him to take an oath. If objections persisted, the poll clerk would note in his book that the vote had been objected to by the person in question. Voters who were suspected of being in arrears with their taxes had to produce

Elected by acclamation, "plain rough Bob Hutchison" was the new city's first mayor.

a tax receipt, without which the name of the voter and the vote were struck from the poll book.

Expectations, if there were any, that incorporation would result in the speedy resolution of the multitude of challenges faced by the community were soon dashed. So, too, was the goodwill extended by many to the new city fathers. Following Robert Hutchison's election by acclamation, he and his 10-member council set about the task of establishing the framework of city government. While 32 by-laws were passed in the first year, the pace of legislation was slow at first. Only four months after the engine of civic administration lurched into motion, the *Examiner* complained that just three or four by-laws had been passed, and that these were "distinguished for nothing at all original or extraordinary." The "filthy streets," "ancient deep and dirty gutters," "rotten and ricketty [*sic*] side-walks," the public squares "lacking traces of progressive civilization" and the "little antiquated" market house proved that "nearly every thing stands just as it did before the Corporation had an existence." In searching for reasons for this inaction, the paper cited as possibilities a slow Recorder who drafted the laws, an inattentive colonial Executive Council that had to review them or City Councillors who had little spare time for official business.[3] The one excuse the paper rejected was the one proposed by the city's administration as the root of inaction: lack of money. The editor believed only evidence of some solid improvement in civic services would justify the increased taxation already being contemplated by the city fathers. Others were not so critical. The editor of *The Weekly Advertiser*, an early opponent of incorporation, was impressed with limited, but welcome, improvements to portions of the Princetown Road and Euston Street, as well as efforts to clean up the vicinity of the market house. Thanks to the presence of a police force, there were also fewer disturbances at night. These accomplishments had been done without incurring debt or increasing taxes.

Although the performance of Mayor Hutchison and his Council had converted some doubters, civic life was still marred by political bickering. Hutchison, a Conservative who had managed to deflect Thomas Heath Haviland, Sr., from running for Mayor in the first election, was no stranger to controversy. His previous activities as

3 The paper was partly correct. W. B. Wellner, who performed clerical tasks for the city, claimed that most of the by-laws were "manufactured" by the mayor and himself because the Councillors had dumped the job on them.

Hutchison asked fellow-Conservative Thomas Heath Haviland not to run against him in the 1855 election. When Haviland decided to seek the office in 1857, he defeated Hutchison handily. Though he sometimes had to be persuaded by supporters to stand for re-election, Haviland remained in the office until his death in 1867.

an opponent of the reform-minded Governor, Sir Henry Vere Huntley, and public feuds involving his service as a Justice of the Peace, marked Hutchison as a doughty political scrapper. He was accused, however, of siding with Liberal interests in his initial term as Mayor. He, himself, claimed that "plain rough Bob Hutchison" was "determined to uphold the rights of the poor so they shall not be trodden upon by the wealthy as they have been" and for that reason had earned the enmity of the town's elite.[4] In the election of 1856, Hutchison was forced to run as a Liberal against John C. Binns and endured a campaign that featured some pretty nasty politics. When Hutchison canvassed William Henry Pope, the latter responded Hutchison could have his vote and many others if he would turn all the dogs and "Monaghans" (Roman Catholic Irish) out of Charlottetown. In an attempt to limit Hutchison's support, Recorder John Lawson denied the franchise to all who were unable to produce receipts for their assessments. Some voters had misplaced the documents; Lawson instructed the tax collector not to issue duplicates. Lawson also tried to block the candidature of John Riggs for Councillor in Ward 1 on the grounds that he was the city auditor and thus ineligible to hold a second paid civic office. Riggs, however, anticipating this, resigned as auditor and paid his £5 penalty for abandoning his duties in time to contest and win the election. Even "the drunken painter," Henry B. Smith, won Ward 5 over Tory stalwart T. B. Tremain.

The victory of "The Monaghan Mayor" and other Liberal candidates for Council prompted observers to conclude that if the Liberals could win the city with a modest property qualification, they could certainly win the city's seats in the colonial legislature with suffrage for all adult male residents. Liberal joy, however, was short-lived. In the election the following year, the highly influential Thomas Heath Haviland, Sr., entered the fray and beat Hutchison. Conservative candidates for Council also did well, giving the Tories the upper hand in city government. The fate of William Murphy is instructive. The manager of the Charlottetown Gas Light Company, a candidate in Ward 2, and, ultimately, a successful member of the civic administration,

4 This was reported in *The Weekly Advertiser* as a heated conversation between Hutchison and Peter Macgowan who was accused of favouring the likes of Daniel Brennen, James Peake and Heath Haviland.

Murphy campaigned on the platform of his work experience in an engineer's office and his lack of affiliation with either political party. He lost. The *Examiner*, perhaps ruefully, noted that the Liberals "wisely" stood aside from the contest because the city's government was so unpopular that there was difficulty finding reasons why a politician would take on work that provided so little thanks in return. Citizens, the paper noted, were grumbling about being overtaxed when the city's services showed no improvement.

Haviland's victory inaugurated a decade-long stay in office, ended only by his death on June 18, 1867. During this period, some steps were taken to improve the level of services in Charlottetown, but effective civic government was hampered by the ongoing restrictions on tax revenue. Even so, Charlottetonians apparently felt that taxes were too high for what they got in return. There was a belief that the administration was wasting money, although the *Examiner* noted that salaries paid to the Mayor, Clerk and Recorder were miserly. That paper, formerly a backer of incorporation, openly questioned the utility of maintaining local government. The former situation, it argued, produced few advancements in services but was at least cheap to run. Voter apathy reflected a general lack of esteem for city offices. Turnouts for the annual elections

This early photograph shows town crier John Hatch and several members of the much-maligned police force outside the first City Hall.

were low — in 1859 only 40 or 50 voters exercised their franchise — and many posts were filled by acclamation. Mayor Haviland, himself, declined to run again in the election of 1862 and only agreed at the last minute to let his name stand when his supporters appealed to him a second time. Towards the end of his time in office, City Council benefitted from two agreements with the Colonial government. In 1865 the Assembly set aside £1,000 for the construction of a new market house, and in 1866 it provided £300 for the purchase of a new steam fire engine.

These grants indicated that the city fathers were finally attempting seriously to address major challenges, such as fire protection and market regulation. Nevertheless, services in these areas tended to be valued most when they were seen to be most needed. For instance, a rash of arson attempts in 1867 provoked a demand for more effective policing. Generally, the few men comprising the police force were dismissed by citizens as buffoons, swelling about town in blue uniforms and bright brass buttons, but incapable of keeping the city's rowdy element or even wandering animals in check. In the face of this new threat, however, the force was expanded. While much of the business of Council remained routine, even trivial, in nature, the flow of requests for road maintenance and installation of streetlights and similar matters meant that by 1868 meetings were being held on a monthly, rather than the required quarterly, basis. That same year, the city received permission from the colonial government to add a special assessment on real estate for road and sidewalk construction. Whether the death of Haviland, a major landowner and opponent of taxes, contributed to the city's willingness to consider increased taxation is a matter of speculation. Three years later, the Legislative Assembly authorized the colonial government to redeem £1,500 of Charlottetown's debentures and to pay another £500 in interest charges and other expenses. As the financial impact and the utility of the city's activities increased, interest in elections and Council proceedings grew somewhat and the tone surrounding discussions of the conduct of city affairs became a bit more respectful.

Looming over all other issues were the twin matters of water service and taxation. In 1874 William Murphy ran again in Ward 2, this time on the issue of water supply. He lost once again, but the following year a group calling themselves the "Water Works Promoters Association" ran a slate of candidates including Murphy, this time in Ward 1, and Theophilus DesBrisay for Mayor. DesBrisay and three of the Association's five candidates for Council, including Murphy, were elected. For the next few years the water issue was hotly debated, opening the split between those advocating civic improvements and others who wanted to keep taxes low. In 1876 changes to the legislation governing Charlottetown gave the city the right to raise revenue to any extent and in any way. This was a major shift in tax policy. At incorporation, the city was given power to tax both freehold and leasehold property, but these were later changed to have taxes apply only to rentals to a maximum amount of one shilling, six pence per pound of rent. Placing the tax burden on the shoulders of tenants, many of whom were poor householders, was a prescription for injustice and civic impoverishment. Faced with the possibility of substantial tax hikes, a group of concerned property-owners banded together in 1877 and nominated their own candidates, including

Jedediah Slason Carvell's first official dealings with the city were in a lawsuit over the boundary line between his property and Pownal Wharf. In 1877 he won election as mayor, and before the end of a remarkable political career also served as a Senator and Lieutenant Governor.

J. S. Carvell to replace retiring Mayor DesBrisay. Their program of retrenchment for the election of 1878 included a call that City Councillors be required to own substantial holdings of real estate as a means of ensuring frugal spending and low taxes. They complained that salaries of city officials were too high and that the police force was now too large. City accounts, which were closed at the end of the calendar year, were incomplete at elections and therefore not of much use to voters considering future expenditures. Taxpayers exacerbated the situation. In 1878 the total expenditures of the city were $60,936.42. Taxes totalling $21,117.54 constituted the single largest source of revenue, but at year's end, $10,777.55 or 49 per cent were unpaid. When $1,919.43 outstanding from the previous year were added, expenditures exceeded income by $11,356.09. The unresolved tension between improvement to services and low taxes became the principal dynamic of civic politics.

URBAN LANDSCAPE

Many factors would mould the physical landscape of Charlottetown after the mid-19th century. The original influence of the surveyors and government officials in determining the shape of the settlement had gradually yielded to the forces of private enterprise — shipyards, workshops and stores — and of individuals building houses and residential outbuildings. To these factors must be added fire, the mortal threat of Victorian wooden cities. Incorporation was a major step in reasserting the place of the state in the town's governance, but in accordance with current attitudes, this role was by no means intended to be a highly active one. While there was much to do to provide the new city with an infrastructure appropriate for its size, the community was still largely contained within its original town plan. Some residences had been established in the Common, but they were largely estates dispersed over a wide area. Intensive development of the Common with new streets and closely spaced housing came only in the last quarter of the century.

Even at the centre of the city, extensive gaps remained in the streetscape. In the early years, especially after incorporation, vacant lots were plentiful. Open vistas abounded where one was able to see complete buildings several blocks away, simply by looking through gaps between the intervening buildings. Most structures, even shops and warehouses, were wooden. Use of brick increased as the 19th century wore

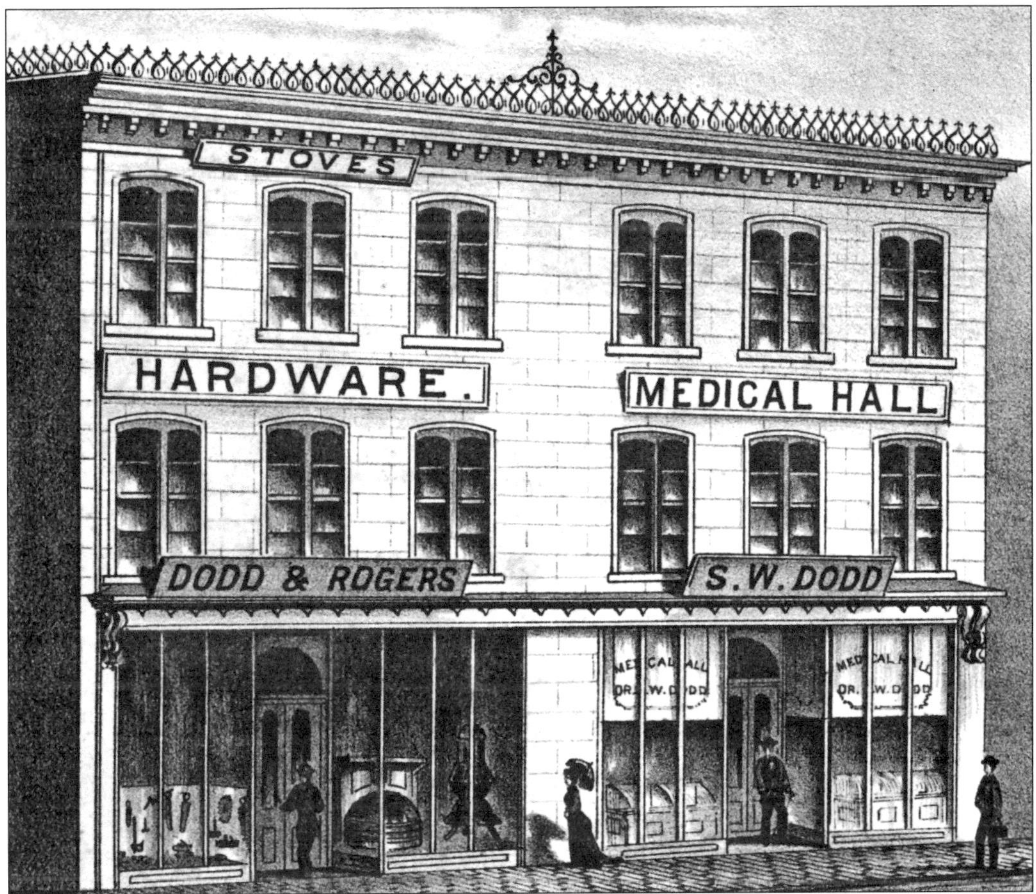

Thomas Dodd and Benjamin Rogers built their brick building in 1867. Thomas' brother, Dr. Simon Dodd, opened the pharmacy seen in this engraving from Meacham's 1880 Atlas.

on, particularly after 1866 when fire cut a swath between Water and Dorchester Streets from Pownal Street almost to Great George Street. Possession of a brick building, however, remained a matter of note and a consumer of scarce capital. A newspaper notice appearing in 1871 alerted the public to the commencement of operations of the Merchants Bank "in their new brick building" on Water Street. Early the next year, an advertisement announced the opening of the Medical Hall, a pharmacy, in "Dodd & Rogers Brick Building" at the corner of Queen and Grafton Streets, and when George L. Dogherty moved his furniture store to the north side of King Square, a newspaper notice positioned it as "nearly opposite Welsh & Owen's Brick Building." Lack of zoning meant that residences, stables, commercial establishments and workshops were jumbled together. King Square, for instance, boasted some very respectable homes, but it was also the location of Archibald White's forge and machine shop, the store of Messrs. Beer and Son and Mark Butcher's furniture warehouse. A bizarre example of the kind of incompatible use to which land could be put was provided by the offer of William McGill to convey a piece of land, free of charge, for use as a temporary fish market. The property adjoined the home of one of the city's doctors.[5]

The first item of business for the new city government was to find itself a home. An inaugural meeting of Council was held on August 11, 1855, at Mayor Hutchison's house on the corner of Sydney and Pownal Streets. Subsequent meetings were conducted in the Supreme Court Room of the Colonial Building. Permanent facilities were needed, and the old John Plaw-designed Court House and Legislature on Queen Square was deemed satisfactory. By 1855 the building had fallen on hard times and was serving as the flour and meal market. When Henry Haszard offered the city a building on Great George Street for the flour market, the old courthouse was cleaned and occupied as a city hall and police station. The first Council meeting held there was on December 21, 1855.

One of the most urgent issues faced by the city in its early days was the state of the market square, as that part of Queen Square was unofficially called. The area had justly earned a reputation as a blight on the civic landscape. Heaps of litter, obnoxious smells and disorder offended the eyes, noses and ears of the citizens. In addition, the colonial government was concerned about the noise and congestion beside its handsome new legislative building, which had been opened in 1847. Within a few weeks of its creation, City Council authorized the employment of one or two workers to "remove the filth about the market house and to improve the sanitary condition of said market house."

The venerable round market house itself was a concern for Charlottetonians. By 1855 it was 32 years old and showing considerable and rapidly worsening signs of age. Two years later, George Lewis, the market clerk, reported that leaks in the roof and under the cupola were causing the plaster to crumble and fall. On one occasion, a large patch fell on a butcher, Joseph Crabbe, spoiling his hat and ruining some of his meat. An equally serious concern was the effect the "dilapidated and inconvenient" building had upon civic revenues. Stalls inside the market could be rented for a sum of at least £4 annually, but this income was in jeopardy if the butchers and others declined to bid and instead joined the hucksters and country butchers who offered their produce for sale outside free of any charge. Moreover, commerce outside the market house was difficult to control, and regulation of the practices and standards of trade in food was one of the important duties of the city government. Whatever his displeasure about his hat may have been, Crabbe renewed his stall rental for another year, as he is listed in 1858 along with nine others paying an annual rent of £4-1-0. Significantly, two stalls were empty. In 1858 Lewis warned that without a charge for vendors in the square, "the revenue derived from the market house must diminish if not fail." He was right; the number of unleased stalls was to grow over the next few years until, by 1864, only three were occupied.

Talk soon turned to the need for a new market building, the city's first major public works initiative. Council favoured putting it near the site of the present one. They were

5 Similarly, two tanneries stood near the Lieutenant Governor's residence.

Though Isaac Smith won the design competition for a new market hall, City Council decided his handsome brick edifice would be too costly to build. Instead they turned to Councillor Mark Butcher, a local furniture manufacturer, to come up with a cheaper design. Butcher's wooden market house opened in 1867.

supported in this by merchants who had opened shops on the surrounding streets, but relocation was also a possibility. After the Lieutenant-Governor in Council rejected their request for a grant of land at the western end of the Square, Council asked for financial aid to purchase land elsewhere. Some public opinion favoured moving the market to the waterfront, where garbage could be deposited into the harbour to be carried away by the ebbing tide. Consideration was also given to a location at the edge of town, and other sites were mentioned, including King Square, Hillsborough Square and a lot at the corner of Queen and Grafton Streets opposite Queen Square. The suitability and expense of available properties were obstacles to a move. Rural members of the legislature, in particular, objected to a financial grant, a factor that, in time, encouraged their support for giving a piece of Queen Square to the city. Country folk, moreover, resented comments about the sights and smells of the market as implied criticism of their presence in the capital. Opponents of a market on Queen Square wanted to fence and landscape the area as a park, thereby providing the city with a refined centre and the legislature with a worthy setting. To offset the cost of purchasing another site, backers of relocation raised a subscription of £1,500. Despite this, in 1861 the colonial government finally approved a site at the westernmost portion of Queen Square, near the round market. Legislators tended to agree with Roderick MacAulay when he commented, "As a comparatively poor community, we should first secure the useful, and afterwards, when our means enable us, we might indulge our taste for the ornamental." Proponents of civic beautification subsequently attempted to have the location switched to a lot adjoining the south side of Queen Square owned by Lady Wood, a daughter of Lieutenant Governor Fanning. They failed, but the cause of beautification was advanced in 1867 by having a new street opened between the market house and the rest of Queen Square. The land on which the market stood then officially became Market Square.

Once the site was settled, the city opened a competition for plans for the new market building. The winner was Isaac Smith, designer of the Colonial Building, who submitted plans for a handsome brick edifice. Smith's market was never built. In a sequence of events that were to become all-too-familiar, the city issued £5,000 of debentures to pay for the work, only to find little demand for them. City fathers blamed the scarcity of liquid capital on the Island and the lack of city-owned land and other property to act as collateral.[6] Alexander Brown offered to take the debenture if it were guaranteed by the colonial government, which the city asked for, and was denied. Legislators feared the colony would end up redeeming the debt. Certainly, opponents pointed to the debt's £300 per annum interest as an intolerably large sum for local taxpayers to bear. Some thought such costs could be covered by reducing civic salaries, but that was easier said than done. Eventually, the colony granted the city £1,000 to help pay for construction. The debate had involved several factions: rural residents who wanted a new market but did not want to help pay for it, the majority of Charlottetonians who preferred a new building on Queen Square and who felt the financial burden for a common facility should be supported from general colonial revenue, and a part of the urban elite who still opposed the selected site and used the argument over money to delay work on the project. The grant was a compromise more or less acceptable to all.

Work commenced in 1865, prompting the *Examiner* to comment "some spell has come over Charlottetown at last." Not only was there to be a new market house, but City Council decided to locate a hay market on King and a wood market on Rochford Square. A fish market was to be installed near one of the city wharves.[7] Completion of the main market house was set for September 1866, but instead of following the expensive Smith plan, one for a cheaper, wooden structure costing £2,000 was used.

---

6 In cities that taxed real property, the property tax base was considered collateral, but taxes on rents denied Charlottetown this option.

7 The fish market was an orphan because of its smell and was moved to various locations. Four years later, the *Examiner* noted that a fish market was to open in the basement of J. C. Pope's warehouse.

Designed by Mark Butcher, a local furniture manufacturer and City Councillor, the new market opened in January 1867. It was a long, narrow, two-storey building with extra spaces in the basement. Centre gables on the long sides facing Richmond and Grafton Streets gave the façade some interest and an appearance that vaguely resembled the Colonial Building to the east. Surmounting the roof was a cupola, the weight of which unfortunately soon caused sagging that needed to be buttressed from below. The ground floor had sections for meat, farm produce, meal and flour. The upper floor was fitted up as an assembly room that could seat up to 800. Although the building was plain, it was large, justifying stall-rental fees at least twice as high as in the round market. To protect the tenants, sale of meat, game, poultry, bulk amounts of farm produce, grain and flour was prohibited except in the market house and, with the exception of stall tenants, people bringing such products to the market were subjected to specified tolls. Even the second-floor hall contributed revenue through rental fees. Income from the market became a significant item in the city budget, rising to almost 11 per cent of the total in 1870.

Income from stall rentals became a significant item in the city budget.

The building was expanded in 1876 to accommodate the city's administrative offices.

In 1872 the civic offices were moved next door to the market house, and the erstwhile city hall was sold and transported to Euston Street. Plans were soon under way to expand the market building to provide better accommodations for the city administration. The municipality asked the colonial government to give it ownership of the old city hall site so an extension of the market could be erected. This request met some hostility from influential citizens worried about the nature and extent of the proposed addition. Consequently, despite the government's approval for the transfer in 1873, construction did not begin immediately. An initial design prepared by David Stirling was set aside, and in 1874 Thomas Alley drafted plans for an extension measuring 75 to 80 feet by 47 feet to sit as a "T" at the western end of the market building. What finally emerged in 1876 was a simple bump extending the market building to Queen Street. Surmounting this addition was a tower for the city's new fire bell, "Big Donald."

Despite the cupola and tower on the market house, church spires remained the dominant feature of Charlottetown's skyline in this period. St. Dunstan's Cathedral, facing Dorchester Street, had a single, prominent spire, which, in 1856 was provided with a clock for the benefit of the townsfolk. Zion Presbyterian, a smaller building, was on Richmond Street facing Queen Square, kitty-corner from St. Paul's Anglican, which sat at the eastern end of the square. The period following incorporation was one of ambitious church construction. The city's Wesleyans constructed a massive new church in 1863-64. Designed by Thomas Alley and intended to seat 1,200, it had a massive façade featuring twin slender spires. In 1872 work was begun on an impressive residence for the Roman Catholic Bishop of Charlottetown, but it was completed only in 1875. Then, in 1878 the old St. James Kirk was replaced with a large new building with a soaring spire. The same year, the Disciples of Christ built their house of worship on Malpeque Road. St. Peter's Anglican on Rochford Square opened the following year, introducing, in both its architecture and liturgy, the precepts of the Oxford Movement to the Island. On December 14, 1879, an entirely different place of worship was opened by the Baptists at the corner of Prince and Fitzroy Streets. The distinctive brick-and-stone building, also designed by Thomas Alley, was octagonal in shape and featured a ceiling supported by 20 groined arches sitting atop pillars. The tower at the front of the church rose 112 feet.

Three other landmarks owed their existence to the Roman Catholic Church. In January 1855, St. Dunstan's College, just outside the city, received its first students. Work had started on the building as early as 1844 and was barely completed by opening day. The poverty of the local diocese caused construction to drag on, but the final structure was imposing enough. It was wooden, three storeys in height and topped by a sharp-pitched gabled roof that was, in turn, surmounted by a cupola. The exterior walls soon rotted and in 1862 had to be replaced with brick cladding. In 1877 a fourth floor, concealed by a mansard roof, was added. Despite the loss of the cupola, a massive main door surmounted by a fanlight and set off by large arched windows above it gave the building an imposing air. A second institution, at the corner of Great George and Richmond Streets, was less grand but still a significant feature on the landscape. St. Patrick's School, as it was christened, was a three-storey brick structure with a large assembly hall on its third floor. Built to educate the city's Catholic boys, its hall was inaugurated by a concert in January 1869, but classes started only in the autumn of 1870. Earlier that year, a new four-storey, red-brick Notre Dame Convent school opened opposite Hillsborough Square. Students had been previously accommodated by an older building at the corner of Sydney and Weymouth Streets. Other Catholic girls attended school in a less imposing structure, St. Joseph's Convent, on Pownal Street. It was a wooden building, the former church at St. Andrew's, which was hauled down the frozen Hillsborough River in March 1864 to take its place in the western reaches of town.

Most of the other primary schools in Charlottetown were small, and some were notoriously decrepit. The Methodists tackled this situation in 1871 when they opened the solid-looking, four-storey brick Wesleyan Day School on Upper Prince Street. Following the passage of the Public Schools Act in 1877, the new Charlottetown School Board addressed the need for an adequate building on the other side of the city and began construction of West Kent School on land at the corner of Kent and Rochford Streets. The cornerstone of this large brick building was laid in 1878.

The recreational needs of the growing population were also reflected in the urban landscape. In August 1871, the cornerstone of the Young Men's Christian Association (YMCA) was laid with great ceremony. The building's front faced Richmond Street opposite Queen Square, and in the opinion of the *Examiner* it would add to the beauty of the square. The two-storey façade was imposing with a large barrel-vaulted door and mansard roof. Around the same time as the YMCA was being planned, a joint stock company was formed to build

Kirk of St. James, c. 1860.

Grace Methodist, c. 1880.

Central Christian, c. 1900.

Charlottetown was a city of church spires. Between the time of incorporation and the early 20th century, all of the city's religious denominations replaced their old, wooden churches with magnificent stone and brick structures.

a winter skating rink. Intended as a commercial operation, it featured live band music and proved to be successful.

In the years immediately following incorporation, the urban landscape remained relatively unchanged by the development of new commercial establishments. A general economic torpor appears to have restrained construction. "It is melancholy to see," a visitor noted, "the number of large shops that are closed in Charlottetown .... You would not require to go far to count a dozen, and the shops that are open do but a small trade." With the passage of time, however, the face of the city began to change, particularly in the commercial district along lower Queen Street. The appearance of new businesses reflected technological change and an expanding economy. They were not restricted to Queen Street. "Steam! Steam! Steam!" screamed an advertisement for Patrick Hickey's woodworking factory. Specializing in the production of cabinets, blinds, sashes and doors, the factory, located on Sydney Street, was the first of its kind on the Island to use steam to power the machinery and to operate a kiln in which wood was dried. Some years later, another furniture manufacturer, Mark Butcher, expanded his premises, and prompted the *Examiner* to comment that "it always affords us much pleasure to notice improvements which are being made by our mechanics."

Along lower Queen Street, a limited number of substantial commercial structures appeared in the years following incorporation. Perhaps the first to open was the Duncan Building at the northeast corner of Dorchester and Queen Streets. Completed in 1855, it was constructed of brick and sandstone and contained two stores with warehouse space on the upper floors. It was followed later in 1857 by a handsome brick building at the southwest corner of Water Street that initially housed two stores and the Bank of Prince Edward Island. Much further up the street, opposite Queen Square, James DesBrisay erected a new two-storey brick building in 1861. Most new construction, however, such as a three-storey brick store, completed between 1862 and 1864 at the corner of Sydney and Queen Streets, was not as far north. Another new commercial venue, the four-storey brick Victoria Building, was erected still closer to the harbour at 57 Queen Street after the Great Fire of 1866. The following year, though, a three-storey brick building was erected by Dodd and Rogers hardware on the southwest corner of Queen and Grafton Streets.

After 1870 a growing number of solid attractive brick buildings appeared along Queen Street. Some of them were in the more developed stretch closer to the harbour. One was on the northwest corner of Queen and Water Streets and opened in 1871, while another, the Queen's Building, was built on the southwest corner of King and Queen Streets in 1873. Still others were erected further up the street. A series of three brick three-storey stores called Heard's Row was built in 1871 across from Queen Square, and two other substantial structures, the Full Building (1874) and the Monaghan Building (1879), appeared on the east side of the street between Dorchester and Sydney Streets. As the period wore on, the number of solid-looking brick stores increased. The progressive spread of such structures up Queen Street gave the city a more impressive commercial streetscape.

The period from 1855 to 1879 was one of active house construction. New homes appeared throughout the town on hitherto vacant lots and sites of buildings that had fallen into decay or been destroyed by fire. In 1855, for example, fire claimed Lieutenant Governor Edmund Fanning's grand mansion on Great George Street. The property was subsequently severed into several lots and a series of substantial row houses arose. The first was built in 1859 by Richard Heartz at the northeast corner of Sydney Street. A second, erected by Martin O'Halloran, appeared in 1865, followed by a third, also built by O'Halloran in 1879. The style of all three was Georgian, with massive lower windows surmounted by stone lintels. Not all of the new homes were as restrained. Alexander Brown built an impressive wooden home in 1872 on Fitzroy Street at the corner of Pownal. Designed in a more contemporary hip-roof style, it featured arched gable windows and a large door with sidelights and glass transom, protected by an ornate portico. Most impressive of all was "Beaconsfield," built in 1877 for James Peake, Jr., a prominent merchant and ship-owner. Constructed by John Lewis from a plan by W. C. Harris, the house featured a large square belvedere, broad verandahs with superb fretwork and ornate interior plaster finishes. From its position at the corner of Kent and West Streets, vistas opened over the harbour and Government House. Next door, Jedediah Carvell built a huge home that boasted five rooms. Although the design was not as noteworthy as Peake's, the house had, like his, hot air heating and hot and cold running water, both a luxury for the times. Unfortunately neither Carvell nor Peake remained in their residences long. Both saw their fortunes eroded by an economic downturn that took hold shortly after the houses were built. Not all new housing was as pretentious. A simple, front-gable, wooden, double house on Sydney Street, for instance, was built by a painter, John Stentiford, around 1860. It was solid and roomy, but it stood right by the street and lacked anything more than a basic stoop at the entranceways.

Proponents of Queen Square beautification were able to rescue little comfort from nearby construction projects. The square had to wait almost two decades for the kinds of improvements that would transform it from an open plot of land to a landscaped park. Described as a "wilderness in the midst of the city," it had a low north side that often flooded, providing a passable skating rink in winter. In 1865 a start was made toward levelling the grounds in preparation for fencing and tree planting. A considerable number of fir, beech, birch and maple trees were located in a "tasteful" plan, but no other major changes seem to have occurred before the 1880s. Thus were incidents possible like the one involving Pat Sweeney's cow. In 1878 this "old and respectable" animal, which had been browsing on the square, became violently ill after eating some loose paper that had been blowing about. The *Examiner* suggested that it must have been a Grit organ because the cow "imitated their *bullying* example and *lied* on the square several hours." Light banter aside, the issue of parks was a significant concern for a number of Charlottetonians.

The first opportunity to acquire a park came with the decision of the British Ordnance Department to retire the garrison grounds in the southwestern end of town below Sydney Street. The colonial government decided to sell the land by auction,

Victoria Park, c. 1900. After years of negotiations, in 1875 the Canadian government agreed to turn over 40 acres adjacent to Government House for use as a city park.

but the city appealed to the British government to have it turned over to it for use as a public park. Evidently this request was unsuccessful. The area was surveyed and auctioned off, and several new streets, Haviland, Union and Dundas Esplanade, were laid out and added to Ward One. While the city failed to gain a park, some of the new landowners developed the shoreline and began to landscape their properties. Some applauded these improvements; others opposed the encroachments onto adjacent water lots which, unlike the land itself, were under civic control.

About the same time, citizens at the opposite end of town, living in trendy new housing adjacent to Hillsborough Square, decided to take matters into their own hands. At a neighbourhood meeting, participants created a committee to arrange for the square to be levelled, fenced, provided with walkways and benches and planted with trees. If the city agreed to fence the square, the committee would collect the money to pay for the rest. These plans were gradually realized, and, two summers later, the park was the setting for band concerts and other public amusements. By 1868, however, the character of the park had again changed. The grass was allowed to grow to provide hay for sale to the highest bidder. Profits were intended to defray maintenance costs, but, to protect the crop, children were no longer allowed to play on the square, and band concerts were suspended. King Square was similarly planted as a meadow. Other favourite recreational areas included Kensington at the eastern edge of town and Spring Park to the north. Both were shady, cool spots suitable for church teas, family outings and picnics. The city purchased the lots containing Spring Park's spring in 1867.

The most important venue for a park, however, was the government farm, part of the land set aside by Lieutenant Governor Edmund Fanning in 1789 as a site for a gubernatorial residence. Much more land had been taken from the Common for the

This engraving from Meacham's 1880 Atlas *shows King Square in one of its tidier phases.*

purpose than was needed, and the colony subsequently established a farm on the bulk of the property. City fathers reckoned that, as the estate had, in a fashion, been taken from the citizens of Charlottetown, a portion should be returned to them as a park. As early as 1869, Council asked the Canadian Governor General, in whose name it was held for use by the Island's Lieutenant Governor, to grant the city a park. No action was taken at the time, but during discussions concerning the Island's entry into Confederation, the issue was raised by J. C. Pope. The Prime Minister, John A. Macdonald, agreed to the proposal, and Pope's government initiated the transfer. Outrage followed when the Canadian government, going back on its word, disallowed the Island legislation. The *Examiner* blamed David Laird, one of the province's six new MPs, claiming that he had intervened to punish his local political opponents.[8] A more commanding reason may have been the possibility that military authorities worried a park might interfere with harbour defences. When 40 acres were finally given to the city in 1875, the gun emplacement at Prince Edward Battery was not included. Even so, it was a generous, open space that would fill the city's recreational needs for years to come, provided, of course, the city could manage it properly. One writer to the *Examiner* sniffed that under the city's care Hillsborough Square had again fallen into a disgraceful condition, and the provincial legislature should pause before entrusting "an incompetent body as the present city Fathers, with the management of any

8 Laird, a Liberal in the Island House of Assembly, stood in opposition to the Conservatives led by J. C. Pope and Lemuel C. Owen. As a newly elected Liberal Member of Parliament, Laird helped to defeat the Macdonald government over the Pacific Scandal in the autumn of 1873. He entered the Liberal federal government of Alexander Mackenzie as Minister of the Interior and was in a position to influence a decision concerning the park. Laird had also been a vigorous opponent of Theophilus DesBrisay over the land question. DesBrisay was Mayor of Charlottetown in 1867-72 and 1875-77.

property which may require ordinary supervision and care." Such carping aside, the *Examiner* got to the heart of the matter by rejoicing, "The western part of Government farm is now ours, and a more pleasant place for a walk could not be desired."

Of all of the challenges facing Charlottetown at incorporation, the state of the streets and walkways was the most intractable. The new city was virtually bereft of sidewalks, and most streets resembled country lanes. In spring and fall and during mid-summer downpours, the red Island soil turned into thick, sloppy goo which bogged down wagons, sucked the shoes off pedestrians' feet and discoloured the hems of ladies' dresses. Once dry, the peaks and hollows hardened into ruts that jarred the bones of drivers and twisted the ankles of unwary pedestrians. Generally, one walked in the middle of the road, the shoulders being especially treacherous as paths running close to the walls of stores or houses posed the danger of uncovered cellar openings or rotting hatches. In dry weather, brisk winds would whip up clouds of dust and litter and swirl them about so that a fine red patina covered any nearby flat surface. In winter, mounds of snow gathered at the sides of tracks opened up by passing sleighs. Merchants and home-owners shovelled passageways in the banks in front of their doors; otherwise, the piles remained to challenge anyone who was moving about town.

City Council authorized the grading of streets and arranged for gravel to be placed in low spots, but progress was slow and elicited complaints that the new city government was not making the improvements that were needed. In fact, in the years immediately following incorporation, the city invested very little in such work.[9] Gradually, sidewalks appeared, usually laid by merchants in front of their shops. They were wooden and prone to rot, but it would be many years before the city attempted to lay permanent sidewalks of concrete or flagstones. In the 1860s, the city began to construct wooden sidewalks and macadamize some of the main thoroughfares and commercial streets. Macadamizing was a method of road construction, named after its Scottish inventor, John Loudon MacAdam, in which various layers of crushed stone were laid down to form a road upon an earthen bed which had already been raised above the surrounding ground level. The largest stones, about eight inches in diameter, were placed at the bottom, followed by another layer of stones about four inches round, and then topped by a third layer of gravel about two inches across. When the stone was pressed into the underlying soil, a hard, durable, well-drained surface resulted. It was a costly and labour-intensive business, involving among other things importing the stone, and the total financial outlay was far beyond the means of the city with its existing revenue.

In 1868 Mayor DesBrisay estimated the bill for macadamizing "the greater part" of the city's streets at £5,000. To cover these sums, increased revenue was necessary, either through higher taxes, which would keep the expense of making permanent improvements on the shoulders of existing ratepayers, or the issuance of debentures.

---

9 In 1857, £65 out of a total expenditure for the year of £1,837 was spent on streets and squares.

Along the street beside Fairholm is a typical, three-plank wooden sidewalk. Sidewalks in commercial sections of the city were often wider.

DesBrisay thought debentures could be guaranteed by the colony and redeemed by a sinking fund administered by the colonial government and created through a modest tax increase. He readily admitted that higher taxes were "not palatable to any of us," and could only be justified by streets which for a large portion of the year were "a positive disgrace." Ongoing restraints on the size of city revenues by Prince Edward Island's Executive Council meant that the progress of road construction was slow. The budget for such purposes nevertheless increased from a mere £338 in 1864 to over £1,000 in 1872. During an outburst of discontent about the streets and sidewalks in early 1874, the city was accused of not collecting all taxes that were due, and, when that charge was proven unfounded, the city was blamed for the appalling state of the streets and sidewalks because it spent too little of its revenue on roads. Even that charge was unjustified.[10] In 1875 the city was reported to have spent $5,186 on the streets and $1,412 on sidewalks, together nearly one-third of its operating budget. The fault lay with the revenue stream itself. The provincial legislature in 1876 finally

10 Real estate and rentals were assessed at 7.5 per cent, of which 2.5 per cent was for macadamizing the roads. The published accounts of the city showed that expenditures for this purpose came to $5,420 in 1873 and $6,597 in 1874.

This sketch from the 1840s shows an ice road across Charlottetown Harbour. The route was "bushed" for safety.

agreed to allow the city to issue debentures for ongoing capital works, such as roadways, thereby relieving the burden caused by a pay-as-you-go policy. That policy had resulted in streets that "had become very bad, and were badly in need of repairs." By 1877 only some of the principal streets had been macadamized.[11]

Besides the streets in the city's centre, by 1877 the four principal access routes from the countryside through the Common and into the city proper were macadamized.[12] Here, once again, relations with the senior level of government had an impact on the pace of work, albeit in this case, at times a positive one. As Mayor DesBrisay pointed out in 1868, the roads and bridges approaching the city were not used by the local residents but by country people coming to town with "vehicles heavily laden with produce." He requested a grant to improve the roads and repair two bridges. The colonial government authorized work on the roads and had a new stone bridge built on Spring Park Road. The mayor and Council pressed its case with respect to the streets in the downtown, arguing that road damage mainly resulted from heavily loaded wagons bringing produce to town or taking limestone from the port to the countryside. Since most of this traffic came from outside of town, the city had a right to some of the general revenue of the colony for the maintenance of its streets. Such claims fell largely on deaf ears, but the demand for a return to the city of a share of Island revenues fairly reflecting the income derived from residents of the city was vigorously asserted.

The city's wharves, like the streets, were used on an everyday basis by Charlottetonians and other Islanders alike. Descriptions from the mid-19th century refer to the prominence of the harbour facilities as one viewed the capital from the water. Many of

11 These included Water Street from Weymouth to Pownal, Queen Street from Peake's Wharf to Kent Street, and Kent Street between Queen and Hillsborough. Also Richmond Street from Pownal to Prince, Grafton Street from Pownal to Great George, and Great George Street from Grafton to Euston were paved, as was most of Peake Street.

12 North River Road and Brighton Street to Black Sam's Bridge, Spring Park Road to Euston Street, Malpeque Road to Euston Street, and St. Peter's Road and Weymouth Street to Kent Street had been completed.

the wharves were owned by private businesses, but two of them, Queen's and Pownal Street Wharves, were given to the city by the colonial government at incorporation. During the 1850s, many more people reached and left the city on watercraft than was the case a century or more later. Merchant and passenger vessels from other colonies and further away, Royal Naval ships, coastal freighters, the Southport and Rocky Point ferries and other boats from across the harbour or up the Hillsborough and West Rivers made the waterfront a bustling place. In winter, the water, frozen over, was a thoroughfare for pedestrians and travellers by sleigh from Southport and more distant parts of the Island. An incident in the early 1870s underscores the significance of the waterfront to the daily life of Charlottetown.

In the spring of 1871, local merchant and future mayor Jedediah S. Carvell brought a suit against the city for its destruction of a newly constructed breastwork extending into the harbour from his property at the end of Pownal Street. Carvell's structure was built adjacent to the Pownal Street Wharf. Reports soon reached Mayor DesBrisay that people coming to town by the harbour ice were being blocked by an impediment being erected at the end of Pownal Street. The "impediment" was Carvell's breastwork, which came so close to Pownal Street Wharf that it inhibited passage of a horse and sleigh, and this was interpreted by the mayor and other officials as an infringement of their right of way. The mayor ordered the impediment removed. Enraged, Carvell replaced his breastwork, this time putting it closer to where he believed his property line lay and protruding even further into his water lot. It virtually touched the Pownal Wharf. He then took the city to court.

In the ensuing case, various witnesses gave evidence of the regular use of the slope at the end of Pownal Street as a means of accessing the city by travellers crossing the frozen harbour in winter. There is little doubt that users were numerous and habitual. In summer, the wharf was also a popular facility for commuters from the surrounding countryside. Ultimately, the city lost its case. Despite the usage of the landing and the city's claim that such use constituted an easement on Carvell's land, if Carvell had not actually infringed on the city's right of way, the court found that the Pownal Street Wharf trespassed on Carvell's property, and he had every right to make improvements to his property.

The case also shed light on the problem of maintaining the wharves. The Pownal Street Wharf had been constructed in 1844 adjacent to the Ordnance Property to facilitate the unloading of supplies for the military. The Ordnance Department sold the property to a private citizen in 1847. Departing spring ice and normal wear and tear resulted in regular damage to the wharf, and the constant reconstruction resulted in its gradual movement westward onto the adjacent water lot. The same was true for the other wharf similarly acquired from the colony: Queen's Wharf. For good reason did the *Examiner* comment, "The wharves, we have heard, have always been a loss and great trouble to the Corporation. Would it not be better to set them up to the highest bidder for a term of years, and have done with them?"

The wharves, however, represented employment and wealth for Charlottetonians. Early budgets reflected their importance. In 1857-58, maintenance of the public wharves was the corporation's largest single expense at over £84. Two years later, Queen's Wharf needed £200 worth of repair work, and, without money available, the city borrowed from the bank and issued debentures for £300. Repair costs rose to almost £243 in 1860, but income from wharfage fees amounted to nearly £266. The income, however, did not make the expenditures more palatable to the city, and the costs put a strain on civic finances. That year, Pownal Street Wharf was in bad repair again, and the city begged the colonial government for financial relief or an end to its responsibilities to maintain it. Part of the requirements was to keep the water surrounding the wharves dredged. To cover such costs, the city had used debentures to pay the dredge-owner, Alexander MacBean. When he eventually refused to accept more debentures, the city in 1862 offered him a promissory note for a portion of his bill. Despite the expenses, the wharves were a substantial part of the city's assets. At an appraised value of $13,000 for Queen Street Wharf and $9,000 for Pownal Street Wharf and breastwork, the harbour facilities were 38 per cent of the City of Charlottetown's total assets of $58,150 in 1874.

Not all of the responsibilities for the physical environment in Charlottetown lay in the public realm. One of the first signs that the urban landscape would undergo substantial change at the hands of private enterprise was the incorporation of the Charlottetown Gas Light Company in April 1853. Many of the town's leading citizens were among the shareholders.[13] By May 1854, 71 individual investors had committed to purchasing 813 shares valued at £5 each. A new gasworks had taken shape on the waterfront at the eastern end of town, with service lines connected to approximately 60 private customers. Gas mains ran along many of the thoroughfares bounded by Prince, Water, Queen and Kent Streets with one extension to Pownal along Grafton and another up Hillsborough Street to Hillsborough Square. Coal gas was produced by heating coal in large retorts and then drawing off the vapour into tubes, cleaning and feeding it into pipes for distribution. The plant and network of service pipes were substantial undertakings. Construction had taken somewhat longer than anticipated, and investors were faced with unexpected cost increases, but that mattered little when, in the evening of June 2, 1854, houses and stores were "lit up with gas and presented a brilliant appearance." This was followed a few days later by "a brilliant exhibition" in front of the Colonial Building.

Service, however, did not extend to street lighting. In an interesting departure from a strategy used by new gas facilities elsewhere, the Charlottetown company targeted private consumers. A similar start-up business in England, for instance, would have secured a contract from local authorities to provide street lighting before initiating such a venture. Indeed, civic governments often made the inexpensive supply of gas for public lighting fixtures a condition for permission to tear up the streets to install gas mains. In Charlottetown, commencement of gas service preceded a city administration. Proponents of civic incorporation saw inauguration of a gas works as a kind

13 Early principal backers included Daniel Hodgson, Ralph Brecken, Charles Hensley, Charles Young, John Rogerson and James McGrath.

The gentleman at the left of this photo, taken at the corner of Water and Great George Streets around 1865, is leaning on one of the early gaslight poles.

of portent of future improvements which would include local government. As it was, the Charlottetown Gas Light Company had neither the security of a guaranteed public market upon which to base its future business nor the obligation to do more than provide "notice to authorities" before tearing up the streets.

Gas service in Charlottetown proved a qualified success. Despite the brilliance of the initial displays, varying supplies of sometimes indifferent grades of gas often meant dim and spluttering lamps which then had to be supplemented by more traditional forms of illumination. Worse still, before the end of the first year's service, unhappy townsfolk were debating a proposed 25 per cent rate increase. The laying of lines also resulted in some controversy about damage to Charlottetown's already rough roadways. Concern was particularly focused on the placement of lines too near the surface, complicating street maintenance and improvement. In 1856 the new city government was presented with a bill from the gas company for damage when workers grading Hillsborough Street accidentally uncovered gas pipes. Council rejected the bill.[14]

14 The gas company took the city to court, and, despite evidence that the pipes were buried only 10 inches beneath the surface, the jury found in favour of the company.

Later, a bill providing for municipal control over the installation of gas and other pipes under the roadways came before the House of Assembly. During the debate, T. Heath Haviland, Jr., successfully argued against conferring a power on the city that would give it the authority to order the gas company to bury its mains four feet below the street surface. This would interfere with the company's chartered rights and jeopardize the investors' capital. Haviland, himself, was not an investor, but he sympathized with many who were. He likely also subscribed to the opinion of *Haszard's Gazette* that a joint-stock venture was unfamiliar to many Charlottetonians, including some of the company's shareholders, yet success for such an enterprise was important to the development of a "young, growing and needy country."

A year after incorporation, Charlottetown's City Council resolved to have Queen Street from the waterfront to Market Square illuminated by gaslight. Civic finances and concerns over the quality of service may explain the lack of action which followed this decision. The main accomplishment was the installation of three lights near the Colonial Building at the expense of the Island's government. Three years later in 1859, the city arranged to have lights installed in the commercial district along Grafton and Queen Streets, with the operating expense being shared equally between the city and private citizens. The following year, Council decided to have the cost of street lighting borne by the general ratepayer and accordingly requested permission of the legislature to impose the requisite additional taxes. By 1861, 50 gas lamps were installed on city streets.

To keep costs low, the lamps were left off until an hour after sunset and an hour before sunrise, as well as during the three nights before and after a full moon if the sky was not heavily overcast. This peculiar piece of economizing caused some disputes between the city and the utility. On one occasion, the glow of the full moon was obscured by cloud, and the lights were accordingly lit. The next night, the fourth after the full moon, the company left the lights off, only to receive a warning from the city that a repetition of such a breach of contract would result in its termination. This was not the only incident involving the hours in which the lamps were burning. In 1875 the city upbraided the company for lighting the lamps at or before four o'clock in the afternoon and leaving them on "considerably after sunrise, causing a waste of gass [*sic*] and perfect loss to the city contrary to the intentions of the agreement."

The cost of providing service rose from less than three per cent of the civic expenditures to about eight per cent in 1870, and it hovered around that mark for the rest of the 1870s. This was a significant concern for the cash-starved city government and caused some bitter arguments between the supporters and opponents of gas street lighting. One of the issues in the otherwise dull election of 1863 was the question of "gas or no gas" and was decided in favour of the gas company. Debates within divided Councils led to some peculiar compromises. The snowy months of January and February 1864 found the city relying upon the reflection of light from other sources to brighten its darkened streets.[15] During other periods of time in the

15 Charlottetown was not alone in facing such situations. In December 1874, Halifax was threatened with termination of service by its gas utility if it failed to accept a steep increase in rates.

1860s and 1870s, the city simply did without street lighting as Council and the gas company attempted to reach satisfactory agreements concerning cost and conditions of service. Use of kerosene lamps was made in locations beyond the reach of the gas pipes. A major adjustment occurred in 1874 when the city was obliged to assume the cost of maintaining the lights in order to extract a condition by which it would pay for the gas that streetlights actually consumed rather than on a flat rate basis. When the contract with the gas company was renewed in 1879, for the last time as it turned out, Charlottetown's streets were lit by 125 gas lamps. By then, the gas company's survival was largely dependent upon its contract with the city.

ECONOMIC GROWTH AND METROPOLITAN DEVELOPMENT

The decades between 1850 and 1880 saw the beginnings of industrialization in many parts of British North America, including centres in the Maritimes. Manufacturing offered employment opportunities and the possibilities of increased wealth. Charlottetown's economic prosperity, however, remained linked to its administrative functions and to its role as a service centre for trade and commerce, rather than its limited secondary industries. The good times waxed and waned during the period 1855-79, and prosperity was not shared equally. The years just before incorporation had benefitted from the generally expanding economy. Reports of slumping retail business suggest a local downturn in the years following incorporation, but an upturn soon followed. Confederation and completion of the railway changed some of the economic equations for the Island, but not the basis of the Charlottetown economy. By the end of the 1870s, a major economic reversal created hardship for some of the city's leading businessmen and cast a pall over the city as a whole. Any optimism felt about the economic future was of the cautious variety.

As the capital of a small but expanding agricultural colony, the city benefitted from the significant number of office-holders who resided there and from hosting members of the legislature when it was in session. While the colonial government was not large by present-day standards, and many functions were filled by persons who received little or no pay, those civil servants who held salaried posts enjoyed a certain security of income that helped to stabilize the local economy. The courts, customs house, post office and Executive Council contributed to this employment pool. Departure of imperial troops just prior to incorporation, except for their brief return in 1865-67 during the Tenant League disturbances, denied Charlottetown the economic benefits their presence may have provided, as well as their contributions to its social life. Personnel connected with the hydrographic survey of the Gulf of St. Lawrence, however, continued to reside in the city throughout this period, and naval officers such as Henry Bayfield and John Orlebar were prominent in the life of the city.

Commerce catering to the needs of both local citizens and rural folk was the city's lifeblood. Its commercial hinterland now reached far beyond Queens into Prince and Kings Counties. Improved roads extended Charlottetown's commercial sway, but travel was still difficult enough to allow other centres, notably Summerside, to prosper. In addition to its general merchant-traders, Charlottetown boasted an array of specialty stores selling jewellery, books, boots and shoes, stationery, hardware, clothing, fabrics, furniture, building supplies and carriages.

Although newspaper advertisements regularly announced the arrival of shipments of manufactured items from Britain and the United States, some products were made locally. Several carriage works were located in the city, as were various furniture factories, tanneries, foundries, breweries, harness-makers and a machinery manufacturer who produced sawmill equipment and potato diggers. Most of these businesses were small and geared to the Island market. They succeeded by using local raw materials and by producing items that were costly to import because of their size and weight. For the most part, beyond the obvious exception of the wooden shipbuilding industry, manufacturing in Charlottetown, and in Prince Edward Island generally, was of secondary importance. A so-called "Industrial Exhibition" held in the Charlottetown drill shed in October 1868 illustrates this fact. It was noteworthy for its "mammoth cabbages, gigantic celery, enormous cauliflowers" and a "magnificent bunch of purple grapes weighing one pound and a quarter." Textiles and knit goods appear to have been made at home. "As no prizes were offered for the products of our mills, workshops and factories, very few of them were exhibited." Two items that were shown, however, were a tin lamp and a mouse trap.

Trade at both the retail and wholesale levels was risky, and the early 1860s, in particular, witnessed a large number of failures. Bankruptcies continued throughout the decade. The *Examiner* noted in October 1867 that "amongst a certain class of trades people" there was "a mania for 'skedaddling' as there was last year for house-burning." One of the more prominent "skedaddlers" was described as "a manufacturer of manifold enterprise, who competed, successfully, it is said, with others in the same trade in Canada — who had a large manufacturing establishment, furnished with all the modern improvements and who enjoyed himself in a handsome villa out of town." Whether the man in question was William B. Dawson or not, the reader is not informed, but the credit reports on Dawson gathered by R. G. Dun and Company suggest this possibility. They reveal Dawson as a "rather speculative" man who frequently overextended himself as a tanner and merchant. Backed by his wealthy father, Thomas, when he started in the early 1850s, by the early 1860s William was unable to secure credit in his own name. He remained in business and in 1863 is reported as having opened an "extensive steam tannery." Two years later he had cleared most of his old debts, but in 1868 Dawson was reported as "swindled and absconded."

Such cases may have been a factor in securing credit, one of the challenges facing Charlottetown businessmen. Hard currency was scarce, and the seasonal nature of commerce, based as it was on agriculture, shipbuilding and the fishery, meant that access to lines of credit was essential for most traders. The demand for credit was in part met by private lenders such as Richard Heartz and James Peake, Sr., but Charlottetown's banks played an essential role in Island commerce. The first to appear might have preceded the city's incorporation except for some wrangling with the imperial

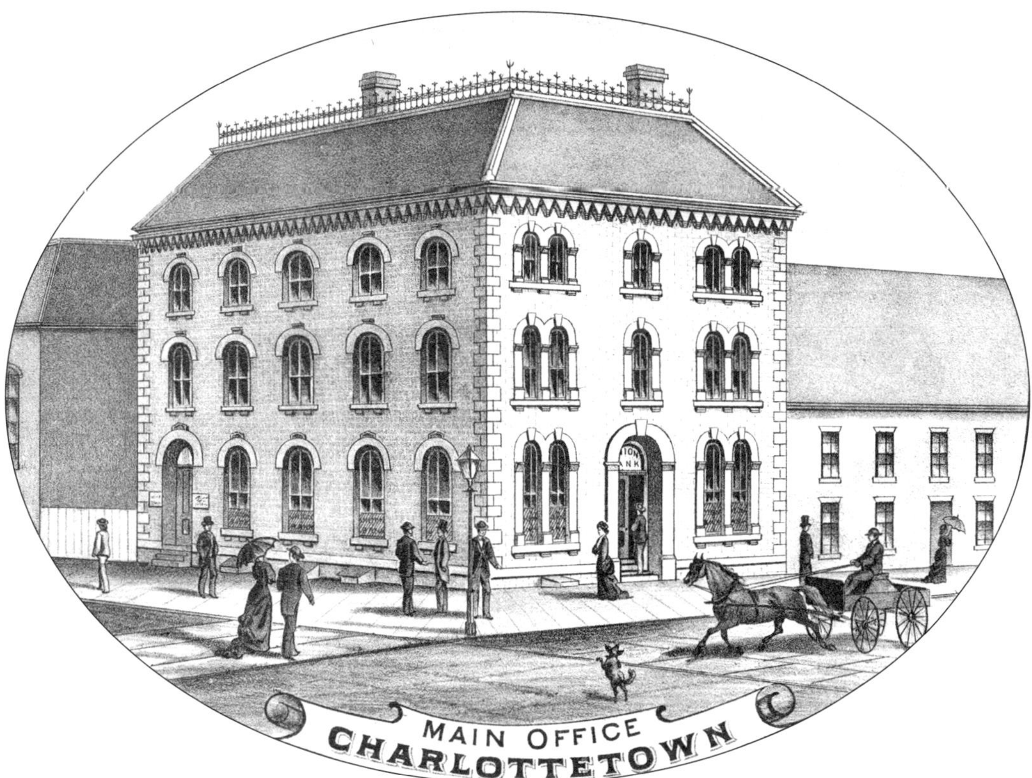

Opening in 1864, the Union Bank was one of the city's three chartered banks.

government about clauses in the bank's charter. Started by a group of nine prominent businessmen, including James Peake, Sr., the Bank of Prince Edward Island welcomed its first customers on August 13, 1856. Despite a shaky start which obliged it to suspend operations during the winter of 1858, the bank proved to be financially prudent and profitable. Its success encouraged the creation of two other Charlottetown banks, the Union Bank, in 1864, and the Merchants Bank, in 1871. These banks, along with the Farmers' Bank of Rustico (1862) and the Bank of Summerside (1866), invested heavily in the local economy and contributed significantly to the growth of the Island's economy. The Charlottetown banks were a major contributor to the city's ongoing domination of the province's commercial life, and when the Bank of Prince Edward Island failed in 1882, its loss diminished not only the fortunes of local investors and creditors but the confidence of the local business community.

The port of Charlottetown in 1867 accounted for just under one half of Prince Edward Island's exports of principal farm crops.[16] In the years immediately following incorporation, exports went to the United Kingdom and to the adjoining British territories. Increasingly, after the Reciprocity Treaty of 1854, Island commodities

16 Farm crops constituted about one-half of the value of Island exports at this time.

entered the coastal trade to New England.[17] Although potatoes were among the exports, the largest farm commodity was oats. Barley and turnips were also major export crops. The cancellation of the Reciprocity Treaty by the United States in 1865 threatened to curtail this trade, and provoked avid interest among Charlottetown's business elite in renewing the trade deal. Representatives of an informally constituted Chamber of Commerce attended meetings of American Chambers of Commerce held in Detroit, Michigan, and in Portland, Maine, which were convened to determine how the commerce of the United States could be revived in the post-Civil War era. Island delegates hoped for the renewal of free trade between the United States and British North America. Such hopes were encouraged by General Benjamin Butler, a prominent member of the House of Representatives, who, in July 1868, proposed a motion in Congress advocating a specific free trade arrangement between the United States and Prince Edward Island. The resolution passed, and Butler was made the head of a committee to conclude the deal. On August 21, an important meeting of "the most influential of our citizens" and leading farmers from Queens County was held in Charlottetown to consider the issue. Chaired by the High Sheriff of Queens County, Francis Longworth, the meeting was addressed by local delegates to the Portland Convention who spoke of the nearly unanimous support for free trade among the delegates in Portland. Many at the Charlottetown meeting shared this sentiment. Just over a week later, on August 29, a vessel carrying General Butler, three other congressmen and other "distinguished gentlemen" steamed into Charlottetown Harbour. Though there were hopes that the issue of renewed reciprocity might be pressed home, Butler's delegation was received cordially by the Island government, tendered a luncheon and sent away with no conclusive results. There the matter ended, a victim of the limited constitutional autonomy of a British colony and the apparent overarching American motive of gaining admission to the fishery off the Island's coast.

Even after commercial banks were established, private lenders like Richard Heartz remained key components in the credit system.

17 Regular steamship service between Charlottetown and Boston, with a stop in Halifax, began in 1864 and continued throughout the period. It was provided by the Boston and Colonial Steamship Company with vessels such as the *Commerce, Franconia, Alhambra* and *Carroll*.

With the entry of Prince Edward Island into the Dominion of Canada and the completion of the Intercolonial Railway, Charlottetown's lines of trade took yet another turn. Connections with the rail network running to central Canada became increasingly important for everyone in the Maritimes. Vessels of the Prince Edward Island Steam Navigation Company, *Princess of Wales*, *Heather Belle* and later *St. Lawrence*, plied between Charlottetown and Pictou, Nova Scotia, Pointe du Chêne, New Brunswick, and other ports in summer, but these links were problematic in winter. After the Island joined Canada, they became critical. Provision of continuous steamship communications with the railway network on the mainland was one of the articles of union. The Dominion government acquired a steamer, the *Northern Light*, which had some icebreaking capacity, to fulfill this obligation, and from December 1876 when it first entered service until its replacement 12 years later, tales of its seasonal misfortunes in the grip of the ice floes of the Northumberland Strait were regular features in Charlottetown newspapers.

Shipbuilding continued along the harbour shoreline and was an important contributor to the city's commercial development. While the pace of construction began to decline about 1855, the early years of the city saw a procession of ships launched into its harbour. The largest vessel ever to be built on Prince Edward Island, the ship *Ethel*, slid down the ways on May 29, 1858, as fascinated townsfolk watched from Ferry Wharf. Unfortunately, the majesty of the event was spoiled when the newly launched vessel lodged itself on a Rosebank sandbar. By the 1860s, the pace of construction slackened. Timber supplies were by then well-removed from the city, and after 1870 few hulls were built in Charlottetown. There was a brisk business, however, in rigging and fitting out vessels built further up the Hillsborough and along the Pisquid River. Many vessels were completed just in time to be loaded with newly harvested crops destined for markets in Great Britain. Ultimately, most of the ships constructed in Charlottetown were sold to owners in Britain or Newfoundland. While profits could be considerable when markets were firm, a loss of a vessel at sea or the weakening of demand for ships in Britain could spell disaster for its owners. One such entrepreneur was Dennis Reddin, a shipbuilder, merchant, tobacconist and baker who in 1856 was estimated to be Charlottetown's second man of property after James Peake. By 1858 he was ruined by his investments in shipbuilding and forced to sell his real estate valued at $100,000. He continued in business in a small way, but when he died in 1864, he was insolvent.

In one respect the harbour was an impediment to commerce. Crossing it in summer from Southport and Rocky Point required the use of ferries that provided service that was sometimes indifferent at best. These vessels were run as concessions granted by the colonial government, which transferred responsibility for them to the city at incorporation. The principal connection was between the capital and Southport. In the early months after incorporation, the operator of this ferry was a temperamental man who one Sunday morning abruptly shut down the operation of his steamboat for no apparent reason, stranding about 25 or 30 churchgoers who wanted to return to their homes across the harbour. When he lost his contract, this same man offered free rides to passengers to disrupt the business of his successful rival. Problems persisted over the years, and in 1871 the Island government purchased the steamer *Ora* and other assets of the contractor and eventually placed larger boats, the *Elfin* and the *Southport*, into service.[18] Even so, commuting proved problematic with numerous groundings and poor waiting facilities. These difficulties underscored the challenges Charlottetown faced in maintaining effective communications with its surrounding hinterland.

One possible resolution of this difficulty came with the tentative appearance of a pillar of 19th-century progress, the railway. Until the early 1870s, Islanders had generally eschewed this form of communication in favour of improving local roads and coastal shipping. Such a strategy made a lot of sense. Most places were close to the sea, and both Charlottetown and its commercial rival, Summerside, were centrally located and had good ports. Then in 1870 came an unexpected explosion of interest in railway construction. The chronicler of the Canadian National Railways system, G. R. Stevens, found the decision to embark on the construction of an Island line inexplicable, as if the government of J. C. Pope, and Islanders generally, had taken leave of their collective senses. He attributes it to an assumption that railways were a good thing and that gravel for road maintenance was hard to procure.

This analysis does some disservice to the decision-makers. As with most undertakings of this nature begun elsewhere at the time, a railway served a variety of interests. Some proponents of the scheme, such as J. S. Carvell, may have glimpsed an opportunity to speculate in land. Contractors had visions of prolonged, lucrative work. Clearly, farmers stood to benefit. The sand bars that obstructed the harbours on the north side of the Island meant that crops had to be hauled overland to the south coast to be loaded onto vessels for Charlottetown, Summerside or Georgetown. The early dates by which Summerside, and occasionally Charlottetown, froze up also complicated the movement of crops to market, punishing urban mercantile interests as well as farmers. Tourist interests welcomed the possibility of travellers getting to Charlottetown from the western part of the Island in four to six hours, or from Georgetown to Charlottetown in one-and-a-half hours. Mostly, however, the practical difficulties of maintaining the roads, bridges and wharves were persuasive. In a speech to the House of Assembly, George Howlan noted that 25 per cent of the colony's revenue went to such public works. Not only was a significant portion of these sums "misappropriated," but the Island soil and the increased traffic of an expanding rural economy soon reduced the roads to ruin again. Moreover, as "A Farmer" pointed out in a letter to the *Examiner*, for those not living in the vicinity of Charlottetown, travel to town through the mud and the pitch dark made a railway an attractive possibility. Even the costs of a fare for a trip by stage coach from Charlottetown to Summerside had increased to the substantial sum of nine shillings. The mutual interest of rural Islanders and urban investors and merchants was a rarity, but it accounts for the widespread political support that the measure attracted.

18 Both vessels were in service by 1878, serving both Southport and Rocky Point.

The train wending its way thorough this engraving is about to do something rare on the PEI Railway – cross a trestle bridge. Bridges were expensive, and to keep costs down the contractor tried to route the line around natural obstacles wherever possible. Though this kept the per-mile costs within budget, it contributed to making the line much longer, and more expensive, than originally planned.

The decision to build a railway "the length of the island" was hailed as a historic mark of progress. Citizens of Charlottetown rejoiced. A torchlight procession consisting of torches outlining the letters "RR" marched from the fire hall on Grafton Street to the Colonial Building. The volunteer band followed, and then more illuminated signs bearing the names Howlan, Brecken, Pope and Cameron. The fire companies followed — not a bad idea under the circumstances — and the whole parade merged with a large, enthusiastic crowd on Queen Square. The total present numbered 3,000-4,000. The nearby Christian Brothers School was illuminated, as were some of the hotels. It was, concluded the *Examiner*, "one of the grandest spectacles ever witnessed" in Charlottetown. The day the first sod was turned for the new enterprise, 75 of Charlotte-town's leading professional and business men sat down to dinner at the St. Lawrence Hotel to celebrate the dawn of a new era.

Once construction commenced, however, problems inherent in building a rail line in a country suffering from limited capital and unlimited politics manifested themselves. The cost of the project had been capped at £5,000 per mile, including rolling stock, although the total length of the line was not set. Nor were the construction specifications precise beyond instructions concerning the angles of slopes and the sharpness of curves. The lack of detailed technical standards encouraged contractors to select the most economical means of completing their tasks. Even at that, costs were soon out of control. Acquisition of the right-of-ways proved to be unexpectedly expensive. At one point, the track as it approached Charlottetown was detoured in a wide arc to avoid land for which its owner was demanding an excessive amount of compensation. Once in the city, the track crossed city streets, and, here again, the railway company was liable for damages. The city claimed £5,000, but the Railway

Though the city boasted numerous hotels, the Revere House, hard by the Steam Navigation Wharf, was ideally suited to accommodate passengers from the Princess of Wales *or the* St. Lawrence. *Though not identified, one of these vessels is probably featured in this engraving from* Meacham's 1880 Atlas.

Commissioners awarded it only $494, a sum set after appeal at $2,404.[19] The cost of the railway had perhaps unforeseen political consequences for the Island as a whole, but it was ultimately completed. Charlottetown was thus connected to its western rival, Summerside, and given full access to the prosperous farming areas of Queens and Kings Counties. The face of the city was also changed. The tracks swept into town past the gas works and terminated in rail yards that ran from Weymouth to Prince Streets. The passenger station was located at the foot of Weymouth and a roundhouse was built at the corner of Prince and Water Streets. Maintenance buildings were located between them, and a substantial wharf facilitated the transshipment of goods from ships to rail cars.

The implications of the railway extended far beyond the development of the rail yards on the waterfront and the installation of new passenger and freight facilities. The anticipated impact on business was immense, with the city's aspirations to become a tourist mecca being one of the chief considerations. The issue of the extent to which such visitors to Charlottetown could be housed had simmered since incorporation. Critics saw the lack of decent hotel space as an indicator of the lack of enterprise on the part of

19 Between the time the railway contract was awarded and work began, the Island switched to the decimal currency system. The conversion rate was roughly $5 to £1.

the business community and a reason for the low level of tourist traffic on the Island. Throughout the 1860s, regular announcements in the press trumpeted the merits of the city's various hostelries. In 1861 Miss Street reopened the Pavilion Hotel, opposite St. Dunstan's Cathedral, furnished "in the best style" and generally able to accommodate the public "in a superior manner." The Globe Hotel on Kent Street, renamed North American Hotel in 1863, claimed to be the largest in the city, although the *Islander* thought that it and the other hotels were not large enough to accommodate the visitors expected to be brought to Charlottetown by the now-frequent steamboat service to the mainland. The *Examiner*, however, pointed out that Charlottetown had a dozen "first class" hotels and boarding houses.[20] Apparently, the *Islander* had the better case, because three years later the *Examiner*, too, was lauding a campaign to promote a public company to open "a first class hotel." The Union Hotel, owned by the O'Neill brothers, opened in 1868, and although it was not the hotel anticipated by the *Examiner*, it boasted a first-class ice cream and oyster saloon and a barber shop. Perhaps, the St. Lawrence Hotel on Water Street, owned by the Misses Street, formerly of the Pavilion Hotel, was typical of such establishments. Three storeys in height, the St. Lawrence had 32 guest rooms, an office, a "fine" sitting room and a dining room that could seat 90. Its competitors in 1869 were Osborne House on Water Street, Miss Rankin's Hotel on Pownal, the North American Hotel and Rocklin House on Kent, the Victoria Hotel on Great George and the Terrace House on King Street. In addition, over 100 private boarding houses offered accommodation to the weary traveller. This was now sufficient, in the opinion of the *Examiner*, to house all who might visit the Island that summer. The paper saw "nothing to prevent the pleasure-seeker from paying Charlottetown a visit."

This, of course, was exactly the point: there was nothing to prevent visitors from coming, but nothing in the way of hotel accommodation to induce them to come. That shortcoming was recognized two years later, when following widespread public discussion of the need for better hotels, the paper concluded that the efforts to accommodate tourists had been "feeble" and reflected "a lack of energy" on the part of the city's investors. It called for the creation of a joint stock company to build a commodious hotel in Charlottetown which, along with a similar one in Summerside, would be an inducement to "pleasure-seekers and invalids" from Canada and the United States to visit. Not only would increased tourist traffic boost trade, but it would encourage real estate markets in rural areas through the construction of cottages along the rivers and attract capital. Four years later, the situation remained much the same, although the Revere House had appeared opposite the Steam Navigation Company wharf at the corner of Great George and Water Streets. Even the arrival of the railway did little to provoke an improvement, with the existing hotels changing hands and the expectation for a new, big hotel resting on the hope that "some public spirited individual will take hold of and push the enterprise."

20 These would have included the Mansion House, which hosted the New Brunswick delegation during the Charlottetown Conference, and the Franklin Hotel, where part of the Canadian delegation stayed. The Nova Scotians checked into the Pavilion.

The quarter-century following incorporation saw Charlottetown's economic position strengthen in some respects and weaken in others. The city's dominance over its Island hinterland was increased by improved roads and the construction of the railway. Its banks buttressed the capital's position as the Island's financial centre. At the same time, commerce was risky and the manufacturing sector tentative. Trade links overseas declined while Confederation brought Prince Edward Island into the Canadian continental economic orbit. Gaining access to this new market became a priority for local businessmen, but the way forward was neither assured nor even clear.

SOCIAL LIFE

The years following incorporation were apprehensive ones for a lot of Charlottetonians. To some extent this angst is surprising. Population growth continued, now largely driven by natural increase rather than immigration. A measure of economic prosperity held promise for the future. A healthy sense of community was sustained by a network of social institutions and organizations. Even so, many citizens felt insecure. Financial worries led to fretting about avoidable expenses. Individually, citizens feared for their security, both of their person and their property. Such concerns were expressed by civic opinion makers. An underclass of the poor, or ill or depraved, lived with insecurity on a daily basis, but their anxieties went largely unrecorded. The sun, of course, shone into the lives of Charlottetonians, and it would be wrong to overemphasize their fears. It is important to note, though, a lingering perception of vulnerability during this era.

Education

Charlottetown's school system remained a fragmented mix of religious and secular institutions after incorporation. The Free Education Act of 1852 provided that the colonial government would pay teachers' salaries if certain conditions were met. One of these involved the provision of school buildings by local inhabitants. Government support was intended to defray much of the cost of attendance, and funding was available for denominational facilities, such as St. Paul's School and the Bog School,[21] connected with the Church of England, as well as the non-denominational Central Academy. Most schools were expected to provide instruction to a level equivalent to today's grade 10. In 1855 St. Dunstan's College was opened by the Roman Catholic Church to provide senior secondary education and university preparation courses to rural students and local "day" scholars. A non-sectarian Normal School was opened in 1856 to provide specialized training for future teachers. This was followed in 1860 by the creation of Prince of Wales College out of the Central Academy to offer similar levels of education as St. Dunstan's. The Catholics, meanwhile, in 1857 had started a small convent school for girls on Sydney Street initially staffed by four sisters of the Congregation of Notre Dame from Montreal. A few years later, in 1864,

21 After 1868, the Bog School occupied a new building at the corner of Rochford and Kent Streets.

Bog School, Rochfort Street, c. 1870 (above). Notre Dame Convent, c. 1915 (left). Denominational schools, like the Anglican's Bog School and the school for girls operated by the Notre Dame Convent, were also eligible for public funds under the 1852 Free Education Act.

St. Joseph's Convent school opened. In 1870 two new Roman Catholic schools were inaugurated: St. Patrick's School overlooking Queen Square for boys and the greatly expanded Notre Dame Convent school for girls opposite Hillsborough Square. St. Peter's Anglican Cathedral opened a school for boys on Rochford Square in 1871, and a girls' school joined it in 1875. In January 1871, the Wesleyans began their academy on Upper Prince Street.

Despite this plethora of institutions, or perhaps partly because of it, a school inspector reported in 1874 that schools in Charlottetown were poorly run and poorly attended. By all accounts, he was right. Attendance varied as some children tended to drift from school to school and felt free to absent themselves. The school buildings were typically small, cramped, stuffy, poorly heated and not well-maintained. Teachers were poorly paid, but some of them, such as Miss Harvie of the Bog School, were highly esteemed and devoted. Even with all the deficiencies, however, some children were receiving sound educations. The accomplishments of the students at exam time attracted considerable interest and were noted in the local newspapers.

One of the principal objectives of 19th-century public education was the inculcation of the community's young with the conventional social beliefs and behavioural standards of the day. Charlottetown was no exception to this rule. Even as incorporation was being considered by the colonial legislature, thought was also being given to the needs of the future city's schools. In the spring of 1855, the government, noting the prevalence of poor, "demoralized" children in the streets of town and before the courts, proposed an amendment to the Normal School Act to provide for a free school for the poor. Not only would such an institution save young waifs charged with crimes, which, it was supposed, they would not have committed if they had received the benefits of an education, it would prepare them for more advanced studies. The government intended that preference for admissions would be given to orphans.

The debate on this charitable initiative was soon aligned along the customary urban-rural divide. Rural members noted that Charlottetown already had ten public and four private schools and felt that the poor should merely be given subsidies to attend one of these. Supporters of the amendment argued that poor children who began in regular schools often dropped out because their sometimes ragged and shoeless condition set them apart from the other students. Impoverished parents also found the small fee of 1s 6d more than they wished to pay. In the end, the legislature agreed to provide £40 a year to engage a teacher to run a free school for poor children aged from four to ten.

Two years later, a much more serious political debate concerning schools was raging, involving an issue that touched upon the very values they were meant to impart. It began in 1856 when John Stark, the Inspector of Schools for the Island's board of education and the first principal of the newly opened Normal School, called for the use of the Bible as a school text. Stark had recently arrived from Scotland, and he sought to emulate the system as it existed in his former home. This proposal broke the delicate balance that had hitherto existed between Protestants and Roman Catholics. Roman Catholics opposed the move because the version of the Bible to be introduced was not sanctioned by their church. Their bishop asked that Catholic children not be required to read a version in which they had no faith, nor to receive religious instruction from persons unskilled in biblical interpretation. No objection was made to Bible study outside of regular hours for students whose parents wanted it. Some opponents of the measure suspected it was an attempt by Protestants to proselytize impressionable, young Roman Catholic pupils. Others believed the proposal was really an effort by the colonial government's political opposition to gain an advantage over its rivals. Whatever the reason, a disruptive religious squabble was soon under way.

At a meeting in Charlottetown addressed by some Protestant clergymen, the Roman Catholics were accused of trying to have the Bible removed from the schools. The Catholic Bishop was characterized as a Bible-hater who wanted it burned. These views were considered extreme, even by many Protestants, but petitions to implement the proposal were sent to the colonial legislature. There, where the Liberal government had just been re-elected with a slim, two-seat majority, the measure made little progress. But the following year the demand was renewed specifically for the Bible's use in the Normal School and Central Academy. In the case of the academy, the legislation governing its operation specified that no religious test was to be introduced into its operation, and use of the Bible was viewed as just such a test. In the Normal School, the Bible already could be read before classes began or after the end of the regular day to students whose parents requested it. Use of the Bible during school hours formed the backdrop of the colonial election of 1859 in which Conservatives ousted the Liberals by espousing the Protestant cause. Once again, the assembly debated the issue. The consensus that emerged was that the original legislation, passed 30 years previously, which sought to ensure peace among Roman Catholics and Protestants over Central Academy, was wise and should not be disturbed. As for the Normal School, so long as there was no prohibition of the use of the Bible, proponents of the status quo argued the interests of all were preserved.

The discussion took an unexpected turn, however, when one of the teachers at the Central Academy, John Kenny, was named headmaster. Kenny was a Roman Catholic, the first to obtain the post, and the same group that had campaigned for introduction of the Bible to the academy proceeded to denounce his scholarly credentials in an attempt to head off his appointment. Their objectives were sectarian rather than pedagogical, but they proposed to subject Kenny to an examination to see if his knowledge was equal to the task. This challenge was not taken up, although the offended Kenny was apparently willing to submit to questioning by qualified examiners. While the Bible debate caused considerable consternation at the time and helped to unseat the Liberals in the general election of 1859, the heat sparked no flames. With the change in government, no immediate effort was made to implement demands for use of the Bible as a textbook. Nevertheless, the relations between Catholics and Protestants in the schools were precarious and liable to ignite at the slightest provocation.

A *modus vivendi* of sorts existed in Charlottetown where Methodist, Anglican and Roman Catholic schools received provincial funding to pay for part of their operating costs. Roman Catholics hoped to adopt this approach generally and establish a province-wide system of publicly supported, religiously separate schools. This issue came to a head in 1876. Both Liberal and Conservative parties were fractured by it, with supporters of both sides crossing party lines.[22] The ensuing Public Schools Act of 1877 was intended to establish a more formal administrative structure for education and to resolve the religious issue finally by creating a single non-denominational system. Following its passage, funding for denominational schools was withdrawn. The province was divided into school districts, and the schools within each were operated as a joint enterprise involving the provincial government and a local board of trustees. The province supervised the schools, licensed teachers and maintained standards of instruction, while local authorities managed school property and funds and employed the teachers. Salaries were paid partly by the province and partly by the district trustees who raised money through the assessment of local ratepayers.

Charlottetown had its own school district and school board. The board was composed of seven members, four appointed by the province and three by the city.

22 Protestant Liberals and Conservatives formed the Free School Coalition, while Catholic Conservatives and Liberals joined into the Denominationalist Coalition, although they ran as Conservatives. The Free School Coalition won the election of 1876 with a majority of 19 to 11. The Public Schools Act followed.

City Council did not welcome this additional responsibility, and consequently the burden to organize the city schools fell to the government-appointed members. The work went ahead with the help of the Principal of the Normal School. Not all of the religious schools were immediately closed, but, by 1880, two important confessional schools had been rented by the city's school board and brought under its jurisdiction. The Wesleyan Academy became Prince Street School, and St. Patrick's was renamed Queen Square School.[23] Although the Christian Brothers, who had staffed St. Patrick's since its opening, by convention it remained Roman Catholic, and its teachers were hired accordingly. This began the practice of maintaining *de facto* Catholic schools inside the city's public school system. Construction began on a third public school, West Kent, in 1878, to serve the children of the western part of town. Roman Catholic girls continued to be educated in the two convent schools as the province refused to license the nuns who staffed them. St. Paul's School and the St. Peter's Schools also remained open, as did St. Dunstan's College, which served Catholics and some non-Catholics, and Prince of Wales College, which attracted mainly Protestant students. Both Protestants and Roman Catholics attended the Normal School, which was joined with PWC in 1879.

Public Health

Not all educational challenges were connected with the organization of the school system. There was much to accomplish in educating the public about matters connected to health and sanitation. Prevailing opinion about disease control in the early part of the 19th century was fatalistic. Recurring outbreaks of typhoid fever, smallpox, cholera and tuberculosis were regarded as calamities to be endured. While medical practitioners could diagnose these diseases with some certainty, cures were less than reliable.[24] The best knowledge of the day held that disease was spread by miasma, or bad vapours produced by swamps, cesspools and rotting plant or animal matter. People who were in a weakened physical or moral state were especially susceptible to infections from such bad air. The answer to the threat of disease was to try to maintain a clean environment and to live a healthy, moral life. When afflicted, the sick were quarantined and given whatever care was possible, but death rates were high. New scientific knowledge based on the understanding of bacteria appeared as the century progressed, but it took time for such knowledge to spread and even longer for whole populations in communities to accept and implement unfamiliar forms of treatment.

Incorporation gave the city the power to establish a board of health with the same powers as the county boards. Council opted to constitute itself the city's board of health with the mayor as chairman. In many ways, the board was a direct extension of the colonial government. The duties of the board were clearly outlined in colonial

23 The Christian Brothers withdrew from the school at this time.

24 Vaccination against smallpox was a well-known procedure by this time, but far from everyone was protected in this way.

legislation, and its expenses were to be borne by the colonial government. Because costs were incurred by one level of government for which another level was liable, there inevitably arose issues of prompt repayment of expenses. The city also was vested with the responsibility for running the quarantine hospital when it was needed. The keepers were paid in kind (an annual supply of firewood), and the insurance on it also involved some financial outlay. Again, the city had to turn to the colonial government to cover its costs. After Confederation, the obligation to pay these bills was transferred to the federal government.

For its part, the hospital was not a matter of high priority with the board of health; yet it was a first line of defence against recurring outbreaks of smallpox, one of the most serious diseases to appear in Charlottetown. While vaccination against this disease was a well-understood precaution by mid-century, not everyone was protected, and, in the minds of some, it was still a procedure that had to be proven.[25] When infections occurred, persons suffering from smallpox were removed to the quarantine hospital as soon as their state was detected.[26] In many instances, the disease was introduced by the crews of visiting ships. When smallpox was reported on an inbound vessel, the board of health could order it to remain anchored offshore and then apply to the Lieutenant Governor to order it to remain in quarantine for a specified period of time. Sites of infection were fumigated with gases, such as sulphurous acid gas, and contaminated clothes and other textiles were destroyed. Even so, quarantine was not always effective. In 1859 the board of health reported that a washerwoman caught smallpox from a seaman's clothes she had taken in for laundering, not knowing that the man was carrying the disease.

There was little clinical provision of health care in the early years of the city's life. Many procedures were performed in the homes of patients or the offices of physicians. An important step forward came in 1879 when the Roman Catholic Bishop of Charlottetown, Peter McIntyre, converted his old episcopal residence on Dorchester Street into the Charlottetown Hospital. It was a small facility offering free medical advice and prescriptions to the poor and was operated by the Sisters of Charity.

Water and Sewerage Services

Diseases associated with contaminated water and poor sanitation posed a greater challenge than smallpox because their sources were always present and their causes were poorly known. Without the knowledge of water-borne bacterial infection, the health benefits of a water works and distribution network were not fully appreciated. A lively debate, however, did arise in Charlottetown about the provision of water, but it was one driven by the aesthetic qualities of piped water and the hope for reduced fire insurance rates. Even so, foul-tasting and smelly, discoloured water was in time linked

25 The cost of vaccination, particularly for large families, would have been a factor for some residents.

26 This facility was located at Battery Point after 1860, but it was destroyed by fire in 1869 and only replaced in 1874.

with disease. The development of a municipal water supply became one of the defining political issues of the post-incorporation period. It pitted those who favoured small, inexpensive municipal government against those who accepted substantial public expenditures as necessary for community well-being. Without the hammer of disease control to decide the issues of clean drinking water and proper sewerage, the debates about them failed to reach a final conclusion before 1880. They nevertheless provided a fascinating view into the mindset of decision-makers and the workings of civic politics.

Note the public pump in this c. 1870 photo of St. Dunstan's Cathedral.

Water for domestic use was hand-pumped from wells scattered throughout the city. These also supplied firefighters but were supplemented for that purpose by large underground cisterns that stored rain runoff. A list of 46 pump locations was recorded nine months after incorporation. Pumps and wells required constant maintenance, such as placing clay around the well to ensure the drainage of surface water away from the source of drinking water, and making repairs to pump handles and water troughs. One of the earliest standing committees of City Council dealt with the numerous complaints about these installations and requests for new ones. In 1857 the city issued a contract to Robert Percival to keep 47 pumps in working order for a fee of £60 per year, a not inconsiderable amount given the city's small budget. In subsequent years, maintenance of the wells continued to be done under contract.

Wells were periodically tested for impurities and contamination. An 1869 report on the well situated in Hillsborough Square found the water to be somewhat saline because of "the proximity of seawater" and polluted by runoff from a nearby cesspool which "had been in constant use by a large number of boys" and never cleaned out "since it was first dug." While the number of wells in Charlottetown had increased to 57 by 1877 and were distributed fairly evenly throughout the city, with the exception of the Bog, the overall quality of water declined due to overuse and contamination. At times, polluted wells could never again be made suitable for drinking water. One such pump on Prince Street was cleaned out, sweetened with charcoal and left in general use with the words "bad water" painted on the pump handle.

An alternate source of drinking water was the freshwater spring found in Spring Park. Charlottetonians made ample use of this source, and in 1868 some local carters

Mayors Dawson (left) and DesBrisay (right) were dogged advocates of a municipal water-works system.

proposed to haul its water to town for sale door-to-door. The city drafted a by-law to regulate such operators. In May, two men were licensed to deliver the water at a charge not to exceed one penny a pailful. To encourage the enterprise, the city forgave a licence fee for any vehicle used exclusively for the purpose. For those who could afford it, this supply of more wholesome drinking water somewhat offset the problems with wells within the built-up parts of the city. Later that year, the municipal health officer, Dr. J. T. Jenkins, showed that an outbreak of cholera in an area near the corner of Prince and Kent Streets was linked to the local well. Following tests by Thomas J. Leeming, the well was closed and others were tested. Clearly, the reliance upon shallow wells was proving to be woefully inappropriate as Charlottetown grew.

Some citizens had looked to incorporation as an opportunity to construct a water system in the city. Despite the best efforts of the advocates of a municipal water works, however, the city's meagre finances frustrated them. Unlike the gas works, there was no possibility that a consortium of private investors would undertake the project. It would have to be built as a public enterprise and paid for through taxes. That made ratepayers extremely cautious. In early 1869, Henry J. Cundall wrote to the city about the need for a "copious supply of wholesome water," and Council asked him, Thomas DesBrisay and Thomas Leeming to compare the elevation of the spring on Brackley Point Road with the one at Holland Grove within the city's boundaries. This investigation led nowhere, as did an enquiry sent to Saint John, New Brunswick, concerning the cost and specifications of the artesian wells that supplied water to that city. The initiatives, however, demonstrate the two possible sources for Charlottetown's drinking water.

In 1870 advocates of pure water prevailed upon the city to hire an engineer, Charles Fairbanks of Halifax, to propose the best way to provide Charlottetown with clean water. He reported that Spring Park, now being built up, was susceptible to pollution and too close to sea level. Use of artesian wells was inadvisable because the bedrock was too soft to ensure good water quality. His preferred solution was a reservoir at Winter River, high enough to permit the water to flow to the city by gravity and, at a distance of five miles, close enough to the city to keep costs reasonable. He praised the quality of the water and estimated that the work could be done for $100,000.[27] This was a huge sum, given the size of the city's, or even the colony's, budget. Indeed, Fairbanks' fee of £169 was more than the city could comfortably afford. He ultimately had to threaten to sue the city for payment and eventually agreed to accept a three-year bond as payment.[28] In March 1871, the colonial legislature was asked to permit the city to raise the money for a water works through the sale of debentures.[29] Approval for the water measure was obtained in 1872.

The issue then became enmeshed in the politics of finance. Some urged caution because of the costs involved, while others lauded the Fairbanks scheme. In 1873 slow sale of the debentures forced the city to ask the now provincial government to guarantee them so as to encourage potential purchasers. The province ultimately agreed but required the approval of the voters in the upcoming civic elections. This was an astute move on the part of provincial politicians who feared they might ultimately be left with paying for the project. In the vote that followed, opposition to the water scheme prevailed. Two years later, supporters of a water works counterattacked. Members of the "Water Works Promoters Association" unanimously resolved to work for the election of any candidate in the upcoming civic elections who would support "a feasible plan proposed and drawn up by a thoroughly qualified civil engineer." In the ensuing vote, pro-water works nominees regained control of Council with the promise to find the cheapest way to reach their objective. Gilbert Murdoch, the water works engineer for Saint John, New Brunswick, was retained as a consultant. The city also decided to engage another engineer to examine the option of sinking artesian wells at Mount Edward. Lack of money dogged these efforts. Mayor DesBrisay pleaded with the province to fund the boring of test wells under a program intended to pay for explorations for coal deposits, but he was apparently unsuccessful and the studies were never concluded. The following year, Council requested permission to issue debentures to pay for the work. Then, in 1880 Mayor W. E. Dawson, a powerful and persistent advocate of a water works, got his Council to agree to have Murdoch

27 This conclusion was tested when Councillors decided to send samples of water taken from the sites specified in Fairbanks' report and others taken from the principal wells in the city to scientists in London, England, and Windsor, Nova Scotia, to be examined and graded according to their suitability for drinking and other domestic purposes. Tests conducted subsequently by Professor Dana Hayes of Boston confirmed the excellent quality of Winter River water when compared to Spring Park water or water drawn from a well in Market Square.

28 These were subsequently converted into 10-year debentures, making the hapless Fairbanks the only off-Island holder of Charlottetown debt.

29 The government was in addition asked to have the engineers working on the PEI Railway assess the Fairbanks plan.

Bird's Eye Map, 1878. The proximity of foundries and tanneries (and their resulting effluent) so close to local water sources contributed to calls for a waterworks.

complete his survey. The increasingly desperate state of civic finances meant, however, that immediate action on Murdoch's report, whatever his recommendation, lay beyond the city's means.

Lack of progress in establishing a water works kept the sewerage question in the background. The two were linked, though, sometimes in the public's mind and cer tainly in practice, because large volumes of water made an efficient means of disposing of effluent necessary. As it was, Charlottetown's method of waste disposal was typical of any community of its size in British North America in the mid-Victorian period. Residences and public buildings had pit privies. Domestic and animal waste and effluent from manufacturers were dumped into cesspools found in low spots throughout the city. A particularly offensive feature was Government Pond, located in the low-lying western end of town between Kent and Euston Streets. All manner of waste was dumped into its waters from various sources, including two tanneries. Occasionally, when a privy was overused or storms or spring runoff swelled a cesspool, contaminants escaped into the general environment, creating a mess, fouling water supplies and assaulting noses.

There was not much that could be done about the waste problem. A city scavenger collected night soil and other noxious litter, and some residents dug dry wells, or pits reaching down into the ground where swill and other liquid wastes would leach into the surrounding earth. By-laws prohibited nuisances, and when situations became unbearable, the city could order them rectified, such as when Dennis Reddin and John Williams were instructed to remove the stagnant water from their property within

48 hours, or have the city do the work for them at their expense. Although citizens were aware of the health and aesthetic dangers of pollution, the worst cases tended to be seasonal or localized and were accepted with complaint. "The blessing of good health," the *Examiner* noted in May 1875, "has been secured to us by a providential withholding of the seasonable rains of spring." On only two or three days had the well water been "of about the same consistency" as the gutter water. Nevertheless, the issue of pollution of the ground water by surface waste was becoming acute. William Heard, in a letter to the *Examiner* in 1876, asserted that "for the last fifty years or more, the soil has been simply a receptacle for every kind of the foulest filth; that not a public sewer exists in the city, and that in some cases the deep wells have been converted into sinks of poison." Charlottetonians were, in Heard's opinion, faced with emigration to another site, importation of pure water, or being content "to accept the periodical visits of those fearful scourges of typhoid and other epidemics, which have already given us gentle intimations of what is in store."

Public Safety

The water supply affected more than public health. It influenced the effectiveness of the firefighters who battled the "devouring element" that was a constant threat to the city. After incorporation, Charlottetown reorganized its volunteer fire department. Companies were trained to man three hand-operated pump engines and serve as a hook and ladder squad. Membership in the fire companies denoted civic leadership, and senior positions were sought after as marks of social standing. Large numbers of men were involved. In 1861 number two company had up to 30 on the squad, and the hook and ladder company consisted of 20 men. Each volunteer was paid £1 per year for his service. Equipment was stored at various places throughout the city; in 1871 fire houses were located on Union Street, Grafton Street and King Square.

Charlottetonians were given to grumbling about their inefficient fire service. In a report to City Council in 1856, Henry Palmer, the Chief Engineer of the Fire Department, recognized this situation by noting that "the public have not yet had a fair opportunity of seeing what these three [engine] companies can do towards extinguishing a fire for the best reason that can be given, *viz*: at each fire as [*sic*] they are invariably fully one half their time idle for want of water."[30] The problem lay, not with the firemen, but with the lack of sufficient equipment, especially carts, to haul water from pumps and cisterns to the engines at the scene of a blaze. The need for hoses, proper housing for equipment and other necessities posed an ongoing financial challenge for City Council, which continually sought additional sources of revenue in the form of grants from the colonial government or permission to augment the small civic budget through increased taxation.

---

30 Palmer's letter also reported that the number one engine, "the Prince Edward," was quite dilapidated. Repairs to equipment, however, were impeded by the same financial restraints which plagued the rest of the civic operations. The letter refers to additional pump engines from the Barracks and from Mr. Coles, which were usually brought to fires.

The "Great Fire" of 1866 ravaged four city blocks.

Beyond the matter of equipment, the simple unavailability of adequate sources of water hindered firefighting. By 1858 H. J. Cundall, Agent for the Equitable Insurance Company, in a letter to Council threatened to recommend his company withdraw from Prince Edward Island unless a "reasonable precaution against fire" were taken. Cundall's letter was prompted by a serious conflagration in a block-making shop in Water Street on December 22, 1857, which spread to a house and a flour and tobacco store. "Owing to the great want of water, and the delay in getting the fire engines in readiness," the fire then engulfed two more houses and a large building which housed a sail loft and another store and warehouse. The current chief engineer of the fire department, Silas Barnard, blamed the inability to contain the flames immediately on the lack of water, a condition, he asserted, that would remain "until proper reservoirs are prepared in the thickly built-up parts of the City." The effectiveness of the fire service thus hinged upon the adequate supply of water for firefighting, and this issue remained a matter of public discussion for some years.

The "Great Fire" of 1866, which ravaged four city blocks, removed any doubt that weaknesses in the system of fire protection had to be immediately addressed. Beginning at the corner of Pownal and King Streets, flames carried by shifting westerly breezes moved southward to Water Street, northward to Dorchester Street and then eastward on a broad front almost to Great George Street. The fire department, volunteer citizens and troops temporarily garrisoned in the city were powerless to halt the ravaging blaze. At its peak, the roar of the flames could be heard for miles around, and the heat was so intense no one could safely approach within 100 yards. Burning fragments of buildings were carried for miles by the wind. In the fire's wake, only heaps of rubble and scorched masonry chimneys remained, along with homeless citizens. Some of the poorest people had to be provided with food and temporary shelter in public buildings. Despite the efforts of the firefighters, this, the greatest of the city's conflagrations, demonstrated how limited were its fire defences. The buckets and hand-pumped fire engines had proven to be hopelessly inadequate, and wells ran dry at the height of the emergency. This knowledge added to the general apprehension about the security of property in the urban core.

The Great Fire was believed to have been started by an arsonist, part of a pattern of incidents that terrorized Charlottetonians in the mid-1860s. Beyond increasing nighttime surveillance of the streets, citizens mobilized to obtain modern firefighting equipment. Following a public meeting, a subscription list was created to record pledges of money from individuals and fire insurance companies for the purchase of a modern, steam-powered pumping engine. Such a machine could draw large volumes of water on its own from cisterns or nearby rivers and discharge a steady stream onto distant targets. Private subscriptions and a special £300 grant from the legislature meant the purchase was made without relying upon the city's meagre regular budget. The engine was ordered from Merryweather and Sons, an English manufacturer, and cost over £1,340. Adapted to allow sea water to be drawn while fresh water was used in its boiler, it was promptly tested after its arrival in Charlottetown towards the end of October 1866. Delighted citizens watched as water, sucked from the harbour, passed through 1,200 feet of hose and was thrown over the old Wesleyan Chapel to a height of 80 feet.

The purchase of a steam fire engine, however, could not solve all of the city's firefighting problems. Several weeks later, the new apparatus proved ineffective at a fire because the large company required to position it and unroll and join multiple lengths of hose lacked adequate equipment and training. Also, at first, the horses needed to haul the engine were stabled in one part of town, the engine house was located in another area, and the man with the keys to the stable lived in yet a third district. It could take an hour to get the horses to the engine. Nevertheless, the new engine proved itself on May 23, 1867, when "the fire fiend" set a small house on Kent Street ablaze. It was in close proximity to a furniture store and the home of Hon. George Coles, but "the Steam Fire Engine was soon on the ground, and poured [water] on the burning roof." Little damage was done to the house. The same cannot be said of Coles. The Premier's premature dementia, exacerbated by his efforts fighting the Great Fire, was further advanced by this latest act of arson. His public life was soon over.[31]

Equipment maintenance and tight finances nevertheless remained significant challenges to overcome. During a fire in 1871 in which the old guard house on the grounds of Government House was destroyed, the steam fire engine broke down as it turned a corner. Its small wooden wheels were dry and brittle and gave way under the strain. Other equipment wore out as well. By the early 1870s, two hand-pumped engines were getting old, and a new one was ordered from England in June 1873 after protracted negotiations over finances with the colonial government. When it arrived following Confederation, new Dominion customs duties were imposed, adding further to the city's woes. When Council subsequently decided to import another engine, it

31 Other factors in Coles' decline include overwork, anxiety and the sudden death of Edward Whelan in December 1867.

resolved to ask both the provincial and dominion governments to pay grants in lieu of taxes on their properties to help defray the costs.[32] With or without such aid, the city was obliged to buy a new steam fire engine in 1875 when the old one almost gave out during a major fire. An American Silsby engine costing $4,000 was ordered and was dubbed "The Hillsboro" when it arrived the following spring. By 1877 the Charlottetown fire department boasted a total complement of 272 officers and men, including a hook and ladder company of 44, and was housed in locations on Grafton, Pownal, Kent and King Streets and on Peake's Wharf. Equipment included five hand-pumped engines and two steam engines.

The challenges confronted by the local constabulary may have been less dramatic than a raging inferno, but the police force faced similar financial and public relations challenges. The force was the main visible symbol of civic authority. Incorporation had reorganized law enforcement by replacing the Board of Magistrates with a Police, or Mayor's, Court consisting of the mayor and one Councillor serving on a rotating basis. Day-to-day policing was undertaken by a small force initially composed of a marshal and six constables.[33] They shared the refurbished Plaw courthouse on Queen Square with the city government and accompanied the city administration in its move to the market house in 1872. The appointment of full-time policemen was necessitated in part by the departure of the permanent garrison of British troops in 1854. But they were also needed to establish a more consistent application of municipal laws. The city force was charged with enforcing the by-laws of the new city covering public health, market regulations, animal control, protection of property and maintenance of moral and orderly behaviour. Serious criminal offences were also attended to, but these were far fewer in number.

Much police work consisted of controlling disorderly drunks and breaking up scuffles — the most frequent charges brought against offenders appearing before the mayor's court. There was a significant level of rowdyism in the 1860s and 1870s, particularly among the city's youth, and considerable property damage resulted. Infractions included theft of fruit from gardens, vandalism of graveyards, harassment of innocent passers-by, and, in one interesting case, the defilement of George Coles' pew by a youth who disliked Liberals. Even the mayor, Theophilus DesBrisay, was roughed up in 1871 on his way home. The *Examiner* complained in May 1871 that "scarcely a night passes without a portion of our City being disturbed by gangs of riotous persons, breaking glass and otherwise destroying property." The paper recommended creation of "Vigilance Committees" in each ward to be made up of householders who would apprehend and punish such offenders. This approach to law enforcement had been tried with some apparent success during the arsonist attacks in 1866. Burglaries were also fairly common occurrences, but these crimes were harder to solve. Charlottetown's

32 Council may have been encouraged in this request by a provincial grant of money for firefighting made in 1874.

33 The number of policemen varied over time and was supplemented by the appointment of night watchmen. In 1868, for instance, there were eight constables and four occasional night watchmen.

functions as a market centre and a port generated illicit activities, including the operation of unlicensed taverns and bawdy houses, the latter apparently centred in the Bog and along Spring Park Road. Crime in the city spiked at various times, such as just prior to the opening of navigation when strangers were visiting the city, in the autumn when the fishermen were in port, and during the regatta, which induced "a large amount of drunkenness and idleness." During these periods, civic authorities appointed special constables if the threats were perceived to be serious.

Not all of the defendants in the Mayor's Court were exuberant youth and visiting sailors. Artemas G. Sims, a Councillor for Ward 3, and William Crabb, the tax collector, were charged with receiving stolen goods. Sims was excluded from Council meetings for six months in 1857 while he pleaded his innocence. Police constables also appeared before the bench, usually on drunken and disorderly charges. In 1860 an officer was fired for his intoxicated behaviour, but in 1866 another policeman saved his job by joining the Order of the Sons of Temperance. In 1862 three city officials appeared in court, charged with falsifying their financial reports. The prosecutor, himself, ran afoul of the law when he stabbed a fellow party-goer in the head. The case was settled out of court with the prosecutor paying the court costs. Occasionally distinguished criminals made their appearance. Ewen Amos, a "notorious" forger who specialized in fraudulent financial notes, was sent to jail in 1859 for two years on two indictments for forgery, although his other criminal actions "for which better men have been hung [*sic*]" went unpunished.

Murder was punishable by death by hanging. One particularly notable execution took place in April 1869 when George Dowie was publicly hanged in the jail yard on Pownal Square for murdering a drinking buddy.[34] Twice Dowie dropped to the ground before he was finally despatched to the great beyond. The large crowd of onlookers was appalled, and the uproar that followed ensured that it was the Island's last public execution. By this time, the severity of the death penalty was having an impact on the public mind. On August 14, 1878, a young mulatto boy, George Kelly, was shot on Fitzroy Street. The 16-year-old had been playing with friends when he was fired upon from a horse-drawn vehicle carrying two young white men. A couple of suspects, Louis Johnston and James Millner, were promptly arrested, Millner at his home and Johnston hiding aboard a vessel moored in the harbour. At the coroner's inquest, defence counsel E. J. Hodgson emphasized the fate awaiting the two alleged murderers if they were named as the persons causing the death. The inquest concluded that the assailants were unknown. During the trial that followed, most witnesses were, like Kelly, coloured inhabitants of the poorest part of town. While several testified they recognized the accused as the men in the wagon, two key witnesses claimed they could not identify them. Hodgson emphasized the degraded circumstances in which the prosecution's witnesses lived and, at the last moment, produced four "virtuous

34 This may have been the last public hanging in what is now Canada. Patrick James Whelan was hanged publicly in Ottawa in February 1869 for the assassination of Thomas D'Arcy McGee. The last public execution in Newfoundland was that of John Flood in 1835.

and undefiled young [white] women" who swore the accused were in another part of town at the time of the murder. The defendants were found not guilty, and no one else was ever charged in the case. Racism was clearly an important factor in the proceedings, as was the drastic penalty if the accused had been found guilty. In an earlier case, Donald McNeill had been found guilty of murdering William Lane and was duly sentenced to be hanged. After a public outcry based upon the belief that he was "a person of unsound mind," the "awful sentence upon the wretched criminal" was commuted to life imprisonment.

The greatest perceived threat to Charlottetown's law and order in its early years came during the Tenant League disturbances. This association, founded in Charlottetown in May 1864, brought together tenant farmers and some urban supporters in opposition to the prevailing system of land ownership, which denied farmers ownership of the land they occupied. Members pledged to refuse payments of farm rents and to act collectively to prevent landlords and the authorities from enforcing the law. In this way, they hoped to pressure estate-owners into selling their land to individual farmers. On March 17, 1865, a crowd of demonstrators, numbering 500 to 600 or more, crossed the frozen harbour from Southport and marched through the streets of the capital to demonstrate their support for the League. It was an orderly procession and few incidents occurred, but one scuffle involving Sam Fletcher, a farmer from Lot 50, resulted in a decision by the colonial executive council to arrest him, using whatever means was necessary. A *posse comitatus*, or body of unpaid citizen volunteers or conscripts acting in support of the county sheriff, was assembled on April 7. The band of around 150 men, many of whom were reported to be sympathizers of the Tenant League, slogged through the spring mud to Fletcher's farm, only to find him gone.[35] On July 26 of the same year, a less peaceful mob attempted to free Charles Dickieson, a tenant leaguer who had been jailed for riot, assault and rescue. Two shots were fired, but no one was injured. The following month, the colonial government recalled imperial troops from Halifax to reassert the rule of law, and by mid-1866 the League had all but collapsed.

Sectarianism was another flash point. The divide between Roman Catholics and Protestants was recognized as a significant factor in politics, education and the provision of social services. For the most part, the forces of moderation held the upper hand, ensuring that compromises, such as the one for education, bridged the social fissures. Infrequently, matters got out of hand. One such occasion took place on July 12, 1877, when Catholic rowdies confronted Orangemen parading home after an excursion. The marchers had reached their hall and raised an orange flag when they were attacked by a group of unruly, and possibly drunk, hooligans. Stones were thrown at the Orangemen, a few of whom, in turn, drew pistols and fired back. No one was seriously injured, and calmer heads convinced both sides to go home. A resumption of hostilities was feared for the next day, but when the two groups reassembled, the

35 At the time, the *posse*, the members of which were all conscripts, was seen as a means of informally punishing Charlottetonians who collaborated or sympathized with the Tenant Leaguers.

police, temporarily strengthened by 100 special constables and backed by a unit of mounted militia, arrested the "street rowdies." General public opinion condemned the violence all around, and the incident was written off as a confrontation between corner loafers and hotheads. What is remarkable is the number of firearms carried by the public and the rapidity with which they could be used. Charlottetown's streets were not necessarily safe places.

The public's overall sense of security was, in fact, quite low, with a general perception that crime was on the increase. Much of this involved the destruction of property, either through random outbreaks of violence or "attempts at incendiarism." Two extra policemen were hired on a temporary basis in 1867 following the departure of the British troops, but the problem remained. "What do we pay a Police for," demanded the *Examiner*, "if it is not to preserve order, and if they cannot keep the peace for a few hours, let them be discharged." In 1871 the force was increased again to eight members, including a sergeant, and the number was further enlarged in 1875 with the addition of another two policemen and a night watchman. In a separate move, also in 1875, the mayor's court was replaced by a stipendiary magistrate, a paid judge who was expected to be an experienced barrister. The new appointee, Rowan R. Fitzgerald, had his work cut out for him, in the opinion of the *Examiner*, which noted that "the evil doers of the town have arrived at such a high state of efficiency and recklessness in rascality and crime, that a considerable amount of magisterial labor will be required ere they are brought to their proper level."

At the opposite end of the law enforcement process lay the prisons. Cells were located in the police station where drunks, rowdies and vagrants were locked up. Offenders found guilty of serious crimes were sent to the county jail on Pownal Square. There they languished in conditions that fell well short of ideal. In 1869, and again in 1876, Mayor Theophilus DesBrisay complained to the Lieutenant Governor about the "evils" found in the prison. Despite the generally commendable efforts of the jailer, circumstances in the facility were hardly conducive to the prisoners' rehabilitation. Inmates were not classified, and juveniles, some as young as seven years old, were locked up with hardened criminals. There were also no facilities in which sentences of hard labour could be imposed in a meaningful way. In some instances, inmates suffering from mental problems were mixed with the criminals; and, in others, paupers were locked up merely because they had nowhere else to go. City Council voted in 1873 to approach the Island government to erect a reformatory for the confinement of juvenile criminals or those whose parents had been imprisoned. If a formal proposal were actually made, no action seems to have ensued.

Public Morality and Social Welfare

Maintenance of the poor and, to a certain extent, care for the mentally ill were, first and foremost, family responsibilities in mid-Victorian times. Paupers without families were given reluctant support by the colonial government, and following the passage of the 1845 Lunatics Act in Britain, public policy favoured treatment of the impoverished insane in publicly maintained institutions. Poor and insane Islanders whose families

Deteriorating conditions at the Lunatic Asylum generated a Grand Jury investigation in 1874. Though no one was brought to trial, the investigation gave impetus to the creation of a new facility, Falconwood, which opened in 1879.

could not provide for them were expected to receive care in the Lunatic Asylum and Workhouse, located at Brighton in the Charlottetown Common. The asylum, like the Queens County Jail, was administered by the colonial government and served needs that were specifically local as well as Island-wide. The government expected that this facility, by housing the poor and the insane together, would aid both groups with a minimum drain upon the public purse. The poor would work for their keep, and the income derived in this way would help pay operating costs and the expense of treating the insane. Problems arose when poor elderly men, who could neither work nor benefit from treatment, collected at the asylum, generating no income and blocking out mental patients requiring care. Nevertheless, at the asylum, overcrowding and underfunding contributed to deteriorating conditions, sometimes deficient patient care, and ultimately to abuses that were documented in 1874 by a Grand Jury headed by J. S. Carvell. The jury's reports resulted in charges being brought against the asylum's keeper, Richard Gidley, and the superintendent, Dr. John Mackieson. In the end, neither was sent to trial, but the scandalous conditions exposed by the report earned the imperial government's censure and a blot on the reputation of Islanders as a compassionate, progressive community. After some further delay, the provincial government began construction of a new facility for the insane in 1877 at Falconwood, northeast of the city. It was completed in 1879.

Unfortunately, much of Charlottetown's underclass could turn neither to the city nor the Island government for help. Those with physical or intellectual limitations often led difficult, sometimes brutal, lives in which aid was only grudgingly given. Age was frequently a factor for those facing hardships. Thomas Pollard was a case in point. For several nights in the depths of the winter of 1856, the infirm 80-year-old sought refuge from the cold in the police station "to the great annoyance of the constables." Ejected from the warmth in the morning, Pollard was lying in the snow in front of the station, as the mayor appealed to the insane asylum for the admission of the "wretched object." The asylum refused and recommended that the city seek help from the colonial government. It is not known if such aid was forthcoming. Nor do we know the fate of John Moore, an 85-year-old resident of Lot 19 in Prince County who had come to Prince Edward Island in 1815 from Newfoundland. He had farmed for a number of years, but surrendered his land because he was unable to pay the rent. He then earned his living as a casual labourer. When he became too old and infirm to work, his son and daughter, who lived in the area, were unable to help with his support. Ultimately, in the autumn of 1868 he boarded the steamer *St. Lawrence* and made his way to Charlottetown where he sought shelter at the police station. Moore was by no means unique, and City Council, faced with an influx of the poor and unemployed from other parts of the Island, drafted a plan to establish a separate poor and work house. Intended to shelter the helpless, oblige the indolent to work and reform youthful delinquents, the proposed institution was never built. Use of part of Victoria Barracks as a makeshift poor house alleviated the situation somewhat until the federal government asked that the building be vacated. Without the resources to act or the influence to convince the Island government to intervene, civic authorities endeavoured to respond to individual cases of need and to suppress the symptoms of poverty. They enacted by-laws prohibiting begging and vagrancy, and, for those unfortunates who met their doom in the streets and whose corpses were deposited on the porch of the mayor's court by helpful citizens, Council passed an order that "no dead bodies shall be placed within the city hall."

The lot of the young could be equally forbidding. Abandoned children posed a perplexing problem. The city's charter made no provision for raising funds for the support of foundlings, and the Island government was slow to respond to such cases. A baby abandoned near St. Dunstan's Cathedral in the autumn of 1871 brought the issue into focus when the mayor and Council unsuccessfully sought funding for its support from the Island government. Money was still a subject of contention three years later when another baby, left at the residence of Benjamin Rogers, was consigned to the care of William Weeks. When Weeks demanded payment for the child's maintenance, Council resolved that the city had no liability in the matter. Provision of support for mentally retarded children who fell under the care of the state was also absent. One young man, who had been brought before the authorities for trespass and for causing a disturbance, could not be confined to the lunatic asylum by the police court, while, at the same time, the Island government refused to provide for his maintenance. Another "idiot boy," aged about 12 years, was assigned to the care of Mary Debbins in July 1872 after he was found abandoned in some bushes near the lunatic asylum. When Mrs. Debbins subsequently asked to be relieved of the responsibility, the city once again turned to the colonial government. Two years later the child was still in the care of Mrs. Debbins, the city still paying two dollars a week for his support while pleading with the colonial government to have him admitted to the lunatic asylum.

Able-bodied children who were neglected by their parents could be taken into custody and assigned to the care of others. Following the receipt of complaints from reputable citizens, hearings were held by the mayor's court to decide if intervention was desirable. Parents of problem children were required to show cause why their offspring should not be bound out as apprentices. Although the fate of the children of one man whose hearing was held in May 1860 is unknown, another was found to have reduced his children to begging because he provided them and their mother with no means of support. He was accordingly ordered to remit regular support payments or be jailed for three months with labour. In April 1871, the two sons of a negligent couple were ordered to be apprenticed to "some fit and proper persons to learn some useful occupation." The boys had been named in complaints as common beggars. One of them, aged 11, was in jail at the time serving a sentence for larceny, and the mayor asked that the balance of the sentence be remitted so that he could be sent to work for a "very respectable" Covehead farmer.

Sometimes civic authorities found it easier to ship out their problems. When a native of Boston appealed for money to pay his way home, the mayor urged he be given a ticket as "he will become a burthen on the Government." Another man arrested as a vagrant had arrived on the Island on one of the vessels of the Steam Navigation

Company, and the city ordered the company either to pay for his upkeep or to return him to his port of origin. Needy persons coming to Charlottetown could expect little sympathy, as one woman, "a lunatic expected shortly to arrive here from Boston," was to discover. Appeals to arrange for her support were denied by City Council. Yet compassion was not unknown. There were instances in which poor widows were exempted from payment of city taxes, and at least one normally law-abiding citizen who had been convicted of a liquor offence was released from jail so that he could provide for his family, while another had a fine remitted because its payment posed too great a hardship for his family.

Liquor Control

One of the more perplexing social issues in the 19th century was the consumption — or overconsumption — of liquor. Regulation of its sale and control of public drunkenness were major tasks facing city governments. Charlottetown was well-serviced with hotels, public houses and saloons, located in all parts of town. They housed weary travellers and refreshed local folk alike.[36] While some outlets were large and well-appointed, others were small and dingy. Sale of spirits was a job of last resort for certain people, including widows, with no other means of support. Importers of liquor, however, included some of the city's leading merchants. Four breweries and distilleries were located in Charlottetown in 1861, including those owned by Thomas Pethick, a founding City Councillor, and George Coles, a Father of Confederation. Municipal licensing regulations distinguished between the individual tipple and bulk sales, with the dividing line drawn at the two-gallon limit. Those selling amounts below that mark were governed by provisions designed to limit personal consumption in a commercial setting and to maintain the comfort and moral tone of such places.

Licences to sell liquor were initially issued by a grand jury. Later, City Council assumed the task. Licences were not handed out freely. An 1861 by-law required an applicant to produce a certificate of "good moral conduct" signed by at least six citizens, and a law adopted in 1872 provided for a certificate of good behaviour to be signed by six of the ten nearest householders. Councillors debated each application, refusing some, accepting others, and at times reversing decisions at subsequent Council meetings. On at least one occasion, an applicant appealed his rejection in provincial court and received his licence. Attempts to stem the flow of applications failed, but Council tried to halt the growing unlicensed trade in liquor by offering informants half the fine paid by convicted illegal vendors.

---

36 F. R. Heartz recounted his grandfather, Richard Jacob Heartz, describing the situation in his childhood home. "When I was very young, I used to see my father and my eldest brother going off to work every day. They were masons and bricklayers and always had a lot of work. They had to have their morning drink before breakfast. Then at 10 o'clock they would throw down their tools and go to the nearest tavern, of which there were many, to have their mid-morning tot. Before dinner they had their noon allowance. At 3 o'clock came the mid-afternoon decoction; before tea, another draw; one right after tea, followed by two or three nightcaps. They were making seven shillings a day and spending considerably more than half of it for grog. They made their money working like horses and spent it like asses."

Those charged with liquor offences appeared before the mayor's court and were handed fairly stiff penalties, with imprisonment if a fine was not paid. Frequently, guilty parties appealed their sentences to the Island government, begging mercy because of extenuating circumstances. On one occasion, a publican, Charles McKenna, was fined £5 for selling alcohol without a licence. He appealed the sentence, and the Colonial Secretary asked Mayor Hutchison for more information. The mayor replied that McKenna had purchased a comfortable house and a stock of liquor and risked financial hardship if he could not sell his wares. Hutchison also affirmed that McKenna, who had previously operated a licensed hostelry, had maintained "a most excellent establishment both as regards dwelling, stabling and persons within his family qualified to conduct it with propriety and respectability." Later, Hugh Quinn was assessed less favourably, having in Hutchison's view kept "a house of resort for characters of the worst description and that gaming and rioting accompanied by robbery and assault took place at the time of the commission of the offence." The plea from a Mary Collins was more complicated. She was reported as selling "a little" rum and was duly convicted, but she claimed in her appeal that she was a poor woman with six dependent children and a husband who was off the Island. Hutchison responded that he had given her a chance to pay half the fine within two weeks and the balance thereafter, and also that her husband had returned to Charlottetown. Mary Collins went to jail.

Despite attempts to control consumption of alcohol and to curb its abuses, illegal alcohol sales were a common occurrence, and arrests for drunkenness could amount to half the total number of charges laid by police in a given year. Public concern about the abuse of alcohol and the social ills such abuse bred led to the establishment of temperance organizations, such as the Sons of Temperance. Support for these groups ebbed and flowed. In 1859 a Charlottetown newspaper noted the Sons, "once a very numerous and respectable body," now numbered only 100 members in good standing. While no one in public life argued for the merits of drunkenness, there was a vigorous debate between those who advocated temperance and the supporters of temperate drinking. The final resolution of the issue required the decision of senior levels of government. Even then, some doubted the likelihood that morality or sobriety could be legislated.

Entertainment

Much of the drinking and revelry that so concerned the city's middle class was associated with the sociability of the poorer members of the community. The exact ways in which leisure time was spent were influenced by the stratum of society in which the participants found themselves. Better-off Charlottetonians, without the modern communications devices that shape today's pastimes, pursued many of the same forms of entertainment as preceding generations despite the technological advances of the age. Descriptions of activities of more prosperous folk as recorded in their diaries and reminiscences conform to the ideals of Victorian propriety. Margaret Gray, daughter of Colonel John Hamilton Gray, focused her activities on the home and church in which

After the Prince of Wales began the trend with his 1860 visit, Charlottetonians welcomed some of Queen Victoria's other children on official visits. This arch was built in honour of the 1869 visit of Edward's younger brother, Prince Arthur.

family members and a close circle of friends played important roles. For Margaret, church attendance was not restricted to Sundays, and on Sundays the day's activities frequently featured more than one service. Church groups also sponsored an active round of picnics, bazaars and teas. At home, leisure time was spent writing letters, reading and receiving guests. Music, including singing, was important, with casual sing-songs at home and more formal choral concerts periodically organized in churches and other public buildings. Efforts at self-improvement could include the study of foreign languages; Margaret took German lessons from Frau Johnsen.

The liveliness that was interjected into Charlottetown society by the presence of British troops was lost with their departure in 1854, but there was still considerable pomp and circumstance arising from the British connection. The visit of the Prince of Wales occasioned much excitement. He arrived in Charlottetown on August 10, 1860, amidst the booming of guns and the cheers of spectators. Meeting him on Queen's Wharf was an honour guard from the 62nd British Regiment and the Island's Prince of Wales Rifles. The prince was welcomed by an assemblage of dignitaries: judges, clergy, the mayor and Councillors, members of the assembly and of the bar, and an array of militia officers. His procession was escorted through festively decorated streets by the St. Andrew's Society dressed in plaid scarves, the Sons of Temperance with broad white collars adorned with rosettes, the Benevolent Irish Society wearing green scarves with gold lace and fringe, and the Masons in their lambskin aprons. One thousand children standing on a raised platform in Rochford Square sang "God Save the Queen" as the guest of honour passed on his way to Government House. Celebrations continued until noon on August 12, at which time the prince departed for his next stop, Quebec City. Nine years later, the prince's younger brother, Arthur, visited the Island as well, and again a considerable stir was created. In retrospect, however, both visits may have been overshadowed by the excitement generated by the performance of General Tom Thumb and his troupe in 1868 "when it appeared that the whole population of the Island – assembled to see these wide world celebrated personages."

Less fuss was made over the visiting delegations from Canada and the other Maritime colonies in 1864 when they gathered in Charlottetown to discuss possible union. At the time, many citizens ignored the event in favour of a visiting circus, which likely received the "merited and generous support" generally given to "popular entertaining companies." Prominent members of society, however, were more engaged with the Confederation proceedings. A round of balls, banquets and recreational outings accompanied the discussions. The arrival of the Earl of Dufferin, the Governor General of Canada, in July 1873 following union of the Island and Canada, elicited more interest. City Council and the provincial government competed for the honour of welcoming Lord Dufferin and ultimately reached an understanding whereby the city fathers met him on Queen's Wharf and presented him with an address, after which he was escorted

In the late 1860s, Henry Vinnicombe organized an orchestra that entertained audiences over the next four decades.

through the city's streets and under a "beautiful arch" in Upper Queen Street, at which point he became the guest of the Lieutenant Governor. Controversy also dogged the 1879 visit by a later Governor General, the Marquis of Lorne, and his consort, Princess Louise, the fourth daughter and sixth child of Queen Victoria. The prospect of a visit of a princess to the small capital by the sea set event planners aflutter in this most loyal of communities — all, it seems, but the provincial government. Despite a roaring cannonade at their arrival, the erection of a series of ceremonial arches, the staging of official welcomes, athletic games, an excursion to the countryside and various sumptuous meals, Premier Sullivan and his colleagues were accused of inhospitality in refusing to upgrade Government House to make it suitable for a princess. She and her husband stayed on board the Canadian government steamer, *Druid*, anchored in the harbour.

Beyond circuses and ceremonial visits, Charlottetonians enthusiastically turned out for concerts, dramatic presentations and illustrated lectures given at venues like the Temperance Hall or the hall of the new market building. An amateur dramatic society flourished between 1866 and 1870, while H. W. Vinnicombe took baton in hand and organized a community orchestra that entertained audiences over four decades from the late 1860s. He often paired with Samuel N. Earle, who directed numerous light operas, plays and minstrel shows. Local performers were supplemented by visiting troupes, including Boston's Wilson and Clark Company, which visited the city in 1869 and 1870, presenting among other plays *The Gipsy Queen*, *Uncle Tom's Cabin*, and *The Green Bushes*. Great public interest existed for slide shows in which large projectors were used to illuminate walls with images up to 18 feet in diameter.

Sporting events, including the Scottish games, which were held in August on the grounds of Government House and attracted competitors from Canada and the United States, and the regattas, enlivened the summer months. Cricket and rifle-shooting were also popular sports. "Base Ball," a sport introduced from the United States in the late 1860s, attracted a growing volume of players and fans, and by the late 1870s was widely played. Horse races took place in September. In winter, there were skating parties held at the Citizens' Rink. One particularly successful party in 1876 followed the trendy form of the fancy dress ball. Participants were costumed as Evangéline, Little Red Riding Hood, Mephistopheles and other figures from fiction, fable, and history as they glided over ice illuminated by the headlights of locomotives. The rink was decorated with banners from various societies, and the militia in full dress put in an appearance.

Joining the ranks of existing fraternal organizations such as the Benevolent Irish and St. Andrew's Societies by the 1860s were a number dedicated to countering the ill effects of alcohol. The Sons of Temperance provided fellowship as well as scope for battling the demon rum. A parallel group, the St. Patrick's Temperance Society, was formed in 1864 to tend to the city's Roman Catholics. This was followed in 1877 by another Catholic organization, the Total Abstinence Society. The Young Men's Christian Association and Literary Institute was founded in 1856 to promote the moral and religious welfare of the young men of Charlottetown. Lectures were arranged on a weekly or fortnightly basis, but provision for physical fitness and sports came only later in the century.

Militia

The militia also had a role as a social organization. Membership was a mark of standing within the community, a kind of certification of respectability and civic mindedness. Each soldier served in a position that roughly accorded with his niche in society. While pride and sociability may have been motivations for belonging, patriotism was not to be overlooked. Charlottetonians were citizens of the Empire, and a sense of being British was widely felt. Britain at this time was being challenged on many fronts. In Europe, fear that the Russians menaced the lines of communication to India and suspicion of their ambitions in Turkey led to the Crimean War of 1853-56. This confrontation was quickly followed by the savagery of the Indian Mutiny in 1857-58. Relations with France, always potentially contentious, were soured in 1858 following the failure of a London-based plot to assassinate Emperor Napoleon III. A war in 1859 pitting France and the Italian state of Piedmont against Austria added to the war jitters and led to British rearmament. In North America, the outbreak of civil war in the United States in 1860 created tensions at sea with the *Trent* Affair of 1861 and the *Chesapeake* Affair in 1863. The Fenian raids, particularly the skirmish on the Maine-New Brunswick border in April 1866, heightened apprehensions among the population. Security concerns, of course, were already acute because of the Tenant League disturbances and were only calmed somewhat by the temporary return of two

After the British garrison departed, shortly before Charlottetown's incorporation, the colony's defence rested in the hands of the volunteer militia.

companies of British regulars in August 1865.[37] Thus, military service was a response to the call of duty as well as an opportunity for comradeship and adventure.

Before Confederation, volunteer companies were organized and outfitted at the expense of individual members and wealthy benefactors. The First Volunteer Guards, organized by Neil Rankin in 1856, were disbanded in 1859. In that same year, an artillery unit was established under the leadership of Captain Thomas Morris and J. P. Pollard. About the same time, two rifle companies, the Prince of Wales Rifles commanded by Captain Rankin and the Irish Volunteers led by Captain John Murphy, were raised. By 1865 the city hosted two more military formations, the Mounted Rifles (Captain John Holman) and the Royalty Rifles (Captain George Wright). The following year, a second city artillery unit was formed under the leadership of Captain Elijah Purdy, and the Prince Edward Rifles, led by Captain Albert Hensley, appeared in the same year. A second Mounted Rifle unit under Captain James Wood followed in 1867. Enthusiasm in Charlottetown for the militia's activities extended beyond mere membership. Drills were held more frequently than required, and they sometimes attracted enthusiastic audiences. The drill hall was initially located on Grafton Street near Pownal, but in 1867 a new hall was opened on Kent Street beside Government Pond. Various reorganizations ensued until 1873, when separate companies were drawn into four, and later three, battalions, one for each county. Much of the cost for maintaining the military formations was then assumed by the Dominion government. In 1878 the Charlottetown Engineer Company was formed.

By 1880 Charlottetown had emerged from its status as an outpost of empire and established itself firmly as a market town and an administrative centre, latterly as a provincial capital. Slowly its physical and social infrastructures were taking shape, although there was still much to be accomplished on both fronts. In terms of the times, the city was a very substantial place. Delivery of municipal services was hampered by inadequate revenue, which was itself the product of rural domination of the legislature and a preference on the part of the city's elite for low taxes. Early in the period, the penury of the civic government compared unfavourably with the generally buoyant colonial economy, but during the 1870s finances became tight for the provincial government as well as its capital. In the years ahead, Charlottetown had to complete the development of its public utilities, secure economic control over its limited, although promising, agricultural hinterland, and establish new economic engines to replace the declining shipbuilding and shipping industries. These were major challenges, but the city's future depended upon successful responses.

37 They were withdrawn to Halifax again in June 1867.

CHAPTER 3

Expansion

1880-1920

At first glance, a city that increased its population by only 7.5 per cent over four decades could hardly be characterized as a growing community. Yet there are measures of civic development other than sheer numbers. In a province that saw its population decline by almost 19 per cent between 1880 and 1920, Charlottetown's ability to hold its own represented a considerable expansion relative to its hinterland. For the capital, those years were ones in which it began to chart a separate course from the rural areas it had long served and upon which it depended. From outpost of empire to market town and commercial entrepôt, Charlottetown now entered the industrial age in which cities were part of a complex network of places that manufactured, shipped and consumed an increasingly diverse array of products.

This new age required more of cities. They had to, among other things, foster economic development, mitigate the effects of crowded housing and industrial pollution, facilitate communications of all kinds, and provide the sort of social and cultural advantages that urban dwellers increasingly expected. In order to accomplish these tasks, municipal governments had to be more robust in their financing, size and expertise. They were obliged to develop different relationships with their citizens and with other levels of government. Civic leaders needed to acquire, in current-day terminology, "attitude." The symptom of success was panache, not caution.

Charlottetown was not untouched by these new circumstances, and the era between 1880 and 1920 is one in which it successfully addressed many of the challenges faced by cities. During these years, the city expanded its physical infrastructure considerably. An array of cultural facilities was acquired, and the economy diversified somewhat. The city government gained new powers and fiscal capacity. Citizens began to feel good about themselves and about the modern state of their community. At the same time, the ingrained caution remained, and with good cause.

Despite the expansion experienced in many areas of life, progress came with a struggle and was overshadowed by what was achieved elsewhere, particularly in Ontario and the West. Some of the solutions found for the challenges of the industrial age were innovative, perhaps even odd, but Charlottetonians remained pragmatic about themselves, their city and the future.

POPULATION GROWTH AND ETHNIC RELATIONSHIPS

After a period of significant population growth in which Charlottetown was able to keep pace with cities of similar size in Canada, the 1880s ushered in an era of stagnation. The city's population in 1891 was 11,374, actually 111 fewer people than in 1881. When growth returned, it was tentative and slow, reaching 12,347 in 1921. This demographic situation obviously was influenced by that of the province as a whole, which lost people steadily after 1891, dropping from 109,078 to only 88,615 in 1921.[1] More Islanders lived in the city. Charlottetonians were 10.5 per cent of the Island population in 1881 and almost 14 per cent in 1921. Where Charlottetown can be seen losing ground most dramatically is in its place in the order of Canadian cities. From 11th position in 1881 when it rivalled Kingston, Ontario, Charlottetown dropped to 15th place in 1891, smaller than St. Henri, a suburb of Montreal, and Brantford, Ontario. In 1901 Charlottetown stood 17th, just after Hull, Quebec, and Windsor, Ontario, and 40th in 1911, trailing Moncton and Port Arthur, Ontario. By 1921 Charlottetown was 46th, just after New Westminster, British Columbia, and Chatham, Ontario, and just leading Belleville and Owen Sound in Ontario.

Ethnically, the population still derived overwhelmingly from British stock. In 1881 the Irish were the largest single group at 35 per cent of the population, followed by the English at 32 and the Scots at 28 per cent. After those listed as French in origin, Acadians for the most part, the next-largest groups were the Germans and the Blacks, each comprising less than one per cent of the population. Both of these smaller groups showed a marked decrease in size by 1921. The Blacks diminished because of outmigration and intermarriage, and the Germans, perhaps, sought identification with other nationalities because of the emotions brought on by the First World War. The English, meanwhile, became the largest segment of the population, 33 per cent, followed by the Irish and the Scots, both with about 29 per cent. The segment of the population which experienced the largest proportional growth was the Acadian community, which rose from two to ten per cent of the population. Although this shift was small in absolute numbers (649), its percentage rise, 302 per cent, was significant when compared to the other communities. The English and Scots grew, while the Irish declined by 11 per cent over the same period.

One new ethnic group to appear in this period was the Lebanese. Identified as Syrians in the censuses, there were no persons of that origin listed in Charlottetown in 1881 and 1901, but by 1921 there was a significant community of 53. Most had come from a few closely situated localities in an area of Syria that is today's Lebanon. The early- to mid-20th century saw an ongoing exodus of Lebanese to various parts of the world. Typically, they were Orthodox Christians fleeing the Ottoman Turks who ruled the area until the First World War or migrants simply seeking a better life elsewhere. Some of the new arrivals in Charlottetown came directly to the Island, while others

1 The population of Canada was 4,325,000 in 1881 and increased 12 per cent to 4,833,000 by 1891. Between 1891 and 1921 there was an 82 per cent jump in the Canadian population to 8,788,000. The data are rounded to the nearest thousand.

had landed first in other parts of Canada. With few skills and limited employment opportunities, the Lebanese became peddlers, selling wares from door to door throughout the province. Those who saved enough money set up corner stores. By 1920 there were a number of such establishments spread throughout the city.

Distinguished by language, customs and skin tone, the Lebanese experienced some discrimination, but less than what might have been expected in a community with such a stable population base. Their growth in number was steady but limited in scope, so there was little fear the city would be flooded with new arrivals. Despite ties reaching back to their homeland, they did not settle in one part of town. Their habit of living over or behind their stores meant they were as dispersed as their businesses. Attendance at Anglican church services facilitated their integration. In addition, the Lebanese were seen as frugal, hard-working and adaptable, all attributes which helped them to live peacefully with their neighbours.

This pattern of integration was followed to some extent by Charlottetown's small Chinese community. In 1904 there were four single males living in the city. All were named Ling and all worked as laundrymen. They belonged to the Church of England, and, unlike the experience of some of their compatriots in other Canadian cities, they could vote and occupy property in the central business district. Like the Lebanese, they experienced some harassment and discrimination, but they also earned a reputation as hard-working, and they provided an important service. When the first Chinese restaurant opened in 1915, it was praised for both its décor and fare. Although the numbers of Chinese in Charlottetown fluctuated, they were never more than a handful before 1920.

Other demographic changes tended to confirm trends established in the decades following incorporation. By 1921 the proportion of Island-born Charlottetonians had increased from 78 per cent to 91 per cent.[2] At the same time, suburbanization proceeded with the percentage of residents living outside the city limits rising steadily in proportion to that of the city and royalty. In 1881 just under 10 per cent lived in the royalty. By 1901 this had grown to over 11 per cent, and by 1921 to well over 12 per cent. The imbalance between males and females in the population continued to widen. In 1881 there were 88 males for every 100 females in Charlottetown (90/100 in city and royalty), and this gap widened until 1911 when it stood at 83 males for every 100 females (85/100 city and royalty). By 1921 the difference was 87 to 100 (88/100 city and royalty). In the same period, the imbalance for the province as a whole was modest, 101 males per 100 females, except as recorded in the 1921 census in which the number of men stood at 103. The gender imbalance in 1921 continued a previously established pattern in which the proportion of males began to drop among teenagers over 15 and decreased for the peak earning years from ages 25 to 50 years, after which an equilibrium tended to be re-established. The data suggest patterns of migration of women seeking employment in the city and an exodus of male workers looking for greater job opportunities off the Island.

2 The 1921 figure was actually down one per cent from a previous high recorded in the census of 1911.

Previous trends in religious affiliations also persisted in this period. The proportion of Anglicans dropped from 15 per cent in 1881 to 10 per cent in 1921. At the same time Presbyterians grew from 19 per cent to 21 per cent and Baptists 4 to 5 per cent. Methodists declined from 22 per cent of the population in 1881 to 16 per cent in 1921. The major gains were amongst the city's Roman Catholic population, which expanded from 38 per cent to 46 per cent. While various factors likely brought about these changes, the continuing migration to the city of rural Islanders, where Roman Catholics, Presbyterians and Baptists predominated, undoubtedly augmented their urban numbers. The now almost-equal balance between the Roman Catholics on the one hand and the Protestants and Anglicans on the other had important implications for the dynamics of politics in the capital.

Charlottetown remained a city in which the prosperous and less well-off lived in close proximity. The assessment rolls for 1921 reveal instances in which one home on a block could be valued at four, five or even ten times that of a neighbour on the same block. Fine homes along Haviland and Water Streets, for instance, backed onto poorer housing on King Street and Union Street. Nevertheless, an overall pattern of economic segregation was beginning to emerge. Perhaps influenced by the location of the railway tracks and the low-lying marshy ground, real estate generally in the eastern blocks of Wards 1, 2, 3 and 4 had the lowest assessed values in the city along with much of the housing in the southeastern section of Ward 5. The preponderance of the best housing lay to the west of Great George Street in Wards 1 to 4 and along the Brighton Road and in the more northerly stretches of Ward 5. Even so, pockets of substantial housing were located in the east along Fitzroy Street from Great George (now University) to Hillsborough Streets, and on portions of Prince and Hillsborough Streets south of Euston Street, while poorer areas were to be found between Pownal and Rochford Squares and adjacent to Government Pond in the western part of Charlottetown.

Professionals, such as physicians, dentists and lawyers, had their homes in widely dispersed parts of town, and by 1921 were increasingly residing outside the city boundaries. Patterns of ownership of automobiles and horses and carriages for personal use, as evidenced by 1921 taxes, reflect the residential property values. Vehicle ownership was particularly high in Ward 5, and this tends to confirm a north- and westward movement of higher-income families. A typical house at the time was valued at approximately $2,500 and contained $350 worth of furnishings and other personal property. Many homes in all price ranges were let to tenants. It was also not uncommon to find residences that also served as the occupant's place of business. Streets, particularly in the older sections of town, exhibited a diversity of lifestyle and activity which differed from the homogeneity which became typical of residential areas later in the 20th century. Thus, while the trend towards more uniform areas of housing had begun, the city still retained much of the 19th-century pattern of intermixture for various income levels and socio-economic groups.

POLITICAL LIFE

By 1880 Charlottetown's administration was facing a fiscal crisis. Under the leadership of Mayor W. E. Dawson, City Council was confronted by the old problem of insufficient financial resources to meet the growing needs of the city. Civic debt exceeded $100,000 and assessments stood at only $25,700. Divided within itself and facing a mounting deficit and deteriorating services, Council voted to ask the provincial legislature, then in session, to give them increased taxing powers. The principal target was persons who lived outside the urban boundaries but did business within them and did not pay taxes. Councillors also wanted changes in the way taxes were collected. To help attain these goals, they suggested a public meeting at which citizens could formulate proposals for change that would then be rolled into a bill for presentation to the legislature.

Not everyone was convinced that the problem lay entirely with freeloading outsiders, or even the revenue stream. "Observer," writing in the *Examiner* nine days after Council issued its call, asserted that the "extravagance and incompetence" of the city administration "should be tolerated no longer." In his opinion, part of the problem was $14,000 in uncollected taxes. He argued that real estate and incomes should be assessed, and the payment of taxes enforced. In addition, costs should be tightly controlled and the number of City Councillors cut from ten to five. In the end, however, he, too, issued a call for a meeting of "representative" citizens to discuss changes to the act incorporating the city.

A private meeting of "leading citizens" was eventually held on April 1, 1880, to suggest amendments to the legislation.[3] Proposals arising from this gathering were far-reaching, and some were controversial. A tax on incomes, as well as real estate, was suggested, and for individuals escaping those forms of taxation, a poll or head tax should be imposed. The concept of a municipal income tax was unusual at the time. Property taxes routinely formed the income base for Canadian cities. Other proposals stated that landlords should pay taxes on their properties and recover the costs from their tenants. All who paid taxes should have the right to vote in civic elections. City Councillors should be required to own property worth at least $1,000 or pay rent of $500 or more. The number of Councillors should be reduced from ten to five, and they should be elected at large, rather than on a ward basis. Elections should be held immediately following passage of a bill in the legislature to implement these changes. Those at the meeting then called upon the mayor to convene a public meeting to discuss their ideas.

Opposition surfaced at once. The *Examiner* argued that elections should be held in January to coincide with the beginning of the city's financial year and deplored the emphasis upon "filthy lucre" rather than "character and intelligence" as a means of measuring a man's right to seek office as a Councillor. Election of Councillors at large, in the paper's opinion, would create confusion and frustrate the

3 Among those in attendance were Patrick Blake, L. H. Davies, John Hughes, John Newson, L. L. Beer, Charles Palmer and Owen Connolly.

objective of having each ward represented in the city government. The tax reforms, however, were applauded. "Fair Play," whose letter appeared in the *Examiner* on April 3, the day of the public meeting called by Mayor Dawson, reiterated the paper's views with respect to the property qualification for Councillors and pointed out "many of our most talented, best educated, and enterprising of our citizens, ... would be debarred from a seat in the City Council under a clause of this arbitrary and tyrannical nature." Despite such reservations, the mayor's meeting largely endorsed the proposals, even though the mayor himself favoured elections in early January.

The ensuing law, passed later in April, was something of a compromise. It provided for real estate taxes to be paid by the city's property-owners irrespective of where they resided, and a maximum tax of one per cent on incomes of $400 or more. Taxes could be imposed upon all residents and businesses or on the income of non-residents employed or conducting business in the city. Income from provincial government appointments and from country bank stock was exempted from this provision. A maximum two-dollar annual poll tax could be levied against all males over the age of 21 who paid no other city taxes. Commercial travellers were also liable to the poll tax. Three assessors were to be given the authority to secure all the information necessary to set fair levies. Taxpayers in default of payment would have their names published for a period of three months, after which time remaining defaulters would have their property seized and sold at public auction. With these new taxing powers came a kind of guarantee against reckless spending. Council was prohibited from entering into a contract for $6,000 or more without first having it discussed at a public meeting of ratepayers. In a separate move, the Council introduced a tax on horses and carriages, although no horse-owner was required to pay for more than two horses.

In the light of present-day dissatisfaction with income taxes, the willingness of Charlottetonians to submit to this form of revenue generation bears comment. Not everyone agreed with the measure when it was debated in the provincial legislature. Opponents believed the tax to be obnoxious and likely to drive "monied men" out of town, but others noted it had been accepted by a meeting of citizens and if rich men opposed it and poor men favoured it, "no better argument could be used to support it." Perhaps the most prescient comment made in the legislative debates was that if an income tax was as distasteful as some thought, "it need only remain in force for one year, and then the citizens could put men in City Council who would discontinue it." In fact, while the records are less than categorical on the matter, it appears that income tax was collected only in the period 1881-83. Income tax assessments were not made in the 1884 financial records, and this form of taxation does not figure in the accounts thereafter. In 1894 the province instituted its own income tax.

The 1880 civic act dealt with matters other than taxation, and among them were clauses covering the qualifications for elected officials and for the franchise. Councillors were required to own property valued at a minimum of $1,000 or pay $200, not

$500, annually in rent.[4] The failure of attempts to have a high rental qualification adopted represented a setback for the interests that sought to exclude less prosperous members of the community from public office. All male British subjects who owned $100 worth of property, or paid $14 in rent, or paid the poll tax could vote in municipal elections. This provision significantly extended the franchise among tenants. Council remained at 11 members, two representatives from each ward, plus the Mayor.[5] Elections were to be held annually on the fourth Wednesday of January, and Council meetings were to be held at least once a month rather than quarterly as heretofore. The terms of the 1880 municipal act indicate that Charlottetown's wealthy elite was losing its ability to influence the Island legislature to its own advantage.

To initiate the new era in civic life, elections were called for May 13, 1880. All seats on Council were to be contested. Incumbent Mayor W. E. Dawson faced off against John Murphy. A slate of some of the city's most prominent citizens was named as candidates at a special meeting held on May 6. It included William Murphy, Owen Connolly and L. H. Davies, with John Murphy as the choice for Mayor. The results at the polls revealed a still-divided community.[6] Four of the ten newly elected Councillors were drawn from the slate while W. E. Dawson retained the Mayor's chair. Calls were subsequently issued for civic politics to be freed from sectarian and party considerations. For his part, Dawson promised to rid the city of the "hole-and-corner meetings" which bred intrigue and rivalries. At the same time, the new administration had to confront a $105,000 debt which only threatened to become worse. The year-end accounts showed that the increased revenue resulting from the new legislation was necessary just to pay for basic services, such as street maintenance and firefighting. To resolve the challenges that lay ahead, Charlottetown clearly would require all of its new taxing powers.

Unfortunately, restructuring the city's financial base did little to address other systemic problems. The tendency of outside political alignments to intrude into civic politics continued. In particular, the educational controversies had the effect of creating factions in the city along religious lines and, after passage of the 1878 federal Scott Act that provided for local plebiscites on the prohibition of beverage alcohol sales, there were divisions along temperance lines. Moreover, the previous decision-making gridlock in Council continued. A clause in the new act obliged the Councillors elected

---

4 These requirements maintained the status quo. In the original act of incorporation, Councillors had to own £200 of real estate or pay £40 annually in rent. Given an exchange of $4.87 equalling £1, the original requirements convert to $974 and $195 respectively. The 1880 act does not mention a property qualification for the mayor, which under the 1855 act was the equivalent of $2,435.

5 In the first election after passage of the city act, all posts were to be contested, and, in the following election, in January 1881, the mayor and five Councillors were to leave office, creating the vacancies to be filled. In subsequent years, the longest-serving Councillor for each ward was to vacate office.

6 Not all contests were determined by policy issues. The contest in Ward 4 resulted in a bitter exchange of letters in the *Examiner* between the successful David Lawson and the defeated Theo. L. Chappelle. Deal-making, betrayal and personal standing in the community seemed to be the determining factors in the outcome.

in May to draw lots to determine one of their number from each ward to vacate office prior to elections scheduled for January 1881. This perpetuated the system in which councils were composed of newly elected and continuing members. Soon there were complaints about the inability of city government to move forward on important issues such as construction of a waterworks or even to meet modest expectations for road construction or provision of sidewalks. Once again, the *Examiner* was lamenting "a do-nothing City Council" in which well-meaning men who lacked clear heads and practical experience prevented things from getting done.

Ironically, part of the difficulty with civic affairs stemmed from the financial situation. Far from completely alleviating the fiscal woes of Charlottetown, the new tax base still left the city strapped for cash. Increasing taxing powers and actually imposing new taxes were two different things. While the Horse and Carriage tax was extended to include all horses, carriages and sleighs in 1881,[7] heavy demands for road maintenance, firefighting equipment and public health, to say nothing of the provision of water and sewerage services, brought elected officials face to face with "the cheese-paring opinions of the more close fisted taxpayers." Budget planners scrimped and saved wherever possible. Complicating matters was the arrangement under which the city was responsible for collecting taxes for the school board. In 1883 teachers were given a pay supplement that was not covered by the city's revenue, and, as a result, the teachers were not paid in full that year. Teachers had first claim on civic revenues, a fact that obliged the city subsequently to juggle accounts and put off other obligations. In the debates over finances, fiscal conservatives banded together in temporary organizations such as the "Civic Protection Association." Those favouring a more expansive role for city government tended to style themselves as "Reformers."

Attention focused upon a proposed personal property tax as a possible means of raising revenue. Under the proposal, the tax would be imposed on household, hall, office and shop furniture, and goods, wares and merchandise. As early as 1881, the legislature considered a request from the city for the power to levy such a tax. It initially rejected the proposal, imposing instead further restrictions to the city's existing taxing powers, but later approved the measure. Assessment records for 1885 contained entries for the kinds of personal property outlined in the proposal.

The election of 1885 represented a kind of watershed in civic affairs. Confronted with ongoing financial difficulties and the lack of improvements in the city's services, the public was once again restless. Henry Beer was elected mayor as an advocate of a waterworks, and four out of five victorious candidates for Council shared his views. Efforts to achieve this goal, however, were sandbagged by their opponents on Council. The city's ability to bear such expenses was a critical factor. In 1886 a new election promised the opportunity to elect more reform candidates. In the run-up to it, reformers highlighted other matters to consider as well. Some called for annual elections for the complete Council, and "Progressist" writing to the *Examiner*'s editor

7 Each horse bore an assessment of $2.00, carriages and sleighs $1.00. Horses and trucks belong to licensed truck men were exempted.

The 1885 election was something of a watershed. Waterworks advocate Henry Beer carried the mayor's office. Four of the five newly-elected Councillors shared his views.

recommended the reduction of the number of Councillors to five.

One important proposal was for the election of Councillors at large rather than on a ward basis. With the passage of time, the residential population in the northern Wards, 4 and 5, had grown in relation to that of Wards 1, 2 and 3, which were becoming increasingly commercial and industrial. The equal representation of each ward left the voters in the three lower wards with more electoral weight than their actual numbers justified. Voting by ward also meant that the influence of a large majority in one electoral division was restricted to that area. Removal of the ward boundaries could cost fiscal conservatives some of their clout. The will of the people, it seemed, was being frustrated by the squeaking wheels of financial self-interest.

Mayor Beer, who had distinguished himself in leading the community during the smallpox epidemic of the autumn of 1885 and had made progress on the waterworks issue, was re-elected in 1886 after a rough-and-tumble campaign with ex-Mayor D. R. M. Hooper, a fervent opponent of a waterworks, but Council remained evenly divided over the water question. Beer used his tie-breaking vote to secure passage of legislation supporting a waterworks. Tragically, he died in September 1886, though not before the success of the water project was guaranteed, and Charlottetown had been set on a course towards a larger role for civic government. The effects of the 1885 tax changes and the prudent financial management of Councillor Simon Crabbe, the new head of the city's finance committee, helped the reform cause. More efficient administration contributed to the improved finances and assured the general taxpayer that waste had been trimmed from the city's accounts. This somewhat allayed public fears about trusting the city with more responsibility, but, in retrospect, it lent some credence to the accusations of inefficiency that had been levelled at City Hall.

The elections immediately following 1886 were comparatively tame affairs in which temperance issues and the relative merits of candidates' personalities played large roles. Simmering beneath the surface, however, was the issue of representation within Council. Various sub-texts characterized previous debates on the matter. The call for elections at large pitted the owners of expensive commercial real estate against citizens of more modest means. The earlier proposal for a $500 annual rental requirement for tenants standing for election as Councillors masked an intention to limit the influence of smaller commercial tenants in the downtown business core. These

(left) In 1886 ex-Mayor D.R.M. Hooper, a fervent opponent of a waterworks, failed to unseat Mayor Beer in a rough-and-tumble campaign.

(right) Simon Crabbe's prudent fiscal management in the mid-1880s helped allay fears that City Hall could not be trusted to manage large undertakings like a waterworks.

people enjoyed the right to hold public office without the obligation to pay high insurance rates on real estate or necessarily the desire to incur taxes for services that mainly benefitted others. The shifts in population gave reformers a new argument for reshaping the "council board," and they pressed it to good effect. In 1891 an amendment to the act of incorporation provided for a City Council consisting of a Mayor and eight Common Councilmen, the latter of which were to be distributed on the basis of one representative each for Wards 1, 2 and 3; two for Ward 4; and three for Ward 5. In addition, the mayor and the whole Council were to be elected biennially at elections to be held on the second Wednesday of February. Before the act came into force, its provisions had to be approved in a city-wide plebiscite.

Passage of the amendments in the legislature caught many Charlottetonians off-guard. The City Council had not been consulted in the matter and, some observers argued, the ordinary citizens were content with the existing system of representation. Formal discussion of the changes began at a public meeting called by the mayor and chaired by Hon. Benjamin Davies on August 9, 1891. Opponents of the measure, including Davies, believed it was unjust to allow people with a small financial stake in the community equal weight at the polls with substantial property-owners.[8] This was despite the provision that allowed multiple votes to property holders, either owners or tenants, who occupied property in more than one ward. Others worried that the influence of Roman Catholics would be undercut when three wards could return only

8 "Citizen" writing to the editor of the *Examiner* asserted that the city corporation was like a joint stock company and the largest shareholders should have the greatest power. The bill as it stood gave three times the power to the poll-tax voter in ward five than the $50,000 real-estate owner in ward one.

Like his father, T. Heath Senior, Thomas Heath Haviland Jr. chose to cap a remarkable career with a long term as Mayor of Charlottetown. After completing the late Henry Beer's term in 1886, he went on to serve until 1893.

one Councillor, likely a member of the Protestant majority.[9] Even so, the ensuing plebiscite endorsed the changes by a wide margin, and they were accordingly implemented.

Following these reforms, Charlottetown entered a quiet period in city politics. Emphasis in the press was on securing candidates of good judgement who would avoid the pressures of party affiliation from the provincial or federal levels and deal with local matters on their merits.[10] Change of office-holders was considered desirable, especially the mayoralty, which was seen by many as a position of honour that should be shared amongst elected leaders whose long service had earned them the privilege.[11] While broad segments of public opinion may have shared these views, they by no means held universal sway. The temperance issue persisted throughout the 1890s, and two long-serving mayors, Thomas Heath Haviland, Jr., and William E. Dawson, held office until the election of political neophyte James Warburton in 1897.[12] The latter then served until 1903 when he entered provincial politics. In that same year, revisions to the act of incorporation linked borrowing powers to revenue, with the corporation empowered to issue debentures equal to five times the taxes collected in the previous fiscal year. The legislature could also, from time to time, permit the city to issue debentures for specific major public works. The leash by which the province controlled the city's finances had been lengthened, but

9 Previously, some Roman Catholics had worried that proposals to abolish the ward system would effectively limit their representation on Council if an election were fought on sectarian lines. In response to those fears, proponents of civic reform dropped their advocacy of the idea.

10 Councils tended to be balanced between the supporters of the two provincial parties, although the alignments were not rigid. For instance, Mayor Beer, a Liberal, was re-elected in 1886 over the opposition of the Liberals and with the support of the Conservatives. On the other hand, Simon Crabbe, an experienced and able member of Council, was defeated in 1880 when his opponent garnered the solid support of one party.

11 Various active politicians espoused this view at a public meeting at which leading issues of the day were discussed. It was also the meeting at which the neophyte Dr. Warburton was officially nominated.

12 Haviland previously held a stunning array of offices of which the most notable were member of the House of Assembly, member of the Executive Council, various posts in the Executive Council before and after Confederation, Leader of the Opposition in PEI, a federal Senator and Lieutenant Governor of PEI.

Meacham's 1880 Atlas *proudly showed off Charlottetown's public buildings, many of which had been erected in the years following incorporation. At incorporation, the most prominent landmark in the city was the Colonial Building. By the 1860s, however, the demand for space for various activities of government resulted in its overcrowding. As the most pressing need was for a new post office and additional court space, in 1869 David Sterling, a Halifax architect, was hired to draft plans for a building to serve those purposes. One possibility was the addition of a wing to the existing Colonial Building, either at the rear or the west side. Some opposition existed to such an expansion as it would reduce the open space on the square, but in the end, Sterling produced a design for a handsome new structure to be located just to the west of the Colonial Building. Completed in 1872, briefly occupied for colonial purposes, it was turned over to the federal government after Confederation and renamed the Dominion Building. The post office remained, to be joined by the customs department, but the provincial courts were again in need of housing. Work began on a replacement law courts building in 1874 according to a plan by Thomas Alley, the province's Superintendent of Works. Located just east of Province House and opened in 1876, the new court house was a solid, Italianate structure with a mansard roof surmounted by a large clock tower.*

the provincial grip remained strong.[13] Overall, Charlottetown was enjoying a period of prosperity in which able candidates offered their services for public office. Following the hotly contested election of 1904, the *Daily Patriot* noted "the deep interest and great activity taken in the elections" that was "in keeping with the general good times prevailing in this city and the optimistic feeling among the people that Charlottetown is progressing."

The era of optimism persisted well into the 20th century and even survived the turbulence of the First World War. Steady progress was made in the macadamization

13 For instance, in 1905 the government allowed the city to issue an additional $25,000 in debentures for the new market house, but it was also required to establish a sinking fund of $100,000 to pay off the debts connected with the market. The money for the fund was to come from revenues from the market in excess of its operating costs, and if those sums were insufficient, from a tax upon ratepayers.

of the roads, street-lighting and the installation of concrete sidewalks. Parks were beautified and efforts made to extend water and sewerage services. All of this, in the view of the *Patriot*, made Charlottetown "one of the finest residential cities in Canada." Yet it was done with a careful eye on finances. Prudent management of the city's accounts combined with ongoing improvements to the city's infrastructure became the boasts of successful civic politicians. Electoral contests were generally followed with enthusiasm, but the candidates were almost universally pledged to stay the familiar course. Occasional interest in investing to develop tourism or to attract new industries was always constrained by the bonds of fiscal responsibility and balanced budgets. Some of the colour went out of city politics as a result, but that was a price citizens and observers alike were prepared to pay for security. The adoption of the secret ballot by the city in 1912 also robbed elections of the excitement of public declarations of political allegiance and made them less predictable.[14] Long service and personal associations counted for less with voters, and, as a result, younger, less-experienced candidates could nudge out their elders on election day. While politicians complained of the poor financial treatment the city received at the hands of the province and the press lamented the disappearance of all-candidates' meetings prior to elections, by the First World War, political life had become relatively serene. "All is harmony within the gates of Charlottetown," waxed the *Patriot*. "There is no automobile question, no liquor problem, no epidemic, no famines and no religious strife to stir the blood of the civic body." Despite the war raging in Europe, the paper noted the "White Dove of Peace spreads its wings over our fair capital."

URBAN LANDSCAPE

Writing in the July 1899 issue of *The Prince Edward Island Magazine*, Horace Haszard sang the praises of Charlottetown's many charms. The city gloried in its water and sewerage systems; well-lit and tidy streets; handsome churches, schools and music hall; splendid stores and shops and "two well equipped and excellently managed hospitals." This view was corroborated a few years later by the American Consul, Delmar J. Vail, who, responding to earlier references to "Sleepy Hollow," declared Charlottetown was "quite a wide-awake city, now." He described "splendidly equipped and stocked" stores, "really fine public buildings," "very creditable gardens in the centre of the city," and "the prettiest natural park that can be seen anywhere."

14 Calls for the secret ballot were made as early as the 1890s. Prior to nomination day, early candidates canvassed their neighbourhoods seeking the support of voters, and, once a vote had been pledged, the voter was honour-bound to cast his ballot accordingly. Occasionally, a subsequent nomination caused a voter to regret his pledge, but his only recourse was to try to persuade his chosen candidate to withdraw from the race. A secret ballot, among other things, gave voters the right to change their minds on election day. In the election of 1912, one candidate found himself with about 500 votes fewer than his canvassing figures indicated. Voters could be challenged as ineligible and could be required to produce a tax receipt to prove their status.

"Unsightly structures met his gaze on every hand / Beside the mansions of the proudest in the land;/ The palace and the hovel forming contrast grand." Corner of Grafton and Rochfort, c. 1904.

Not everyone was so favourably impressed. John A. Cooper, writing in 1901 for *The Canadian Magazine*, claimed that Charlottetown was "the dingiest and most unprogressive city in the east." It seemed to him that "the whole place had given up on itself in disgust." Even Delmar Vail noted that Charlottetonians "cannot be persuaded to spend money in beautifying their town." Harshest criticism, however, came from native commentators. "Rambler," in a poem published in the *Examiner*, described a city in which "Unsightly structures met his gaze on every hand / Beside the mansions of the proudest in the land; / The palace and the hovel forming contrast grand." Another poem, "The City of the Dead (Dedicated to Charlottetown)", opened: "Upon a wide and lonely street, I stood with fear and dread, No sign of life around me, all active scenes had fled."

In truth, the record for the period following 1880 demonstrates considerable progress in many areas of civic life. One small measure, the introduction of street numbering in 1887, was an indication that urban growth and increased numbers of visitors made assistance in finding specific locations in town essential.[15] Citizens were, by and large, aware of the positive changes around them. While care was taken with finances, a general optimism, based on the assumption that the future would bring greater prosperity rather than less, encouraged investments which changed the physical face of the city.

15 The streets were re-numbered in 1907. Any consideration of the built heritage of Charlottetown in this period can benefit from a close reading of Irene L. Rogers' finely detailed study, *Charlottetown: The Life in Its Buildings*.

Public Buildings

City Hall was a case in point. In March 1885, the fire department made representations to City Council that it was inefficient to station its equipment in various locations across the city. The two steam fire engines, for instance, were housed apart, one on Grafton Street and the other on King Street. Concentration of firefighting engines at one place would improve service and save money. With remarkably little debate, Council requested its finance committee to find a suitable site for a fire department building in the vicinity of Queen Square. It took only eight days for the committee to locate a satisfactory piece of land and receive authorization to begin planning a new building. In this brief time, the concept changed to include civic offices as well as the fire department. One month later, Council unanimously agreed to have the committee buy land from Edward Love and to give the architectural firm of Phillips and Chappell a contract to draft plans for a fire hall and civic offices. On May 15, 1885, Phillips and Chappell submitted their plans. William Harris also made an unsolicited proposal, but Council asked Phillips and Chappell to draft specifications in accordance with their plans and agreed to call for tenders for the building's construction. By this time, the project was going ahead with less-than-unanimous support from Council, and, in July, when the tender of William Fraser was proposed for acceptance, Council was evenly split on the matter, with Mayor Beer casting the deciding affirmative vote.

The speed with which this undertaking advanced was breathtaking when compared to the earlier construction of the market hall or the decision concerning a civic

City Hall, decked out to greet Governor General Lord Aberdeen in 1894.

waterworks. Yet progress slowed, perhaps because Council became divided and unruly over the waterworks and street-lighting issues or because of the substantial expenditures that those other undertakings might entail. The Council minutes are silent on the matter. In any event, over a year and a half passed before work on the new City Hall commenced.[16] The inaugural meeting of Council in its new quarters took place about a year and a half after that. Though the meeting was recorded in the press, the Council minutes do not mention the significance of the occasion.

Impressive in its design and detailed finish, the brick-and-stone structure featured three storeys capped by a slated mansard roof, an 80-foot tower in which to hang fire hoses and lodge the city's fire bell and three doors facing Queen Street for the fire engines. The main entrance faced Kent Street, and the police station was located to the left of the entrance. Five cells were in the basement and a sixth, for women, was on the first floor. The Council chamber was on the second floor and reached by an impressive oak staircase.

City building projects were not limited to City Hall alone. After years of complaints about the smell of the fish market in the centre of town, Council voted in March 1887 to erect a new market on the wharf at the foot of Pownal Street. The design was prepared by Phillips and Chappell, and the contract to build the market was awarded to John W. Cox. Its site was subsequently switched to Queen's Wharf. When completed, the market was rented by tender. In 1888 the fish market was again relocated, this time to market square,[17] and in 1900 it was transferred into the main market building, although regulations restricted the time fish vendors could be in the area. Just two years later, on December 17, 1902, the wooden "Butcher" market house burned to the ground. Steps to replace it were taken at once. To provide an interim facility, Council hastily authorized construction of a "market shack." There may have been some question about rebuilding on the same site. The *Guardian* newspaper felt the market seemed "out of keeping with its surroundings," but its loss would be keenly felt "by both citizens and our country cousins," and recommended its quick replacement. The *Patriot* had no such quibbles: "The new market house, which like the old, will be one of our chief attractions, should in all respects be worthy of its central position." The request for designs was answered by three architects: C. B. Chappell, W. C. Harris and John P. Nicholson. On this occasion, William Harris prevailed over his old competitor, Chappell, but only after his plans were modified to make them more economical. With the design finally selected, Council awarded the construction contract to the Maritime Contracting and Mining Company.

The new market was significantly different from its predecessors. Nearly square in shape, it featured Gothic revival flourishes in its gables and small buttresses

16 Council issued a second call for tenders but did so only after a tied vote was broken in the affirmative by the mayor. Again, William Harris attempted to have his plans considered, and, as in 1885, William Fraser was selected to build according to the Phillips and Chappell plans.

17 The reason for the switch was the savings the city could realize if the same individual were given the contract to collect tolls at both the market house and the fish market, something that was impossible if the two markets were not close to each other.

with added touches of Romanesque revival in its window and door treatments. It had concrete floors and walls constructed of Island sandstone. The trim over the windows and doors were of contrasting Wallace freestone. Inside, market stalls were located on the first floor and in the basement. The second floor of the new building, like the former one, was reserved for use as a public hall. It had a capacity of 1,300 with room for 300 more on its large stage. Completion of the market building gave the city a facility which in appearance was worthy company for its neighbours on Queen Square.

The federal government also contributed to Charlottetown's stock of substantial public buildings. Chief of these was the Dominion Building on Queen Square. An earlier structure, which housed the post office and customs department, had been imposing, but its shingle roof and surrounding wooden cornice made it vulnerable to fire. On February 20, 1884, a conflagration broke out in a commercial establishment across Richmond Street, and, as the fire grew, flames spread to the post office. A couple of attempts were made to save the building, although there was a shortage of water and the firemen felt a greater obligation to save the private properties since the government had refused a grant to the fire department for fire protection, but the blaze destroyed the Dominion Building. The Post Office Department engaged

The new post office, c. 1895.

The new railway station, c. 1908. Note the steam roller to the right.

Several Charlottetown congregations undertook major building projects in the late 1800s. After erecting a stone rectory in 1888, the congregation of St. Paul's Anglican undertook a new church, seen here nearing completion c. 1896. In 1905 St. Paul's capped its building program with a sandstone Sunday School.

The new market house, on a market day, c. 1910.

William Harris to design a replacement. He spent several weeks in Ottawa working on the project. The completed plans featured a mansard roof and arched windows, combined with a massive façade that tended to overpower its neighbours, Province House and the Butcher market house. One of the purposes of federal buildings at this time was to announce the presence of the federal government and underscore the practical value of Confederation to the ordinary citizen, and the Cabot Building, as it was christened, had that effect on the Charlottetown landscape.

The Prince Edward Island Railway was operating out of an inadequate wooden building on Water Street when, in 1905, plans were completed for a more prestigious station. This formed part of a larger project to construct a rail link to Murray Harbour, including a bridge over the Hillsborough River. Situated at the foot of Weymouth Street adjacent to the railway yards, the three-storey terminal was constructed of red sandstone with Nova Scotia freestone trim and capped with a mansard roof. The reported cost was $150,000, a substantial sum at the time. Though built on marshy land, much to the dismay of some Charlottetonians, the station provided a modern, impressive facility to welcome visitors and serve the travelling public generally.

As in the previous period of Charlottetown's development, new churches were prominent features of the changing cityscape. Continuing the ambitious round of construction begun in the decades following incorporation, various religious communities undertook major building projects. The first of these occurred beside St. Peter's Cathedral, in the years 1888-89. There, a small stone chapel was erected according to a William Harris plan. Squat and simple on the exterior, with small windows and a diminutive entry, the richly finished interior of carved wood and stained glass was highlighted by a series of paintings by Robert Harris. The chapel was dedicated to the memory of Rev. George Hodgson, the first rector, who died in 1885. Work on this little gem continued for many years; the final painting was installed in 1917. The congregation of the city's other Anglican church, St. Paul's, also began a building program in 1888. Beside the church and facing Richmond Street, they erected a rectory of Island sandstone. Designed by W. C. Harris, this project was followed by a new sandstone church, again designed by Harris and built by H. & S. Lowe. Its distinctive octagonal sanctuary, innovative electrical lighting and lavish wood finishing evoked considerable praise when it opened in 1896. Finally, in 1905 St. Paul's built a sandstone Sunday School at the corner of Richmond and Prince Streets. This structure was designed by C. B. Chappell and built by Lowe Brothers. It completed a remarkable block of architecture that demonstrates the mature state of Island design and construction.[18]

Charlottetown's Baptists were unexpectedly obliged to construct a new place of worship when their decade-old church was severely damaged by fire. It was replaced by a substantial, rectangular brick-and-stone building designed by C. B. Chappell, featuring an 85-foot tower and slate roof. The inaugural service was held on January 11, 1891. In the first decade of the new century, the congregation of Zion Presbyterian decided to replace its venerable wooden building with a larger, more substantial place of worship. A site was selected at the corner of Grafton and Prince Streets, and C. B. Chappell was named as the architect. Work commenced in 1911 and was completed in 1913. Constructed of red brick with stone highlights around the windows and doors, the façade featured three massive arched windows and a prominent tower.

In 1896, after years of planning, the city's large Roman Catholic community began work on a new cathedral. The old wooden church was removed from its site facing Dorchester Street and deposited near Queen Square School, where it was used until the basement of the future cathedral was capped and fitted up as a makeshift church. The alignment of the new stone structure was changed so that the doors of the nave faced Great George Street. Construction proceeded over the next decade and was completed in 1907. With its gothic design and two soaring spires that dominated the city's skyline, the new cathedral was deemed to be an apt witness to the faith and financial prosperity of the Roman Catholic community on Prince Edward Island.

Unfortunately, it was not to be an enduring witness. On March 8, 1913, fire swept through the cathedral, leaving only a blackened, gutted shell. Worship continued in the former Zion Presbyterian Church on Richmond while plans were made to rebuild

18 One notable exception to this pattern of expansion was the decision of the congregation of Grace Methodist Church to merge with the First Methodist Church in 1917.

St. Dunstan's College, as it looked prior to the addition of the new wing and annex.

the cathedral.[19] John Marshall Hunter, a Scot who had formed a partnership with C. B. Chappell in 1912, was selected as the architect. The design was ambitious and called for a bigger, more majestic edifice. Not only were the horizontal dimensions expanded, but the elevation was lengthened. The gothic style was retained, and each spire reached 200 feet into the sky. The Miramichi freestone walls sat upon Wallace stone foundations. Grand as the exterior was, the interior was even more sumptuous. Marble columns, vaulted ceilings and ornate stucco work complemented an impressive rose window above the high altar. The church was completed in 1919, except for the rose window which arrived two years later from Munich, Germany.

Charlottetown's two centres of higher education also undertook significant building projects in the period 1880-1920. Both St. Dunstan's and Prince of Wales Colleges were housed in facilities dating from the second quarter of the 19th century. St. Dunstan's had been rebuilt with brick exterior walls in 1862. Neither institution was large, but both experienced gradual growth which accelerated in the immediate aftermath of the First World War. By 1898 St. Dunstan's enrolment had expanded to the point where more space was needed, and the college turned to C. B. Chappell to design a four-storey wing to house dormitories, a refectory, a chapel, a library

19 Services were subsequently moved to the basement of the new basilica when it, as its predecessor, was made ready for the purpose.

and science rooms. Work on this extension was finished in 1899. At the same time, Chappell was busy designing a new stone building to replace the wooden structure that had been occupied by Prince of Wales. Plans called for an imposing façade featuring two prominent gables, arched windows and doors and horizontal layering. Construction, begun in 1898, was completed in 1900. Two years later, Chappell was at work on another project for St. Dunstan's, a two-storey annex to house a community of Sisters brought to the college to provide domestic services. He was then commissioned by Prince of Wales College to design a new wing to house an assembly hall, physical education facilities and three classrooms associated with the Normal School. The considerable costs of the project, which was completed in 1907, were underwritten by Sir William Macdonald, the Island-born tobacco magnate. Then, in 1917 Island fox rancher and financier Charles Dalton provided some of the funds needed for a new residence at St. Dunstan's. The four-storey brick building, named for its benefactor, had stone trim around the windows and doors and an exuberant façade and roofline suitable for "a monument to Dalton's generosity and a mark of [the college's] prospects."

Commercial Developments

The drift of commercial activity away from the harbourfront to the centre of the city, begun in the post-incorporation period, continued after 1880. The central axis of this shift was Queen Street, but the focus of development came to rest on the streets bordering Queen and Market Squares. Not all commercial development occurred in these areas. The large warehouse on Pownal Street built for Owen Connolly in 1886 is an example of activity elsewhere. These construction projects typically involved the erection of substantial brick buildings, usually three storeys in height with architectural flourishes on the front façade to provide visual interest. There was little use of prefabricated commercial façades, such as were found in many other North American cities at the time.

As elsewhere, fire was a major factor behind the reshaping of Charlottetown's commercial cityscape. Not only did fear of it encourage the use of flame-resistant materials, but its occurrence removed older buildings, making room for the new. For instance, the February 1884 blaze on Richmond Street which gutted the post office also destroyed all but two buildings on the south side between Queen and Great George Streets.[20] Among the properties lost were the premises of Mayor Henry Beer, an event which may have fuelled his commitment to creating a waterworks. The sole survivors were St. Patrick's Hall at the corner of Great George and Richmond and a building owned by the Stamper family at the corner of Queen and Richmond. Gone were a variety of shops and offices, including the British Warehouse and "Cheapside," a store, perhaps promisingly, named to differentiate it from competitors on "Sunnyside" across Queen Square.

20 Two major fires in 1887 and another in 1888 destroyed substantial lines of buildings on Kent Street and some adjoining properties, and a large fire on Queen Street in 1890 cost the life of one of the firemen.

Fire was a major factor in reshaping the urban landscape. Perhaps the most striking example of this is the portion of Richmond Street known as Victoria Row.

Replacement of the burned-out buildings began almost at once. Initially the property-owners gave some consideration to the construction of one long building in which individual segments would be separated by arched gangways, but this concept was ultimately set aside. In hindsight, this was a fortunate decision, for the varied, yet compatible, series of buildings that rose from the ruins has provided a rich architectural legacy. W. C. Harris received the commission to design the first building, the Cameron Block: a brick, three-storey structure composed of three symmetrical units in a pleasingly uncluttered design. It was completed by February 1885, to be followed a few months later by the Brown Block, a line of three individually designed brick buildings planned by Phillips and Chappell. W. C. Harris was the architect for the Newson Building, next to St. Patrick's Hall. Also a three-storey building, its brick façade was relieved by the use of stone on the first floor. Phillips and Chappell designed the Morris Building which was erected between the Newson and Brown Blocks and opened in 1890 to complete the reconstruction of the area destroyed by the 1884 fire. Finally, in 1892, the Stamper property was rebuilt according to a plan of Phillips and Chappell that called for the use of Nova Scotia freestone as trim for the brick façade. Taken together, the line of harmonious buildings came to be known as "Victoria Row" and constituted a streetscape that reflected artistic flair and entrepreneurial optimism.

The part of Queen Street that faced Market Square complemented this nexus of commercial development. Many of the buildings date from before 1880, but Beer Brothers added an imposing new façade to their store in 1888, and the Medical Hall on the southwest corner of Queen and Grafton Streets was improved and expanded several times between 1888 and 1904. Further down Queen Street, the two lines of mostly brick buildings erected before 1880 were augmented by the McDonald Building in 1893 and the Owen Connolly Building, designed by W. C. Harris and completed in 1900.[21]

On the north side of Market and Queen Squares, the vista along Grafton Street was rather motley. Throughout the period, smaller wooden buildings pockmarked the block between Queen and Great George Streets.[22] Nevertheless, a splendid three-storey brick and freestone "ornament to the city" rose at the corner of Queen and Grafton Streets in 1901. Designed by W. C. Harris, the DesBrisay Block housed a drug store on the ground floor and its architect's office on an upper storey. Rival C. B. Chappell had already designed two other brick buildings near Great George Street which opened in 1896 and 1897.

The scene changed less around the corner on Great George Street between Grafton and Euston Streets. There, small wooden shops continued to predominate throughout the period. They housed an array of businesses from taverns to general stores, saddlers to tin smiths. On Kent Street, in the blocks adjacent to Great George Street, change was more apparent. A particularly significant addition to the commercial area was a large brick store and office of Massey-Harris Company Limited, farm implement manufacturer, completed in 1918. As a whole, the commercial district along Queen Street and surrounding Market and Queen Squares conveyed an image of commercial vitality which lent credence to some of the more positive descriptions of Charlottetown at the opening of the 20th century.

Residential Housing

Early photographs of Charlottetown's residential areas show wide open vistas. Prior to 1880, vacant lots were found liberally sprinkled throughout built-up areas. Trees were remarkably absent. Occasionally, property-owners selling houses well-removed from the water would claim splendid, unobstructed views of the harbour or river. The densely treed, tightly packed avenues that now typify the original town plan stem from developments in the decades following 1880. In that era, many empty spaces were filled with new construction. The first Arbour Day, May 24, 1884, signalled the early stages of the greening of Charlottetown in which freshly planted trees appeared along many streets.

Although new houses sprang up throughout the city, infill development was particularly active along Cumberland, Fitzroy, Kent and Pownal Streets. More

21 Completed after Owen Connolly's death, it features a bust of the owner on the façade, a somewhat ironic flourish for a generally retiring personality.

22 A note about street names may be helpful here. Until 1971, Great George Street was found on both sides of Queen Square. The upper end of the street ran from Grafton Street to Euston Street where it joined Malpeque Road. In the summer of 1903, the stretch of Malpeque Road between Euston Street and the northern limit of the Common was renamed Elm Avenue. The author wishes to thank Catherine Hennessey for this information.

extensive developments occurred along Brighton Road and the adjacent part of Euston Street and in the Common along, and just off, North River Road. The western end of Grafton Street and the eastern reaches of Richmond Street also experienced a lot of construction activity, as did the northern stretches of Hillsborough, Prince, Rochford and Weymouth Streets. While some of these new homes were modest, some were very substantial and architecturally distinguished. The familiar names of William Harris and C. B. Chappell are associated with numerous big projects, but other architects were active in the period: John Corbett, Richard Weeks and E. Stirling Blanchard. Dundas Terrace, a multi-unit residence at the western end of Water Street, is a fine example of a Harris design. It was built in the neo-Queen Anne style in 1889 and was designated a National Historic Site in 1990.

Many houses were the products of builders who prepared their own designs. Firms, such as Parkman and Crabbe, Thomas and Benjamin Seller, Trainor and Hughes, Charles McGregor and William H. Fraser, left their mark on the city's residential landscape. Lowe Brothers was a particularly prominent builder and enjoyed a sound reputation. In 1882 a local newspaper commenting upon the new house of pharmacist C. D. Rankin stated, "when we say it was designed and erected by Lowe Bros., the public will understand that the work throughout is first class ...."

Because of its stable demographics and the absence of large-scale industries, Charlottetown did not see the construction of extensive clusters of cheap tenements for workers, although there was inexpensive housing, particularly in the east end of the city near the rail yards. Charlottetonians, however, did believe in recycling and

Dundas Terrace, seen at the foot of Water Street in this 1893 photo, is a fine example of a William Harris design.

reusing buildings for housing purposes. An old Methodist chapel and a workshop, amongst other non-residential structures, were made into homes. Sometimes buildings were moved before they were converted. The Revere House was hauled from the wharf at the foot of Great George Street to Brighton Road in 1890 to be transformed into two tenements. The old manse of St. James Presbyterian Church was moved from Pownal Street to Brighton Road in 1906 to become another tenement. Even the house that became the first Charlottetown Hospital was taken in the 1890s from its site on Dorchester Street near St. Dunstan's Cathedral to a new location on Haviland Street where it was converted into apartments.

For the early decades of the period 1880-1920, an overall taste for more ornate housing designs predominated. High-style houses featured gables, turrets, façades with wings and indentations, ornate fretwork and prominent verandahs. The drab grey and brown paints of the earlier era gave way to brighter, more varied colours with contrasting trims. After the turn of the 20th century, the trend shifted to less angular, more balanced, square-shaped designs with hipped roofs. White became the almost-universal colour of choice. Gradually the housing along residential streets closed ranks as vacant land was built upon, and the focus of sightlines became increasingly confined to what was near at hand. The housing stock in general, however, was more varied and interesting than it had been earlier, even if some of the older and the more basic residences were beginning to deteriorate and even decay. Whether there was a sufficient supply of housing for the whole community, either showcase or merely decent, is another matter. In the aftermath of the First World War, housing stocks in Canada generally were in short supply. The federal government instituted a program of low-interest loans to the provinces for the construction of new housing. City Council passed an address to the provincial government urging it to take advantage of the offer.

Parks

Interest in the care of Charlottetown's squares and parks had been sporadic in the 25 years following incorporation. Hillsborough Square, for instance, had been improved so that it was "a beautiful spot and a credit to the city," but it had been allowed to lapse into a state that was "a disgrace to the century and a standing memorial of the incapacity or neglect of men who have been placed in responsible [civic] positions ...." In the 1880s, however, there was a renewal of concern about the maintenance and beautification of the city's open spaces. This may have been linked to international thinking about ways to make cities more attractive and wholesome, or perhaps to worries about the effects of the increased density of development in the original town plan, or merely to a desire to keep up with standards found in other communities. Of course, a segment of the population had always wanted Queen Square to be suitably landscaped. For whatever reasons, an Arbour Day committee was formed at the instigation of A. B. Warburton and R. R. Fitzgerald, and a concerted attack was planned on the barren parks and waysides of the city. The work was carried out on May 24, 1884, Charlottetown's first Arbour Day. On that occasion alone, a reported 800 trees

One can see the impact of the Arbour Day movement in these two views of Grafton Street, taken from the top of Province House less than a decade apart. Right - 1883. Above - 1895.

were planted in the city. The following spring, the *Examiner* announced the majority had survived the winter, the cows and boys who "never think of breaking a tree now." With time, it concluded, "our city trees will soon be a conspicuous ornament — a shade for the body and a solace for the mind."

Special attention was given to the squares, each of which had its own committee. Under the leadership of Arthur Newbery, a group of volunteers prepared a design for the planting of trees on Queen Square. Other parks received similar attention. P. Weeks headed the Hillsborough Square committee; J. Ball, the King Square; and William Harris, the Rochford Square. Though Harris's mother declared her son's plan to be the best, no one was as persistent and untiring in his efforts as Newbery. In the years following 1884, under his guidance, gardens, sidewalks, a fountain and a band shell appeared in Queen Square, and what had formerly been forlorn, untidy grounds were gradually transformed into a showplace for the entire provincial capital.

Victoria Park, which so charmed Consul Vail, posed different challenges in its management. The principal of these was access for vehicles from the central part of town. A road was proposed as an extension of Kent Street, but opposition in the provincial legislature delayed passage of the requisite act until 1887, and, even then, the city was further delayed by unco-operative Lieutenant Governors who denied the legal right of the city to claim the clearance for the roadway along the shoreline.[23] Several years passed before the dispute was settled in 1896, and the city was able to commence the construction of an embankment and landscaped drive. Horace Haszard was later given much of the credit for securing the right of way for the city. The carriageway opened on May 24, 1897, Queen Victoria's Diamond Jubilee. The road was eventually extended in 1899 around Duchess Point to join Brighton Road.

While the park was a wonderful, natural setting with lush vegetation and ample wildlife, efforts were made to improve it both cosmetically and functionally. Drives and walkways were laid out, fallen trees and old roots were removed and new trees were planted, some areas were levelled, bath houses were installed along the shore and cricket pitches and tennis courts were established. A high board fence near the embankment in front of Government House was removed in 1899, and in 1902 Government Pond was defined by the erection of a stone wall at its northern end and an embankment on the south. An additional 16 acres adjacent to Prince Edward Battery were added in 1905. Part of the park was used by local militia units as a parade ground. Tensions arose between those who sought to protect nature and those who advocated further development of recreational facilities. While over the years the emphasis swayed back and forth between the two approaches to administration of the park, the contradictions between them were never satisfactorily resolved. Even so, the sight of the citizenry enjoying themselves in the park would, in the view of one observer, cause "the thoughtful spectator" to conclude "that Charlottetown is not, after all, such a 'poverty-stricken hole' as a certain large class in our community delight in representing it."

Streets and Sidewalks

The roads and walkways of Charlottetown continued to inspire both fury and satisfaction in the hearts of its citizenry throughout the period 1880-1920. Substantial improvements had been made to the streets with macadamization and the installation of sidewalks, but inevitably the cost of such public works was wearing, and taxpayers at times sought relief. One such occasion came right at the end of the century. Some of the victors in the election of 1898 fought campaigns calling for economy in civic affairs, and other politicians soon realized that this was popular with the electorate. "Consequently work on the streets has been gradually lessened, the sidewalks have been neglected." Critics saw such cutbacks as ill-considered attempts to achieve an advanced level of city management in order to produce barely noticeable savings. Clean streets, they argued, made the city more attractive to tourists, and road construction meant the construction crews would avoid idleness, vagrancy or emigration.

At other times, the mood was more expansive. In 1902, of the 11½ miles of streets in the city, only 3 3/10 miles were macadamized. In the Common, 1½ of the

23 In the period, three Lieutenant Governors held office: Andrew A. MacDonald, Jedediah S. Carvell and George W. Howlan. Problems seem to have started with MacDonald.

7½ miles of roads were paved. By 1910 citizens were fairly buoyant about the condition of the city's streets and sidewalks. By 1920 Charlottetown was laying asphalt on its streets. This was a relatively new road-building technique, but, even so, City Council discussed the purchase of a used asphalt plant in 1919, and in 1920 spent $50,000 on asphalting the city's roads. City officials believed the money was well-invested although the source of the revenue was a matter of concern. Rather than having costs borne solely by the existing ratepayers, Council believed that the tax base should be as broad as possible. To that end, the provincial government was asked to amend the act of incorporation to provide that "no exemption should be allowed on any real property in the city from contributing a *pro rata* share of the cost of permanent streets or permanent street improvement." Charlottetonians also voiced strong objections to the provincial government's tax policies. The press occasionally urged the return of a fair portion of the revenue from the income tax, and Council opposed a 1920 provincial poll tax proposal because "a poll tax is already being collected and the citizens of Charlottetown are now being heavily taxed to keep their own streets."

The Harbour

In the years following 1880, the wharves below Water Street remained busy with ocean-going and coastal trade. This diminished over time as internal travel by road and rail increased and the local economy became more closely aligned with markets in the rest of Canada. The municipally owned wharves had proven expensive to manage and maintain, and the corporation had adopted a policy of leasing them to

Wharves at the foot of Great George Street, c. 1895. The wharves below Water Street remained busy in the years following 1880. There was talk of extending the railway along the entire waterfront. Note the ferry on its way to Rocky Point.

The caissons for the Hillsborough Bridge were assembled at the end of Water Street on what was by this time known as Paoli's Wharf.

commercial operators. Although the railway had become a key factor for the continuing vitality of the harbour, ultimately the port that would benefit the most from the railway would be the home to the ferries that carried freight cars to and from the mainland. Competition for this prize was fierce, but the decision to construct the New Brunswick and Prince Edward Island Railway between Cape Tormentine, New Brunswick, and the Intercolonial Railway's main line, and the completion in 1916 of a major ferry terminus at Carleton Point, Prince Edward Island, meant that the point of arrival and departure by train on the Island would irrevocably be located not in the capital, but at Borden.

Although it was to become one of the agents of its downturn, the railway, at first, contributed to the activity on Charlottetown's harbour. Produce from distant parts of the province was brought to the capital for transshipment, and imports arrived to be distributed to customers across the Island. To facilitate that process, rail lines were extended along the waterfront as far as Great George Street. A proposed right of way envisaged tracks running beyond that point as far west as Connolly's Wharf at the bottom of Haviland Street. Discussions about extending the railway along Lower Water (Peake) Street persisted. If installed, the tracks would service local businesses and encourage the opening of additional warehouses. The seaward-looking harbour where hotels, warehouses and stores intermingled with imposing and modest residences was giving way to an industrial waterfront of rail yards, repair shops and manufacturing plants. A new roundhouse was erected in the train yards in 1909, and Bruce Stewart and Company, an important Island manufacturing enterprise, was located nearby.

The railway also reduced the significance of the harbour, as it created a barrier to the southeastern part of Prince Edward Island. Rail travel from Charlottetown east followed the Hillsborough River to Mount Stewart and on to Georgetown and Souris. Roads from Murray Harbour and Vernon led to Southport and a ferry ride across the harbour. Besides the *Elfin* and the *Southport*, in 1894 the *Hillsborough* was added to the service, which also crossed the West River. The passage from Southport to Charlottetown during the navigation season was not always reliable nor pleasant as numerous accounts testify. In winter, the crossing by ice was far from comfortable. As early as 1855, a plan had been developed to erect an iron bridge across the Hillsborough, but at an estimated cost of £100,000, it was unaffordable. Later, a scheme to construct a tunnel under the water was proposed but rejected as infeasible, and in 1890 the topic of a bridge was resurrected, but again with no definitive outcome.

All of this indecision ended in 1905 when the federal government undertook to finance a branch line to southeastern Kings County. Part of the project involved construction of a bridge across Charlottetown harbour. A used bridge that once traversed the Miramichi River in New Brunswick was purchased, cut into sections, and brought to Charlottetown where it was reassembled on piers that stepped across the Hillsborough from Kensington Range to Southport. Planks laid beside the rails permitted vehicular traffic. A swing span midway across the river permitted movement of vessels. This original fixed link served for over 50 years as a vital part of the Island's transportation structure. On the water, the *Southport* was retired, to be followed by the *Elfin* within four years. The *Hillsborough* continued operating on the run to Rocky Point.

Utilities

Until the latter part of the 19th century, Charlottetown's skyline was uncluttered by telephone and power wires and their attendant ranks of supporting utility poles. A few telegraph wires trekked their way through town, but one of the distinguishing features of the modern cityscape had yet to appear over local rooftops. All of that changed in 1884 when Robert Angus, a Scot, was sent to Prince Edward Island as the representative of Bell Telephone of Canada, and began to canvass for subscribers for telephone service. His task was to find 25 customers willing to pay $30 a year for the new technology. In actual fact, he initially located only 11 — the railway took seven telephones, and the Roman Catholic Bishop subscribed for two, as did Judge Edward Hodgson. An exchange was put into operation at the law offices of Palmer and MacLeod in 1885 with a total capacity of 50 lines. By then, the Bell company had sold its interests on the Island to a group of local investors.[24] It was the newly

24 The group was headed by Charles Palmer, Malcolm MacLeod, Thomas Dodd, Benjamin Rogers and John Ings.

formed Telephone Company of Prince Edward Island, then, which maintained the lines that connected the various pioneer subscribers. By 1890 demand for service was brisk, and wires were appearing everywhere in the city.

Not many months passed after the installation of the telephone wires before power lines joined them overhead. In 1885 the Royal Electric Company of Montreal had been invited by the city to bid on a contract to provide street lighting. The company subsequently offered to supply 32 arc lights to illuminate the main thoroughfares.[25] The city accepted, and by Christmas of that year installation of the new lights was complete. Soon Royal Electric was also locally incorporated, in this case as the Prince Edward Island Electric Company, and, in the years that followed, more lamps would be installed and electricity would be extended to homes and businesses.

Each of the telegraph, telephone and power companies used a single-wire distribution system. Unfortunately, the electrical lines created static on the telephone network. This prompted the phone company in 1908 to convert to a two-wire system with a central energy supply, thereby improving the clarity of sound and eliminating crank phones and batteries from subscribers' premises. Charlottetown became the third city in Canada to be served by this superior technology. By 1911 it could boast of having 560 telephones. The tangle of wires that characterized Canadian cities in the 20th century had emerged in the Island capital.

Towards 1920, another harbinger of modern urban life appeared fleetingly. Thomas Adams, a Scottish city-planner working for the Canadian Commission of Conservation, delivered a lecture at Prince of Wales College on the benefits of planned development. Noting that a bad environment impaired or destroyed human resources and thus undercut production, he called for government leadership to ensure proper planning. While the original plan for Charlottetown was one of the best in Canada, the city in recent years had "fallen from grace" with the new railway station and its approaches. It would take more than one speech, however, to change some of the haphazard land-use practices that had become firmly entrenched.

ECONOMIC GROWTH AND METROPOLITAN DEVELOPMENT

Charlottetown's functions as a provincial capital continued to be one of the mainstays of the local economy in this period. A Victorian preference for small government continued well into the 20th century, although the range of administrative activities gradually eased upward. Some of this expansion was in response to the notion that government could improve the economy by setting standards for the production and processing of farm, forest and fishery products and educating the public on how these standards might be attained. The same trend could be observed for the limited federal presence in the city.

---

25 Arc lamps emit light by means of an electric arc bridging the gap between two carbon electrodes. The light is bright, but it creates noise, and the electrodes burn away quickly with the result that the lamps have to be replaced frequently. Incandescent bulbs produce light by heating a filament inside a vacuum. They are smaller and last longer than arc lamps, but they are not as bright.

A key to Charlottetown's prosperity was its role as a provider of goods and services to the farming community. This could work the other way, as well. Robert Bridges had a 48-acre farm on the Brackley Point Road, "2 miles from Charlottetown." There he raised pigs, cattle and sheep ...

The opening of the Charlottetown Experimental Farm in 1909 was an example of growth in government. For decades, there had been a provincial farm at Falconwood, where livestock were bred and sold, and some crop experimentation was undertaken. In 1901 the Island government created a department of agriculture but discovered it lacked the resources to expand the experimental program at Falconwood. It requested the federal department of agriculture take on this responsibility, but Falconwood was deemed unsuitable for the purposes by Ottawa. Eight years later, the province purchased the Pope property, "Ravenwood," on Mount Edward Road and offered it as a suitable site.

The first superintendent of the station was J. Artemus Clark, who had a small staff of seven employees plus temporary farm hands. Some of the initial tasks involved improvements to the buildings and fields, but cereal, fruit and forage crops were soon planted and a livestock program was instituted. After 1913, poultry breeding was undertaken, and the Charlottetown facility eventually became one of the sites for annual egg-laying contests sponsored by the dominion agriculture department. Such activity encouraged the expansion of the Island's egg and poultry industry, some of it Charlottetown-based, and contributed to employment in the city. The 1921 assessment rolls, for instance, noted several candlers among the ratepayers.[26]

26 The candlers may have processed local eggs sold as surplus to domestic needs. Many eggs coming into the city would have arrived packed and graded. Egg producers and grading stations were eventually found throughout rural Prince Edward Island.

Much of Charlottetown's wealth, however, continued to be derived from commerce. The city remained throughout the period the focus of Island business, even if there was some rivalry with other centres, particularly Summerside, and places like Halifax and Saint John. The emphasis in trade, though, shifted away from primary products, either at the wholesale or the retail level, to retail sales of manufactured goods. Increasingly, these products were imported. This was the age in which brand names and mass distribution were emerging as forces in the marketplace. Demand was influenced by widespread advertising, and tastes were shaped by fashion and women's magazines, many of which were American in origin. Consumers sought reliable quality, competitive prices and a wide selection of goods. Merchandising was a competitive business. As well as battling each other, shopkeepers had to contend with travelling salesmen and mail order catalogues. Beyond Canadian giants, Eaton's and Simpson's, after 1909 Charlottetonians could select items from catalogues issued by Holman's of Summerside. In response, Charlottetown merchants upgraded their stores and business practices. There was more entrepreneurial flair. For instance, Prowse Brothers, a dry goods firm formed in the late 1880s, employed aggressive marketing techniques designed to appeal to rural folk and to people with modest incomes. Referring to themselves as "The Wonderful Cheap Men" or "The Farmer's Boys," boasting how they "slaughtered" prices, they also organized promotions such as bean-counting contests and exhibitions of black bears to attract customers. By the turn of the 20th century, they were one of the largest stores of their type in the city, and soon afterwards opened a branch in Sydney, Nova Scotia. Conversely, growing numbers of branch businesses were also present in Charlottetown. The locations where these firms were headquartered reflected the shifting structure of the Canadian economy. In 1881 there were six Halifax-based businesses in Charlottetown, but, by 1911, the Halifax companies were gone and instead there were eight with head offices in either Montreal or Toronto. Although still a small segment of the local economy, outside businesses became connected to the national centres rather than regional ones. On that level, Charlottetown's links were increasingly with Toronto. By 1931 the city was host to 26 branch businesses, all from Toronto.

... and sold pork, beef and mutton at his store on Hillsborough Street.

Manufacturing

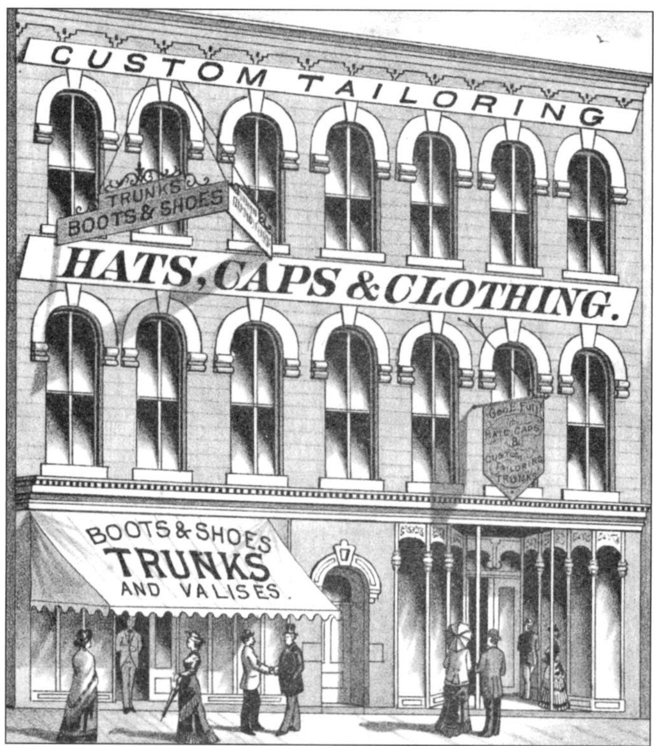

George E. Full, from Meacham's 1880 Atlas. *Though the emphasis was beginning to shift to the retail trade ...*

Virtually no wooden shipbuilding took place on the shores of Charlottetown harbour after 1880. Of the 132 vessels built there between 1810 and 1907, only eight were completed between 1870 and 1900. Some of the city's shipbuilders, however, continued to build vessels at Mount Stewart into the 1880s. This provided some ongoing business for the city's outfitters, but, by 1890, construction of ships at Mount Stewart had also ceased. An attempt to have the federal Department of Public Works construct a slip in Charlottetown harbour for the repair and cleaning of Island ships appears to have fallen upon deaf ears. Although a certain amount of work remained for ship chandlers, the future of the city's manufacturers lay elsewhere.

Unfortunately, there was no single product that could become the mainstay industry. Lobster canning apparently absorbed much of the Island's capital that had hitherto been invested in shipbuilding, and the 1880s saw an explosion of canneries across the Island. Most of these businesses were located in rural areas, close to supplies of lobster and to inexpensive female labour. By 1900 there were two lobster processors, George D. Longworth and James E. Grant, in the city, along with the Portland Packing Company. In 1920 O'Leary and Lee, as well as Simpson Roberts and Company, continued in the business from their respective Water Street premises. Other forms of food processing also occurred in the city. Charlottetown had four pork-packing firms in 1900, plus a condensed milk factory, a brewery and an entrepreneur who shipped oysters. By 1920 there also was a cold storage facility for products such as eggs, poultry, meat and cheese. The food processing sector at this time included the condensed milk factory, brewery, five meat packers and a lobster packer and two creameries.

There were, of course, some small-scale manufacturers serving local markets. They specialized in consumer products and had quite a broad range of goods, including carriages, furniture, tobacco, aerated water and beer, woollens and boots and shoes.

... there were still some small-scale manufacturers serving local markets. (McKinnon and Fraser Carriage Builders, Sawing and Planing, from Meacham's 1880 Atlas.*)*

In 1901, 31 of the Island's 334 factories were located in Charlottetown.[27] Their output, valued at $900,000, accounted for 39 per cent of the Island's total manufacturing output. Obstacles to transportation with the mainland offered these local firms some measure of protection from outside competitors, but as communications improved, the ability of small, locally owned factories to compete in their own marketplace declined. Enough impediments to commerce remained, though, to frustrate most attempts of Charlottetown manufacturers to develop off-Island markets. Thus, the manufacturing sector of Charlottetown's economy remained small and vulnerable.

Metal fabrication was, to a certain extent, an exception to this rule. Charlottetown maintained a number of foundries throughout the period 1880-1920. Products ranged from farm equipment to boilers. The most notable firm was Bruce Stewart and Company, founded in 1890 and producing cast and machined iron and steel products. Stewart's "Imperial" marine engines became a mainstay of the east coast fishing fleet and enjoyed sales across the country. The company also turned out a popular line of beater diggers for potato farmers and an array of other agricultural equipment. In 1919 the value of products exported by the Stewart company was $80,000.[28] The completion of new railway shops in 1906 provided a capacity to manufacture railway cars and locomotives and provided work for a large body of skilled labour. The railway shops, however, were not always busy, and in 1912 the Board of Trade attempted to

27 According to the 1901 census, the average annual output of a factory in Charlottetown was $29,032, while factories elsewhere had an average annual output of $4,646.

28 Equivalent value in 2008 would have been $924,800.

win some business for them by appealing to the Prime Minister to have them used to make the locomotives and rolling stock required by the Island railway when it was converted to standard gauge. Little seems to have come of this initiative since it was repeated in 1917 and again in 1919.

The outbreak of the First World War seemed to offer some prospect for the expansion of manufacturing in Charlottetown. The *Guardian* anticipated new markets for food and greater opportunities for fox farmers freed from competition from Russia. The struggle, in fact, became one of unprecedented proportions, consuming vast quantities of supplies of all kinds. In March 1916, a conference of businessmen and professionals was held to look for ways to improve the province's economy, transportation and education. After this meeting, an aptly named General Committee of Twenty was established, with Frank R. Heartz, a leading businessman and capitalist, as chairman. It had six members each from Charlottetown, Kings and Prince Counties and two from Queens County. As part of its activities, a "New Industries, Undeveloped Resources Sub-Committee" was created. It identified some specific prospects for new manufacturing, such as the establishment of canning industries using an improved type of can made in Charlottetown. Despite some optimistic comments from politicians and other leaders, the attitudes about new wartime ventures remained cautious. In a report on industry produced in 1917, Percy Pope noted that public attitudes constituted the greatest barrier to the establishment of new industries. He argued that there was a widespread fear that success by any one individual came at the expense of others in the community. Pope recommended the exploitation of currently unused natural resources as well as co-operation to ensure that local products were preferred in the marketplace over products from away.

The war years, however, underscored the vulnerability of the manufacturing sector of both the city and the province. Munitions were produced in Canada on an unprecedented scale by an organization called the Imperial Munitions Board. At the height of its operations, the IMB's budget matched that of the federal government, yet not a cent was spent on the Island. In 1917 some members of the Board of Trade discussed the possibility of organizing a company to operate a munitions plant, but nothing was done. That was just as well, since the IMB did not favour placing orders in the Maritimes and would have certainly rejected any overtures from Charlottetown.

Charlottetonians, like other Canadians, had been caught up in the fervour of the Great War. Many in the community suffered personal loss and hardships in the process. In common with other Canadians, they sought an explanation for this trial by fire, and the answer they found was in the expected purification of the social and economic order. Victory brought the promise of reform. The social inequities and economic torpor experienced before the war were to be overcome. This theme was taken up by politicians, and community and religious leaders across Canada, and even writers and artists. Charlottetonians did not escape the emotional tide, and they anticipated the fruits of peace with enthusiasm. "Old things are passing away," proclaimed the *Evening Patriot* in January 1919, "and many things are becoming new."

> *We have entered upon a period which will tax to the utmost the courage, enterprise, knowledge and experience of our business and professional men, if we are to keep pace with these stirring and restless times.*

Faced with the challenges of a new age, the city's business leaders responded by developing new strategies for economic prosperity. The time had come to rectify the lack of industrial development. A beginning was made in 1917 with the creation of a Development Commission, based upon the General Committee of Twenty and headed by Frank R. Heartz. After due deliberation, the commission issued a thoughtful report that highlighted assistance to agriculture, improvements to the educational system and creation of manufacturing enterprises as the means to achieve greater prosperity. The most promising new industries, the report suggested, would be ones connected to the Island's primary resources. An example of such a business was the manufacture of field drainage tiles. Unfortunately, after the report's appearance, there was no immediate follow-through. The Development Commission set the stage, though, for the next attempt to jump start manufacturing in the city.

On January 15, 1919, a Citizens' Industrial Promotion Committee was founded, composed of three members of City Council, including the mayor, three representatives of the Rotary Club, three delegates from the Great War Veterans Association, seven members of the Retail Merchants Association and the entire council of the Board of Trade.[29] Those who were inclined to adopt "a pessimistic, not to say rather sneering attitude" were advised by a supportive *Evening Patriot* to consider the membership of the Committee — all substantial community leaders. As for the *Patriot* there were few doubts. The paper believed "a new era has dawned" and "young, vigorous and enterprising professional and business men of this community" had taken hold of the situation and would "not only advocate and stimulate the interest of our people in these undertakings" but also would "invest part of their own earnings and surpluses." The consequences of industrial development were momentous: larger population, greater prosperity and the opportunity for Islanders to remain at home and prosper.

Where to start was the problem. Ideas were plentiful: factories for broom handles, dried fruits and vegetables, potato flour and starch, fish by-products, biscuits and confections, spices and boots and shoes were only some of the suggestions. To generate additional concepts, the committee sponsored as essay-writing contest on the theme, "New Manufacturing Industries for Prince Edward Island." The winning entries, published in the *Evening Patriot*, provide an interesting view of current ideas about industrialization and perhaps incidentally the predisposition of the contest judges. Many of the proposals referred to advantages derived from PEI's setting. A mixed farming economy capable of supporting milk condenseries and seed-packaging operations was seen as one natural advantage. Rich clay soils suitable for the

29 Within this organization were three standing committees: one for publicity to encourage local support for new industries, another for investigation of promising developmental prospects and a third to recommend action to responsible elected bodies and specific business groups.

production of sugar beets and flax, which in turn would support processing plants, fisheries with waste products suitable for fertilizers, and nearby iron and coal mines supplying the raw materials for an agricultural implements industry were others. While the concept of Charlottetown becoming the "Belfast of Canada" must have seemed far-fetched even then, many of the suggestions reflected an awareness of the factors of resource availability and market demands. Moreover, there seemed to be little doubt about the desirability of industrialization or the ability of local entrepreneurs to achieve their goals.

One other aspect of the various scenarios bears comment. They contained a strong element of nativism. Industrial development was to be supported by local consumers who would discriminate against products from away. D. L. McKinnon, first-prize winner of the essay contest, exhorted merchants to ask themselves whether "the goods I import and sell [can] be manufactured at home" and decried local investors who sank their money into "empty oil wells, fake gold mines and boomed real estate out West, to say nothing of stock on margin." The *Patriot* echoed these sentiments in an editorial which noted, "all these proposed industries will require the backing of our people, not only in the way of capital, but particularly with regard to patronage." "Encourage home industry," it continued, "patronize local organizations and in every way try to keep as much as we can of our wealth within the province ...."

Not everyone was swept away by this enthusiasm. The owners of the St. Peter's Starch Company noted that the Japanese could manufacture, ship, pay duty and still profitably undersell Canadian starch manufacturers in the domestic market. Exporters to the large American market faced a twenty-dollar-per-ton tariff and found unsold supplies in their warehouses. A returned veteran worried that boosting a particular industry might keep down the wages of returned soldiers because of the absence of competition. Another cold voice of reason enquired after the fate of previous industrial ventures and suggested that the principal weakness of past attempts was the lack of finances. "If the financial men of the country want to do any good," "Friend of Island Industries" noted, "let them give financial aid to the existing industries as well as starting new ones and let them not take cold feet at slight failures ... but stick to it with earnestness ...."

As 1919 wore on, there was a marked and steady diminution in the activities of the Citizens' Industrial Promotion Committee. Talk of industrial development, like the belief in the regeneration of mankind, was dissipated by the complexities of everyday peacetime life and the decline of jointly shared wartime goals. Patriotic fervour was redirected to preparations for the visit of the Prince of Wales, and old strategies reasserted themselves. Premier Arsenault called for a campaign of thrift, which would reach "every man, women and child," to drive home the message that "the savings of the many are infinitely better than the hoardings of the few." A delegation from the Canadian Manufacturers' Association visiting in October was confronted with a synopsis of general ills that closely resembled traditional Board of Trade complaints about transportation and communications. By the new year, community leaders had decided the thrust of the CIPC was inappropriate. R. E. Mutch, outgoing President of the Board of Trade, noted that the results should have been more directed towards agriculture. The *Patriot* agreed, asserting that while large industries should be given encouragement insofar as possible, the focus of economic development should be on farming and fishing.

Even so, the immediate postwar economic situation was not all bad. Charlottetown had been relatively untouched by "the financial and industrial storms which swept over other cities," and had seen some substantial investments in local businesses. The CIPC had given support to Bruce Stewart and Company, a marine engine manufacturer that was the city's third-largest employer, with the result the company went ahead with a plant expansion financed by a stock issue. Discussion of a need for a central creamery to provide greater efficiency for the processing of Island milk presaged the opening of such a facility several years later. A new milling company opened, and a start was made on the seed potato export business. Nevertheless, these were slim pickings compared to expectations. The explanation for this situation was undoubtedly in some measure to be found along the lines proposed by Mr. Mutch. "Friend of Island Industries" probably was also partly right when he questioned the seriousness of the committee. "The business men are as usual meditating on something. But! why can't they start something in earnest."

Lack of investment capital may be seen as one possible answer to this question. A situation that developed early in the autumn of 1919 pointed in this direction. At that time, the owner of the Victoria Hotel, the principal hostelry of the city, decided that he would sell or close the establishment. Shares were offered to the public at $100 each. They were promoted as safe investments, but 600 shares had to be marketed by the owner's deadline of September 20. Sales were sluggish, and the attempt to keep the hotel open became a race against time. An extensive advertising campaign accompanied by active arm-twisting was necessary before the required sum was raised, and even that was reached just under the wire. Significantly, the persons spearheading the effort were not the ones most closely associated with the CIPC. Shortage of capital was not the issue. Those with money to invest might have just been pragmatic analysts of what ventures were realistic locally, and risk aversion was likely an important factor.[30] This possibility is suggested by the spectacular results of the Victory Loan drives during the war. Patriotism and local pride may explain part of the success, but not all. Bonds were truly safe and secure investments.

Banking and Finance

By 1880 Charlottetown's status as the Island's business centre was in part demonstrated by its domination of the province's commercial finance. Initially, individual lenders had provided critical investment capital, but subsequently a network of banks

30 For instance, at the same time there was a proposed aerial transportation venture in which a large British company promised to provide two-thirds of the capital if local investors came up with the balance. Charlottetown investors were even promised preferred status on the dividends, but potential backers still wanted provincial guarantees that they would receive a six per cent return on their capital. Those investors who were prepared to take risks may have preferred stocks in incorporated fox farms.

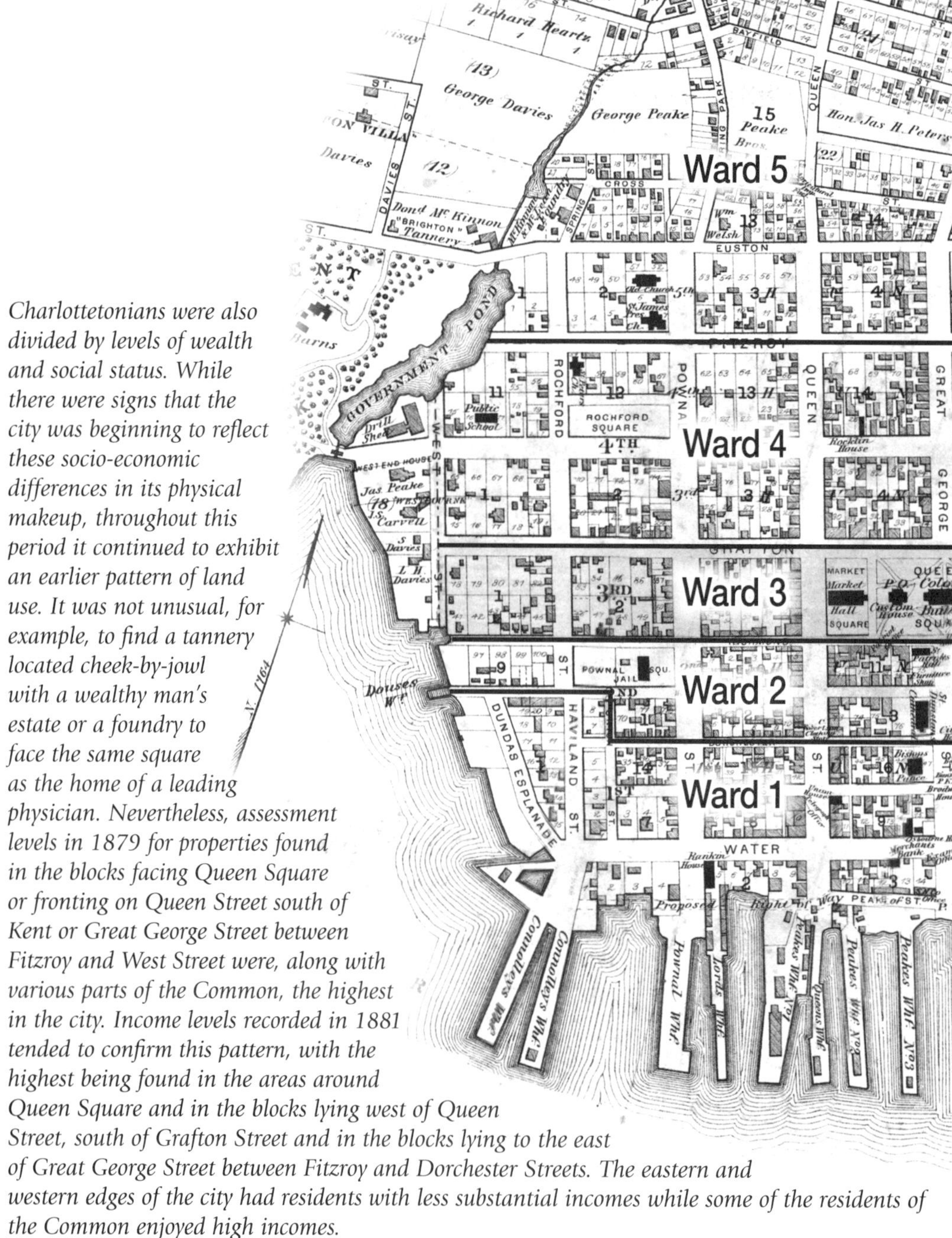

Charlottetonians were also divided by levels of wealth and social status. While there were signs that the city was beginning to reflect these socio-economic differences in its physical makeup, throughout this period it continued to exhibit an earlier pattern of land use. It was not unusual, for example, to find a tannery located cheek-by-jowl with a wealthy man's estate or a foundry to face the same square as the home of a leading physician. Nevertheless, assessment levels in 1879 for properties found in the blocks facing Queen Square or fronting on Queen Street south of Kent or Great George Street between Fitzroy and West Street were, along with various parts of the Common, the highest in the city. Income levels recorded in 1881 tended to confirm this pattern, with the highest being found in the areas around Queen Square and in the blocks lying west of Queen Street, south of Grafton Street and in the blocks lying to the east of Great George Street between Fitzroy and Dorchester Streets. The eastern and western edges of the city had residents with less substantial incomes while some of the residents of the Common enjoyed high incomes.

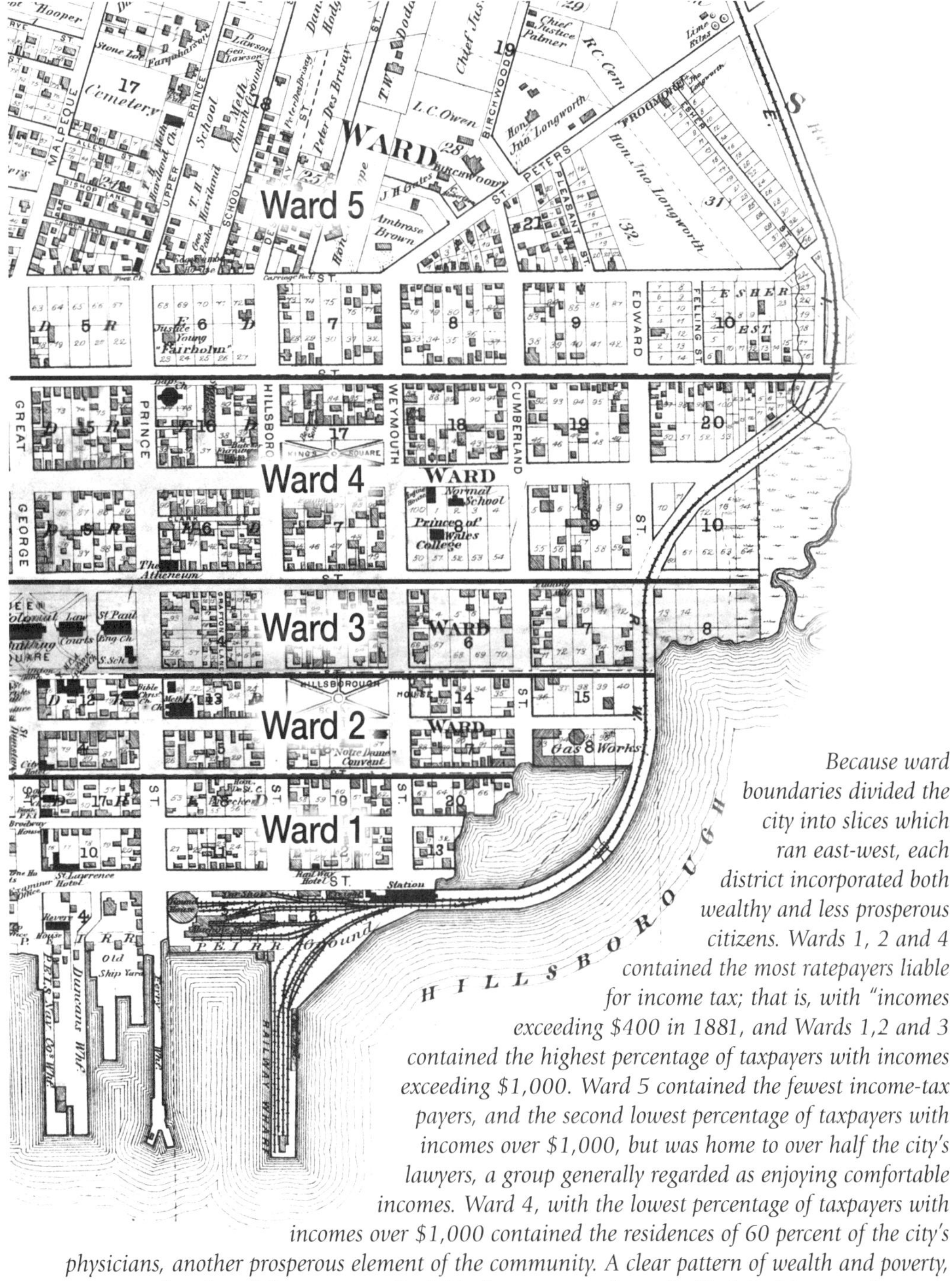

Because ward boundaries divided the city into slices which ran east-west, each district incorporated both wealthy and less prosperous citizens. Wards 1, 2 and 4 contained the most ratepayers liable for income tax; that is, with "incomes exceeding $400 in 1881, and Wards 1,2 and 3 contained the highest percentage of taxpayers with incomes exceeding $1,000. Ward 5 contained the fewest income-tax payers, and the second lowest percentage of taxpayers with incomes over $1,000, but was home to over half the city's lawyers, a group generally regarded as enjoying comfortable incomes. Ward 4, with the lowest percentage of taxpayers with incomes over $1,000 contained the residences of 60 percent of the city's physicians, another prosperous element of the community. A clear pattern of wealth and poverty, therefore, fails to emerge. Each block or even portions of a block had its own character, and the differences between the economic prosperity of their residents in the same neighbourhood could be considerable.

had sprung up. Of Prince Edward Island's five banks, three were headquartered in Charlottetown, including the oldest, the Bank of Prince Edward Island. The Bank of Prince Edward Island and the Merchants Bank invested heavily in the shipbuilding industry, while the Union Bank catered more to retail business. Despite the existence of the commercial banks, private bankers, such as Richard Heartz, continued to conduct a brisk trade after 1880.[31]

During the relative prosperity of the 1860s and 1870s, local financial institutions had served their clients and shareholders well, although an economic downturn and some imprudent investments had obliged the Bank of PEI to suspend operations in the winter of 1857-58, and similar circumstances prompted the Merchants Bank to do the same briefly towards the end of 1878. The more severe reversals in the economy were experienced after the late 1870s, when the effects of the worldwide trade downturn, which finally reached the Island,[32] proved the undoing of Charlottetown's banks. First the Bank of PEI succumbed to the pressures of defaulted loans secretly issued to unreliable clients by the bank's cashier, Joseph Brecken. Between the moment when Brecken fled the province in November 1881 and the submission of a petition of bankruptcy in May 1882, the economic uncertainty and destruction of personal fortunes suppressed investment in trade and industry and eroded confidence in the other local banks. Shortly afterwards in 1883, the Union Bank amalgamated with the Bank of Nova Scotia. The Merchants Bank soldiered on, but increased competition from mainland banks that opened branches in Charlottetown and elsewhere on the Island, and lingering doubts about the vulnerable position of the local bank, led to its merger with the Canadian Bank of Commerce in 1906. It was the last of the autonomous Island banks.

The disappearance of local banks had significant implications for the Charlottetown economy. It became increasingly dependent upon decisions made by outsiders who had little knowledge of the community or loyalty to it. More importantly, the large integrated banks sought to maximize the return upon the capital they commanded, and Charlottetown found itself in competition for investment with the rapidly expanding centres in Central and Western Canada. Local banks had tended to invest their deposits and other assets locally, while merged banks transferred capital out of the city to more lucrative markets. While depositors had some greater assurance that their money was safe in the larger institutions, and borrowers were not subjected to some of the favouritism practiced by the locally owned banks, the interest of the banking system in local development diminished and the ability of local entrepreneurs to obtain investment capital became circumscribed.

31 Inherently cautious banks tended to favour well-established clientele. Those of more modest means could turn to private lenders and could open a savings account at a Post Office Savings Bank.

32 The $800,000 loan, guaranteed by the federal government and dispersed under the Land Purchase Act of 1875, may have helped to shelter the economy from the early effects of the depression because a lot of the purchased land was Island owned, and some of the money would have been invested locally.

Economic Promotion

In July 1887, 12 years after the disappearance of the short-lived Chamber of Commerce, Charlottetown business-leaders gathered to form a Board of Trade. The early membership of the Board represented a broad swath of the local business community and included J. S. Carvell, George R. Beer, L. E. Prowse, George E. Full, L. C. Owen, Benjamin Rogers and John Ings. Physicians and politicians and architect W. C. Harris also were members. The first president was Lewis Carvell. In the initial burst of enthusiasm, meetings were frequent and the range of topics discussed was quite broad, running from trade issues to immigration, communications, rail and steamship service and promotion of the city and tourism. After 1887, interest waned, and meetings became less frequent. At the general meeting held on January 8, 1890, a membership report revealed that of the 120 people who had joined the board since it was inaugurated, 51 had quit, 35 were behind in their dues and only 34 were members in good standing. By the mid-1890s, membership stabilized, but there were only about 10 to 15 actively participating in the board's affairs. In subsequent years, numbers edged upwards; by 1904 there were 104 members, including Premier Arthur Peters who declared to the annual meeting that there was a time when he "considered the Board of Trade a thing of small importance but that day is now past." Some of the subsequent years, however, may have been lean ones since board minutes in 1914 noted that the current membership of 115 was "a very considerable increase over former years."

The period from 1880 to 1920 saw rapid urban development across most of North America. Expansion was not continuous since the economy was characterized by downturns as well as bursts of prosperity, but, especially after the turn of the 20th century, certain cities blossomed. To a degree, growth was understood as a competition in which municipalities battled to attract the entrepreneurs and capital required to drive the economy and to build a vibrant industrial base. Leadership was a critical factor in this struggle, and the "booster," the optimistic promoter of a community's virtues, became the hallmark of successful growth efforts. Charlottetown had its share of boosters, as well as a number of less charitable "knockers," but the city's business and political leaders exhibited caution in pursuing growth. In particular, many were suspicious of offering grants or similar concessions, such as "bonusing", to attract new businesses. The *Guardian* summed up this sentiment when it commented on ambitious promises of civic improvements: "We know the quantity of cloth we have and we know that even that is liable to shrinkage .... The only question is how to make the best of what we have, how to prevent what we have from deteriorating and how to prepare for the future." Even so, others concluded: "If ever Charlottetown is to become a city of increased population and greater activity, then, there must be more industrial works established here." The solution was to encourage manufacturers to come and make what they could with profit in the city.

City Council had arranged to exempt new industries from taxation a couple of times before 1885, when permission was sought from the province to exempt backers of "a worthy first-class Hotel" from taxes for 15 years.[33] After that time, the city occasionally encouraged economic development through grants to specific businesses of free water or exemption from taxation.[34] While tax breaks, free water and even free building sites were used to encourage new businesses, bonuses remained rare, despite the avowal of James Paton, Mayor from 1906 to 1908, that Charlottetown should encourage industries by granting them. The issue of bonusing sparked a lively debate in 1902 in connection with a pork-packing plant. An old established firm, Rattenbury's, had been acquired by the Dominion Packing Company. It proposed to expand the business and asked for assistance in the form of tax exemptions and government guarantees for its interest charges. The Board of Trade opposed the measure unless it were approved in a plebiscite. Its council resolved that "capitalists should be encouraged to come to Prince Edward Island to engage in business and every opportunity should be afforded them to do so [but] upon equal terms with our own people." William S. Stewart, a future mayor, writing in *The Prince Edward Island Magazine*, denounced the move as the work of "a few, able oily-tongued strangers" who threatened to shipwreck provincial finances for their own benefit. The company obtained sufficient concessions for the project to go forward, but clearly some Charlottetonians were uneasy about bidding to attract investors.

Pragmatism — or perhaps limiting caution — was apparent in other responses to issues connected with Charlottetown's economic development. Outmigration had halted population growth, and this was identified by the city's businessmen as one of the factors that inhibited economic expansion. Immigration was a possible solution, but the city, along with most of the Maritimes, was being bypassed by new arrivals to Canada. In 1887 the Board of Trade called for the establishment of a real estate agency to contact potential migrants advising them of properties available in the city. Fourteen months further on, the proposed agency had still not been organized. Later, in 1902, the board linked the lack of effective exploitation of the cod fishery by Islanders to the absence of full-time fishermen and requested the provincial government to invest money in attracting such people. This motion may have indicated the sentiments of the members, but it left to others the burden of action. In both of these instances, business seemed content to advocate rather than act.

Similarly, stands taken on tariffs and trade failed to reflect decisiveness and determination, but they did show some consistency. Discussions by the Board of Trade in 1887 concerning a call for commercial union with the United States were a case in point. An initial categorical resolution in favour of such a policy was met with a counter-proposal to reject commercial union for reciprocal free trade and later for "a fair settlement of all differences ... through the removal of all tariff restrictions."

---

33 Exemptions were granted to John Dorsey and R. Goff for a new boot and shoe factory and to the Charlottetown Woollen Factory. Tax exemptions initially ran for five years and guarantees were secured that $5,000 per year would be paid in salaries and the business would not vary from what was described in the applications for exemptions. In arguing in favour of extending the city's power so it could exempt a hotel from taxation for 15 years, Neil MacLeod commented that a hotel that will attract business to the city would "be of as much benefit as any new industry."

34 In 1905 the city received permission to exempt the Charlottetown Condensed Milk Company from taxation for a further 10 years because the company was planning to improve and enlarge its plant.

Eventually, the board agreed to support reciprocal free trade on "the broadest possible basis." In 1897 the board declined to support tariff protection for the iron and coal industries of Nova Scotia and New Brunswick, or preferential free trade within the British Empire.[35] Over 20 years later, Charlottetown commodity exporters with an eye on the American market revisited the tariff issue. Potential sales to the United States of a glut of Island potatoes were impeded by an 8¢ to 10¢ a bushel tariff imposed by the Americans. This barrier responded to a similar one put in place by the Canadian government, and the Board of Trade asked the province to lobby the federal government to scrap the Canadian tariff, thereby freeing Island potatoes from the American duty and opening that market to them. Premier Arsenault promised to do so. These efforts were successful, and the offending tariff was removed.

While Charlottetown's business community was somewhat ambivalent about government economic intervention, city politicians were more open to the idea. A willingness to become involved in the delivery of essential public services was demonstrated in the prolonged debate over the provision of electricity in the city. For years, there had been widespread unhappiness over the deficiencies in the gas street lamps. "Light! Light! Light! More light is what is required," the *Patriot* proclaimed as it condemned the gas lighting in the autumn of 1884. The *Herald* agreed, remarking that "what we should aspire to in Charlottetown is the Electric Light which would be found not only to be more efficient, but ... far cheaper in the end," adding, "it behooves us to keep pace with the times and not remain forever in our 'sleepy hollow.'" In 1885, despite pleas that the gas company was a local firm that invested locally and provided employment, City Council awarded the contract for the provision of street lamps to the Royal Electric Company of Montreal. The *Examiner* had cautioned that the city fathers should ensure electricity was "here to stay," and when the somewhat unexpected decision was made, commented sardonically that Council had secured "the advantage of those latest products of science," and "in a month or two we shall step about in the brilliantly lighted streets ... with all the vanity of a half-clad Indian rejoicing in a new ornament." Before that fateful moment arrived, citizens were obliged to grope through the muddy streets at night in the absence of any lighting at all. When the electric street lamps were switched on, finally, the focus of discussion shifted to the source of the electricity and the extent of service.[36]

Two years later, City Council asked the agent of Royal Electric what it would cost the city to acquire the electrical plant.[37] This did not happen. Instead, two years

35 Just three years previously, the board had protested Ottawa's duty on British tea.

36 Henry Cundall described in his letterbook how the gas lamps were extinguished by the end of October and dismantled well before December 19 when the electric lights were first turned on. The disapproving tone of his comments may have been due, in part, to the fact that he had invested in the gas company. A number of prominent businesses were among the first subscribers. They included W. A. Weeks and Company, Watson's Drug Store, Beer and Goff and Theo. A. Chappelle.

37 Royal Electric had previously had discussions with the gas company with a view to having the local firm gain control of the electrical company. Significantly, the new City Hall was lit by gas. Electricity was not installed for over a decade.

later, the Charlottetown Gas Light Company had its charter amended to permit it to produce and furnish electricity for lighting, heat and other purposes.[38] Royal Electric, which became the Prince Edward Island Electric Company, fulfilled its initial five-year contract for street lighting and was renewed in 1890 for another five-year term. By then, it was in competition with a second power provider, the Full Electric Company. When the street lighting contract was again up for renewal in 1895, Council once more considered acquiring a municipally owned electricity plant. Some opposed the step as running counter to the spirit of private enterprise, while others believed that electric power had, like water, become an essential service and should be under public control, if only to ensure that rates were kept reasonable. Still others wanted more street lights installed and believed a civic utility would accomplish this end.

Discussion of municipal ownership of a power plant continued off and on between 1895 and 1901 when Charlottetonians, ignoring the long-standing and repeated urgings of Mayor Warburton, rejected the idea in a plebiscite.[39] The debate pitted those who feared increased civic debt and favoured prudence until electricity was past its experimental stages against those who believed public ownership promised better street lighting at no increased yearly cost.[40] That same year, Full Electric, PEI Electric and Charlottetown Light and Power, a company formed in 1898 to take over the gas company,[41] combined to form a new business. Now a monopoly, the conglomerate, operating as Charlottetown Light and Power, raised residential electrical rates.[42] Fearing similar price hikes for street lighting, City Council continued to investigate the cost and technical matters connected with providing municipal power. Service had also deteriorated because of the power company's obsolete plant. Supporters of a public utility noted that municipal ownership was common in Great Britain and the city authorities had already demonstrated with the waterworks that they could effectively manage a large enterprise. Some opponents of a city-owned utility claimed that the citizens as a whole would incur the cost of a new plant while, beyond street lighting, only the rich would benefit from improved service. Others referred to the increased

---

38 Even so, the gas company was unable to break into the new energy field and suffered such great competition that the shareholders were obliged to rescue what they could by winding up the business. Henry Cundall recorded in his diary the decision of the gas company to dispose of its works.

39 The electorate also rejected a proposition to abolish the city's wards.

40 This was a debate that was being waged widely across Canada, with varying outcomes. Cities such as Ottawa, Guelph, and Hamilton, Ontario, embarked upon municipal ownership of power. In both Ottawa and Hamilton, private power companies continued to serve commercial and industrial clients. In 1916 Truro, Nova Scotia, began a municipally owned power company, followed in 1919 by Kentville, NS. In Halifax, the privately owned Halifax Power Company, Limited continued to operate, although, after 1917, the city could own shares and lend the company money.

41 Members of the corporation included William Weeks, Lemuel Beer, Benjamin Rogers, Benjamin Heartz, John Ings, Henry Lordly, William Beer, A. E. Ings, Lemuel Prowse, and four New Brunswickers. Little progress was made in the provision of electricity by this third company before it merged with the others.

42 Operations of the combined company were centralized at the old gas works site in the east end of town.

taxes that would be needed to pay the debt on the new facility.

The issue was again presented to the public in a plebiscite held on February 18, 1905. Debate had focused on rates, which, in the opinion of one citizen, should provide "the best possible light at the lowest possible price." This time the proponents of public power won handily. By May, the city had sought and received permission from the provincial legislature to get into the electricity business. The city, which was embroiled in negotiations over the renewal of the street lighting contract and unhappy with the rates being charged by Charlottetown Light and Power, had acquired a strong lever. Intimidated by the possibility of municipally owned competition, the power company offered to sell its property or renew its existing contract with improved service and lower rates. Council opted to extend the contract, subject to the approval of a general meeting of citizens. The threat of public ownership proved effective in keeping power rates low, and in 1910 Council renewed the contract until 1921 with provision for only modest price increases. By 1913 City Council was again calling for municipally owned power when Charlottetown Light and Power received an acceptable take-over offer from the Maritime Trust Company, but their plans went unrealized. A general meeting of citizens failed to endorse the city's proposal.[43] An essential pragmatism to the management of the city's power supply typified the community's mindset. In an age when some municipalities were turning to cheap, publicly owned power as a means to attract industry, Charlottetonians were content to choose the less venturesome route of private power if they could obtain rates they were prepared to pay.

A widely acknowledged consequence of this approach was the fate of public transport. As early as 1887, amendments to the gas company's charter granting it the right to generate electricity foresaw the use of electricity for "motive power." By 1896 a syndicate interested in building a street railway approached the city, and Council appointed a committee to consider the matter. In 1898 the charter of the Charlottetown Light and Power Company included details of the construction of a tramway. Four miles of track were to be laid within three years. While there would be a five-year tax exemption for the streetcar service, the city would have the option to purchase the facility after 20 years. The trams never materialized, but civic authorities continued to investigate the possibility of building a street railway into the new century. Since the city was still small enough for people to get around by foot, the appeal of urban transport likely had more to do with a desire to appear modern than with practical need.

In 1906 another company, the Charlottetown Electric Transit and Power Company, was incorporated partly to build a trolley car system, and again nothing came of the project. Construction of a street railway by what could be a potential rival for the general electricity market was opposed by the Charlottetown Light and Power Company. This opposition became an issue when the company was discussing its acquisition with

43 The meeting attracted 400-500 people and appeared to be evenly divided amongst supporters and opponents of municipal ownership. Persons present refused to vote on the proposal, and the meeting ended "in a fiasco."

outsiders a few years later. Proponents of municipal ownership of the power utility argued that their policy would facilitate the provision of streetcar service. With the newest rejection of the option of a municipal electrical utility, the hope for streetcar service became slimmer, although it never absolutely died.[44] Even so, the inability of the power company to see any financial advantage to investing in a tramway and its opposition to attempts by others to provide one ensured that Charlottetown was to do without municipal transportation for the foreseeable future.

Communications

In its first 33 years, the Board of Trade debated many issues having to do with local development, public administration and the conduct of trade. Overwhelmingly, the board was concerned with getting people and goods to and from the city, by rail or by sea. In fact, just over half of all topics brought up for formal discussion between 1887 and 1920 dealt with either railway or steamship service. When related topics, such as harbour development, construction of a tunnel to the mainland, or building a bridge over the Hillsborough River are included, the only subject that arose frequently that was not connected with transport was trade policy.

By the 1880s, the age of the wooden sailing ship was, for the most part, over. Steamships were playing an increasingly important role in communications between Charlottetown and destinations both near and far. The advent of stronger iron-clad, and later iron-hulled, steamers lengthened the shipping season of the port but failed to resolve the problems of the annual freeze-up entirely. New shipbuilding technologies, moreover, largely spelled the end of local ownership of the means of communication with overseas markets. Iron-hulled steamships were costly to produce at a time when important Charlottetown merchant houses faced reverses. James Duncan and Company went bankrupt in 1878; James Peake became personally insolvent in 1882; and other businesses, such as Carvell Brothers, were in reduced circumstances. Charlottetown's traditional shippers were thus unable to remain heavily involved in the shipping business as owners. Instead, they became dependent upon the availability of vessels owned elsewhere to get their goods to and from markets.

There were two aspects to Charlottetown's ongoing struggle to maintain connections with its commercial partners. Of prime importance were the links with nearby ports in Nova Scotia and New Brunswick and through them with the Intercolonial Railway and commercial centres on the mainland. Overseas links posed a different problem. They were not as busy or, indeed, as critical to the life of the city and the province in general, but they were important to the export of the Island's agricultural produce and lobsters and to the general prosperity of many farmers, fishermen and merchants. While day-to-day life depended upon the connections across the

44 A columnist in the *Patriot,* for instance, looked forward to a publicly owned bus or electric car service. In 1914 some Charlottetown businessmen attempted to bring streetcar service to the city, but the plan failed. One reason for the failure was the short duration, 10 years, in which a $50,000 tax break on real and personal property would apply.

Northumberland Strait, timely departures of steamships during certain seasons, especially the autumn, were necessary for an export-oriented farm and food processing economy with overseas markets.

For much of the period 1880-1920, service between Charlottetown and the neighbouring provinces during the open seasons of the year was provided by small, privately owned, steam-driven vessels. The Charlottetown Steam Navigation Company remained the largest operator into the 20th century with its vessels *Empress* and *Northumberland*. Destinations varied from year to year, but Pictou, Brule and Shediac were the principal ones. City businessmen pressed for speedy service, frequent departures and seasons that began promptly at the spring break-up and continued until winter ice in the strait made further use of the port impossible. Subsidies intended to offset shortfalls in revenue from traffic were a critical component of service on some routes. For instance, service between Charlottetown and Cape Breton required help, and the Board of Trade issued requests for a subvention for service to Glace Bay in 1904 and for a connection with Cape Breton and Newfoundland in 1909. Such appeals sometimes failed. In 1907 a subsidy for steamship service on the Three Rivers (Cardigan Bay), Pictou and Halifax route was lost because the call at Charlottetown drew business away from the Island railway. The following year, when the Three Rivers Steamship Company replaced the *Electra* with the larger and more powerful *Enterprise*, it proposed to cut the stop in Charlottetown. Service to the capital continued, but in 1913 the connection at Charlottetown was ended despite strong opposition from local businessmen and demands for an increased subsidy.

Winter transportation was particularly problematic. With the advent of cold weather, an ice-breaking steamer was assigned to the run between Charlottetown and

For much of the period 1880-1920, service between Charlottetown and the mainland was provided by private steamers like the SS Northumberland.

Pictou. When ice in the strait finally blocked the passage of ships to Charlottetown, service commenced between Georgetown and Pictou. Frequently, long delays were experienced in loading the vessels at either port and in transshipping goods to the trains. This often entailed storage and increased handling costs. In addition, shippers found that the capital could suffer from discriminatory rates in the winter season. Even if departures from Charlottetown were possible after ice closed Georgetown or Summerside, the routine transshipment points, carriers charged a premium for service to the capital, and the Island railway cancelled through rates for goods leaving the city for connection with the Intercolonial.

In the worst circumstances, service was interrupted completely. The *Northern Light*, assigned by the federal government to the run between Georgetown and Pictou, was a wooden ship built for service in the St. Lawrence River. She was severely underpowered and frequently got stuck in the ice; in the winter of 1881, for instance, she was stranded in transit for three weeks. A shortage of provisions eventually forced passengers to abandon ship and complete the perilously cold and icy trip by boat and on foot. The *Northern Light* was replaced in 1888 by the *Stanley*, a new steel icebreaker designed for service on the strait. Though more reliable and capable, the *Stanley* was also frequently unable to complete the crossing.

Frustration mounted. Such delays were more than an inconvenience, they were considered a breach of the terms of Confederation that promised uninterrupted communications between the Island and the mainland. In his presidential address to the Board of Trade in January 1891, President Carvell called for another solution: construction of a tunnel under the Northumberland Strait. A version of this idea had been popular in the mid-1880s, but had been dropped when the federal government undertook to build the *Stanley*. Now it was back. A committee of the board was appointed to press the idea upon the Dominion government. An English engineer, Sir Douglas Fox, was asked to complete a current cost study of the project. At the urging of the Board, the provincial government sent Senator George Howlan to England to discuss the scheme with Fox. Howlan returned to report that there were three options, ranging from a tunnel that was 11 feet in diameter to one that was 18 feet across. The costs ran from $5,376,000 to $11,262,500 plus interest. Despite the fervour with which Islanders pressed their claims for a tunnel and the politeness with which they were heard by federal politicians of both parties, the concept of a tunnel remained just that. New icebreaking steamships were cheaper to complete.

A second steamer, the *Minto*, was constructed to join the *Stanley* in 1899. Larger and more powerful than the *Stanley*, the *Minto*'s presence considerably improved the flow of commerce, but did not resolve the problems entirely. In 1903 the *Stanley* became trapped in the ice, and when the *Minto* went to free her, she, herself, was frozen in. Both vessels remained stuck for almost three weeks during which time the province reverted to the use of iceboats for communications with the mainland.[45] Obviously,

45 The *Stanley* became stuck on January 13, and the *Minto* was trapped when she broke down on February 25. They were finally freed on March 17. The *Stanley* had been stuck for a full nine weeks.

Winter service relied on government steamers like the Stanley, Minto, *and* Earl Grey. *SS* Stanley *c. 1905. Note the iceboats being carried in the lifeboat davits.*

this was far from satisfactory, and angry demands, including those of the Board of Trade, were promptly made for a third even more powerful ship. After much delay, the *Earl Grey*, designed to overcome severe ice conditions, made her inaugural run between Charlottetown and Pictou on December 30, 1909.

Although the combined service of the *Earl Grey* and the *Minto* made travel more reliable, the cost of shipping remained exorbitantly high. Handling goods three times as they moved from the Island railway to the ferry and back onto the standard-gauge trains on the mainland made commerce expensive and slow. Use of standard rail cars coupled with a ferry especially designed to transport them across the Northumberland Strait could partly rectify the situation. The election of a new Conservative federal government under Robert Borden in 1911 augured well for change. Borden had pledged to improve communications with the Island, and in 1912 plans were announced to build a railcar ferry and to reconstruct the Island railway to accommodate standard-gauge stock. It would take years to accomplish this improvement fully. In the meantime, with the advent of the First World War, the *Earl Grey* and then the *Minto* were sold to the hard-pressed Russians for use in their Arctic seas. The arrival of the new car ferry, *Prince Edward Island*, and the return of the *Stanley* to Island service in 1915 compensated for this loss, although it was not until April 1917 that the use of winter iceboats was finally ended. For a short period, Charlottetown enjoyed the advantage of the *Prince Edward Island* service running from the city to Pictou because of the lack of proper docking facilities at Carleton Point. Completion of the terminal at the newly named Port Borden permitted reliable, daily service between the Island and Cape Tormentine on the mainland.

Regular all-season service from Borden ended Charlottetown's aspirations to be the Island's year-round entrepôt. Local businessmen had persistently pressed for service between Charlottetown and Pictou to continue even when ice partially blocked the strait. "Whatever is done with respect to the running of the winter steamers, the fact should not be lost sight of that Charlottetown is the Capital, the centre of population and where ½ to ¾ of the shipping business of the province is done, [and] has just claim on the services of these steamers," declared President Auld of the Board of Trade in his annual address to members in January 1903. In part, concern reflected the presence nearby of condensed milk factories, pork-packing and other meat industries, and the need to get their products quickly to market. The requirement of these goods for refrigerated holds prompted the Board of Trade to call for the federal government to assume operation of the ferry service, both winter and summer, using government-railway-operated refrigerated ships. The prospect of the car ferry prompted the board to suspend its agitation for service to Charlottetown in favour of a route deemed by the federal government to be the most advantageous for the province. Members did not want to place any obstacle in the way of the project. The opening of service between Borden and Cape Tormentine did not immediately provide all of the anticipated benefits. Goods still had to be transferred between PEI Railway cars and standard-gauge cars at Borden, and that situation continued until the Island railway was converted to standard gauge. The changeover began on the main line between Charlottetown and Summerside in 1918, and the first standard-gauge train reached the capital on September 14, 1919, but full completion of the project was realized only in the 1920s.

Efforts to obtain reliable steamship service for overseas traffic experienced a similarly frustrating history. The traditional link between Charlottetown and Liverpool was

When the Prince Edward Island *began reliable, daily service out of Port Borden in 1917, Charlottetown's aspirations to be the Island's year-round shipping port ended. This photo of the "Prince" is from the 1960s.*

Henry Plant's "Plant Line" sailed out of Government Wharf at the foot of Great George Street. The service, maintained from 1885 until 1916, was nick-named the "Boston Boat."

threatened continuously by a lack of frequent departures, particularly by ships with refrigeration to conserve loads of potatoes and pork. Calls for subsidies to make the service viable were interwoven with demands from the Board of Trade for cold storage facilities in which to hold produce awaiting shipment. Persistent representations were made with the Minister of Marine throughout the 1890s to obtain five direct departures a year for England. The federal government experienced difficulties in finding a company that would send a vessel so frequently. In 1899 the only direct steamship service to Great Britain was provided by the autumn departure of the *Gaspesia*, and in 1901 by the *Dalton Hall*, which left in December with a cargo valued at $150,000. Uneven volumes of goods, the need to dredge Charlottetown harbour and the Boer War were variously impediments to better service at this time.

A breakthrough occurred in 1902 when Manchester Lines agreed to provide service between Charlottetown and its home port in England. Unfortunately, the first ship to leave Charlottetown, in July, experienced difficulties at the Railway Wharf, and in 1903 the company offered only two departure dates, in October and December. Trade on this route diminished to the point where, in 1908, direct service was not needed, and the subsidy was left unused. It was removed from the 1909 federal estimates. Efforts were made to include Charlottetown in the schedules to other destinations as well. The Elder Demster Steamship Company placed the city on its route from Canada to Cuba and Mexico in 1906. Less exotic, but of more economic importance, were ties to Newfoundland. These were secured after 1918 by including Charlottetown in the Montreal to St. John's run of the Canadian Government Merchant Marine service. Steamship service also extended to Boston and was provided by the Boston and Colonial Steamship Company until 1885 when that line, as well as the PEI Steam Navigation Company, was purchased by Henry Plant. The Plant Line maintained service on the Boston run until 1916. Overall, however, port clearances declined in this period. In 1911 there were 2,465 departures from Charlottetown, by both steamer and sailing ship, and by 1917 that number dropped to 1,694.[46]

Problems with rail service compounded the communications difficulties. A principal concern for Charlottetown businessmen was the co-ordination of arrival and departure times of trains and steamships. Mail crossing at Georgetown and Cape Traverse sometimes had to wait almost a day before it could be loaded onto a train bound for the capital. The problem persisted throughout the period, and demands for special mail trains were issued by the Board of Trade from time to time, sometimes successfully, frequently not.

The schedules for train service within the province itself were no better.[47] From the business point of view in Charlottetown, departures from the eastern and western ends of the line were best if passengers were not obliged to rise too early but were provided with enough time in the city to conduct their affairs and then return home the same day. A five-hour stay between a mid-morning arrival and a late-afternoon departure was deemed ideal. Often, however, visitors barely had time to grab a bite to eat. Delays were rampant as trains were frequently halted so the engines could shunt cars on and off sidings and spurs. In the summer season of 1914, for instance, the train from the west was on time only 43 days out of 196. The difficulties were virtually intractable. Meetings between the Board of Trade and the Board of Railway Commissioners in Moncton occasionally produced promises of improved scheduling, but deficiencies remained. Charlottetonians were told plainly that the railway was being managed to keep expenses down and to maintain efficiency. That did not necessarily translate into convenient service.

Not only was rail service at times unpredictable, but it was expensive. The issue of freight rates was a sore point throughout the Maritimes, and nowhere more so than in Charlottetown. The Board of Trade sought rate reductions for Island produce on the Intercolonial. When well-placed contacts, such as Sir L. H. Davies, could be drafted to support such interventions, rate adjustments were sometimes obtained. On other occasions there was no relief. The extent of the disadvantage faced by Charlottetown merchants in 1907 was demonstrated by the cost of shipping a quantity of feed from Chicago to the city: $120 for the distance from Chicago to Pictou and another $90 for the final leg to Charlottetown. Despite constant representations to both the railway and federal government, the issue remained a live one throughout the period.

Increasingly, the challenge of doing business involved movement of information as well as people and goods. The period 1880-1920 saw the emergence of a number of technological advances that would revolutionize communications. Already, the

---

46 Historian Mary K. Cullen points out that goods were no longer carried to markets by fishing boats and coastal vessels, thereby placing additional burdens on the railway for transporting agricultural products.

47 Travel times and costs of a one-way trip to Charlottetown in 1900 were as follows: Tignish 6½-8 hours, $3.50; Summerside 2½-3 hours, $1.45; Souris 3-4½ hours, $1.80; Georgetown 2½-3 hours $1.40.

telegraph had made getting in touch with contacts beyond the city, and even the province, virtually instantaneous. The introduction of the telephone in 1884 and the extension of service to rural areas the following year were major advances. The appearance of Marconi wireless technology soon after the turn of the 20th century offered yet another way of breaking the bonds of geography.

As with travel by sea and land, modern telecommunications service to Charlottetown fell short of local expectations. There was a realistic fear that the telegraph cable laid across the Northumberland Strait would break. Repairs could take a week or more, and if such a break were to take place during the winter, service would be disrupted for months. Then, "no calculation could estimate the loss and inconvenience" to business. The solution in the opinion of the Board of Trade was to install a second cable. Even when the system was running normally, which was most of the time, it was deemed deficient. The problem lay with rates and hours of operation. In 1889 the board wanted the telegraph offices in Charlottetown and Sackville, New Brunswick, to remain open from 8 a.m. to 8 p.m. Complaints about short hours and other matters were sent to the Anglo-American Telegraph Company's management in London, as well as to politicians in Ottawa, with apparently little satisfaction. The inability to send night messages, a surtax on messages and delays in service eventually prompted some local businessmen to call for the Dominion government to take over and operate the telegraph as a public service. In 1904, with the payment of a subsidy of $5,000 for five years, the telegraph company agreed to reduce its rates, keep its Charlottetown and Sackville offices open all night, and extend the hours of the Summerside office. This satisfied Charlottetown's business community and relieved the pressure on the government to act more aggressively. Federal authorities nevertheless laid two cables across the strait, and in 1917 almost tripled the subsidy for the service. Even so, by 1919, rates charged for messages to the Island remained higher than for similar service in the rest of Canada.

The provision of telephone service across the Northumberland Strait was also a costly matter. In 1907 the Telephone Company of Prince Edward Island began a well-orchestrated campaign to get the Dominion government to install a cable for use in a new long-distance telephone service. Working with Island politicians, the Nova Scotia Telephone Company and the Bell Telephone Company, executives of the Telephone Company of Prince Edward Island extracted an agreement from Ottawa that the work would be done if the money could be found.[48] Instead, in 1910 the Nova Scotia firm, which had re-baptized itself the Maritime Telegraph and Telephone Company, laid a twin-wire cable from Caribou, Nova Scotia, to Wood Islands. While service, at first, was restricted to the hours of 7 a.m. to 5 p.m., except for emergency calls, the new cable opened up an important link with the mainland. Yet, its cost demonstrated the kinds of investments Island telephone interests faced to expand their service. Less than a year later, the Island company sold out to Maritime Telegraph and Telephone

48 Members of the executive in 1906-7 were Benjamin Rogers, president; W. A. Winfield, general manager; and A. E. Ings and H. J. Palmer, directors.

Company. Subsequent experience with costly breaks in the cable because of ice and tidal damage showed the wisdom of an association with the larger, better capitalized company.

Such disruptions made the new Marconi radio technology particularly appealing. Business circles in Charlottetown were assessing the advantages of wireless service at least as early as 1901. Ongoing reliable service, however, did not appear for a couple of decades. Instead, unless a steamer was in port, messages from Charlottetown had to be telephoned to the wireless station at Cape Bear for transmission. The Board of Trade wanted a station at Charlottetown. For two years, a winter wireless network was established, involving the stations at Cape Bear and Pictou and a wireless set on the car ferry *Prince Edward Island*. Unfortunately, in 1917 the equipment and the operator were removed from the ferry, breaking the network. Even as they campaigned to have the link re-established, Charlottetown business interests must have realized that whatever the potential of wireless technology might be, it was not an immediate solution to their communications problems.

Tourism

In 1880 tourism was still tied to the annual exodus of prosperous urban dwellers that occurred during the sweltering summer months. Migrants made their way to cooler seaside destinations where they took up residence in summer homes or grand hotels. Some with more modest means followed the same route and stayed in less imposing facilities, but tourism, especially for locations such as Prince Edward Island which were somewhat removed from larger urban centres, depended upon the well-to-do. Thus the business community of Charlottetown fussed about the quality of the rail cars found on the feeder lines to the ferry connections at Pictou and Point du Chêne, near Shediac, and especially about the perennial matter of a first-class hotel. The city was graced with a number of small, perfectly respectable establishments, but lacked the kind of accommodation that would entice tourists to "spend weeks and months in our midst."[49] Limited space also curtailed business. Delegates to the Maritime Board of Trade meeting in Charlottetown in 1897 were instructed to book rooms in advance or lose out to visitors in town for the annual exhibition. Matters came to a head in 1904 when the owner of the Hotel Davies announced that he was selling his property and furniture for $30,000. Spurred on by anxiety of not having space for "several parties of important individuals" due to visit the province and for visitors to the exhibition, the Board of Trade hastily arranged the creation of a Tourist and Improvement Association. This new group continued the tradition of calling for others, such as the railways, to make improvements that would facilitate summer travel to the city. Meanwhile, visitors had to content themselves with the modest hostelries despite the incorporation of the Charlottetown Hotel Company in 1916.

---

49 *Baedeker's Canada* tourist guide for 1900 notes that a new summer hotel was located at Langley Beach near Southport.

Though urban promoters urged the development of a "first class" hotel and other amenities, they also had to deal with the fact that most tourists in the early years of the industry were coming to enjoy the country and seaside at places like Stanhope's Point Pleasant Hotel.

The nature of the tourist business began to change with the dawning of the 20th century. Travel was destined to be less exclusive and more responsive to diverse interests as general levels of prosperity increased and railways and roads improved. New kinds of tourists were identified and cultivated. One obvious target group was the expatriate Island community in Boston and other east-coast American centres. Emigrants were encouraged to return for "Old Home Week," an event instituted in 1905 which ultimately became a high point of the tourist season. Efforts were made to distribute tourist literature broadly, to attract conventions and to have steamers stop in the port for a day so passengers could visit the city. The beauty of the city's natural surroundings and its healthy climate remained the key assets to draw tourists, but its modern civic services were frequently cited as an attraction in the new century.

Charlottetonians were also able to observe the use of celebratory observances to promote travel. The 400th anniversary of the arrival of John Cabot in 1897, the 300th anniversary of the arrival of the Acadians in 1904 and the founding of Quebec in 1908 demonstrated the appeal such events could have. Charlottetown, of course, had hosted the conference which eventually

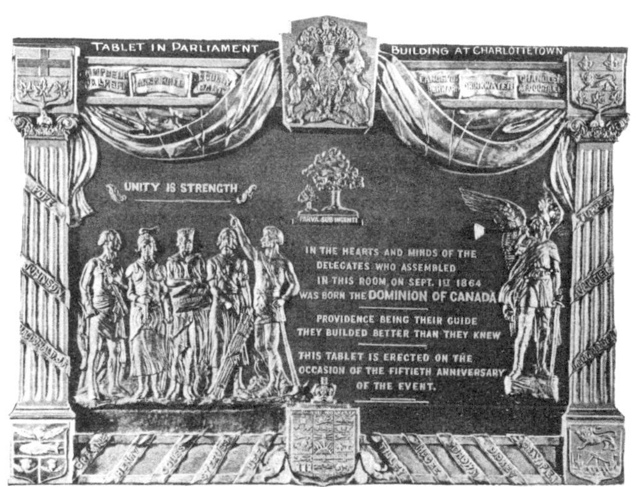

As 1914 approached, provincial and civic promoters began planning for the 50th anniversary of the Charlottetown Conference. Though the war disrupted most of the planned events, the theme would prove durable.

gave rise to the Dominion of Canada. The Charlottetown Conference had created a flutter in official circles when it was held in 1864, but its anniversaries had been largely ignored since. As 1914 approached, the provincial government and city tourist promoters began to plan for the meeting's 50th anniversary. The Board of Trade printed 10,000 copies of a tourist brochure, and struck a management committee to make preparations for a grand celebration. Incoming mayor R. H. Sterns remarked upon this and the upcoming Canadian Track and Field Championships as being "the means of bringing a large number of visitors from all parts of Canada and the neighbouring republic" to the city. That was the last mention of the Confederation festivities in the City Council minutes. Instead, on September 14, a month and 10 days after Great Britain declared war on Germany, Council called for a moment of prayer for the soldiers and sailors of the empire.[50] The Confederation celebrations would have to wait.

SOCIAL LIFE

The lack of significant growth in the population of Charlottetown during this period was a mixed blessing. Stagnation robbed the city of a sense of vitality and of substantially increased revenues generated by a larger commercial tax base and more residential property-owners. This dampened public enthusiasm for the kind of investment that would increase the quality of life within the city, and it forced politicians and civic administrators to keep a watchful eye on the bottom line. At the same time, the city's existing range of social services and facilities, while less than optimal, were not scandalously inadequate. Without the pressures of accommodating a rapidly increasing population, Charlottetown was able to move ahead gradually with the development of new and expanded social programs for its citizens.

Education

The school system demonstrated these circumstances well. For most of the period, the city had three public schools: Prince Street, Queen Square and West Kent. The size of their student bodies remained remarkably stable. In 1885 Upper Prince had 512 students; Queen Square 274; and West Kent, 405, comprising 734 boys and 457 girls for a total of 1,191. There were 26 teachers, three Principals and two Vice-Principals. By the turn of the 20th century, there were 1,312 students and 35 teachers and principals.[51] By 1916 that number had dropped to 1,171 students and 30 staff. The spotty attendance of the early years of the period — only 68 per cent of total enrolment on a daily basis in 1883 — improved as time went on. By 1901-2, daily attendance was 84 to 86 per cent; this high rate was likely because of a general concern about truancy. The city's share of

50 The track and field championships were also cancelled.

51 The breakdown by school was Prince Street, 577 pupils, 14 staff; Queen Square, 319 pupils, 9 staff; and West Kent, 423 pupils, 12 staff.

The Anglican Church maintained the Bog School until the 1890s. After that, the closest school for the city's small black population was West Kent. West Kent School class c. 1900.

the school board's costs was $16,540 in 1885,[52] while it allotted $13,970 for education in 1915 and $18,672 in 1917. The latter increase in part reflected the expense of renting and operating Rochford Square School beginning in 1917, but it may also have resulted from inflation since the amount increased again in 1918 and subsequent years. Low funding levels resulted in shoestring budgets for everything from building maintenance to teachers' salaries. The result by 1920 was outmoded facilities and staff unrest.

The School Act of 1877 had provided Prince Edward Island's publicly funded schools would henceforth be non-denominational. Beneath a veneer of conformity, however, Charlottetonians crafted a school system which circumvented, if not amended, the education laws. Queen Square School, the former Roman Catholic St. Patrick's boys school, continued to cater to Catholic boys and was staffed mainly by Roman Catholics. Prince Street School had a student body consisting almost entirely of girls,[53] and West Kent, although in principle co-educational, had relatively few girls because of the reputed rowdiness of the boys. In practice, Charlottetown had a public school for Catholic boys, a public school for Protestant girls and a public school for Protestant boys. Many Roman Catholic girls continued to attend one of the two convent schools, for which their parents had to pay tuition. These institutions had substantial enrolments. In 1883, for instance, St. Joseph's had an average daily attendance of nearly 200 pupils. In 1917, however, it entered the publicly funded system and became Rochford Square School.

52 The City School Board was authorized to raise money as well. That sum was set in 1894 at $10,000.

53 At this time, all the teachers were women, although by 1916 one man was on staff. Some of the pupils must have been boys because the size of the student body at Prince Street School exceeded the total number of girls in the system.

Roman Catholics were not alone in operating schools outside the public system. The Anglicans kept St. Paul's School and the Bog School open until the 1890s, and the St. Peter's schools operated throughout the period, although the boys' school ended its senior classes in 1900. A non-denominational girls' school was opened by a Miss Russell on September 1, 1890. The subjects offered there included English, Latin, French, German, mathematics, drawing, music and calisthenics. Two years later, the school was described as being "in a very highly flourishing condition."

The religious accommodation between Catholics and Protestants within the public school system moderated the rivalry between the two communities, but not without the occasional outbreak of ill feelings. Catholics resented the inequity of funding the convent schools, and more than a few parents found the added cost of sending their daughters there burdensome. Various Protestants, for their part, were suspicious of Catholic intentions with respect to education. The appointment by the provincial government of A. A. MacDonald, a Catholic, to the school board in 1882 evoked some adverse comment in the city. The fact, however, that at the time two of the three trustees appointed by the city were Catholic and three of the four provincial nominees were Protestant indicates a desire to have the school board fairly representative. Similarly, in 1884 a Catholic teacher was dismissed from his position at West Kent School. "Catholic" writing to the *Examiner* in 1886 characterized this firing as "unmistakable evidences of deeply rooted prejudice," as a Protestant activist continued to teach at the same school. "Justice" retorted that the Catholic's dismissal had less to do with bigotry than with teaching ability. Whatever the truth of the matter, religion was clearly an educational sore point. Efforts were made by authorities on both sides of the divide to soothe antagonisms by, among other things, including members of various faiths as examiners during the public testing of students, a practice which was a feature of academic life in the later Victorian years.[54] By the end of the period, conciliatory gestures and the simple acceptance of the prevailing situation had considerably diminished sectarian tensions in education.

The curriculum in the schools followed the traditional pattern of developing literacy and numeracy in the primary grades and enriching the content of more advanced years with the study of literature, history and geography, science and languages. A strong sentiment that emerged by 1890 was that public education should "conduce towards the oneness of patriotic sentiment," although there was less agreement that students should generally be educated in more than the three Rs. In 1900 a manual training centre was opened on the third floor of Queen Square School. Financially supported by Sir William C. Macdonald, a graduate of Central Academy who in later life made a fortune in the tobacco industry, the centre allowed 20 boys from both

54 The public examination of scholars, and the accompanying entertainment and presentation of awards were the subject of considerable comment in the press and attracted a varied audience. In 1889 the visitors at the Queen Square examinations included the Lieutenant Governor, politicians, leading citizens and Catholic clerics. A similar event at the St. Peter's Schools drew a large crowd that included prominent citizens, the principals of two public schools and Protestant clergy.

Queen Square and West Kent Schools to learn basic woodworking and other skills.[55] Parallel domestic science classes for girls were begun at Prince Street School in 1917. Despite these concessions to contemporary pedagogical thinking about the importance of practical skills, there was debate about the need to teach farming in Charlottetown's schools, even though recognition of the importance of the Island's rural economy prompted its inclusion in the provincial curriculum in 1882. Nevertheless, by 1901, classes in agricultural science were being given to secondary students at Prince of Wales College, and in 1920 an agricultural and technical school opened in Government House. For some within an urban environment, clerical training was of greater use, and in 1880 the Charlottetown Business College opened its doors for "such as have enjoyed the best educational advantages, but also for those whose education is deficient from want of early training." Classes were often held in the evening, and included courses on bookkeeping, commercial arithmetic, penmanship, typing, shorthand and correspondence.

The Charlottetown Business College ad from McAlpine's 1904 Prince Edward Island Directory.

Charlottetown's two colleges were buffeted by the same economic storms besetting the elementary system. Each was controlled by an ungenerous master, the provincial government in the case of Prince of Wales College and a cash-strapped Diocese of Charlottetown for St. Dunstan's College. Circumstances were so bad at St. Dunstan's in the early 1880s that it was in danger of closing. Only 30 students were enrolled in 1881-82, but its strength recovered, and the number of students increased to about 80 by the end of the decade. Prince of Wales, its ranks swollen by teachers-in-training from the newly amalgamated Normal School, had about 137 on the books around the same time. Both colleges continued to grow fitfully as the century progressed and by 1900 had 120 and 246 students respectively.

55 In 1903 Macdonald also funded a consolidated school at Mount Herbert on a trial basis. Although deemed a success and attracting students from a broad area, the Macdonald School closed in 1912 when the provincial government declined to pay for its ongoing operating costs.

The curriculum in both institutions also evolved. To the classical diet of Greek, Latin, philosophy, mathematics, history, English and French literature and some science, Prince of Wales incorporated teacher training, and, after the turn of the 20th century, agriculture, physical geography and more intensive courses in chemistry, physics and botany. St. Dunstan's added music, art and commerce in the 1880s, and later instituted a fuller commerce program including bookkeeping, banking and commercial law courses. It also enhanced science training. Academics at St. Dunstan's were strengthened by that institution's affiliation with Laval University in 1892, a move that required some adjustment to the college's curriculum. An attempt by PWC to duplicate that move through an affiliation with McGill University was frustrated in 1907 when the government withdrew the requisite legislation. Opposition from impecunious farmers was blamed at the time, but a future PWC principal, Frank MacKinnon, believed that behind-the-scenes machinations by the Roman Catholic Church played a part. If this were true, the Catholics were not without complaint because ongoing efforts to have their graduates deemed eligible for teachers' licences were being frustrated. St. Dunstan's did gain an advantage, however, in 1917 when it was given the right to grant university degrees in its own name.

In an era when public libraries were beginning to appear in many cities across Canada, the readers of Charlottetown lacked a similar municipal institution but were not without a similar service. Some private libraries existed, as did libraries in the two colleges, and in 1902 the YMCA opened a library.[56] The principal resource in the city, however, was the legislative library which had been established in 1773. As in many provinces, it was open to visitors and "rightly or wrongly" was by the early 20th century practically a public library. It had a somewhat limited and specialized collection, a fact that concerned the Provincial Librarian, W. H. Crosskill. He hoped to add works of history, science and literature to benefit the public schools and the population at large. A means to this end soon appeared.

In 1900 Thomas W. Dodd left a bequest of $3,500 for the establishment of a public library. This amount grew to over $5,000 by 1905. The trustees of the estate, H. J. Cundall and F. L. Haszard, then joined with Crosskill to accomplish both his ambition and the wishes of their benefactor. The bequest was placed in the hands of the provincial government, which was to hold it in trust. An initial $1,000 was to go to the Legislative Library for the purchase of books, bookcases and accessories. Regular supplements resulting from interest accrued on the balance of the bequest would follow and be used for the same purposes. The Legislative Library agreed to provide additional space in its rooms on the second and third floors of the provincial building to serve the visiting public. All assets purchased by the Dodd bequest were to be marked as belonging to the Dodd Library. If a Charlottetown Library Association was formed and the association raised $20,000 for a new public library, the province would

56 The impetus for increased interest in a public library was the donation of a set of the *Encyclopaedia Britannica* by T. A. Lepage of Prince of Wales College. William Dodd later made a bequest of $500 for a YMCA library.

return the books and other assets, as well as the principal sum of the Dodd trust for use by a new public library. In the interim, the Legislative and Dodd Library became Charlottetown's *de facto* public library. It opened in February 1906 and soon saw its holdings augmented by 300 volumes sent from the library of St. Paul's Church. The city thus obtained a library without it costing the municipal exchequer a cent.

Public Health

Of all the areas of social policy, perhaps the most critical for the well-being of the community was the provision of health services. By the late 19th century, medical practice was becoming increasingly professionalized, and physicians were beginning to cloak themselves in the mantle of omniscient science. The accomplishments of modern medicine notwithstanding, the pattern of increased longevity experienced in the 20th century was almost entirely due to improvements in public health. On both sides of

Both the Prince Edward Island (above) and Charlottetown (right) hospitals moved into new buildings in the 1890s.

the equation, however, advances were made in Charlottetown, but often in a hesitant and slow fashion. The creation in 1879 of the Charlottetown Hospital opened a new era for health care in the city. For the first time, both wealthy and less prosperous patients had access to the co-ordinated services of several physicians, nursing staff and specialized equipment. Although fees were charged, those unable to pay were still served. Occasional appeals were made on behalf of the hospital by the Bishop of Charlottetown to the clergy and people of his diocese for financial assistance. The first annual report of the 14-bed hospital indicated that 61 patients had been admitted by October 1880, and of that number 21 were cured, 20 were "much improved," 9 were found incurable, and one died. Twenty-five patients were Charlottetonians; the balance came from rural parts of the province. The small number of patients clearly indicates that the vast majority continued to receive treatment at home or in less appropriate facilities, and some of those might well have benefitted from hospital care.

While patients and practitioners of all religions were welcome at the Catholic institution, some Protestants preferred what they termed a "non-sectarian" hospital. With this in mind, a group of influential citizens, including Henry J. Cundall and W. E. Dawson, organized the establishment of a second hospital in the city.[57] The Prince Edward Island Hospital was located in a converted house, the former home of Henry Haszard on Longworth Street, and had an initial capacity of 12 beds. Among the appointments to the staff was Dr. T. J. Leeming as the "analyst" and "microscopist." This heralded the arrival in the city of a new branch of medical science, one in which bacteriology and clinical pathology played a large part. The Prince Edward Island Hospital in its first year treated 56 patients.

Both of the two hospitals soon outgrew their original quarters, and in 1891 the Charlottetown Hospital moved to a new building on the former Owen Connolly property on Dundas Esplanade. Two years later, the Prince Edward Island Hospital occupied new facilities on Kensington Road. Whether the public might have been better served by a single larger hospital is a moot point. Religious affiliation mattered greatly, and both communities were jealous of their own. Unfortunately, neither hospital would in the beginning care for patients with infectious diseases, and this was a critical shortcoming for the city as a whole.

This became apparent when on November 12, 1885, the city's health officer, Dr. Richard Johnson, identified nine cases of smallpox in a stretch of houses on Long Street in the city's north end. For some time, Charlottetonians, along with other Maritimers, had watched the spread of a smallpox epidemic from Montreal to communities down the St. Lawrence River. Islanders were hopeful the plague would pass them by; vaccination against the disease had been compulsory since 1862, and for those who had ignored the regulation, the salubrious climate served as protection. Events proved otherwise. A carrier reached the city in October and passed the disease to a hotel employee who in turn infected his family. Within days, Charlottetown was

57 This was, in effect, the Protestant hospital, although people of all faiths were treated.

in the grips of a full-blown epidemic. Churches and schools were ordered closed, stores were fumigated with sulphurous gas and the residences of stricken patients were quarantined and then fumigated.

The struggle against the disease was led by Mayor Henry Beer, assisted by a citizens' committee, and volunteers who entered every home in the city to ascertain whether anyone had not been vaccinated. They found over 1,100 unprotected people who were then obliged to receive preventative treatment. Many who had already taken ill were consigned to the former lunatic asylum. The building had been vacant since it had been abandoned as unfit for the care of the mentally ill, and it seems to have been similarly unsuitable for smallpox patients. Some died, contributing to an overall death toll exceeding 50, about one-quarter of all deaths in Charlottetown in 1885.[58] By the end of December, the crisis had abated. In its wake, the smallpox epidemic left an exhausted mayor, civic debt, disrupted commerce, recriminations concerning the social ills that were alleged to have permitted the outbreak,[59] and lingering apprehensions about the security of the city's public health. The provincial government later gave additional powers to the board of health to enable the city to respond better to similar emergencies, but the need for a proper quarantine hospital went unaddressed, despite the urgings of Dr. Johnson. Outbreaks of diphtheria in 1886 and typhoid fever in 1889, and the reappearance of smallpox in 1902, did nothing to change this shortcoming.

As in other cities, an awareness gradually grew that death through the spread of infectious diseases could be reduced by better sanitation and higher standards of food inspection. Events in Charlottetown were heavily influenced by Richard Johnson, who persistently lobbied for improvements to the city's physical environment and monitoring of disease. His annual reports containing statistics outlining the causes of death were designed to teach basic epidemiological lessons. Slowly, progress was made. In 1887 the city hired a sanitation officer to try to enforce the sanitary by-laws,[60] and in 1907 the registration of births and deaths was made mandatory, thereby facilitating review of the city's health standards. An Anti-Tuberculosis Society was organized in 1906 to combat a scourge that had long been a major killer. That disease alone accounted for almost half as many deaths in 1885, for instance, as the

58 The *Examiner* newspaper reported the number as 52, but other sources, quoting the *Report of the City of Charlottetown, 1886*, set the number at 53. Unfortunately, that report has recently been unavailable at PARO. During the epidemic, 80 persons were treated at the smallpox hospital, and 25 were treated at their homes, for a total of 105. Thus, the death rate was 50 per cent. There were 207 deaths in the city during the year.

59 Disease was imperfectly understood in the Victorian era, and many believed that moral imperfections, including drunkenness and prostitution, encouraged pestilence. The appearance of smallpox in one of Charlottetown's seedier areas signalled the need to strengthen community morality. The outbreak cost the Board of Health $13,494.98 — a considerable sum for the time — and the city had to issue debentures to cover $8,000 of the cost. The provincial government agreed to pay half the cost for medicines, medical attendance and removal of nuisances.

60 The reports of Sanitary Officer Duncan McRae, and his successor, outline the inspection of privies, cesspools, slaughterhouses, and substandard housing and the remedial actions that were ordered. One area of improvement in subsequent years was the extent to which deep water closets were cleansed and filled in.

smallpox epidemic. Due to the efforts of Dr. S. R. Jenkins and the TB society, a free dispensary was later opened to provide the poor with medicines to fight tuberculosis and other diseases. This was followed in 1915 by the opening of the Dalton Sanatorium in nearby North Wiltshire.[61] A year later, the school board was empowered by the province to conduct medical inspections in the schools with the expectation that it would encourage better health and increased attendance among the students. Nothing much happened, however, until 1920 when the Anti-Tuberculosis Society insisted that such inspections proceed.

The appearance of the Spanish Influenza epidemic in the city in September 1918 found the city almost as vulnerable to mass contagion as it had been during the smallpox outbreak of 1885. Even the best public health system, though, could not have resisted the pandemic. Charlottetonians succumbed by the hundreds; the hospitals were soon clogged, and medical staff, overworked and often ill themselves, were unable to cope with the volume of patients. Again, schools and churches were closed. Public meetings were banned, and on October 23 even public funerals were prohibited. The crisis reached a peak in the fourth week of October and subsided in early November. While the capital was safe, the disease migrated to rural areas of the province where it persisted until February 1919. The flu wrought unprecedented hardship upon the city and province and served to show that disease respected neither class, nor age, nor location.

Water and Sewerage Services

Despite the fact that the way disease spread was imperfectly understood, the value of a supply of pure water to the public's health was becoming increasingly appreciated by the 1880s.[62] So, too, was the desire to control fire insurance rates by having piped water service. Unfortunately, a waterworks was an expensive proposition, and its construction at public expense would be a dramatic departure from the administrative norm for the city. Although Ottawa obtained piped water only in 1873, water service was inaugurated in Toronto in 1843, in Halifax in 1848, and in St. John's about the same time, while Charlottetown clung to its pumps and water carts. The question of whether to establish a municipal water service provoked much political discussion in the 1870s and early 1880s.

This debate continued with less intensity after W. E. Dawson was deposed from the mayor's chair in 1882 by supporters of D. R. M. Hooper, an opponent of a municipal waterworks. Some public consideration of the issue persisted, though. Councillor William Murphy raised the possibility of a privately owned company undertaking the task. This option met with arguments that pointed to unsatisfactory British experiences

61 Designed to serve the whole province, the sanatorium was a gift of Sir Charles Dalton. It was closed in 1922 when the provincial government refused to pay the operating costs.

62 The persuasiveness of the health argument in favour of a waterworks was undercut somewhat by statistics from the city's health officer that showed Charlottetown was relatively safe from disease.

with such enterprises. Concerns about reliable water quality and inadequate drainage systems were significant objections to such a scheme. The matter simmered until February 1884, when the conflagration on Richmond Street galvanized the city's fire insurers. The heavy insurance claims prompted threats of massive rate increases unless significant improvements were made in fire protection. Adequate water supplies for the fire engines were a key component of any such change. Seven large cisterns and four wells were available to supply the steam fire engines with water, but the limited capacity of the tanks and location of the wells could result in water shortages at major blazes. A waterworks and street hydrants were an obvious remedy.

With the revival of intense interest in the issue, consideration was initially given to having a utility built by a local firm, the Charlottetown Water Works Company. Founded in the wake of the fire with the support of such prominent business leaders as John Ings, James Peake Jr., and W. E. Dawson, the company's incorporation was stalled in the provincial legislature by opponents. But the insurance underwriters would not back down in their demands. Faced with the choice of paying for a waterworks or for insurance coverage, opponents, such as Councillor William Ladner, changed their minds. In his view, "there was a change of opinion in the city, and the electors want water."[63] The question was how to provide it.

In his annual report for 1884, Mayor Beer commented that the choice facing Charlottetonians was whether the waterworks would be built as a private business or a public utility. Not all were convinced. Council was evenly divided over a plan by "a first-class contractor" to do the work. A hotly contested election in 1885 returned a pro-waterworks Council, but a year later Beer was dead and so, too, was the plan for a privately operated utility. Attempts to revive the effort to build the system with private capital failed when not enough local investors could be found. Moreover, extensive investigations by City Council revealed strong preferences in cities that already had a waterworks for a publicly owned system. Practically and politically, there was only one course of action open to the city.

Thomas Heath Haviland, Jr., who in 1886 stepped in to complete Mayor Beer's term, was slower than some to recognize the necessity of moving ahead on the issue, and, in the election of 1887 he was initially opposed by an old proponent of a water utility, W. E. Dawson. Dawson withdrew once Haviland came out in clear support of a city-owned waterworks. After that, events moved quickly. The election results produced a Council clearly in favour of the scheme, and a large public meeting in April approved the report of a citizens' committee that advocated creating an independent water commission made up of three commissioners elected by ratepayers. Based upon the systems in place in Ottawa and Hamilton, Ontario, the commission would be responsible for the construction, management and operation of a publicly owned utility. In May the provincial legislature passed an act vesting the commission with the powers to accomplish their mandate. The following month, David Laird, John Kelly and Alexander MacKinnon were elected as the first Commissioners of Water Supply.

63 As it turned out, property-owners paid for both a waterworks and higher insurance rates.

The frugal citizenry had not, however, thrown financial caution to the wind. The custom of the open ratepayers' meeting was invoked to ensure that the commissioners did not make financial commitments exceeding $3,000 without having prior approval from another public gathering. City Council also exercised control over the Commission, which had to submit annual budgets. Council likewise had to agree to the issuance of debentures before the commission could raise additional money for capital expenditures. In the years ahead, Council would exercise its right to block such fund-raising efforts, thereby effectively controlling the pace at which installation of services occurred.[64]

The commissioners began their work immediately. They hired M. M. Tidd, a civil engineer from Boston, Massachusetts, to plan the system. Despite the various opinions on the merits of drawing water from the Winter River versus the use of wells, after examining the streams and their watersheds within eight miles of the city, Tidd recommended the sinking of several test wells 2½ miles north of the city, close to the Upper Malpeque Road. They all provided copious discharges. A site near Crabbe's Dam on Three Mile Brook was selected as the location of the main well. Later, a high point of land on Mount Edward Road was chosen as the place for a clay-lined reservoir. Water could be pumped from the well to the reservoir and then carried by gravity to hydrants and consumers in the city. Water mains would follow Mount Edward Road, Longworth Avenue and Weymouth Street to Richmond Street. From there, smaller lines would distribute the water within the area lying between Water Street and Euston Street. In December, the plan was presented to an enthusiastic citizens' meeting where it was heartily endorsed. Work began on the reservoir, pumping station and installation of the mains, with a target date for the commencement of operations set for October 31, 1888.

Completion of this work marked a beginning as much as an end. After 1890, service was extended to additional streets, and in 1900 the pumping station on Malpeque Road had to be rebuilt when it was destroyed, ironically, by fire. Fortunately the pumps were not damaged and water held in the reservoir ensured that service continued despite the fire. Attention turned next to the location of additional water sources when a summer drought in 1901 revealed that maximum levels of consumption exceeded the production capacity of the well. In addition, the reservoir, which was found to have leaks as early as 1889, was by 1901 deemed unserviceable.[65] A new covered concrete reservoir was completed in 1902. This resolved problems of water loss and also the growth of algae which occurred in the open reservoir.

The need to find additional water supplies remained, however, as did a long-standing proposal to construct a second main water line to the city. The additional

64 The city itself was constrained by provincial legislation limiting the amounts for which debentures could be issued for water and sewers. Legislation passed in 1901 also required the city to use profits of the service above and beyond the maintenance and operating expenses to pay the interest on the loans. The remaining financing costs were to be covered by taxes as a separate charge from general civic expenses.

65 In places where the weight of the water had ruptured the clay lining, so much water was allowed to leak into the porous underlying rocks that there was a danger that a neighbouring quarry would be flooded.

Note the fire hydrant in this c. 1885 photo of Apothecaries Hall, corner of Kent and Prince Street.

pipe, to run along Malpeque Road from the pumping station, would ensure service would not be interrupted by a break in the original line, and it was hoped that it would prompt reductions in fire insurance rates. City Council had blocked the project in 1892 and subsequent years by refusing to issue debentures to pay for it. Finally, in 1903 Council relented, also agreeing to build an auxiliary pumping station near the Lower Malpeque Road. Linked to a new source of water and to the main pumping station, it could bring that additional water on line in periods of peak demand. By the end of the year, the commission's chief engineer was able to boast that he knew of no other place "that has a system which is more complete for its requirements." Alas, the situation was not to continue. Despite the installation of additional wells, including a whole new cluster near the North River, by 1920, water consumption was again beginning to tax the system's productive capacity. Citizens had long been warned to economize, and now with water shortages looming, plans were made to install meters on some large consumers.

The installation of water mains did not mean that everyone in Charlottetown had water service. Initially, only 80 fire hydrants and some wealthy citizens were hooked into the system. In 1889 there were 1,018 connections, of which 935 were dwellings; the rest were mainly commercial and manufacturing establishments, public buildings and stables. By 1894 this number had risen to 1,465. An annual fee was charged for domestic water service based upon the number of rooms and occupants. They varied from $6 for a house with 8 rooms and 8 occupants to a maximum of $10 for a 14-room house with 12 occupants.[66] These were considerable sums at the time and were for only one tap. Additional charges applied for extra taps and for bathtubs and toilets. Other rates applied for different categories of buildings. In 1891, 110 houses with water connections did not use the service. The perplexity felt by the water commissioners over such a state of affairs could not be explained by a preference for well water. The commissioners knew that the city's pumps and wells were so bad that City Council in 1891 had asked them if some arrangement could be made to supply the poor with water from the waterworks.[67] The reasons some potential consumers declined service were largely economic.

Another possibility might have been difficulties in disposing of the water. If so, the problem was soon addressed. Opponents of a waterworks persistently indicated that it would necessitate the expensive installation of sewerage. A citizens' meeting in January 1886 recognized this and urged the two systems be studied as a unit. Insurance rates had motivated Charlottetown's decision to install water service, but the loss of life due to diseases associated with contaminated wastewater proved to be less persuasive with respect to sewerage. With the arrival of water service, more dry wells were bored to drain moisture from cellars, but the use of water closets threatened to overwhelm existing methods of handling human waste. Already, Government Pond had been fouled beyond the endurance of the average nose. In 1892 Council hired American sanitary engineer George E. Waring to visit the city and offer some advice concerning the installation of sewers. He found that a suitable waste system could be put in place for $150,000. By comparison, the water system had cost $192,521 by 1890.

The prospect of even more debt and the higher taxes to pay for it intimidated many taxpayers. Charles Heartz exclaimed, "It is too great for our poor city. Our people are poor and cannot afford such taxation ...." In the 1894 election, the prospect of a candidate campaigning in favour of a sewerage system prompted "A Large Tax Payer" to complain that it was undoubtedly citizens who did not own property who would support the measure. "Elector" agreed, urging his fellow citizens to vote against any candidate who was "in any way tainted in that direction." Mayor Haviland's supporters asked him to promise not to take action on the provision of sewers before having the issue decided at the polls. In any event, W. E. Dawson was re-elected Mayor, but clearly the time to move ahead had not been reached. Four years later, the public mood had changed. Both mayoralty candidates supported the installation of a sewerage system and a plebiscite to decide the issue was won by supporters by a wide margin. Why had opinions changed so drastically? One would like to think a greater understanding

66 Adjusted for inflation, these fees roughly approximated $125 to $205 in 2008 dollars.

67 In August 1890, the commissioners agreed to extend service to the Poor House and to provide water free to the inmates. In addition, with the approval of the owner, families without water service would be allowed by the commission to take water from a consumer's tap for a $3 annual fee.

of disease and sanitation was the prime factor, but it is more likely that citizens were feeling prosperous enough to afford the costs. The world economy was improving, and Canada was entering a boom. Optimism was growing. Sitting politicians boasted of a small surplus and were ambitious to improve the city's infrastructure and image. Charlottetown could afford to be modern.

Changes were accordingly made to the legislation governing the Commissioners of Water Supply to make them responsible for a new sewer system. A new Chief Engineer was hired, and the 1892 Waring plan was revised. The new plan called for a large sewage reservoir to be built close to Pownal Wharf. Waste from many parts of town would be carried by gravity through sewers to this point. Lower parts of the city to the east and west would be served by smaller underground reservoirs, one at the corner of Cumberland and Fitzroy Streets and the other near Government Pond, and the waste would then be pumped to more elevated points where it would flow to the main reservoir. Sewage would be discharged into the centre channel of the Hillsborough River where currents would carry it out to sea. Work was scheduled for completion by February 1901, but, by December 1900, only 170 houses and stores were connected. Even so, work continued. Surprisingly, it was found that a large number of homeowners rejected connection to the sewers because of a $10 fee. As with water service, the ability to pay was a factor for some. Although new buildings had to be joined to the system, years passed before all older houses were hooked up. Construction of the sewer system nevertheless went a long way to resolving one problem, but in doing so created two others. In the short run, the steady increase in water consumption required higher volumes of fresh supplies, and ultimately, of course, there were ecological consequences for the water in the harbour.

Public Safety

The construction of a waterworks had a significant impact upon the operations of the volunteer fire department. Men and equipment were centralized at the new station in City Hall rather than dispersed among local depots spread around town. Some antiquated equipment was discarded, although the two steam fire engines remained. It was only in 1916 that the department acquired its first motorized vehicle, a combined chemical and hose truck. Recourse to the use of buckets to supplement water supplies became a thing of the past, and hydrants allowed for shorter response times. Small hose reels were placed in different parts of the city where they could be promptly connected to hydrants even before equipment arrived from the central station. In 1890 the fire department's Chief Engineer, A. N. Large, proclaimed, "Our water supply is second to none, which Charlottetown has much to be thankful for." He went on to say that had it not been for the plentiful supply of water, he was sure that he "would have to report some very serious fires during the past year."

The period to 1920 was nevertheless marked by some spectacular blazes. Following the massive 1884 fire on Richmond Street, there was a major conflagration in 1887 at the Kent Street furniture factory formerly owned by Mark Butcher, which resulted in the destruction of nearby buildings on Hillsborough Street. The next year, the Excelsior

Some of the city's fire equipment can be seen in this c. 1895 photo of City Hall.

Skating Rink on Kent Street near Prince was destroyed and flames spread to the Baptist Church and other structures. In 1890 the year in which Chief Large noted an absence of serious fires, a fireman died fighting a blaze at a Queen Street stable. The 1867 Butcher market house burned in 1902, and in 1913 a spectacular blaze gutted the virtually new St. Dunstan's Cathedral. Such catastrophic losses did not mean that water mains and fire hydrants were of no consequence. Things would have been much worse in their absence. Regrettably, with or without a waterworks, fire remained a clear and present danger.

Crime persisted as well. Some observers even feared, at times, that it was about to overwhelm the community. In the mid-1880s, there was a spate of incidents involving firearms, some of which involved loss of life. In one such incident, the master of a ship in port discovered a drunken sailor molesting a boy. When the captain intervened, the drunk objected, and the captain, in response, shot at him, hitting him in the chest. The drunk died, and the captain was sentenced to four years in prison for manslaughter.[68] A few months earlier, a homeowner fired at a burglar, wounding him in the leg. Other incidents involved stray bullets narrowly missing people or, in one case, fatally striking a 13-year-old boy in the stomach. In 1885 and 1888, there were also fatal stabbings. Such violence was a matter of serious concern. "There has been an alarming increase in serious crime in our city of late," thundered the

68 This was the case of Captain John Walsh of the *Claribel* and seaman Thomas Ottree of the *Moselle*, May 10, 1887.

Guardian in 1904. "Murder," the paper continued, "and the murderer still at large ...,[69] theft, housebreaking and only last evening the dastardly burglary and murderous attack upon Mr. MacEachern in the very heart of the city"[70] were some of the reasons why "many people are afraid to venture abroad and women and children feel themselves at peril even at home ...." Taxpayers have a right to feel safe, the *Guardian* concluded, and "they do not feel safe as things are now."

Was public safety as threatened as all that? At times, it appeared so, and certainly the small police force was kept busy. By the early 1880s, it was composed of the city marshal, two sergeants, a courier and four constables, and in 1904 there were still only eight policemen. They worked two twelve-hour shifts, during which two men were assigned to the office, one to make emergency calls and one to remain permanently there. That left two officers on each shift to patrol the streets. Even though temporary watchmen were engaged from time to time, the force remained small throughout the period.[71] Their day-to-day routines, however, paint an entirely different picture from the one depicted by the *Guardian*. Most of a police officer's duties pertained to the woof and warp of everyday life. By-law transgressions, petty arguments, and control of wayward children, street-corner loafers and stray animals, along with the drudgery of the foot patrol, were interspersed only occasionally with more noteworthy incidents.

Statistics show that by far the most common cause for an appearance in Charlottetown's Police Court was drunkenness.[72] In 1880 drunkenness accounted for over 60 per cent of convictions and, although this amounted to only 43 per cent in 1919, it hovered in the area of 50 to 60 per cent for most of the period, and stood at 70 per cent in 1914. When related convictions for offences against the Canada Temperance and the Prohibition Acts are included, alcohol and its use and abuse were clearly the principal challenges to law and order. Assaults, not infrequently related to

---

69 Miss Harriet Drake Warren, a seamstress, was struck and killed with an axe near the Charlottetown Hospital as she was walking home. Her body was found almost immediately, and a witness reported seeing a tall, middle-aged man, with whiskers and wearing dark clothes and a cap, fleeing the area. Two men were soon arrested. Neither matched the description of the man running from the scene. The evidence against the two in custody seems to have been circumstantial, and a Coroner's Jury, meeting in secret, was unable to agree upon a finding. The case was turned over to a magistrate for a preliminary hearing. At this point, a third man was identified as the one who fled the crime scene. The magistrate found the evidence concerning all three men to be contradictory, although the first man to be arrested was the prime suspect. Even though Pinkerton detectives assisted the Charlottetown Police, there appears to have been insufficient evidence against that man, and the case did not go to the Supreme Court for trial. He was freed in early December, and the murder of Harriet Warren seems not to have been solved.

70 McEachern was attacked by one of two men who mistook him for the owner of their boarding house. They had been out drinking and returned to the wrong residence. When they found the door locked, they slept on McEachern's porch. He was then beaten "quite severely" and "thrown from his house" for locking them out. The victim identified his assailant who was jailed for six months.

71 In 1920 the number of police per 1,000 population in Charlottetown was .4, the lowest of the six major centres in the Maritimes. This compared with .7 for Moncton and 1.2 for Halifax.

72 The most frequent transgressors of the law were generally labourers, farmers, building trades workers and other members of the working class.

drinking, were the next most common cause of court appearances. Unspecified by-law offences, and even less significantly theft and vagrancy, accounted for relatively few convictions. Break and entry was infrequent, a case or two a year, except for 1904 when 20 convictions were obtained. The reasons for the spike in this kind of crime and the consequent concern of the *Guardian* are hard to fathom. Equally perplexing is the sudden return to normality. The following year only seven such charges were laid, and all were dismissed. Perhaps all the guilty parties had been apprehended or had fled town, because burglary then returned to its customary levels. Charlottetown, thus, was typically a generally safe, if not a particularly sober, society. Fortunately, the 1904 murder case or the celebrated 1890 attempted murder of the wife of a Liberal member of the legislature by her husband's lover, a well-known widow, were uncommon.[73]

The police force and policing still remained an area of active public concern. Serving officers were held in somewhat higher esteem than had been the case in the early years following incorporation, but they were subject to intense public scrutiny. Religion and personal deportment mattered. In 1894 City Council received a petition from citizens concerned that the traditional balance of Roman Catholics and Protestants on the force had been lost when Council recently approved the appointment of four Catholics and only two Protestants. A number of years previously, Thomas Flynn, the long-serving city marshal, was forced out of office by supporters of prohibition on the grounds that he was slack in enforcing the Canada Temperance Act. His replacement, George Passmore, who was a member of the Sons of Temperance, was in turn sacked in 1887 for drinking while on duty. In a cost-conscious city, salaries were carefully watched, and Council ensured that they remained at modest levels. Constables earned $400 a year in 1892 and sergeants $450. This income was supplemented by occasional fees, such as the customary "premium" paid by officers of visiting naval ships for the arrest and return of absentee sailors.

Those convicted of serious offences elicited little sympathy from the general public. While opinion on penal correction may have softened somewhat after Mayor Dawson commented that "a taste of the 'cat'" might be as "wholesome and salutary" as a reformatory for the correction of juvenile offenders, prisoners faced arduous circumstances while in custody. The cells in the police station were described in 1894 as dirty, poorly ventilated and lacking a water closet.[74] Inmates of the Queens County jail on Pownal Square were in worse circumstances. Sweltering in summer and cold and drafty in winter, this "dismally ugly" building was described as squalid and dirty and infested with rats and bedbugs. Prisoners spent their days breaking up limestone in the jail yard. By 1907 the dilapidated jail was generally regarded as "unfit for use,"

73 The politician was said to have had a relationship with the widow of his former law partner, which was "too intimate, indeed scandalous." The gossip was recorded by Margaret Gray Lord in her diary. The widow was accused of adding arsenic to the intended victim's medicines. While the evidence was insufficient to convict her, the MLA's political career was over. He resigned in 1891.

74 To its credit, City Council did seek ways to improve these conditions.

and the province adopted legislation providing for its replacement. That change came only in 1911 when a new jail was built at the corner of Longworth Avenue and Mount Edward Road. Under the 1907 legislation, Charlottetown provided the new site in exchange for ownership of the old, which was to be used as a public square and known as "Waterside Park."[75]

Public Morality and Social Welfare

The frequency with which cases involving alcohol appeared in the Charlottetown Police Court was a clear symptom of the widespread availability of liquor in the city. Passage of the 1878 Canada Temperance Act or "Scott Act," and the application of its provisions to prohibit the sale of alcoholic beverages in the rural areas of the province, did little to stem sales in the capital.[76] Even when drinking establishments were officially banned, sale of spirits for medicinal purposes ensured none would go thirsty. "Men go there [to a drugstore] with a certificate of their own manufacture with an imaginary doctor's name on it and get as much as they want," commented a local journalist in 1882. The Charlottetown Temperance Society, the Women's Christian Temperance Union, and similar organizations vigorously promoted temperance as a prominent issue in civic politics throughout the 1880s and 1890s. While many citizens regarded drinking as a matter of temperance versus excess, others saw it as one of abstinence versus moral decay. This was clear in the 1888 election in Ward 4 where promoters of the Scott Act denounced opponents as "supporters of the rum candidate." Triumphant in that contest, prohibitionists lacked the essential grassroots support required to make their policy effective. When temperance advocates pressed Council to have the city marshal or some other person assigned to prosecute offenders under the Scott Act, other taxpayers objected, and Council narrowly declined to make an appointment. Frustrated prohibitionists offered to prosecute offenders themselves when city officials did not, and in 1890 after several tries, the WCTU successfully lobbied City Council to have the fines collected for breaches of the Scott Act used for its enforcement.

All was for naught. The *Examiner* noted in June 1889 that "liquor shops are found in every part of town" and "everyone who cares to sell, sells; everyone who wants to drink, drinks." When a woman was imprisoned for selling an intoxicating beverage, City Council adopted a resolution denouncing the sentence as "an act worthy

---

75 The name was subsequently changed to Connaught Square in honour of Prince Arthur, Duke of Connaught, the third son of Queen Victoria and Governor General of Canada from 1911 to 1916.

76 The prohibition movement was an extremely powerful lobby in Canada during the late 19th century, but political support varied from place to place. Even some governments were loath to lose the revenues derived from the sale of beverage alcohol. The Canada Temperance Act, sponsored in Parliament by Sir Richard Scott, hence the name "Scott" Act, was a compromise intended to placate all parties. Under its provisions, a municipality (city or county) could hold a plebiscite on the prohibition of the sale of alcohol within its boundaries. A vote would be held if 25 per cent of electors requested one, and a simple majority of those who voted would carry the day. A "yes" vote lasted for three years. Within jurisdictions that had opted in, anyone who engaged in the trade faced stiff fines and possibly imprisonment.

of the days of the Star Chamber and Jeffreys."[77] Councillors asserted the prohibition law was not supported by public opinion, was contrary to British freedom, justice and liberty, and the beverage was used by all from the Queen who is Head of the Church and Defender of the Faith down to her most loyal and dutiful subjects. By 1891 the public was ready to try another approach. A "Free Rum" policy made the sale of alcohol possible in licensed premises. Sixty-seven such establishments were inspected in 1892, a testament to the thirst of Charlottetonians and the profits of the business. The stock and ambiance of liquor stores were rudimentary, to say the least. Only liquor, cigars, tobacco and oysters could be sold, and seating typically consisted of a chair or two or a couple of stools or boxes. Unfortunately, observers noted that "'free rum' in the town tends to debauch the country," and the press soon recorded an upswing in convictions of rural visitors for drunkenness. By 1894 the Canada Temperance Act was readopted by the city for this and other reasons, but the same pattern of official non-enforcement and private prosecutions by prohibitionists emerged. Citizens reversed themselves again in July 1897 and returned to the system of licensed sale of alcohol.[78]

In the end, it was admitted by moderates of both sides that neither the Canada Temperance Act nor the controlled sale of liquor had their desired effects within the city. The very first article in the initial issue of *The Prince Edward Island Magazine* bore the title, "Is There Any Practical Way of Dealing with the Liquor Problem in Charlottetown?" In it, the author reviewed the failure of both the licence system and the Canada Temperance Act. Under the act, not only did youth commence to drink and thus perpetuate the evils of the bottle, but also popular support was lacking and hence enforcement was lax. Prohibition's opponents were motivated not only by their own willingness to tipple but by a belief that it was class legislation and was not applied equally to the rich man's club and the tavern. A solution was to make the sale of liquor in Charlottetown a provincial government monopoly in which outlets would be austere government premises staffed by bonded government employees. Profits from the trade would then be invested in comfortable coffee houses supplied with free literature and offering free lectures to provide a counter-attraction to the present drinking establishments. While somewhat naive, this suggestion had aspects that were innovative and far-sighted.

---

77 These references relate to two separate occurrences in English history, the special court established under King Henry VII (1457-1509) which operated as an extension of the King's Council and was later viewed as arbitrary and harsh, and the judge at the "Bloody Assizes" following the Monmouth Rebellion (1682) that imposed excessive punishments for those who rose against King James II.

78 The sale of alcoholic beverages under the Liquor Regulation Act was controlled by limits on the time of sale, among other restraints. In 1899 these were amended to prohibit sales between 6 p.m. on Saturday and 8 a.m. on Monday. To protect the rural folk, on market days (Tuesdays and Fridays) sales were prohibited from 7 p.m. until 8 a.m. the following day. Under the same amendments, gratuitous treats of another to liquor in a tavern were prohibited, and fines were provided for physicians who issued bogus prescriptions for liquor.

The provincial government, however, envisaged its role somewhat differently. Armed with Supreme Court rulings that confirmed prohibition as a provincial responsibility, in 1900 the government passed its own legislation that stated bluntly, "no liquor [is] to be sold" except to druggists and physicians for medicinal use and to clergy for sacramental purposes.[79] As of June 5, 1901, the taverns in the town were thus finally closed. This law initially applied solely to Charlottetown, at the time the only jurisdiction on the Island that had not opted for prohibition under the Scott Act.[80] From then, the city, like the rest of the Island, was officially dry. The city fathers, miffed that they had not been consulted concerning the legislation, showed little interest in prosecuting offenders. Most deemed the Scott Act unworkable and feared the city might be held liable for damages if it enforced provisions of the new act that were subsequently declared unconstitutional.[81] Drinking continued, and the bootlegger took his, or her, storied place in the life of the community. During the First World War, federal regulations issued on March 11, 1918, under the War Measures Act further strengthened the restraints on the manufacture and trade in alcohol, but, in the wake of peace, traffic resumed.[82] So, too, did efforts by the provincial liquor commission to stamp out illicit medicines, such as Wilson's Invalid Port Wine, and the issuance of bogus medical prescriptions.

While liquor and temperance were deemed to be the great social issues of the age, they were not alone. Challenges involving poverty, homelessness and physical and mental incapacities existed as well. For the neediest Charlottetonians, at the beginning of the period, the provincial government provided the Poor House, a converted army barracks adjacent to the old Lunatic Asylum. It had only the meanest of accommodations. In 1882 a Grand Jury described them as four small, poorly heated rooms with low ceilings in which 45 men and women lived, ate and slept. Some inmates were diseased with "ulcerated and cancerous sores" and would have been more appropriately placed in a hospital. Improvements were unlikely since the annual expenditure on the facility was only $1,600 and had not been increased in years. Consideration was given to moving the paupers into the vacant Lunatic Asylum, but that would have required some expense for renovations. In the end, a pavilion was built on the grounds of the new Falconwood Hospital for the Insane, and the inhabitants of the Poor House were transferred there in 1884.

For those unable or unwilling to seek shelter in the Poor House or its successor, the Infirmary, the provincial government provided some measure of support. Those granted relief were usually blind, deaf or mildly retarded and had to have their request

---

79 The act delayed implementation for one year to allow sellers time to dispose of their stock of liquors.

80 Under the act, it applied only in locales that had opted out of the Canada Temperance Act, and Charlottetown was the only such place. By 1906 the rest of the province had chosen to come under the provincial Prohibition Act, a stricter regulatory regime.

81 The issue seems to have revolved around whether the provincial prohibition act infringed federal jurisdiction over trade and commerce.

82 Federal emergency controls ended at the end of 1919.

for aid supported by a member of the House of Assembly. Again, funds were distributed sparingly. Between 1880 and 1900, the government consistently ran deficits, a circumstance that compelled fiscal restraint in all areas of expenditure and ensured that poor relief would be meagre. Civic officials tried to evade any responsibility for helping the destitute, and on only rare occasions did they extend some form of help. In 1889 a young, unmarried mother without a known family was granted assistance until a respectable couple could be found to adopt her baby. Councillors believed the girl would get work quicker if she were unencumbered by family responsibilities. The next year, Council granted a dismissed employee $20 after he fell ill and could not provide for his family. When he died three years later, Council gave his family another $20. In the winter of 1890-91, the city authorized the distribution of firewood to the poor when severe cold weather prevented a shipload of coal from reaching port. Reluctant as City Council might have been to deal with poor relief, it eventually had the task thrust upon it. In 1918 Premier Arsenault informed Mayor Wright: "the town has certain obligations to fill" and henceforth no Charlottetonian would be admitted to Falconwood Hospital or to the Infirmary except upon application of the mayor, and no grants would be given directly to indigent townsmen.

This left the fallback of private charity. There were individual benevolent acts, such as the decision by Mrs. Charles Nicholson to take home a sick, destitute orphan who could not walk but had been refused entry to both the hospital and the Poor House. Mrs. Nicholson fed and nursed the girl, who nevertheless died two months later.[83] Perhaps the most renowned charitable gift occurred in 1916 when Henry Cundall left his substantial fortune to be an endowment for the maintenance of his residence as "a Refuge and Temporary home in Charlottetown for the care and training in industrious and Christian ways of friendless young women and girls [newly arrived in the city] and thereby enable them to lead lives of usefulness and respectability." Cundall, alas, was not present to hear his good works hailed. Others were more fortunate. Margaret Gray Lord records that despite feeling poorly, she was able to make a cake for the Poor House festival at Thanksgiving in 1890 and to attend the event which went off "very well." Organizers were rewarded by "short speeches from several of the men, expressive of gratitude ...."

Most charity was funnelled through organizations, often connected with a church. The Wesleyan Dorcas Society and the Ladies Benevolent Society of the Kirk of St. James were leading charities, but other churches had similar bodies, as did the Masons and the YMCA, which organized Margaret Lord's Poor House festival. Often charities catered to their own, but the Dorcas, Saint Vincent de Paul and Ladies Benevolent Societies extended their work to the community generally. Recipients of benefits from the Dorcas Society were "the distressed poor of Charlottetown and royalty." They were not necessarily Methodist, but they were usually deserving, meaning very ill or unavoidably out of work but ultimately employable. Such charities looked to their congregations for encouragement and financial support, as the 1889 report of

83 Mrs. Nicholson then asked City Council to reimburse her $30 for her expenses.

the Ladies Benevolent Society makes clear. Occasionally, assistance was offered by cultural groups that organized fund-raising events. Lest their beneficence be abused, however, steps were taken by charities to ensure gifts were used for life's essentials. Virtually all expenditures went towards the purchase of groceries or medicines or the payment of rent rather than cash in hand. There was no desire to contribute further to Charlottetown's drinking problem.

Not much pity was spared for the indolent, immoral or inebriated, but some concessions were made for their humanity. The Prince Edward Island Hospital admitted patients, performed surgeries and provided medicine and medical care free of charge to patients unable to pay. The city paid for the vaccinations of anyone who could not afford the vaccine and medical fee. Council recognized the plight of the poor when planning a civic clean-up campaign in 1906. Councillor D. J. Riley felt the poor should not be put to the hardship of cleaning or being charged for the expense if the city performed the task. Instead, Councillor Daniel Stewart thought, property-owners and landlords should be responsible for cleaning the yards of their impoverished tenants.

Children were a special case. "Cannot those who are blest with means," asked "Sympathy" in 1889, "put some of it to good interest by doing something permanently for the good of the poor, especially the poor children." The writer felt the training of children in habits of industry and honesty was waiting only for effective leadership. Nothing much was done, however, in the 19th century. Some wards of the state were placed in private homes either in the city or rural areas, while others were shipped off to the Halifax Industrial School or the St. Patrick's Home in Halifax. Still others were sent to institutions in Quebec. Services improved after the turn of the 20th century. In 1910 the Catholic Church established St. Vincent's Orphanage. Located on Malpeque Road across from St. Dunstan's College, it was staffed by the Sisters of Charity from Quebec. The Charlottetown Children's Aid Society was organized in September 1909. It dedicated itself to act upon the provisions of the PEI Children's Protection Act, passed in 1910, and to lobby against factors that robbed children of their right to grow up "in an atmosphere of purity and moral cleanliness." Other objectives included the prosecution of parties who contributed to delinquency, the establishment of a personal service corps and the education of the public about children's aid.

The task was daunting. In the first year of operation, the society's agent, L. W. Watson, found some appalling conditions. Children were living in extreme poverty, the home of one family being "more like a kennel than a human habitation." In one case, a retarded, mute and practically blind boy was discovered abandoned and was admitted to the infirmary, while in another, a 10-year-old boy was surviving as a vagrant. Three children lived with a mother who was suffering from tuberculosis. Although the jail and police station cells could be pressed into service, a refuge that would operate more like a home than a penal institution was needed. The owners of a house on Cumberland Street agreed to provide two rooms as a "detention home" for delinquent children at a cost to the society of 50¢ per child a day.[84] In addition, arrangements were made with a Montreal Reform School to accept Roman Catholic boys from Charlottetown. For Protestant boys, a similar deal was struck with a Shawinigan, Quebec, Boys Farm. Corrections to the problem of child poverty were slow in coming. In 1912 the society reported that truancy levels in local schools were down due to the efforts of agent Wilbert McDonald, but truancy continued to be mentioned in the society's annual reports. Lest one think only boys were a concern, it was reported that "certain girls" frequented the wharves when steamers arrived. Much work remained to be done: the basic needs of some children still had to be met, better statistics were required, and changes had to be made to a justice system that arrested boys and tried them in police court.

The use of public money to generate employment for the jobless was a largely unexplored concept in the period, but unemployment among veterans in the aftermath of the Great War prompted some thinking along these lines. One innovative response was a proposal to build a Victory Highway running from Souris in the east to Tignish in the west. The road would be a living war memorial incorporating symbolic tributes to the men who died and markers listing the various battlefields of the western front. Electrical power facilities could follow the route, and military pensioners and their dependents could settle along it, thereby reviving local market gardening and specialized crop production. Construction would provide employment for returned soldiers. Best of all, 40 per cent of the expense for the project would be borne by the Dominion government under its newly announced road construction program. Despite these advantages, the proposal was not acted upon, and the unemployed were left largely to their own devices.

Efforts to deal with labour issues, including unemployment, were not heavily influenced by the activities of labour unions. This might come as no surprise to anyone familiar with the limited industrial development of the city, but it was not an indication of the absence of labour organizations. Union activities in Charlottetown went back as far as 1898 or 1899 when the Trades and Labour Congress of Canada issued a charter to a local of railway employees.[85] By 1901 this group was squabbling with representatives of the American Federation of Labor, which had organized unions of carpenters and joiners, painters and decorators, iron workers and railway trackmen. Tobacco workers, labourers and teamsters were soon organized as well. In 1902 the seven American unions formed a local Trades and Labour Council. Although generally successful efforts were made to smooth over the differences among the various unions, the Charlottetown locals were not overly vital. Ten union locals in Charlottetown in 1903 dwindled to six in 1904 and then to five by 1907. By 1911 the Trades and Labour Council was defunct, but there were eight union locals functioning, including an independent "truckman's" union. Organized labour in Charlottetown failed to develop the robust following found in larger industrial centres, and the activism that characterized

84 The Children's Protection Act specified that the City of Charlottetown would provide one or more places of refuge entirely separate from penal institutions or institutions for paupers.

85 The local was called the PEI Railway Employees' Federal Labor Union No. 10, Charlottetown.

unions in places like Hamilton or Winnipeg was absent from the Island capital during this period. Workers continued to band together, however, with a home-grown body, the Labourers' Protective Union, attracting the most widespread support.

Entertainment

Entertainment in Charlottetown was also largely home-grown before 1920, despite the appearance of some modern means of communication. Many amusements were created by the individual or focused on the family — quiet hours spent reading, making crafts and playing games. Phonographs may have made their appearance, but the piano remained a principal source of music in the home. Considerable emphasis was placed on acquiring the skills needed to pursue music and hobbies. There were, of course, differences based on economic and social status, and the preference of some members of society to congregate at drinking establishments or at street corners and in parks was frowned upon by those who possessed more comfortable, if not necessarily more congenial, surroundings to while away their hours. "The monotony of Charlottetown life" may also have enticed some drinkers to the liquor saloons. At least that was the opinion of "Plug," a young man temporarily resident in Boston, who wrote home to advise that more be done to entertain youth with "greater attractions."

Sports played an important role. The old tried-and-true activities remained popular, and none surpassed skating in appeal and community involvement. Newspapers regularly commented upon the quality of the ice and the size of the crowds at the Citizens', Excelsior or Hillsborough Rinks and at Government Pond. Special attention was paid to events such as the "Scratch Match," a 20-lap race, or the "50 miles go-as-you-please" contest. Carnivals were "always anticipated as one of the most delightful entertainments of the winter season."[86] The one held at the Excelsior Rink in January 1887 drew skaters from Summerside, Georgetown, Montague and Crapaud. The rink was decorated with Chinese lanterns, and entertainment was provided by the Brudder Gardiner and Lime Kiln Club minstrel troupes, trick ponies and clowns from Hindpaugh's Circus and the band of the 82nd Battalion. In summer, cricket was played at Victoria Park where contests between local clubs or pick-up matches between informal teams such as "Law and Medicine" and "Allcomers" attracted considerable public attention. Occasionally, players ventured further afield: in 1884 the Charlottetown Cricket Team went to a match in New Glasgow. Rugby retained its popularity, with frequent games involving the Prince of Wales College Football Association, the Abegweit Football Club and other clubs, as well as groups like "English" who battled "Allcomers" in a game at Victoria Park in August 1891. Charlottetonians also took to the water in yachts and smaller craft during the warm months, and various associations were formed, including the South End and Hillsborough Clubs in the 1890s. Regattas were major events, though not always scheduled as reliably as some wished.

86 Inevitably, there were rules that governed what could be worn. One held in 1882 prohibited the personification of clergymen, volunteers, firemen, or any objectionable character.

Horse racing was better organized, and sweepstakes could even be held in winter. In 1887, for instance, the 20-member Hillsborough Driving Association prepared and maintained a mile-long track on the ice. Harness racing, though, was at its best on dirt tracks, and on October 2, 1889, it got a permanent home when the Charlottetown Driving Park and Provincial Exhibition Association opened its new facility in the east end of the city. Designed by W. B. Fasiz of Cleveland, Ohio, the track was built on the former Kensington Range, marshy land that had to be protected from flooding by a causeway that became the extension of Grafton Street.[87] Horse racing has continued at this site and enjoyed a remarkably enduring popularity ever since.

New sports came to share this widespread appeal as Charlottetonians enthusiastically pursued the latest trends in recreational activities. In this they were not alone; Canadians generally embraced the late-Victorian and Edwardian ideals of rugged manliness and muscular Christianity. Hockey, a sport organized in Montreal in the 1870s, spread quickly to the Maritimes where it first became popular in Halifax. By 1886 the *Examiner* announced that "hockey is at last to the fore." By 1890 matches were regularly held on indoor natural ice at the Hillsborough Rink. Games took place between informal teams, such as "Sir John" and "Laurier," held during the federal general election of 1891, or the 1893 match of "English" against "Scotch." Club play soon emerged, and in 1907 the Charlottetown Arena was built to accommodate contests between the Victoria and Abegweit Hockey Clubs and teams from places such as Summerside and Halifax. In the off-season, and even in the depths of winter, some Charlottetonians

87 The land cost $9,000, somewhat less than half the $22,400 in stock issued by the association to this date.

turned to roller skating. A roller rink was opened in July 1885, drawing "enthusiastic" audiences to races and carnivals on rollers. About this same time, baseball, an American import, began to attract increasing interest. Early games were played in Victoria Park. By 1890 various baseball clubs had sprung up and interclub competitions were arranged, occasionally involving teams from Summerside or Pictou. The Charlottetown Baseball Club was formed in June 1896 and won the first Island championship, held that year. After 1903, competitive play became centred at the Abegweit Amateur Athletic Association diamond, although the association itself did not field a team until 1905. By 1912 baseball was popular enough in the city to support three leagues. The Scottish game of golf was rapidly becoming known in Canada in the 1880s and 1890s, and, after 1902, the Charlottetown Golf Club established a course at Belvedere at the edge of town. Lawn tennis also enjoyed a wide following and considerable social standing. Games were played in Victoria Park, or even on the grounds of Government House,[88] and teams sometimes travelled to other cities for matches. Curling was officially organized in 1887 when the Charlottetown Curling Club was created largely at the instigation of George MacLeod. Play initially took place at the Citizens' Rink and later the Excelsior and Hillsborough Rinks. In January 1914, a rink built especially for curling opened on Grafton Street. For those with time and

Though traditional pastimes like snowshoeing remained popular, newer ones like baseball and golf caught on in the period between 1880 and 1920.

88 A match between the Micmac and Fitzroy Lawn Tennis clubs was held in the latter venue in June 1883 on the invitation of the Lieutenant Governor and before a large audience.

energy remaining, the press noted other sports, including tobogganing in Victoria Park, lacrosse, boxing, bowling, cycling, sleighing and shooting.

An important element in the emergence of sports as a focus of community life in this period was their formal organizations. The earliest and perhaps chief of these, the YMCA, was created originally for more passive endeavours, but by the late 1880s, it had recognized the effectiveness of appealing to young men through sport. In addition to securing its own future, the "Y" saw a role in offering an alternative to the city's numerous sports clubs, some of which were earning reputations as places "where youthful morals were being deteriorated." A gymnasium was built, and soon newspaper notices were informing the public it was open in the evenings.[89] Despite the fact the YMCA was dedicated to young men who were communicants of "an evangelical church," exercise classes for seniors appeared by 1893, and classes for ladies started around 1901. By1904-5, there were 484 members, including 120 full members, 83 boys, 47 ladies and 84 sustaining members, among others. Although annual reports mentioned the number of religious meetings and Bible classes that were held, organizers acknowledged the importance of physical development by declaring that "we stand on the threshold of an era when healthy bodies, clear minds and pure thoughts are blessings for all." Various sports, including track and field, rugby, baseball, basketball and after 1910 when two alleys were installed, bowling, provided appealing additions to callisthenics and Indian club swinging as means of increasing physical fitness. Membership ebbed and flowed over the years, but the "Y" with its focus on physical, social, mental and religious growth retained a central role in the development of young athletes in the city.[90] Towards the end of the period 1880-1920, a YWCA was established in Charlottetown. On May 22, 1919, the organization dedicated its new home in Beaconsfield, former home of Henry Cundall who died in 1916 and left the house to be used as a residence for young women.[91]

An important milestone in the development of sport in Charlottetown was reached when the Charlottetown Athletic Association was organized in 1891. Structured as an umbrella organization along the lines of the Montreal Amateur Athletic Association and the Halifax Wanderers Club, the CAA was intended to nurture sports and physical fitness generally. Its focus was too wide, so a reorganization in 1897 into the Charlottetown Amateur Athletic Association brought with it a specific mandate to construct a facility for track and field, cycling, baseball, rugby and other summer sports. This was accomplished by September of that year, for the first time giving Charlottetown

89 "The gymnasium will afford a means of many, healthful and wholesome recreation and amusement for our boys and be a strong counter attraction to the liquor saloons, and billiard halls and bowling alleys at which too many are apt to waste their time, their money, their bodily health and their good moral characters."

90 In 1904 there were 434 members and a typical physical education class had 84 attendees, including 11 young men, 4 businessmen, 9 working boys, 13 students, 13 intermediate boys, 22 junior boys and 12 ladies.

91 Beaconsfield also was to serve as a nurses' residence.

a comprehensive outdoor athletics complex. It was located at the northern end of Upper Prince Street.

Soon afterwards, three of Charlottetown's many athletics clubs, the Abegweit Rugby Club and the Crescent and the Anchor Athletic Clubs, merged to form a multi-sport organization, again along the line of the Montreal and Halifax sports clubs. Initially called the Abegweit-Crescent Athletic Club, it became the Abegweit Amateur Athletic Association by 1902 and provided an organizational focus for sport in the city. Specializing in rugby, hockey and track and field, the AAAA also fielded baseball and basketball teams. The success of the teams in the early 20th century earned the club a distinguished reputation and nurtured many talented athletes, including Bill Halpenny, a pole vaulter who received a special bronze medal at the 1912 Olympics.[92]

In addition to sporting events, Charlottetown enjoyed an active round of social occasions, everything from strawberry festivals in June and July to summertime moonlight excursions on steamers where live band or dance music was provided. Picnics were popular from June to August, while the spring and autumn seemed to have been the best times for bazaars. Many of the events were fund-raisers for the organization that sponsored them, but on occasion they were held to help others. Mr. and Mrs. John J. Davies, for instance, organized a ball at the Hotel Davies in February 1891 for the benefit of the poor, and a July 1885 concert and strawberry festival was intended to raise money for improvements to Queen Square. Members of the Scottish community were ready to assemble throughout the year, with the highlight event, Caledonian Days, attracting visitors from considerable distances. Old Home Week, held in July 1905 to commemorate the city's golden jubilee, tried to capitalize upon a multitude of homesick Islanders to widen such gatherings beyond Scots and congregated firemen.[93] The success of the event planted the seed of tourism based upon an appeal to expatriates and led to its repetition in subsequent years.

In June 1881, Henry W. Vinnicombe was presented with "a very fine old violin" in recognition of his contribution to the music scene in Charlottetown. Vinnicombe, a musician, piano tuner and conductor, directed the Charlottetown Philharmonic Orchestra and would continue to play a prominent role in the city's cultural life for another three decades. Frequently, he would team with S. N. Earle to produce light operas and vocal concerts. Vinnicombe was not a wealthy man, as a benefit concert held for him later that year attests, but the respect shown to him was testimony to his contributions and the importance of music to many of his fellow citizens. Music was seen as a "brightening influence" that could dispel the gloom that lay about some households, a force that "more than gold" elevated tastes and refined natures. Such "education and refinement of the citizen as an individual" were regarded as "among the most powerful influences to revise intemperance and immorality." Not

92 He was forced to withdraw from competition after he set a new Olympic record but broke a rib because of inadequate cushioning in the landing pit.

93 The firemen's procession, planned for April 1884, was anticipated to be the "grandest ever witnessed in the Maritime Provinces."

The Opera House ...

that everyone appreciated its charms. The "most brilliant" concert ever rendered by the Quintette Club failed to fill the hall to overflowing, "a remarkable display of lack of appreciation and culture" on the part of the populace. Even if an audience was "a fine one," the conduct of the "boys" might involve too much "stamping with feet and thumping with sticks." But on the whole, Charlottetown's cultural life was buzzing with music, drama and other forms of live entertainment.

As with sports, theatrical and musical groups were constantly emerging and disappearing. Many met "to organize in the fall only to go to pieces as summer approach[ed]"; others, such as the Philharmonic Society and Orchestral Club, enjoyed long, productive lives. For many years, the Academy of Music both performed and sponsored concerts. Churches spawned associations of youthful entertainers such as "The Band of Hope" and "The League of the Cross," and the militia, colleges and private individuals formed concert bands. Theatrical companies proliferated in the late 19th century. In 1885 the Union Dramatic Club, forerunner of the BIS Dramatic Club and Lyceum Comedy Club, was formed. The Dramatic Club of St. Dunstan's College appeared in the 1890s, and the Charlottetown Dramatic Club was organized in 1894. At times there appeared to be too much going on for some. Formation of an Anglican Literary and Dramatic Club brought the caustic comment that the church should instead initiate a mission series to "lead to the salvation of never-dying souls."

... was the setting for both professional and amateur theatre. Cast of "Robert Emmett," 1894.

"We are just now being attacked," observed the *Examiner* on another occasion, "by street musicians, having no less than a piano on wheels, a hurdy-gurdy and a harper and violinist 'doing' the city."

Every kind of performance seemed to have its clientele, but Gilbert and Sullivan's HMS *Pinafore* was a perennial favourite, as were minstrel shows. Talent from "away" was frequently on the bill. Dean, the "World's Greatest Ventriloquist"; Bosco, the "Renowned Magician"; Madame Camilla Urso, the "Greatest Violinist on this Continent"; and Stuart Rogers, the "Great Character Impersonator," were just some of the acts that joined Leon W. Washburn's Circus, the Kickapoo Indian Medicine Company and Hazlie and Ryerson's Comedy Company on the list of visiting entertainers over the years. Some visitors were particularly distinguished, including the Boston Comedy Club, Madame Albani, Oscar Wilde, John Philip Sousa and E. Pauline Johnson. The Market Hall, YMCA and the St. Patrick's and Benevolent Irish Society Halls were popular venues at the beginning of the period, followed later by Lyceum Hall on Prince Street and the Opera House on Grafton Street. Smaller events occurred in educational and church facilities, including St. Peter's schoolroom, St. Paul's schoolroom and St. James' Hall. Although live performances enjoyed vast popularity well into the 20th century, new forms of entertainment appeared, including motion pictures. The Market House built in 1904 contained a hall that could be used as a cinema. Jessie Hogg's "Wonderland," a concert hall and movie theatre that occupied this space, boasted low ticket prices and popular programming. The name was changed to the "People's Theatre" in 1910 to underscore the trend towards a broader audience that was to increase as the century wore on.

Public lectures were also prominent features on the Charlottetown entertainment scene. Many speakers were clergymen of various denominations, supplemented by a sprinkling of academics, such as the august John Caven of St. Dunstan's and, later, Prince of Wales College; physicians; and others such as philanthropist Henry J. Cundall.[94] Some presentations were made in aid of a charity, and others were part of a series sponsored by organizations like the YMCA and St. James Church. Subject matter was frequently related to the professional concerns of the lecturer, so titles like "Moses, the Great Hebrew Statesman, Legislator and Poet," "The Church in Council," and "Christianity and its Founder," abounded. Travel enjoyed popular appeal, and over the years, talks were given on "The Palaces of the French Kings," "A Trip to Thunder Bay," and "To and Fro in Scotland" — the latter advertised as "illustrated with choice views." Presentations on Prince Edward Island were common, and topics covered included "Red Sandstone," "Early History," and "Scraps of History." Lectures occurred in the same halls as musicals and dramatic productions, and attendance could be large and enthusiastic, although not invariably so. Rev. Dr. O'Brien's talk on "The Early Stages of Christianity in England" was given to a capacity crowd at the capacious market hall, and A. A. Bartlett held his audience in "almost breathless attention" during his presentation of "The Conquest of Mexico." On the other hand, Charles Watts, "the celebrated English Philosopher and Lecturer," attracted only small numbers to his lecture about "The Religion of Secularism."

This was also an age in which fraternal and ethnic societies flourished. Some of the more active were long-established, but even these showed new life after 1880.[95] Freemasonry was the oldest and one of the most robust organizations, with roots that went back to 1797, but a new temple was begun in 1892, and the 1890s saw the introduction of the Knights Templar and Scottish Rite Masons. In 1825 one of Charlottetown's most enduring and active associations, the Benevolent Irish Society, was created, in part to work for the perpetuation of Irish sentiment. It remained vital into the next century. Just prior to the city's incorporation, in 1849, the Orange Order was organized to assert the Protestant Irish tradition, although members had other origins as well. Incorporating people of various social strata, the local "Boyne" Lodge was active in the current period and proved to be an irritant to some local Catholics. The Sons of Temperance, the Charlottetown branch of which was founded in 1848, had known good times and some poorer ones before 1881 when better leadership expanded and mobilized its membership for what was hoped to be a definitive battle in the war for general sobriety. Members of the Scottish community formed the Caledonian Club in 1864 to preserve their heritage in sport, music and dress. By the 1890s, the club had a large membership, and the annual sports competitions had become one of the most

94 Cundall's wealth gave him the time and means to indulge a long-standing passion for photography. He took up photography as a young man and helped to found a camera club. Eventually, his magic lantern shows became famous.

95 Entries in D. A. MacKinnon and A. B. Warburton's *Past and Present of Prince Edward Island*, 1903, attest to the vitality of such organizations, but they do not exhaust the list. Newspapers mention other groups, such as the Irish National Land League and the St. Vincent de Paul Society.

anticipated events on the calendar. The Odd Fellows, with a lodge dating from 1869, saw similar growth, with the opening of a new Alpha Rebekah Lodge in 1896.

To this list of long-standing organizations were added newer names. They included the Sons of England Benevolent Society, 1891; Independent Order of Foresters, 1892; Catholic Mutual Benefit Society, 1893; Knights of Pythias, 1899; Ancient Order of United Workmen, 1900; Knights of Columbus, 1903; and the Rotary Club, 1917. Although fellowship was important for most of these organizations, they also sought to promote the general welfare of the community and to perform charitable acts. A significant feature, and one that might have been the prime consideration for many members, was mutual assistance and particularly insurance. The Masons, Odd Fellows, Foresters, Sons of England, Knights of Columbus and Catholic Mutual Benefit Society offered forms of life and sometimes medical insurance. In doing so, they provided an essential service at modest cost to urban families who in the event of the loss of income through illness or death could be left economically vulnerable without the community support often available to country dwellers.

Militia

Unlike the previous decades when adventuresome Charlottetonians and other Islanders were obliged to enlist in the armies of Great Britain or the United States to seek paths of glory, the years after 1880 provided that opportunity within Canadian battle formations. At this time, the capital was both the centre point in the province of enthusiasm for military service and the principal source of recruits for Island units. By the turn of the century, the 82nd Battalion of Infantry, organized after Confederation, was composed of eight companies with a total strength of 367, the bulk drawn from Queens County, and in particular the capital. Most of the 244 complement of the 4th Regiment of Canadian Artillery, formed in 1882, was also drawn from Charlottetown, with the balance from Kings County. The Charlottetown Engineers, organized in 1878, consisted of two companies incorporating 166 officers, non-commissioned officers, and men, but early in the new century, it was merged with the artillery regiment. Regular militia drills, as well as the annual 12-day field training exercises held at Camp Brighton on the outskirts of town, took on a practical tone in 1885 when a contingent was mobilized to help suppress the Riel Rebellion. Troops were mustered in Charlottetown and ready to proceed to the West when word was received that the uprising had been quelled. This false start was not to be repeated.

In 1899 Britain's imperial adventure in Africa brought it face to face with two small, independent republics established by the Boers, descendants of largely Dutch settlers. Gold, diamonds and the dreams of a British Cape-to-Cairo railway provoked the conflict. When war broke out, an upsurge in patriotic fervour swept across the empire and found a strong resonance in many parts of English-speaking Canada, including Charlottetown. The Island capital buzzed with excitement and expressions of loyalty, and local militiamen coveted places in the small contingent of 1,000 that Canada undertook to send to help the mother country. In the end, Islanders were allotted 30 spots on the force, and the selected volunteers left Charlottetown on October 25, 1899,

The 4th Canadian Artillery Regiment, based mostly in Charlottetown, was a frequent champion at national gunnery competitions.

with a heroes' send-off and a gift of money. The anticipated cakewalk instead proved to be an anguished struggle of attrition that ultimately involved 450,000 British troops of whom 125 came from Prince Edward Island. The original contingent returned to the city on November 2, 1900, and received a tumultuous welcome, marred only by the knowledge that two local boys had perished in the conflict.[96] A grateful citizenry raised money for a war memorial to bear witness to the loyalty of Islanders and to the valour of its warriors.

In the aftermath of the South African struggle, service in the city's militia had considerable appeal. Within a few years, three more militia units were formed: the Prince Edward Island Light Horse, the Medical Corps and the Signalling Corps. Island units did well in the annual efficiency assessments, maintaining a tradition of excellence that, particularly in the case of the artillery, stretched back to the 1890s. Despite this enthusiasm and apparent competence, reorganization of the military stripped the province of its status as a separate military district in 1911, when it became part of Military District Number 6 centred in Nova Scotia.

As war clouds gathered in Europe in 1914, Charlottetonians again rallied to the flag. On August 7, three days after the declaration of war, the 4th Regiment held a special drill and enlisted 30 men on the spot. The excitement of the times resulted in the cancellation of many social events, and the *Guardian* promised to post news updates on special boards twice a day and to add important stories as they were received. By August 21, some volunteers had already departed for training on the mainland, while local women had gotten busy knitting and sewing for the Red Cross. The surge of enthusiasm waned somewhat as 1915 progressed. One reason, apparently, was the lack of a distinctively

96 Roland Dennis Taylor and Alfred Riggs.

Island component of the Canadian Expeditionary Force. This was subsequently remedied by the creation of the 105th Battalion (PEI Highlanders). The 1,250-strong unit was a source of local pride, and when it departed for overseas on June 13, 1916, "practically the whole City was on the streets while flags waved from many buildings in honour of the Island's first regiment." Unfortunately, the unit was broken up after its arrival in England so its members could reinforce other regiments decimated by battle.

Two small Island formations, however, did fight under their own colours. The artillery regiment provided a good base upon which to mobilize an active battery, and recruitment began in 1915 and progressed to the extent that training commenced at Camp Brighton in September of that year. Only a minority of the enlisted gunners were Charlottetonians, but the city turned out *en masse* to bid the 2nd Canadian Siege Battery farewell as the men paraded from their barracks to the Steam Navigation Wharf on November 28. Another siege battery, the 8th, was raised and sent off to England in less than a year. Both of these units saw heavy battle. August 1917 was a particularly gruelling time for the 8th battery. Its positions were subjected to gas attacks, and on August 11, 34 were listed as "wounded and gassed." Fifteen were from Charlottetown. News of these casualties followed shortly on the heels of the announcement of the death of a local man, Gunner W. B. VanIderstine, who died after being gassed in April.[97] On August 15, news was received of further losses from the 8th battery due to gas attacks. Perhaps in response to these setbacks, Lieutenant Governor A. C. MacDonald announced on August 24 that Government House would be made available as a convalescent hospital for wounded soldiers.

By this point in time, the grim reality of battle was apparent to all. On August 6, 1917, the third anniversary of the outbreak of war was observed with special church services that were well-attended. Returned soldiers were met at the waterfront and taken in a motor cavalcade to Victoria Park where a large crowd had gathered. In his first appearance as Premier, A. E. Arsenault declared that "we must win the war, nothing else matters." Mayor P. S. Brown made the soldiers "the guests of the Mayor while in the city." He also moved a resolution affirming "that on this third anniversary of the declaration of a righteous war, this meeting of the citizens of Charlottetown records its inflexible determination to continue to a victorious end the struggle in maintenance of those ideals of Liberty and Justice which are the common and sacred cause of the Allies." These observances were not the only tributes paid to veterans. In September, a pilot, Lieutenant H. R. Large, "one of the original six to leave Charlottetown," returned to a hero's welcome and three months' leave, after sustaining chest injuries and severe burns that resulted from the crash of his aircraft following an attack on an enemy zeppelin.

The human cost of war by mid-1917 was driving politics, certainly at the federal level. Dissident Liberals joined with the Conservatives to form a Union Government under Robert Borden in October. Its principal objective was to implement conscription as a means of ensuring a constant flow of new recruits for the military. In the

---

97 VanIderstine had been serving with the 2nd Siege. Though his cause of death was attributed to a gas attack, he actually died of influenza.

ensuing federal general election, local Unionist candidates, Donald Nicholson and Alexander Martin, faced Liberals, Alexander B. Warburton and John E. Sinclair, in a contest in which the need to win the war was not an issue, but the route to that end was. The *Patriot*, a Liberal newspaper, supported conscription, yet argued that victory could best be achieved by returning Sir Wilfrid Laurier, who opposed conscription, to power. The *Guardian* demanded to differ, heaping scorn on the Liberals and accusing Warburton and Sinclair of concealing their position on conscription in a "false and contemptible" effort to be "all things to all men." Initial returns posted victories for both Warburton and Sinclair, but with the subsequent addition of the soldiers' vote, Nicholson, who had run on his party's accomplishments since 1911 as well as conscription, displaced Warburton. This mixed result was an indication, perhaps, of a public that appreciated the subtleties of the wartime situation more than politicians and editorial writers.

Before heading overseas, the 2nd Siege Battery showed off its tallest and shortest members — both from Charlottetown and area. Ferguson Robertson (6'5") was from Marshfield. Rowland Beck (5'1"), was a recent emigrant from England who had settled in Charlottetown before the war. Both men lived to tell their tales.

In other ways, popular opinion was similarly divided. This was shown to be the case with the Victory Loan campaigns. The bond drive of 1917 was advertised as the biggest financial undertaking ever made by the Dominion government, with an overall objective of raising $150 million. The Island's share was $1 million. The campaign in Charlottetown started on November 12, with a chorus of church bells and factory whistles. Canvassers began their rounds under the leadership of C. H. B. Longworth, J. O. Hyndman, W. K. Rogers, Frank R. Heartz and other community notables. After the first day, the *Guardian* announced that very few refusals were received at the door. Merchants backed the campaign, including W. W. Wellner, who promised to accept bonds in payment for merchandise. A large dial on the window of the Eastern Trust Building, the campaign headquarters, marked the progress. In the days that followed, the indicator crept ever closer to its objective, eventually surpassing the target handily.

Although Islanders eventually subscribed to more than twice their quota, they had the second-lowest participation rate in the country and the smallest purchase per capita. The average subscription, however, was $440, placing provincial investors fifth among the nine provinces. Yet another Victory Loan drive followed in 1918, again headed by C. H. B. Longworth. This time, the Island's participation rate was by far the lowest in the land, but the average subscription at approximately $557 was the third-highest. The objective for 1918 was $2.5 million, and the subscriptions amounted to a little more than $3 million. Clearly, fewer Islanders on a proportional basis purchased bonds, but those who did made relatively large investments. In all likelihood, the proud bondholders were urban dwellers from Charlottetown and, to a lesser extent, Summerside.

By the time the results of the 1918 Victory Loan campaign were announced, the war was over. On the last day of battle, the Canadian army re-entered Mons, the scene of the original British defeat in the war. Just over a month later, Sir Arthur Currie reviewed his troops as they crossed the Rhine River to occupy Bonn and Cologne. An announcement had been made by then that repatriation of the Canadian Corps would begin at an estimated rate of 30,000 per month. Most of the soldiers did not return until 1919; sadly, some never did. Overall, somewhat less than 4,000 Prince Edward Island residents joined the armed services during the Great War. Approximately another 3,000 Islanders living in other parts of Canada served.[98] A significant number, more than 520,[99] had made their home in the capital, and they bore their fair share of discomfort, injury and death.[100]

---

98 See Edward MacDonald, *If You're Stronghearted*, Charlottetown: PEIMHF, 2000, for an excellent treatment of the First World War years. MacDonald notes that 3,696 people enlisted within the province but 7,168 Island-born Canadians signed up. Both figures were low by national standards, a reflection of low numbers of unemployed single males and British-born residents. Those two groups typified volunteer enlistees in the Canadian Expeditionary Force.

99 It is virtually impossible to say exactly how many Charlottetonians saw service. This figure is an extrapolation from the percentage of Charlottetonians among a specific list of Islanders for whom attestation records are found in the National Archives. That percentage, 14.5, was roughly the city's proportion of the provincial population. About one-half of the specific list was native Charlottetonians living off-Island, a figure that accords with the overall split of Island residents and expatriates who saw service. Since about 50 per cent of the Charlottetown residents on the list were born elsewhere on PEI, an estimated 260 locally born Charlottetown residents joined the military.

100 One estimate put the number of Islanders who perished at about 400. The official Canadian count identified 318 of the dead as having PEI addresses. *The Guardian* claimed that 503 Islanders died in active service, and a recent estimate arrived at a total of 793. Figures are somewhat vague, because Islanders living away who volunteered and served are hard to identify.

The roar of the guns of August 1914 which rolled over the hills of Belgium had echoes in the gentle slopes and quiet lanes of Charlottetown. Fear for the future, anxiety about the safety of sons and neighbours, and anguish following the receipt of telegrams of condolence ruptured the city's sense of safety and serenity. In the war's wake came the harsh reality of a new and brutal age. Wartime prosperity waned as the country returned to "normalcy." A prolonged, spirit-destroying economic depression settled across the whole of the Maritimes and, except for a brief period, was unrelieved by the prosperity that was experienced elsewhere during much of the 1920s. The east coast had been largely overlooked in plans to perpetuate war-based industries by converting them to peacetime endeavours, although that made little difference because these attempts were poorly organized and haphazardly implemented. For Charlottetonians, the return of peace brought economic stagnation, lower commodity prices and their consequences: unemployment, poverty, some social dislocation and sagging public morale. The years of progress in the provision of services and of confidence in public life were over. The grim necessity of managing hard times was about to begin.

CHAPTER 4

Recession

1921-45

As it entered the postwar era, Charlottetown, like other Maritime centres, was still in the twin shadows of the industrial dominance of the central provinces and the rapidly expanding West. This was a time of transition, but it was more the end of an era than the beginning of one.

Unlike many other Canadian cities, the basic mix of people in Charlottetown remained pretty much the same as it had been. Immigrants mostly went to the interior reaches of the country. There was some population growth, but this was generated locally. A consciousness of the population's roots in the British Isles and a loyalty to the imperial connection was widely shared. Limited physical expansion of the city occurred, with Brighton developing as a new, prestigious housing area, but extensive suburban growth was still in the offing. Municipal politics was similarly measured and generally placid except for a few years in the 1930s. Economically, the period was more tumultuous. Early reverses and discontent gave way to a dash of prosperity and optimism in the late 1920s. That in turn was followed by a plunge into economic despair as the city, province and nation were swept into the vortex of the Great Depression. Socially, the city was shucking off the tatters of isolation. Better communications by rail, road and sea, while generally acknowledged to be less than adequate, served to connect the city more closely to its rural hinterland and to the rest of Canada. New technologies in the form of passenger aircraft, radio and motion pictures brought the world to Charlottetown's streets and living rooms. If there was some loss of self-sufficiency and local distinctiveness, there was also opportunity. Citizens would learn to use modernity as well as merely to seek it.

POPULATION GROWTH AND ETHNIC RELATIONSHIPS

Between 1921 and 1945, Charlottetown continued its relative decline in size compared to other Canadian cities, even though its actual population moved upward. Growth during the 1920s was considerable, from 12,347 in 1921 to 14,101 in 1931, a 14.2 per cent increase. The following decade saw the population move 32.1 per cent to 17,356.[1] The city was the 46th largest in Canada in 1921, 50th in 1931 and 55th in 1941. By comparison, Timmins and East Windsor, Ontario, were just a little larger

1 These figures are for the city and royalty.

than Charlottetown in 1931 while Galt and Belleville, Ontario, were a bit smaller. By 1941 Galt and North Bay, Ontario, were the next largest cities and Lethbridge, Alberta, and Granby, Quebec, were the next smallest. Within the Island context, however, Charlottetown maintained its persistent growth. Since Prince Edward Island's population declined between 1921 and 1931, the capital's increase moved it from somewhat less than 14 per cent of the population to slightly more than 16 per cent. During the next decade, the provincial population grew by 7,009 due to a slowing of outmigration and the return of some previous emigrants to their homes. Even so, Charlottetown's growth meant that its inhabitants represented over 18.3 per cent of the Island's population by 1941. Urbanization continued on Prince Edward Island as elsewhere in Canada during this period, apparently impervious to the effects of the Depression and the hardship that a shrinking economy imposed, particularly upon the city's labouring class.

Without massive immigration, the ethnic mix of Charlottetown appeared to remain stable during this period, but closer examination reveals significant movements in the balance of the old-stock population. People of English origin were still the largest component of the population at 33.9 per cent in 1931 and 34.4 per cent in 1941. They were followed by the Scots with 28.7 per cent of the population in 1931 and 27.8 per cent a decade later. Persons of Irish background represented 24.9 per cent of Charlottetonians in 1931 and 24.8 per cent in 1941. Those claiming mixed origins also remained stable — 8.3 per cent in 1921 and 8.6 per cent in 1931. Thereafter, this category was not tracked by the census. The real shift was among the population with French origins. They increased from less than 7 per cent of the total in 1921 to 9.8 per cent in 1931, before inching up to 10 per cent in 1941. Overall, the English segment of the population expanded by 23.8 per cent between 1921 and 1941, the Scots by 16.7 per cent, the Irish by a mere 1.8 per cent, while the French (Acadian) numbers leapt ahead by a substantial 72.2 per cent. The apparent stagnation of the Irish component of the population invites speculation: do these data reflect changes in self-identification rather than actual numbers, or reality? If the latter, did the relative decline of the Irish result from out-migration or smaller families? One possible explanation is that the Irish, typically less prosperous than the English and Scots, were more likely to move for economic reasons. People of other origins represented minuscule proportions of the population. The largest of these census groups in 1931 and 1941 was "Other Oriental," which likely included the Lebanese and a handful of Chinese, among others. Next came the Germans, Welsh, Dutch and Scandinavians in 1931, and the "Africans,"[2] Welsh, Dutch and Germans in 1941. All of the smaller groups together represented only 2.7 per cent of the population in 1931 and 3 per cent in 1941.

Trends established previously among the adherents of major denominations persisted in this period. Anglicans dropped to 9 per cent of the population in 1931 and 1941. With church union, the proportion of Methodists/United Churchmen rose

2 This category appears in the census of 1921 and 1941, but not 1931. Its overall size of the city's population is small, 29 people in 1921 and 52 in 1941, but its specific increase is substantial, over 79 per cent. With such small numbers, changes in self-identification would have a substantial impact.

to 19 per cent in both decades, while the numbers of Presbyterians dropped to 16 per cent. The proportion of Baptists crept up to 6 per cent at the same time. Roman Catholics grew to 47 per cent of the population by 1931, reaching 48 per cent in 1941. All other religions and those unaffiliated with any faith represented 3 per cent of the population in 1931 and 2 per cent in 1941.

Another trend, predictable given the passage of time and the relatively small numbers of new arrivals, was the continued shrinkage of the proportion of non-Islanders in the overall population of the city. Locally born folk accounted for about 89 per cent of the total population in 1931 and 90 per cent in 1941. People born in the rest of Canada contributed almost another 6 per cent in both decades, leaving the balance shared among British-born[3] (2.5 per cent in 1931 and 2 per cent in 1941), Americans (1.7 per cent and 1 per cent) and all other foreign-born (0.62 per cent and 1.8 per cent). In 1931, 1,740 people lived in the royalty as opposed to the city proper. This was 12.3 per cent of the population for the whole area or an equivalent of 14.1 per cent of the city's population. By 1941, 2,535 people lived in the royalty — 14.6 per cent of the region's total population or a number equalling 17.1 per cent of the city's residents. Suburbanization thus continued during the 1920s and '30s, albeit at a slower pace.

The economic reverses of the Depression decades altered one demographic trend, however. After a long period in which the gender balance in the city weighed heavily in favour of females, the relative number of males began to increase. There were 89 males to every 100 females in the city in 1931, and the figure rose to 91 when the royalty was considered. The figure dipped slightly to 88 per 100 in 1941,[4] reflecting, no doubt, the effects of recruitment for the armed forces during the Second World War. Even so, the rise in the male portion of the population between 1921 and 1941 returned the male-to-female ratio to the levels experienced in the years before 1881. It indicates a slowing of the pace of outmigration of working-age males in response to fewer opportunities elsewhere and also, perhaps, fewer rural females coming to the city to work in service jobs.

Charlottetown was also shedding the way in which various social groups and economic activities mingled geographically. The Victorian intermixing of classes and land uses had not disappeared, but the lower wards were now more consistently given over to commercial and industrial activities, and the eastern end of the city was increasingly working-class in nature. With the exception of pockets in Ward 1, the western end of Charlottetown housed relatively few families with marginal incomes. In Ward 5 above Euston Street, housing was still mixed economically between Upper Prince Street and Longworth Avenue, and more consistently modest in the areas from Malpeque Road over to Spring Park Road. Further west, Brighton was steadily becoming a haven for the middle-class and wealthier Charlottetonians.

3 British-born includes British possessions, including Newfoundland. In 1931, 88 Newfoundlanders lived in the city.

4 This 1941 figure is for the city alone, and not the city including the royalty, for which data were not given.

POLITICAL LIFE

The period between 1921 and 1945 was not one of great political innovation in Charlottetown. Rather it was a time in which established approaches to governance continued on their course. The political arena continued to be filled for the most part by merchants and a lesser number of professionals, such as lawyers and medical doctors who were, of course, themselves in business. Businessmen and wealthy property-owners benefitted from having the right to vote in any ward in which they owned property, giving some multiple ballots in civic elections. Such plural voting was a much more common feature of municipal politics in the West and Ontario than it was in the Maritimes. It evolved as a response by property interests to balance a widening franchise and the diminishing effectiveness of property qualifications to screen office-holders. In 1935 the municipal franchise was extended to non-residents who had commercial addresses in the city. Needless to say, Council remained responsive to the interests of business.[5] Various representatives claimed to be the "friend" of labour, and a few of them were even labelled as such by workers themselves, but no one in these years had a concrete link to the city's labouring class. Competition for places at "the council board" was brisk, if not avid, and the mayor's chair remained in the mind of the electorate an honour to be shared in rotation by men who had earned that recognition by long civic service. Between 1920 and 1946, only one mayor, B. Roy Holman, was returned a second time. In the same era, there was but a single instance of someone being elected mayor without serving a substantial political apprenticeship, and that, the term of W. S. Stewart, was not a happy one.

A step towards widening the involvement of citizens in the political process was taken in 1927 when women were given the vote. This came five years after women got the provincial franchise, and it was a cautious advance. Only those who owned freehold property valued at $500 (equivalent to $6,422 in 2008) qualified. While this was not a huge sum, it tended to ensure these women would likely be drawn from the same circle as the existing political establishment. At the same time, electors whose taxes were in arrears saw their vote suspended. In 1932 the requirements for the franchise were further loosened when both men and women who were 21 years old, British subjects and owners of property valued at $100 or who paid the poll tax of $3 qualified,[6] as did men who were tenants paying rent of $14 a year. Taxes, however, still had to be paid in full. The issue of the loss of the franchise because of back taxes came to the fore during the Great Depression when it was a common enough

---

5 The already formidable influence of business and professional circles at City Hall could be buttressed if circumstances required. In the winter of 1944, a joint committee of Charlottetown service clubs appeared before Council to urge expenditures for supervised parks. These clubs were made up of 150 "leading business and professional men" including "some of the largest tax-payers" and their members were concerned with children playing in the streets and thereby putting themselves at risk and sometimes engaging in anti-social behaviour. The minutes of the meeting noted Council was in "one hundred per cent unanimous support of this Committee."

6 The poll tax was raised to $5 in 1935. Non-residents meeting these requirements could also vote.

condition. The Labourers' Protective Union asked the city in 1934 to rescind the offending by-law, only to be told that, despite its desire, Council could not act unilaterally. An amendment to the act of incorporation would be required from the provincial legislature. In 1938 the LPU again called for universal male suffrage even for those who had defaulted on the poll tax, and the next year this demand was modified to seek the vote for those who were up-to-date with their taxes for only the current year. Little progress was made with the matter.

A possible structural change was averted in 1929 when Council considered reforming the ward system. Instead of five wards with varying numbers of Councillors depending upon their population, a proposal called for six wards, each with a single representative plus two Councillors elected at large. Although this would have left the same number of elected members, Council was comfortable with the existing arrangement, and so the matter was never acted upon. Nor was there any follow-through with a 1934 resolution to take over the duties of the directly elected water commissioners. The ostensible reason was to control city expenditures, but the public and, it seems, most politicians were generally satisfied with the service and administration of the Water Commission, and the political will to end its arm's length relationship with the city government was not there. Neither was there any certainty that the change would actually save money.

Another issue to arise in the 1930s involved municipal administration and the handling of the city's business. There were not many full-time bureaucrats to be found at City Hall. Management of various responsibilities, such as finance and roads, was parcelled out to a system of committees, each of which was composed of a number of Councillors. Their mandate extended beyond policy formation to the actual administration and supervision of work done in their areas of responsibility. In a sense, some of the duties of the unpaid committees were executive in nature, and others were functional, in which members filled roles now often associated with paid employees. In some cases, the activities of the committees reduced the ambit of civic officials. The Public Works Committee and the Market Committee reduced the role of the City Clerk with respect to the market and other public property, and the Street Committee performed some of the tasks formerly undertaken by the City Surveyor. The overall performance of the committees depended upon the dedication and abilities of their members, particularly the chairmen, and these differed considerably. There were inevitably details that were neglected or simply overlooked by the politicians. These tended to end up in the lap of the City Clerk.

In 1932 Mayor W. S. Stewart tried to change the management of civic affairs. He urged the appointment of a City Manager to take over the purchase of city supplies and the hiring and supervision of all non-permanent employees. Noting that Charlottetown had "an antiquated and wasteful system of civic administration by eight separate Council Committees," Stewart claimed committee members had "little or no time apart from their own private business to spare on that of the City." Most Councillors dismissed the idea of a City Manager. Some resented Stewart because he had never spent time on Council before being elected Chief Magistrate, and some feared the appointment would threaten their grip on power and their ability to distribute civic funds. After an acrimonious debate, the proposal died, but the resentments it engendered lingered for the remainder of Stewart's term. The complaints about the diligence of Councillors persisted as well. In his annual report for 1942, Mayor B. Roy Holman urged his Council to attend meetings more faithfully and to devote more time to running the city. He noted that Councillors tended not to be overly concerned with the everyday affairs of the city unless the business at hand pertained directly to them.

Mayor Roy Holman

Many of the matters that came before City Council were highly routine in nature, including paying bills, appointing minor officials such as bath house attendants, and the receiving of complaints and requests for civic services. Other topics generated more discussion and were more newsworthy. The ongoing debate between the province and municipality over finances was one such issue. It was an old bone of contention that involved the Island government's wish to restrict the city's spending and revenue demands and Charlottetown's need and desire to gain back from the province a larger share of revenue raised within its limits. An occasion to debate these differences arose in 1926 when the federally owned Canadian National Railways acknowledged its responsibility to pay provincial and municipal taxes. In recognition of this obligation, the company gave the province a grant of $40,000. The province rebuffed the city's request to obtain a share based upon the extensive properties the railway owned within its boundaries. A sullen Mayor Leonard B. Miller responded that the city was "disenchanted with this decision" and argued that in future the money should go directly to Charlottetown. The next year, the same request met a similar fate, although by then Miller had widened the city's claim to half the amusement taxes raised, a sum that "would considerably swell the grants to our Hospitals and Orphanages." The claims of the two jurisdictions for the same revenue constituted an intractable difference and one that was bound to grow. As Mayor Samuel Kennedy noted in 1935, "the purchase of any city property by the Dominion or Provincial governments deprives the city of taxes thereon." A satisfactory resolution of the problem from Charlottetown's perspective was unlikely as long as the city was under-represented in the provincial legislature. The city was certainly entitled to more than its two members.

On other matters the city was given its head. In 1936 interest was once more revived in municipal ownership of electricity. Resolving that the advantages to the city and citizens generally of civic ownership and operation of a power plant was becoming "increasingly obvious," Council asked the legislature for the authority to set up its own utility, which was duly granted that same month. The city, however, did not exercise this new power. Perhaps civic politicians were more concerned with the greater problems of unemployment and poverty. An evocative letter from "Citizen" delineated the situation in 1933 when he or she wrote that "many strong, willing workers are sitting on our parks and squares all day long with apparently no prospects of work this summer." These were neither faceless nonentities nor strangers. "Ninety-five per cent of the unemployed men and their families are native citizens who lived here all their lives. In many cases their forefathers lived all their lives here and spent all their earnings in this city." "Citizen" went on to make the point that City Councillors should be "big and brave enough" to stand up and undertake to do something on behalf of the unemployed. The need to respond to the economic crisis and pleas for help, such as the regulation of unreasonably high rents, was clearly the most important challenge to face politicians. All others paled in comparison.

Mayor Ira Yeo

In the interwar period, the city government had a significant role to play in the lives of Charlottetown's workers. It worked effectively with the Labourers' Protective Union, a unique organization that initially represented the city's stevedores and longshoremen and later expanded to include other occupations. As the principal voice of organized labour in the 1920s, the LPU enjoyed admiration, even at times affection, from other elements of society. In return for moderate policies, the union was able to negotiate employment conditions with employers and civic officials. One example was a minimum wage for labourers within the city limits — $3 for a nine-hour day in the 1920s.[7] The rate had declined to 30¢ an hour by 1930, and, in the face of the impending economic crisis, the LPU approached City Council and Mayor Ira Yeo to increase it to 35¢. Yeo was termed "a true friend of labour" and the LPU expressed confidence that the proposal would have his support. Yeo was about to step down as mayor, but the going wage rate was eventually set at 35¢ an hour for labourers and 45¢ for skilled trades such as carpenters.

Attempts by contractors, particularly those from outside Charlottetown, to undercut these wage levels were met with resistance by the union, often with the sympathy and open support of city politicians. In 1936 a dispute at the building site of the new Metropolitan store arose because wages were pegged at the going rate for the contractor's home city of Moncton. A City Councillor prevailed upon the contractor to raise the pay to 25¢ an hour for labourers and 35¢ for carpenters, but this failed to satisfy the LPU whose members then walked off the job. The union pushed the city to claim the authority from the province to enforce local pay scales within the city. In the face

7 This was not a huge sum, equivalent to about $38 in 2008.

of the labour stoppage, wages went up to the accepted standards and work resumed at the building site. Even so, the city requested and received permission from the provincial legislature to enforce its minimum wage upon all contractors or others acting as contractors within Charlottetown.

Hardship arising from the economic conditions of the Great Depression were a far greater challenge for Charlottetown's political leadership. The first response to unemployment by city politicians was to try to discourage competition for work by outsiders. This even predated the 1930s. A by-law passed in May 1926 required "non-residents" who did "transient" labour to obtain a licence at the cost of $5. Failure to do so could result in a $20 fine or 30 days in jail. Once the worldwide Depression hit, efforts to this end were stepped up. Mayor T. W. L. Prowse asked the government to order the Provincial Police to bar non-Island hobos from entering Prince Edward Island at Borden. Complaints that the Island Fertilizer Company was employing non-resident single workers prompted a visit by Prowse to the company's manager who agreed that henceforth local men would be hired and married men would be given preference. Because outside contractors might bring their own labour, the city adopted a by-law in 1931 requiring all non-resident contractors doing work in the city to pay a tax.

Mayor T. W. L. Prowse

As conditions worsened, City Councillors promised that no one except citizens of Charlottetown would be given work generated by unemployment relief projects or would receive any direct relief. When a committee of clergymen proposed a scheme whereby indigent non-residents would be given food and rest prior to being sent off to their home communities, one Councillor protested against the provision of any relief to transients. Attempts of the crew of a visiting Canadian Government Steamship to secure casual work while in port in late 1932 outraged local labour and led to a protest in the press. Two years later, with the persistence of interlopers among the city's labour force (Mayor W. S. Stewart estimated 25 to 40 per cent of the unemployed were from outside the city), attitudes hardened. Stewart proclaimed that "our slogan must be a Back to the Land Movement, for those who have come in from without, who are a charge upon us ...," and Councillor B. Roy Holman promised that no outsider would be given work that winter until "every unemployed citizen is working." The city tried to make good on this undertaking. Council eventually obtained from the provincial legislature confirmation of its right to license non-resident workers, and, as late as 1938, activity was halted at a major make-work project until the contractor agreed to give preference in hiring to city labour. While outsiders doubtlessly were able to get jobs in Charlottetown at times, the intention of the city government was clearly to limit such occurrences. Any non-resident seeking work or welfare was encouraged to leave.[8] Targets of these efforts included residents of the surrounding country districts as well as Island-born American citizens returning to their birthplace.

Concern about joblessness provoked Charlottetown's unemployed workers to create the Unemployed Workers' Association in May 1932. At its organizational meeting, 137 unemployed or marginally employed workers signed the register. As a display of community solidarity, the association's constitution declared it to be non-partisan and non-sectarian and provided for the Lieutenant Governor, the Mayor, the Premier, the Rector of St. Dunstan's Basilica, the Pastor of Trinity United Church and the President of the Labourers' Protective Union to be advisors. The association was dedicated to the provision of winter employment, payment of a minimum wage of 30¢ an hour for those labouring on make-work projects, and the operation of an unemployment office that was funded by the city and headed by managers who held their position for only a month at a time. After asserting that they were not asking for charity, the men voiced fears about out-of-town labour flooding the job market and taking work from residents and complained about the uneven distribution of employment and relief. Significantly, they adopted the view that, to date, federal-provincial unemployment relief funds had hindered rather than helped the jobless, and such funds should be used to pay a living wage to the unemployed and to provide direct relief for those unable to secure work.

Initially, this collaborative approach worked. At a meeting in June 1932, speakers included a provincial cabinet minister, two MLAs, a City Councillor and the secretary of the LPU. In turn, the association suggested that a committee, preferably of clergymen, be appointed by the government to deal with the unemployment situation expected the following winter. There seem to have been no hard feelings arising from the city's decision to eject the association from its office near the entrance to the market building because unemployed men milling about created congestion. Later in the fall at a meeting to reorganize the association, now with a membership of 600, a suggestion was made to drop "unemployed" from its name. This proposal was rejected, possibly to avoid a perception that the unemployed workers were in competition with the LPU. The association's mandate was to secure relief and work for the jobless, and any intention "to run counter to any other organization" was renounced. The LPU, for its part, promised to help the association in any way possible. At a subsequent meeting, local merchants were thanked for donating furniture for an office to be maintained by the association, which announced plans to organize a benefit show and hockey games to raise funds for the needy. Clearly organizers had no intention of stirring up dissent.

Cracks appeared in this alliance, but it never broke completely apart. The meeting in mid-October 1932 was not attended by any official representative of City Council, and the city and province had begun to feud over the extent of their respective contributions to relief. Various Councillors were also at odds over the subject. In November, a mass meeting of the unemployed held at the Strand Theatre attracted only a few clergymen

8 In 1936 the city paid the province $150 for its help in deporting the Culpeck family.

or members of the city's relief committee. One complaint aired there was about the stingy level of relief being offered. Mayor W. S. Stewart and his Council were suspected of allowing concerns about the city's finances to stand in the way of meeting the needs of the unemployed. This prompted a suggestion that a labour candidate should be fielded in the next civic election. Nine months later, another meeting of jobless men threatened to get out of control when some participants called for a march and others demanded a "rough demonstration." In the end, committees were appointed to investigate the administration of welfare. Even as unemployment increased, Charlottetown's jobless remained orderly overall. This was acknowledged by Norman McLeod Rogers, Minister of Labour, who stated in the House of Commons that Charlottetown's unemployed did not occupy the post office or other public buildings as had occurred elsewhere. Compared to Vancouver, Charlottetown was "a sensible community."

The Second World War solved the problem of joblessness for Charlottetown as it did in the rest of Canada. With the end of the war, however, the threat of unemployment returned with the demobilized soldiers. City Council made sure that the onus of responding to the challenge of supporting those without work was not, once again, thrust upon the city. Determined there would be no repetition of the epic struggles of the 1930s, the municipality despatched delegations to both the provincial and federal governments to line up financial support if unemployment rose.

The stresses of managing welfare during the Depression inevitably had a serious impact on the workings of the city government. Even before the problem was acknowledged as catastrophic, its influences were being felt. Mayor Ira J. Yeo was fortunate to escape office well-regarded by the establishment and labour alike and unscathed by the effects of the economic downturn. His successor, T. W. L. Prowse, undertook a series of projects to generate jobs, including repairs to the breastworks at Victoria Park, a restoration of City Hall and construction of an annex to it. Prowse explained these undertakings were a means of honouring his election promise to help the unemployed. This rationale did not shelter him from criticism in the press for extravagance and losing control of the city's finances. Nevertheless, two Councillors who aspired to succeed Prowse promised to continue in the same vein.

Not everyone agreed. "Elector" in a letter to the *Patriot* demanded to know the extent of the city's debt and called for an independent audit of the city's books, a concern echoed by W. P. Doull, a City Councillor. "Caution" warned about the operations of the Water Commission and predicted "the city would be ruined" unless people paid more attention to it. W. S. Stewart, a retired county court judge and frequent commentator on current events, complained in a series of letters to the press about the rapid increase in civic debt. This was accompanied by raised assessments, which, he charged, were not equitably imposed. Increases were due, in part, to costs resulting from sloppy administration of the make-work projects. As an example, he cited a sweetheart deal between the city and the executors of the Cundall estate involving work along the shoreline by the Cundall Home.[9]

9 His accusations were later shown to be wide of the mark.

Although Stewart had initially claimed his interest in civic affairs did not reflect any political ambitions on his part, he had soon changed his mind and decided to run for mayor in the upcoming election. His campaign focused on his accusations concerning waste and inefficiency, and he promised that he would discontinue street work until financial "credit" was re-established. This would be accomplished by putting adequate sinking funds in place to repay the city's debt. Stewart perceived a resentment of him as an outsider by sitting Councillors and responded by calling for the injection of new life into a "closed corporation." Although civic finances and assessments were not the only issues in the election — Councillor B. Roy Holman raised the matter of a low-cost contract with Maritime Electric — the electorate were overwhelmingly impressed with Stewart's arguments. He won handily with 1,265 votes over Councillors Blanchard and Foster with 850 and 442 votes respectively. Even the *Guardian*, which was not well disposed to Stewart, admitted that he had captured the public's mood. Events and personality combined to make his mayoralty worthy of detailed examination.

Mayor W.S. Stewart

Mayor Samuel Kennedy

Once in office, Stewart failed to make good on his promises. He did cut back on relief payments, but the money that was expended was not used to best advantage when poor communications with the province, which was also providing support, resulted in duplication of aid to some welfare recipients. Stewart also unsuccessfully opposed a decision of the Finance Committee to have an independent audit of the city's accounts. When the auditor, Donald S. Hart of Halifax, submitted his report, Stewart trivialized the findings, even though they agreed with his contention that the debt was growing and the city should cease to finance public works with borrowed money. The audit similarly confirmed the need for beefed-up sinking funds. Rather than feeling vindicated by these results, Stewart seemed to resent having to pay the auditor for his work. The mayor found little new in the observation that taxes raised for capital projects should not be used as general revenue, although he did approve of the suggestion to establish debenture and coupon

The 1928-30 City Council contained three future Mayors. In the centre is City Clerk G.P. Nicholson.

registers. The Finance Committee itself largely ignored a recommendation to adopt modern methods of municipal accounting. Overall, Stewart dubbed the report "useless." In a commentary destined to become ironic, he praised the financial management of City Clerk George P. Nicholson. Referring to him as "a valuable City asset," Stewart wrote in his annual report that there was neither a hint nor a suggestion "that there was anything wrong or inaccurate with the accounts." Now safely in office, the mayor saw Charlottetown's debt grow during his term and, in due course, a range of relief measures were instituted.

If Mayor Stewart lacked consistency in his pursuit of fiscal discipline, he was unfortunately more constant in provoking opposition. His early reservations about relief alienated the Unemployed Workers' Association and some of Charlottetown's clergy. His proposal to have a City Manager was interpreted as an attack upon the City Engineer and the finance and property committees, and other administrative changes he suggested were characterized as attempts to get rid of opponents and install his own supporters. A somewhat bizarre speech to the Rotary Club — one that made him appear to advocate Maritime Union — added to his growing reputation as a loose cannon. He was blunt and confrontational in debate and derisive of dissenting opinions. Relations with other members of Council deteriorated, most notably with John F. Whear. A stormy confrontation with Whear at the last meeting of Council prior to the municipal election of 1934 resulted in Mayor Stewart abruptly declaring an end to proceedings. He stormed out of the chamber, but without a proper adjournment, and the meeting continued with Councillor Samuel Kennedy in the chair. This development was welcomed by other Councillors with comments of "let's see how you fit" and "you might as well take it now as later" amidst much laughter.

The jokes were pointed. In the ensuing election, Kennedy opposed Stewart's bid for re-election. The incumbent renewed his alarms about overspending and promised to balance the budget "soon." He complained his policies to correct the situation had been blocked by opposition on Council and hoped that fresh candidates for Council would step forward to support him. Stewart described himself as an advocate of fair assessment and the friend of the working man. In portraying himself as someone who would not mindlessly boast about his city, he promised not to shirk his responsibility to identify problems and tackle them. For his part, Kennedy charged that Stewart never had a clear policy to cure the ills he had diagnosed and argued Council could not obstruct what did not exist. Administratively, it was not the time to rock the civic boat. He offered a stand-pat approach to government and promised co-operation and economy in the conduct of civic affairs. Kennedy believed that Charlottetown was coping quite well when compared with other centres. Newspaper reports noted that Charlottetown had the seventh-lowest funded debt out of 54 Canadian cities, and the lowest accumulated tax arrears per capita of any Canadian city. "I stand as a booster for the city not a knocker," he proclaimed at a public all-candidates meeting, "that should be the attitude of every citizen especially its governing officials."

Clearly the audience shared these sentiments. When Stewart kept bobbing up to confront accusations hurled at him by others, he was booed and told to sit down. This anticipated the decision of the electorate. In a vote conducted in a severe storm, Stewart went down to defeat by Kennedy 471 to 790. The low turn-out may have reflected the smaller electoral list as well as the weather because loss of the franchise due to unpaid taxes had reduced the number of qualified voters to 1,932 from 2,564. Even so, such a result cannot be interpreted as anything but a repudiation of the person if not his policies. Both newspapers suggested that Stewart's defeat partly arose from the belief that the honours should be passed around, a view Kennedy summed up himself when he quipped "one term as Mayor should be sufficient for any man." In any case, the transaction of business at City Hall returned to its accustomed manner, but the question of Charlottetown's accounting practices was soon to reappear.

Throughout the city's history, Charlottetonians had preferred to keep tax rates low. In a community with little industry, the burden of taxes fell upon property-owners and merchants, the same people who wielded the most influence politically. At the same time, the city traditionally was prepared to carry a little more debt than was typical for other cities in the Maritimes. Faced with the Depression, a strategy of borrowing the money to fight its effects was most suitable for large Central Canadian cities which had the hope of taxing industry once the economy revived. There would be no such salvation for Charlottetown's taxpayers, a fact of which they were fully aware when they faced the choice of paying now or borrowing now and paying later. In response, they opted for the middle course — a bit of both.

Tax rates increased by one-quarter of a per cent in 1936, and the civic debt moved upwards at an average year-over-year rate of 4.4 per cent between 1930 and 1937. In the same period, expenditures had grown at an average rate of 4.7 per cent from year to year in a pattern marked by wild fluctuations. Another perspective can be gained by comparing Charlottetown's expenditures in 1930 over 1929, a substantial 12.1 per cent increase, and then comparing the outflow in the succeeding seven years with the 1930 base. In 1931, 1935 and 1936, spending actually decreased, but substantial increases were made in the other years giving an overall increase for the period of 21.4 per cent. At the same time, the year-over-year increase in real estate values ran at 1.7 per cent, although the pace of change varied greatly. Personal property values in the same period actually went down in three of the seven years but posted an overall year-over-year average gain of .04 per cent. An examination of assessed real estate and personal property values shows Charlottetonians were modestly richer in 1937 than in 1930. Real estate posted a 7 per cent increase in 1930 over 1929 and then gained another 12.3 per cent over the years 1930–37. Personal property values did not match these advances. They increased 27 per cent in 1930 over 1929, but then registered gains averaging 3.1 per cent until 1937, with the poorest showing coming in 1937, when personal property was assessed at only 0.1 per cent above 1930 levels. Clearly, expenditures were rising in the years between 1930 and 1937 faster than the tax base. For some rate-payers, the burden was unsustainable, and the list of defaulters grew.[10] The concern about the city's rising debt and its ability to repay it was quite understandable.

When a new Council was elected in February 1938, the city debt exceeded $2 million or $150 per capita. The Mayor warned that the rate of indebtedness could not continue as it had for the last four years. The finance committee chaired by Councillor R. C. Chandler resolved to reverse the trend by planning a balanced budget, and to that end a tax increase of .25 per cent was imposed. City Clerk Nicholson was asked to prepare detailed monthly statements of revenues and expenses for the coming year and to gather similar accounts for 1937. The committee hoped that comparing past spending to current trends would help control costs. At the end of December, they seemed to have their objective within reach. To complete their annual report for the city's full fiscal year ending on January 15, 1939, they asked Nicholson to provide them with anticipated expenses for the two-week period in the new calendar year. Anticipated revenue based upon the previous year was added to income with the result that a modest surplus seemed probable. To verify their findings, the committee asked the city's banker to provide statements of all of its accounts. When these were

10 Between 1931 and 1933, the amount of back taxes owed by Charlottetonians to the city rose 149 per cent.

returned, they bore little resemblance to the statements provided by the Clerk. When asked about the discrepancy, the Clerk suggested that moneys were deposited into the wrong accounts. He would review the books and explain the differences the next day. The following day, the Clerk was nowhere to be seen at City Hall; he was home sick. After a few days' absence, Councillor Chandler was summoned to Nicholson's home and informed by him that earlier statements had been incorrect. There was a $33,439 deficit, including $27,000 in tax arrears.

The surprised and alarmed committee decided, with Nicholson's approval, to commission a special audit of the city's accounts. The ensuing report by D. F. Archibald and W. A. Morrell revealed grave irregularities, some of which had been foretold in the Hart report of 1932. There were at least 20 deficiencies in the city's finances, including forged endorsements on vouchers and paid cheques, debenture issues from which the city received no revenue, and hidden income and overstated account balances. W. S. Stewart had died on February 11, 1938, and was thus unable to learn that he had been right about assessments and unfunded debt. Assessment books were a mess, but the auditors found reductions had been handed out arbitrarily and in some cases illegally. Unauthorized tax breaks amounted to $10,778 in the period 1934–39. As for the sinking funds, they were considerably short of the amount needed to retire the principal of the city's loans, perhaps in part because some of the revenue from their investments had been siphoned off to cover annual interest payments. Stewart would have been less gratified by Archibald and Morrell's conclusion that failure to act upon the Hart report cost the city thousands of dollars. As for the overall effect of the misappropriation of city funds, the juggling of accounts and neglect and falsification of records, the city was short $69,436 (equivalent to $1,056,158 in 2008). In the words of the auditors, "During the investigation we have found more types of fraud than we have ever seen or heard of in one office ...."

The fall-out from the special audit was immediate. Nicholson was summarily fired. The Institute of Chartered Accountants of Prince Edward Island revoked his membership for unbecoming conduct.[11] Steps were taken to collect the surety bond maintained for the City Clerk, and the auditors' report was turned over to the provincial attorney general for review. Nicholson, who was still ill at home, was examined by a medical specialist to determine his fitness to stand trial for the financial irregularities. The city advertised for a new City Clerk and a City Accountant. Calls resurfaced in the press for the appointment of a city manager. Some of the interest that might have been generated by this scandal was deflected by the excitement surrounding the visit of King George and Queen Elizabeth, followed by the celebrations of the 75th anniversary of the Charlottetown Conference. A lively exchange of opinions did, however, occur in the newspapers.

As it turns out, there was considerable sympathy for Nicholson. John Anderson, a correspondent writing to the *Patriot*, characterized him as a war veteran and "a nervous wreck" who had been ill for 4½ years, was subject to bouts of insomnia, and who

11 Nicholson was well-respected and one of the charter members of the Institute.

worked night and day including Sundays. When his errors were discovered, his wife signed over her life savings of $6,367 to help repay the losses. Others felt that some of the blame lay with the politicians who oversaw finances. They were portrayed as either lacking the capacity to manage the city's finances or willing to allow such irregularities to occur. "Taxpayer" wrote to the *Guardian* and urged that Nicholson not be condemned too readily. He offered a possible explanation for the discrepancies in revenue from the sale of debentures and suggested that instead of being a goat, the Clerk might be "a kid among the goats." Gradually suspicion of Nicholson abated. One writer concluded that city officials seemed not to have profited from their misdemeanours. "Taxpayer" pointedly asked about the cause of the "underlying secret division" in the city government during W. S. Stewart's term and, in particular, the identities of those who demanded the 1932 audit and those who opposed it. Attention came to rest on the non-collection of taxes and under-assessment of certain taxpayers. The conventional wisdom eventually became that Nicholson was inept but well-intentioned and not corrupt. "Taxpayer" had the final word on the matter. The City Clerk's insistent approval of the special audit, he wrote, was "conclusive proof that his conscience was clear ... of any wilful wrongdoing."

As part of their audit, Archibald and Morrell took steps to collect back taxes. The city then proposed a review board to adjudicate appeals, a move that sparked considerable opposition from some citizens. Various other improvements were made to the administration of the city's finances. The accounting system was revised; proper control accounts were instituted; a bond register and arrears ledger were opened; cancelled cheques, redeemed debentures, paid dividend coupons, vouchers and other financial papers were filed; and an easily audited system of purchase orders was set up. The intent was to distribute responsibility to make dishonest practices more difficult. A new City Clerk and City Accountant, both existing civic employees, were appointed, and a chartered accountant was named as an external auditor. "Taxpayers," the *Guardian* opined, "will breathe more freely and sleep more soundly than they have done for months." By then, Charlottetonians had other matters to keep them awake at nights, and these concerns tended to overshadow the ebb and flow of battle in the civic political arena.

URBAN LANDSCAPE

The economic reversals of the era after the First World War might have been expected to have had a dampening effect upon the transformation of Charlottetown's urban landscape. To a certain degree that may have been the case, but the period 1921–45 is also marked by significant additions to the city's skyline and to its geographical expanse. Old factors, such as fire and limited city budgets, remained significant influences on the process of shaping the city, but new ones emerged, including the isolation of the workplace from the home and the broadening scope of the tourism industry. The Victorian eclecticism of land use began to give way to zones dedicated to single activities.

Public Buildings

Nowhere were these changes more apparent than in the construction of the city's first public library. The Dodd and Legislative Library, which had served the city's needs for two decades, was outgrowing its quarters in the Provincial Building. In 1927 there was some thought of moving it to the Market Building. Nothing came of the idea, but the next year everything changed. Part of the agreement between the province and the Dodd trustees envisaged establishing a separate public library if the funds could be raised. In 1927, following the death of Mrs. Robert Harris, her heirs announced a $20,000 bequest from the estate for the creation of a library and art gallery. The original idea saw the facility near the Harris family home in Brighton, but a widespread preference amongst the public for a central location resolved the matter in favour of a site at the north end of Market Square.

Charlottetown would finally have a purpose-built library located in the precinct housing most of the city's principal institutions. The decision had the additional advantages of placing the library on publicly owned property, thereby avoiding the purchase of land and reducing future operating costs by connections to the market's heating plant. To complete the financing, the city contributed $10,000 to the project, an amount matched by the province. Work began promptly. Designed by James Harris, a nephew of W. C. Harris, the solid, if not majestic-looking, brick building with some ornamentation over the front entrance lacked the flair that characterized his uncle's

Designed by James Harris, a nephew of W.C. Harris, the Harris Memorial Art and Library Building opened on February 6, 1931. This photo was taken in 1958.

Erected adjacent to Government House in 1918 to serve as a convalescent hospital, the Rena McLean Memorial Hospital was later used as a technical school. It may not have been well-built, if the decided backward lean seen in this photo is any indication, and was demolished in 1925.

architecture. But it did provide a second-floor gallery space for his more famous uncle Robert's art. The library occupied the main floor, and the basement was set aside for a museum of "local antiquities." The collection and staff of the Dodd and Legislative Library transferred to the new Harris Memorial Art and Library Building in time for an opening on February 6, 1930.

Other major construction projects involved the city's hospitals. A blaze that damaged the Charlottetown Hospital in 1920 led to the erection of a new building on the existing site. Designed by architects Chappell and Hunter in an eclectic, faintly Italianate style, the buff-coloured building featured a central façade with twin, two-storey columns flanking the main entrance. A domed tower surmounted the façade. The architecture was far from contemporary, but when the 80-bed building opened in August 1925, it provided the city with modern treatment and recovery facilities.

The old, wooden, fire-damaged building was not lost from service. In a Herculean engineering feat, the structure was severed into three 120-foot sections, each of which was rotated and then hauled over greased railway ties to a new site opposite Pownal Square. Reconnected and positioned on new foundations, the building was used as a temporary hospital until its replacement was complete. After that, it became the Sacred Heart Home for the aged and infirm. This was not the only example of relocation of hospital buildings. The Rena McLean Memorial Hospital, erected adjacent to Government House in 1918 to serve convalescing soldiers, was subsequently used as an agriculture and trade school, but was abandoned and demolished in 1925. The nurses' residence that had been associated with it was divided into two and hauled to Brighton Road to become private homes.

While all this was happening, the trustees of the Prince Edward Island Hospital were struggling with overcrowding at their building on Longworth Avenue. Plans were eventually laid to erect a new hospital on six acres severed from the Government House grounds facing Brighton Road. Although preparations for the project were begun in 1930 during challenging economic circumstances, a fund-raising campaign secured $200,000 in cash and pledges. Nevertheless, financing was tight, so the building's design was functional — boxy with little adornment. Construction began in 1932, and the new hospital was opened on July 4, 1933. With a capacity of 104 beds, it was initially deemed by many to be too large, although at least one observer praised the planners as being "ten years ahead of your time." It joined another newly built medical facility, the Provincial Sanatorium on McGill Avenue, which opened in June 1931. Designed by E. S. Blanchard, it featured large verandahs on its west side.

On December 14, 1931, fire struck the venerable Falconwood Hospital for the Insane. Nine people died, and although the building was not completely destroyed, extensive reconstruction was needed. Patients were temporarily housed in the old PEI Hospital. A restoration design, produced by a Halifax architect, C. A. Fowler, called for the repair of the east wing and construction of two other wings, along with two convalescent homes, a doctor's residence and a central heating and power plant. The buildings were steel-framed and brick with stone trim in construction. Work proceeded in 1933–34 with the province bearing the costs. The result was a modern, fire-resistant facility capable of providing state-of-the-art treatments, such as hydrotherapy.

Prince of Wales College with the addition financed by Sir William C. Macdonald in 1907...

... and just after the fire that destroyed it in February, 1932.

Fire also intervened at Prince of Wales College on February 6, 1932. The substantial stone and brick building was gutted, and college authorities were faced with the task of erecting an entirely new school. The Toronto architectural firm of Marani, Lawson and Morris drafted plans for a handsome, expansive replacement. The brick with stone trim design reflected contemporary taste in educational buildings but was hailed as retaining "the atmosphere of colonial days." By the time the institution reopened on February 16, 1933, the expenditures involved had become a matter of widespread comment and some political cost to the ruling provincial Conservatives. Construction in 1944 of a vocational school at the corner of Grafton and Cumberland Streets was less controversial, although the loss of the site of PWC's outdoor hockey rink caused consternation in some quarters. PWC's cross-town rival, St. Dunstan's, avoided any charge of extravagance when it opened a new science building in 1940. The small, three-storey brick structure, erected according to a frugal design by James Harris, was financed by the priests of the Roman Catholic diocese and their parishioners. The opening of the new building realized a steadfast ambition of college officials to strengthen their institution's commitment to science.

There was less construction for the junior levels of education. Annexes were added to West Kent and Prince Street Schools in 1920, and an addition was built onto Queen Square School in 1930. Similarly, the feverish rate of church construction that played such a prominent role in altering the face of the city in the previous period abated after 1920. One new church, the Roman Catholic parish of Holy Redeemer, was established to serve the city's west end following the arrival of the Redemptorist Fathers in 1929. Built at the corner of Upper Queen and Bayfield Street, the unprepossessing design

The new Prince of Wales College building opened just a year after the destruction of its predecessor.

of the low-slung structure surmounted by a stubby bell tower was faintly reminiscent of Spanish mission churches in the southwestern United States.

A long-standing need in another area of activity was filled on December 9, 1930, when the Charlottetown Forum opened for business.[12] Until that time, winter sports were played on natural ice frequently plagued with surface defects and constantly vulnerable to fickle weather conditions. The new arena, along with only two others in the Maritimes, had artificial ice. Promoters boasted it was one of the finest rinks on the continent. Located on Fitzroy Street, the new "ice palace" had an arching façade with art deco ornamentation and towering windows. Although the Forum, with a capacity of around 3,000 people, did not rival another Depression-era project, Maple Leaf Gardens, in size or fame, its impact upon sport and entertainment in its own locale was just as profound. For decades to come, the Forum was the scene of memorable hockey battles, colourful ice shows and other spectacles.

Commercial Developments

As might be expected during times of economic uncertainty, there were few remarkable changes to Charlottetown's commercial building stock in the interwar period. Early on, the Bank of Nova Scotia opened new premises at the corner of Grafton and Great George Streets (now University Avenue) to replace its old quarters at the corner of Richmond and Great George. Designed by Sharp and Horner, architects, of Toronto, this addition to a long-established streetscape was intended to harmonize with its surroundings. The façade facing Grafton Street was buff-coloured brick and stone with imposing columns. Large windows with rounded tops lined the Great George

12 The opening performance was by a Toronto-based group called Mardi Gras Abandon. News reports suggested that the performers experienced some difficulty with the new ice surface.

Street side. Construction began in 1921 and was completed the following spring. A new Metropolitan Store appeared in 1936, and the Tweel Block was expanded at about the same time.

One of the most significant changes to the commercial life of the city came after a dramatic fire on January 12, 1929, destroyed the Victoria Hotel on Water Street. Losing its largest hostelry exacerbated Charlottetown's chronic shortage of visitor accommodations. In the wake of the disaster, all eyes immediately turned towards the Canadian National Railways, owner of the PEI Railway and a large chain of hotels, including the soon-to-be-opened Nova Scotian in Halifax. The Board of Trade called upon the railway to build a new hotel in the vicinity of Charlottetown, and a delegation was sent to Montreal to present the case to Sir Henry Thornton, the railway's president. Beyond the obvious need for rooms, the delegation emphasized the rise in the tourist trade and the stated desire of the central and western provinces to help the economically besieged Maritimes in a substantial way. Thornton responded well to the submission.

The following June, six railway representatives visited the city to examine six possible building sites. Much to the delight of the board and Charlottetonians generally, the railway announced on July 2 that a new hotel would be built on the Knights of Columbus grounds on Kent Street, just a few steps from City Hall. The new building was larger than expected and luxurious in design. Architects John Schofield and G. F. Drummond drew up a five-storey Georgian-Revival style building combining the conveniences of a "modern hotel in a large city" with the atmosphere "one would

The new Bank of Nova Scotia premises was one of the few major additions to Charlottetown's commercial building stock in the interwar years.

expect to find in a city with the old-world charm of Charlottetown." On April 14, 1931, less than a year after the contracts were issued, the new hotel was officially opened. The Canadian National Hotel, as it was called, was more than a hotel for Charlottetonians; it was the realization of a long-sought dream.[13] Its opening, glowed the *Guardian*, "marks the beginning of a new era socially in the history of the province." The new hotel was "evidence of the farsightedness and confident courage of the leaders of the general community in the development of the Province along its most attractive and remunerative lines, vis: that of a tourists' playground and a natural health resort."

Residential Housing

Before the First World War, most of the available housing space within the old city boundaries had been occupied, and construction was spreading well north of Euston Street and Brighton Road. With the return of peace, house-building resumed in these areas. New subdivisions also opened up outside the city limits along the St. Peter's and Kensington Roads. In parts of the older areas, the quality of some of the housing stock was eroding, and more people were crowding into the available spaces. The deterioration of some houses led to their demolition in 1929 by order of the Board of Health. There were exceptions to this pattern, of course. George DeBlois, for instance, erected a substantial two-storey Georgian-style home on West Street in 1940 after stepping down as the province's Lieutenant Governor. Overall, though, the city experienced a lack of decent, affordable housing. The shortages were exposed with the return of soldiers following the war and were compounded by the ongoing migration of rural residents to the city. The postwar economic downturn and the Depression of the 1930s merely increased and entrenched the problem.

City Council looked to the Federal Housing Plan of 1919 as a way to fix the shortage of adequate housing. Under this program, cities, provincial governments and the Dominion government worked jointly to provide financial assistance to those intending to build single-family houses. Numerous Charlottetonians expressed an interest in the subsidy, and Council repeatedly urged the province to join with them and the national government to access the federal assistance, but the province steadfastly refused. In 1923 Mayor R. H. Jenkins estimated that over $400,000 could be made available to citizens of Charlottetown, but likely none of this money would be forthcoming. Eventually, some funds were provided, and by the end of 1923, $15,000 was available. With $12,500 of this, five dwellings were built. By 1927 approximately $50,000 had been disbursed, and a total of 19 units were constructed under the Federal Housing Plan.

The key to this limited success was the Charlottetown Housing Commission appointed in 1922. Nominated by City Council, three commissioners, Henry Craswell, John McKenna and John Henderson, were assigned to work with officials from the

13 The name was changed to "The Charlottetown" in 1939.

federal housing plan and to regulate other new house construction.[14] This early effort to create more and better housing ended on a sour note when the commissioners sued the city for compensation as provided under the plan.[15] New commissioners were appointed in June 1927 on an unpaid basis, but shortly thereafter the city's participation in the plan came to an end.

While the houses built with federal and provincial aid alleviated the housing shortage to a certain extent, they did not change the problem fundamentally, and the impact of the Depression worsened the overcrowding, high rents, poor maintenance and improper sanitation that characterized the worst of the city's housing stock. A report prepared by the Health Officer, Dr. Creelman, in 1931 detailed slum housing of the worst kind. A series of six houses on Rochford Street, for instance, were in bad repair and without sewer connections. Residents threw their garbage into cellars that were no more than pits. The sanitary conditions were "deplorable," and, in Creelman's opinion, the houses should be closed. At the corner of Union and Sydney Streets, four families used one privy — "a menace to the neighbourhood" — while two families shared a house at the corner of Cumberland and Sydney Streets which was "beyond saving." Such pockets of degraded housing not only blighted the urban landscape but fostered social problems and harboured disease.

Parks

As the most prominent green space in the city, Queen Square had passed its prime by the 1920s, but its significance in the consciousness of the public remained undiminished. Almost inevitably, it figured in discussions concerning a cenotaph to commemorate the fallen of the First World War. Immediately after the conflict, various options were considered as an appropriate memorial, including a trans-provincial highway and a clubhouse or home for veterans. An early proposal came from Milton MacLeod of Charlottetown who wrote to the *Guardian* on November 15, 1918, urging that two "Hun" cannon be obtained for display on Queen Square. When Prince Edward visited the city in 1919, a temporary cenotaph was erected in Market Square and a ceremonial arch raised before the entrance to Province House. This focused public interest on a permanent monument. More functional tributes, it was feared, would see their commemorative meaning fade with the passage of time. "People lose interest in anything," the *Patriot* commented, "even the war." Funds continued to be raised by private citizens for a memorial, and, at the beginning of 1922, the Board of Trade called upon the provincial government to erect a cenotaph in Charlottetown at a cost of no more than $15,000. Plans finally moved forward after Council created a special committee to develop a specific proposal. It was to be erected on Queen Square at the head of Upper Great George Street. George W. Hill of Montreal was awarded the commission, with a budget of $16,000. After its unveiling on

14 John McKenna was later succeeded by Peter McQuaid.

15 Council agreed to pay them a combined total of $400.

"The Soldiers"

July 1, 1925, the bronze memorial — "The Soldiers" — quickly became one of the most cherished landmarks in the city.

As Charlottetown grew and density of land use increased, so, too, did the significance of Victoria Park and the adjoining Government House grounds as the city's largest green space. At times, the importance of the park as a civic asset seems to have been overlooked, such as in 1922, when Council proposed turning a strip of land along Brighton Road into residential building lots. The bandstand became so deteriorated the City Engineer condemned it in 1927. Automobiles, which were generally banned from the park, became such a problem that Council had to appeal to the Lieutenant Governor to exclude them from all roads except the one running across the park from just west of the armouries to the Brighton Road. This ban continued until 1932 when cars were also permitted on the waterfront roadway — at a 12 mph speed limit. A by-law change in 1937 removed the speed limit but retained the ban for all roads except this route and the north-south cross thoroughfare.

For the most part, there was a sustained effort to maintain the park's facilities and improve the quality of the setting. In 1925 a new baseball diamond was built, and in 1929 Council approved an expansion to the girl's bath house on the southern waterfront. Improvements were made to the bath houses in 1936, and in 1942 Council considered installing new ones at the western end of the park where the shallow water made the area safe for small children. The city's girl guides were permitted to start a wildflower sanctuary in 1939, and, by 1943, the Knights of Columbus were providing recreational facilities for the city's youth. Government Pond was the target of various measures to prevent it from flooding, reduce its pollution and make it better for winter ice-skating. Trees and shrubs were planted around the pond and lights and fences were installed. In 1936 the stone retaining walls were reconstructed and Black Sam's Bridge joining Euston Street and Brighton Road had its abutments extended. Attempts were made to have the federal government restore the battery at Prince Edward Battery and either repair or remove the two 36-pounder cannons located there. This took some time, but finally yielded results in 1938 when the site was improved and turned over to the city.

Electric car in Victoria Park, c. 1905. When this was one of the few automobiles on the entire Island, banning or regulating their access to the Park was not an issue.

The principal concern was the breastwork facing the harbour. By 1930 Council was receiving complaints about the state of the park's shoreline. The railing around the perimeter had deteriorated and was in need of repair, but when the work was tendered, the bids were all too high. Council decided, instead, to have the work done by day labour. In 1931 Council agreed to pay two-thirds of the cost for breastworks

Government Pond c. 1930. This postcard image was taken before the work on the pond and Black Sam's Bridge was done.

in front of the former Cundall house, with the Cundall estate paying the balance. These improvements soon became part of the city's job creation strategy during the Depression. When Councillor B. Roy Holman found that the employment costs of such work were chargeable to the federal government's unemployment relief fund, the rehabilitation and repair of the Victoria Park shoreline became an ongoing endeavour. Work had begun on the breastwork, when high tides in November 1934 washed away part of some recently completed sections, underscoring the importance of sturdy retaining walls. In succeeding years, as reconstruction of the breastworks continued, the road ringing the park was improved as well. Repairs began in 1933, and in 1937 the roadway was paved with asphalt. Further grading of the roadsides and median was completed in 1938, and in 1942 the lighting was renewed. Not only had the Victoria Park roadway become a source of employment for the city's jobless, but it ultimately evolved into a pleasantly landscaped scenic drive that was featured in tourist promotions.

Streets and Sidewalks

The return of "normalcy" foreshadowed a renewal of the perennial battle to improve roads and walkways. There was good reason. Well-paved streets facilitated commerce, both within the city and between the city and countryside. Increasingly, horse-drawn transportation was being displaced by motor-powered vehicles. Greater speeds and complex mechanisms demanded smoother road surfaces. Macadamized and clay surfaces were unable to match the performance of asphalt. The city consequently acquired an asphalt plant, erecting it on Pownal Wharf. The apparent extravagance of the investment was offset by the savings of acquiring construction materials at cost. The outside contractor also used local labour instead of bringing workers from away. In commending Mayor Wright and his Council, the *Guardian* noted, "These supplies were not purchased in a haphazard way; they were purchased as cheaply here as they could have been elsewhere and whatever benefits accrued from them came to the merchants and the city."

The strongest impetus for an ambitious plan to lay asphalt streets came from a federal postwar reconstruction program, the Canada Highways Act. Under its provisions, 40 per cent of the cost of provincial highway construction was to be provided by the federal government. To turn this program to the city's advantage, in 1923 Council transferred to the provincial government jurisdiction for roads connecting provincial highways to the railway depot, the wharves and other shipping points. Mayor R. H. Jenkins and Councillor Rattray also secured from federal authorities an immediate grant of $34,617 for road construction and a promise of further payments to come. By 1929, in the opinion of Mayor I. J. Yeo, Charlottetown had become "a modern City through the construction of permanent pavements, the extension of street surface drainage to all parts of the City, the practical elimination of wooden sidewalks and their substitution by concrete, the gravelling and betterment of secondary streets ...." To this list he added street-cleaning apparatus and motorized snow ploughs.

Much changed with the Depression. The importance of road construction to local workers had long been recognized. As early as 1920, the Board of Trade noted that "the building of the streets will mean the employment of a great many laboring men and therefor[e] very much improve labor conditions." The 1930s brought maintenance projects that were justified more for the work they provided than the smoother streets they produced. In 1934 Mayor Samuel Kennedy noted that money spent on roadwork would not have been disbursed directly to the unemployed "only as relief measures." As Percy W. Turner asserted in 1937, "it is far better to spend money for public works, and thus furnish the means for the worker to maintain his self respect, and earn the necessities of life by the sweat of his brow, rather than he should prostitute his manhood by accepting a mere pittance in order to keep body and soul together." Whatever the merits of this attitude, it was widely held in the community, and resulted in opening new streets and repairing the old. Sidewalks were also reconstructed, and, by the end of the 1930s, the shoulders of some main thoroughfares were being levelled and covered in concrete to create parking spaces. Those who were not required to preserve their manhood by working on the streets increasingly were riding about in automobiles on the fruit of this labour. Indeed, traffic control was becoming a challenge for the city. During the Second World War, road construction abated, and only necessary maintenance and repairs were undertaken, this being "the proper and patriotic course" in wartime. Further improvements would await the return of peace.

The Harbour

During the festivities to mark the 400th anniversary of the arrival of Jacques Cartier on Prince Edward Island, a large delegation of French mayors and officials led by Foreign Minister, and soon to be Prime Minister, Pierre Etienne Flandin, visited Charlottetown. Although they were hospitably received, the large ocean liner on which the delegation was travelling, the SS *Champlain*, was forced to anchor four miles outside the harbour.[16] This event underscored the shortcomings of the harbour and its facilities as a deepwater port. It was an old problem. Conditions were so bad at the railway wharf in 1926 that a member of the Board of Trade charged it was unsafe to berth a vessel there, and charter brokers knew the situation, thereby hindering trade in the port. The CNR subsequently repaired the wharf and frost-proofed its warehouse. The next year the federal Department of Public Works took over the property and was about to transfer it to the Department of Marine when fire destroyed the warehouse. Repairs to the wharf and warehouse were begun, but, with the election of the R. B. Bennett government in 1930, the pace of public works slowed. Some wharf maintenance continued, and plans to dredge the harbour were announced in 1934 prior to the upcoming federal election, though too late for the *Champlain*. Several years later, the city rebuilt Lord's Wharf, adjacent to Pownal Wharf. This improvement

16 When launched in 1932, the *Champlain*, at 28,124 gross tons, with a length of 641 feet (195 metres) and breadth of 82 feet (25 metres), was the largest, fastest and most luxurious passenger liner afloat.

"St. Dunstan's Cathedral Today Nothing But a Pile of Ruins," read the headline on March 8, 1913. As one newspaper reported, W.B. Prowse, a prominent Protestant, signed a cheque on behalf of Prowse Brothers for $5,000 "by the light of the still burning fire." The new cathedral, designed by J.M. Hunter, was finished in 1919.

Hon. James H. Peters
POND
Edward Bayfield
W. R. Watson
Mrs. Ralp Peake
Wm Welsh
OLD LINE BETW. ROYALTY &
SUPPOSED LINE OF CITY
George Lewis
Hon. James H. Peters
"SIDMOUNT"
James Mc Gill
Theo. Des Brisay
"SPRING PARK"
26 acres
Old Asylum
5TH
Hon. James
H. Peters
Hon. James H. Peters
Benj Heartz
Wm Weeks
Matthews
Allen
Admiral Bayfield
"BRIGHTON LODGE"
ADMIRAL ST.
GREEN ST.
Sir Robt. Hodgson
Geo. Peake
F. T. Newberry
Richard Heartz
Capt. Freeland
18 acres
James Des Brisay
George Davies
George Peake
Peake Bros.
Jno Ings
Jas. Currie
Hon. W. Sullivan
Henry Palmer
Geo. Bremner
W. Murray
Henry Palmer
VILLA ST.
"BRIGHTON VILLA"
George Davies
YORK LANE
Hon. W. W. Sullivan
F. W. Hyndman
Major Cropley
"WATERMERE"
F. W. Hyndman
Henry Palmer
VICTORIA BARRACKS
Brewery
C. A. Hyndman
Artemas Lord
Donl. Mc Kinnon
"BRIGHTON" Tannery
DAVIES ST.
NORTH RIVER RD.
BRIGHTON ST.
DOUGLAS
BAYFIELD
SPRING
CROSS ST.
LONG
EUSTON
FITZROY
ROCHFORD
POWNAL
ROCHFORD SQUARE
KENT
QUEEN
GOVERNMENT POND
GOVERNMENT PARK
Barns
GOVERNMENT HOUSE
Res. of T. Heath Haviland Lieut. Gov.
Drill Shed
Public School
WEST
WEST-END HOUSE
Jas Peake
S. Davies
J. H. Davies
PARADE GROND
PROPOSED LAKE
VICTORIA PARK
CRICKET GROUND
PT. EDWARD BATTERY
POWNAL SQU.
JAIL
HAVILAND ST.
DUNDAS ESPLANADE
Dauses Wf.
Connolleys Whf.
N. 17½°
CHARLOTTETOWN HARBOUR
RIVER
HORN
COMMON
4TH
3RD
2ND
1ST
St. James Ch.
Old Church

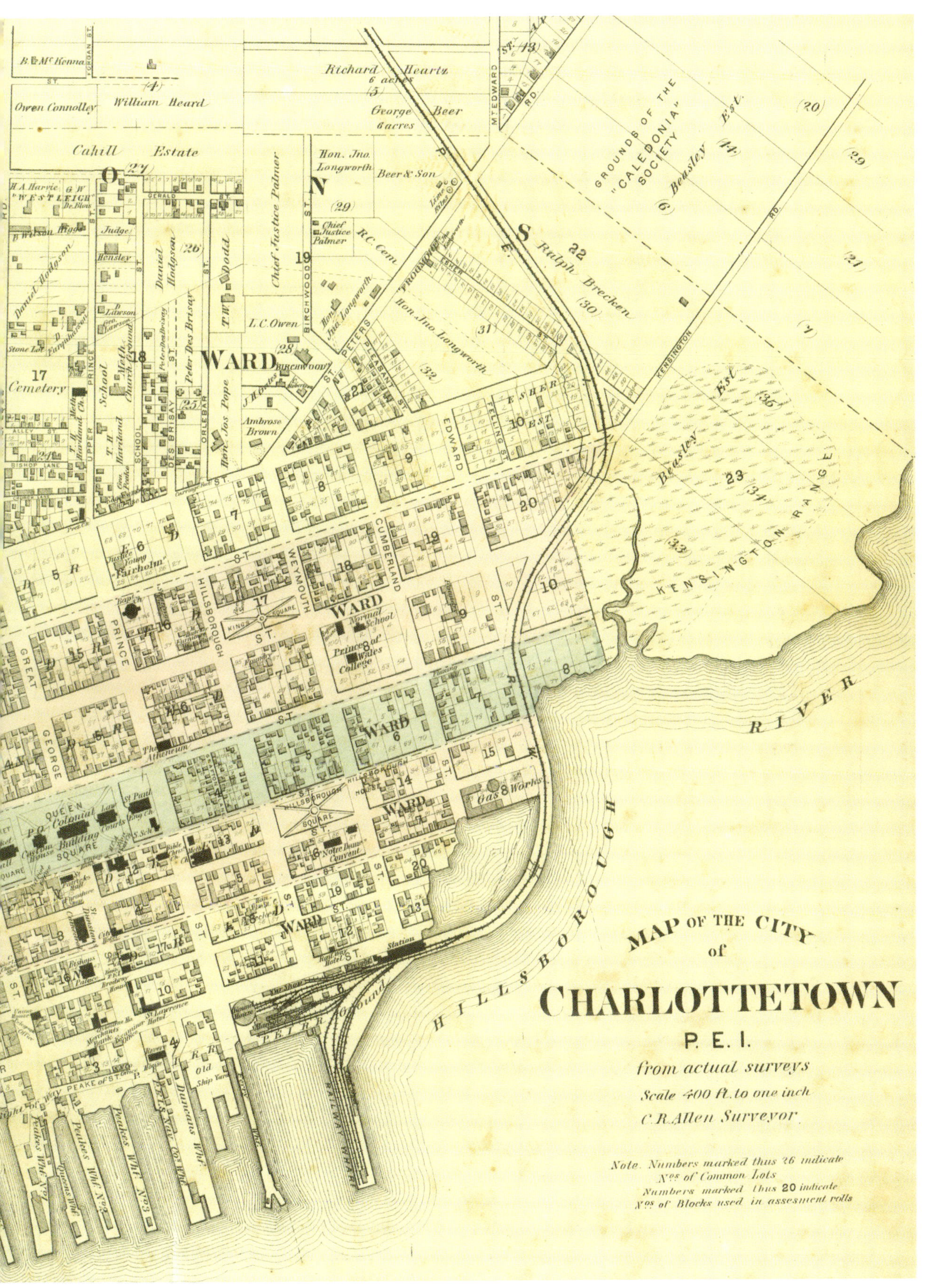
MAP OF THE CITY
of
CHARLOTTETOWN
P. E. I.
from actual surveys
Scale 400 ft. to one inch
C. R. Allen Surveyor.
Note. Numbers marked thus 26 indicate
Nos of Common Lots
Numbers marked thus 20 indicate
Nos of Blocks used in assesment rolls
HILLSBOROUGH
RIVER
KENSINGTON RANGE
GROUNDS OF THE "CALEDONIA" SOCIETY
Ralph Brecken
Hon. Jno. Longworth
Cahill Estate
William Heard
Owen Connolley
Richard Heartz
George Beer
Beer & Son
Chief Justice Palmer
Daniel Hodgson
Peter Des Brisay
Ambrose Brown
L. C. Owen
Cemetery
KINGS SQUARE
QUEEN SQUARE
HILLSBOROUGH SQUARE
Prince of Wales College
Normal School
Colonial Building
Atheneum
Gas Works
Station
Old Ship Yard
RAILWAY WHARF
GREAT GEORGE
PRINCE
WEYMOUTH
CUMBERLAND
EDWARD
HILLSBOROUGH
BIRCHWOOD ST.
KENSINGTON RD.
WARD

The toboggan run was one of the first features in Victoria Park.

The city found it difficult to maintain two band stands – one on Queen Square and the one pictured here. By 1927 it had become so deteriorated that the City Engineer condemned it.

The carriageway opened on May 24, 1897, Queen Victoria's Diamond Jubilee. The road was eventually extended in 1899 around Duchess Point to join Brighton Road.

Though pretty to look at, for many years Government Pond, at the entrance of Victoria Park, was used as an industrial waste and sewage outlet, and was considered more nuisance than attraction.

Architect E.S. "Bones" Blanchard's elevation for the Charlottetown Forum, which opened on December 9, 1930. At the time, it was one of only three rinks in the Maritimes that boasted artificial ice. Long before hockey gripped the popular imagination, skating was a popular winter pastime.

Built in the 1880s in conjunction with the Charlottetown Driving Park harness racing facility, the Provincial Exhibition Building featured a huge display floor surrounded by a broad mezzanine.

In addition to casual users, Victoria Park was also the site of more organized activities like sports, militia exercises and camps like this YMCA meeting in 1908. While over the years, the emphasis swayed back and forth between the two approaches to administration of the park, the contradictions between them were never resolved to everyone's satisfaction.

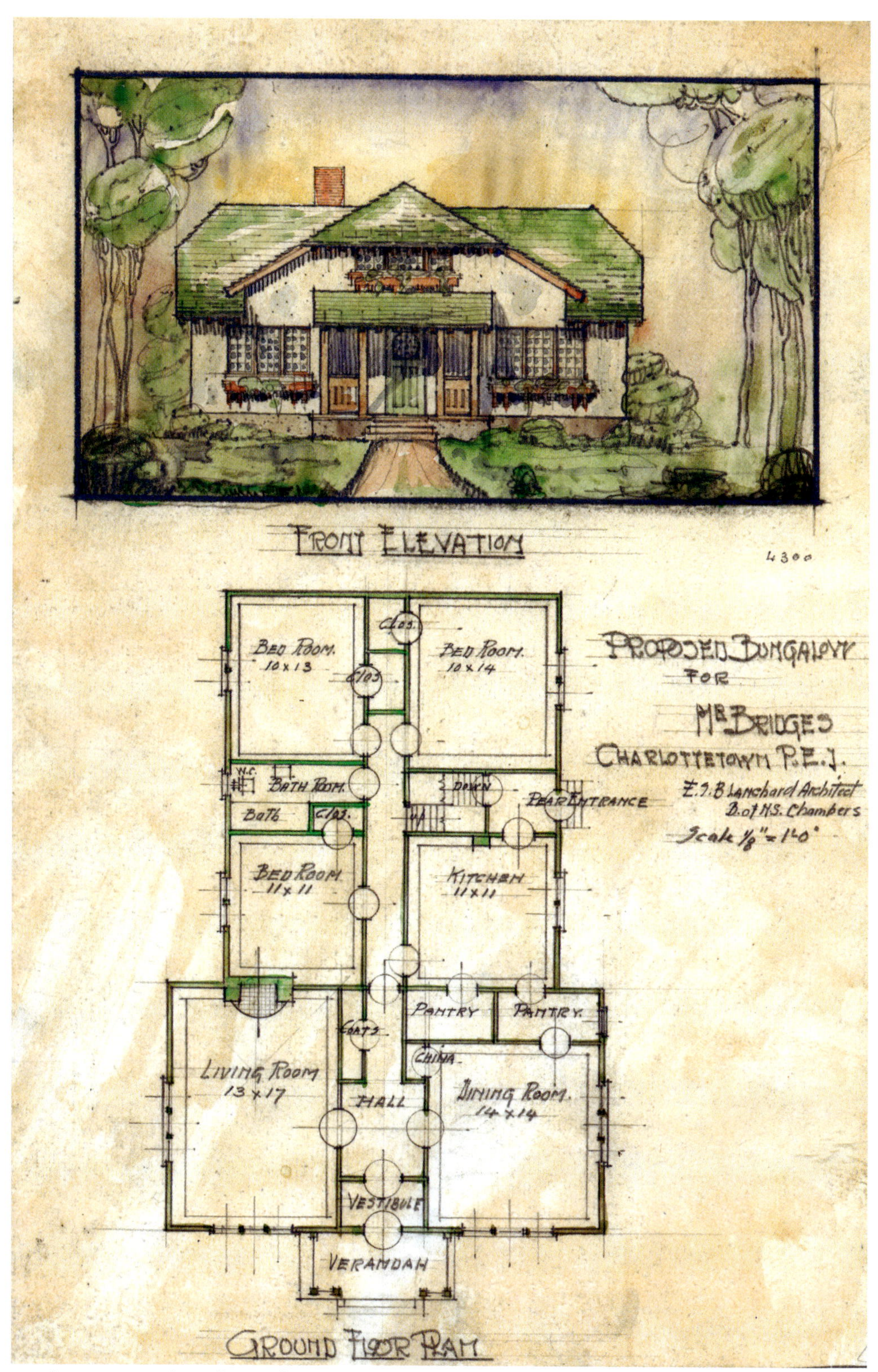

In the 1920s, when "Bones" Blanchard drafted this elevation for "Mr. Bridges Proposed Bungalow," the concept of a "bungalow" had not yet settled into the version that would be featured so prominently in later housing developments.

Though it was constructed for train traffic, the Hillsborough Bridge was becoming a major motor route. Note the plank decking used by motor vehicles.

may have encouraged the Charlottetown Yacht Club to erect a new clubhouse, but it failed to remedy substantially the limitations of the port facilities.

About this time the ongoing significance of the harbour became a matter of public debate. This was within the context of discussions about a new North River bridge. A correspondent in the *Guardian* advocated harbour improvements even at the risk of delay to the bridge construction. "Islander," replying in the *Patriot*, retorted that some improvements had been made and with some dredging the harbour would be serviceable. He ridiculed the assumption that a better harbour would generate business. Only increased production that attracted marine traffic would do that. Meanwhile the existing road crossing was narrow, antiquated and unsafe, and should be replaced.

While the Board of Trade regularly, if not frequently, discussed the harbour, particularly after 1927, in this period its members also found other matters clearly more pressing — particularly railway service. Major changes to harbour installations had to wait for another day, but the 1920s saw the end of the prolonged discussions over the extension of the railway tracks along the waterfront. Concerns about safety and inconvenience to certain businesses were overcome by 1927, and Council cleared the way for the Canadian National Railways to run their tracks as far west as Pownal Wharf. Hopes to complete the transit of the harbourfront by connecting the wharves at the foot of Haviland Street to the tracks at Pownal Wharf went unrealized. The same may be said about major improvements to the Hillsborough Bridge, which spanned the harbour. By 1928 the venerable structure needed strengthening in order to support the heavier standard-gauge railway cars. The narrow span — not designed for automobiles — was increasingly unable to handle motor traffic. By the end of the Second World War, the day when a replacement was necessary was coming into sight. And the harbour itself was losing its critical role for the city's commerce. In 1943 only 14 seagoing and 59 coastal vessels entered the port, a testimonial to the increasing importance of the railway and car ferry to the Island's trade and commerce.

Mayor Percy Turner

Utilities

Improvement of utilities in Charlottetown was incremental during the 1920s. Council regularly received and generally granted petitions for new streetlights, particularly in the expanding Brighton area. By the early 1930s, the rising cost of providing such services was once again causing concern, and this led to questions about the legitimacy of rates charged by Maritime Electric. Mayor Samuel Kennedy revived the call for public ownership of the electricity supply in 1934, and in 1937 a thorough review of the physical and financial assets of the power company by a committee of Council led to prolonged negotiations with the firm about its rate structure. This ultimately produced an arrangement that lessened electrical costs and allowed the city to contemplate more and stronger street lamps. In the process, some politicians, including Mayor Percy Turner, revived the link between civic services and modernity, and, by implication, modernity and self-respect. For Turner, increased street illumination was required if Charlottetown was to be modern. Subsequent progress in this regard was held up, however, after Maritime Electric announced that wartime restrictions prohibited further installation of street lights.

Telephone service also expanded in the 1920s, with telephones making their way into an increasing number of homes and offices. By 1929 almost half of the Island Telephone Company's phones were assigned to the capital city. The wires connecting them intensified the overhead clutter that appeared along virtually every street. A decision by the telephone company to purchase new equipment and improve their accommodation led to the construction of a three-storey brick building at the corner of Queen and Fitzroy Streets in 1930. It was opened with great fanfare by Mayor T. W. L. Prowse on October 4, 1931.

Planning

The visual clutter of the overhead wires was a foretaste of the ills connected with the lack of planning regulations. Unlike many cities and towns, including Saint John,

As Brighton became one of the most attractive of the city's new neighbourhoods, this and adjacent streets would soon look much more crowded than in this c. 1900 photograph. Note the fire hydrant.

Halifax, Ottawa, Calgary and Vancouver, which drafted master plans in the 1920s, Charlottetown did little to regulate development. A brief encounter with Thomas Adams, an apostle for town planning in Canada, failed to spur local authorities. A small first step was taken in 1923 when Council passed a by-law providing for rules governing the inspection and erection of buildings in the city. The purpose of the legislation was to curtail fire losses. The next year, the province augmented the city's powers to establish fire districts within which rules governing inspection and construction of buildings could be enforced. Nothing much more was heard about planning until 1937 when some residents in the Brighton neighbourhood asked Council to require that new residences in their area cost a minimum of $3,000.[17] While this amount was the equivalent of a little more than $45,039 in 2008, it was many times the annual average income and, thus, clearly intended to maintain a fairly substantial standard for new house construction. The request for a restricted building zone was passed with blinding speed by both City Council and the provincial legislature.

17 The measure was accomplished in April 1937. It allowed the city to set standards for construction, appearance and completed worth within such zones. The average annual income in Canada for 1937 was $448. In 2001, the average income was $29,770. It would have taken 6.7 years of labour at the average rate to earn $3,000 in 1937. In 2001, the same amount of labour in the same time at the average income level would have produced an income of $199,353. A similar building restriction in 2001 would, therefore, call for a minimum value of around $200,000. This would be equivalent to $241,588 in 2008.

Residents living along less prestigious Longworth Avenue who wrote in 1939 to ask for a restricted building zone in their locale, on the other hand, were unable to duplicate this success.

When the City Council petitioned the provincial government for powers to create restricted building zones, one of the stated purposes was to regulate the establishment of businesses in areas where they had hitherto not existed. This power was not conferred by the legislature, and this may explain why the request from the Longworth Avenue residents failed since their intent was to preserve the residential character of the street. In March 1940, Council asked for powers to regulate the location and operation of automobile repair garages in order "to protect public safety and ... prevent nuisance in or detriment to residential sections." The legislature approved it in May 1940 and corresponding city by-laws were enacted the same month. This was an important step forward for Charlottetown in its evolution away from the chaotic land use that had generally prevailed since incorporation. Even so, the city was not ready to undertake planning in a major way. Passage of a provincial town planning act in 1945 conferred powers to establish municipal planning boards and prepare comprehensive plans, but Council refrained from embarking upon the task. It did, however, ask for and gain annexation of a small section of Spring Park which had been conveyed to the city by Edward Jarvis. Still, the years of suburban sprawl, territorial growth and eventually comprehensive zoning lay in the future.

ECONOMIC GROWTH AND METROPOLITAN DEVELOPMENT

The period from 1921 to 1945 was a trying one for the city. It expanded physically, improved its infrastructure, and attempted to boost its prosperity. Business and civic leaders supported regional agitation for a better deal within Confederation and pressed for every conceivable boon that could be of local advantage. The economic obstacles were familiar, and the responses to them were time-tested. New challenges arose, in particular an international depression of unprecedented gravity, and these required some innovative responses, but change was approached cautiously. The cartoon of the fat cow feeding in the West, being milked in Ontario and leaving its droppings on the East Coast, still seemed an apt metaphor for the economy.

Administrative Functions

Government continued to play a stable but important role in the city's economy. Employment for federal employees was provided by the post office and the customs, fisheries and agriculture departments, including the experimental farm. The range of opportunities within the provincial bureaucracy was wider, but the province still kept its staffing as short as possible, and services in certain areas were understaffed or non-existent. The number of civic employees varied with the year and the season, but municipal government was also kept lean. There was certainly an appreciation by the business leaders in Charlottetown that a healthy public sector was of considerable economic benefit to them. If, for instance, more clerical work connected with the local operations of the federal department of marine were done in the city, staff, and hence potential customers, would increase proportionally. Conversely, centralization of the accounting office of the CNR in Moncton was viewed with alarm because of the loss of jobs it entailed for Charlottetown. The economic challenges of the 1920s, followed by the Great Depression, ensured that substantial bureaucratic expansion was unlikely, although the years 1939–45 saw growth in certain areas connected with the war effort.

Commercial Activities

Commerce retained a critical role in the city's economy, but the times were anything but booming for the retail sector. The number of stores remained about the same, as did the number of employees, although the volume of business inched upward. In 1931 there were 221 stores employing 609 people selling $5,800,000 in goods. More than one-third of the establishments — 88 shops — sold principally food. Another 23 dealt in clothing and footwear. There were as many drug stores as restaurants — 9 each. Six gas stations and 2 garages serviced vehicles sold by 10 automobile dealers. Candy (11), variety (2), dry goods (2), hardware (3) and tobacco stores (2), along with lumber (4), coal (8),

At the turn of the 20th century, if you did not make your own, you could purchase a bottle of jam or syrup locally made in a local store. By the 1930s, you were as likely to buy a national brand from a national chain store.

radio (3), home furnishing dealers (5) and farm suppliers (9) accounted for most of the rest. A decade later, 240 establishments had 683 employees moving $6,786,000 worth of merchandise. Thus, while the average size of the businesses was the same with respect to employment, their volume of trade increased almost 8 per cent. Significantly, the number of businesses in Charlottetown compared to the provincial total increased by over 3 per cent, but their share of all provincial sales was virtually static. Stores outside the capital posted an average income growth of nearly 12 per cent during the decade.

There was also competition within the city's marketplace. Some local firms were quite robust, such as Prowse Brothers, a venerable dry goods, clothing and home furnishings business which by 1930 was reputed to be one of the largest of its type in the Maritimes. But the commercial sector was becoming more diverse. In 1923 R. T. Holman of Summerside established a branch store, and in 1929 one of the large national retail chains, Metropolitan Stores, opened its doors in the city. Outside retailers were as likely as not to have their head office in Toronto, as Charlottetown, by 1931, had fallen into the economic orbit of the Ontario metropolis. In addition, catalogue merchants took a share of sales. As early as 1925, Eaton's and Simpson's were posing a serious threat to the vitality of local stores. Beyond their catalogue service, Simpson's had an agent, F. A. Stewart Jones Company, which sold Simpson's merchandise in Charlottetown. In 1928 Eaton's opened a branch in a building that formerly housed a grocer, Jenkins and Sons. In 1939 another growing national chain, Canadian Tire Corporation, got a foothold in the city by opening a sub-dealership on Kent Street.[18] Local merchants defended themselves against these intrusions as best they could, but their options were limited. One modest gesture taken by City Council in 1931 on behalf of home-grown entrepreneurs was to impose a licensing requirement on non-residents retailing goods in the city.[19] And at least one city business began to extend its reach into the countryside, as Maritime Electric undertook the slow process of consolidating the generation and distribution of electricity across the Island.

Manufacturing

In the decades following the First World War, it became widely accepted that there was little hope for a substantial industrial sector in the Prince Edward Island economy. Conditions within the province worked against the development of manufacturing, and the centralization of capital doomed traditional businesses which made carriages, ploughs and parts for farm machinery. "Industrial life has been more or less throttled," proclaimed the *Guardian* in 1925, "and almost extinguished in P.E.I. as far as manufacturing is concerned." In 1941 a study of the province's economy concluded, "with the limited supplies of capital, skilled labor, rather low per capita wealth and income, and very slowly increasing population, the Province is not destined to have

18 A full-fledged franchise opened a decade later on Great George Street.

19 Peddlers' licences required in earlier times could be seen as forerunners of the current impositions.

any great increase or change in its manufactures." Data substantiated this pessimism. Employment in manufacturing dropped 65 per cent between 1900 and 1920, and the sector continued to shrink thereafter. In 1917 there were 411 manufacturers with 1,556 employees and a gross production value of $4,838,000, but this dropped to 249 establishments providing jobs for 991 producing $2,776,000 worth of goods in 1933. By 1943 the number of businesses had declined to 230, although the number of employees rebounded to 1,552, and the value of goods had increased substantially to $9,577,000, or a 98 per cent gain since 1917.

In the midst of this mixed overall picture of decline and subsequent growth, Charlottetown's manufacturing sector showed a modest but steady increase. In 1925 there were 27 firms making products valued at $1.6 million. This grew to 34 plants with products worth $1.5 million in 1936, and 36 with $2 million in production by 1941. Some of the manufacturers included processors of milk and other dairy products, meat packers, woodworking factories, fox biscuit makers, soft drink bottlers, metal works and a tobacco manufacturer. Some of these businesses supplied the surrounding rural areas, such as the fox biscuit manufacturers and a new fertilizer plant, built in 1930. Others processed primary products, including a woollen mill owned by William Landrigan and William Condon which began production in 1931 and a canning plant set up by J. Arthur Lewis in 1943. These successful ventures gave Charlottetonians some cause for hope for their manufacturing sector, but as the Depression lifted, the province's industrial output seems to have become less focused on the capital.

Throughout this period, business leaders were receptive to development opportunities even if they were at times improbable. In 1925 the Optical Development Corporation of New York inquired about a possible location in the city for an eyeglass lens factory. It was called "one of the most important communications the board [of trade] has received for some time." Lt. Gov. Frank Heartz preferred an alternate approach, one that built upon areas of existing economic activity. He suggested industries such as flour and other grain mills and canneries for vegetables and other products. In the depths of the Depression, H. K. S. Hemming saw merit in pursuing both new and traditional product lines. Fruit, vegetables, fish and meat and dairy products could be processed, but, in addition, bricks, imitation stone, or fabric bags also could be manufactured.[20] The key to success was modern equipment, efficient management, able, affordable labour and high-quality materials. With this combination of assets, locally produced products would find favour in outside, particularly British, markets. In addition, hopes for an oil industry periodically surfaced, and some exploration was done, including a test well bored on Governor's Island in 1927 and surveys of Hillsborough Bay undertaken between 1940 and 1943. The results were not encouraging.

Bonusing remained a device for promoting industry. Even as the Depression deepened, City Council granted the National Candy Company an exemption from all civic taxes on real estate and personal property. In 1930 the Island Fertilizer

---

20 Bricks were made in Charlottetown as early as 1827.

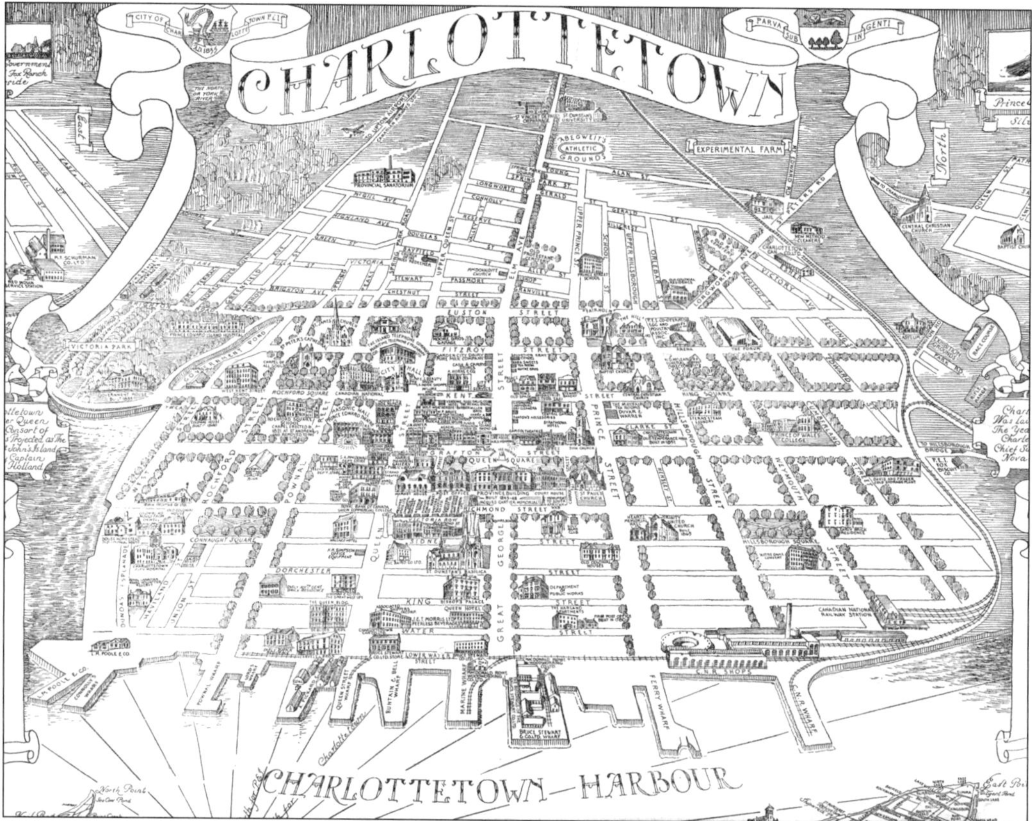

This detail from a promotional map issued by the Dominion Fox Company of Summerside highlights the Charlottetown manufacturing and business districts in the 1930s.

Company petitioned for a five-year tax relief. The best example of bonusing as a means to secure industry proved to be William Landrigan and Company, a manufacturer of woollen goods and yarn in Souris, Prince Edward Island. Following a decision to move the mill to Charlottetown and enlarge it, the company asked for, and received, a five-year civic tax exemption. The money was well-invested. Though now closed, the mill operated for over 50 years.

There were also sporadic efforts to promote the sale of the city's manufactures at home and abroad. The Board of Trade wanted Island products well-represented in an exhibition of Canadian goods planned to tour France in 1922. Closer to home, the board worked to ensure Island products were promoted at the Provincial Exhibition and was active in establishing the Prince Edward Island Manufacturers' Association and the mounting of a campaign to encourage Islanders to buy locally.

The Second World War seemed to offer an opportunity to increase the manufacturing sector. In early 1940, Council urged the provincial government to press the city's claims for war contracts. Mayor B. Roy Holman asserted it was "only fair" that the province and city receive a share of munitions contracts because more Islanders had volunteered for active service per capita than any other province. Holman received promises of business from the federal government in April 1941, but had to report that nothing had resulted by the end of that year. This set a pattern. Strong representations by the mayor and others to have the railway shops used for war contracts were given "a very civil and polite hearing," but little was promised and nothing was delivered. Indeed, the railway had begun to centralize the repair of its equipment in Moncton as early as 1922, causing staff reductions in Charlottetown and protests from the business community. Though viewed as gravely detrimental to the local economy, the removal of shop work to Moncton was renewed in 1942. A City Councillor charged that it constituted a breach of the Confederation agreement, and the *Guardian* proclaimed opposition "will not stop until the shops are again used." Eventually Bruce Stewart and Company received munitions contracts, but an economic bounce in the city's economy resulting from the war was due to construction rather than manufacturing.[21]

One wartime economic casualty was a long-standing hope that a dry-dock would be established in Charlottetown harbour. During the previous World War, the federal government had proposed constructing a ship repair facility at Southport sufficiently large to accommodate the car ferry *Prince Edward Island*. Plans were drawn up, but the facility was never built, although a dry-dock scheme was revived by the R. B. Bennett federal government. With the onset of the Second World War, Canada embarked upon an ambitious program of shipbuilding, focused on the inland Great Lakes and Upper St. Lawrence. "With all this shipbuilding going on," opined the *Guardian*, "isn't it strange that the capital city of this Island province isn't humming with activity?" Suggestions included an installation that could repair the ferries, or build ocean-going tugs or floating docks. Despite the city's best efforts to pressure the federal government through James Ralston, a federal cabinet minister elected in Prince County, a shipbuilding facility in the harbour was not built.[22]

Economic Promotion

The successful promotion of Charlottetown as a place to live and do business also proved an arduous challenge. Council made sporadic efforts to this end. In 1925, for instance, it sent circulars to retired government and railway officials extolling the attractions of the city as a place to live. For the most part, though, the Board of Trade remained the main advocate of economic development. Unfortunately, throughout the years 1921-45, there was a gradual weakening of the association's vitality. The principal problem was membership, which declined about 30 per cent during these years. By the late 1930s, this had become a concern to the board, and by 1945 was a topic of discussion in the press. The heavy commitment of time required of members

21 The difficulties faced by Charlottetown in securing munitions contracts mirrored the experience of the First World War and the situation faced by the Maritimes generally in the Second World War.

22 Ralston, however, may well have been instrumental in the establishment of five British Commonwealth Air Training Plan bases on the Island — four in Prince County.

who volunteered for various committees and the emergence of other organizations competing for the time and attention of businessmen explained some of the slackening interest. Although the board's existence was not in peril, there was concern that its ability to influence government policy might be undermined. Even so, the stream of resolutions on various economic matters continued unabated. Overwhelmingly, these bore on the issue of transportation, either within the province by train or between the province and outside destinations by steamship, railway or aircraft. Related topics, such as the harbour or communications in general, also were frequent topics of discussion. Trade was the only other subject that regularly made the agenda. Matters having to do with development, including industrial development and tourist promotion, received less attention. A surprisingly small amount of time was spent on labour matters, highways and immigration, while strictly local concerns such as store hours, daylight saving time, public works and suburban development attracted almost no attention.

One issue that dealt with labour was a proposed workmen's compensation act. The proposal came before the provincial legislature in early 1932 and provoked concern among the membership of the board. There was a belief that such a law would be a burden on industry. Local reservations were buttressed by the Maritime Board of Trade, which cautioned against any changes at the present time. The board contacted Premier Stewart to make their objections known, and the bill was quietly dropped. Similarly, the board saw little merit in the provision of unemployment insurance in Canada. Workmen's compensation legislation re-emerged as a possibility in 1938, despite the opinion of Hon. B. W. Lepage, the President of the Executive Council in the Thane A. Campbell Liberal government, that it would not succeed. Immediate steps to enact such legislation were not taken although the board monitored it carefully.

The business community, nevertheless, continued to look to government, particularly the federal government, to act for the common good as they, themselves, defined it. Most local businessmen were predisposed to low tariffs even in the face of American trade barriers that significantly reduced markets for products like Island potatoes in the United States.[23] At the same time, the Board of Trade turned to the federal government to try to locate replacement trade partners. One such possibility was Cuba, once a major consumer of PEI potatoes and, in the view of the board in 1937, potentially one again if Canada could negotiate a trade agreement with the Caribbean nation. Prior to that, board members had seen potential in increased trade with the British West Indies. Within the realm of provincial jurisdiction, the Board of Trade went on record in 1921 as favouring a utilities commission to set telephone rates and oversee the relations between the various companies operating in the province. Major development initiatives were viewed as the proper domain of government. Planning for reconstruction to follow the Second World War attracted little active involvement of members of the Board of Trade. Although there was a strong sense that

23 An agreement that provided easy access for PEI potatoes to the American market ended in 1921.

agriculture would be the basis of the future economy, diversification was desirable. When it came to defining the most essential projects for the postwar economy, the board threw its support behind rural electrification, highway construction between Charlottetown and the ferry terminals, and the long-awaited dry-dock. Implicit in this approach was an acceptance that the key to economic development was held by others, particularly the provincial and federal governments.

Not all government intervention was welcome. In response to a questionnaire from the Canadian Chamber of Commerce concerning marketing boards for agricultural, forestry and fishery products, the board generally favoured their implementation with the proviso that they would not be financed with public money, nor would they use government funds to compensate for losses sustained in exporting, storing, or withholding products from markets. Similarly, the board wanted reconciliation of the federal government's programs with regional needs. The Farmers' Creditors' Arrangement Act, designed to allow farmers to apply to the courts for an adjustment of their debts, including arrears of taxes, meant that credit-worthy farmers were having difficulty obtaining loans, so the Board of Trade asked that the provisions of the act be suspended for the Island.

Charlottetown business also seems to have become more actively engaged with the general needs of agriculture, and, to a lesser extent, the fishery. The board tried to convince senior levels of government of "the absolute need of a properly equipped soil laboratory and a trained soil chemist" to advise Island farmers on the application of fertilizers. In 1925 the board tried to encourage sugar beet cultivation on the Island, in part by distributing sugar beet seed. In 1931 it endorsed resolutions in support of improvements to the skills of fishermen and fish plant workers, and to harbour facilities. Board of Trade members also promised to co-operate "in any way necessary to further fishery development."

In 1928 the board appealed to the federal government to give special consideration to promoting immigration to the province as a means of reinvigorating the farming industry. It suggested people from Great Britain, Denmark and other parts of Scandinavia as potential migrants, as well as expatriate Islanders, and proposed a provincial department of immigration and colonization. The board subsequently lobbied to support the so-called Hornby Immigration Plan, a scheme to bring British immigrants to Canada and establish them on fully equipped farms at no expense to either the provincial or federal governments — the imperial government was expected to subsidize the venture. During the Second World War, it called for a military discharge depot in Charlottetown so that demobilized Islanders would not be tempted to settle elsewhere.

Communications

The long-awaited introduction in 1917 of regular service between Borden and Cape Tormentine by the car ferry *Prince Edward Island* did not resolve all the communications problems facing Charlottetonians. While travel in winter became fairly reliable, the volume of traffic soared, and, consequently, by the early 1920s, the need for additional shipping capacity became apparent. In addition, there were concerns about the economic fallout if the *Prince Edward Island* broke down or had an accident. It also left the matter of adequate connections to destinations outside the Maritimes unresolved.

Overall, the city's business interests were ambivalent about their overseas links. On the positive side, Canada Steamship Lines operated a route from Montreal to St. John's, Newfoundland, via Charlottetown. Links to this traditional market were dependent upon federal subsidies and the economic policies of the Newfoundland administration.[24] In 1942 a weekly service was established. Coastal ships and the occasional deep-sea vessel also called at Charlottetown, but these became fewer as the period progressed. Coastal trade, in particular, suffered from railway and road competition. To lengthen the shipping season in the early 1920s, an icebreaker operated in the harbour until heavy freeze-up occurred. Potatoes were a principal outward-bound commodity, with a substantial share of the Island's potato crop passing through the port. During the peak season from October to December in 1927, 11 vessels carrying 681,043 tons cleared Charlottetown compared with 10 ships loaded with 351,677 tons from other ports.[25] Loss of the frost-proof warehouse on the railway wharf in June 1928 posed a threat to trade, but the federal government quickly began to restore the facility.

Another potential danger to the port's prosperity was labour. In the early 1920s, the Labourers' Protective Union enjoyed a comfortable relationship with the city's business elite and even a degree of admiration and affection from the public at large. This gave the union a sympathetic hearing when it sought to establish wage rates for longshoremen. Generally, shippers tolerated the expense in return for the union's co-operation during peak periods of export activity. By the end of the decade, however, the relationship was becoming frayed. Shippers complained of the cost and size of the work gangs, while longshoremen complained of inadequate port facilities. In 1930 shippers agreed to pay 4¼ cents to load a ninety-pound bag of potatoes, an amount that exceeded costs elsewhere.[26] When shippers threatened to use other ports, the Board of Trade tried to arbitrate, but without notable success. A proposed increase of hourly wages from 55¢ to 60¢ in 1936 drew protests from at least one carrier, the Canada Newfoundland Steamship Company, which said its sailings would be affected. There were complaints that Charlottetown was "the most expensive port in Eastern Canada to load or unload a ship." The LPU, in response, laid the blame for lost business on improved facilities at competing ports. Nevertheless, it became clear that Charlottetown was losing business to its competitors.

---

24 Newfoundland lost its autonomous status because of the economic impact of the Depression. In 1933 it requested that it revert to colonial status, and a Commission of Government was appointed in 1934 to administer the island.

25 Five ships left Summerside with 140,941 tons, while another five carrying 210,736 tons departed from Georgetown.

26 The rate at Summerside, for instance, was 3½¢.

The Labourers' Protective Union, which represented longshoremen like these, enjoyed a comfortable relationship with the city's business elite in the 1920s. Relations grew more strained in the 1930s.

Some services could not be operated profitably from Charlottetown. In 1921 Canada Steamship Lines rejected the possibility of connecting the city to Boston with stops in Halifax and Saint John. There were fewer than the necessary number of tourists to make the trip, and markets in the United States were "cheaper" than expected. Five years later, another attempt to get regular weekly sailings between Charlottetown and Boston apparently met a similar fate. In 1935 the federal government subsidized a trial service linking Charlottetown, Cape Breton, Halifax and Boston. The experiment ended with the subsidy the following year. A decade earlier, a Montreal company asked for $15,000 to operate a coastal vessel, the *Gaspé Trader*, connecting Charlottetown and Summerside with ports in New Brunswick and the Gaspé. Despite prodding from the Board of Trade, the federal government refused to consider any such support. What was particularly interesting about this latter scheme was that it consciously tried to revive connections formerly provided by sailing vessels. In the future, communication with communities along the gulf coast would be via rail or road.

Connections with the mainland — always important — thus became increasingly critical to the city's postwar economic success. In particular, the rapid transit of passengers and mail on the Borden-Cape Tormentine run, with prompt transfers to through trains at both ends, was desirable. Charlottetown business interests also wanted direct

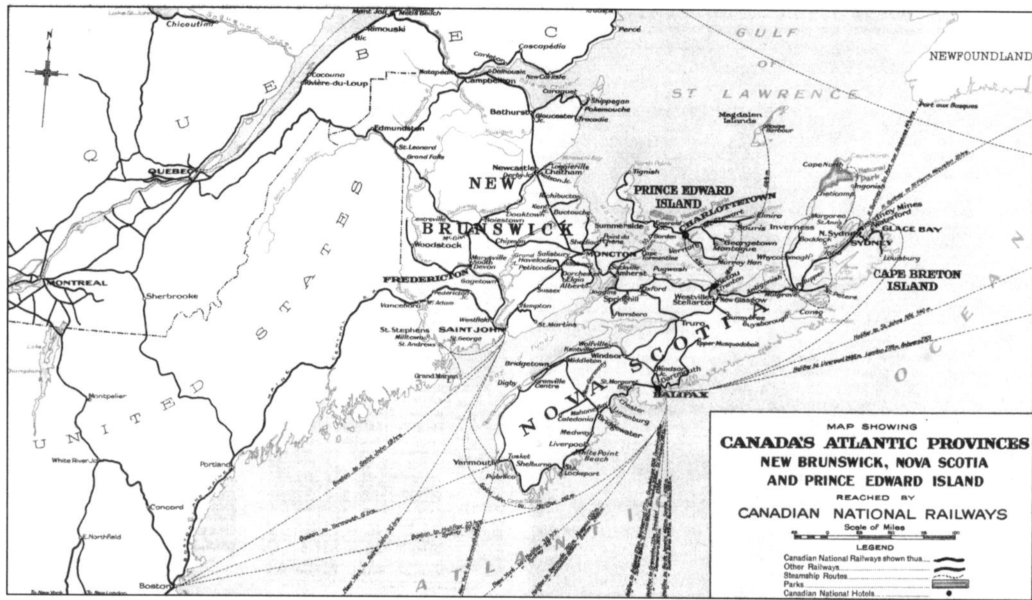

In To Everywhere in Canada, *a promotional brochure from the late 1930s, Canadian National highlighted numerous steamship and railway connections to the Island. It is not known how much solace those who fought constantly to maintain and improve such connections took from the railway's claims.*

service to Pictou outside of the winter months. Neither of these expectations were being met in the early 1920s. The vessel on the Pictou run was seen as deficient in size and comfort, and the winter service at the capes at one point was denounced as "rotten" and "damnable." A better steamer, the *Hochelaga*, was found for the Pictou service, but it, like the car ferry, operated at a loss.[27] Although the federal government provided a subsidy to support the Pictou connection, the Canadian National Railways financed the car ferry, and this siphoned off revenue from its PEI division. By 1924 the business community was pressuring the federal government to pay these deficits out of general revenue and, in addition, provide a second car ferry. Traffic volume certainly justified the second ferry. For example, the month-over-month increase in the number of rail cars crossing between Borden and Cape Tormentine in October and November 1926 was 75 per cent.[28]

Links to the mainland became one of the major grievances Prince Edward Island brought before the Duncan enquiry, a Royal Commission established in 1926 to investigate the Maritime provinces' claims for better treatment within Confederation. Because of the importance of the matter to Charlottetown's business community, the

27 The *Hochelaga* had been built originally for an Austrian archduke and was capable of carrying 12 autos.

28 In October 1926, there were 2,252 railway cars and in November, 3,936; 105 on November 6, and 187 on November 21 alone.

Board of Trade worked with the provincial government to prepare the case. Speaking for the province in his brief on transportation, Donald MacKinnon asserted that transportation facilities on the Island should be equal to those found in the rest of the country. Hence, a second car ferry was needed to ensure that heavy freight traffic and scheduled maintenance to the existing ferry did not delay the timely flow of passengers and mail. This was particularly necessary because the connection between Borden and Cape Tormentine carried the huge bulk of the province's commerce, when in former times much of it had departed by other water-borne traffic. To revive or sustain such alternate trade links, harbours should be improved and provided with rail service to the docksides, and government should foster visits by cargo vessels even if subventions had to be provided until the routes became well-established.

The Royal Commission largely accepted the Island's claims. In his report Sir Andrew Rae Duncan, a British civil servant and politician, judged the car ferry service to be inadequate. A second boat was needed, and service should be administered as a separate unit of the CNR and not part of the railway operation. Moreover, significant improvements were prescribed for Island ports to facilitate potato exports. That work, the commission noted, should be done by the Department of Public Works and not the railway. William Lyon Mackenzie King's Liberal administration agreed to implement the report's recommendations.

A start was made with the survey of the harbour, wharves and storage facilities. Even so, by early 1928, the Board of Trade was clearly unhappy with progress, calling again for a second car ferry, improved loading facilities and better steamship connections.

The SS Charlottetown, *seen here departing Cape Tormentine, was larger and more powerful than its predecessor, the* Prince Edward Island, *and could accommodate 40 automobiles as well as 16 rail cars.*

By late 1928, plans were being prepared for a new icebreaking ferry, and the following year work started on reconstructing the railway wharf. The pace of public works slowed when the Bennett Conservatives replaced the King Liberals in 1930, but during the election campaign Bennett promised to complete the contract for a new ferry the Liberals had awarded before the election. When the SS *Charlottetown* was launched in 1931, an era of improved service seemed to have arrived. It was larger and more powerful than the *Prince Edward Island* and could accommodate 40 automobiles as well as 16 railway cars, thereby acting as a link to both the nation's highway and rail systems. Ironically, despite the declared intention of the King and Bennett governments to run two ferries between Borden and Cape Tormentine, the appearance of the *Charlottetown* heralded the retirement of the well-worn *Prince Edward Island*. The railway also blocked the creation of a separate account for its ferry service, although the costs of operating it were eventually removed from the CNR and charged directly to the federal government.

Disappointment set the tone for the rest of the decade. In the Board of Trade's opinion, Charlottetown's harbour was so neglected by the federal government that it was fit only for small coastal vessels. In addition, the new car ferry proved unequal to the increased volume of traffic, and the Board wanted it to be joined by a refitted *Prince Edward Island*.[29] Submissions to the Royal Commission on Financial Arrangements between the Dominion and the Maritime Provinces, headed by Sir Thomas White (1935), and to the Royal Commission on Dominion-Provincial Relations chaired by N. W. Rowell and J. Sirois (1937–40), mirrored the complaints made before the Duncan Commission. By 1938 some Islanders were again calling for a tunnel to the mainland. This idea, or a causeway, had been briefly considered by the federal government in the late 1920s as an alternative to a new car ferry, but was dismissed as too expensive to build. The Rowell-Sirois Commission was likewise unsympathetic. In 1944–45, the federal government again looked at the tunnel's feasibility and once again rejected it. Nevertheless, the persistence of the concept testified to an enduring Island belief that continuous communication, as guaranteed by Confederation, meant literally what it said and that nothing less than a fixed link across the Northumberland Strait could guarantee such a result.

The one bright spot in the transportation scene at this time was the decision in 1937 by a private company to launch a cross-strait ferry service between Wood Islands, Prince Edward Island, and Caribou, Nova Scotia. This initiative had the full support of Charlottetown's business community, even though it would result in losing the direct link between the city and Pictou. The latter service had become costly and inconvenient; the new one offered more frequent crossings. Moreover, it could accommodate automobiles and trucks. At the time, virtually no trucks carried commodities across the strait. The boat to Pictou was too small, and the railway-operated ferry service had

29 Suggestions called for it to be fitted with oil-fired engines and facilities to allow the loading of automobiles under their own power. Previously, they had to be loaded onto railway flatcars and shunted on board.

no interest in helping the competition.[30] The Board of Trade wanted the Wood Islands route to be served by a steel-hulled vessel capable of operating late into the autumn, early in spring, and even throughout a mild winter. Fares should be low so the service would operate as a subsidized public utility. Hopes to have the route in operation by 1938 were unrealized, and further delays resulted when the ferry and then its replacement were seized by the government for war purposes. Service finally commenced on June 28, 1941, with the *Prince Nova*, imported from the Great Lakes.

The 1940s at first seemed to offer the promise of better communications. Plans were made to enlarge the railway wharf and dredge the adjacent harbour, but they were subsequently shelved because of the war. Then, disaster struck elsewhere. On June 18, 1941, the *Charlottetown* hit an underwater obstacle on its way to Saint John for scheduled maintenance and sank. With no better option, the venerable *Prince Edward Island* was hastily refurbished and returned to the Borden-Cape Tormentine run. Its limitations were obvious, and soon calls rang out for a new vessel and immediate provision of a winter back-up service. Even so, the aging ferry provided an essential link in the Island's transportation network during the war. As a safeguard for interprovincial commerce in the event of a mishap befalling the *Prince Edward Island*, the Board of Trade urged the federal government to improve Charlottetown's port facilities. In addition, a new car ferry was absolutely necessary, particularly if the Island were to contribute fully to the war effort, but considerable lobbying on the part of the Board of Trade, the city and the province was still required to prod the federal government into constructing a replacement. Meanwhile, note was ruefully made of the comparison with Vancouver Island. With a population of only one-third more than PEI, it was served by "a fleet of 9 to 14 palatial steamers." Work finally began on the project in early 1944, but the new ferry — "the best science can produce" — did not enter service for another three years. Meanwhile, the *Prince Edward Island* laboured on at the Borden-Cape Tormentine crossing while service at Wood Islands was handicapped by inadequate terminal facilities, a deficient steamer and unpaved access roads. The period ended, as it began, with Charlottetown facing major challenges with its marine communications to the outside.

Much the same could be said about railway service. In the early 1920s, three of the issues that plagued it in the prewar era remained sore points: long stretches of narrow-gauge track, high freight rates and poor schedules. Added to this list was an insufficient number of cars for late autumn potato shipments, congestion during that same period along the tracks and loading areas, substandard roadbeds and antiquated equipment. The Board of Trade regularly passed resolutions demanding improvements but to no apparent avail. They expressed similar concerns to Sir Henry Thornton, President of the railway, when he visited Charlottetown in 1924.[31] Yet, as of January, 1926, only 130 of the 276 miles of track had been widened to standard

30 The fee to carry a truck from Borden to Cape Tormentine, return, was $42.65. The Board of Trade calculated this was equivalent to the same vehicle travelling 1,422 miles on the highway.

31 The board chose to emphasize the issues of narrow gauge, freight rates and schedules.

gauge. Virtually all of it east of Charlottetown was narrow gauge, severely hampering the export of crops and imports of coal.

Scheduling problems within the province meant prolonged journeys for travellers to and from the capital, particularly on mixed freight and passenger trains. Passengers and mail coming to the province via Cape Tormentine frequently were held back almost a day because no train was available to carry them from Sackville to catch the last ferry. Suggested solutions included diesel commuter cars for the Island service, an adjustment of freight rates to remove discrimination against shipments of commodities entering and leaving the Island — particularly the rates that favoured Summerside over Charlottetown — and either an extra train or an early morning ferry departure to accommodate travellers and mail coming to the province via the car ferry. The Charlottetown businessmen clearly felt they were the victims of discrimination, a charge the railway denied.

As with shipping, the Royal Commission on Maritime Claims found the complaints to be justified. Sir Andrew Rae Duncan recommended an immediate 20 per cent reduction of freight rates on shipments originating or terminating in the Atlantic Division of the CNR. He called for better service to PEI from Moncton, and a survey of the tracks on the Island to find what upgrades were needed. Funds for the latter improvements, he ruled, should be made available "in the shortest possible time." Again, victory before the Duncan commission proved hollow. Within a month, the Board of Trade was protesting unacceptable delays in railway schedules, and a month after that was expressing "emphatic disapproval" of an apparent plan not to implement the proposed freight rate reductions. The need for rate reductions remained an important part of the Board's representations throughout the Depression. The competitiveness of the city's meat packing plants, for instance, suffered in comparison to similar businesses in Moncton because of the extra charges for shipments from Charlottetown. In fact, with the exception of the conversion to standard gauge, completed on September 29, 1930, virtually all the demands of the 1920s continued to be made into the Second World War years.[32] One improvement, the twice-daily connections with through trains at Sackville, was reduced to one again in 1931. As before and not for the last time, Charlottetown businessmen protested discrimination.[33] In this instance, Prince Edward Island was disadvantaged in relation to the other Maritime provinces as well as with the rest of Canada. The history of the campaign for better railway service provided substance to Duncan's quip, made at his Commission's hearings in Charlottetown, that "resolutions do not get you very far."

Furor over the railway service tended to obscure the increasing importance of road travel within the province. Better roads were widening the catchment area for Charlottetown business. "Since the introduction of automobiles," the *Examiner*

32 See, for instance, protests against the cancellation of Pullman car service to the Island. City Councillors were quoted as feeling that PEI was being treated as a county and not a province.

33 Twice-daily service continued in Nova Scotia and New Brunswick.

The increasing use of automobiles emphasized the shortcomings of the Island's roads. Of special interest to Charlottetown were nearby highways like this one in West River.

noted in 1921, "local merchants have been able to reach customers in ever increasing [numbers] .... Car owners 20 miles away now shop in the city with regularity and comfort."[34] Rural roads and highways, however, were notoriously dusty in fine weather, and an "uncertain quantity, depending altogether on weather conditions" in the spring and fall. The clouds of dust and soggy potholes slowed travel and hindered economic growth, making rural roads and their condition increasingly a matter of urban concern. So, too, was access to all parts of the surrounding countryside. In particular, two bridges, one over the North River at Brighton and another over the West River, came to be regarded as badly needed improvements to communications. The Board of Trade in January 1936 called for their construction, and in the following month City Hall hosted a citizens' meeting to discuss the projects. An early advocate of the idea, J. O. Hyndman, rather ungenerously pointed out that the board had been "lukewarm" earlier, although City Council had been receptive. Now, the idea had general support, including from people representing rural districts that had "long suffered regarding transportation." Although the meeting unanimously urged that the work commence in the coming summer, not until 1944

34 The paper also thought an efficient streetcar service would bring similar convenience to suburbanites without them having to use automobiles. A bus service was eventually established. In 1933 the Lewis and Farley Bus Company advertised a single route serving the principal parts of the city. By 1938 Island Motor Transport Limited created an extended route that reached out Spring Park, Upper Queen, Elm, Gerald and Upper Prince Streets to the housing areas in the northern sections of town.

did the provincial government announce that the North River bridge would be built, and its realization took even longer.[35]

Equally significant for Charlottetonians were the roads leading to the ferries. As soon as the new Wood Islands crossing was proposed, the Board of Trade called for a paved highway to the ferry via the shore road through Belfast. It would, in some measure, compensate the city for losing its subsidized steamship connection with Pictou. An additional road was needed to connect the highway with the terminal. At the time, travellers had to cross a half-mile of unimproved road and a mile of sand beach to reach the dock. The provincial government was unmoved. It decided not to pave the route for the peculiar reason that it was heavily travelled; when done, it would have to be done well. By May 1941, the paved stretch still ended well short of its destination, but the route was at least being marked with signs.

In any case, the road to Borden in the west was even more important. The provincial government was not overly sympathetic to the wishes of travellers going in this direction either. Plans to pave the highway from Charlottetown to Searletown to connect with the road from Summerside meant commuters between the capital and the ferry at Borden would have to go 36 miles out of their way. The Board of Trade "strongly urged" the provincial government to build a paved road directly from Albany to Carleton, a distance of 2.6 miles, to avoid the proposed circuitous route. On discovering that this connection would be hard to keep clear in winter, the board changed its demand to a paved link running from Tryon to Carleton via Augustine Cove. This could be kept open in winter except in very severe weather.

While the roads brought the country to the city, modern communication was bringing the city to the country. The telegraph, and subsequently the wireless telegraph, had diminished the impact of geographical space and made the exchange of information between distant places enormously easier. Now, telephones were making ongoing access to rapid communication increasingly available to ordinary Islanders. After the rapid expansion of the network in the 1920s, however, usage dropped off during the Depression as hundreds of customers returned equipment to the Telephone Company of Prince Edward Island. Radio broadcasting, on the other hand, promised the greatest potential to link large numbers in a way never before realized.

Radio service began in the early 1920s in a small way, and it soon blossomed into a major influence on the lives of Charlottetonians. Key to this revolution was station CFCY. It was started by Keith Rogers in his living room in 1921 with a 10-watt, battery-powered transmitter broadcasting for an hour a day. The station began licensed operations with an official call number in 1925. By then the station's power had grown to 100 watts, and the broadcast day to three hours. A second Charlottetown station opened in 1928, but it, like a small Summerside station, was outdistanced by CFCY, which had a coverage that extended to parts of the mainland. In 1930 the Board of Trade urged licensing authorities to approve a further increase in the power

35 One significant transportation improvement that was achieved was the replacement of the aging Rocky Point ferry *Hillsborough* with the *Fairview* in 1935.

of Charlottetown stations to 500 watts, even up to 10,000 watts if the transmitters were located far enough from town to avoid interference with other frequencies. Rogers increased his station's output to 500 watts and further broadened his audience within the Island and beyond.

The schedule was largely home-grown at first, with programs to suit a wide range of interests. Children's shows, an *Outports Program* that featured old-time music, and live broadcasts of hockey games from the Forum reflected local taste, but offerings of country-and-western music introduced new influences from away. CFCY became a creative force in the country-and-western music field by featuring musicians such as "Tex" Cochrane, Ches Cooper and Don Messer and His Islanders. Although Rogers complained about unfair competition from Canadian Broadcasting Corporation stations in 1939, he reached a *modus vivendi* with the public broadcaster in which CFCY became an affiliate. Not only did this bring network shows to the parlours of Charlottetown and its hinterland, but it made Canadians familiar with Don Messer, Ches Cooper and announcer Loman McAulay. In a strange and unexpected way, a new form of communication was bringing the world to Charlottetown and exporting the Island to the whole of Canada.

Air travel was also beginning to help bridge the gap between Charlottetown and mainland centres. Ever since Cecil Peoli, the "Bird Boy" of New York, made the Island's first airplane flight over the exhibition grounds in September 1912, the potential of aircraft as a means of rapid transportation was recognized. Islanders, the *Examiner* announced, could look forward to the day "when that nine mile strip of water dividing us from the mainland need no longer be a barrier in the way of continuous communications summer or winter." In particular, the usefulness of the airplane could be seen in relation to mail service, a fact that was demonstrated seven years later when a flight carrying first-class mail arrived in Charlottetown from Truro, Nova Scotia. By 1926 John MacDonald, MP for Kings, was proposing an air service to Prince Edward Island to carry mail, passengers and light baggage. He made little headway, and a call for air-mail service by the Board of Trade in 1927 met with outright refusal from the Postmaster General. An accident involving the *Prince Edward Island* in October 1929 changed all that. It resulted in a reduction of car ferry service to only one crossing a day for mail and passengers, and led to a request from the board for an airmail service to handle late-day business. Surprisingly, this was granted. The special service continued throughout the winter and was generally renewed thereafter during the winter months of reduced ferry service.

The need for a proper airfield for Charlottetown soon became an issue, as a flying club, established in 1929, searched for a suitable site. Before the end of the year, a federal inspector identified several possibilities in the Charlottetown area, and two years later an airfield finally opened at Upton on the northwest edge of town. Built with the help of the provincial government, but significantly not of the city, on land provided by local aviation enthusiast Dr. J. S. Jenkins, the field became the terminus for regular passenger flights to Moncton. After 1932, the service was provided by Canadian Airways Ltd., and it quickly proved its worth "in contradistinction to the delays imposed upon other means of transportation by reason of our insular position."[36] By 1936 the Board of Trade was advocating twice-daily flights so that passengers and mail could connect with both through trains running between Montreal and Halifax. This was still to be achieved by 1939.

By then, the city had decided to address both the unemployment situation and a need for improved landing facilities by constructing a municipal airport. Since space for expansion at Upton was limited, the city asked the federal Department of Transport for advice on alternative locations. In 1938 the City bought a 300-acre parcel on the Brackley Point Road with the province's financial help. By that August, a construction contract was signed with the Department of Transport, and site preparation began. The airport was officially inaugurated on July 20, 1939, with the arrival of its first transcontinental flight. At the outbreak of the Second World War, the city offered the federal government free use of the airport for air defence. The gesture was both patriotic and astute. The government quickly erected six hangars, plus numerous other buildings to serve an establishment of 700 men,[37] and constructed three paved runways. Training operations were subsequently turned over to the Royal Air Force under the Commonwealth Air Training Plan. Then the facilities were used by the Royal Canadian Air Force as an air navigation school. While all this was going on, the airport continued to serve civilian flights to the city.

By the late 1930s, complaints long associated with shipping and railway service began to develop with civilian aviation: flights were not frequent enough and their schedules failed to meet significant business needs. The creation by the federal government of publicly owned Trans-Canada Airlines in 1937 and the expected introduction of TCA service to the Maritimes implied the displacement of Canadian Airways from the Moncton-Charlottetown route. While this would integrate the city into a national aviation system, it jeopardized the late-afternoon flight that brought mail and passengers from Moncton. At the same time, hopes were raised that passenger fares might drop by half to typical mainland levels. Appeals to the Minister of Transport initially seemed to have had little effect. The TCA flight that was finally scheduled to connect with Moncton had a planned departure time that was too early to avoid a twenty-hour delay of Island-bound passengers and mail arriving in the New Brunswick city by train. Business interests demanded restoration of a late-day car ferry run if the air schedule could not be adjusted. When a second, later flight was subsequently planned, it was not expected to carry general first-class mail, just airmail, and that still failed to provide a level of service that the Board of Trade, for one, considered to be the continuous communication promised by the articles of Confederation. Nevertheless, when TCA began service on April 15, 1941, there were two scheduled flights a day to and from Moncton. By September, the national airline wanted out, and arrangements were made with Carl Burke and Associates to provide connections to

36 The desired service on Sunday was a single round trip.

37 During the summer of 1940, 36 buildings were erected at the airport.

Moncton. The Board of Trade insisted upon continuation of TCA service at standard Trans-Canada rates to demonstrate that Prince Edward Island was still a province of Canada with transcontinental air service to other parts of the Dominion. It was not to be, but Carl Burke's Maritime Central Airways was destined to become a major player in the airline industry.

Burke soon turned Charlottetown into the centre of a cluster of routes that served the Maritimes and the Magdalen Islands. Continued success, however, depended upon an adequate airport, and by 1943 the limitations of the Charlottetown installation were already becoming apparent. City Council determined that the runways needed lengthening, and Mayor B. Roy Holman tried to mobilize public opinion to advocate the improvement as "an essential war measure." It was perhaps more an essential economic measure. By early 1944, express packages were shipped to and from Prince Edward Island by air, but matter destined for Charlottetown moved via Summerside because the runways at the Charlottetown airport could not handle the aircraft involved. A proposal to move the air navigation school to Summerside in 1945 was seen as a severe threat to the further development of the Charlottetown airport and resulted in a vigorous protest to the Minister of National Defence by City Council, the Board of Trade and local members of Parliament and the provincial legislature. The protests were successful; the move did not take place, and the fear that Charlottetown would be reduced to an economic backwater by Summerside waned.[38] Airport improvements came after the war, as the importance of air communications to the city's economy continued to grow.

Tourism

The end of the First World War also brought renewed interest in developing the tourist industry. One mechanism to achieve this goal was the PEI Tourist Association, founded on November 27, 1923, by a group of Charlottetown citizens and subsequently renamed the PEI Publicity Association. Railway and steamship companies had already recognized the value of running tourist offices, and several attempts had been made to establish a tourist bureau, but until this point in time the Island was the only Canadian province to be without one. Soon after its creation, the city granted the tourist association $500; Council also provided a grant to A. Dudley Corelli to prepare tourist brochures to be distributed via the two transcontinental railways. The city's support for tourist promotion by the association continued until 1932, when Mayor W. S. Stewart grumpily asserted, "it was impossible to discern whether [tourist promotion] made any addition to the Island's tourist population." He deemed it "a miscalculation to suppose that this Province will become a great tourist centre." Others were not so sure. One businessman attributed slackness in the tourist trade to bad roads, high ferry rates, the prevailing liquor laws and the lack of advertising. The

38 Councillor T. B. Rogers lamented that "We are very quickly reaching the status of Fredericton, N.B. Summerside will be the Saint John of P.E.I."

Board of Trade worked with the Publicity Association on tourist promotion until this responsibility was taken over by the provincial government on January 2, 1940. Even the city showed renewed interest in 1945 when it and the Board of Trade produced a promotional booklet.

Unlike Stewart, most Charlottetonians after the First World War persistently looked to tourism as a major prop to the local economy. The arrival of a new steamship on the run between the city and Pictou was seen as a means to recapture prewar tourist traffic. Complaints about the poor railway road beds and antiquated running stock mirrored concern that tourists would be discouraged by substandard travel conditions. Lack of high-quality accommodation prompted the Board of Trade to lobby the Canadian National Railways for a new hotel even before the Victoria Hotel was destroyed by fire. Although the completion of the Canadian National Hotel resolved the problem of accommodation in the capital, there remained a need for an upscale summer resort. The nearby Beach Grove Inn, a 60-room establishment with a view of Charlottetown Harbour, offered swimming, tennis, billiards and a dance floor, but it was not "high class" in local opinion. There were other impediments to a flourishing tourist industry. Increased automobile travel emphasized the importance of frequent scheduling and convenient loading and unloading of motor vehicles from the Borden-Cape Tormentine car ferry.[39] Unpaved highways forced disgruntled motorists to trail one another through billowing clouds of dust. The asphalt surfacing of major roads proved to be a boon to tourism.

The cost of travel was a bone of contention. In particular, automobile and passenger fares on the Borden ferry were considered exorbitant. The Board of Trade cited an example in 1934 of a Toronto tourist driving a Ford hauling a small two-wheeled trailer and carrying two passengers. The total fare was $14.95 (equivalent to $240 in 2008). After a lengthy struggle by the board and local politicians at the provincial and federal level, the fare for automobiles was subsequently cut to $2 one-way or $3 return ($32.11 and $48.17 in 2008). Demands for a second Borden ferry capable of carrying automobiles during the tourist season, and protests against the proposed sale of the SS *North Star*, the last cruise ship making regular stops at Charlottetown, were intended to ensure easy access to the city by tourists.

Of course, getting there was only part of the tourist puzzle. Another major piece was the motivation to visit. The city's picturesque setting and pleasant summer climate were two important draws, and the opening of the nearby national park and Green Gables golf course in 1939 promised spillover business, but more was needed. One encouraging initiative occurred in 1929 when the city, province and National Fox Breeders Association sponsored a major fox exhibition in Charlottetown.[40] The

39 The *Charlottetown* permitted automobiles to drive directly on and off, but the *Prince Edward Island* required autos to be loaded onto railway flat cars. Special structures were eventually built at the terminals to allow motor vehicles to drive directly on and off the flatcars without going into reverse. Later a passenger deck was converted into an automobile deck.

40 Contributions were National Fox Breeders Association, $1,000; PEI, $2,500; and Charlottetown, $250.

The 60-room Beach Grove Inn was not, in local opinion, "high class" enough to be the upscale summer resort that many thought the city needed to offer.

four-day event was a huge success attracting more than 2,000 spectators on one day alone to view about 470 foxes. Visitors came from as far away as Europe, making the show "the greatest ever held on the continent." Unfortunately, such successes were hard to replicate.

On the eve of the Second World War, a major celebration provided a model for future marketing efforts. In 1938 the provincial government began to plan for special observances to mark the 75th anniversary of the Charlottetown Conference. It appointed Justice A. E. Arsenault, President of the Publicity Association and a renowned booster for the tourism industry, to convene a "Confederation Celebration Committee" to oversee preparations. His selection signalled the desire of the government to have the festivities generate publicity for the Island and to attract tourists. The celebrations were to be national, not merely local, in scope. An agreement with the Canadian Broadcasting Corporation to air a national broadcast from Charlottetown and the presence of federal politicians, members of the armed forces and premiers or their representatives from other provinces reinforced this profile.

Various events were scheduled to occur throughout the week of July 16–21, but the most significant for the city were the ones stressing the history of Confederation and the pivotal role Charlottetown played in early discussions leading to the union. Plaques were unveiled, parades and religious services were held, and a spectacular pageant called "The Romance of Canada" was produced for a crowd of 8,000 crammed into the exhibition grounds. The performance highlighted the Confederation proceedings of 75 years before and the virtues that made Canada great, and organizers were careful to include references to all provinces. The celebrations of Confederation Week were a spectacular success at both the local and national levels. Tourists flooded in, but, more importantly, Charlottetown was sanctified as the birthplace of Confederation and the spiritual home of Canada's nationhood. In the years ahead, the city worked assiduously to confirm its role as a national shrine. By doing so, tourism was made an essential part of the local economy.

SOCIAL LIFE

The economic turbulence experienced in the years between 1921 and 1945 had its parallel in the social life of the community. Charlottetown emerged from the Great War with a sense of cautious optimism. The feeling of well-being from before the conflict was expected to grow with the return of peace. While some of the trappings of small-town, rural-dominated life remained, the face of the city and its people had been gradually altered by developments expected by a modern, 20th-century urban society. More of this slow transformation was anticipated. The unwelcome postwar economic reverses eroded the momentum of change, however, and, as the crisis deepened in the 1930s, the city was forced to respond to new challenges in unexpected ways. Concerns also arose about an apparent decline in social behaviours, as reflected in spiralling rates of venereal disease and underage smoking. Even so, Charlottetonians clung to the belief that the city and its inhabitants should keep pace with the ever-changing standards of modernity, whatever they may be.

At this time the wider social context in which Charlottetonians were living their lives was in flux. The traditional urban family structure in which men earned income and women presided over the home was being modified by the processes of urbanization and industrialization. The urban home was a residence for a nuclear family, in contrast to the home's role in the countryside as a base for production by an extended family. For the most part, boys were still treated differently than girls. They took some different subjects at schools, played some different games and had substantially different career expectations. As men, they sought employment while their wives undertook domestic work and child care. Women who had paid jobs could expect fewer promotions and poorer salaries. But girls had comparatively wider opportunities for education and recreation than their mothers, and women were establishing new social networks and standards for personal success. The era marked by the Great Depression and the Second World War represented a watershed for society, in Charlottetown as elsewhere in Canada.

Education

The period was one of consolidation for the city's schools. At the primary level, the four existing buildings continued to be relied upon to meet the needs of the city's expanding school-age population. Additions were made to Prince Street and West Kent Schools in 1922, but overcrowding remained a serious concern. By 1931 enrolment had reached 2,198 pupils, an increase of almost 88 per cent in less than 15 years. In addition to a shortage of classrooms, the schools lacked many of the trappings envisaged by modern educational standards. There were no gymnasiums, auditoriums, or sports fields, for instance, to support the non-academic aspects of education; nor were there any school libraries or domestic science kitchens. Students were expected to use the Dodd and Legislative Library and later the Harris Memorial Library, and in 1940 the school board made arrangements for the girls from Prince Street and West Kent Schools to use the kitchen at Prince of Wales College. In an effort to sort out

Grade 5 class, Prince Street School, 1927. Though additions were made to Prince Street and West Kent Schools in 1922, over-crowding remained a serious concern.

these kinds of difficulties and to provide some direction to the administration of the schools, the school board, in 1926, appointed a Supervisor of City Schools, Lloyd W. Shaw. He concluded that a new high school was needed to siphon off the older students, thereby relieving the crowded conditions for the primary students, but got little support from the administrations of the four schools. In any case, nothing came of the idea at the time.

Problems extended beyond congested facilities. For starters, teachers were unhappy with their inadequate salaries. Although pay levels in the city were higher than in the rural areas of the province, they prompted a three day strike in 1929. Truancy, another unresolved challenge, persisted until long after it had ceased to be regarded as a regrettable but unavoidable reality. The Children's Aid Society, charged with the enforcement of the truancy laws, worked with school authorities to establish night classes in an effort to accommodate different needs within the student body. In 1926, the first year for such courses, 200 youths applied to enroll. Meanwhile, concerns expressed by the Women's City Club and the Rotarians about the need for additional manual training facilities or enhanced safety programs went unheeded by the appointed board.

Frustration with some of these circumstances perhaps spurred the formation of Charlottetown's first Home and School Association. It was started at Queen Square School in 1933, with a focus on nutrition and fire safety. A decade later, the School Improvement League was created to campaign for better physical facilities, improved lighting, sanitation and fire safety.[41] Most of the members of these organizations were women, and educational concerns were regarded as areas in which they could

41 Curriculum matters were rarely addressed.

At St. Dunstan's, the Depression caused enrollments to decline by a third. In 1934 its administration contemplated closing.

legitimately express their opinions. These volunteer groups were to become a launching pad for efforts to obtain membership on the school board, and, as such, were a toehold for women in the city's political arena. Despite these activities, substantial change had to wait until after the end of the Second World War. In 1945 a provincial advisory reconstruction committee recommended the creation of a composite regional high school to offer academic, commercial and technical training to older students. Despite the School Improvement League's endorsement, no action was taken.

The circumstances faced by the city's two colleges were somewhat more fluid. During the Depression, enrolments dropped off. St. Dunstan's declined by up to one-third, and in the fall of 1934 its administration contemplated closing. Prince of Wales College lost students, too, although the Normal School swelled its population somewhat.[42] Both institutions were cash-strapped. There were, even so, small steps forward. The Carnegie Corporation, as part of its efforts to improve education in the Maritimes, began in 1929 to provide each college with grants to develop their libraries. Prince of Wales also received a substantial endowment to establish a chair in economics and sociology, a move that allowed it to offer a complete range of second-year university courses and thereby claim the status of a junior college in 1934. At the express wish of the Carnegie Corporation, the new appointee, Dr. J. T. Croteau, also

42 PWC was considerably larger than SDU. Including the Normal School, which Catholics attended as well as Protestants, PWC enrolments were in the range of 600 students in the 1930s, of which around one-quarter were from Charlottetown. SDU had enrolments ranging from 170 in 1930–31 to a low of 115 in 1935–36.

taught at St. Dunstan's. This latter institution, in turn, improved its science program and finally invoked its right to grant its own university degrees in time for the May 1941 convocation.

A less happy fate awaited the provincial Agricultural and Technical School that occupied Fanningbank and its outbuildings. Launched in late 1920 to provide practical education as a postwar rehabilitation measure, the school was funded on a cost-shared basis with the federal government. The province paid one-third of the expenses, and the federal government contributed the balance. Tuition was free, although some out-of-town students had housing expenses. Night classes were also offered, and these proved to be very popular with Charlottetonians. The courses focused on agriculture, motor mechanics, carpentry and, after 1923, home economics. Short courses were also offered for occupations such as lobster packing and butter or cheese processing. While specific educational prerequisites were not established, the course content prepared some agricultural students for admission to the Truro Agricultural College. Unfortunately, the federal program under which the school was funded had a finite life span, and, when the money ran out in 1924, the school closed. A limited number of short courses were thereafter offered from time to time in the Agricultural Hall on Fitzroy Street or at Prince of Wales College, but an early venture into the field of technical training on the Island had essentially come screeching to a halt for the usual budgetary reasons.

Another significant and more encouraging development occurred in the area of library service. The Carnegie Corporation as early as 1922 had identified a shortage of books as an impediment to public education in Prince Edward Island. The main resource in the province was the Dodd and Legislative Library, succeeded by the Harris Memorial Library, but public funding for these facilities was parsimonious. The city, for instance, gave no support beyond the provision of "a very small nominal sum for upkeep." The American philanthropic body was actively trying to increase the availability of books in all of Canada. In a 1930 survey of the Canadian library system, it found that Prince Edward Island was "a perfect unit" in which to demonstrate how a program of book circulation should operate. In the view of one corporate advisor, it was "compact, self-supported and self-respecting; its people are believers in education."

After Prince of Wales College burned down in 1931, the Carnegie Corporation in the Maritimes decided to make the rebuilt school the base for a library demonstration project on the Island. In January 1933, PWC received a substantial grant to purchase books and to hire two new librarians. Operating out of the basement of the new college building, the project circulated books to schools across the Island. City Council even agreed to pay for an assistant to help with the work. Despite the Depression and a concomitant fear of higher taxes, there was general support for the initiative because of "a widespread realization that the establishment of free books next to the existence of free schools is the greatest contribution that can be made to the educational system of the province." The Carnegie-funded project was scheduled to run for three years, and before it concluded the province had passed legislation to create a Library Commission to promote and manage library facilities on the Island.

Once the demonstration project was wrapped up in 1936, the books and staff were moved to the Harris Memorial Library, which assumed the obligation to circulate books to various parts of the Island. The city and the province split the building's maintenance costs, and the province provided the salaries of the two librarians. The city undertook to pay for a third librarian. Charlottetown had finally taken on some responsibility for a public library, but the province still bore two-thirds of the cost. It was a good deal for the city. As a report to City Council concluded, the bulk of the benefit of the library went to Charlottetown and the overall cost to the city was small by Canadian standards.

Public Health

The provision of health care in Charlottetown during this period was marked by both encouraging and discouraging developments. Each of the hospitals obtained new buildings — the Charlottetown Hospital in 1925 and the Prince Edward Island Hospital in 1933 — and some new equipment, such as new X-ray machines for the PEI Hospital in 1926. The improved facilities supported modern diagnostic and surgical services, but the ability to pay for treatments varied from patient to patient. Individuals were often admitted without particular regard to their financial resources, straining the institutions' finances.[43] During the Depression, in particular, this burden made hospital budgets extremely tight. There was limited investment from provincial and municipal governments, which, to keep taxes low, left private charities, service clubs and citizens to compensate for meagre state commitments for health. The provincial government provided a $2,000 contribution to the PEI Hospital in 1927, and in 1928 the city agreed to make an annual grant of $1,000.[44] The Charlottetown Hospital got equivalent sums. Early on in the Depression, the possibility of a provincial health tax was discussed to fund free public hospital care,[45] but the idea went nowhere at the time. As it was, the largest portion of the money to operate both of Charlottetown's general hospitals was raised privately within the local community. Much less support came from most of the rural areas of the province, although the hospitals were expected to serve the countryside as well as the city.[46]

Despite the fact that the hospitals were the settings for surgeries and other significant medical procedures, the bulk of health care was still delivered by individual physicians in their private practices. An interesting departure from this pattern occurred in 1925 when three young medical doctors opened the Polyclinic. Each of them had a distinct

43 In 1927, 45 patients, a significant number for the time, were treated at the PEI Hospital free of charge.

44 The city's grant went up to $1,500 by 1932 and to $2,000 by 1933.

45 The participants were W. M. Lea, Liberal Leader of the Opposition, and Dr. W. J. P. MacMillan, the Minister of Education and Public Health.

46 A report on the annual meeting of the PEI Hospital in 1922 showed that 53 per cent of the patients came from rural areas, but less than 33 per cent of private donations came from there. About 100 school districts failed to donate one dollar.

In 1915 fox magnate Charles Dalton built a 25-bed sanatorium in North Wiltshire with the intent of giving it as a gift to the province. Instead it was loaned to the Canadian government as a facility to treat consumptive soldiers. The federal government expanded it to the size seen here, but when it tried to give it back to the province in 1921, the province refused to accept it. Instead it reverted to Charles Dalton, who had little alternative but to order its demolition.

specialization as well as a general practice.[47] Shared practices were not commonly found even in larger centres at this time, and this one was deeply resented by solo practitioners who did not appreciate the added competition. The Polyclinic, located in a refurbished house on Prince Street, boasted a "beautifully finished and furnished" large waiting room, examining rooms in which minor operations could be performed, and a laboratory. In 1929 the clinic added a fourth specialist; two more physicians joined it during the 1930s. Besides providing medical care to their patients, the partners in the clinic expanded the city's limited range of medical technology through the purchase of specialized equipment for installation at the PEI Hospital.[48]

One of the greatest health challenges throughout the 1920s and 1930s was tuberculosis. In 1922 the mortality rate in Prince Edward Island from this disease was the highest in Canada. In 1929, 15 Charlottetonians died from tuberculosis. A sanatorium had been built prior to the First World War in North Wiltshire, 15 miles north of the city, by Charles Dalton, a wealthy fox breeder, but provincial funding of it sparked a heated controversy. With some relief, in 1916 the provincial government turned the facility over to the federal government for use as a sanatorium for consumptive soldiers. In 1921 the federal government was ready to give the now-enlarged hospital back to the province. Premier John H. Bell, a long-time opponent of the sanatorium, refused to have the provincial government pay its ongoing costs, and the building reverted to Dalton in 1922.

47 They were J. Wendell MacKenzie, internal medicine; R. F. Seaman, surgery and gynaecology; and F. W. Tidmarsh, obstetrics and children's diseases. They were subsequently joined by J. Lantz, eye, ear, nose and throat; and D. Campbell and C. Houston.

48 The "P" in Polyclinic, along with the "P" in Prince Edward Island Hospital, like the "C" in the Charlottetown Hospital and the future Charlottetown Clinic, was reputed to be code for the main target clientele. The Protestants used the "P" institutions; the Catholics, the "C." In practice, there were crossovers. The equipment was a Basal Metabolic Rate (BMR) machine and Electrocardiogram (ECG) machine.

Nine years after it refused to accept Charles Dalton's sanatorium, the province opened the 48-bed Provincial Sanatorium on McGill Avenue.

The Charlottetown Anti-Tuberculosis Society challenged this neglect of a vital public health issue. It had championed the cause of the sanatorium throughout its existence, but where similar organizations in other parts of the province had supported the Charlottetown group's efforts before the war, it fought the postwar battle to save the hospital alone. Subsequently, the provincial Red Cross Society intervened and, with the help of the Anti-Tuberculosis Society and various branches of the Women's Institute, worked to convince the provincial government of the need for a new sanatorium. In 1929 the administration of A. C. Saunders agreed to establish one, with the proviso of a major contribution raised by public subscription. The fundraising campaign exceeded its goal, and a new 48-bed sanatorium finally opened in 1931 at the corner of North River Road and McGill Avenue. The crucial role of volunteer organizations in this process underscored the basis upon which public health services were provided in Charlottetown and throughout the Island.

Pressure from the city's Anti-Tuberculosis Society and other public health advocates provoked various public health advances. In 1935 Dr. B. C. Keeping, the Provincial Health Officer wrote, "almost all the efforts for the improvement of public health [in the years following 1910] can be traced to the work of the Anti-Tuberculosis Society" and related Charlottetown groups. In 1938 a speaker at the annual meeting of the patrons of the Free Dispensary listed various advances in which the society had been instrumental. They included, amongst others, provision of pure ice to city buyers, improved school sanitation, an anti-spitting by-law, appointment of a provincial health officer, medical examinations of school children and establishment of a disease-free area for cattle. In addition, the society continued to furnish drugs, clothing and food to stricken citizens through the Free Dispensary, although lack of funds sometimes hampered this project.

Successful agitation for improved public health standards resulted in increased civic regulatory activities. These included appointing an inspector of milk and meat and a sanitary officer to inspect privies and yards; granting small subventions to hospitals, orphanages and charities; and enacting and enforcing by-laws governing the bottling and later pasteurization of milk and the wrapping of bread sold within the city. Milk inspection was an important task in an era before universal pasteurization. In the 1920s, city inspectors examined dairy farms supplying Charlottetown with milk; tested the product; and checked the conditions of the stables, milk houses and the handling methods. They also monitored local citizens who kept a cow to ensure untested milk was used solely for personal consumption. A 1922 by-law required milk retailers to deliver their product in stoppered bottles. Grocery stores were checked to see if they were equipped to handle milk in a sanitary way, and at times the police were delegated to collect milk samples for testing. Another concern, odd to modern ways, was the keeping of swine in the city, a practice that drew the ire of the Health Officer throughout the 1920s and into the 1930s. In 1932 there were still 110 local pig sties, a fact that must have contributed a distinct odour as well as potential health hazards. It was not until June 8, 1940, that all persons owning pigs were required to remove them from the city. The city dump at the Kensington Range was further concern, particularly when fires were started illegally. The Health Officer wanted an incinerator, but by 1944 had yet to achieve this goal.

The provincial Red Cross Society provided additional services. This organization waged a campaign in the early 1920s to improve health care and sanitation, an effort that was Island-wide but focused on Charlottetown. Objectives included a provincial laboratory, a health organization and a nursing agency. In 1921 it opened a health centre in the Market House to provide nursing services to expectant mothers and to children. During the 1920s, the society worked with community activists and agencies from outside the province to promote an awareness for improved health care. An examination of the children at Prince Street School by a Red Cross health inspector in 1921 found that 95 per cent had a physical defect that required attention. In addition, there were the ongoing menaces of tuberculosis, smallpox and childhood diseases such as diphtheria. In 1927, for instance, 11 cases of smallpox were reported in Charlottetown. Efforts were made to control the disease through the vaccination of all school children; by 1924, 85 per cent of Charlottetown's school children were vaccinated. By contrast, a survey of 210 country schools in 1927 found that at 90 of them none of the pupils was vaccinated. The society also advocated other public health programs. In 1930 weekly chest clinics were held in Charlottetown to combat tuberculosis, and a campaign against diphtheria inoculated 1,347 school children and 346 preschoolers.[49]

49 By 1938 practically all public school children were inoculated against diphtheria.

Lack of co-ordination among health agencies, however, hampered the effective delivery of such services, particularly outside of Charlottetown. In December 1920, a meeting was held at Charlottetown to organize a Child Welfare and Public Health Association for the province. Although delegates attended from across the Island, half came from the capital. They represented churches, the hospitals, the YMCA, service clubs, charities, groups already involved in public health and the government. Beyond establishing a child welfare bureau, many at the conference wanted the creation of a provincial department of public health. The provincial government of John H. Bell showed remarkably little interest in addressing issues of public health. Meanwhile, the city's Health Officer, Dr. W. J. P. MacMillan, entered provincial politics as a Conservative. Following that party's victory at the polls in 1923, he convinced Premier J. D. Stewart to extend financial support for Red Cross programs.

Yet the standards of public health service still lagged behind what was found elsewhere, and so, in 1929, the concept of a single public health organization was resurrected. It came in the form of a proposal to establish a full-time health service for a five-year trial period. The initiative would involve government, the Red Cross and the Canadian Life Insurance Officers Association. Following persistent pressure from public health advocates, in July 1931, the provincial government, now led by Premier Walter Lea, created a Department of Health to provide amalgamated health services. The experiment was funded on a 50-50 basis between the province and city on the one hand and the Canadian Life Insurance Officers Association on the other. There was an understanding that the department would continue after 1936

Junior Red Cross group, c. 1925. In the 1920s, the Red Cross became an important factor in public health in the province.

with provincial or civic backing. Under these arrangements, the provision of various public health services was consolidated, with the bulk of Charlottetown's health unit being transferred to the new department along with a payment from the city for ongoing services. The municipality retained its food inspector and sanitary officer. This rationalized administration facilitated additional public health projects, such as the creation of a venereal disease clinic in 1931 and a program in 1940 to inoculate children against scarlet fever.

The city and its service clubs were still involved in health protection, though, as evidenced by the establishment of a dental clinic for needy children in 1935. It was part of an initiative by the Department of Health, but the department could not provide all the finances, so the city made office space and equipment available and the Gyro Club and Rotary Club helped pay for some of the expenses.[50] Success with the sanatorium and other efforts to promote public health services for the province would not have been possible without the intervention of outside agencies as well as active support from across the Island. A crucial impetus for reform came from Charlottetown's professional, religious and business leaders. Although some of the responsibilities for public health services were taken over by the new department, there was much that remained to be done by charitable organizations.

Water and Sewerage Services

Unlike public health matters, municipal water service failed to evoke much concern from Charlottetonians in the early 1920s. The city had become accustomed to ample supplies, and citizens had developed little concern for conservation. Shortages that appeared in 1920 prompted the Water Commissioners to urge the public to economize in their water consumption, but these went largely unheeded. Additional wells at the North River site increased supplies, but continued periodic shortages indicated that more than gentle prodding was needed to trim water usage. The installation of meters was discussed, but the generally moist temperate climate and the costs involved discouraged this step until 1925, when the Water Commission decided to install meters on large consumers. They also launched a number of surveys to locate additional water sources. In 1924 sea water flooded inactive springs near some of the city's supplementary wells at North River. This temporarily gave water a brackish taste, and the springs were subsequently plugged and dams built to hold back the high tides. The summer of 1929 was different. It was dry, very dry, with little significant precipitation from late May until the end of November. During the worst of the drought, Charlottetown's drinking water began to remind citizens of the saltiness experienced in 1924. Now the taste was back but for a different reason. The drought of 1929 left little doubt that the city had to find more fresh water.

In 1930 the Water Commission asked City Council for the authority to borrow money to develop one of two possible sites: one on the Brackley Point Road, about

50 The need was great. In 1936 all but 2 per cent of school children had defective teeth.

5½ miles north of the city; the other on the Union Road, 1¼ miles east of the Brackley site. The rock formations at the Union site were less promising, so approval was sought for a project at the Brackley location. Once permission was received from the city, work proceeded at a quick pace. Over 70 acres were purchased at the upper reaches of the Winter River to protect the purity of the ground water; and by December four miles of pipe were laid from the new wells to the reservoir on Mount Edward Road. Half of Charlottetown's water was now drawn from the Brackley wells, with most of the balance coming from the Malpeque station. The North River wells were used only to meet peak demands. With these resources, the city's water supplies were adequate until the end of the Second World War. Increased consumption by 1945, however, renewed concern for the future. To meet immediate needs, a new deep well was sunk at Malpeque, but ongoing expansion of demand and the tendency of the shallow wells to be affected by prolonged dry weather meant further sources would be required in the next few years.

Water quality was another concern. From its inception, the Water Commission pumped untreated water into people's homes. Groundwater contamination was always a potential threat, and in many parts of Canada the purity of raw water was indeed compromised. Chlorine treatment gradually became the norm for Canadian municipalities. Tests of Charlottetown's supplies put the city's water within the safety limits established by the federal department of health, but these tests were not done on a daily basis, and the possibility existed that on certain days, particularly in dry periods, the bacteria count might exceed permitted limits. In 1938, in response to studies done by the provincial health department the previous year, chlorinators were installed at the Brackley and Malpeque pumping stations.

Pumping Station, c. 1900. The drought of 1929 left little doubt that the city needed to expand the waterworks developed 50 years earlier.

By the 1920s and 1930s, connecting to the city water and sewer systems had become a matter of necessity for many homeowners and businesses. People in the newer parts of town, particularly Brighton, clamoured for these services. Unfortunately, the weak economy and Charlottetown's relatively high debt levels made City Council reticent about approving a rapid expansion of public utilities.[51] Resistance came from homeowners as well. By 1940 there were still several hundred outdoor privies in the city. In 1930 the Water Commission asked for permission to expand its system to Brighton and other outlying areas. The administrators of the new sanatorium intervened with City Council by supporting this request so that services would reach the new health facility. Without them, the health lobby argued, the hospital might not be able to house its tuberculosis patients, and returning ill people to the community would create "a public menace as well as a menace to their own families." The work went ahead. Providing water and sewerage services in residential zones beyond the city's boundaries was more problematic. Generally, non-residents were permitted to tap into the water mains running along both Malpeque and Mount Edward Roads, but they had to pay supplementary fees. On two occasions water lines were extended at the owners' expense to facilitate hook-ups. Even so, the civic administration strongly felt that suburban residents should not benefit from an infrastructure for which they had not paid.

Public Safety

Unlike the low profile of the water issue, fires continued to make headlines between 1920 and 1945. The fire that tore through a building at the corner of Kent and Great George Streets on April 28, 1923, was guaranteed to make the news, since it housed the *Guardian*, one of Charlottetown's leading newspapers. On January 12, 1929, the Victoria Hotel, Charlottetown's largest and finest, went up in flames, as did the Falconwood Hospital for the Insane in 1931, Prince of Wales College in 1932, the Agricultural Hall on Fitzroy Street in 1941 and the Exhibition Building in 1945. In between there was a plethora of smaller blazes, proof that fire was still a danger even in a city that was mainly serviced with water hydrants and increasingly constructed of brick.

Fires were popular public spectacles. Inevitably, onlookers were drawn to the conflagrations, and with the widespread appearance of automobiles, firefighters began to find their access to the scene blocked by curious citizens. In 1940 the Fire Chief threatened to have charges laid against people who impeded the passage of his men and equipment. Composed of a nucleus of full-time firefighters and a larger number of volunteers, the department remained centralized at City Hall. Ranks were smaller than in former times — about 24 members in 1937.

Equipment had changed as well, with the arrival of motor vehicles. An American LaFrance fire truck was purchased in 1929, and by 1937 three trucks sat in the bays

51 In 1920 Charlottetown's debt stood at 12.24 per cent of the tax base. By way of comparison, it was 10.2 per cent for Halifax and only 2.45 per cent for Saint John.

facing Queen Street. Economy remained a watchword, however, in this as in many other aspects of civic life. A modern pumper truck was purchased in 1941 only after the local fire underwriters assured City Council that they would lower insurance rates sufficiently to make the acquisition a profitable move for citizens.

Slow change was similarly taking place in the area of law enforcement in the interwar years. A particularly significant development occurred in 1932 when the RCMP assumed duties for policing the province. Policing within Charlottetown was largely left to the city force, which retained substantial responsibilities. These included patrolling the streets; enforcing city by-laws, highway traffic laws and the liquor control act; tending to automobile accidents; as well as investigating crimes committed in Charlottetown.

Enforcing liquor regulations was particularly troublesome since the laws were widely flouted, even though the sale of beverage alcohol had been prohibited since 1901 and the importation of liquor into the province was banned in 1923. In 1931, for instance, 370 people were convicted of offences involving liquor, including 13 instances of impaired driving, 88 cases of drunken and disorderly behaviour and 269 occurrences of being drunk and incapable. Alcohol had gotten out of control in the opinion of "Alarmed Citizen" who proclaimed in a letter to the editor of the *Patriot* that Charlottetown "is becoming a veritable Sodom." Undaunted, bootleggers

When the Guardian *office burned down in 1923, the fire department was still horse-drawn.*

continued to operate in the city, patronized by a wide spectrum of the population. In 1945 Council concluded that the municipality should be excluded from the provisions of the provincial prohibition legislation. Charlottetonians had consistently opposed the law, which, in the opinion of Council, encouraged crime and delinquency while discouraging tourism. Prohibition, however, would remain on the books for several more years. Meanwhile, police played a cat-and-mouse game with those who ignored its strictures.

More serious crimes were considerably less common. In 1932 two arrests were made for keeping a brothel, eight for breaking and entering and two for robbery with violence. Crime increased enough towards the end of the decade, however, for the *Patriot* to issue a report headed "The Crime Wave," about a grand jury's investigations into widespread crime in Charlottetown. In it, remarks about "theft, breaking and entering, burglary and even armed robbery" prompted the paper to conclude that unless something was done, "the Island is in a fair way of losing her reputation as a law-abiding community." The January 1941 murder of Peter Trainor was one of the most sensational crimes in Island history. Trainor, a butcher, had been viciously attacked in his shop at the corner of King and Pownal Streets. Fred Phillips and Earl Lund were discovered at the scene and charged soon afterwards. The case went to trial in June, and the defence built its arguments around the absence of a murder weapon and the sighting of an unknown third person at the location of the crime at about the same time as the killing. Found guilty of murder, the accused were hanged in the yard of the Queens County Jail on August 20, the last people to be executed on the Island.

Public Morality and Social Welfare

Charlottetown remained throughout the 1920s, 1930s and the Second World War a small, relatively homogeneous community with generally unremarkable social concerns. Complexities found in larger centres with more diverse populations appeared in muted form in the Island capital or not at all. Nevertheless, there were cleavages along economic, religious and social lines. While workers struggled to secure a wage rate of 30¢ an hour,[52] some professionals and businessmen enjoyed buoyant incomes. Degraded housing was condemned and torn down as, elsewhere, mansions, such as the home of George DeBlois on West Street, were built. Most of the population was affiliated with a church and was about evenly divided between Roman Catholics and Protestants. A *modus vivendi* kept the relations between the two groups civil if not always cordial.[53] An air of propriety suffused the city, but there was also the occasional whiff of

52 Purchasing power of this wage was equivalent on the average to $4.08 in 2008. The low point was 1921 with an equivalency of $3.33 and the high point was 1933 with a value of $4.79. The purchasing power of this wage was the same in 1926 and 1946 ($3.73) and virtually the same in 1931 and 1941 ($4.06 and $4.15).

53 Not all was well concerning inter-religious relations. Neil A. Matheson, a Protestant, recalled that he was contacted by a member of the local Ku Klux Klan in 1932 to tell him that his application to the Charlottetown Police Force was being supported by the Klan. As it happened, Matheson was not hired by the police, and he went on to become a sportswriter for the *Patriot*. Another resident, Woodrow Wheatley of Mount Edward Road, recalled that as a boy he saw a burned cross early one morning beside St. Peter's Road.

venal pleasure. The biggest challenge facing Charlottetonians was the impact of the Great Depression of the 1930s. Even here, ironies could be found. A significant proportion of the city's population was thrown onto welfare while the Charlottetown area reported a greater increase in income tax receipts than any other in Canada. Some city folk starved, and farmers left the countryside where food could be grown for a chance to find employment in town. A municipal government that prided itself with budgeting within its means was obliged to assume the burden of providing for large numbers of people who could no longer support themselves. The municipal reflex to economize in matters of civic concern was tested as never before.

The Depression started slowly on Prince Edward Island. In 1929 agricultural prices were up over 1928 and more tourists visited the province. Demand for farm commodities and fish products slackened in 1930, but unemployment was still not too severe. This deviation from the worldwide picture of economic chaos was observed with some complacency by Islanders. All of that changed in 1931 when soft markets and dry weather reduced the value of the province's agricultural crop. Next year, conditions were worse.[54] Charlottetonians found themselves facing widespread unemployment, spiralling welfare rolls and increases in unpaid taxes. The number of families on relief reached 465 in April 1933, rose to 583 one year later and stood around the 500 mark in February 1935. That meant about 2,000 people, or 15

54 Some protection for the local workforce had been provided until 1931 by the construction of the Canadian National Hotel and the Provincial Sanatorium. Although two other major building projects began shortly thereafter at the PEI Hospital and the Falconwood Hospital, they could not fully compensate for job losses elsewhere.

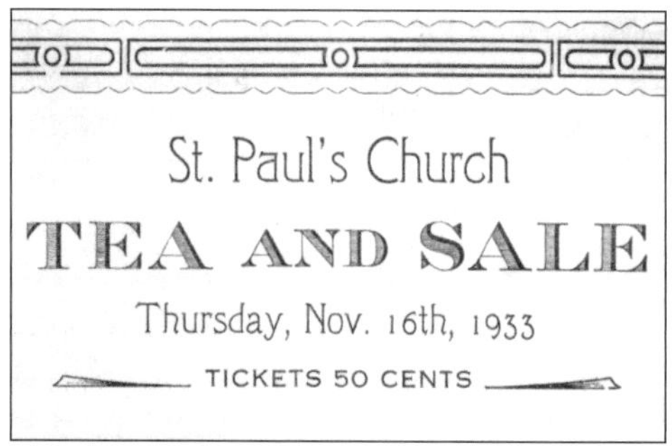

In the area of social welfare, Charlottetonians left much to private initiative. The Depression would prove, though, that charity teas and church suppers could only do so much.

St. Vincent's Orphanage, opened in 1910 across the Malpeque Road from St. Dunstan's, shared the task of sheltering vulnerable children during the Depression.

per cent of the population, were on charity. Back taxes rose from $40,000 in 1931 to $99,548 in 1933. Circumstances remained dire until after 1938.

In the area of social welfare, Charlottetonians left much to private initiative. Long ago, churches and to a lesser extent benevolent societies had assumed the task of bringing support from the community to its weakest and most vulnerable citizens. Churches were widely regarded as having the closest associations with the most people and being the most effective agents for social action. This approach was typical for the age, but it would be challenged during the 1920s and 1930s. Unprecedented circumstances, particularly during the Great Depression, tested the limits of the conservative concepts of self-reliance and charitable voluntarism and, ultimately, even the ability of the municipal government to provide for the welfare of its citizens.

As always, children and the elderly were the most vulnerable members of society, and the city's indigent and orphaned children were especially a problem. Some came into the care of the Children's Aid Society when one or both of their parents were jailed for breaking the prohibition act. Others were deserted by their parents or lost them through accident or illness. In 1921 the PEI Protestant Orphanage was established at Mount Herbert, just east of the city, to offer shelter and support for unparented children who could be neither adopted nor placed into a foster home. The facility was a community project backed by the various churches and their ladies auxiliaries, and, interestingly, the Loyal Orange Lodge. Later, support was received from the Masons, the Gyro Club and the Benevolent Irish Society. The institution shared the task of sheltering vulnerable children with the St. Vincent's Orphanage, a Roman Catholic institution that opened in 1910 on Malpeque Road. Less was done for the aged. Of the 90 inhabitants of the Provincial Infirmary in the mid-1920s, 80 per cent were elderly and mentally incompetent. Other seniors had to be admitted to the Falconwood psychiatric hospital for "humane" rather than "curative" reasons because they had neither family nor "Christian" friends to care for them.

Concerns about unemployment and poverty began during the economic doldrums of the 1920s, well before the Great Depression. One of the arguments J. A. Messervy, MP for Queen's, used in advocating federal policies to encourage cargo ships to call at Charlottetown was that "the bringing of steamers to Charlottetown would enable our longshoremen, labourers, and truckmen to find work, and they want it badly." Conditions worsened as the Depression deepened after 1931. The city's annual report for 1932 noted that, for the first time in its history, the city needed to organize for the relief of the unemployed. Two years later, the city admitted that, even if industrial conditions improved generally, "there was little hope that work could be found for the unemployed" in the Island capital since it "had practically no industry."

Much of what was done in the city responded to programs developed by senior levels of government, particularly the federal government. Initially, money was provided under the federal Unemployment Relief Act of 1930 for both public works to create jobs and direct relief to aid those without income.[55] The program was a cost-shared arrangement involving the federal and provincial governments and municipalities. Each paid one-third of the cost of direct relief, and the two senior levels of government split half the cost of public works, leaving the other half and administration to the municipalities. In 1931 a new program allowed for public works projects to be undertaken as a means of employment, with the federal government picking up half the cost. Charlottetown borrowed $50,000 to spend on civic improvements. Mayor T. W. L. Prowse explained, "this money was all used to alleviate suffering and unemployment, and every dollar spent, we received value for it, and 50 percent of it came from … the Unemployment Relief Fund." The next year, more emphasis was given to direct relief with each level of government responsible for one-third of the costs, although the provincial and federal governments would split the cost of any expenses the city could not meet.

While direct relief was deemed the cheapest way of handling destitution, it was stop-gap, and, in response to requests from the provinces, the federal government made money available again for public works in 1933. The emphasis remained on direct relief until 1934, however, after which time a more balanced long-term approach was adopted. This extended federal assistance for provincially administered direct relief and funds for municipal and provincial public works projects. Special assistance was available to provinces as required. Rather than paying one-third of the

55 Direct relief involved the provision of bare essentials, including food, fuel in winter and items of clothing. Food might include molasses and codfish but no meat, and there was great reluctance to provide help in summer when jobs were more available.

cost of municipal relief, the federal government provided lump sum payments that gradually increased as the Depression wore on.

The actual provision of relief to Charlottetonians hit hard by unemployment and poverty took various shapes as the city responded to shifting policy environments and levels of need. In the early stages, payments were kept to a minimum with direct relief provided by charities, including the Dr. Jenkins Coal Fund,[56] and the city through the City Clerk's office. In October 1932, the city agreed to pay relief to persons named by the province, but only so long as the province received unemployment relief funds from the federal government.[57] Council decided in 1933 that aid requests had to be reviewed by a clergyman or the social service nurse at the Dispensary to ensure they were justified. Approved requests were then presented to the City Clerk who checked on the prices charged for the required supplies and directed the business evenly among the city's merchants. The authorities later concluded that direct relief would be most efficiently handled if it came from one source that could purchase welfare supplies at wholesale prices. With this in mind, in May 1933 the city gave religious leaders responsibility for distributing relief and helped them in the process with grants of public funds. By the summer the need for direct relief exceeded the available funds. The province claimed it would match anything the city undertook to pay, but the city indicated that direct relief should be curtailed as much as possible for the summer months.

The winter of 1933–34 was particularly arduous. By February, volunteer charities were overwhelmed, and the city resumed responsibility for direct relief. By April, a despondent City Council resolved to stop unemployment relief at the end of the month. Emphasis was increasingly placed upon job creation after 1934 rather than the dole. Some direct aid was inevitable, but in 1936 the city made welfare recipients liable to perform work in return for their relief.[58] Anyone who refused such work could be sent to jail for a period of up to 30 days. Direct relief continued as a supplement to a steadily increasing stream of employment-creation projects. The preference for this strategy was based on the perception that work gave welfare recipients a sense of independence and cash incomes benefitted merchants in general. Public works schemes also leveraged money from senior levels of government. The extent to which direct relief remained part of the welfare formula can be seen from the following table. It is interesting that payments for the necessities of life continued until 1941.

56 The Dr. Jenkins Coal Fund was established by Dr. J. T. Jenkins to receive donations from individuals and companies to purchase coal for the needy. Donors' names were publicly acknowledged. The fund was perpetuated in the 1930s by a grandson, Dr. J. T. Jenkins, and lists of contributors made regular appearances on the front page of the *Guardian* in this era.

57 City Council resolved to have the understanding between the city and the province in writing with specific mention that the city's responsibilities for payments to the poor ended with the discontinuation of unemployment relief to PEI.

58 Relief was prorated at the prevailing scale of wages.

Payments ($) Made to Suppliers for Necessities Provided as Direct Relief*						
	1936	1937	1938	1939	1940	1941
Winter: December to February**	20,817	22,447	26,210	15,983	19,521	7,098
Spring: March to May	19,470	19,374	21,414	31,032	25,538	10,589
Summer: June to August	1,520	2,073	4,391	5,875	5,553	90
Autumn: September to November	1,709	2,161	2,333	2,720	2,794	0

* Commodities supplied at city expense as relief included milk, flour, coal, potatoes, vegetables, etc.

** Winter includes expenses for December of the preceding year, except for 1936 which includes expenses only for January and February of that year.

There was some initial hesitation in Charlottetown to use public works as a means of creating jobs, but, in 1931, $10,000 was spent for that reason on repairs to city streets. Even with access to funds from the senior governments, the financial challenges facing the city were greater than it felt it could manage. During the difficult winter of 1933–34, a proposal to have work done at Government Pond and the Victoria Park roadway was held in abeyance until Council learned whether federal and provincial money dedicated to direct relief could be used for make-work projects. When this was permitted, the work proceeded. This was significant in that it demonstrated the city's preference for public works over direct relief as a means of helping the unemployed. After 1934, public works, the objective of which was in whole or in part the provision of employment, provided a measure of relief to the city's jobless and destitute. The city's economically disadvantaged, nevertheless, continued to endure soul-destroying misery.

Twenty per cent of the city's population was on relief at one point in 1937. As joblessness worsened, the city conceded that unemployment was a national problem in which a city could only help senior governments. Much the same was expected in 1938, but the decision to build the new airport offered some hope. When the project began, officials acknowledged that a principal objective was the provision of jobs. In fact, during the summer of 1938, the composition of work crews was changed every two weeks to spread the income around. In October, 796 were working at the airport, a figure that rose to 1,014 by December. Despite these developments, the city and the province considered the burden of social relief unsustainable. There was a sense that the aid was never enough, and "the employment and relief question" got "harder to face every year." Although it was not known at the time, the worst was past by 1938. In the aftermath of the Depression, there was a considerable legacy: roads were repaired, Government Pond was cleaned, Lord's Wharf was rebuilt, the breastwork around the western end of Victoria Park was renewed, the exhibition grounds were graded, and, most significantly of all, a new airport was constructed. There was also a sense of vulnerability that would linger for years.

Entertainment

The Eaton's catalogue offered the floor model of the "Lyric" for $39.50.

Economic hardship had a major impact on the ways Charlottetonians spent their leisure time. A night out at a charity bingo at the Little Theatre, Holy Name Hall or the IOOF Dance Hall offered inexpensive entertainment with the chance of some gain. Other pleasures could be costly. Access to radio programming, for instance, could be constrained by the price of the equipment. An inexpensive "Lyric" table model radio on sale at Holman's in the winter of 1934 cost $19.50, down from $24.50. The reduced price was still hefty, equivalent to $313.08 in 2008. The classy "All Wave" floor model with short-wave reception was reduced from $154 to $144, still a substantial sum equal to $2,312 in 2008.[59] The squeeze was tighter on some than others, of course, and those with a dependable income may have actually seen their standard of living rise. For most, irrespective of income, the pervasive atmosphere of want during the Depression shaped sensibilities and confirmed the instinctive financial caution that was shared generally by Charlottetonians. With financial restraints on entertainment, much leisure time continued to be spent in the home. Family fun included all of the old pastimes and a few new ones, such as an animated session of Monopoly, a game that began appearing on store shelves in 1935.

Religion endured as an important dimension of family life. Church attendance remained high and almost everyone professed an affiliation with one or another Christian faith. For those unable or unwilling to rouse themselves on a Sunday morning, CFCY broadcast a service, followed by reflective programming, such as readings from James Allen's *As a Man Thinketh*. A major rupture within two of the city's major Protestant groups occurred in the 1920s during the debate over the union of the Presbyterian, Methodist and Congregational churches. The topic had been actively considered prior to the First World War and was resurrected at the national level in 1920. In Charlottetown, the Methodists supported union, and the idea initially elicited some interest from the pastor of Zion Presbyterian, although his counterpart at St. James Presbyterian would not hear of it. Large segments of both Presbyterian congregations opposed union, feeling that it was a change driven by the national leadership and contrary to Presbyterianism's democratic traditions. In the end, the

59 Sales on credit with easy payment terms softened the blow in some cases.

The Elders of Zion Presbyterian and about a third of the congregation favoured Church Union ...

elders at Zion Presbyterian favoured union along with one-third of the congregation, but the minister and the balance of the membership dissented. Opposition was even stronger at St. James. Both congregations retained their affiliation with the now substantially reduced Presbyterian Church in Canada,[60] but a significant number of communicants and their financial resources transferred to the new church. One of many results of this debate was the influx of Presbyterians to the massive First Methodist, soon re-baptized, Trinity United Church on Prince Street. Even more than before, that church's Heartz Memorial Hall, built in 1910, proved to be a focal point for lectures and musical entertainment, as well as religious events.

As in former years, the city's churches were centres of considerable social activity. An active round of bazaars, concerts and teas helped build a sense of community, not only within particular congregations but Charlottetown as a whole. A typical event might have been a garden party and tea held by the Women's Missionary Society of the Kirk of St. James on a "delightfully fine day" in the summer of 1933. Bonnahinley, the home of Chester McLure, MP, was a magnificent venue for the occasion with stately trees, velvety lawns and beautiful flower gardens. The tea brought together a

60 The legalities of the situation impaired the Presbyterian right to use the name "The Presbyterian Church in Canada" until 1939, and as late as 1947 in PEI.

... but the majority at Zion and an even larger proportion of those at St. James decided to remain part of the substantially reduced Presbyterian Church in Canada. Fortunately, the massive First Methodist Church (above) was able to absorb the influx of former Presbyterians as it became Trinity United. Note: Trinity's twin spires have been taken down to roof level.

large number of out-of-town visitors, local residents and members of the church, both ladies and gentlemen. The annals of the church for this period are full of notations concerning lectures, sewing sessions, bake sales, candy sales, banquets and amateur plays, as well as regular meetings of women's groups held at the homes of various members. During the Second World War, some of the customary events were replaced by practices in setting up emergency hospitals, first aid posts and relief kitchens, and, happily, in 1945 a welcome-home party for returned servicemen and women. With slight variations, similar stories emerged from the city's other places of worship.

The return of military personnel from overseas following the Great War helped to reinvigorate the sporting life of the provincial capital. Cyclists, swimmers and fishermen resumed their pastimes with a gratitude based on a renewed appreciation of life. There was also the volunteer time and money to revitalize sports programs within the YMCA and the city's churches. The "Y," the Roman Catholic League of the Cross and the Church Athletic League sponsored by the Anglicans, Baptists, Methodists and Presbyterians offered an array of activities including basketball, volleyball, bowling, baseball and hockey. Badminton and soccer appeared in a significant way in the mid-1930s. Interschool sport also attracted numerous participants at both the public school and college levels. The naval reserve received a budget for sports, and, during the 1930s, this, along with training cruises, proved a powerful magnet for

A. CHANDLER Hoc. Com.
F. HENNESSY Hoc. Com.
T.W.L. PROWSE. Pres.
Dr. I. J. YEO. Hoc. Com.
G. L. PROWSE. Secy.
W. HALPENNY
F. BROWN
P. RODD. L. Wing
F. PROWSE. L. Wing
J. GORDON. R. Wing
F. CRONIN. R. Wing
CHAMPIONS
MARITIME
PROVINCES
1922 1923
J. McEACHERN. Centre
R. PROWSE. Centre
C. CAMPBELL. Def.
F. KELLY. Capt. R. Def.
F. MOORE. L. Def.
H. MORGAN. Goal
CLUB RECORD 1921-22-23 GAMES WON 30 DRAW 1 LOST 1
ABEGWEIT
HOCKEY TEAM
Bayer Photo.

recruits. Lawn tennis, golf and curling prospered with the benefit of their own private facilities, even in the face of the Depression that undercut participation in some other sports. Sailing, which had traditionally enjoyed a large following in the city, equally weathered the economic storm, and with the incorporation of the Charlottetown Yacht Club in 1938, local sailors obtained a secure berth for themselves and their craft.

In the 1922-23 season, the "Abbies" successfully defended the NB-PEI Hockey Association championship they'd won the previous season. As the Falconwood Women's Hockey Team suggests, though, hockey was a popular game at all levels.

Enthusiasm for sports whetted the appetites of spectators who turned out in large numbers to cheer local teams. The famous Abegweit Amateur Athletic Association senior hockey team was reorganized in 1920, but the absence of serious, in-province competition (from other than Summerside) forced it to play most of its away games on the mainland. During the 1921–22 season, the Charlottetown team won the NB-PEI Hockey Association championship and subsequently the Maritime senior championship, defeating the Nova Scotia titleholders before an ecstatic hometown crowd. Repeating this triumph in the 1922–23 campaign, the Abbies were a recognized powerhouse in Canadian hockey. In 1931 they joined five New Brunswick teams in a league that set aside local residency rules for players and permitted some team members to be paid. By 1935 Charlottetown was in a circuit with teams from Saint John, Moncton and Halifax. Unfortunately, later that year, pressure from the Canadian Amateur Hockey Association over the incipient professionalism of the "Big Four" teams led to the league's collapse. A new senior league operated between 1937 and 1939 with two teams from Charlottetown, the Abbies and the Rangers, but it lacked the spark of the earlier groupings. Not all was lost, though. The excitement generated by the previous senior Abbies teams had stimulated the rise of various women's and junior clubs. In 1934 the junior Abbies played in the Memorial Cup finals and the Royals made it to the eastern semifinal round of the Memorial Cup in 1939. The advent of the Second World War disrupted organized hockey, but junior play continued with the Royals winning the Maritime championship in 1940 and 1941. Meanwhile, teams from St. Dunstan's and Prince of Wales pursued a separate but ardent rivalry at the college level.

Of course, there was much more to organized competitive sport than hockey, and most alternatives attracted widespread support in the interwar period. Track and field was revitalized in 1921 when the Abegweit Amateur Athletic Association lured Bill Halpenny back to Charlottetown as a coach. The effects were almost immediate, and although few succeeded as spectacularly as Philip Blake Macdonald and Barney Francis, the club showed well at regional and national meets throughout most of the 1920s. Rival League of the Cross Amateur Athletic Association produced accomplished stars of its own, including Elliot McGuigan who won four gold medals at the Maritime championships in 1924. The 1930s were less kind to the large integrated sports associations, but track and field found new sponsors in the form of the YMCA, the fire department and the *Patriot* newspaper, and Charlottetown competitors continued to do well at meets throughout the Depression.

The economic doldrums of the 1930s had a similar effect on baseball, which had boomed as a popular sport in the 1920s. Here again, powerful Abbies teams were prominent, but Charlottetown boasted other successful ball clubs, and vigorous rivalries at various levels of play continued into the early Depression years before baseball's fortunes waned. Rugby also went through a cycle of waxing and waning, with teams from the Abegweit organization and St. Dunstan's College battling for supremacy before large crowds of supporters every autumn in the 1920s. The financial collapse of the Abegweit team in 1933 left St. Dunstan's in competition with Prince of Wales College and a new rival, the Nomads, but, by 1938, SDU had to seek opponents in New Brunswick.

Horse racing fans had no worries about the future of their sport. Charlottetown remained a principal harness racing centre in the Maritimes. Events at the Driving Park attracted large crowds, and Charlottetown-owned horses ran to victory in important events outside the province. Horse racing, in fact, was considered to be the Island's favourite sport. Noted Island sports historian Charlie Ballem has observed that the principal movers and shakers behind the driving park and horse racing generally were influential members of society. This kind of leadership and financial commitment kept racing vibrant even as the Depression sapped vitality from other sports.

In a tart commentary on the state of cultural activities in Prince Edward Island, a report on the libraries noted, "there is also little interest shown, outside of Charlottetown and Summerside, in music, art, poetry, or gardening, although interest in the last mentioned is increasing." Whatever the merits of this view is for the Island generally, it at least concedes that the capital city retained its interest in the arts and in various forms of public entertainment. Undoubtedly, the author of the report had in mind the more cerebral and refined forms of cultural expression, but a popular definition might have wider limits, and the city, in fact, boasted of a wide variety of entertainment.

For many years, Charlottetown had been a regular stop in the circuit of performers and athletes who trekked through the Maritime provinces in search of a living. Improved communications and an appetite for professional entertainment increased this flow. Boxing and wrestling matches were held at the Palais De Danse, otherwise known as the Lyceum. Other venues also hosted events, such as the "Big Time Wrestling" (to be followed by a dance) featured at the Sporting Club in June 1939. Admission was 50¢ for

Renting space in the Market Hall, the Strand was Charlottetown's main movie theatre in the early 1920s. Now showing in this c. 1920 photo is The Furnace, *directed by William Desmond Taylor, who in 1919 also directed the first film adaptation of* Anne of Green Gables.

gentlemen, 25¢ for unaccompanied ladies and free for ladies with a male escort. One feature of the annual entertainment calendar grew in significance as the 1920s wore on. The Exhibition became increasingly venturesome in its productions and brought new and better acts and vaudeville shows to the fairgrounds. Performers were brought from as far away as Europe, and local audiences were treated to "every worth while act shown in the larger centres of the U.S. or Canada with the exception of the Zacchinis Cannon act." These performances continued throughout the 1930s, but after the outbreak of the war they were made part of the Old Home Week festivities. As such, they broke Maritime attendance records for outside entertainment in 1944 and 1945.

There was still avid interest in local talent. A performance at the Prince Edward Theatre in August 1939 by Don Messer and his Backwoods Breakdown Five, featuring Charlie Chamberlain, "the singing lumberjack," was deemed a crowd pleaser. More than one fiddler could be found in town, however, and on March 30, 1926, a large number of them turned up at the Strand Theatre for a "mammoth" fiddling contest. Unfortunately, local talent played second fiddle to the winner, Neil Cheverie of Elmira, who went on to take second place at the world championships in Boston. There were lots of opportunities for amateurs to find a stage and an audience at the

Prince Edward, too, and it was a popular site for musical reviews. A January 1932 concert featured an orchestra, a pipe and drum band, highland dancers, step dancers, solo singers, duets and quartets. Live entertainment and concerts were also held at Heartz Memorial Hall. After its reconstruction, the Prince of Wales College Hall hosted various productions, including a "good, old-fashioned minstrel show" that attracted "a large attendance" in the winter of 1934. Even the exhibition, despite its pursuit of big-name talent, had room for locals. Evening presentations, in particular, were extravaganzas in which members of the driving club "properly attired and with perfectly turned out mounts" took their places under the lights at centre field in front of the grandstand. In January 1939, the Dominion Drama Festival was held at the Prince Edward. Newspapers reported, with not a little pride, that the Charlottetown Little Theatre Guild acquitted itself commendably in the competition.

The cinema grew as a popular diversion, and blossomed in the 1930s. The two main movie houses were the Prince Edward Theatre and the Capitol Theatre. Films such as *The Common Law* with Constance Bennett ("Love painted the portrait, Love wrote this story") and *Let's Go Native,* starring Jack Oakie and Jeanette MacDonald, appeared in 1932. Viewers to the latter production could hear Oakie sing "I've Got a Yen" and see "Sweet Jeanette Make Tropical Love." A few years later the big screen at the Prince Edward was filled with Clark Gable and Jean Harlow in *Saratoga*. Ostensibly about horse racing, *Saratoga* was the sixth film to pair Gable and Harlow in a smouldering romance. Those Charlottetonian horse-lovers with tamer tastes could line up at the Capitol for Dick Foran with Jill Valkis in *Blazing Sixes* in which the lead had "a song on his lips … and a price on his head!" A familiar, local story appeared in 1934 when *Anne of Green Gables* was released by RKO Radio Pictures.[61] It starred Dawn Paris as Anne and was successful enough to prompt Paris to change her screen name to Anne Shirley. She went on to make *Anne of Windy Poplars* in 1940. Locals were thrilled in 1938 when *Heart of the North* opened with the sponsorship of the Canadian Legion. It featured Dick Foran, Gloria Dickson and Island native Bruce Carruthers in a tale of the RCMP set in "a million miles of wilderness." In July 1939, the Prince Edward hosted the Eastern Canada première of *Goodbye, Mr. Chips* featuring an imposing cast led by Robert Donat and Greer Garson.

Most of the fraternal societies and similar organizations that sprang up in previous decades continued to play a part in the social life of Charlottetown from 1921 until 1945, but the more recently established service clubs seemed to have captured the spirit of the times most effectively. Significantly, one of the more robust traditional groups, at least in terms of press coverage, was a women's service organization, the Imperial Order of the Daughters of the Empire. Two new "fraternal" societies responded to the larger role that women were playing in society in the postwar world. The Order of the Eastern Star that began its chapter in Charlottetown in 1921

61 This was not the first Anne movie. That distinction is held by a silent film produced in Hollywood by Realart Pictures Corporation in 1919. It starred Mary Miles Minter and had a grossly distorted storyline. Fortunately, it quickly faded from the big screen.

admitted both men and women, and the Pythian Sisters, begun in 1923, was a women's auxiliary of the Knights of Pythias. For men, the Rotary Club, established in 1917, was particularly active in the 1920s and '30s, attracting large audiences to hear addresses on timely topics. The Canadian Legion was organized in 1926 to provide fellowship and act as an advocate for veterans of the war. It took over from the Great War Veterans' Association that had purchased a house in 1919 to serve as a social centre. In 1927 the Gyro Club was founded. It had a mandate to perpetuate friendships established in the early stages of adulthood and focused on social activities such as summer dances at the Beach Grove Inn. Although in philosophy Gyro left charitable work and community service to other organizations, in practice the Charlottetown group engaged in such projects, including charitable fund-raising, selling Christmas seals and giving gifts to orphans at Christmas. In 1937 a Charlottetown branch of the Kinsmen Club was instituted. This distinctively Canadian organization was dedicated to young men under 40 and combined the objectives of fun, community service and personal development. An emphasis on youth was also apparent in the establishment of the Junior Board of Trade in 1938. In 1944 a joint committee of the city's service clubs was created to provide co-ordinated backing for various civic projects. Worthy undertakings would be more likely sanctioned by politicians and supported by the public as a whole if they had the backing of over 150 "leading business and professional men of the city" — or so it was believed.

It is not surprising, given the spirit of the age, that young Charlottetonians found an opportunity for companionship and personal development in the burgeoning scouting movement. There were attempts to establish a Boy Scout troop at the YMCA in 1910 and again in 1914, but both had foundered. After the end of the Great War, scouting flourished at various city churches. The first troop was formed at St. Dunstan's Basilica in 1919. It was followed by a troop at St. Peter's Cathedral based upon a nucleus of boys from the Otter Patrol of the old YMCA troop. In 1922 a troop was established at the Kirk of St. James and soon thereafter at Zion Presbyterian and First Methodist. First Baptist Church followed suit in 1927, Holy Redeemer Catholic in 1930 and St. Paul's Anglican Church in 1932. The troop at First Methodist lapsed in 1925 but was reconstituted in 1934 after the church had become Trinity United.

Typically, these organizations seem to have had about 40 members in the early years and, with a brief decline in the late 1920s, grew subsequently. In addition, new categories of members were drawn into the movement: Girl Guides for girls, Wolf Cubs and Brownies for younger boys and girls, and a Rover Crew for older boys. During the school year, members engaged in various training programs emphasizing woodcraft, teamwork, character skills and athletics. The scouting season was capped by a camp, and occasionally there was a jamboree that brought together troops from across the Island and even beyond. Scouts, guides and cubs soon were allotted roles in public ceremonies and even had their activities featured in a column, "Scout News and Notes" in the *Guardian*. A visit by the World Chief Scout, Lord Robert Baden-Powell, in 1935 was a highlight of the interwar period. A Grand Rally was held at the exhibition grounds in which 14 units from all parts of the province engaged in a whimsical "circus" parade of fictional or imaginary animals, in addition to sporting and skills demonstrations, a concert and a patriotic closing. It was an impressive display of youthful energy, Christian outreach and imperial loyalty.

The stir surrounding the visit of Lord Baden-Powell, however, was a foretaste of the pomp of the Royal Tour of 1939. The visit of King George VI and Queen Elizabeth to Canada was an event of immense social and political importance that excited Canadians from coast to coast. The presence of the king-emperor elicited an outpouring of loyalty, nowhere more than from the Island capital. In the days leading up to the visit, scheduled for June 14, the occasion was cited as justification for all manner of improvements to make Charlottetown as modern as other cities. "Citizen" writing to the *Patriot* noted the absence of street signs at most intersections and called for their installation "particularly now when His Majesty the King is coming and this ... is sure to bring visitors to this city, who always look to street corner signs for proper direction." Closer to the event, paint stores urged residents to spruce up their properties to make a good impression on the royal tourists. Entrepreneurs erected grandstands at various spots along the parade route and sold single seats for $2.50 (equivalent to $38.03 in 2008). Particularly loyal observers, wanting to watch the procession coming and going, could reserve their perch on some stands all day for $4.

June 14 dawned cloudy, and intermittent rain fell throughout the day, but the weather failed to dampen the spirit of the crowds. "Words can hardly describe the sentiments of loyalty and enthusiasm with which the people of Prince Edward Island are waiting to welcome" the King and Queen, reported the *Guardian*, noting that 6,000 children were expected to line Great George Street. Other children formed part of the parade as Boy Scouts and Girl Guides. At 12:30, HMCS *Skeena*, the vessel carrying the monarch, arrived at Marine Wharf, and the royal couple proceeded directly up Great George Street to the Provincial Building. After a brief stop, the procession moved on through streets decked out in flags and bunting to Government House where between 1:30 and 4:00 p.m. they mingled with the Island's dignitaries and social pillars.[62] The return to the ship took a half-hour as departure time was at 4:30. "The oldest residents recall nothing remotely approaching the tremendous demonstration witnessed in the Island Capital during the four hours' visit," proclaimed the *Guardian*." Charlottetown had done itself proud as visitors were "enthusiastic in praise of the street and building decorations, and the splendid appearance" that was presented in honour of the occasion. And the patriotism of the crowds was manifest. Soon, those same feelings would be called upon to be demonstrated in a far less festive way.

The world was a dangerous place in the 1930s. Headlines in the *Guardian* and *Patriot* screamed out news of Japanese incursions into Manchuria, turmoil in the Soviet Union and sinister developments in Germany. British power seemed threatened in the

---

62 The route followed was Great George Street to the Provincial Building, Richmond, Queen, Grafton, Prince, Fitzroy, Upper Great George (now University Avenue) and Kent Streets to Government House and a return to the ship via the Victoria Park driveway, Brighton Road, Rochford, Kent, Queen, Richmond and Great George Streets.

Far East and in Europe, while at home the domestic economy wreaked havoc upon the personal security of millions of Canadians. Amidst all the gloom, optimistic forecasts of increased prosperity and the improbability of war and assertions of the military preparedness of the Empire if the worst happened offered hope to stressed readers. Coverage of the Confederation celebrations and of the annual exhibition broke the sequence of reports on military deployments in France and Poland during the summer of 1939, but, as the season wore on, the news became increasingly ominous. Even so, various experts assured a nervous public that war was unlikely. They were wrong. In the early hours of a September morning in Charlottetown, Britain declared war on Germany over its invasion of Poland.[63] Canada did not immediately follow suit, although there was no doubt it would do so. As Robert Menzies, the Prime Minister of Australia, commented, "where Great Britain stands there stand the people of the entire British world."

Headlines in the local papers announced the news. "Britain at War" proclaimed the *Guardian*, while a secondary headline, in a foretaste of things to come, bore the news, "British Liner Torpedoed." The same newspaper noted that "Charlottetown is once more a military city, the uniform being the fashion for men." Memories of the previous conflict with Germany still lay at the surface, and old sentiments sprang readily to one's lips. "Slackers will be as unpopular today as they were in 1914," the *Guardian* asserted. The editor understood his community; Islanders would proportionally volunteer in greater numbers than any other Canadians. By the war's end, half of Island males between the ages of 18 and 45 would serve, many of them overseas. But, for the moment, life also continued on normally. Dorothy Dix's column advised her female readers that "Unless You Are An Expert, Don't Attempt to Keep Your Husband Dangling at Your Side by Keeping Him in a Jealous State of Mind." *Going Places* with Dick Powell and Anita Louise was playing at the Prince Edward and *The Mysterious Miss X* featuring Michael Whalen, Mary Hart, Chick Chandler and Mabel Todd was on at the Capitol, but, by September 13, *Confessions of a Nazi Spy*, starring Edward G. Robinson and Paul Lukas, had opened at the Prince Edward to jam-packed crowds that caused the movie to be held over.

The flow of recruits began immediately. Volunteers were motivated by various sentiments including patriotism and a desire to find employment and relief from relief. The army converted the Beach Grove Inn into the Beach Grove Army Basic Training Centre and began the process of converting peaceful civilians into fighting soldiers. Prospective naval personnel found their way to the Naval Reserve Division located in a former furniture factory and meat-packing plant at the corner of Kent and Hillsborough Streets. Those wanting to enter the air force had to go to the mainland to volunteer. Charlottetonians who were already members of the Prince Edward Island Highlanders left within days for garrison duty in Halifax and Cape Breton. A number of them joined the North Nova Scotia Regiment and were sent to Britain in July 1941.

63 War was declared at 11 a.m. London time on September 3, 1939.

Keeping the car shops open and well-booked with work was a constant struggle, as the railway had begun to centralize its repair work in Moncton as early as 1922. During the Second World War, the Mayor among others made strong, though unsuccessful, representations to have the car shops used for war contracts.

Others from the city enlisted in the Prince Edward Island Light Horse, an armoured company, or in one of two artillery batteries, a field ambulance formation or a signals unit. For some, going to war was the first time they had been off the Island.

Collapse in 1940 of Allied resistance to the Germans in France and the Low Countries kept the city's soldiers out of action in the early part of the war, but members of the Highlanders were drafted into other units overseas. The 2nd Medium Battery, descended from the 2nd Siege Battery of the First World War, departed for England in January 1940 and the 8th Battery followed in August 1941. The 2nd Battery served in Italy in 1943 and 1944 before going to Northwest Europe in 1945. The 8th Battery remained in Britain until the Normandy invasion in June 1944.

If Charlottetown's service personnel were, for the most part, removed from the conflict in the early stages of the war, its effects were brought home to the city in various ways. The arrival of the Royal Air Force's No. 31 General Reconnaissance School at Charlottetown Airport in January 1941 brought noise, the machines of war, and a sense of engagement. An air navigation school opened seven months later. These installations injected a welcome buoyancy into both the economy and social life of the community. In 1940 daylight saving time was adopted by the city after 10 years of debate.[64] Nine Victory Loan campaigns were waged, with the first one in June 1941. To raise interest in one campaign, a mock assault on the naval barracks was staged. Two companies with a field gun using blank ammunition attacked across King Square under cover of darkness as crowds watched the flashes from the weapons. Gas rationing was also begun in 1941, and practice blackouts were organized. In 1942 a Civilian Defence Committee was established to co-ordinate the execution of such exercises. On January 7, 1942, two aircraft from the Commonwealth Air Training base at the city's airport collided in mid-air over Southport and crashed into a nearby field, killing all on board. A few months later, on September 11, 1942, HMCS *Charlottetown*, a Flower-class corvette, was torpedoed and sunk in the Gulf of St. Lawrence, taking with her the captain and six seamen. Other local military accidents included the crash of an RAF Anson bomber on the frozen sea off the north shore in January 1943, but in this case the flight crew was rescued when Carl Burke made multiple trips in a small Department of Transport plane to pluck them off an ice floe. The ultimate cost of war was brought home in its starkest reality when telegrams of regrets began to arrive at the doors of the city.

News of the death of one native Charlottetonian evoked pride as well as sadness. Frederick Thornton ("Fritz") Peters, the son of former Liberal premier Frederick Peters, was a Captain in the Royal Navy when he was assigned the deadly task of breeching the defensive harbour boom at Oran, Algeria, during the Allied landings in North Africa. On November 8, 1942, Peters' vessel, the *Walney*, an ex-US coast-guard cutter, facing withering enemy fire, managed to break through the barrier and reach the enemy jetty before sinking. Peters was the only survivor on the bridge. He was captured but liberated a few days later when the Allies took the town. Ironically, he died soon after in a plane crash as he was returning to England. He was posthumously awarded the Victoria Cross.

Others also served with distinction. Sergeant Charles A. MacGillivary, a Charlottetown-born member of the US Army, was awarded the Congressional Medal of Honor for his single-handed assault on four enemy machine-gun positions during the German Ardennes offensive in January 1945. Clarence Higgins was awarded the Distinguished Flying Cross after he piloted his twin-engine bomber as if it were a fighter in strafing a German infantry column during the Normandy campaign. Two local men, W. W. Reid and David Stewart, rose through the ranks to command army regiments. Stewart, to his immense credit, lost his command when he refused to expose his men to needless danger during the dying days of the war.[65] Most who served,

64 A resolution to adopt such a measure between June 1 and August 31 had been approved by Council in 1930 over objections that it would be an inconvenience to country folk who wanted to shop in the city. In 1932 a plebiscite on the issue of summer daylight saving time resulted in rejection by the voters. Now the pressures of war changed the balance of the debate.

65 The incident in question involved Major-General Chris Vokes, commander of the Canadian 1st Division. Vokes, an unimaginative leader who was not afraid of taking casualties, ordered Stewart to have his Argyll and Sutherland Highlanders patrol aggressively in the wake of the retreating Germans. Stewart, showing perhaps "undue concern for his men," declined to proceed as ordered and was subsequently reassigned to a new regiment in Canada.

however, did so with less notoriety, if not less courage. Meanwhile, at home their families lived with the nagging anxiety that accompanies an unwelcome absence and uncertain fate of loved ones.

Beyond such apprehension, the conflict had a major impact on the social life of the community. An influx of personnel for training and other purposes provided extra patrons for restaurants, theatres and other places of entertainment, and companions for some of Charlottetown's belles. A housing shortage developed, and employment vacancies created by departing servicemen were filled by women, including housewives who never expected to work outside the home. Renewed economic activity brought prosperity, but also shortages of consumer goods and hefty price increases until federal wage and price controls were introduced in December 1941. Food rationing followed the next year. In an interesting turn of events, the presence of thirsty outsiders intruded into the renewed debate over prohibition. A plebiscite was to be held in 1940 to determine whether liquor could be again sold in the province. Arrayed in opposition was a formidable alliance led by the United, Baptist and Presbyterian churches and the United Church's Social Service Secretary. The opponents of alcohol won the day, but the city favoured its sale. The "drys" saw their objective somewhat frustrated when City Council allowed servicemen to have wet canteens. Despite criticism from a number of clergymen, Councillors were sympathetic to the wishes of military personnel.[66] In this they demonstrated a tolerance of beverage alcohol consumption that mirrored the attitudes of Councillors of 40 years earlier.

Born in Charlottetown, a member of the West Kent Cadet Corps, W. W. "Bill" Reid was one of two Charlottetown militiamen who rose to command a combat regiment.

The balance in the war shifted towards the Allies in 1943, and by the spring of 1945 their armies were advancing rapidly towards victory across Europe. Triumph came for the Canadian Army in Holland and Northern Germany on May 4, 1945,

66 The Presbyterian Synod, meeting in Summerside, called for total abstinence and closure of wet canteens for servicemen.

Except for some of the church spires, the roof of the Charlottetown Hotel offered the highest vantage point in the city. During the war, Civil Defence lookouts were stationed here.

after a battlefield surrender of German forces was arranged with Field Marshall Bernard Montgomery's 21st Army Group. The official surrender of the enemy facing the 1st Canadian Army occurred the next day. Surrender of the remaining German forces followed two days later, and an official day marking victory in Europe was set for May 8. Charlottetonians reacted in "shocked, stunned amazement" and, like other Canadians, took to the streets in celebration after the news broke in the afternoon of May 7. Mayor James E. Blanchard proclaimed that "by the Grace of Almighty God, through the medium of our gallant leaders and men, the world has been freed of the scourge of the Nazi gangsters," and declared May 8 a civic holiday. But the celebrations had already started and continued through intermittent rain until a strong wind drove revellers indoors.

V-E day opened with the ringing of bells and blowing of whistles at 9 a.m.[67] Church services followed at 11 a.m., and at 2 p.m. there was a patriotic rally at Victoria Park. Afterwards in what the *Guardian* called the "biggest demonstration of spontaneous enthusiasm" since the Royal Tour, huge crowds surged back into the city where they lined the streets in dense ranks to watch "one of the largest and most colourful [parades] seen here for many years." Columns of the Reserve Armoured Regiment, Naval

67 A 40-gun salute was planned but cancelled on orders from Ottawa.

Personnel, Cadets, Scouts and Guides, a detachment of the 8th District Signals and the Fire Department were followed at the end by a truck bearing a gallows, a hanging effigy of Adolph Hitler and a sign reading "Crime Does Not Pay." The next day, newspapers recorded the death of a boy who accidentally slipped under the wheels of that truck while headlines told of the riots in Halifax. On June 17, the first contingent of returning veterans reached Charlottetown.

For the second time in 25 years, war had rent the pleasant quiet of Charlottetown life. Unlike the previous conflict, victory this time was complete and unequivocal. Canada emerged from the struggle immensely more powerful than when she had entered. Her adversaries were shattered, and many of her allies were broken and impoverished. Canadians, with their economy enriched and confidence restored, were positioned to reap the sweet spoils of victory. Despite fears of domestic unrest and, soon enough, the perception of a new mortal threat from abroad, Canadians were on the threshold of unprecedented prosperity. A tide of change that was about to transform the economy and society of the Dominion would flow over Prince Edward Island and its unimposing capital, bringing fundamental transformation in its wake. In the years that followed 1945, Charlottetown and its citizens inched out of the shadow of the stringent past towards the promising glow of a new era.

CHAPTER 5

Recovery

1946-84

In contrast to the First World War, the end of the Second brought more than a promise of change. There was less ambivalence about the future. Following the First World War, the desire to create the new Jerusalem was neutralized by a yearning for a return to "normalcy." After the Second, the optimism of the victor prevailed. The aftermath of the First brought economic downturn and a dreadful influenza pandemic. The cessation of hostilities in Europe and Asia in 1945 left the economies and physical infrastructures of the vanquished — and many of the winners — in tatters. The few exceptions included Canada and the United States. The "Great Dominion" with its new factories, improved communications networks and undamaged cities made the best of a trading situation in which many competitors were handicapped. Its citizens, including demobilized service personnel, had pent-up savings to spend. The country's doors were thrown open to thousands of displaced persons from Europe. Returned soldiers and their new wives, some of whom were war brides from overseas, soon created a crush at the maternity wards. Massive public works, widespread urban growth and increased prosperity for the ordinary citizen provided some credence for the confident expectations of political leaders.

It was not to last, of course. Not everyone shared in the fruits of victory, and, by the 1960s, reconstruction in Europe and the Far East put Canada back into the second tier of world economies. Economic downturns and the resurgence of old concerns about national unity agitated the waters of progress, but change persisted. The ballooning population of young Canadians indulged themselves with novel forms of music, bizarre clothing styles, freer social mores and expectations of more of whatever good the world had to offer. It was an age of liberation: women assumed new roles and youth of both genders "took off" to explore exotic corners of the world. Traditional loyalties to faith and empire weakened — to be replaced by new nationalisms — while restructured immigration policies began to change the complexion of the country. The 1982 charter of rights and freedoms fundamentally altered the relationship between the citizen and the state. By the mid-1980s, Canada had drastically changed, its population culturally sophisticated but politically insecure. Its economy had grown massively since 1945 but was vulnerable to upheavals beyond its control. The country had embraced technology but many of its people pined for the simplicity and honesty of old ways. Change proved a fickle mistress, alluring and yet at times bitter.

The pressure of change pierced the isolation of Prince Edward Island's capital. While its citizens reflected the traditional population base, their numbers were swollen by migrants from the rest of the province and even other parts of Canada. Increased numbers brought fresh challenges in the areas of housing, employment and governance. These developments were reflected in a livelier, more issue-oriented political life. The city grew physically. Suburbs spread. With them came car-centred shopping areas and road construction. Within the downtown, impressive public buildings, unusual in extent and significance for a place of Charlottetown's size, rose from the red mud. At the same time, there was a growing awareness that the old commercial and residential fabric, a gift of the economic somnolence of previous eras, held significant cultural and economic opportunities. City planning, the concepts of which were being espoused across the country, was begun in Charlottetown, too. The city was tidied up. Its people sought to welcome outsiders as pilgrims to the birthplace of the nation. In turn, Charlottetonians became connected to the outside as never before. Modern communications brought them in touch with their fellow Canadians and people beyond the nation's boundaries. The strange became familiar, and influences from "away" blended into the streets, the homes and the lives of the city's inhabitants. After generations of seeking to be up-to-date with the advances thought to characterize progress, by the 1980s Charlottetonians had generally achieved their goal. There was a price to pay, of course, but for most people modernity was worth it.

POPULATION GROWTH AND ETHNIC RELATIONSHIPS

After decades of lethargic growth, the rate of population growth in Charlottetown accelerated after the Second World War. At first, although the numbers were substantial, they continued to lag behind those registered in many parts of Canada, but, by the 1970s, the increases were becoming more dramatic, and the city was more than holding its own in relation to comparable communities. In 1951 the population of Charlottetown and royalty was 20,387 (15,887 for the city only), an increase of 3,031 or 17.5 per cent over 1941. By 1961 the figure stood at 23,132 (city: 18,318), a growth of 13.5 per cent. By 1971 the population was 26,671 (city: 19,130), an increase of 15.3 per cent, but the Island capital, as elsewhere in Canada, was beginning to experience significant growth at the fringes of town. To capture this demographic reality, statisticians measured population agglomerations based on economic affinities rather than political boundaries. By this way of reckoning, the number of people living within the overall Charlottetown urban area jumped considerably by 1981. In the census of that year, Charlottetown and the communities located within the old royalty had a population of 26,100. Those living within the official city boundaries decreased from 17,063 in 1976 to 15,282 in 1981. Growth had stalled in Sherwood and Parkdale as well. The addition, however, of the rapidly urbanizing communities of Cornwall, Southport and Lots 31 (Meadow Bank to North Wiltshire), 32 (Cornwall

In the century since Meacham's 1880 Atlas, *the city's demographics steadily shifted northward. In 1881, only ten per cent of Charlottetown's 11,485 residents lived in the Royalty. By 1981 the population was 26,100, but only 15,282 lived within the official city boundary.*

to North Milton) and 33[1] raised the population total to 36,315. Counting everyone in the census area, the population had soared to 44,999, an impressive 68.7 per cent increase over 1971. The population of the Charlottetown agglomeration was growing substantially, and most of the increase was at the fringes of town.

These changes can be put into perspective by comparing the city with other Canadian centres. In 1951 the city stood in 71st place in the order of Canadian communities by size, just behind Fredericton, New Brunswick, and Joliette, Quebec, and just ahead of North Vancouver, British Columbia, and Woodstock, Ontario. By 1961 Charlottetown had dropped to the 99th spot, smaller than Brampton, Ontario, and Leaside, Ontario, a suburb of Toronto but larger than Mimico, another suburb of Toronto, and Riverside, a community in the Windsor, Ontario, area. Charlottetown's relative size dropped further by 1971 when it was the 125th largest, smaller than Sorel and Beaconsfield, Quebec, and Kelowna, British Columbia, but bigger than Thompson,

1 Lot 31 ran from Meadow Bank to North Wiltshire; Lot 32 included the land from Crosby Point and North Point to Springvale and North Milton; and Lot 33 incorporated properties facing the Winsloe, Brackley Point and Union Roads between the Royalty Road and the North Shore.

Manitoba, and Newmarket, Ontario. By this time, the need to record the demographics of urban areas together with their adjacent suburbs made two other classifications of cities important for statisticians. The census metropolitan areas represented Canada's 18 largest urban centres while 31 census agglomerations covered smaller urban clusters. Charlottetown was the smallest of the census agglomerations, just behind Baie Comeau and Thetford Mines, Quebec, and Port Alberni, British Columbia. In the 1981 census, there were 25 census metropolitan areas and 87 census agglomerations. Charlottetown and its adjacent municipalities was the 51st largest census agglomeration, a little smaller than Granby, Quebec, and Belleville, Ontario, but larger than St. Jerome, Quebec, and Vernon, British Columbia.

Nevertheless, the proportion of Islanders living in Charlottetown's urban area grew in a significant way. In 1951 just under 21 per cent of Islanders lived in the capital. This rose to 22 per cent in 1961, dropped to 17 per cent in 1971, but rose to 23 per cent when the adjacent communities were included. The 1970s saw the greatest change. By 1981 approximately 37 per cent of Islanders lived in the Charlottetown urban agglomeration. Thus, as the postwar period wore on, the centrifugal pull of the capital on the province's population intensified.

Between 1946 and 1984, little changed with respect to the city's ethnic mix. If anything, the existing population structure was consolidated. The 1951 census failed to record the specific sizes of the English, Scottish, Irish and Welsh communities, lumping them together as British. They constituted fully 86.5 per cent of the population, down slightly from 87.3 per cent in 1941. The French proportion of the population was just over 10 per cent, up marginally from 1941. The next largest communities were the Dutch, Germans and Scandinavians at 0.6, 0.4 and 0.2 per cent respectively. Other ethnic groups were very small, although an undifferentiated "Other Oriental" category accounted for 1.3 per cent. This excluded the 18 who were listed as Chinese, but included the Lebanese and others from the Middle and Far East. Racial minorities other than Europeans and Orientals, including Blacks, were entered into a "Not Given" category that totalled 0.37 per cent of the population. The 1961 census returned to the practice of tracking the various British backgrounds, although their cumulative total of 85.6 per cent continued a slight downward trend. The English were almost 31 per cent, the Scots comprised 29.5 per cent and the Irish made up 24.1 per cent. In comparison with 1941, these figures show a modest decline for the English and a slight gain for the Scots, with the Irish holding their own. The Welsh were less than one per cent of the population. Even so, they were more numerous than those of German (less than 0.7 per cent), Dutch (0.55 per cent) and Scandinavian (0.5 per cent) origins. The "Other Oriental" category represented 1.1 per cent, down slightly from 1951, while the Chinese community more than doubled to 38 and there were 45 people of African origin. Census results following 1961 provide less precision on the individual ethnic backgrounds of Charlottetonians but trace the blending of backgrounds through intermarriage. In 1981 over 81 per cent was British in origin; over 2 per cent were a mix of British and "Other"; barely more than 6.1 per cent were French; but nearly as many, almost 5.4 per cent, were of British and French extraction. The Dutch and German groups were small, 1 per cent and 0.83 per cent, and all others together constituted 3.3 per cent of the population. This small group of "Others" represented a slight increase over 1961 when the figure was 2.8 per cent. After the Second World War, Charlottetonians were becoming more ethnically diverse, but only to a very limited degree.

Charlottetown's stable ethnic mix makes the relative stability of religious affiliations unsurprising. Despite this apparent continuity, some trends were highly significant, if tentative. The Anglicans continued their gentle slide in their share of religious adherents, losing about a percentage each decade. Baptists grew in numbers, virtually overtaking the Anglicans by the 1980s. Affiliation with the Presbyterian Church generally remained stable. Not so the membership in the United Church. It had increased somewhat by 1951 from its earlier level of 19 per cent, sagged in the middle of the 1960s, but recovered throughout the 1970s to include virtually 25 per cent of the population by 1981. The percentage of Roman Catholic Charlottetonians peaked around the 1951 census and dropped significantly by 1961. The 1971 census recorded a rebound in the Roman Catholic segment, but, by 1981, their numbers had subsided to levels not experienced since the first decade of the 20th century. Roman Catholics remained, however, Charlottetown's largest religious community by far. Two other trends of interest that appeared towards the end of the current period were the increased diversity of smaller faith communities and the gradual, but significant, growth of the segment that professed no religious faith. These trends are elaborated in the table below. The data refer only to the city for 1951, 1961 and 1971 and to the census agglomeration for 1981.

Table One — Percentage Population by Religion

Religion	1951 per cent	1961 per cent	1971 per cent	1981 per cent
Anglican	8.1	7.4	6.8	6.0
Baptist	4.7	6.4	6.0	5.9
Pentecostal	0.3	0.5	[1]	0.8
Presbyterian	12.8	11.6	11.6	11.8
Roman Catholic	50.1	44.4	49.9	42.7
Salvation Army	1.1	1.0	0.8	[2]
United	21.3	20.9	20.4	24.5
Other/Not Given/No Religion[3]	1.6	7.8		
Other Protestant/Not Given			2.9	1.9
Other			0.4[4]	2.8
No Religion			1.2	3.6

[1] Included in Other Protestant/Not Given.
[2] Included in Other Protestant.
[3] Includes a Jewish population of 3 in 1951 and 13 in 1961.
[4] Includes Jehovah's Witnesses (60), Jews (5) and Mormons (10).

While an examination of the data from the 1981 census suggests that there are some differences in the proportion of the population claimed by the various religions in the urbanized core, as opposed to the fringe areas in the Charlottetown census agglomeration, the overall trends were generally consistent.[2] In matters of faith, Charlottetonians were becoming a little more diverse, a little less religious and a little less attracted to ritual and tradition, but not much so.

As a relatively small, demographically self-contained community, Charlottetown had long been characterized by the fact that a large proportion of its residents were natives of Prince Edward Island. In 1941, 90 per cent of the population was born in the province. Despite the influx of outsiders during the war, over 88 per cent of the city's residents called the Island their province of birth in 1951. Another 6.9 per cent hailed from the rest of Canada, principally Nova Scotia, New Brunswick and to a lesser degree Ontario. Foreign-born came from the United Kingdom (1.7 per cent) and the United States (1.2 per cent). Only a sprinkling came from other countries. By 1961 Islanders comprised 87 per cent of the population, and other Canadians had grown to be 9.1 per cent. Residents born in the UK and US maintained their share, 1.5 per cent and 1.1 per cent respectively, and Charlottetonians born in Europe were 0.6 per cent of the population. By 1971 the importance of the inflow of other Canadians revealed by the 1961 census was clear. The proportion of Island-born had dropped to approximately 83 per cent, and those born in the rest of Canada had increased to almost 13 per cent. People born in Great Britain and Ireland made up 1.5 per cent, Americans 1.3 per cent, Europeans 0.8 per cent and Asians 0.6 per cent of the population. These trends continued throughout the 1970s, so that by 1981, native-born Islanders were down to 76.7 per cent, while Canadians born in other provinces represented 18.8 per cent of the population. Although Nova Scotia, Ontario, and New Brunswick contributed the most people, there were citizens with birthplaces in all other parts of Canada except the Yukon Territory. Britons made up 1.6 per cent, Americans 1.4 per cent and those with other origins, 1.5 per cent. In an increasingly mobile society, internal migration was bringing other Canadians to the city. Their influx did not extensively alter other demographic characteristics, such as ethnicity and religion.

Women in Charlottetown with marriage on their minds still had a problem in the postwar era. Since the 19th century, the departure of working-age males to the mainland and arrival of single females from rural areas had created an imbalance of women compared to men within the city. The Great Depression reversed the situation somewhat, but the census of 1951 revealed that females again strongly outnumbered males in the 15 to 35 age range. The effects of the post–Second World War baby boom, on the other hand, tended to counter this gender imbalance. Children aged from less than a year to five years old, and those over five and under ten, were the

2 The main difference was that there were significantly more United Churchmen and fewer Roman Catholics in the fringe areas than the urbanized core.

two largest segments of Charlottetown's population,[3] and within these groups boys had a small overall majority. For Charlottetonians as a whole, there were almost 84 males for every 100 females in 1951.[4] Ten years later, within the under-25 age group, the number of boys and girls aged 14 and under was relatively balanced, while the number of females aged 15 to 24 exceeded that of the males. This latter imbalance was greater for some age groups than others. The overall ratio was 86 males per 100 females. Following the boom of the 1960s, in 1971 the imbalance of females to males was beginning to even out. For the population generally the ratio was almost 92 males for every 100 females. Although there was a substantial balance in favour of women aged 20–24, the prime working years from 25 to 55 exhibited reasonable equivalencies between the numbers of each sex. This trend continued in the suburban parts of the Charlottetown census agglomeration where there were 97 males for every 100 females in 1981. In the city itself, the proportion of males plummeted to 79 per 100 females. The ratio for the whole urban area was 88:100. Within the city proper, a diminution of children as a segment of the population and an increase in the number of the elderly who were predominantly women influenced the population profile. Suburban areas contained largely two-parent families with children, accounting for the gender balance found there.

Charlottetown also began to change in the way people and the economy were organized spatially. The mingling of the various social strata in residential areas and the overlapping of residential, commercial and industrial land use, which had characterized the city since incorporation, diminished in the postwar era. The older parts of the city below Euston Street lost population to the expanding suburbs. Although pockets of fine homes remained in the central core, much of the older housing stock was wearing out, and its occupants were less prosperous than in other parts of town. Large areas of the centre were given over to commercial, institutional and some industrial use. Charlottetown developed discrete areas of economic activity and social standing. Two bellwether occupations that indicated the location of desirable residential areas were physicians and lawyers. In 1950 physicians could be found living in broadly dispersed locations in the older part of the city, although significant clusters had taken up residence along Upper Prince Street, Brighton Road and North River Road. Lawyers were also sprinkled along the streets of the inner city and in the area north of Euston from Upper Prince to the east, but they, too, were beginning to gravitate to the Brighton Road and North River Road areas. By 1975 much had changed. The physicians had virtually abandoned the older parts of town, such as Upper Prince Street, to crowd into Brighton and the new areas further north. Lawyers maintained a presence in the central core and a few lived in Sherwood and Parkdale, but for the most part they were in Brighton or north of it. Brighton Road, Queen Elizabeth Drive, Prince Charles Drive and North River Road and adjacent streets were

3 Census statistics broke the population into clusters of five years, such as under 1 to 4, 5 to 9, 10 to 14, etc.

4 Part of the imbalance might be explained by deaths of servicemen during the Second World War.

clearly the desirable residential locations. As a rule of thumb, locations in the west of Charlottetown were more prestigious than those in the east.

Other locations became notable in exactly the opposite way. A survey of Charlottetown's housing written in 1962 pointed to the Jordan Crescent area adjacent to the Experimental Farm. "Within a matter of twenty years or so an utter and terrible slum — a lot of Charlottetown — has materialized." The same study reported that other decay was rapidly spreading on the fringes of the city's centre. Some housing had deteriorated to the extent that the tax assessor had to add a fourth category — "very poor or derelict" — to the existing system of classification of good, fair and poor. Many of the worst buildings faced poorly maintained streets "very often next to a non-residential population of disturbing quality"; that is, commercial and industrial buildings. The report explained that residential housing was creeping into areas hitherto used for other purposes. These blighted areas were significant in extent and housed some of Charlottetown's most marginal citizens. Although the city was not large by contemporary standards, it was beginning to exhibit some big-city characteristics in terms of where people lived.

POLITICAL LIFE

Politics became livelier in the postwar years, and the old tradition of mayors staying in office for only one term was firmly and finally laid to rest. Growth, particularly in suburban areas, posed challenges that could only be resolved by either extending municipal boundaries or establishing new administrative structures. As events transpired, both occurred. Although some political concerns were uniquely local, others involved issues commonly found in other communities at the same time. Increasingly during this period, the city's distinctiveness faded in the face of homogenizing social, economic and technological change. Politics and politicians began to sound and operate like those in other Maritime and Canadian centres.

Vestiges of restrictions on the franchise were removed, particularly in the 1960s when the winds of political inclusiveness were blowing strongly. A curious initiative involved the removal of the disadvantage faced by incorporated businesses compared with privately owned enterprises. A change to the act governing Charlottetown allowed a representative of a corporation to vote in the ward or wards in which the corporation qualified as an elector. In 1961 citizens, mainly women, who lost their ballot when they turned 65 and were exempted from the educational tax, regained the right to register as voters. In 1968, as part of a wider package of electoral reforms, the property qualification for office-holders was ended, so tenants were allowed to nominate candidates and run themselves. The franchise was widened in 1972 when the voting age was lowered to 18. Under the same legislation, the one person, one vote principle was adopted, and corporate voting ended. In the realm of cosmetic change, "alderman" was adopted for use in 1971 as a replacement for "councillor." Like corporate voting, this would be short-lived.

Changes were also made to the terms of office. The mayor and Councillors from Wards 4 and 5 who took office after the 1962 elections had three-year terms, while

Two political trends that typified then 1960s — greater involvement of women in municipal politics and more social activism by civic politicians — coalesced in the person of M. Dorothy Corrigan.

Councillors from the other wards were elected for two years. Thereafter, all terms were to be three years. Staggered terms were intended to provide continuity during the key centennial year of 1964, an indication of just how important city politicians thought the event to be. That objective may have been achieved, but elections had to be held more frequently. The system was abandoned in 1968 when Council voted to have elections for all members every three years. Voting day was then set for the first Monday in November with the new Council to take office the following February. At that time, consideration was also given to electing Councillors from the city as a whole rather than from individual wards, but there was concern among Councillors that city-wide voting would result in over-representation of districts such as Brighton. Although the concept had some supporters on Council, a majority favoured the existing ward system. Discussions about reducing the number of Councillors from ten to six or eight also stalled in 1974.

Two political trends that typified the 1960s — greater involvement of women in municipal politics and more social activism by civic politicians — coalesced in the person of M. Dorothy Corrigan. In 1960 Corrigan became the first woman ever elected to Council. She soon demonstrated an acute interest in matters affecting women and the city's underprivileged — particularly adequate housing for the poor. In 1966 she was named Deputy Mayor. The novelty of having a successful female politician amongst them was underscored by some good-natured remarks by her male colleagues, but everyone may not have been supportive. During one Council meeting when Deputy Mayor Corrigan was presiding, two visitors who wished to address Council declined to speak until the mayor arrived. Corrigan was elected mayor in 1969 and served one term. Her record in office was marked by efforts to help the disadvantaged and defend the city's interests against discriminatory provincial policies.

One of the most complex matters facing the political establishment between 1946 and 1985 was the city's relationship with the neighbouring suburban communities. The Second World War was not yet over when a peculiar situation arose regarding the Charlottetown's northern boundary. A benefactor named Edward Jarvis had conveyed a segment of land that he owned in Spring Park to the city. Council successfully petitioned the provincial legislature to have it annexed to its territory. Soon afterwards, the fate of the rest of Spring Park, as well as the village of Parkdale, came under public scrutiny. Both were nestled in the rural landscape of the royalty, to the north and northeast of the city respectively. These communities had essentially been settled by Charlottetonians seeking affordable homes. As the use of Charlottetown's core was given over increasingly to business, industry and public administration, pressure on the remaining residential areas and on land costs increased. The city needed to expand to retain its population and provide affordable areas for development.

This population shift created inequities in services and taxation. Suburban residents required basic services such as water, and police and fire protection. Meanwhile rate-payers left in the city proper had to pay for these same services with relatively fewer numbers to share the tax burden. For the capital, it was a prescription for financial disaster. In time, increased costs with no new sources of income would require higher taxes. More residents would flee to the suburbs, heightening the need for essential services there. Financial deficits in the city would be parallelled by service deficits in the suburbs. Although non-residents who worked in Charlottetown paid an annual $25 fee, those living in town felt that more of the burden of municipal finances should be borne by the suburbanites. Moreover, all three communities faced higher-than-necessary fire insurance rates because their water services failed to meet the standards set by the underwriters. With these factors in mind, the Board of Trade arranged a meeting of interested parties on May 28, 1951, to consider the merits of amalgamation. Nothing much arose from this first gathering, but the idea of drawing the city and suburbs under one administrative umbrella persisted.

In April 1950, a delegation from the Board of Trade asked Council to consider annexing Parkdale. Council appointed a committee to look into the matter, and the following year a meeting was held to consider the amalgamation of Charlottetown, Parkdale and Spring Park. Little progress was made, but, in November 1956, the three municipalities along with the Board of Trade formed a Metropolitan Committee to discuss common problems and to collaborate in resolving them.[5] Both the committee and the provincial government's Director of Town Planning, Claude Smith, encouraged expansion. Although discussions proceeded with both Spring Park and Parkdale, by the end of 1957 only Spring Park remained interested in amalgamation. Consequently, it became part of Charlottetown in April 1958 and was designated Ward 6 for electoral purposes.

The annexation left a part of the former Spring Park school district in limbo. Stretching from the new city limits north to the Trans-Canada Highway, it soon was tagged as "No Man's Land" and represented a kind of administrative void. The area's citizens formulated a series of demands the city would have to meet before they would accept amalgamation. These included installing water and sewerage, favourable assessments, adequate police and fire protection, pavement for North River Road, a separate seat on Council and guarantees concerning road maintenance, snow removal, parks and playgrounds. In his 1962 re-election platform, Mayor Walthen Gaudet promised

5 The Board of Trade, traditionally influential within the realm of civic politics, suggested in 1952 that the Mayor and City Clerk be given *ex officio* status at meetings of the Board of Trade in exchange for allowing two Board members to attend City Council meetings. Mayor David Stewart accepted the offer.

In his 1962 re-election program, Mayor Gaudet promised to expand city services into the administrative "No Man's Land" of Spring Park.

to do everything he could to effect this further expansion of the city. Once re-elected, Gaudet pressed ahead with efforts to amalgamate with No Man's Land and succeeded later that year.

In 1962 the Suburban Study Committee, led by Judge C. St. Clair Trainor, examined the possibility of further amalgamations with West Royalty, Sherwood and Parkdale, but the concept made little headway for most of the decade. Parkdale was the principal sticking point. Sherwood had voted to amalgamate in 1958, but Parkdale formed a physical barrier between that community and Charlottetown. In 1969, when the province began to consider granting town status to both Parkdale and Sherwood, interest in mergers with Charlottetown revived. Many observers believed that the province had long-range intentions to deal with the metropolitan area as a single unit. A piecemeal approach to the provision of education, roads, recreational facilities and especially sewage treatment would be onerous for local taxpayers. Perhaps believing time was on their side, City Council adopted a wait-and-see attitude.

By the 1970s, the separate jurisdictions were beginning to be seen as a hindrance to development. Speaking in Charlottetown in 1971, Harold C. Shipp of the Housing and Urban Development Association of Canada noted that the Central Mortgage and Housing Corporation did not make mortgage money available in areas serviced by septic tanks. The lack of sewerage in the suburban communities was thus an impediment to obtaining housing. Mortgage concerns may have influenced residents of West Royalty, for a large number of ratepayers who attended a community meeting in early 1972 supported talks with the city about amalgamation. They saw this step not so much as entering a courtship as exploring whether a courtship should be undertaken.

The big advantage for the city was access to undeveloped land that would permit economic growth. A resulting increase in the tax base would help to meet rising costs for existing services. Civic leaders had to be careful not to appear too eager since that would create the impression that the city was "trying to take over." From the perspective of West Royalty, amalgamation was "a dollar and cents" question. Citizens there had essentially the same shopping list as the residents of No Man's Land. If a merger would provide these benefits at the lowest cost, it stood some chance of success. Sixty per cent in a plebiscite would have to conclude that West Royalty's gains justified the loss of local autonomy.

A fruitful outcome to any negotiations on amalgamation needed the involvement of the provincial authorities. Their stand on the matter appears to have been in flux. In early 1972, Community Services Minister Robert Schurman said the advantages of amalgamation of the city with West Royalty outweighed the disadvantages. Yet less than two years later, the government was perceived as opposing the union. Active consideration of civic mergers died, despite an effort by Charlottetown mayoralty candidate Norville Getty in 1977 to revive the issue. The surrounding communities responded to the prospect of amalgamation with reactions ranging from vague interest to adamant hostility. Hopes to merge municipalities in the Charlottetown metropolitan area would have to wait.

Education was another area beset with controversy. An observer noted around this time that the most important functional unit of local government in the province was the school board, not the municipality.[6] While this may have been true generally, Charlottetown was an exception in that the school board co-existed with a civic government that had an avid interest in educational matters. The city appointed some of the trustees, and the municipality was ultimately responsible for the costs incurred by the school board. Municipal leaders were justifiably concerned with the financial implications of operating a school system with large and costly physical plants. The rapid expansion of the educational system in the 1950s and early 1960s required unprecedented expenditures. Cost-conscious municipal politicians were anxious to ensure that any financial liabilities related to schools were minimal.

Who should pay for education was one issue that arose. The city raised most of its revenue through property taxes, but the school board believed that everyone of voting age in the community should contribute to education. Needless to say, this approach was popular among property-owners and had support on City Council, including that of Mayor David Stewart. As a result, an educational tax was imposed on all male and all gainfully employed female residents. In reality it was a poll tax, and while it was theoretically sufficient to cover the costs of education, it was notoriously difficult to collect. By 1969 an estimated 25 per cent of the tax was uncollectible and a consultant's report recommended it be scrapped. By that time, the province was making substantial teachers' grants, but Charlottetown was convinced that the city still paid a much larger share of its educational costs than did rural areas. To observers, this was one more symptom of the perceived fiscal imbalance between the province and the city.

Financial considerations made their weight felt in all aspects of education, most noticeably in the decision to erect new schools. In the early 1950s, cost considerations drove the decisions being made over creating a new high school. Initially, Council preferred to expand existing accommodation, and in January 1953 instructed the school board to investigate what this would cost. There was also talk of purchasing Prince of Wales College, which could be stripped of its higher educational role and

6 This opinion, contained in a consultant's report written in 1969, had been voiced by Frank MacKinnon in his study of the government of PEI, published in 1951.

used strictly for secondary education. Later in the year, consensus was reached that a new school had to be constructed, but that opened yet another sensitive issue.

The city had achieved a *modus vivendi* between Roman Catholics and Protestants by informally identifying its various schools with one religious community or the other. If there were to be a single high school, how would that duality be maintained? Should there be two high schools? The school board had two options: a single 900-student school for $770,000, or two 500-student schools for $910,000. Council, which had to this point been actively engaged in school affairs, chose to tread lightly. Opinion was balanced about whether to favour a single school for financial reasons, but the resolution that finally passed referred vaguely to opposing extra expenditures for buildings to meet the wishes "of any particular group."[7] In rejecting the two-school option, Council included a disclaimer that it had no authority to advise the school board in matters of policy. It promised nevertheless to seek legislative approval from the province to raise the necessary funds for the school building program. Not to be deterred, the Roman Catholic Episcopal Corporation offered to build a second high school for the school board, which would then furnish and maintain it. In the end, the religious balancing act in the school system endured until a single senior high school was added in 1966.

The way in which City Council handled this confrontation revealed one of the shortcomings of a non-elected school board. The board could provoke issues that would fall into Council's unwelcoming lap. As early as March 1945, the city had petitioned the province to make the city school board elected instead of appointed. No action was taken. During the 1960s, when Council was actively pressuring the province to assume more of the financial burden of Charlottetown's schools, it raised again the need for an elected school board. A serious concern by this time was the threat of burgeoning bureaucratic control as the province took a larger role in education. Trustees concluded an elected board would be more effective in preserving local school board autonomy. When the province took direct control of education in 1971, the school board got what it wanted — and less. Although members would henceforth be elected, their schools would not constitute a stand-alone unit. Charlottetown schools were merged into a larger Unit 3 that included schools from the surrounding rural areas. The provincial government saw this as a way to spread the city's higher educational standards beyond the urban area. Supporters of a separate Charlottetown board thought the city was losing an asset in which it had invested its own resources and was being condemned to pedagogical stagnation while the rest of Unit 3 caught up to its standards. Some viewed the changes as a non-democratic exercise in which technocrats were imposing their priorities. The process, however, proved irreversible.

Between 1946 and 1984, perhaps the most heated issue in municipal politics across Canada was the question of whether or not to fluoridate drinking water. The

---

7 Council was evenly divided on an amendment calling for the removal of the sentence that registered its opposition to an additional building and it was passed with the deciding vote by Mayor Stewart.

controversy arose in Charlottetown in 1952. At a meeting of City Council, during which a motion to sell the city's horses was defeated, Dr. B. J. O'Meara, Director of Dental Public Health, made a pitch for adding sodium fluoride to the municipal water supply. This was, at the time, a new way to fight dental caries, and Council was very receptive to the idea, and asked O'Meara to report back with the cost implications. Whether he did so is unclear, but more than a year later, Dr. O'Meara was still agitating for the proposal to be implemented. He claimed that at the four main city schools, only six per cent of the pupils had no tooth decay. The problem could be reduced by two-thirds with this public health measure. The cost of treating the water was, he asserted, a modest 15¢ per capita.

Initially, city officials and Councillors appear to have generally supported the measure, but the water commission that was actually responsible for municipal water services was less interested. It studied the question but declined to give fluoridation serious consideration. Meanwhile, opposition was mobilizing. When a proposal came before Council in June 1954, it was initially adopted, but that approval was rescinded because federal health authorities were still examining the merits of the treatment. In August 1954, when Council resumed discussions of the issue, there were worries that medical experts seemed to be divided over the safety of sodium fluoride. Although children would benefit, there were fears that others drinking fluoridated water could be harmed. The proposal was defeated. About this time, two of the three water commissioners had come out in opposition to fluoridation for mainly cost reasons.

Supporters of fluoridation proved persistent. A number of citizens and some schools subsequently asked Council to reconsider and support the measure. Council responded to this pressure by procrastinating: in February 1955 it asked the water commission for details on how to integrate fluoride into the system. By this time, the controversy was growing and attracting wider involvement. Writing to the *Guardian*, the Mayor of Yarmouth, Nova Scotia, described how his Council had resisted attempts to force fluoridation on the town. Speaking in the Provincial Legislature, MLA Dr. Lorne Bonnell took the opposite view. Others cited the experience of other Canadian cities that had either adopted the measure or rejected it as evidence of whether fluoridation was effective or not. When the water commission took a wait-and-see approach, the Home and School Association, the provincial medical society and dental association, provincial health officials, and others mobilized to convince them to proceed. Torn between opposing forces, in August 1955 City Council narrowly agreed to ask the water commission to begin fluoridation.

The water commission refused to proceed without public endorsement. This raised the spectre of a plebiscite and the ire of supporters of fluoridation who argued that public health measures should be decided by those in authority who could understand expert advice. The *Patriot* begged to differ, charging the measure was a push by the Aluminum Company of America to market its sodium fluoride. The paper also pointed out that a reward promised to anyone who could prove that sodium fluoride was not poisonous had never been collected. "We are afraid of it," the paper exclaimed, "and will continue so until the medical profession unanimously agree that the fluoridation of water is safe." With people like Dr. Leo Spira arguing in his book, *The Drama of Fluorine: Arch-enemy of Mankind*, that fluoridation involved a deadly poison, there was little likelihood of that happening soon. The *Guardian*, for its part, was convinced by arguments in favour of fluoridation. So, eventually, was City Council, which in September 1958 unanimously approved a motion urging the water commission to implement the measure "at an early date." In response, the commission asked that a plebiscite on the issue be held during the 1960 municipal election.

In the ensuing debate all the old arguments were repeated. The medical and dental establishment and public health authorities advanced the case for acceptance, and an array of opponents raised fears concerning mass medication of the population with a poison that would make the water taste bad. One opponent believed that fluoride softened the brain and made personalities malleable, which explained why Soviet leader Nikita Khrushchev and his henchmen backed the concept. Organized labour, on the other hand, supported the measure because lower dental bills would benefit working people. Although proponents were hopeful, the measure was defeated by a narrow margin of 23 votes. Although the forces were essentially balanced, only five of 16 polls voted in favour and none of these were in the poorer Wards 1, 2 and 3. Health experts took an "I told you so" approach to their defeat, lamenting that a plebiscite should never have been held and the people who rejected fluoridation were the ones who would most benefit from it. Less sympathetic observers noted the controversial nature of the debate over an issue that was still unproven. They pointed to the role of emotion rather than fact in the campaign and identified a growing feeling among the public against enforced general public medication.

Advocates of fluoridation refused, however, to take "no" for an answer. The Department of Health promised to continue to promote it. Topical treatments of the teeth of a limited number of needy children was offered as an interim measure in 1966. Finally, in the municipal elections of 1967, another plebiscite was held on fluoridation, while E. W. Coady ran for the position of Water Commissioner on a platform favouring the measure. Supporters pointed out that one-quarter of the Canadian population already drank fluoridated water. The dental and medical groups and health officials at all levels of government were vigorous in their advocacy. Charlottetown's doctors and dentists published a signed advertisement of support in local newspapers. The Health League of Canada also placed a pro-fluoride ad. Opponents traded on fears, including the accusation that "mongolism"(Down Syndrome) was associated with fluoride. The contest was lively and at times bitter, but in the end the "yes" side won, 1,139 to 1,002. Some observers credited the influence of the medical community and health authorities with the victory.

The opponents of fluoridation proved to be as stubborn. They launched a court challenge with a petition bearing 2,500 signatures, and it was only after the Appeal Court rejected the suit that the Lieutenant-Governor in Council proclaimed the results of the plebiscite. Water treatment duly began in April 1968. This did not end the opposition. In October 1968 a 20-member delegation of the Pure Water Association descended upon City Council demanding another plebiscite. The meeting had, the

Like most municipal politicians in the 1950s and '60s, Walter Cox had to deal with the issue of fluoridation. In 1968 he temporarily quieted the anti-fluoridators by challenging them to field a candidate in the next civic election.

Guardian claimed, "all the ingredients of an old fashion political gathering," including "shouts, accusations, name-calling, interruptions, displays of temper, finger pointing and sometimes confusion." The association's brief said the recent plebiscite was undemocratic, unfair and discriminatory because only property-owners had the right to vote. A local chiropractor, W. R. Carson, accused the water commission of subterfuge and improper procedures in applying the fluorides. Mayor Walter Cox temporarily ended the matter by challenging the Pure Water Association to field a candidate in the next civic election, but as late as the spring of 1977, a convention of the Catholic Women's League approved a resolution asking for a ban on the addition of sodium fluoride to Island drinking water.

In the midst of the debate over fluoridation, another controversy sprang up over the status of the water commission itself. The commission had been established as an independent body at a time when the merits of the utilities were hotly contested at the municipal level. Since then, they had become proven necessities like other municipal services, such as fire and police protection and road maintenance. Although independent, the commission relied upon the city financially. Even so, the fluoride issue demonstrated that co-operation between the Commission and Council could be problematic. In December 1957 Council concluded that water and sewerage should come under its jurisdiction. It petitioned the provincial legislature to amend the city's charter and reduce the water commission to a purely advisory body. The Legislature considered the petition, but failed to pass the amendment before the session ended.

In its defence, the water commission questioned the sincerity of Council, particularly the renewal of its request for changes in April 1958, just before the end of the legislative session. It noted how little effort had been made to settle the question during the recent civic elections. The commission also adopted an "if it ain't broke, don't fix it" approach, noting that the sewer and water services paid their way and were a municipal asset. On May 21, 1958, the matter was put to a plebiscite. The water commission emerged victorious. Apparently voters were content with the present set-up and the good intentions of the commissioners. A few years later, Council accorded them salary increases of 240 per cent to give them parity with City Councillors.

Relations between civic authorities and the provincial government could also be difficult. Although the two agreed on the issue of fluoridation, the same could not be said for daylight saving time. Charlottetown began to advance its clocks one hour during the summer of 1940 as a wartime measure. Citizens liked the extra hour of daylight in the evenings and wanted to maintain the practice once the war was over. Provincial authorities rejected attempts to bring in daylight saving time on a province-wide basis. Year-round standard time was legally mandated, and the Liberal government of Walter Jones blocked suggestions Charlottetown and other urban areas might simply advance their schedules by one hour during the summer months. The interests of farmers were politically paramount. They employed a large number of seasonal labourers who worked from 8:00 a.m. until 6:00 p.m. Haying could not begin until the dew was off the fields, usually around 10:00 a.m. If daylight saving time were imposed, haying could start only at 11:00 a.m., imposing a loss of an hour that farmers could ill afford. For their part, urbanites argued that daylight saving time provided people with an extra hour of healthy relaxation after long sedentary winters.

During the civic elections of 1952, a canvass of the various wards showed that Charlottetonians were strongly in favour of daylight saving time. After the subsequent election in 1954, City Council voted to introduce summer time in defiance of the province's uniform time act. The Attorney General censured the city for its illegal move, but the retail merchants' association, organized labour and the banks backed it. Although one Liberal minister suggested that the choice could be made a matter of local option, the government finally confirmed its opposition. In 1956 the legislature resolved that any municipality breaking Atlantic Standard Time would lose its financial grant. City politicians could only reiterate their case and call upon MLAs to change their minds.

By 1960 the arguments in favour of summer time and its widespread acceptance elsewhere in the Maritimes and the rest of Canada had made some impression on the provincial government. "Fresh air and sunshine are the best medicine the Lord has given us," proclaimed Dr. George Dewar, the Minister of Education, as the Shaw Conservatives instituted uniform daylight saving time in 1960. Mayor Gaudet sent the Premier and the two city MLAs flowers, but the reaction of farmers was bitter, and the story did not end there. The Farm Federation suggested that the change should be regarded as an experiment. It proposed that the following summer, standard time should remain in effect and that early opening and closing hours should be promoted instead. Shaw's government agreed; in 1961 the province stayed with standard time.

Now some urbanites were incensed. Mayor Gaudet took the situation in stride, calling the complainers "spoiled children." Dorothy Corrigan lamented the inconvenience imposed on housewives. Then, with the written support of the Board of Trade and the promised co-operation of the School Board, the chartered banks and the federal and provincial governments, Council resolved that normal working hours in the city would be from 8:00 a.m. to 4:00 p.m. Individual citizens could decide whether or not to advance their clocks one hour. As the step was recommended by the Premier, the city was assured it would not be penalized by the provincial government. The "experiment" was repeated in 1962, but by then the weight of public opinion and the practicalities of the Island's location adjacent to Nova Scotia and New Brunswick

As both a municipal politician and MLA, David Stewart urged the province to increase its financial support to ease the burden on the city's ratepayers.

made themselves felt. Uniform daylight saving time came to Prince Edward Island. Farmers grumbled that their interests were being sacrificed for the convenience of tourists. That was an oversimplification, of course, although by the early 1960s tourism was the second industry of the province and an important element in the Island's hope for economic renewal.

The hour of the day was not the only bone of contention between the city and the province. Of the various areas of dispute, finances were perhaps the most enduring and perplexing. Inadequate revenue and the controlling hand of the senior level of government had bedevilled the city since incorporation. The root of the jurisdictional struggles lay in the Island's rural character. Farmers feared they might be stuck with some of the cost of maintaining their urban cousins, while the province's small, dispersed population retarded the creation of municipalities generally. Charlottetown, as the province's only city, and the Town of Summerside, along with some smaller communities, accounted for only 31 per cent of the population in 1958. The balance looked to the provincial government to provide many of the services normally handled by municipal governments. Frank MacKinnon in his landmark study of the government of Prince Edward Island noted that many of the newer activities, particularly in the area of social services, were administered by the province, and it preferred "to spend the money and direct the enterprise." In its pastoral Island setting, Charlottetown was an anomaly, and little provision was made for that fact. Suggestions that the city might merit an official representative in the provincial cabinet made little headway. The mayor served as that link, and his effectiveness depended almost entirely on how well he got along with the premier.

When it came to finances, personal rapport greased few wheels. Pressing the provincial government for more money was generally fruitless. It was tried in 1951 with little result. After a new Council was elected in 1952, the city renewed its claims. Though the province increased its grant by 25 per cent, Mayor Stewart felt that was not adequate and promised to go back for more. He went back in 1953 and was disappointed. Stewart had better luck with the federal government, which agreed to "a very substantial" increase in its grant in lieu of taxes for its properties in the city. Unfortunately, the province hesitated to pass other federal grants on to the municipalities. Charlottetown's per capita grant from federal-provincial transfer payments was many times lower than those of municipalities in other provinces. Growth of the city, particularly through amalgamation, had the effect of lightening the provincial financial burden and shifting it to the city. The province made some progress in increased grants to cover the costs of extended municipal services, but in the city's view this was not enough. By 1967 David Stewart, by then an opposition member of the legislature, was still urging the government to increase its support to ease the burden on the city's ratepayers.

An examination of the revenue sources for Charlottetown between 1950 and 1980 shows the slow and uneven progress made in revenue-sharing between the province and city.

Revenue Stream	1950	1955	1960	1965	1970	1975	1980
Real Estate Tax	53.6	50.9	46.0	56.1	56.9		
Real Estate and Business Taxes						71.7	62.1
Personal Property Tax	23.8	23.2					
Personal Property and Business Tax			22.2				
Business Tax				16.9			
Motor Vehicle and Business Taxes					23.9		
Poll Tax	3.5	9.2					
Educational Tax			8.1	4.9	3.9		
Automobile Tax				5.1			
Sewer and Water Charges	5.9	4.4	2.7		3.3		3.6
Debt Charges Collected							4.1
Per Capita Grant	4.4	4.8	16.7	8.7	6.9	21.8	15.3
Special Agreement / Program	3.6						4.1

In updating its taxation policies, the city made several modifications to the terms under which it collected revenue. The personal property tax was converted into a business tax, and the poll tax, which went to support education, was renamed an education tax. The tax on automobiles and other motor vehicles which had been added to the personal property tax in 1940 re-emerged in its own right in 1964. Both motor vehicle and education taxes disappeared after 1971 because there were no provisions for the collection of such taxes after the province took over responsibility for education. Such measures failed to obscure the basic inability of the city to tap revenue streams that were fully adequate for its apparent needs. The refusal of the province to grant Charlottetown an equitable share of provincial revenue, a substantial portion of which was raised within the city, was an irritant that continued well beyond 1984.

Politics in Charlottetown reflected the changing circumstances of the city. Throughout the period 1946–84, the Island capital took on a greater role in the socio-economic life of the province. It was becoming increasingly the engine of prosperity and the focus of cultural life. A centrifugal force was being created that drew productive activity and people into it. The city was growing and with the growth came urban problems typically found in other modern Canadian cities. Charlottetown was a bigger, more sophisticated place in 1984 than it had been in 1946. This, of course, was true of many communities, but, in Charlottetown's case, this transformation may have been more dramatic than most. The challenge for municipal politicians and officials was to keep pace with these changes and to offer the leadership and competent administration that the times and circumstances required.

URBAN LANDSCAPE

Time, the Great Depression, the stresses of the Second World War and neglect had left their marks on the face of Charlottetown. In the 1940s and '50s, the surging Canadian economy that was rapidly changing cities in central and western Canada was less apparent in the Maritimes. In the postwar era, newness reflected progress. Throughout much of Canada, new roads, new skyscrapers, new residential subdivisions with their attendant new schools, parks, recreation centres and churches profoundly altered the urban landscape. In Charlottetown, as in most other Maritime centres, there was less that was new and more that was old. It would be a while before Canadians would appreciate the cultural and aesthetic value of heritage districts. Meanwhile, the response of outsiders to the wearing fabric of the Island's capital may have been typified by a member of the foundation responsible for the future Confederation Centre of the Arts when he commented, "Charlottetown … is a mess. Shabby houses with broken windows, broken sidewalks, weeds and general untidiness. I think we should make it known in some way that we take a dim view of having the magnificent memorial buildings surrounded by appalling shabbiness." Justified or not at the time, a similar observation would have been impossible 20 years later. In that period, Charlottetown grew more prosperous, but, more significantly, the city began to reshape itself as a place with a future as well as a past.

Public Buildings

Fire continued to do its own reshaping, returning with a vengeance on April 30, 1958, when it swept through the 54-year-old Harris market house, completely gutting it. There had been other conflagrations in the city since the Second World War. On the night of October 10, 1946, the Bruce Stewart and Company plant was almost totally consumed by flames, as was the Island Fertilizer plant. In the same year, much of Davis and Fraser's meat packing establishment on Grafton Street went up in smoke. In 1951 several buildings in the block bounded by present-day University Avenue, and Kent, Prince and Grafton Streets were razed by fire on the night of August 18. More fires followed the market blaze. Two separate blazes in 1959 ravaged the grandstand at the exhibition grounds, and, in January 1976, flames roared through the Law Courts Building on Queen Square, severely damaging the interior and destroying the clock tower. During the night of January 29, 1979, an apartment building at the corner of Water and Pownal Streets was gutted, and a number of families were left homeless. But the market house fire was different. It changed the face of the city forever. The

"Charlottetown ... is a mess .... Shabby houses with broken windows, broken sidewalks, weeds and general untidiness." Corner of Kent and University Avenue c. 1965.

building was not replaced. Instead, the blackened shell was demolished and the site was used as a parking lot. Even before the fire, the market's importance as an outlet for farmers' produce had declined. Although a few stalls and a meat and a fish market remained in operation in the 1950s, much of the market building served as a tourist bureau and a bus terminal. Its loss did not seriously affect the commercial life of the city, but the forlorn gap left in the streetscape offered the possibility of future development. Some years would go by before construction in this prime urban setting actually began.

When a new purpose was finally found for the site, it had massive implications for the economy and cultural life of Charlottetown as well as its cityscape. The community had long required improved facilities for concerts and live theatrical performances. Efforts to plan for this goal dated back to at least 1946,[8] and Frank MacKinnon, Principal of Prince of Wales College, in his presentation to the Massey Royal Commission on the Arts, Letters and Sciences in 1950 recommended such a facility be built. The need increased in 1956 when the Prince Edward Theatre was destroyed by fire. Loss of the theatre space in the market building was a further blow to the city's cultural infrastructure. Within three months of the destruction of the market, MacKinnon was setting the stage for the creation of a new arts centre on the site. Due to the combination of remarkable abilities of persuasion and management, the political evolution of Canada, a shared vision of Canadian history and sheer happenstance, MacKinnon and his close associate, Calgary oil millionaire Eric Harvie, eventually attained their

8 The *Guardian*, on November 16, 1946, noted that a committee was being organized to "canvass ways and means of developing a permanent Community Art Centre."

objective. Market Street was closed, motor vehicles were literally and figuratively driven from Market Square, the decaying 1887 Cabot Building was demolished and the cramped Harris Memorial Art and Library Building torn down. In their place rose the imposing Confederation Centre of the Arts.

Five years passed between the fire at the market house and the opening of the Dominion Drama Festival that marked the inaugural use of the new arts centre. Much of the time had been spent mobilizing support, financing and planning. Fortunately, some of the backers of the Centre, including Eric Harvie, had deep pockets. The very best advisors were consulted. Eric Arthur, a distinguished Toronto architect and heritage activist, drafted the design specifications, and Sir Basil Spence, the celebrated Scottish architect of the new Coventry Cathedral, guided the selection process as an outside appraiser. Forty-seven proposals were received. The winning concept was submitted by the Montreal firm of Affleck, Debarats, Dimakopolous, Lebensold and Sise. Although the building was massive in scale, it deferred to nearby Province House. Even before a winning design had been chosen, a decision was made to have the centre clad in the same Wallace sandstone that faced the legislature. As the old Nova Scotian quarry was nearly exhausted, enough stone to realize the project was purchased in advance of funding guarantees. The new building also respected Province House by having the façade of the memorial hall face the west side of the legislature. Viewed from inside the Hall, the original meeting place of the Fathers of Confederation is framed by the sweeping staircase leading downwards to a glass curtain wall surmounted by the names of Canada's founding statesmen. The historic setting of the conference was complemented, not overshadowed, by the memorial to the event.

Fred Lebensold and his colleagues produced a strikingly innovative "Brutalist" design, and Pigott Construction of Hamilton, Ontario, won the contract to build it. Actual construction began in February 1963. The building was intended to house a memorial hall, a 1,100-seat theatre, an art gallery, a library and archives and supporting work areas. Its bulk was partially hidden by setting the building into the ground so that the visible elevations were compatible with its neighbours. Light was admitted by soaring corner windows, a sunken atrium and extensive skylights. The memorial hall was crowned by a novel glass roof resembling an egg crate through which light poured to be reflected off the marble walls below. However effective the architecture might have been, it was accompanied by both conceptual and technical difficulties. With respect to the theatre, the architects initially omitted a box office and failed to recognize that the most convenient access point for the public would be from Queen Street. A secondary entrance and admission wickets were subsequently inserted into the plans at the northwest corner of the theatre foyer. Weather also proved a challenge. The glass roof of Memorial Hall, suitable for drier, sunnier climates, leaked when melting slush built up around the windows. It was eventually made watertight, but years passed and the leaks elsewhere were never completely stopped. Despite the inevitable flaws and disparaging comments from some locals,[9] the project was

9 The building was known as the "tomb" or the "potato warehouse" by some.

Construction of the Confederation Centre began in February, 1963. The building was completed, on time and on budget, the following year, and was officially opened by Queen Elizabeth II on October 6, 1964.

completed on time and on budget. When Queen Elizabeth II opened the Fathers of Confederation Memorial Building on October 6, 1964, Charlottetown had not only a modern civic cultural centre but an architectural landmark that was national, and even international, in significance.

Although the Confederation Centre was the most imposing addition to Charlottetown's streetscape in this period, it was far from the only one. The first important building to be completed was the Dominion Building, which opened on Queen Street in 1956. Intended to supplant the Cabot Building as a post office and working space for the federal civil servants in town, it was designed by the Department of Public Works in Ottawa and erected by Anglin-Norcross Maritimes Limited, Halifax. While its architecture was considered to be practical and modern — "P.E.I.'s most imposing building and one of the finest and most modern of its kind in Canada" — it soon came to be regarded by some as lacking "neighbourliness" and being a "living testimony of … 'architectural engineering.'" In 1965 Affleck, Debarats, Dimakopolous, Lebensold and Sise turned their hands to designing a complex of provincial buildings to be built on Rochford Street between Kent and Fitzroy Street. Adjacent to partially filled-in Government Pond, the marshy site posed some technical challenges, but the boxy architecture of the concrete buildings was pleasing enough and in scale with the surroundings. The two parts of the complex, opened by the Queen Mother Elizabeth on July 17, 1967, were eventually named after two Conservative premiers: Walter Shaw and W. W. Sullivan. In 1972 the Jones Building, a five-storey, red brick office block commemorating former Liberal Premier J. Walter Jones, was put up on the southwest corner of the property.

Other impressive developments followed in subsequent years. The fire which ravaged the courthouse in 1976 made a new court building necessary, and this coincided with plans to redevelop the city's waterfront. The Charlottetown Area Development Corporation (CADC) undertook the project, having identified a solid old warehouse on Water Street as suitable for conversion. Cochrane Forsyth Pickard of Halifax and Charlottetown were hired as architects, with Williams Murphy and MacLeod as their contractors. The plans incorporated the building's existing wooden floors and massive wooden beams while the wood and red brick façade was surmounted by an expansive, sloping, green-coloured, copper roof. CADC leased the three-storey building to the provincial government to house the provincial supreme court and the federal court. When opened in 1979, the Sir Louis Davies Law Courts building was, the *Guardian* boasted, "one of Canada's most modern and unique courthouses." Adjacent to it was a much more prosaically designed provincial court.

Decentralization of some federal government departments paid dividends for Charlottetown when Ottawa decided to relocate the Department of Veterans Affairs to the city. Its new headquarters occupied much of the block bounded by University Avenue and Kent, Prince and Grafton Streets. Although the five-storey, reddish-brown brick, glass and black-metal Daniel J. MacDonald building was massive by local standards, its architects, Consortium Designers and Consultants, made it compatible with its neighbours. A two-storey podium opened onto Grafton Street while elevations facing Kent Street were stepped back from three to five storeys. The contractor, Schurman Construction, completed the building by 1984.

The health sector also loomed large in the transformation of the built environment. Although both of the general hospitals were enlarged in the postwar years, by

In 1965, work began on a complex of provincial buildings designed by the same firm that crafted the Confederation Centre. The two-part complex, named for former Conservative premiers Walter Shaw and W.W. Sullivan, opened in 1967.

the 1970s they were in need of modernization. In an era of consolidation, the delivery of health services was heavily influenced by the trend to have fewer and bigger medical facilities. Instead of investing more in the existing institutions, the province decided to build a new, 330-bed, regional general hospital. Construction began in 1979 on a site in the east end of town on Riverside Drive. The design of the metal and glass building included elements of structural expressionism, a novel element in the architectural mix of the city. A. W. Cluff and P. J. Cluff, Toronto, were the architects, and Thomas Fuller Construction, Ottawa, was the principal contractor. The Queen Elizabeth Hospital (QEH) opened in the spring of 1982. Other hospital construction saw an attractive yellow and brown brick and stone School of Nursing and nurses' residence built for the Charlottetown Hospital in 1959. In 1962 the Sacred Heart Home abandoned its old location for a new five-storey, brown brick and concrete building at the corner of Water and Haviland Streets. At the time, the home was one of the tallest structures in the city. A new active treatment psychiatric facility, the Riverside (soon to be renamed Hillsborough) Hospital was opened in 1957. The low-rise, two-storey, red brick and stone structure with pleasing bay windows looked more like a school than a mental institution, unlike Falconwood Hospital, which it replaced. It was followed in 1962 by the Sherwood Home for children with developmental disabilities.

The city's expanding population eventually prompted the construction of new schools. The first was Queen Charlotte Junior High on North River Road, opening in 1954. Birchwood Junior High on Longworth Avenue followed in 1957. Three new elementary schools came shortly thereafter. A new Prince Street School was erected on the grounds of the old, now antiquated building, which was subsequently torn down. West Kent School was relocated to a new facility on Viceroy Street. This followed the recommendation of Walter P. de Silva, the Provincial Planner, who noted that in 10 to 15 years, the population served by the school would be located well north of Euston Street. St. Jean Elementary, on Upper Queen Street, was created to house students from Queen Square and, after its closure in June 1975, Rochford Square School. Spring Park, an elementary school on Dunkirk Avenue, was built just prior to the area's amalgamation with the city. It was "up-to-date in all respects" and continued to house its existing population for some years. The crowning achievement of Charlottetown's baby boom school construction program was the completion of Colonel Gray Senior High School in 1966. Built on Spring Park Road, it accommodated Grade 11 and 12 students who had formerly been educated at Prince of Wales College and St. Dunstan's University, as well as Grade 10 students from Queen Charlotte and Birchwood Junior High Schools.

There was school construction as well beyond the city proper. A badly needed Provincial Vocational Institute opened on Enman Crescent in Central Royalty in 1964. It served mainly as a vocational high school for students from Charlottetown, Parkdale and Sherwood. An older elementary school, built on Parkdale's Linden Avenue in 1937, had become overcrowded by the 1950s. In 1956 a new school opened on Confederation Street to house Grades 6–10, while the younger pupils stayed at the old facility. By the late 1970s, after the older grades were transferred to other schools in the area, and the junior grades were moved to the Confederation Street site, the building on Linden Avenue was closed. Increased numbers of school-aged children were also found in Sherwood, which was school district 84 before the area was incorporated as a village in 1960. To accommodate this expanding population, Sherwood Elementary School was built on Maple Avenue in 1956. Stonepark Junior High opened at the end of December 1973 on Pope Avenue. Charlottetown Rural High School, one of a series of consolidated senior secondary schools built by the province, opened on Burns Crescent in 1964. The architecture of all of these school buildings reflected the conventional designs of their time, and they injected an element of predictability into the built landscape of the city. Charlottetown was nevertheless provided with a modern system of schools supporting then-current educational practices.

The boom in school construction also extended to the college and university levels. In 1960–61, Prince of Wales built its first residence, Montgomery Hall. Located at the northeast corner of Cumberland and Kent Streets, it was designed by C. A. Fowler and Company of Halifax and built by the provincial department of public works. The generally uninspiring architecture of the rectangular, four-storey, brown brick, glass and metal building was relieved by the gracious lines of a two-storey wing. Some years earlier, Memorial Hall had been erected at St. Dunstan's to serve as a residence and tribute to the financial sacrifices of the University's backers. Started in 1946 and finished in 1947, the three-storey red brick building had a plain, almost austere façade softened by a central projection rising the full height and topped by an ornate gable. This was the first step in a construction program that saw a new chapel and dining room open beside Main Building in 1950 and an alumni gymnasium follow in 1951.

"Proposed Charlottetown High School, North River Road, 1953." Architect E. S. "Bones" Blanchard.

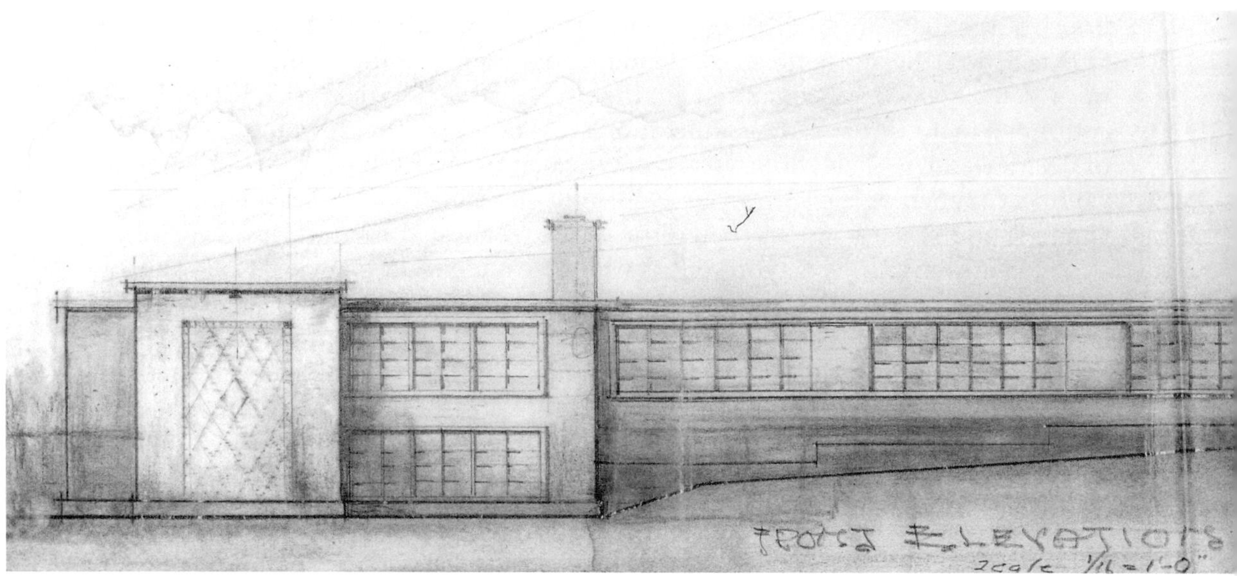

With increasing enrolments and larger numbers of young women pursuing higher education, St. Dunstan's built a badly needed women's residence, Marian Hall, in 1959. A four-storey red-brick structure sitting closer to Malpeque Road than the other university buildings, its uncluttered "neo-Georgian" design was adorned with a few architectural flourishes reminiscent of Memorial Hall. It incorporated a chapel, dining hall and some teaching areas, as well as the dormitory rooms. The Kelly Memorial Library, designed by Alfred J. Hennessey, followed in 1963. Placed next to the Science Building, it extended the central quadrangle towards Malpeque Road to be in line with Marian Hall. Boxy in design and clad in red brick, the library introduced a more contemporary if blandly functional appearance to the campus. A smaller Student Union building, with a low square red-brick façade, opened in 1965. The next year, an important new science facility opened. Named after Dr. St. Clair Duffy, whose financial support made the project possible, the building's recessed entrance and first floor added visual interest to its three, otherwise-unadorned, red-brick storeys. A second women's residence, Bernardine Hall, the last construction undertaken by St. Dunstan's, was completed in 1967. Located to the south of Marian Hall and closer to Malpeque Road, it was contemporary in design, with its façades broken and given visual interest by inset tiers of windows.

Following the merger of Prince of Wales College and St. Dunstan's University to form the University of Prince Edward Island in 1969, a new round of construction was begun at the Malpeque Road campus. Prudently, the first structure was a central utility building. Functional in every respect from design to purpose, it was finished in 1972 and supported the expansion of other facilities. The following year, work began

on Blanchard Hall, a co-ed residence, and the spacious Robertson Library. The residence was completed in 1974; the library followed in 1975. Blanchard Hall contained apartment-style suites and looked like thousands of low-rise apartment buildings found anywhere in Canada at the time. Robertson Library was more distinctive. A massive structure, it was recessed into the landscape to preserve a low elevation and avoid overshadowing the other buildings on campus. Sloping roofs muted the long rectangular walls and a large skylight animated the interior with natural lighting. An entirely new element was introduced into the architectural mix of the university when a planetarium was opened. The design of the structure was inspired by Buckminster Fuller's geodesic dome, a perfect shape for the purpose, and it resembled a giant, grey golf ball on the exterior. Intended partially to attract tourists in the summer, the planetarium ultimately failed to generate sufficient revenue to remain in operation and was removed from the campus. In February 1983, an announcement that a veterinary college would be opened at the University guaranteed the continuation of the transformation of the built environment of the campus in the years ahead.

In the period immediately following the war, construction for the state far outpaced the creation of new church buildings. Generally, Charlottetown's growing suburban population did not immediately translate into a plethora of new places of worship at the edges of town. Many of the faithful commuted to the well-established churches in the centre of the city. This practice resulted in some expansion and renovation of existing church buildings, such as the modification of the Central Christian Church in 1974. The work involved the removal of a wall between the church proper and an annex to provide more seating space. Earlier in 1958, the same congregation converted an old building at the corner of Kent and Hillsborough Streets into an education centre.[10]

As migration to the suburbs continued, however, the situation changed. People preferred to worship where they lived, and the presence of churches became one of the hallmarks of a well-established community. A Free Presbyterian congregation organized after the Second World War built a church on Birchwood Street in 1954. The Christian Brethren assembly, which had met in the Sons of England Hall in 1954 and 1955, began building the Charlottetown Bible Chapel at the corner of Cumberland Street and Longworth Avenue in 1955, and held their first meeting in it in January 1956. A new Roman Catholic parish to serve the Parkdale area, Pius X, was created in 1956. First Baptist Church dedicated a new building on Prince Street in May 1959. Park Royal United Church in Parkdale was built in 1958, and the continued growth of the congregation prompted it to open an education centre in 1966.

That same year, 1966, the Salvation Army inaugurated a new Citadel, Barracks and Welfare Bureau on Great George Street. Meanwhile, in 1964 Holy Redeemer Roman Catholic parish erected a replacement for its overcrowded building. The design of

10 The building had formerly been used variously as a furniture factory, meat packing plant, candy works and naval barracks.

the new structure on Spring Park Road was prepared by a parishioner, Alfred J. Hennessey, and featured a soaring conical dome over the chancel. The Roman Catholic Sisters of St. Martha also erected an expansive new motherhouse off Mount Edward Road in 1964. Spring Park United Church and the Christian Reformed Church on Mount Edward Road were opened in 1965, to be followed in 1970 by the Sherwood Church of Christ. By the early 1970s, the assembly at the Charlottetown Bible Chapel had expanded to the point new quarters were needed. An expansive new chapel was opened in Sherwood in 1975. Later, in 1978, Grace Baptist Church occupied its new building on Kirkdale Road in West Royalty. The Pentecostal community established the Calvary Temple on Prince Street in 1960, quickly outgrew it, and so opened a massive, new building at the junction of the Trans-Canada Highway and Malpeque Road in 1980. Faith Bible Church on St. Peter's Road was also built in 1980. In 1984 the Mormons, who had been meeting in the Y Centre since 1973, moved to their new home on the Northridge Parkway at St. Peter's Road.

These and other places of worship made distinctive statements of faith on the built landscape of the city. The gothic idiom that dominated church architecture in previous periods was largely absent from the new buildings. A need to provide educational and recreational space for the many baby boom children imposed a certain functionality to some of the designs, but allusions to conventional architectural features, such as the steeple and the arched window, marked their purpose and set them apart from the unadorned linear boxes that characterized so much of the commercial and institutional construction of the period.

Commercial Buildings

Expansion of the commercial and retail space in Charlottetown also began slowly after the Second World War. Much of the construction was small in scale and located in the centre of the city or along the principal commercial arteries leading to the downtown. The pace of construction on a grander scale picked up gradually in the 1950s. Holman's Department Store, for instance, opened its "Little Shop" on Kent Street in 1950 and made plans to enlarge its main store later. A spacious new Eaton's store also on Kent Street welcomed its first customers in 1955. Zellers subsequently located a branch next door. In 1957 a new two-storey Tweel Building opened.

The most dramatic developments came in the 1960s, however, when commercial activity spread outward from the city core to the emerging suburbs. Much of it responded to the use of automobiles by suburban and rural residents to commute to stores and other places of business. Shoppers and business people had already demonstrated a marked preference, even expectation, for parking adjacent to their destinations. It made sense to take commerce to the edge of town to meet them and to provide ample parking space for their cars. The new business office of the water commission, which opened in 1965 on Kirkwood Drive in the north of the city, was an example of this commercial relocation. Another was the Island Telephone Company's new service centre built in 1974 on Belvedere Avenue. In 1980 Island Tel erected an impressive headquarters, also on Belvedere Avenue. With its contrasting horizontal and vertical features, this new landmark immediately ranked as one of the most attractive modern buildings in the city.

When the Dairy Queen ice cream store opened in 1960, it heralded the arrival of drive-in restaurants to the city and to its main access road from the west (now University Avenue). An A&W restaurant at the corner of Belvedere Avenue and Malpeque Road, near St. Dunstan's, followed in 1964; a Colonel Sanders Kentucky Fried Chicken outlet opened in 1969, and in succeeding years other similar fast food operations appeared nearby. Their garish signs soon festooned the thoroughfare as it worked its way past the University, Spring Park Square and the Experimental Farm towards downtown.

Large-scale commercial development followed in 1965 with the decision of the local Co-op to build a shopping mall on Elm Avenue. The Royalty Mall was the first of its kind in Prince Edward Island and only the third in the Maritimes. Besides the supermarket, the mall attracted a Stedmans variety store, bank, pharmacy and a number of smaller enterprises. In addition, the Canadian Tire franchise moved from its old premises on Queen Street to the mall and its acres of customer parking. In 1969 S. S. Kresge Corporation announced plans for a K-Mart to be located at the corner of Malpeque Road and Belvedere Avenue. A new-format big-box retailer that sold both groceries and general merchandise, the K-Mart sat well back from the streets behind an expansive parking lot. The plaza also included a mall along its south side. Local developer Bernard Dale continued the march of commerce to the periphery in 1974 when he built an even bigger Towers Mall further down University Avenue[11] in West Royalty. Typically, these linear, low-rise buildings were characterized by expanses of store windows fronted by covered walkways, backed by featureless stretches of wall, and surrounded by huge, well-lit parking areas. In the case of the Towers Mall, the store fronts faced inwards towards a central concourse so that the backsides of the businesses formed the exterior façades. Only the occasional entry pierced the uninviting bulwark. The new shopping plazas offered convenience and efficiency but lacked charm and distinctiveness.

In an effort to compete with the suburban commercial developments, a group of downtown merchants banded together to make the mall concept work for them. The proprietors of stores facing a block bounded by Grafton, Queen and Kent Streets and University Avenue agreed to cover over the properties behind their stores and erect an adjoining office tower to form a large enclosed shopping and commercial concourse. By creating a central core for the block, the owners provided new space for stores and a food court, the latest concept in new fast-food service. After some delays, the project went ahead in 1979. The complex, known as the Confederation Court Mall, provided Charlottetown with its equivalent of Toronto's Eaton Centre and went some distance towards sustaining some vitality in the city's commercial centre.

---

11 Upper Great George Street, Elm Avenue and Malpeque Road were known as University Avenue as of midnight December 30, 1970. Prior to this, the transition between Elm Avenue and Malpeque Road occurred just north of Kirkwood Drive and Allan Street at the southern edge of the Experimental Farm.

The CADC was instrumental in developing Harbourside, a multi-faceted restoration of the city's waterfront lying south of Water Street between Queen and Pownal Streets. An important component of the project was the provision of prime commercial space for offices and stores. Several new three-storey buildings were designed to fit into the well-established setting and blend with renovated, historic buildings. This initiative, which began in the late 1970s and was completed by the early 1980s, reversed several decades of economic stagnation and physical decay in the area. It achieved, in the words of the 1978 community profile for Charlottetown, the re-emphasis of the "traditional relationships between the waterfront and the city, reinforcing [the] existing character and functions of the area."

Visitor accommodation in Charlottetown followed a development pattern similar to other commercial infrastructure. After the Second World War, the Canadian National Hotel, renamed "The Charlottetown" in 1939, was the largest and most luxurious hostelry in the city, but smaller, older places, such as the Revere Hotel on Kent Street and the Queen Hotel on Water Street remained in operation. The motor car as the vehicle of choice for many travellers, however, began to change the dynamics of the hospitality industry. Competition arose from motels and tourist cabins established along major routes into town. When the Kirkwood Motel opened on Elm Avenue in the mid-1950s, it represented what was considered to be the best of this new trend with free parking in front of each unit, a no-tipping policy and special rates and facilities for commercial travellers. MacLauchlan's Motel on Grafton Street and the Islander Motel on Pownal offered the same amenities when they opened. These establishments were long, low buildings with large parking lots, but the Inn on the Hill that opened on Euston Street in 1972 departed from that format. While it was five storeys in height, the motorist was still provided with ample free parking.[12] By then, air travel and guided bus tours were again restructuring the marketplace. When the Prince Edward Hilton Hotel was built in the early 1980s as part of CADC's waterfront redevelopment program, it featured a parking garage and two levels of dining, shopping and convention facilities, as well as eight storeys of guest rooms.

Restoration of the waterfront beginning in the late 1970s signalled the abandonment of the long-time approach to industrial development that concentrated activities along the harbour. Warehouses, railway tracks, the Canadian National repair shops, oil storage facilities and various manufacturers were clustered there. With the reorientation of transport from sea and rail to road travel, and a steady decline in vitality of businesses along the waterfront, planners turned to other sites in which industry could settle. Three prime locales, the West Royalty Industrial Park and locations in the north end of Sherwood and northeastern Parkdale, all of which lay beyond the city's boundaries, emerged as preferred areas for new development. Ample serviced land with quick access to principal highways attracted businesses that needed

12 The owner was H. Douglas Hill, making the hotel's name a pun as well as an apt description of its location.

cost-efficient space and few associations with their neighbours. This phase of economic growth began in the mid-1970s and produced estates of light industries that differed very little in architecture and layout from others found throughout North America.[13] One business that fought the trend was PEI Energy Systems, which opened a district hot water heating plant on the harbour in 1983. It used local fuels, including wood waste and municipal garbage, to provide thermo-energy to nearby customers.

Residential Housing

Charlottetown emerged from the Second World War with much of its housing stock battered and worn. Brighton and pockets of well-maintained homes in the older parts of the city reflected pride of ownership and the income to support it, but there was a large number of "blighted and obsolescent" rental properties that yielded "small tax revenue to the city but at the same time sizeable incomes to their owners." New construction occurred in Brighton, but its nature changed somewhat. Between 1946 and 1950, over 60 houses were erected, and new streets were laid out, but properties were typically reduced in size to resemble conventional suburban lots rather than estates. There was additional housing built east of Brighton, and after the demise of the Abegweit Athletic Association, homes were put up on the old sports fields. In the 1960s, housing inched towards the city's northern limits, and subsidized housing projects were opened in areas along Upper Queen Street in 1968 and Belmont Avenue in 1972. In the immediate postwar era, many of the single homes being built were semi-bungalows, and in the later 1950s and 1960s, popular taste favoured the ranch and high-ranch bungalow design. The subsidized developments contained two-storey row houses.

There were only a few apartment buildings erected before the late 1970s. Several were clustered on Ashburn Crescent and nearby Belvedere Avenue; others were found on Euston Street, Wendy Drive and other locations sprinkled around town, including the Harbourside development. At the end of the period, an expansive townhouse development appeared in the fields opposite UPEI. Most of this housing was conventional in design and construction and left the newer areas of Charlottetown with few elements of local distinctiveness. Some of the homes appearing in Brighton, however, were exceptions to this rule and helped to maintain the area as prime real estate turf. The Harbourside apartments, which were adjacent to the marina and included some two-storey units, provided resort-style accommodations in buildings with designs compatible with the historic neighbourhood.

From the 1950s onwards, much of the home construction took place in the suburbs. Parkdale was the oldest of these settlement areas; plans for its subdivision were

13 This is not to say that there were no controls on what was built and how. All indusries that purchased plant sites in the West Royalty Industrial Park, for instance, had to meet design standards established by Industrial Enterprises Incorporated with respect to size, layout and other details including materials used.

originally made in the 19th century. Housing was well-established there before the Second World War, and further development followed the war. By the late 1950s, the town was a mature middle- and working-class community of single-family homes in a village-like setting. Zoning changes arising from the provincial housing act of the late 1960s prompted a trend away from low-density family housing to more multiple-family housing and commercial development. Development came later to Sherwood. A few homes dating from before the Second World War were sprinkled throughout the area, but development only began in earnest in the late 1950s. For the most part, potential homeowners brought their own designs to developers who had acquired and subdivided blocks of land. Because the land was unserviced, lots were large, usually with 100-foot frontages and 150-foot depths to accommodate wells and septic systems. As sewers were introduced in the early 1970s, lot sizes diminished to 75 feet by 100 feet.[14] Nevertheless, the sense of spaciousness that still characterizes Sherwood had by that time been firmly established. By the late 1970s, a slower growth rate and maturing population prompted planners to call for more multiple-family units and denser housing patterns.

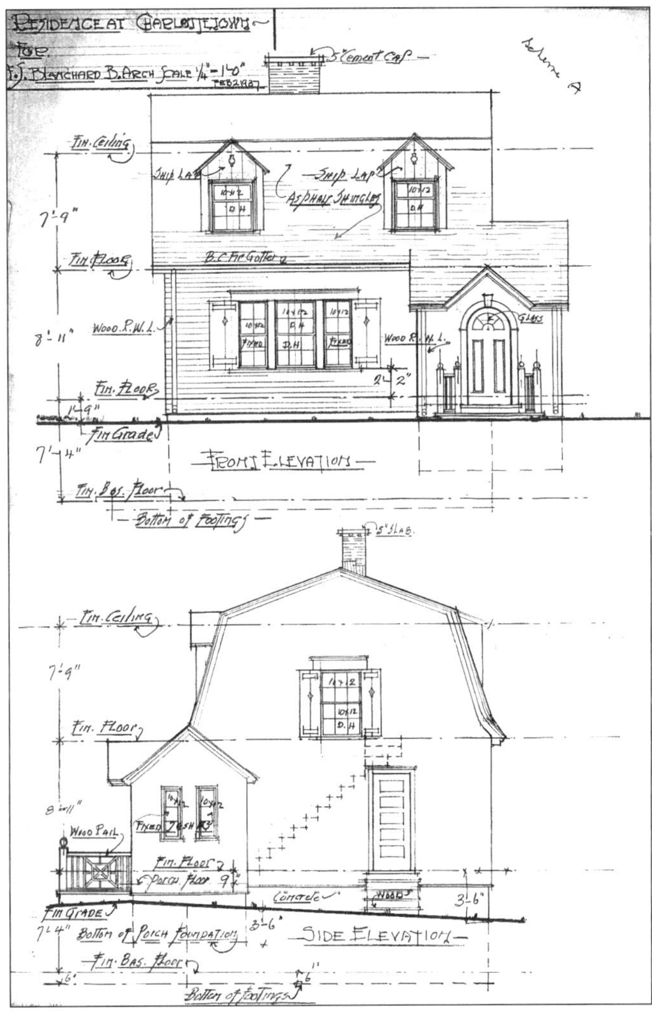

"Proposed Dominion Housing Act Residence," E. S. "Bones" Blanchard, 1937. By the time the post war housing boom occurred in Charlottetown, popular taste favoured the ranch and high-ranch bungalow design.

The Hillsborough Park development represented a departure in the building of suburban communities. Created by the province out of farmland in East Royalty as a

14 The standard 100-foot lot in many Canadian communities had a 40- to 60-foot frontage.

planned community, it was intended to be self-sufficient with its own schools, churches and mini-mall. None of these facilities materialized in this period, but the province installed water and sewer services. The first homes in Hillsborough Park were begun in 1971 under the auspices of the housing co-operative movement. In the years that followed, various co-operatives were founded, each with its own approach to house construction. Some preferred that homes be largely owner-built; others had contractors excavate the basements, pour foundations and frame the houses before owners proceeded to complete the structures. By the late 1970s, the co-op phase of development was largely over. A period followed in which contractors constructed houses on order or speculation. Building was brisk. In 1977, 32 units were erected; the following year the total was 98, and another 59 went up in 1979. Throughout the development of Hillsborough Park, emphasis was placed upon the provision of affordable housing for people with modest incomes. Designs were generally for modest-sized homes on 75- by 100-foot lots, giving the community an unpretentious consistency.

Although the other areas surrounding Charlottetown were largely rural until the 1970s, some non-farm residences were completed before then. By 1976 there were an estimated 310 housing units in East Royalty and 314 in West Royalty.[15] From that point on, the pace of construction of homes in these areas picked up. Between 1976 and 1981, 245 new residences were built in East Royalty and 156 in West Royalty. Most were single-family dwellings although some multiple-family units were built. Development was not dense because the absence of water and sewerage services necessitated larger lots. House design and the layout of residential districts were typical for the period, while the semi-rural setting made the Royalties, particularly West Royalty, desirable residential areas. A similar pattern occurred in Winsloe after it was incorporated in 1971. Again, the absence of water and sewerage services dictated large lots. Areas of development were spread out with a concentration in the northern reaches. As a bedroom community intended to appeal to young families, Winsloe had little commercial or industrial development. Projects were typically small and undertaken by builders such as Alexius McQuaid, Arlie Jay, Howard Douglas and MacPherson and Johnson. Stresses arose between those whose interests were rural and the suburban commuters. The southern, more agricultural part of the community separated from the housing area in 1985, leaving the latter isolated at the fringe of the Charlottetown region.

Parks

Although the streets of Charlottetown bustled with automobiles before the Second World War, the automobile age really arrived with the general economic expansion that peace brought. One of the peculiar consequences of widespread car ownership was an assault on the city's green spaces. A planning study completed in 1962 noted

15 By way of contrast, there were 5,470 units in Charlottetown, 655 in Parkdale, 1,475 in Sherwood and approximately 102 in Hillsborough Park.

that mature trees lining the city streets had been razed to provide parking. Grass strips bordering some of the streets were also paved over for the same reason. The city's squares and Victoria Park, which for years had provided opportunities for recreation and relaxation, were no longer adequate for the population's needs. Not only was the ratio of approximately five acres of parkland per 1,000 persons inadequate by modern standards, but shifting residential patterns meant that a considerable number of people lived a mile or more from the nearest park. To reach the open spaces, many children had to cross busy streets.

The inadequacy of Charlottetown's parklands arose despite a number of attempts to meet the city's recreational needs. A substantial, almost-10-acre playground was established in the Desbrisay Crescent area, and in 1954 City Council set aside 2.35 acres in Spring Park as a playground and public park, mainly for the benefit of people living beyond the then-current city limits.[16] In 1947 a major outdoor sports complex to accommodate baseball, track and field and rugby was created in Victoria Park. Dedicated to the memory of athletes who died in the two World Wars, Memorial Field provided a much-needed venue for organized recreation. New lighting was installed in the park in 1951, extensive work was done on the sea wall in 1954 and 1956, and the old bathing houses were taken down and replaced with new ones in 1961. In November 1955, an organization called "The Council for the Beautification of Charlottetown" was established to oversee planning of the city's green spaces. Landscaping was subsequently completed in Victoria Park, Prince Edward Battery and Queen Square, although Government Pond continued to defy attempts to clean it up. All of this activity, of course, did nothing to expand the extent of the recreational areas.

A tool empowering the city to meet its need for more parks came in 1962 when the act of incorporation was amended to allow the city to acquire a 7 per cent share of any new subdivision for use as parkland or playgrounds. As an alternative, the developer could pay the city an amount equivalent to 10 per cent of the total assessment of the area. Ten years later, the act was again changed to make it clear that land acquired for such purposes would be free of all encumbrances, and the 10 per cent tax was for the provision of open spaces elsewhere in the city. While land could be made available for recreation, not everyone was enchanted with the presence of such facilities in their neighbourhood. Residents of Brighton, for instance, were concerned about the prospect of a hockey rink facing North River Road. They feared the steel structure would blight their prestigious part of the city.

The suburbs offered fewer obstacles to establishing parkland. Since these communities were just taking shape, land was available, and the young families that settled there expected to have parks and playgrounds as part of the local infrastructure. The oldest community outside the city, Parkdale, was obliged to address the need for recreational facilities first. In the early years, existing open spaces and ad hoc arrangements sufficed. The "old 36" (or "36 Marsh"), a marshy field lying between St.

16 As part of the arrangement, the non-residents were expected to bear the costs of improving the land.

Peter's Road and Kensington Road opposite the Driving Park, provided space in which children could play and men could fish and hunt ducks. In the 1960s, a spring and creek were covered over, and low-lying ground was built up to provide more gentrified parkland. The grounds surrounding Ravenwood House were the venues for fêtes and tea parties, and, in the 1950s, airline owner Carl Burke set up a lighted outdoor hockey rink and a tennis court at his home on Mount Edward Road. A community hall erected by the Women's Institute in 1944 was enlarged in 1949, and it hosted a variety of recreational organizations and activities.

The development of nearby Sherwood prompted a change to the approach to recreation in Parkdale. It made sense to embark on shared projects. Sherwood had ample green spaces with up to 10 per cent of new development, or its equivalent in cash value, set aside for this purpose. In 1967 the first park, aptly named Centennial Park, was developed on land that in 1860 had been graced by the Prince of Wales as he relaxed during an outing from Charlottetown. Volunteer agencies were encouraged to organize recreational activities in the community. The Women's Institute of Central Royalty operated a recreational hall that was turned over to the community in the 1960s. It was used for various sports and youth activities, but the village still lacked a fully developed recreational infrastructure. Following a decision by Charlottetown to reserve its ice-skating facilities for city residents, Sherwood and Parkdale formed the Community Caravan of Sports, Inc. to build their own indoor rink. After skirmishes among various local interests, a collaborative citizen-based approach led to a successful fund-raising campaign and the construction of a new arena, which opened in 1973. With this model of community co-operation now firmly established, Sherwood later struck a deal with Parkdale to take over the arena and extend the partnership to the provision of recreational services generally in the two communities. The Sherwood-Parkdale Recreation Committee was then created with a broad mandate to manage the arena and create other sports infrastructure.[17] Sherwood assumed 60 per cent of the costs and assets and Parkdale, 40 per cent. The committee worked with local schools to develop nearby vacant land into soccer and baseball fields and also to utilize school gyms after hours. Its principal facility, however, remained the Sherwood Sportsplex which included the indoor rink and the Maplewood Room for community events.[18]

The smaller suburban communities also developed their recreational facilities, but each had its own approach to the task. Hillsborough Park began modestly, building an outdoor rink and baseball diamond in 1974 with Local Improvement Program funding. In May 1975, the first playground was opened on Patterson Drive. In 1978 work began on the community centre, which officially opened in 1979. Two years later, the playground was moved there. Bleachers were added to the baseball diamond in

17 The committee was incorporated in 1979. Although it included two Councillors from both Sherwood and Parkdale, its operations were separate from the municipal administrations.

18 The Sportsplex was renamed the Cody Banks Arena in honour of a dedicated supporter of minor league hockey and recreational sports who died suddenly in a construction accident.

1984. Neighbouring East Royalty had long benefitted from the presence of Heartz Hall, but the expanding population made it too small by the 1970s. In November 1977, a new community centre was opened with a playground located nearby. West Royalty favoured small neighbourhood parks throughout the community. This provided a good ratio of green space per thousand population while keeping it accessible at the very local level. Winsloe similarly had ample parklands, but they tended to be more clustered at the southern end of the community. The Winsloe Lions Club served as the community centre.

Streets and Sidewalks

Unlike former times, streets and sidewalks seem not to have been a matter of paramount importance in the post-Second World War era. It was not that roads no longer mattered. Charlottetonians had come to expect that the city would attend to the maintenance of the thoroughfares as a matter of course. True, citizens never ceased to badger politicians and city officials about them, and a steady stream of requests flowed into City Hall, but the topic generated less passion, and streets got paved when time and budget allowed. There remained, however, much to do. In 1945 some roadways were still clay, and some of the sidewalks wooden. While the decision to pave all streets with asphalt was made by 1946, it was not until 1949 that the city finally resolved to abandon wooden sidewalks for cement ones. Improvements demanded costly equipment. A steam engine, boiler and kettle for the asphalt plant were purchased in 1948, and a cement mixer in 1949. A spurt of growth in the late 1940s left the city further behind than usual in street construction. This led the Street Committee in 1950 to suggest the city's pay-as-you-go policy be abandoned in favour of a "programme of permanent work" even if the city's debt was "oversized." A decade later, when virtually all streets were paved with asphalt, the city reverted to its old pay-as-you-go policy. This put off the day when the major improvements contemplated by planners, such as bypass routes and new scenic drives, could be realized.

First to receive attention were the main arteries to the city's commercial centre. In 1954 Queen and Pownal Streets were widened, and the following year work was begun on Elm Avenue as part of the Trans-Canada Highway project.[19] The financial burdens of some road work were lightened in 1958 by an understanding in which the federal government picked up half the cost of improvements to roads that were part of the Trans-Canada, while the city and province split the remaining half between them. An alternative route into the city from the west was agreed upon in 1961 when the city accepted $100,000 from the province in return for rebuilding North River Road. The city also accepted responsibility for the sections of Malpeque Road and Belvedere

19 The additional traffic flow and resulting congestion on Elm Avenue prodded the city into proposing that Upper Queen Street be turned into the principal entry route from the west, with Elm Avenue serving as the main way out. Action was not taken on this proposal, and it was abandoned the following year.

Avenue within its limits. Roads in the suburbs remained a provincial responsibility, although Parkdale paved its own streets.[20]

The eastern entry to the city emerged as another major problem in the immediate postwar era. The old Hillsborough Bridge was proving increasingly inadequate. It was narrow, only 14 feet wide, making the passage of two trucks difficult, and falling into disrepair. By 1958 planning for a new bridge was under way. This was timely; in 1960 a fire broke out in the old bridge's wooden planking, and the span was subsequently closed to vehicular traffic for several weeks. In 1961 the new wider and sturdier concrete Hillsborough Bridge opened. The old one was then quietly closed and removed.

Increased use of motor vehicles was behind much of the street construction in the postwar era. More than smooth road surfaces were required, though. For starters, there was the problem of snow clearance. There was some embarrassment in 1944 when Charlottetown's new plough truck, borrowed to clear an ice-racing track on the Hillsborough River, fell through the ice. Following that unfortunate incident, the city purchased additional equipment, including a tractor to clear the sidewalks and a grader with a snow plough. Hopes that city crews could handle snow removal on their own were dashed by major storms in the late 1950s. The city had to hire construction companies to help with the job, and later rented the necessary equipment. Snow clearance proved to be a costly responsibility and a frequent source of complaints from the residents.[21] Traffic congestion and inadequate parking in the downtown core were also concerns. Parking spaces nibbled away at the sidewalks, and the curbs of downtown streets became lined with car bumpers. Market Square became a parking lot after the market house fire. Resistance from many merchants to the creation of the Confederation Centre was based partly on the fear that precious parking spaces would be lost. A consultant found in 1967 that the centre of the city was being ruined by the attempt to "park too many cars on the street." Over a decade passed before construction of the Queen Parkade lessened the pressure on curbside parking.[22]

The Harbour

The triumph of the motor vehicle in the postwar era had huge implications for Charlottetown's harbour. Once a central point of entry, its facilities had lapsed into decay by the 1950s, superseded, in part, by standard-gauge railway cars using the ferry at Borden. Motor transportation exacerbated the problem. By 1960 Council expressed concern about the shortage of cargo space and shipping facilities at the waterfront. Faced with an exodus of manufacturing to the suburbs, the city initially considered a revitalized harbour as a means of safeguarding its economy. It discussed different approaches, including one that envisioned recovering 70 acres from shallow water

20 The first streets to be paved in Parkdale were Hawthorne, Connolly (now Linden), Beasley and part of First Street in 1953 and Confederation, Gower, part of Allen and Kensington Road in 1954.

21 Snow clearance in suburban communities, including Parkdale, was done by the province.

22 The Queen Parkade was opened on July 15, 1979, by Mayor F. J. Moran.

Lower Queen Street, looking north, 1964. The industrial and transportation infrastructure that had characterized the waterfront for more than a century would disappear relatively quickly as the harbour became more of a recreational asset.

lying between Railway Wharf and the Hillsborough Bridge. Such schemes proved costly, and ran counter to the current trend in which transportation and manufacturing were located along major roads approaching the city. An admission that the harbour was becoming more of a recreational asset than one for shipping and industry came in 1964 when the city agreed to make additional waterfront available to the yacht club. Five years later, the city promised to allocate even more space for a marina. The subsequent development of Harbourside both dramatically changed the appearance of the waterfront and underscored the new role it was destined to play in the city's life and economy. Landscaped walks, residences and commercial buildings would replace the docks, sheds and factories that had lined the water's edge for over a century. One countervailing development was the reconstruction of Queen's Wharf in 1964. After its official opening in 1965, it became the Charlottetown home for the Canadian Coast Guard. In 1980 the Coast Guard erected a new administrative building nearby.

Utilities

Charlottetown's long-lasting struggle to have city streets adequately illuminated faced major setbacks in the immediate postwar years. By November 1946, periodic blackouts left roadways in darkness, causing some Councillors to demand Maritime Electric be fined for not providing enough energy. Council had resolved that all parts of the city should be served with lighting, and, despite the power shortages, requests for new installations flowed into City Hall. Throughout the late 1940s and early 1950s, the system was widely expanded. A survey conducted in May 1956 concluded the city was fairly well served, but by then the old incandescent lamps were considered inadequate. Experiments were conducted with mercury vapour and fluorescent fixtures, and the 1960s saw a program to convert from the old bulbs to improved lights. Though there were plans to bury the wires in the downtown core, overhead wires remained a part of Charlottetown's streetscapes throughout the period and beyond. Replacing old lighting units and providing service to new areas kept the pace of installations brisk throughout the 1960s and 1970s. In an effort to placate dissatisfaction among the voters, Council invited citizens in 1966 to report poorly serviced areas to City Hall by telephone. Perhaps embarrassed by the response, the following year persons making requests for lights were instructed to contact the city comptroller, who would then turn the applications over to the lighting committee. After touring the areas in question, committee members either approved or denied the requested installations.

The appetite for service in Charlottetown was symptomatic of the increased demand for electricity across the Island. Maritime Electric was obliged to expand its generating capacity following its decision in March 1945 to serve the countryside, and that, in turn, had implications for its plant on the waterfront. Throughout the postwar period, as new generating equipment was installed, the sprawling facility, or the adjacent fuel oil tanks that fed the boilers, was frequently expanded. This continued until cables laid under the Northumberland Strait connected the province to the New Brunswick power grid. The plant in Charlottetown thereupon became a secondary source of power, used at peak periods and in emergencies.

Telephone service matched the growth of energy consumption. Automatic switching equipment was installed at the main building at Queen and Fitzroy Streets in 1953, and to accommodate it a third floor and an addition were added to the building. Some telephone wires had begun to disappear underground as early as 1919, and in the 1960s Island Telephone began a program to bury all of its wires. While much had been achieved in this respect across the Island by the 1980s, telephone wires continued to grace the city's skyline. There they were joined by other markers of technology, including the communications towers of various kinds that began to pierce the sky in the postwar era. In 1958 a tower on the roof of the telephone company's main building announced the commencement of microwave telephone service. Various aerials required for commercial mobile phone communication began to appear above companies such as Maple Leaf Taxi and Northumberland Ferry Service. They joined the antennae erected by homeowners hoping to trap the signals from the ATV station in Moncton. Most of these television aerials were taken down when cable television service brought clearer pictures and a greater selection of stations into the living rooms of the city.

Planning

Up until the Second World War, there was not much urban planning in Charlottetown. Attitudes began to change, though, in the postwar years. While the original city plan had been carefully laid out, in the newly built-up areas "there has been no civic planning at all," and the results were "almost disastrous," at least in the *Guardian*'s opinion. In 1946 City Council established a planning committee, and at least one meeting was held with the province to co-ordinate planning in the greater Charlottetown area. The effectiveness of this initiative was questionable, however, and in 1955 the Board of Trade asked the city to create a Town Planning Board. Council instead created an advisory body. In 1960 the provincial government hired a town planner, Walter de Silva, and two years later he completed a report on the various issues that could best be addressed by a city plan. Over the next few years, there were some attempts to grapple with some of these concerns, but much of what passed for town planning in the 1960s consisted of reviewing and approving requests for subdivisions. A master plan, however, was completed in 1965, and the following year the federal government produced a model plan for the city. With that in hand, Council resolved to apply to the Central Mortgage and Housing Corporation for an urban renewal study, but the early 1970s revealed a city government that was stalled on the issue. It was not until 1980 that a formal, official plan for civic development was adopted.

Sydney and Pownal Streets, looking East.

By 1975 the town planning committee was exploring the Neighbourhood Improvement Program designed to revitalize run-down but architecturally significant sections of Canada's cities. In July a manager for Charlottetown was appointed, and in September the area bounded by Water, Great George, Richmond, Rochford and Haviland Streets was selected as the first to be planned under NIP. Work on implementing the plan in this area began the following year, and the city prepared to widen the program to a larger Area 2. Work began on some of the projects in this second area in mid-1977. From these initiatives emerged the quarter now known as "Olde Charlottetown." Many heritage homes, small office buildings and historic landmarks, such as St. Peter's Church, were successfully rehabilitated under the program or by property-owners who had been encouraged by the improvements. Advocacy organizations contributed significantly to the cause. Heritage Canada provided funds to reconstruct the fire-damaged Heartz-O'Halloran houses on Great George Street, while, at the other end of town, the PEI Heritage Foundation restored the well-worn Cundall Home, which reopened in 1973 as the foundation's headquarters. Fittingly, the mansion's name reverted to its original "Beaconsfield."

Many heritage homes and historic landmarks were successfully rehabilitated under the preservation and planning initiatives of the late 1970s. Photos taken in 2008, when compared to the planners' vision in 1978, indicated that traffic and overhead wires remain an issue. Sydney near Pownal looking West.

Meanwhile, following an agreement among the city, the provincial government and the Charlottetown Regional Planning Board, Charlottetown appointed Kenneth Zahara as a town planner in November 1975. He came from an assignment in Corner Brook, Newfoundland, where he had drafted city plans and zoning by-laws, and his experience with zoning was an asset. Zoning had traditionally responded to active lobbying by residents and various interest groups and had resulted in piecemeal legislation, such as a 1950 by-law to restrict building around Brighton. The city's management of land use and construction was tightened gradually. A new zoning by-law was passed in 1954, and in 1960 Council decided to adopt a version of the National Building Code. Firmer zoning regulation set the stage for skirmishes between advocates of competing visions for various areas of the city. Some of these differences resulted in heated battles. They underscored the recognition by all citizens that regulation of land use was a fact of life for the future and that certain activities were decidedly incompatible with others. This was a far cry from the acceptance of undifferentiated land use that had long characterized the city.

In this, Charlottetown may not have been much different from similar-sized or larger cities in Canada. It is worth mentioning, nonetheless, the passage of the city from a compact community governed by legislation — at times disjointed — administered by elected officials and volunteers to a larger community with more formalized administration by civil servants with technical expertise. The city was a more handsome, orderly place in 1984 than it had been in 1946. These years were also marked by a shift in the city's economic underpinnings. Charlottetown's passage from its first century of incorporation into its second saw the arrival of larger arts and educational institutions and more public administration and tourism. This allowed a greater number of people deriving better incomes to live in comfortable suburban homes and shop in convenient nearby locations. Ironically, the changes also reduced local distinctiveness and spurred the exploitation of what remained distinct in the built landscape to market the city to outsiders.

ECONOMIC GROWTH AND METROPOLITAN DEVELOPMENT

From the perspective of governance in Canada, the aftermath of the Second World War differed profoundly from that of the First. Many of the administrative lessons and techniques that had been learned during the 1914–18 conflict were promptly forgotten after the armistice. Similar lessons were retained after 1945, and, in particular, governments were anxious to continue their involvement in the economy through the management of growth and the operation of state-owned enterprises. While the national plants created to produce war supplies during the first conflict were promptly closed, federal crown corporations created during the second struggle lived on to become the tools of an expanding national economy. Indeed, governments at various levels became imbued with the sense that economic prosperity depended upon their intervention.

Although there were few traditions of government intervention on Prince Edward Island, the province was not immune to the new trend. In 1949 the Prince Edward Island Industrial Corporation was created with "wide powers" to assist the development of industry. The corporation was headed by a provincial cabinet minister and a board of directors of "assorted deputy ministers," but the results of its efforts were unimpressive, even "disastrous."[23] If little came of that initiative, there were other attempts to stimulate growth within the region, including the creation in 1954 of a federally incorporated, non-profit research agency, the Atlantic Provinces Economic Council, funded largely by the private sector. By the 1960s, government was taking concrete measures to spur economic growth. Many were directed towards the rural economy, including federal programs under the Agricultural Rehabilitation and Development Act (ARDA, 1961) and the Fund for Regional Economic Development (FRED, 1965). Industrial expansion

23 In a 1965 entry in *Canadian Annual Review of Politics and Public Affairs*, Frank MacKinnon wrote that bureaucrats lacked business experience and were responsive to political interests. What was needed instead was a "public utility trust" type of administration operating on business principles, a model he employed in his various public initiatives.

was encouraged by the Area Development Incentives Act (ADIA, 1965). Impressed by these innovative development schemes and Nova Scotia's Industrial Estates Limited, the Conservative government of Walter Shaw established Industrial Enterprises Incorporated (IEI) in 1965. Although IEI was not intended specifically to benefit Charlottetown, its objectives, including provision of serviced industrial sites and factory buildings for new or expanding manufacturers, certainly worked to the city's advantage. This was underscored several weeks later when APEC recommended Charlottetown become one of eight Atlantic regional growth centres, the only one on the Island.

By then, government investments were flowing to various sectors of the economy, with more planned. In Charlottetown, the search for an industrial park site was spearheaded by the Board of Trade's Industrial Development Committee. For most people, however, hope for economic development lay in a revived scheme to join Prince Edward Island to the mainland by a causeway. Discussed throughout much of the 1950s and given credence by the opening of the Canso Causeway in 1955, Prime Minister John Diefenbaker promised one to the Shaw government on the eve of the 1962 federal election. Thereafter, the project was studied, re-promised and delayed. Nevertheless, during the 1960s, the causeway, actually a combination of bridge, tunnel and causeway, was regarded as the best way to address the perennial problem of inadequate connections to the mainland. When the federal government finally decided that the cost was too great, alternate strategies for economic expansion were required. In March 1969, within two days of cancelling the causeway, Ottawa announced its intention to undertake a Comprehensive Development Plan for Prince Edward Island. Critics complained that something with substance like rocks, mortar and steel was replaced with something "more ephemeral," in the form of economic progress through social change and adjustment. Despite such reservations, the development plan changed Prince Edward Island in ways that were barely imagined at the time, and became the single most powerful influence in shaping the economy of Charlottetown in the last third of the 20th century.

The key to the development plan was precisely its comprehensiveness. Intended to do more than spur economic growth, it was designed to attack the weaknesses in infrastructure and in social development that underpinned poor economic performance. The federal and provincial governments pledged $725 million dollars to be spent over 15 years on everything from provision of adequate water supplies and waste disposal to urban renewal and the improvement of living conditions and technical skills.[24] The first step in preparing the plan was to examine the travel patterns of people obtaining goods and services over a seven-day period. On the basis of these observations, discrete socio-economic areas were identified. Charlottetown and its environs was one such area. Knowledgeable people in the area were then asked to identify community

24 Interestingly, one of the matters that fell under the development plan was the ongoing investigation into the proposal for a Charlottetown industrial park. The studies and delays continued into the 1970s, demonstrating that decisive action was easier anticipated than realized, even in an energized planning environment.

leaders. Those named were put onto a list, and from that list the provincial department of development selected a balanced, representative committee. One academic described the kind of public participation found in the Charlottetown committee as "neither desirable nor honest," and believed it was susceptible to manipulation by government officials. Even so, in the words of a planning document, "This committee, once formed, would be responsible for recognizing the needs and problems of the area with respect to development of the total resources, whether physical or human, and making appropriate recommendations for either government or private action in allocating or reallocating those resources to meet the needs in adjustment and development to help solve the problems." Although this explanation may have been somewhat obtuse, the general intention was understood.

Faced with producing a plan to develop the economic and social life of the area, the Charlottetown Area Development Committee commissioned a development opportunity analysis by Stevenson Kellogg Limited, a large management consulting firm. The study, conducted between 1972 and 1974, proposed three structures that could be used to guide redevelopment. The one finally chosen was the development corporation, and the Charlottetown Area Development Corporation was duly formed on December 5, 1974, with the province holding 75 per cent of the shares, the city 15 per cent, and the Charlottetown Planning Board 10 per cent.[25] CADC was expected to act as a commercial company in the planning, development, financing and temporary management of industries and other businesses, but it was also to work in concert with federal and provincial government departments, Heritage Canada and similar agencies. Although it was initially expected to run a deficit, CADC was intended to be self-sufficient. During the formative period, operational funds came from the federal and provincial governments, of which 90 per cent came from the Department of Regional Economic Expansion (DREE)[26] and the rest from the province under the development plan.[27] CADC became, in effect, the focal point for various developmental initiatives of a public or quasi-public nature. This collaboration among CADC, the local community and the federal and provincial governments proved fruitful.

---

25 The provisional directors were John H. Maloney, Minister of Development; Clive Stewart, a civil servant; Ronald H. Atkinson, Brian R. Cudmore, David Darby, Ivan J. Doherty, and Fred E. Hyndman, all businessmen; and George Smith, an architect.

26 The Department of Regional Economic Expansion of the Government of Canada was charged with promoting economic development and enhancing earned incomes and employment opportunities. It was renamed the Department of Regional Industrial Expansion (DRIE), and in 1987 the Atlantic Canada Opportunities Agency (ACOA) was created and eventually assumed DRIE's development responsibilities for the Atlantic region.

27 Eventually CADC received $493,400 between 1975 and 1980 as follows: $75,000 (1975–76); $130,000 (1976–77); $115,900 (1977–78); $97,500 (1978–79); and $75,000 (1979–80). Note: These figures apply to the operations of CADC only, not the total CADC budget. For the years December 1, 1974, to March 31, 1981, CADC had a total budget of $24,452,073 of which $7,256,945 came under the development plan (90 per cent federal, 10 per cent provincial). Of the balance, the largest amount was raised from the sale of preferred stock ($17,100,000), from the city ($919,899) and the province ($322,633). The accumulated debt by the end of the 1980–81 financial year was $2,452,073.

Administrative Functions

More government involvement in the economy was inextricably bound up with bigger bureaucracies. This reality was reflected in all three levels of political administration. Government became a growth industry. At one time, appointments to office ensured the economic security of a favoured few. By the 1970s, a robust public service helped to provide the economic underpinnings of whole communities.

In the municipal arena, population growth meant more civic employees to administer routine business and to plan and provide technical advice on the increasingly complex issues connected with maintaining physical infrastructure. This expansion was well under way by the 1970s. Co-ordination of the various municipalities in the greater Charlottetown area through bodies such as the Regional Planning Board made further demands for administrative support. The number of city employees — a stable total of 300 in 1961 and 1968, jumped to 400 in 1976 — documents this evolution.

Centralizing social services at the provincial level, added to the burdens of guiding economic transformation, caused significant expansion within the provincial government. The greatest bureaucratic growth, in fact, occurred at the provincial level. In 1960 there were 500 provincial employees living in Charlottetown. By 1968 that number had grown to 800, and, by 1976, it had ballooned to 2,600.[28] Big government led to some disgruntlement and with some reason, as the number of PEI public servants per capita was the highest in Atlantic Canada.[29] From the city's perspective, there was the challenge of ensuring these new employees worked and, to the greatest extent possible, lived within Charlottetown.[30] When new buildings were required to house provincial government employees, the city strenuously worked to have them near the downtown core. These efforts included selling the site of the old West Kent School to the province for one dollar.

The presence of the national government in Charlottetown also had a major economic impact. In the immediate postwar years and into the 1950s, municipal authorities pressed the federal government for subventions in lieu of taxes on its extensive property holdings. After Canadian National Railways, a federal crown corporation, agreed to this in January 1949, Mayor Earle MacDonald took it as a sign of the city's "right to tax Dominion Government property," and hoped that in the near future "municipalities will be receiving revenue from all Dominion Government buildings." This expectation was gradually realized as the level of federal grants increased during the 1950s.

The federal government created jobs locally, but it could take them away. Beyond administrative personnel for local operations, Ottawa based some regional services in Charlottetown. Gradually, these latter operations were trimmed back in the 1960s.

---

28 Approximately seven out of every ten provincial public servants were based in Charlottetown.

29 The ratios of public servant per 1,000 population in 1972 were 32/1,000 in PEI, 21/1,000 in New Brunswick, 24/1,000 in Newfoundland and 26/1,000 in Nova Scotia.

30 Charlottetown acted decisively within its own realm: municipal employees were required to live within the city limits.

Such reductions were viewed with increasing concern. Rumours abounded that a division of the Department of Transport, including CGS *Wolfe*, was destined for transfer to Halifax. Council protested, as did the local Member of Parliament, Heath Macquarrie, who commented that the phasing-out of federal operations generally "is a dreary and unwelcome trend and seems scarcely sensitive to the expressed concern for regional disparity." Such pessimism may have been unwarranted, since the federal presence steadily increased in the period 1960–76.[31]

Then came the policy of decentralizing federal government operations in the 1970s. Public servants, who once referred to Toronto as the "boonies" and declared their career ambitions were bounded by Bronson Avenue and Elgin Street in Ottawa, were being told to pack their bags. In Prince Edward Island, Charlottetown was promoted as the first and logical choice to receive a decentralized department. In the view of the provincial government, "the addition of a federal unit to the employment structure of a relatively small community could assist in stabilizing population, reducing outmigration and stimulating further industrial and service growth." Announced in 1976, a decision was made to transfer the Department of Veterans Affairs and 600 jobs to the Island capital. Immediate employment opportunities were created in the construction industry with the erection of a new office building in the city's core to house 500 employees and the provision of new housing for the public servants who chose to move. Employment for Charlottetonians and other Islanders would follow when Ottawa-based personnel refused to relocate. By 1979 it was clear that the federal government would become one of the main props for the local economy through direct employment. The city's labour force totalled 21,835 in 1981, of which 2,930 were classified as working in public administration and defence. Ultimately, an estimated 900 staff positions moved from Ottawa to Charlottetown, an increase of over 4 per cent of the total labour force and a whopping 31 per cent increase in the public administration and defence sector.[32]

Commercial activities

Charlottetown emerged from the years of postwar economic transition with a remarkably robust retail sector. In 1947 the city was home to 247 stores with overall sales of $6.8 million. This constituted approximately 30 per cent of the stores within the province and 45 per cent of all sales. Four years later, there were a few more stores, 251, but sales had trebled to almost $21 million. Retail establishments employed between 986 and 1,212 people. Charlottetown stood out as a rich market with unusually high sales volumes compared with other Canadian cities. Not only did the trade reflect the city's role as a commercial hub for the Island, but also its relatively high level of local

31 In terms of employment for the province as a whole, federal employees numbered 900 in 1961, 1,400 in 1968 and 2,000 in 1976.

32 In the end, less than 5 per cent of the incumbents of the transferred positions actually moved with their jobs. This development provided the economy with a hoped-for increase in employment opportunities.

incomes. The *Guardian* reported the average family in Charlottetown earned $3,177 in 1950 compared with $2,262 nationally.

Despite this prosperity, there were a few problems. Door-to-door salesmen were taking business from local merchants and occasionally taking advantage of their customers. As a counter-measure, the Board of Trade agitated for a by-law to regulate hawkers and peddlers. The city was also overly serviced with commercial establishments. One estimate claimed there was in some areas twice as much retail frontage as required. Initially, lack of zoning permitted commercial establishments to pop up along streets radiating from the city's core, and when the city subsequently zoned the land facing those streets as commercial, financing for residential construction there became impossible. Consequently, "the only person who could use [them was] the man prepared to work eighteen hours a day and live in the back of the shop."

Significant changes occurred by 1961. There were far fewer stores in Charlottetown by then, only 198, and they employed about the same number of people as a decade earlier, 1,138; but sales had risen to $29 million. Adjusting for inflation, this was just under a 17 per cent advance in sales in the preceding 10 years.[33] Charlottetown's retail outlets were by then only 23 per cent of the Island's total and they represented only 37 per cent of all sales. Thus, local businesses were larger and fewer in number than 10 years earlier, and they had expanded their sales somewhat, but their dominance over the provincial economy had eroded.

In some respects, the 1960s seem not to have altered much for the city's retailers. By 1971 there were 200 stores employing 1,312 people. There was, however, one significant change. Charlottetown stores again accounted for 45 per cent of all retail sales on the Island. And the city's stores were efficient; in 1971 they generated $59.10 per square foot in sales compared to a national average of $40.49 per square foot. While the number of hardware and home furnishing stores remained about the same for the two decades between 1951 and 1971, the number of clothing stores declined modestly, and the establishments catering to the automobile increased. The most significant shift occurred in the number of retailers marketing food and beverages. They declined 45 per cent in the 20-year period.[34] Clearly, the era of the "mom and pop" corner store was coming to an end.

By the mid-1970s, Charlottetown still enjoyed a 42 per cent share of provincial retail sales with a value of $115.3 million. The official per capita income in Prince Edward Island by then was 27 per cent below the national average, a fact that tended to depress sales generally. Incomes in Charlottetown were, however, 38 per cent higher than the provincial average.[35] This relative affluence and the tourist trade explain why per capita sales on the Island lagged the national average by only 8 per cent. Officials

33 With inflation over the decade, $21 million was equivalent to $24.85 million in 1961.

34 For the years 1951 and 1971, the principal kinds of retail establishments numbered as follows: food and beverages, 127 and 70; automotive, 24 and 37; clothing, 37 and 28; hardware and furnishings, 10 and 12.

35 The figures were based on reported income and officials recognized that agricultural incomes were "understated." Summerside also had incomes above the provincial average but slightly lower than the capital.

expected more retail consolidation in Charlottetown in the period 1976–81. Expansion of the capital's commercial reach and strengthening of local tourism thus were critical factors for the health of its retail economy.

The trend to fewer and larger stores in the 1950s, 1960s and 1970s was not without controversy. Store hours were a hotly contested and prolonged issue. In 1955, when merchants decided to remain open Friday evenings and close Saturday afternoons, they were criticized for ignoring the needs of farmers. In the words of one commentator, "After all this is a farming country and we must cater to that trade if we city folks want to live." Five years later, there was a movement to re-establish Saturday afternoon shopping while retaining Friday evening. Most merchants, other than grocers, were opposed, saying that the extended shopping was unnecessary and "would not be worth the havoc wrought upon store employees' personal lives."

Regulation of store hours remained a matter to be decided by the merchants themselves. During the 1960s, larger retailers tended to keep longer hours, and many smaller merchants had difficulty in matching them. In April 1965, City Council considered the possibility of establishing a committee drawn from itself, the Board of Trade and local business to make recommendations for regulating of store hours within the municipality. Objections to this proposal ranged from a lack of jurisdiction to concern for free enterprise and the need for corner stores to remain open to catch the night trade. In the end, Council opted to do nothing and leave the matter for the Board of Trade. Following the opening of the new Stedmans store, which offered extended hours, both the city and Board of Trade again came under pressure to regulate hours of opening. Mayor Walter Cox was unsympathetic, as was Council generally, and even the Board of Trade felt the matter was best left for the merchants to resolve.

The issue came to a head in 1969 when the S. S. Kresge Company announced the opening of an expansive K-Mart store at the corner of Malpeque Road and Belvedere Avenue. Kresge stressed that its success hinged upon the implementation of "progressive merchandising policies," including extended shopping hours. A group of disgruntled merchants soon mobilized to have regulated store hours imposed. In the absence of support from either City Council or the Board of Trade, they formed the PEI Merchants' Association and obtained the support of Harold Smith, a Liberal MLA, who introduced a private member's bill calling for regulations. Under the proposed law, known as Bill 15, night shopping would be limited to two nights a week for nine months of the year for all but small family businesses.

A vigorous debate ensued both in and outside the Legislature. S. S. Kresge Company, supported by Stedmans, Sobeys, Royalty Mall Limited and Archer and MacDonald Limited, opposed Bill 15. Kresge threatened to terminate its plans if the bill passed. Council entered the fray and decided by a narrow margin to ask the legislature either to drop the bill or exempt Charlottetown from its provisions. Many private citizens expressed their opposition, but the Co-op stores and the PEI Federation of Labour backed the bill. After the Legislature approved Bill 15 in principle on April 1, Kresge announced that it would abandon its plans for the store. Public opinion as expressed in the press generally deplored regulation. Whether it was this reaction or the threat from Kresge, Smith moved to "hoist" the bill for six months, effectively killing it. K-Mart Plaza was subsequently built, and Charlottetown entered the era of the big box store.

The debate over store hours masked another matter of greater long-term consequence: the development of shopping malls. In 1962 the city considered and then rejected a proposal to re-zone a stretch of Belvedere Avenue to permit the construction of a shopping centre. Despite accusations that downtown merchants forced the decision to avoid competition, Councillors eventually turned down the proposal because Walter de Silva and other planners convinced a majority there was already a surplus of unused commercial land. Some businesses, de Silva noted, sought out less expensive areas and appealed for zoning changes. The proposed site was also too close to established commercial areas downtown and at the Sherwood and Parkdale end of Belvedere Avenue. Even so, three years later, the Royalty Mall was begun on Elm Avenue closer to the downtown, to be followed by the K-Mart Plaza and then the Towers Mall on Malpeque Road in West Royalty.

Charlottetonians were ambivalent about shopping malls. They liked the increased tax revenue and modern, convenient shopping, but were concerned about the drift of commerce to the outskirts of town and increased traffic. Although Royalty Mall was approved in 1965, a proposal to construct a large Sobeys supermarket on Longworth Avenue was rejected after a citizens' meeting voted against it. The reasons were problems for pedestrians and increased traffic on one of the most convenient routes to the downtown.

An even bigger controversy erupted in 1973 when the Roman Catholic Episcopal Corporation asked to be allowed to sell 86 acres of its land on University Avenue to Sherbrooke Plaza Inc. for a new 300,000-square-foot shopping centre. The $25 million project envisaged a mall, offices and housing. Sherbrooke then sought zoning changes. In response to concerns about anticipated traffic problems, the company offered to allow space for the extension of Upper Queen Street to the Trans-Canada Highway. Council initially liked the proposal, in part because costs of providing services were to be borne by the developer while the city would expand its tax base. Since two-thirds of the land was for residential purposes, the character of the neighbourhood would be preserved.

Yet opposition to the project grew. Some wanted the city to buy the land to use as a land bank for residential development. Others worried about traffic flow, increased loads on the water and sewer systems, and increased costs for police and fire protection. The Downtown Business Association noted the proposal flew in the face of the Stevenson Kellogg report which stressed the preservation of a vibrant downtown. In the end, Council decided that the potential problems outweighed the potential gains and voted six to four against re-zoning the land. The developer behind Sherbrooke Plaza, felt he was the victim of discrimination because he was an Islander. "If you are an outsider, you get the best of everything," he complained, "just look at K-Mart." Some, however, appear to have had other considerations in mind. Alderman Morris pointed to downtown redevelopment, where the infrastructure already was

Highlighted on this c. 1975 aerial photo is the block that would become the Confederation Court Mall and the site of the all-important parking garage that accompanied it.

in place, as desirable and "long overdue." This was where he thought action should really occur.

Morris did not have long to wait. Within three years, plans were announced for the Confederation Court Mall. The initial concept was suggested by the Charlottetown Area Development Corporation, and most of the effected merchants, led by Michael Arnold, owner of Holman's, "liked what they saw." Brian Cudmore claimed, "if the go-ahead is given … the project will keep the centre of the city from dying and will also encourage other business people to settle in town." It would enable merchants in the downtown to compete with the malls.

The local merchants got the planning process going, and the general assumption was that the project would be their responsibility. A holding company, the Dyne Corporation, was created to undertake the development. Mayor Frank Zakem announced there would be no civic financial commitment. CADC claimed to be only interested in implementing some of the strategy of the Stevenson Kellogg report and perhaps the development of some of the areas surrounding the project. Premier Alex Campbell, while stating, "historical areas should be restored and used as living places," affirmed that his government would be "quite deliberate in not taking the lead."

By the autumn of 1976, these intentions were being reconsidered. The promoters had completed preliminary planning and purchased some of the properties involved, but Dyne faced major investments for construction and upgrades, and businesses run by non-shareholders were liable for heavy costs as well. Total project costs, estimated at $4.5 million, would place the promoters at considerable risk. Studies had shown, in addition, that the paucity of parking in the area threatened the project's viability. The city looked at public transportation as a potential solution, concluded this would not resolve the issue, and so established a parking authority. The parking authority, in turn, found a site on Queen Street for a parking garage, but the cost of construction was considerable and financing was a challenge. Both Dyne Corporation and the city turned to CADC for help.

CADC responded positively. With money provided under the Comprehensive Development Plan by DREE, CADC loaned $300,000 to purchase the land for the mall project. CADC also agreed to locate $5 million in funding at advantageous rates for Dyne Corporation. The federal government's $300,000 made this task easier. Meanwhile, the province loaned $500,000 to construct "public open space" in the proposed mall. For its part, the city paid $500,000 for the land on which to build the parking garage. The $1.5 million facility would provide 380 parking spaces. Merchants in the mall undertook to help cover its ongoing costs, but CADC built the parking garage, assisted in part by provincial funds. What had begun as a private development had become heavily subsidized by all three levels of government.

This use of taxpayers' dollars was not welcomed by all. The Merchants' Association of the Charlottetown Mall (the replacement name for the Towers Mall) complained of "discriminatory government intervention in the market place." Bernard Dale, one of Charlottetown's largest commercial landlords, expressed concerns about existing vacant space in the city's centre, claiming he had 31,000 square feet of commercial space vacant in prime downtown locations. Dale, nevertheless, offered to co-operate with CADC "in programs which other developers might be reluctant to undertake." DREE, for its part, replied to its critics by noting: "its efforts ... [we]re intended to stimulate the economy and to encourage self-sufficiency." The office tower to be built in conjunction with the shopping concourse also disturbed landlords who suspected the construction costs were being partly underwritten by CADC, using provincial and federal funds, to drive down rents on commercial office space. Assurances were provided by the provincial industry minister, John Maloney, that such fears were baseless; CADC was not a financial contributor to the office tower component.

September 1978 saw the start of construction. The parking garage was first, followed by the National Bank Tower and then the covering of the interior court. Touted as a spark plug that would ignite a round of new building valued at $20 million over the next two years, the Confederation Court Mall was, in fact, only one of several undertakings that was transforming the face of central Charlottetown.

This revitalization of the central business district instilled a sense of confidence among area businessmen. In 1979, when plans were announced for another major shopping mall in West Royalty, reaction downtown was muted. Little concern was expressed about the additional competition. In the perhaps ironic words of Ronald Orton of the Downtown Businessmen's Association, "no businessman is ever against competition."

This sense of security was perhaps misplaced. During the controversy in 1973 over re-zoning for the Sherbrooke Plaza, there was a concern that refusal might drive mall development outside city limits. This fear also emerged in the Stevenson Kellogg report that said new suburban shopping centres should be discouraged and existing ones should not be allowed to expand. "Control over this distribution [of retail space]," the report noted, "should be recognized by public authorities as an instrument for both furthering the goals of the [development] plan and improving the presence of the Charlottetown area." In 1978 the Charlottetown Area Regional Planning Board studied how new retail facilities would impinge upon existing retail centres.[36] The conclusions were striking. Even though the city would require significant increases in both general merchandising and food retail space by the early 1980s, the proposed West Royalty mall would result in an excess of space. The four existing malls[37] could expect reductions of about one-quarter in their ratio of sales to floor space as a result. In the downtown core, sales could drop one-fifth by 1981 but recover thereafter, although curtailing projects planned for the central business district could lead to an exodus of businesses. Curiously, a public opinion survey indicated that 46 per cent of Charlottetonians wanted commercial expansion downtown, while 35 per cent favoured Southport. Less than 5 per cent preferred mall development in the Royalties.

The effect of this report was to encourage the West Royalty Community Improvement Committee (the equivalent of the town council) to turn down the proposed mall. Frank Johnston, the project's driving force, accused planners of "conning" the politicians and produced a study of his own that disparaged the planning board's document. He then began an advertising campaign to force the politicians to reconsider. Unfortunately for him, the development would breach the provincially accepted official plan for West Royalty. This plan had previously been sanctioned by local residents at a public meeting, and unless the plan were overturned by the public in another meeting, the province, which had final authority in the matter, would back the decision of the CIC.

---

36 It is interesting to note that in 1977 City Council approved an application of the Rocca Group to build a mall on University Avenue. The decision was made with some trepidation because the development would aggravate traffic problems in the area, but the land was zoned commercial. After the planning report was completed, Council discussed the possible reconsideration of the Rocca permit, but decided to allow the permit to stand even before aldermen had examined the report carefully.

37 Charlottetown Mall, Royalty Mall, K-Mart Plaza and Ellis Brothers Plaza.

Johnston then persuaded the Land Use Commission to order the CIC to grant him the permit. Prompted by this precedent, the Dale Corporation, which had been frustrated in its plan to expand the Confederation Mall, decided to appeal to the Land Use Commission as well. The West Royalty CIC responded by challenging the LUC's ruling in the Supreme Court. Public opinion appeared split. A West Royalty Citizens' Committee demanded a public meeting to discuss the issue and claimed to have a petition signed by 250 residents who wanted the mall built. The West Royalty CIC, however, was far from sure that the community as a whole shared this viewpoint. Pushed and pulled by public opinion and various interests, the CIC wanted to preserve its right to plan the community. In a strange twist, an individual property-owner, whose house would have been nearly surrounded by the mall property, obtained a Supreme Court injunction against the building permit. In its final ruling, the Supreme Court found that the Land Use Commission had overstepped its authority, concluding there was a likelihood of bias and a conflict of interest on the part of some LUC members. Only the CIC, the court declared, could change the official plan to allow for the mall's building permit.

Touted as a sparkplug that would ignite a round of new building and revitalize the downtown, the Confederation Court Mall opened in the summer of 1981.

Before this ruling came down, the province had imposed a two-year moratorium on the construction of shopping centres or retail stores of over 6,000 square metres.[38] During the spring of 1979, opposition to unrestricted mall development had been mobilized throughout the Island. Charlottetown's downtown merchants, the Summerside Chamber of Commerce and the Official Opposition came out in favour of the moratorium. As the province had twice as much retail space per capita as the national average, it made sense to apply the brakes to development for the

38 Six thousand square metres equals 64,584 square feet.

moment. Announcement of the moratorium prompted Frank Johnston to comment, "I don't know where I stand now. I don't know what they've done to me now." Despite the setback for Johnston, plans for the construction of new malls at the periphery of Charlottetown continued. The trend in consumer preferences was apparent. While a moratorium provided a respite, established shopping areas would be challenged sometime in the future by new retail developments at the edge of town.

After imposing the moratorium, the provincial government commissioned a study of shopping centres, which concluded that unchecked development fostered "inefficient, expensive and unattractive" suburban sprawl. Planned developments that respected other land uses and existing and proposed services and scaled to the size of the immediate surrounding market "can be an asset to any community." The problem lay with the flurry of shopping centre proposals that threatened to double the square footage of the province's malls. "Even the most optimistic market analyst," the report concluded, "could not imagine where the market for these new facilities would come from."

A study completed for the Downtown Business Association amplified concerns about malls. It asserted that the Island had accumulated more retail space in the period 1965–80 than it had throughout all of its previous history. The ensuing competition failed to reduce prices, increase tax assessments or significantly improve the choice of goods, but reduced employment in the retail sector and among suppliers to independent retailers. Local merchandisers were being squeezed, traditional downtown shopping areas were being weakened and "the majority of profits" from retail trade were now leaving the province. Shopping centres also made demands on municipal services, required improvements to roadways and ate up land. The business study called for provincial planning regulations to provide for "a modicum of sane development."

Charlottetown, in fact, was in the grips of a classic struggle between local business and large integrated outside retail interests, such as Woolworth's, Metropolitan Stores, Eaton's, Stedmans, Zellers, K-Mart, Canadian Tire and Sobeys. Even so, a 1969 study concluded that control of the city's commerce was "distinctly in the hands of local businessmen managing local firms staffed predominately by local employees and selling to a local market." The concept of "Charlottetown Square" was intended to buttress such home-grown enterprise. In order to accomplish this end, the Stevenson Kellogg report advocated the establishment of a farmers' or fishermen's market along the waterfront, as well as shops, boutiques, outdoor cafés and other taverns and restaurants that would keep the downtown abuzz with activity. The extent to which this vision would succeed remained to be seen. The failure in 1985 of Holman's Department Store, the principal Island retailer and the anchor store for the Confederation Court Mall, did not augur well. Fortunately, the business continued to operate as Holman's of Prince Edward Island, with individual owners running sections of the store, until 1989. The extra four years ensured the survival of the mall project. But in the mid-1980s, the future was far from clear.

Manufacturing

The end of the Second World War left Charlottetown with some lingering benefits from wartime activities and ongoing ambitions to expand its manufacturing sector. The former, in particular, meant ship refitting at Bruce Stewart Limited. In 1947 the city was home to 37 plants with an overall output of $4.5 million. A total of 604 employees earned $850,000 in wages. Although the manufacturing establishments were only 14 per cent of the Island's total, Charlottetonians comprised 32 per cent of the province's industrial work force, collecting 42.5 per cent of all industrial wages paid. In 1946, keen to see more manufacturing, City Council appointed a special committee to encourage businesses to settle in the city and secure appropriate industrial sites. In its first year, the committee, working with the provincial government, arranged for a pickle plant to begin operations and provided land for a soft drink bottling plant and distribution centre. Such sites were scarce, however, and virtually nothing was available that combined railway access with water and electrical services. The President of the Board of Trade proposed as a solution that the experimental farm be moved to provide suitable industrial sites.

The enthusiasm for industry was mixed with realism and even some doubt. In his 1947 presidential speech to the Board of Trade, Carl F. Burke, founder of Maritime Central Airways, stressed that he wanted a "better" Charlottetown, not necessarily a bigger one. The city should avoid encouraging indiscriminate growth, but should seek light industries, particularly those connected with the products of farm and sea. His successor favoured small industries, and Eugene Cullen, owner of a local dairy and provincial Minister of Industry, also linked smallness and the processing of farming and fishing products. Some set their sights even lower. R. E. Mutch, a member of the Board of Trade, cautioned against theorizing about more industries while neglecting improvements to the "all ready made and available" tourist business. And then there were those who viewed industry from the "NIMBY" ("Not In My Back Yard") perspective. When Hall and Stavert wanted to establish a new foundry on Elm Avenue, residents asked City Council to refuse unless there were assurances that the foundry

Producing everything from engines to engine parts to horseshoes, Bruce Stewart and Company remained the city's flagship industry until 1949. The fire that levelled the machine shop that year resulted in 200 layoffs.

would not create smoke, noise, nuisances and street obstructions. Despite promises from Hall and Stavert that the foundry would not be a nuisance, Council declined permission.

Market size was clearly an inhibiting factor when it came to Charlottetown-based industries. A brick manufacturer assessed the possibility of establishing a plant in Prince Edward Island in 1946. The clays were suitable, but fuel costs were high and markets limited. A plant in New Glasgow could meet local needs more cheaply. The American Can plant that began operations in 1945 and had taken over a local business, Charlottetown Can, closed in 1952 when expected markets failed to develop and several customers were lost. Nor does there seem to have been a concerted effort to market local manufactures outside the immediate area. E. D. Reid, President of the Board of Trade in 1953, suggested that the biggest handicap to local industries was the uncertainty of support from Islanders. He noted not a single Island exhibit was to be found in a recent trade fair in Toronto. Perhaps Charlottetonians — and other Islanders — had become inured to absence of a robust manufacturing economy.

If that were the case, they were not prepared to give up completely without a struggle. The flagship industry locally was, of course, Bruce Stewart and Company. It had its hopes raised for postwar prosperity by the promise of C. D. Howe, the federal Minister of Reconstruction and Supply, of considerable work for the company's dry dock refitting and repairing tug boats, dredges and scows. Those contracts failed to materialize, the *Guardian* complained in January 1946, but the company was undeterred.[39] In October 1949, a fire that levelled everything but the machine shop resulted in 200 men being laid off, and in 1951 the business was taken over by Ferguson Industries of Pictou, Nova Scotia. Although the new owner promised to expand operations by making brass and iron fittings for its internal consumption, only one member of the new board of directors was a local person; the rest were Nova Scotians. The Royal Canadian Navy ordered some work, but failure to secure ongoing government contracts resulted in renewed layoffs of 200 men in 1953.[40] By 1957, when Ferguson Industries sold the business to Charlottetown Marine Industries, the work force had shrunk to 20 from a peak of 250 in the early 1950s. H. E. MacDonald was the new president, and Frank Sobey of Sobeys grocery stores was the vice-president. The new owners hoped to win government contracts, but such plums remained elusive.

Equally rare, it seems, was any tangible aid from the city by way of corporate bonuses or tax relief. In 1954 a group of citizens contemplating the establishment of a second abattoir requested a temporary tax reduction. Councillors were divided on the merits of the proposal, but the Board of Trade was "generally opposed" to such exemptions. The company withdrew its application for a tax exemption and instead

39 It looked at the possibility of installing a marine slip at its facilities.

40 There was some suggestion that failure to win contracts had something to do with the local members of parliament being in opposition.

requested a yearly grant. Some Councillors supported the proposed company because of its community base and association with other local organizations, but this was not enough. The request was filed. Despite hesitancy to grant subventions, the Tourist and Industrial Development Committee continued to recognize the potential need to entice small manufacturing plants to the city with tax concessions.

By the end of the 1950s, Charlottetown had 21 businesses classified as manufacturers that employed 10 or more. Most serviced the agricultural sector or processed its products. In addition to drycleaners, a laundry and the power plant, there were two machine shops, two woodworking shops and a woollen mill. Food processing was the principal activity, along with two dairies, two bakeries, two frozen food processors, one meat packing plant and the aforementioned pickle factory. There were also two soft drink bottlers, a tobacco manufacturer and a fertilizer plant. The years since the end of the war had been frustrating, and in the midst of high unemployment, the future of industry in Charlottetown appeared to be discouraging.

The 1960s began, however, on the upbeat. During the municipal election campaign in February, the incumbent mayor, Walthen Gaudet, promised to improve the economy by attracting new industries to Charlottetown. By year's end, he reported several successes: Enheat, the Enamel and Heating Company, a New Brunswick firm that worked on aircraft repair; Texaco, a major American oil company; and the Arnold

By the late 1950s, most of Charlottetown's manufacturers and many of its businesses serviced the agricultural sector. Turner Farm Implements on Fitzroy Street was the local Cockshutt dealer.

In 1981, the largest business cluster in the city involved food processing. Perfection Dairy, c. 1950.

Brick Company.[41] The Enheat plant was located at the airport, attracted by the length of the runway. This burst of initiative was relatively short-lived and was followed by a period of lesser accomplishment. Criticism of the city's performance led to the renewal of the Industrial Development Committee in April 1962 to liaise between Council and firms interested in starting operations in Charlottetown. The committee faced two impediments, the absence of permanent staff for its operations and the lack of suitable industrial land for potential clients. Before much progress was made on either of these issues, the closure of the Enheat plant was announced due to fewer military contracts. A delegation from the province and city made the customary trek to Ottawa to appeal for more business, but to little avail. C. M. "Bud" Drury, Minister of Industry and of Defence Production, suggested that industry based on agriculture or tourism that was "continuous" was needed, not something that relied on "the whim of the various services."

Shortly thereafter a second blow appeared ready to fall. The possible closure of the venerable Bruce Stewart plant generated considerable bitterness among employees and city politicians because the province apparently was making no effort to keep the plant going while providing financial aid to new industries in rural areas. Eventually, an infusion of new capital allowed for the expansion and modernization of the plant. Besides winches, lobster rollers and potato harvesters, the company began to manufacture boilers for domestic and industrial use. Mayor Walter Cox also embarked upon a campaign to secure the long-sought-after marine slip for the waterfront. "We

41 Discussions continued with Arnold Brick until 1965 when "it was decided that nothing could be done for the industry."

are not asking for handouts the way others are," the mayor asserted, "but our only hope for industrial survival is to fight to have some of these things established in Charlottetown, then we will work out our own salvation."

Perhaps he had in mind the kind of innovations made by William Rix of Charlottetown Metal Products. Rix assumed control of a company in 1959 that made culverts and highway guard rails, then branched into the manufacture of horseshoes.[42] In February 1966, he announced the launch of a new product, stainless steel tiles for homes and institutions. Since Charlottetown Metals was the sole domestic supplier of both the tiles and horseshoes for the Canadian market, the company prospered. Its 1,000-square-foot plant grew to 14,000 square feet by 1968. By then, too, the company was rebuilding and designing fish-processing equipment.

After 1965, the city's economic future was influenced by the active planning of the long-sought permanent link to the mainland. A fixed link was bound to stabilize energy and transportation costs and possibly stimulate industrial growth, provided there were sites for new industries. All three available locations were problematic. One was along the waterfront, but the expense of filling in part of the harbour and constructing breastworks was high. The Jordan Crescent area was too small without added land from the experimental farm, an unlikely prospect. The best option was a piece of pasture land adjacent to St. Dunstan's University. It was near the railway and easily serviceable. In 1967 a study commissioned by the Atlantic Development Board came up with possibilities in Parkdale, north of the exhibition grounds, in Sherwood and in Beach Grove.

To compete for new businesses, the city set up the Charlottetown Industrial Development Commission in 1967.[43] Drawn from City Council, the Board of Trade, the Town Planning Commission and the general public, this new body had the mandate to publicize Charlottetown's advantages, encourage new businesses to establish themselves in the city, and to help with the expansion of existing industries. The new commission received a ready-made model to facilitate their work. A recent seminar held at St. Dunstan's University outlined four kinds of industry suited to the region. Resource-based industries relied on local natural resources. Market-based industry could exist when transportation costs were low in relation to the value of the products. Footloose industries would focus on high-value, low-weight and dense products, such as clothing, but they were liable to drift to other locales. Home-grown industries would produce items needed locally and would remain based in the community. This latter category was deemed worthy of "every assistance and encouragement." In selecting target industries, the commission decided to assess possibilities according

42 Although Charlottetown Metal Products pioneered a process that used aluminium and titanium in metal fabrication, the steel horseshoes gave it a quaint air. William Rix subsequently commented that horseshoes accounted for 12 per cent of his profits and "practically all of my publicity."

43 The city's previous Industrial and Tourism Development Committee had been replaced by a Public Relations Committee in 1958. Councillors concluded that rather than re-establishing a separate industrial development committee, a joint body with the Board of Trade that drew upon the city's Town Planning Committee would be more expedient; hence, the commission.

to six criteria: potential growth, availability of inexpensive raw materials, skill level of the required labour, reasonable initial investment, inexpensive product shipping costs and potential demand for the product.

Once identified, suitable industries would be contacted and informed of the advantages of the city. This strategy was felt to be superior to a shotgun approach in which a pitch was directed to industry in general. To deal with the lack of available industrial land, the commission urged the city to acquire property near the waterfront and along the railway lines. Yet another study, this one completed in 1969, however, undermined these aspirations by dismissing the significance of municipal boundaries in the selection of a site for an industrial park and even questioning the immediate need given Charlottetown's limited industrial base. The study concluded that a 200-acre site should be located "outside the perimeter of the future residential area."

In 1969 the environment for economic development changed once again. The Northumberland Strait causeway was shelved and succeeded by the Comprehensive Development Plan. The focal point of the plan was not industrial expansion, although some attention was given to the issue. Manufacturing created non-seasonal jobs and diversified employment opportunities beyond those in resource-based activities. More processing capacity would be needed to handle the expected increase in agricultural output. DREE expected metal manufacturing to be a potential growth area. Activities would include all aspects of metal fabrication and making of machinery and equipment, including ventilation and heating equipment; fisheries, farm and food-processing equipment; restaurant and retail store fixtures; marine hardware; and transportation equipment. The development plan called for 10 per cent industrial growth per annum.[44] An industrial development fund was established to assist in training, technological upgrading and the consolidation of existing plants and the creation of new ones. Forgivable loans to assist with capital costs were to be provided. The long-anticipated industrial park in Charlottetown was part of the strategy.

The base on which to build was still small. Despite the efforts of Charlottetown and the provincially owned Industrial Enterprises Incorporated, there was not a lot more industry in the city in 1971 than a decade earlier. A total of 29 plants employed 642 workers and had a gross output of $21 million ($7.6 million net).[45] This was 19 per cent of the number of factories and 24 per cent of the work force in the province. About half of those employed were engaged in food and beverage processing. The next three largest areas of employment were building supplies, publishing and allied trades, and metal fabrication and hardware.[46] The city's production was 33 per cent of the Island's gross output (net 35 per cent). Wages from Charlottetown's industries totalled $3.6 million, or 33 per cent of the provincial industrial wage income. Although the city had increased

---

44 Three per cent would be normal expected expansion, 2 per cent would be "induced" growth in existing industries and 5 per cent would be new industry.

45 The Stevenson Kellogg report stated 1,150 worked in light manufacturing.

46 These latter figures may be based on data for 1973 instead of 1971.

its share of the province's plants since the postwar era, it had a smaller portion of the work force and industrial wages. Moreover, the city actually had eight fewer plants than in 1947 and only 40 more industrial employees. The total salaries, however, were 103 per cent higher even after adjustments for inflation. Still, after a quarter-century of effort to bolster its industrial economy, Charlottetown had little to show for its efforts.

And the prognosis for the future was not overly promising. The Stevenson Kellogg report concluded in 1973 that there were no major opportunities in the industrial sectors of light manufacturing and resource support for the Charlottetown area. Investigators saw Charlottetown, itself, remaining essentially a tourist and service centre. They suggested four potential niche areas of business: building supplies, such as trusses and wall panels; replica pine furniture; skim milk powder; and handcrafts like pottery. Any new enterprises in the industrial parks would likely be small light manufacturing firms, examples being makers of food and beverages and metal fabricators. This outlook sat well with the provincial government, which according to Premier Alex Campbell wanted to avoid factories that belched smoke and pollution. Manufacturing, the Stevenson Kellogg report suggested, should be mainly located in industrial parks outside of Charlottetown. That meant future industrial expansion and its related population growth would take place principally in the suburbs.

Although the Parkdale Industrial Park could take some of the expansion, more space would be needed. The report proposed setting aside an additional 100 acres. In March 1974, Industrial Enterprises Incorporated bought 100 acres of easily serviceable, prime farm land in West Royalty for this purpose. John A. Simmonds, IEI Chairman, envisaged the new park as a functional showcase for Island business, blending in with, and enhancing, the local environment. To that end, site use would be restricted to businesses whose operations were totally contained within a building and would not produce obnoxious noise, smells, smoke or fumes. Any commercial use that related to manufacturing would be permitted, including warehousing, storage and trucking terminals, as well as the automotive business, with the exception of scrap yards. All premises were to be landscaped, and advertising was to be low-key.

The process of ramping up Charlottetown's industrial sector started slowly. In 1973–74, eight small businesses received a total of $78,760 of DREE funding and added 37.3 jobs to the labour force. In addition, four metal products firms got $14,350 and expanded by 18 employees. This funding was part of the "base period" of development in which relatively little change took place. A "growth period" followed in which significant expansion was planned, both in terms of the number of enterprises involved and in the range of their products. Much more job creation was anticipated in this phase. New businesses were described as ones not requiring a highly skilled and educated labour force, nor needing a lot of electrical or petroleum energy. They would use local materials and market the products locally or make a product that could be shipped easily, efficiently and economically. Despite DREE expectations that new industries would be small, locally managed and would distribute their profits locally, a marked distinction appeared between the occupants of the West Royalty Industrial Park and industries in the city proper. Park businesses were less likely to be locally owned, and their plants were intended to serve national and international markets. City firms catered more to the local market. Firms in the park were much more likely to have received financial aid from government agencies and departments than the city's established businesses. Although this disparity generated some dissatisfaction within Charlottetown, considerably more criticism emanated from other parts of the province. Community leaders across the Island felt the capital was receiving favoured treatment from the federal government, which was becoming too heavily involved in non-resource-related manufacturing in Charlottetown at the expense of agricultural and fisheries processing in smaller centres. There was a widespread belief that the West Royalty Industrial Park was a potential white elephant and that a similar investment in the primary and processing sectors would produce better results.

Yet the expansion of industry in the short term was significant. In 1981 there were 77 firms that could be considered secondary industry in the Charlottetown area; half were in the suburbs. The largest business cluster involved food processing. Twenty-one enterprises produced a range of items that included meat and meat products, baked goods, seafood, milk and dairy products and soft drinks. There were nine companies making manufactured metal products, and another nine were engaged in printing, publishing and design. Seven firms produced precision and other equipment. Six made wood products; four, textiles and clothing; and three, both concrete products and electrical equipment and electronics. There were two window manufacturers and two makers of horse-racing gear. The remaining eleven businesses made a range of products as varied as paint, fertilizer, skis, chemical products and modular homes. Interestingly, all of the precision equipment plants and half of the textile and clothing plants and metal fabricators were located in the West Royalty Industrial Park, as was a ski manufacturer and a producer of medical and bio-chemical products. Leading names in the park included Northern Telecom, Paderno, and Hall and Stavert, which had relocated from the city. Charlottetown Metal Products meanwhile had migrated slightly further afield to Milton. The bulk of the food processing and printing establishments remained within Charlottetown proper.

Even with this growth, in 1980 the proportion of the population working in manufacturing was virtually the same as in 1960. During the same period, the segment of workers in the retail sector expanded significantly.[47] The era of hyper-inflation in the early 1980s claimed a victim when Canada Packers announced that it would close its Charlottetown operations in 1983. The provincial government, stung by the prospect of the Island's livestock industry losing such an important facility, stepped in and announced the construction of a new "kill and chill" plant in Sherwood. Even with a forced wage rollback for the workers, the economics of the plant were shaky. For this, as with the results of the drive for industrial expansion, the question was whether the enterprise would survive in the long run.

47 The labour force by sector in 1961, 1972 and 1980 was for manufacturing, 877 (11.8 per cent), 1,080 (11.4 per cent), 1,500 (11.7 per cent); for retail trade, 1,424 (19.2 per cent), 1,950 (20.5 per cent), 2,900 (22.7 per cent).

Communications

Efficient communications with the mainland was another important challenge for Charlottetonians in the postwar era. The promised delivery of the new MV *Abegweit* seemed a long way off in July 1946 when Mayor B. Earle MacDonald complained of "the great hindrance" to the city's trade imposed by the "deplorable" service provided by the existing ferry operations. Others criticized the unhappy conditions at the terminals, particularly Wood Islands, and the effect they had on the tourist industry. Even with the arrival of the *Abegweit* in 1947, capacity was less than needed for the volume of traffic. An inadequate ramp at Borden added to the problems by delaying the loading of heavy vehicles. The fact that the Borden crossing was still operated by the Canadian National Railways was underscored by the need to load larger trucks onto rail cars because the lower deck of the *Abby* was not level with the train rails. Further, the departure times from Borden and Cape Tormentine were geared to the railway schedules, not the flow of automobile, bus and truck traffic. Of course, there was no incentive for the railway to provide efficient service for the trucking industry, and for that reason the Board of Trade called upon the Royal Commission on Transportation (the Turgeon Commission) to recommend that the ferries be operated by the federal government. Turgeon failed to act on this idea, even though a paralyzing railway strike shut down the service at Borden while his report was being prepared.

During the strike of 1950, a segment of local opinion turned against the railway union, claiming that "the control of the operation of our car ferry is a determined objective of the C[anadian] C[ongress] [of] L[abour]." For its part, the union regarded arguments to take management of the ferry away from CNR as "an obvious attempt to prevent organized Labour from carrying on collective bargaining." At the core of the issue was "the solemn Confederation contract" of continuous communications between Prince Edward Island and the mainland. A second railway strike occurred in 1966, and again commerce was tied up and tourists fled. A third strike, 10 days long, ironically took place in the middle of the centennial celebrations that proclaimed the Island "the place to be in '73." Between 1950 and the mid-1960s, the lack of adequate service remained a concern in the city. The province persistently used the constitutional provision to lever improvements in the ferry service. Ottawa provided subsidies to contain the rise in ferry charges, and new boats were gradually put into operation on both runs. Although a causeway was proposed, studied and tentatively begun, when the project was abandoned in 1969, a new round of agitation over ferry service did not occur. By then, improvements to the existing shore facilities and additions to the numbers and size of vessels, particularly the huge *John Hamilton Gray*, which replaced the venerable *Prince Edward Island* in 1968, had made service acceptable to most Islanders. The appearance in December 1982 of an ultramodern and powerful MV *Abegweit* as a replacement for its namesake seemed to guarantee reliable connections to the mainland even in the depths of winter. What remained was the frisson tardy commuters sometimes felt as they raced down the Trans-Canada Highway, the occasional speeding ticket dished out by a Borden policeman concealed behind the

Though the arrival of MV Abegweit *in 1947 was a great improvement, civic and business leaders still found much to criticize in the ferry service — especially the railway's failure to accommodate more truck traffic.*

town's railway station, and, for some, comfort in the knowledge that the province's distinct way of life was sheltered by a 45-minute ferry ride.

The progress made in improving ferry links to the mainland was not matched by marine communications to other destinations. Although road travel had reduced the significance of Charlottetown's harbour in the overall scope of commerce, it remained a significant, if outdated, asset. In its submission to the 1949 Turgeon Royal Commission, the Board of Trade noted the wharves were too small for large, modern vessels and asked that the harbour be dredged, adequate docks built and construction started on the Chignecto Canal through the isthmus joining Nova Scotia and New Brunswick. If built, the canal would cut 485 miles off the sea journey between Charlottetown and Boston. As it was, the principal destination of goods that cleared the port was St. John's, Newfoundland. In the late 1940s, a ship left for there every three weeks. By the mid-1950s, two cargo vessels chartered by the PEI Industrial Corporation were making the trip to Newfoundland. The service, which included a cold storage facility for Island produce, ran an average annual deficit of $30,000. This loss notwithstanding, pressure mounted for additional connections to the north shore of the St. Lawrence River and to Corner Brook, Newfoundland. By 1967 Charlottetown was a port of call on runs that went to Sept-Iles, Quebec; Pictou, Nova Scotia; the Magdalen Islands; and St. John's. In that year, there were 201 port clearances by coastal vessels and 21 by ocean-going ships. A couple years later, 239 calls were made at Charlottetown by vessels that unloaded 568,540 tons of cargo and took away 186,896 tons. Clearly the port was more important as an importer of products, including oil, than an exporter. Activity connected with the export of Island goods was fairly quiet in the early 1970s and focused principally on the runs to the Magdalens and St. John's, but it picked up in the later part of the decade.

Improvements to the port's facilities were sought; some were actually realized. Extensive renovations to the railway wharf were undertaken in 1946 and 1947, although the changes failed to remedy the deficiencies of which the Board of Trade complained in 1949. More work was done on the railway wharf in the early 1950s, and by the end of the decade plans were announced for a new federal Department of Transport wharf. Subsequently, in 1961 Heath Macquarrie pressed the case in the House of Commons for a new railway wharf. Hopes for a sea wall running from the railway wharf at the eastern end of the waterfront to the new Queen Charlotte naval establishment on the site of the Paoli's Wharf at the western end surfaced from time to time in the 1940s and 50s. The chimera of a marine slip persisted during the late 1940s and 1950s. Championed until 1953 by W. C. S. McLure in the House of Commons and by Bruce Stewart and Company at home, the idea resurfaced in the 1960s. In the early 1970s, changing technology resulted in calls from the Chamber of Commerce and City Council for construction of a container installation. By then, facilities had fallen so far behind current standards that a single tanker in port would prevent the berthing of other cargo ships.

A meaningful promise of improvements resulting from the Comprehensive Development Plan gave rise to concerns about the nature of the impending changes. Modernity could be menacing, particularly for heritage activists passionate about safeguarding the Island's connection with the past. There was a legitimate concern that the city's indigenous charm could be displaced by artificial expressions of the picturesque. Alderman Doherty, for instance, warned City Council against having "a San Francisco restaurant on one of our wharves." Others feared the implications of changes to the harbour. The Chamber of Commerce fretted that the waterfront could be lost to commerce. It opposed the rumoured use of the area for the new Department of Veterans Affairs headquarters and threw its support behind extending the port's truck and rail infrastructure and building a container facility. Influential business interests continued to view the port as a key commercial asset. A study completed for DREE found that local private enterprise was anxious to be free of government involvement elsewhere in town and recommended CADC turn its attention to major port developments on land owned by Canadian National and the Ministry of Transportation. The third phase of the development plan foresaw port expansion and additional industries along the waterfront, but the incentive to improve the harbour would come from cruise ship tourism. Eleven such vessels stopped at Charlottetown in 1980, and ten were expected in 1981. More were possible. One New York company was forced to cancel nine proposed visits partly because of problems with the port.

Similarly, rail service continued to be an irritant to business in Charlottetown during much of the period. The transportation of animal feed was problematic in the late 1940s when rail cars were not always available. To remedy the situation, a somewhat impractical suggestion was made to build a grain elevator at Charlottetown to store grain shipped by sea from Churchill, Manitoba. Whether the Island could use a whole ship-load of feed grain at a time was a large question. Another legacy of wartime restrictions was the practice of purchasing commodities in small quantities. This was the result of scarcities during and immediately after the war and the resulting high costs that made large-scale storage by farmers and their suppliers uneconomical. Unfortunately,

The 1905 bridge, prior to its demolition. You can see the approach to the new bridge at the right.

orders of less than a car load were subject to additional charges. Freight rates were also increasing after 1948, and although the Board of Trade asked the Turgeon Royal Commission in 1949 to roll them back, little headway was made.[48]

Within the city itself, as late as 1950, standardization of the gauge of railway tracks was not complete in the terminal works. An even greater worry was the state of the Hillsborough Bridge. The structure was in such poor condition that freight trains to the southeastern part of the province were routed through Mount Stewart. Passenger service continued over it until safety considerations prompted the railway to stop all use by trains in 1951.[49] Instead, the railway proposed to run buses as a replacement. This was part of a plan by CNR to abandon all passenger rail service on the Island except for the line between Charlottetown and Borden.[50] The idea failed to take into account fierce winter weather that frequently closed roads, so the railway promised to run trains when the buses could not operate. These arrangements were put into effect on the route between Charlottetown and Murray Harbour in 1951. Whenever weather made road travel perilous, a train would bring passengers to Southport to board a bus or taxis for the final leg of the trip across the bridge. Passenger service was retained elsewhere in the province, but as road conditions improved, travel by rail became less economically competitive and was finally ended on October 25, 1969. Freight service remained, but as income suffered over the years from increased competition from trucks, CN allowed its system to deteriorate through poor maintenance. By the 1980s, rail transport on Prince Edward Island was reaching the end of the line.

As the railway waned in importance, roads became increasingly critical. Highway improvements begun in the prewar era continued throughout the 1940s and

---

48 Freight rates soared after wartime price controls were removed: 21 per cent in 1948, 8 per cent in 1949 and 20 per cent in 1950. These increases were presented to a subsequent royal commission on transportation, the MacPherson Commission, in a brief by the Maritimes Transportation Commission in 1960.

49 Concern about the bridge's load capacity prompted CNR in 1947 to assign the first diesel locomotive on the Island to the Murray Harbour line. It was lighter than the steam locomotives.

50 There was potential for conflict between the railway and provincially licensed bus operators. In the event of duplication of routes, the CNR would surrender the route to its competitor and operate whatever train service the federal Board of Transport Commissioners decided was needed to meet the "convenience and necessity" of the public.

A consultant found in 1967 that the centre of the city was being ruined by the attempt to "park too many cars on the street."

1950s, spurred on by postwar prosperity that spread the use of automobiles. Federal assistance in the construction of a Trans-Canada Highway offered the prospect of a transportation spine running from Borden to Wood Islands through Charlottetown. A new bridge across the Hillsborough River was part of the scheme announced in the autumn of 1950. Initial discussions included the railway, perhaps because CNR's participation would lessen the province's half-share of the construction costs, but the railway wanted nothing more to do with the Hillsborough crossing. After 1951, it was kept open for motor vehicles.[51]

By 1955, 3,000 automobiles crossed the narrow, decrepit Hillsborough Bridge every day. In April of that year, a federal Order-in-Council transferred ownership of the bridge from CNR to the federal Department of Transport. For reasons of safety, the department ordered the railway to close it completely. The railway complied on July 8, only to see its barricades torn down at the insistence of an angry premier A. W. Matheson who then sought a legal order to keep the bridge open. The new bridge that eventually replaced the old railway span had two lanes, each 12 feet wide, and four-foot-wide sidewalks on both sides. It ensured that Charlottetown remained the focal point of the province's highway system and was easily accessible for Islanders

51 The bridge cost the province $10,000 a year for payments in lieu of user tolls.

and tourists alike. For those who expected bus service to replace passenger rail service, disappointment lay ahead. Connections between Charlottetown and Tignish and Charlottetown and Elmira provided by Island Motor Transport proved to be money-losers. In April 1975, IMT announced that operations would cease without a government subsidy. This was refused. In the era of the broad highway, the car was king.[52]

Cars created their own problems. From the 1950s, Charlottetown had suffered from congestion in the city centre with parking spaces at a premium. In 1960 Mayor Walthen Gaudet proclaimed the parking problem "Public Enemy Number One." By the mid-1970s, it was estimated that the number of parking spaces in the downtown core would have to more than double by 1991 to meet demand. That figure was for only long-term parking. Casual parking for shoppers was also in short supply, placing businesses at the centre of town at a competitive disadvantage with suburban malls. The future prosperity of the central business district thus depended on the resolution of the parking problem. Hopes for relief ultimately were placed in the construction of parking garages.

Urban transit, frequently mentioned as a solution, was a difficult sell in Charlottetown. A company started in 1960 by Fernando Vidal to provide bus service in the metropolitan area failed, and an attempt begun in 1975 to provide shuttle service from parking lots at the periphery of the city to downtown had limited success before it, too, succumbed. Even Robert Murray, who piloted the project, referred to it as "a Band-Aid approach to our parking problems." When federal grants under a new Urban Transportation Assistance Program became available in 1980, Andy Jamieson formed a company to try again to provide the city with transit service. Despite initial signs of commuter support, the business was ultimately not viable. The essential weakness, beyond an ingrained preference of shoppers and commuters for their automobiles, was the treatment of urban transit as a business rather than a public service. Spending restraints, rooted in part in the lack of funding from senior levels of government, choked off support from the municipal government. Charlottetown remained the only provincial capital without a bus service. Citizens who did not own a car either walked, took a taxi or stayed home.

Travel around town may not have been getting easier, but changes in the world of telecommunications were reducing barriers over long distances. Wartime innovations included the development of a "pulse time modulation" or "microwave" system. The first commercial application of microwave technology was established between the Maritime Telegraph and Telephone Company and the Island Telephone Company on November 19, 1948. Land-based communications service began to give way to satellite links on November 10, 1972, when Canada's Anik I was launched from Cape Canaveral, Florida, on a NASA Delta rocket. The capacity of this and subsequent space-based links to carry television and radio programs, telephone messages and, in due

52 Subsequent to the termination of IMT service, a group of nine community co-operatives set up runs between Tignish and Charlottetown and Souris and Charlottetown using school-type buses. They lost money, but for a while the province provided a subsidy to keep them going.

A vast improvement on Upton Airfield, Charlottetown Airport (top photo) *became an important asset in the years following World War II.*

course, computer data had the effect of shrinking space and overcoming many of the obstacles that had plagued earlier generations of Charlottetonians. As the telecommunications revolution unfolded during this period, barriers of distance, time and place diminished. The city joined the mainstream of the nation and the world and prepared to adjust its economy accordingly.

Air transport, of course, likewise held great promise as a means of communications, and it, too, expanded rapidly after the Second World War. At first it was not completely apparent that passenger travel would become popular. Carl Burke of Maritime Central Airways thought the short distances between centres on the east coast and their small populations could make local passenger service unprofitable. As Trans-Canada Airlines had the monopoly of long-haul flights, Burke concentrated his efforts on the commercial cargo business and eventually prospered during the construction of the Pine Tree and DEW radar lines. Nevertheless, Charlottetown's airport became an important asset in this era. The city had purchased the site during the Depression, but the federal government had expanded and operated it during the war. The Department of Transport assumed responsibility for its maintenance and operation in 1946, and municipal authorities were anxious to have them take over complete ownership. By 1949 the runways needed extensions and improvements to handle increased freight volumes, and the city much preferred to have others foot the bill. An example of the potential of air freight was the shipment of 171,600 pounds of fresh strawberries from Charlottetown to Moncton in 1948. MCA operated three routes out of the Island capital in 1949: three daily flights to Summerside and Moncton, one to New Glasgow and Sydney, and two flights a week to the Magdalen Islands. As facilities expanded, larger aircraft took lobster and other Island products to cities in the United States and Central Canada.

By 1952 agitation for airport expansion was at full throttle. J. A. MacLean pressed the case in the House of Commons, and Mayor J. David Stewart urged citizens to voice their support for the cause. A longer runway permitted aircraft the size of DC-3s to land, but new ones were needed for the larger DC-4s and C-46s. By 1953 shipments of cargo were booming, and 23,000 passengers passed through the airport. MCA, however, moved its main operations to Moncton. Discussions with the federal government thus took on some sense of urgency. A new Progressive Conservative government was receptive to these appeals. Transport Minister George Hees officially opened a 7,000-foot runway on April 29, 1960. He described it as a "tremendous boon" to the province, and, indeed, it was a factor in the establishment of the Enheat plant in the city. MCA also was able to upgrade its fleet to larger and more modern Handley Page Herald aircraft.

In 1963 MCA was sold to Eastern Provincial Airlines. This brought an end to a particular chapter in Charlottetown's entrepreneurial history but not to the increasing importance of air travel to the city. A considerable volume of trade was done by air with Newfoundland and the Magdalens, and EPA applied to broaden its reach to include Bathurst, New Brunswick, and Montreal. Both the city and Board of Trade supported this proposal, which ultimately proved successful, and service to Montreal with a stop at Charlo, New Brunswick, was inaugurated on October 27, 1968. This opened the wider markets for Island products and increased passenger travel. EPA introduced Boeing 737 twin-jet aircraft with much greater passenger capacity than the Handley Page Heralds. While runways were again a concern, the most pressing need was new terminal facilities to replace the wooden, Second World War structure. The terminal building was designed to receive 25 to 30 passengers, but by the late 1960s, 90 to 100 travellers were disembarking at one time. Though the Department of Transport promised a new building, it managed to construct only an 82-foot-long enlargement of the existing structure in 1970 that included space for airline offices, ticket counters and a waiting area with rest rooms. Two 32-foot extensions followed, one in 1971 and another in 1973. Another addition in 1974 for a new passenger lounge and washrooms prompted the *Guardian* to ask, "Why don't they put up the new terminal and be done with it?"

In a repeat of the earlier experience with railway service, the frequency and connections of passenger flights became an issue. The Council of Maritime Premiers prodded EPA to establish connections among Charlottetown, Halifax and Fredericton, and, to help ensure the routes were profitable, the Island government encouraged its travelling bureaucrats to make their trips to other provincial capitals by air. The service proved unsustainable. Five years later, to reach Fredericton, a high-flying Island public servant had to go to Halifax and switch to an Air Canada flight that stopped first in Saint John. The trip took four hours and cost an estimated 6 per cent more than a direct flight. That fare may have been wishful thinking. In 1974 the cost of travel by air to Fredericton from Charlottetown was only $10 less than the flight to Montreal. Direct flights to Central Canada, particularly Ottawa and Toronto, were also needed. An Air Canada flight to Ottawa and on to Toronto was begun in early 1975, but convenient air travel out of Charlottetown remained elusive.

Business was brisk enough, though, to highlight the terminal's inadequacies.[53] The Department of Transport finally prepared a master plan for the complete renewal of the airport, including a new terminal to be built by 1978, plus a new 5,000-foot runway. In 1976 the project was put on hold as part of a federal budgetary restraint effort. While politicians such as Heath Macquarrie pressured the government to move ahead with construction, other voices rose in opposition. The plan called for an 800-acre buffer zone, and landowners in East Royalty objected. The National Farmers' Union demanded the estimated cost of $21.5 million for the whole project be put into road and rail improvements instead. EPA and Air Canada were reported to favour upgrading and extension of the existing runway rather than the new 5,000-foot strip. They foresaw the need for an 8,000-foot runway within a few years. EPA also disliked the increased landing fees that a new runway would trigger. This would add to the 40 per cent rise in such costs sustained since 1975. Back in Ottawa, officials were having concerns about costs themselves, and, in October 1978, began to trim the size and design of the terminal. After $800,000 was chopped out of the $5.8 million budget for this part of the project, government was ready to proceed. Construction began in 1979 on a new Combined Services Building, ramp, taxiways and sewer and drainage lines. In 1980 a final 16 feet for luggage handling were tacked onto the old terminal, and preparations were begun for the balance of the project. When the old runway was resurfaced in 1983, Air Canada and EPA were required to transfer their operations to Summerside for two months. Passengers were taken to and from the air base by bus. The control tower and 5,000-foot runway were finished in 1984, and the new terminal opened in March 1986. The total cost of the airport renewal, including a new access road, parking facilities and re-routing of the Union Road, was $30 million. Charlottetown finally had an airport that met its needs and its status as a provincial capital. Whether airline service matched this standard would depend upon the economic vagaries of the travel industry.

53 Usage of the airport increased 320 per cent between 1966 and 1977.

Tourism

Service responded to demand, and travellers, in turn, had to be drawn to the city. The striking success of the 1939 Confederation Week Celebrations revealed the extent to which well-orchestrated tourist events could attract visitors. With the onset of the Second World War, tourism declined, but picked up after 1942. By the time victory was won in Europe, the number of visitors to Prince Edward Island had pretty well returned to prewar levels. Most still visited the province for the pleasant landscape and the beaches rather than the urban centres. The question for Charlottetonians was how to entice visitors to the city and gain maximum impact from the tourist industry. At one end of a list of possibilities was the suggestion to build two bridges across the West River to link the city to south shore vacation areas between Borden and Rocky Point. Although one of the proposed links, a bridge at Brighton, was extremely costly, it had supporters, including MP W. C. S. McLure. He and other advocates had to content themselves with the second connection, a causeway at Meadow Bank. For its time and place, this project was "gargantuan." It was planned as a 1,800-foot-long causeway with a 60-foot bridge to allow tidal flows to pass. Work began in 1956 and was completed in 1958. After it opened, the trip between Charlottetown and Rocky Point was shortened by four miles but the water quality of the river above the causeway began to deteriorate. Reduced tidal rises and higher water temperatures degraded both the fishery and the aesthetics of the area upstream. Problems persisted until 1993, when a new opening was created in the causeway and a 300-foot-long bridge erected. At the other end of the list of promotional methods for the city was the printed brochure. The provincial government unfortunately showed a dismaying lack of interest in promoting tourism in the early years after the war, so less costly strategies prevailed. City Council agreed to place some promotional information in booklets on Charlottetown produced in 1950. It also gave its approval for a Board of Trade effort to establish a tourist bureau in 1953, and helped the PEI Travel Bureau publish a city map in 1954.

These tentative steps gave way to a more ambitious strategy for 1955, the centenary of the city's incorporation. A Centennial Committee was established, chaired by Lieutenant-Colonel Frank J. Storey with Councillor A. Walthen Gaudet, who was also Secretary-Treasurer of the PEI Innkeepers Association, as General Manager. Fourteen other members were responsible for everything from public relations to decorations and floats. Frank MacKinnon, Principal of Prince of Wales College and a committee member, headed a list of contributors to a substantial souvenir booklet published by the committee. Merchants sold and redeemed 25¢ souvenir paper currency, and a new "civic centre" was opened in the market building to house the tourist bureau, the bus terminal and a display area. Various organizations, including the Canadian Freight Association, the Canadian Standards Association, the Maritime Masons and the Maritime Dental Association, were lured to Charlottetown for their annual meetings. Three R.C.N. vessels visited the port in July. The Acadians "celebrated" the 200th anniversary of their expulsion. In July and August, organizers tried to have something going on every day. Celebrations peaked around natal day, August 8, with a parade and historical pageant. While allusions were made throughout the year to the birthplace of Confederation theme that so heavily influenced the 1939 observances, another distinguishing feature of the Island's identity also appeared. The Charlottetown Little Theatre presented *Anne of Green Gables*, the cherished story by Lucy Maud Montgomery of a spirited orphan girl who underwent the joys and heartbreak of growing up in late-Victorian rural Prince Edward Island

Civic officials and citizens generally were well-pleased with the results of the centennial observances. To build on that success, the city took out a membership in the Canadian Tourist Association, and planned a celebration of the 25th anniversary of inter-provincial air mail service for 1956. These observances, too, were pronounced completely successful. As a means of capitalizing on the momentum from the centenary, City Council established its Industry and Tourist Development Committee in 1956. Other ideas to boost Charlottetown's marketing appeal followed. In 1957 two Councillors visited Shubenacadie, Nova Scotia, to inspect the animal and bird sanctuary there. Some thought was given to establishing a similar attraction in Victoria Park, but too much time was needed to get it up and running for the current year. The Industry and Tourist Development Committee was replaced by a Public Relations Committee in February 1958 only to see its cause set back when a large amount of promotional literature was destroyed by the market house fire. Meanwhile, the

As in 1914, when the 50th anniversary of the Charlottetown Conference was eclipsed by the growing war in Europe, the 75th anniversary in 1939 was overshadowed by an impending world war. In an era of surging nationalism, the 1964 centennial celebrations were able to capture public attention, firmly fixing Confederation as a central theme in Charlottetown's tourist offering.

province was beginning to acknowledge the full potential of the travel business. David Stewart, the former mayor and Provincial Secretary in the newly elected Conservative government, remarked at a Board of Trade meeting that tourism could well become the Island's premier industry. Changes, such as six months of daylight saving time and "enlightened" liquor laws, would help attract and hold more visitors. So would special events. Stewart called for one major event in both June and September and one every week during July and August.

Clearly the effectiveness of well-organized celebrations was recognized. When a group of "interested citizens" met with Mayor Gaudet to discuss a possible celebration of the centenary of the Charlottetown Conference in 1964, City Council promptly set up a permanent Convention Committee to work with various service clubs. The Board of Trade followed suit six months later with its Centennial Committee. The role of the city as the birthplace of the nation was one that Charlottetown had long claimed and one that had generally been accepted, although some interlopers appeared as 1964 drew nigh. Furthermore, in an era of surging nationalism, the meeting that gave rise to the Canadian federation was capturing public attention anew. This fact was underscored by the appearance in the city of a crew from the Canadian Broadcasting Corporation to film a program on Confederation. The opportunities offered by such free publicity were not lost on city politicians. In 1961 Council decided to send a float to the Grey Cup parade in Toronto as a means of drawing attention to the celebrations in Charlottetown scheduled for 1964. A float was again entered in the 1962 parade, again in Toronto. The festivities surrounding the Charlottetown Conference that ultimately unfolded featured a series of events and re-enactments, including a Dominion-Provincial conference in the Confederation Chamber of Province House. The opening of the Fathers of Confederation Memorial Building by Queen Elizabeth on October 6, 1964, crowned the year's proceedings. As in 1955, these centennial celebrations drew various organizations to the city to hold their annual meetings. Mayor Gaudet, while appropriating much of the credit for both sets of successes, proposed the city hire a manager to promote Charlottetown as a convention city.[54]

Although business travel represented a significant opportunity, summer tourism offered the greatest potential. In this regard, the new Confederation Centre would play a key role. Even before its official opening, the Centre had hosted the Dominion Drama Festival in May. This was followed by a series of nationally known performers, including Maureen Forrester, Lois Marshall, Jon Vickers, Wayne and Shuster and companies such as Spring Thaw, the Halifax Symphony, the Royal Winnipeg Ballet and the Neptune Theatre. It was a line-up that showcased the best in Canadian culture and entertainment, and it was an artistic and commercial triumph. But could such success be sustained? The answer to that question rested with Mavor Moore, the distinguished author, director and producer, who was named to head both the Centre and its theatre. He concluded that an annual summer featuring Canadian artists and

54 The mayor's enthusiasm was not shared by all. Councillor MacNeill believed more effort should be directed instead to attracting small industries to town.

works was both desirable and practical. The success of the 1964 program proved the viability of the concept. At the core of the festival's line-up would be a musical, a form of entertainment that was flexible, suitable for audiences of vacationers and sustainable by Canada's talent pool. For the opening feature, Moore commissioned a production of *Anne of Green Gables*, written by Don Harron, directed and choreographed by Alan Lund, with music by Norman Campbell.[55] The response to this original creation was overwhelming. It cemented the Charlottetown Festival as a destination point for summer travellers and set the standards for other productions that followed. In marrying the concepts of a special summer event, the birthplace of Confederation and the land of Anne, the Confederation Centre and its festival provided Charlottetown with the appeal to draw travellers from away.

Such an accomplishment did not come without costs. While the Centre and its festival had drawn thousands of visitors to Charlottetown, contributing handsomely to the local economy, the festival itself experienced financial difficulties. The Centre's trustees were required to appeal for help from both the city and the province. The city provided a grant, and the Centre was given the status of a charitable organization to encourage donations. Trustees recognized that the public would want to know why, with all the talk of success, money was needed to cover a loss. "Publicity must be prepared now," wrote businessman Alan Holman, "to educate our people on the financial as well as cultural benefits that a festival brings to the community; on the fact that no festival pays its way; and that a community must help to defray these financial expenses either by civic contributions, business contributions, or personal contributions." The Centre hired a director of public relations. Trustees also successfully lobbied the Atlantic Development Board for grants to complete the complex. To support their case, they noted the employment generated — 50 permanent and 125 seasonal employees — and a 20 per cent increase in tourist traffic.

Charlottetown's tourist strategy was bolstered by Comprehensive Development Plan. The Greater Charlottetown Area Development Committee identified the natural environment and historical heritage as important assets for the development of local tourism. With the increasing leisure time available to individuals and the emphasis employers were giving to employee training, the committee proposed making Charlottetown a destination point in Eastern North America for individuals and corporations desiring recreation, convention and seminar facilities. They called for a convention and seminar centre on the waterfront or in "some other blighted area"; a central sports complex near the University that would include an NHL-sized rink and an Olympic-sized pool; improved infrastructure including high-speed access to the city from the airport, a by-pass for the Trans-Canada Highway, better port facilities, the burial of overhead wires and development of a central municipal services building. Realizing these proposals, together with other goals, such as a pollution abatement program, would draw visitors and make the area a good place to live. This, in turn, would attract head offices and possibly light industry.

---

55 Lyrics were by Don Harron, Norman Campbell, Mavor Moore and Elaine Campbell.

The first phase of the development plan did not place any special emphasis on tourism in Charlottetown, preferring instead to enhance the attraction of places outside the axis running from the city to the north shore beaches. A later study returned to the issue of enhancing the city's appeal to visitors. Consultants from Kates, Peat, Marwick and Company noted that almost one-quarter of all travellers to the province visited Charlottetown, but only 17 per cent spent a night in the city. Even so, the summer peak accounted for half the room rentals. Since a hotel room had to be occupied 100 nights to pay for itself, expanding accommodation capacity required more trade in the off-season and especially the "shoulder" seasons in June and September. The report affirmed that Charlottetown — and Summerside as well — could play a substantially larger role in the tourist industry than they did at present, but expansion required both considerable investment and meticulous planning. An investigation by the accounting firm of Laventhol, Krekstein, Horwath and Horwath into Charlottetown's potential as a convention centre concluded that growth was possible. Its report, completed in 1973, noted that problems with accommodation, convention facilities and accessibility were offset by the city's charm and "special characteristics." Charlottetown would not be able to compete with larger centres, but a revitalized downtown and another hotel with 150–175 rooms and meeting space would create an appropriate market niche. Stevenson Kellogg, in its report, endorsed this concept, calling

Most of the new accommodations after World War II were built as motor lodges, often on the outskirts of the city. This helped fuel calls for a "first class" hotel and convention centre be built as part of revitalizing the downtown.

for a 175–200-room hotel at the city core or waterfront that was part of a national or international chain, plus a "first-class" restaurant. The pedestrian-oriented Charlottetown Square historical zone, a small theatre to be associated with the Confederation Centre and a retail outlet to sell Island handicrafts completed this vision of how the city could develop market appeal as a convention centre.

Confirmation of the potential and importance of conventions came in 1973 when a record-breaking number were held in town. There were 55 national, 57 regional and 5 international meetings that drew an estimated total of 17,400 delegates in that year. The occasion of this influx was another well-promoted centennial, this time marking the entry of Prince Edward Island into Confederation. It was a province-wide celebration with emphasis on grassroots participation. The committee that oversaw the festivities, however, was heavily endowed with Charlottetonians, and heritage was a focus of activity.

During years without special celebrations, Charlottetown was demonstrating some improvement in widening its tourist appeal, but progress was slow. In 1965, 24 per cent of visitors to the province came to its capital and 17 per cent percent stayed overnight. By 1978 these figures had increased to only 27.5 per cent and 23.3 per cent respectively. More was required to move the city towards its objectives for tourism. Calls to develop a hotel in the downtown area commanded particular attention. In response, the Dale Corporation joined with Hilton International to propose a hotel and convention centre on the waterfront adjacent to Harbourside. An economic downturn halted work in 1982, and, when it was resumed, relations between Dale and Hilton were strained. The hotel could be made to pay its own way, but the convention centre weighed heavily on Dale's finances. In 1984 the two partners split. Shortly thereafter, the Dale Corporation collapsed, leaving the provincial government to weigh its options.[56] The province stepped in and rescued the operations, in what some declared to be an ill-advised move. By then, the desirability of dedicating so much effort and investment towards tourism was being questioned by a vocal segment of the public. This debate would continue in the years to come. Meanwhile, Charlottetown had its tourist infrastructure largely in place. It remained to be seen whether, having built it, tourists would come.

SOCIAL LIFE

The destiny of a people unfolds at its own pace. Periods of calm and social stability may be followed by crises and frenzied change. For much of its history, Prince Edward Island and its capital had known relative tranquility. In Charlottetown, a familiar lifestyle and well-established familial and community relationships served as a backdrop to daily events. This was by no means a unique phenomenon, but the extent to which set patterns of life were characteristic of the place before the Second World

56 Ironically, about a year after Dale Corporation failed, the federal government set up a program that basically paid for the construction of such facilities.

War was unusual. This was especially true when the city is compared to larger centres that received more migrants and had become more industrialized. With the return of peace came change. Many of the assumptions that had hitherto underpinned society were eroded by factors largely beyond local control. The demise of the British Empire and the potency of the ties to Britain, the rise of Canadian nationalism and American popular culture, the demographic earthquake of the "baby boom," the sexual revolution of the 1960s, the secularization of community values and the brave new world of electronic communications were just some of these developments.

There was nothing distinctive about the impact of such transformations upon the citizens of Charlottetown and the Island, nor the resentment that some felt about the disruptions. To a degree, it was the muted form these changes took that was remarkable. The economic buoyancy that characterized postwar Canada was less apparent. This frustrated Islanders and stood as a challenge to the technocrats and planners who typified the new activist governments taking root in postwar Canada. Conventional social attitudes dating back generations were identified as an important cause of economic underperformance. The Comprehensive Development Plan was not seen by planners as revolutionary in essence; it sought to introduce new concepts rather than displace socio-economic patterns established over 200 years and deemed to "have value." As one background report put it, "all the plan does is to indicate how improvements may be made in the productive use of Island resources and how waste can be lessened by greater efficiency among those working on the Island, whether they be civil servants or fishermen." The consequences of such adjustments, however, were to be far-reaching.

Education

The end of the Second World War had a profound influence on education in Charlottetown, as elsewhere. Returning servicemen and servicewomen were anxious to get on with their lives, which at that time meant a job, marriage and children. The consequences of the resulting demographic phenomenon are still being played out today. In the postwar era, the schools were some of the first institutions to feel the impact of this change. Even before the baby boomers reached their doors, they were adapting to new circumstances. Returned veterans with incomplete educations needed further training. Many joined existing programs, swelling classes to unprecedented sizes. The province's reconstruction advisory committee proposed four new classrooms be added to Prince of Wales College to provide adult education with alternatives to academic fields of study. The Vocational School was a response. It opened in 1945 as a joint dominion-provincial initiative to give veterans vocational and technical training. By 1948 civilian classes were being formed as veterans completed their studies.

The war also accelerated changes to the status of women in the community. In 1945 the first female appointees took their places on the School Board. "The modern woman has more leisure time," the *Guardian* commented; "their horizons have been widened." With that in mind, the paper gave its support to "mothers on the school board." The replacement in 1950 of one of the first appointees, Mrs. Gordon MacDonald, by a man came as a shock. Members were usually renewed, and this step was deemed to be unfair and "a slap in the face" to the School Improvement League. Seven women appeared before City Council and demanded to have two women on the nine-member board.[57] Although Mayor B. Earle MacDonald resented the intrusion, there was support elsewhere on Council for women on the board, and it eventually became standard procedure.

Creating a high school was another idea that gained support as the war wound down. The Reconstruction Advisory Committee suggested it, and both the School Improvement League and Kinsmen Club endorsed it. Proponents envisioned a composite school that would service the city, Rustico, Hunter River and New Haven. In response, the province said it would erect a building, if the Dominion government paid for it. Not surprisingly, federal financing failed to materialize. Undeterred, a large delegation representing a broad swath of Charlottetown's society delivered to the provincial

Auto mechanics and cooking were just two of the many trades taught at the Provincial Vocational Institute wing of PWC after it opened in 1945. In 1964, PVI moved to a new facility in Central Royalty.

57 The city board of school trustees consisted of nine members; four, including the chair, were appointed by the province and five were named by the city. Efforts were made to balance Roman Catholics and Protestants. The city regularly named two Catholics and three Protestants.

government in April 1947 a brief which argued that educational levels, while excellent, should be raised further.[58] There were enough children, 3,215, in Charlottetown and the surrounding area to justify a regional high school, and paved roads meant rural children could be transported to it efficiently. The new school would even make a fitting war memorial. Despite similar representations to Council by "the most … awe inspiring delegation," no action was taken. By 1949, however, the city school board had decided to proceed and began planning for a facility that would offer both academic and vocational education for grades nine and ten.

This development was long overdue. A review prepared for the School Board by John C. Matthews of the Department of Education of Fenn College in Cleveland, Ohio, revealed many shortcomings in Charlottetown's school system. Between 1950 and 1952, he polled five groups of people, including a representative sample of citizens (334 people), a smaller selection of 32 community leaders who were "keenly interested" in education, members of the 1934 Grade 1 class who still resided in town, the teachers and current high school students. Matthews expected that in a city "consisting of those races that inhabit Charlottetown," one would find "a high degree of educational development," but his findings suggested otherwise. Improvements were needed throughout the system, particularly in the school buildings, the curriculum and educational materials.

Public funds maintained the four existing schools, but 63 per cent of the city's residents were tenants, and past experience proved that "the owners of tenant-occupied dwelling units are more inclined to react negatively to school improvement programs than are those people who own and occupy their own homes." The schools were substandard and overcrowded. They offered 1,665 spaces with a maximum short-term, or "emergency," capacity of 2,300, but current enrolments came to 2,415. None had a gymnasium or library. Assembly rooms were on top floors accessed by wooden stairways, making them fire traps, but none of the buildings was constructed of fireproof materials. They lacked exit lights and signs, and one had no fire extinguishers. None of the schools had adequate playgrounds, and their science facilities were "appallingly limited" and lacked sufficient equipment for instruction. There were bright spots, however. Matthews found Rochford Square School clean and attractive, and the teachers had provided equipment, plus four pianos and a movie projector. Overall, the physical plants were obsolete and no longer suitable for housing a modern educational program. Matthews suggested safety upgrades but not massive alterations. Instead, new schools were needed.

Major curriculum changes were also required. The whole thrust of the course work was to prepare students for entrance examinations to the senior high school grades at Prince of Wales College.[59] Yet this elitist agenda did little for the 90 per cent who never progressed beyond high school. In fact, only one-third completed

58 The delegation, led by Dr. W. J. P. MacMillan, included the Mayor, representatives of the School Board, Charlottetown Teachers' Federation, Women's Institute, School Improvement League, the Board of Trade, Canadian Legion, YMCA, Knights of Columbus and other service organizations.

59 St. Dunstan's University offered high school courses, and PWC provided two years of secondary education. Both institutions were, thus, at this time part secondary and part post-secondary institutions.

Grade 10. Another third failed to reach Grade 7. The 32 community leaders interested in education strongly supported the idea that the curriculum should be geared for those who were not planning to go to university by offering training in the industrial arts.[60] This practical attitude encouraged Matthews to urge more citizen participation in education. He applauded the board's efforts to forge an independent constituency by working with citizens' groups. As it was, the school board was an instrument of "state" rather than "local" power. Appointees, while nominally independent, were actually subject to political pressures that intimidated and stultified "even the most dynamic and courageous members." Removing board offices from civic buildings and schools to a separate site, the report noted, would facilitate an autonomous school board. The trustees' attention was mostly directed to administrative matters rather than policy discussions, so Matthews recommended a superintendent be appointed to deal with administration. This proposal was acted upon when K. A. Parker was made Superintendent of Schools in 1952.

Other observations and conclusions touched upon two of the most sensitive details of Charlottetown life: religious balance and nativism. The religious split in the schools, the report concluded, bred "mistrust, scepticism and even prejudice" among the staff. Barriers were erected that had more to do with emotion than reason, and the staff as a consequence failed to function as a co-operative group with common purpose and ideals. All but two of the 80 teachers were native Islanders, and all but three lived in Charlottetown. They were poorly paid in relation to other teachers — a point often made by the teachers themselves — and only four had university degrees. The report recommended that teachers should be hired only if they had at least two years of post-secondary education and urged present staff to begin to work on their Bachelor of Arts degrees part-time.

A major conclusion called for the construction of a comprehensive high school for 700–1,000 students in grades seven to twelve, to separate elementary and junior high grades and offer a broad selection of courses. Matthews recommended that course streams include academic, general, vocational and commercial subjects. The cost to the city would not be insignificant, but the report pointed out that the city had not made an investment in schools in the last 75 years that required assessment of major properties. City and school revenues had increased but had failed to keep pace with inflation. During the previous two decades only 20.5 per cent of city taxes went for education. It was now time to do more.

To its credit, the School Board had already concluded as much. In no small measure, the Matthews Survey seems to have been commissioned to advance this goal. The board decided to proceed with the new school with one major modification: it would incorporate only grades seven to ten. The final two years of secondary education would remain at Prince of Wales College. Matthews proposed a site for the school on

---

60 Premier J. Walter Jones would have approved. He once stated, "I don't think we should train a man too much. The first thing you know, he's a professor and gone off to Upper Canada and we've had the expense of training him."

the west side of Elm Avenue just outside the city limits.[61] The location finally selected was in the western end of the city near Brighton and recently established suburbs. The construction contract for Queen Charlotte High School was let in 1953, and the first students were admitted in September 1954. Birchwood High School followed in March 1958. The traditional duality of Charlottetown's educational system was observed as Protestants mainly attended Queen Charlotte and Roman Catholics, Birchwood. New elementary schools opened in rapid succession: Prince Street (January 1962), St. Jean, (September 1962) and West Kent (January 1963). Colonel Gray Senior High School, which rounded out this flurry of development, brought change on two fronts. The school board now offered the final years of secondary education and offered it to both Protestant and Catholic students together. Spurred on by advancing enrolments and increasing prosperity, more was accomplished in education in the 14 years between 1952 and 1966 than in several previous generations.[62]

New buildings did not correct all of the problems facing schools in the postwar years. Matthews also highlighted deficiencies in course offerings. K. A. Parker reiterated this in his first report as Superintendent of Schools. He found the curriculum far too narrow. It was particularly important to serve the 90 per cent of pupils who did not go to university. Although two teachers had been hired in 1947 for the instruction of the mentally handicapped, by 1959 there was still a shortage of classes "for boys and girls with low mental abilities" who could not cope with the regular curriculum. The school board noted that four classes with twelve children in each were required to serve this clientele adequately. The vast majority of non-academic students had no need for such special arrangements, but progress in extending appropriate vocational education to them was equally slow. Particularly acute at the secondary school level, this shortcoming was filled by the opening of the new Provincial Vocational Institute in 1964. It was an innovative combination of a trades and occupational training school and a vocational high school. The curriculum included four-year high school courses in English, mathematics, science and social studies, as well as classes in 15 different trades, including navigation, cooking, electronics, drafting and stenography.[63] An estimated 65 to 75 per cent of the students were from Charlottetown or suburban Parkdale and Sherwood.

Teaching standards were an ongoing problem, as was supply. The war had drawn away some prospective teachers; in 1945 there were only 38 trainees in the Normal School at Prince of Wales. Low salaries subsequently perpetuated a teacher shortage, as did young women deciding to start families and remain at home to raise the children.

---

61 A previous suggestion was to use the Vocational School at Prince of Wales College as a wing of the new high school. Another idea that briefly surfaced during the political discussions that swirled around the decision was to convert the college itself into a high school.

62 Rochford Square School continued to operate until the early 1970s, as did the non-public Notre Dame Academy. The last class graduated from Notre Dame in 1971, when the Roman Catholic Church ended its involvement in education. Another school, François-Buote, opened in 1983 to serve the Francophone community. Initially, it was located in the Spring Park United Church Hall.

63 When the new school opened, instruction in the building trades remained at the old Vocational School.

By 1950 the college was training 76 teachers, but a province-wide shortage persisted into the 1950s. Furthermore, the prevalence of under-qualified teachers was acute. While this was particularly apparent in rural schools, the "status" of the courses at Prince of Wales College made it difficult for teachers trained there "to meet the needs of the City's Grade X students." In March 1957, Monsignor John A. Sullivan, Rector of St. Dunstan's University, reopened the long-dormant issue of teacher training at his Roman Catholic institution. He argued that teachers' salaries and working conditions should be raised and teaching standards needed to be improved by higher professional and academic training. He offered his university's help to that end.

This did not come as a surprise. Already in 1956, the Anglican Diocesan Church Society had expressed concern that "a sectarian body" would be granted the right to act as a normal school. Although the provincial government appeared to welcome Monsignor Sullivan's proposal, opponents were not hard to find. The Loyal Orange Lodge objected to the Catholic university having the same status as the (theoretically) non-denominational PWC, and the Ministerial Association expressed concern about having teachers in training, 75 per cent of whom were currently Roman Catholics, educated in a sectarian school by a sectarian staff. SDU graduates would receive degrees rather than PWC diplomas, a distinct disadvantage for the latter and a strong incentive for it to seek university status. Despite strong resistance, the province's department of education gave St. Dunstan's its approval. By 1960 the University had a complete bachelor's degree program in education.

Few would have guessed at this point that in the near future a far greater struggle would occur, this time involving the very survival of both St. Dunstan's and Prince of Wales. Both schools experienced a period of development in the early 1960s. Creation of regional high schools and the arrival of the first baby boomers at university age expanded enrolments. In 1962 a newly formed citizens' committee began to lobby for the elevation of Prince of Wales College to a university, and in 1964 the provincial legislature gave it degree-granting status. The new university was to be strictly non-sectarian and autonomous with its own board of governors and senate. Since the vote on the bill followed an acrimonious debate in which the governing Conservative Party was split, the legislation provided that the act would be proclaimed only after a provincial royal commission had investigated the whole issue of higher education on the Island. Although the royal commission subsequently recommended that PWC be made a university, it urged the two institutions of higher learning to co-operate closely and to keep in mind the possibility of federating into a University of Prince Edward Island.

The commission also anticipated that both Island universities would phase out their courses for senior high school students and concentrate exclusively on post-secondary education. That meant Charlottetown would be required to provide facilities for its senior high school pupils. Planning for this got under way with some sense of urgency. Nearby Charlottetown Rural High School had already begun to prepare to accommodate the senior students from its district. The decision to build Colonel Gray Senior High School came after "a great deal of study and assessment." One important issue involved funding. Because the province provided funding for schools outside

Charlottetown and Summerside, the school board wanted some of that aid to flow to the city. The municipality eventually applied for a loan under the provincial development and loan act of 1963. When built, the new school would offer classes for city students in grades ten to twelve. Grades seven to nine would continue to attend the junior high schools. Colonel Gray Senior High School opened in September 1966.

Meanwhile, PWC's Principal Frank MacKinnon was planning for new facilities, including a gymnasium, library and a concourse or rotunda to link the existing academic building to the vocational school. He was also exploring innovative pedagogical approaches, and envisioned a small liberal arts university with high academic standards along the lines, perhaps, of Trent University in Peterborough, Ontario. At the same time, others were experiencing second thoughts about having two universities in such a small province. In 1964 a "university study group" of about 21 physicians, clerics, lawyers and educators from both sides of the religious divide was formed to reconsider the merits of the single university concept. They concluded that one university made the most sense financially and academically. More to the point, the new Liberal premier, Alex Campbell, was eventually convinced that they were right.

Clearly there were problems with the existing structure of higher education. Both institutions were operating at a loss while paying the lowest salaries in Canada. Although only 8 per cent of Islanders between 18 and 24 were attending university in 1968, the province had the highest percentage in Canada of students enrolled at an out-of-province university. Courses and facilities were being duplicated while applied and technical arts were neglected. The government's severe budget problems left little room to manoeuvre. Campbell's government had to get "interim financing" from Ottawa to pay its employees during its first summer in office. The fact that the provincial government had been given full control of federal funds dedicated to higher education provided it with the leverage to impose its will. Development Plan officials also backed the one university approach. On April 2, 1968, Campbell introduced a white paper on higher education. It proposed a single, non-denominational university and a college of applied arts and technology. All government funding would be directed to those institutions.

Both existing universities had reached the end of the line. Reaction at St. Dunstan's was muted at first, and most students backed a single, secular university.[64] Not so at PWC where there was a belief that its academic excellence and non-denominational nature fulfilled the requirements to become the single, secular, provincial university. Principal MacKinnon resigned as did 16 faculty members.[65] Many students openly

64 Eventually a group of laymen, "The Catholic Committee for a Just Community," reacted to the plans by calling upon the church to keep control of St. Dunstan's. The issue was resolved when a Department of Religion was created and chaplains were appointed. The province, although nearly bankrupt, purchased the St. Dunstan's property for $5.7 million.

65 MacKinnon's departure was inevitable given the lack of consultation between the government and PWC and the ultimate direction of the government's policy. Many sympathized with his position; some gloated. MacKinnon had alienated a number in the community by his drive, ambition and seeming lack of modesty. He left the province for Alberta, prompting former premier Walter Shaw to comment, "We have lost one of the most accomplished men we have ever produced here."

demonstrated their outrage. Premier Campbell claimed that the decision was in the best interests of the taxpayer and dismissed charges of government infringement on academic freedom as the opinions of those who were "either uninformed, badly misled or simply ignoring the rapid changes which have taken place in society." All protests were for naught. In September 1969, the new University of Prince Edward Island welcomed its first students at the site of the former St. Dunstan's University. Holland College, a community institution of applied arts and technology, began operations in the former Prince of Wales College the same year.[66]

The reformed structure of higher education made economic and administrative sense and met the educational needs of the province, but there were hidden costs to pay. Supporters of PWC lamented what they regarded as the loss of its distinctive academic tradition, while those affiliated with St. Dunstan's mourned the loss of "soul." Detractors on all sides agreed that the new university failed to connect with the grassroots of Islanders. As for Holland College, it served a utilitarian purpose but lacked any kind of tradition. Yet time would reveal certain advantages. Holland College was well-positioned to obtain the right to house the Atlantic Police Academy. Headed by an ex-RCMP officer, W. J. R. MacDonald, it opened in 1971 to serve all of the region's police forces.[67] Similarly, UPEI had not completed the first phase of its development plan before beginning a campaign to have a veterinary college for the Maritimes placed on its campus.[68] City Council and the Chamber of Commerce actively supported UPEI's cause. While higher education's structural reform was undertaken with the interests of the provincial exchequer and students in mind, the economic and social advantages of two expanding institutions in the city were not lost on local political and business leaders.

Public Health

The administration of public health in Charlottetown tracked postwar changes in attitudes towards the role of government in social issues. At first, the medical challenges were familiar, and the solutions involved the traditional approach of isolating the ill and treating them in institutions. Tuberculosis continued to plague the province, and in 1945 the provincial government added a new wing to the sanatorium. In addition, medical advisors to the provincial government's Reconstruction Committee recommended a laboratory be installed there. Outbreaks of infantile paralysis, or poliomyelitis (polio), were a widely dreaded threat. In 1946, an epidemic year, space was made available at the sanatorium for the care of crippled children.

---

66 In April 1977, the Provincial Vocational Institute and Summerside Vocational High School were integrated with Holland College. The College began to widen its offerings to more than post-secondary students in 1975.

67 In the first graduating class, nine of the cadets were from PEI, four of whom were Charlottetonians.

68 In 1975 Dean H. G. Howell, of the Ontario Veterinary College, along with the Maritime Provinces Higher Education Commission, recommended the installation of an Atlantic School of Veterinary Medicine on the UPEI campus.

Conventional wisdom still held that the disease was waterborne, so beaches, puddles and water fountains were to be avoided. In truth the root cause of the disease was poorly understood as were appropriate treatments. Significantly, postwar medical advisors urged that various public health officials be appointed to deal with matters as diverse as sanitation, venereal diseases and care of the newborn and children. That advice presaged greater efforts at health maintenance through public health measures and better preventative medicine.

The 1950s were a decade of significant progress for public health. New drugs were cutting the death rate from tuberculosis to a point where the closure of the sanatorium could be anticipated, and new infections were reduced through efforts such as the widespread testing program that began in the city in January 1957. Polio subsided after 1955 with the development of effective anti-viral vaccines by Drs. Jonas Salk and Albert Sabin. The willingness of government to intervene to ensure adequate provision of health care was likewise becoming apparent in the mid-1950s, to the extent that the city's health officer declared complete state medicine was only "one step away." Although comprehensive state medical insurance was, in fact, years away, significant progress to that end was being made. A city-operated dental clinic was established by the early 1950s, and a second dentist was hired in 1959 to cope with demand. Children received treatment free of charge, ensuring a basic level of oral health. By the early 1960s, those unable to afford medical insurance had their expenses covered by the Hospital Commission and the Department of Health and Welfare.

In an effort to be proactive, City Council in 1952 decided to work with the province to establish a municipal board of health charged with, among other things, the inspection of milk, meat, fish and other foods.[69] There was much to do in this area, particularly in monitoring the production and serving of food. A 1947 survey had revealed a wide variation in the quality of milk produced in the city. This situation was addressed by a corrective by-law passed in February 1949. By 1953 sanitary inspectors regularly visited the plants of the six milk processors that sold their products in the city, taking samples for evaluation. Although 99 per cent of the milk supply was being pasteurized, problems continued. In 1961, for instance, two dairies were found to be producing sub-standard milk. On the other hand, the city's Health Officer, Dr. W. L. MacDonald, told Council that meat inspection would accomplish little other than to appease complainers. Later in 1959, Council rejected an offer by a veterinarian to inspect stores selling fresh meat.

Food production was not the only concern.[70] Inspections of restaurants, hotels and other eating establishments turned up numerous shortcomings.[71] In May 1961, only two of the city's restaurants managed to meet health standards. This revelation

69 Eventually many of these duties were passed to the equivalent provincial agency.

70 The Health Officer noted in 1956 that barber shops needed to be cleaner.

71 This work was conducted after 1957 by the Sanitary Engineering Division of the provincial Department of Health and Welfare under an agreement with the city.

produced considerable controversy in which demands for the restaurants to be named were countered by protests that such publicity would hurt the restaurant business. Compliance improved after offenders were finally named, but when cleanliness declined again in September, the Health Officer suggested that this time delinquents should be named, charged and fined.[72] This possibility seemed to have prompted a sustained improvement. The following year, most restaurants were safe. As more opened, the sheer number and variety of establishments to police eventually became a problem according to the Health Officer.

Garbage collection was another concern that grew increasingly troublesome in the postwar era, a sign perhaps of impending throw-away consumerism. Refuse, abandoned on private property and left in the streets, was a long-standing complaint. Waste collection was done on a private, voluntary basis in 1947, when Councillor David Stewart announced that he had prepared a by-law for compulsory garbage collection. Such service remained an individual obligation and one that some shirked. In 1957 the Health Officer suggested that the city assume full responsibility for garbage collection. After much delay,[73] action was taken in December 1963 when the city awarded a contract for city-wide garbage collection to the Jenkins and Clark Company. With this new service came regulations on how citizens were to dispose of various items, but few complained. The move was fairly popular with the citizenry as a whole.

Collecting waste was one matter; getting rid of it was another. A properly managed disposal site required a landfill to minimize the rat problem, an incinerator to reduce the volume of accumulation and controlled access to monitor what was discarded. Charlottetown's dump had none of these requisites. By May 1946, it was an obvious environmental hazard. City Council made plans to open a new dump. Councillors also investigated the purchase of an incinerator but did not pursue the matter. In 1950 a major pollution problem was eliminated when Canada Packers was prohibited from using the old dump for manure and other wastes. Other problems persisted. A privately owned site at the north end of the city on land forming part of the Connolly estate was closed in July 1953 after a disagreement between Council and the Department of Health. By 1959 the facility near Parkdale was filling up and fires were becoming a menace. Council began to discuss the need for an alternate location and the use of clay fill to suppress some of the worst nuisances. Little was done, essentially for reasons of cost, but in August 1961, after a fire had burned at the dump for a week, Council again looked at the purchase of an incinerator. By then, the dump was nearly full.

The dump, in the opinion of the Health Officer, was an "eyesore and a disgrace." It and summer street litter showed "a lack of civic pride." In May 1962, the city purchased a farm that it thought would, with the use of an incinerator, fill its needs for a

72 Twelve establishments were operating without a licence.

73 No decision to this effect was made in 1957, and in 1962 calls were still being heard for the institution of compulsory collection.

century, but residents in the area complained, and the province blocked the project. Instead, a site up the Hillsborough River from the Riverside Hospital was selected in 1964, and a teepee-style incinerator was erected. Soon, newly arrived neighbours in Hillsborough Village were complaining about smoke from the incinerator. The dump was expected to serve suburban communities as well as the city, producing the inevitable problems of political co-ordination. Then high energy prices sparked a change. The PEI Energy Corporation installed a heating plant for the new Queen Elizabeth Hospital which used municipal waste for fuel. The dump was closed and covered over to be turned into a park. This did not end the problems of garbage disposal in Charlottetown, but it did move the city from the position of just coping with waste management to that of being a cautious innovator.

The same prudent innovation can be seen in the provision of health care services. In its 1946 report, the advisory committee on reconstruction noted that there was a particular need to focus on mental health in the province. Conditions at Falconwood in the late 1940s were not good, and, until 1949, the number of mentally retarded children was not even known. In 1952 a mental health clinic opened in Charlottetown as an effort in "preventive psychiatry." It functioned on a part-time basis and would soon include the services of two psychiatrists, a psychologist, a social service worker and a guidance consultant. The following year, at the request of the province, representatives of the American Psychiatric Association inspected the Falconwood Hospital and Provincial Infirmary. They found many shortcomings. Some of the needs included a separate school for children with mental retardation, and special facilities for disturbed patients, for patients with tuberculosis and for geriatric patients. The upshot of this report was a new hospital, Hillsborough General, which featured "the very best treatment for early and relatively acute psychiatric ailments." Nearby Falconwood was renamed Riverside Hospital, partly in the hope of shedding some of the negative connotations associated with the old name. Next, the provincial government created a new institution to provide treatment and training for "mentally defective children," the 21-bed Sherwood Hospital which opened in March 1962. It was a combination of hospital, home and school for mentally handicapped children up to 19 years old who could benefit from short periods of care and for those who could no longer remain with their families.

In some respects, even greater changes were in store for the Charlottetown and Prince Edward Island Hospitals. The widespread use of Blue Cross hospital insurance in the years after the Second World War made it possible for more people to be hospitalized when such care was required and to stay longer once there, putting additional pressure on the two general hospitals. Matters worsened after 1959 when the province implemented a health insurance plan that covered paediatric and out-patient services. A 1958 survey investigated ways in which the two institutions could rationalize their services. In 1965 representatives of both hospitals discussed the possibility of a single paediatric unit. As a result, the boards of the two hospitals began to consider the possibility of a merger to end the duplication of expensive equipment and highly trained personnel. Both institutions required substantial upgrades. The wing of the

PEI Hospital built in 1933 needed replacement, and the Charlottetown Hospital's radiology and physical therapy departments were inadequate.

Although amalgamation intrigued the boards and was favoured by a 1967 consultant's report, there were impediments, such as "overcoming ... old religious prejudices and changing patterns of hospital service and practice." In the words of the report, there was a need "to cultivate support of the medical community and the clergy." In particular, the ongoing role of the Sisters of St. Martha in the new institution would be important to resolve. There was also the question of where to build a combined hospital. The Charlottetown Hospital site was too small. While it could fit onto the site of the Prince Edward Island Hospital, the consultants favoured a location across from St. Dunstan's University. In any case, the time was not right for amalgamation.

The need for improved medical facilities soon became acute. The province's universal medical coverage came into effect on December 1, 1970, and with it even greater demands for service. Charlottetown's two hospitals drew patients from across the Island, and this clientele added significantly to demand. In 1971 a Department of National Health and Welfare study found obsolete mechanical and electrical equipment and problems connected with the structure, plumbing and fire equipment at the Charlottetown Hospital, with similar shortcomings at the PEI Hospital. A joint committee of medical staffs and board members from the two hospitals, struck in 1970, favoured a new, combined institution. A further National Health and Welfare report, completed in 1972, confirmed this as the best option. A committee with representatives from the provincial government, the two hospitals and professional consultants began to plan the new facility, and a Board of Trustees was appointed. In August 1974, Mayor Elmer M. MacRae met with the Minister of Health, Catherine Callbeck, to discuss where the hospital could be constructed. The most likely site was near the existing Hillsborough Hospital. Plans went forward in 1974 even though the government was beginning to waver on the issue.[74] Declaring that the hospital was not the government's project nor the government's hospital, the medical community pressed its case, but there was a lot of bravado in their proclamations. The proposed $29 million project was the largest in Island history at the time. The province was expected to pay $24 million; the federal government $1.5 to $2.5 million; and $3 million was to be raised from the community by subscription. Until it was clear that the province would participate in the financing, the city was cautious about becoming involved. Newly elected mayor Frank Zakem and his Council feared the hospital might become a financial dead weight. By the summer of 1975, however, the hospital board appeared ready to call for tenders, but abruptly, in September, the provincial government withdrew its funding support, claiming public indifference,

---

74 Plans followed the "Best Buy" concept developed in the United Kingdom. This approach involved the implementation of three criteria for the project: the utmost economy in construction that is consistent with accepted medical and nursing standards, standards of design and construction that are no higher than are necessary, and design that provides for efficient internal layout and full amenities for patients and pleasant working conditions for staff.

medical apathy and uncertainty on the part of the federal government. The province also had a tight budget.

The medical community retaliated by forming "Doctors United for a Single Hospital" to argue that the new hospital was not for the physicians but for the patients. The issue was not so much the need to increase the number of beds over what existed in current facilities, but to provide expensive equipment and back-up services in one place. Dr. Harry Callaghan declared in a letter to the *Guardian* that a new hospital would be "the major advance in health care in a generation." Dr. K. C. Grant argued that the cost of a new hospital was $20 million less than bringing the two existing facilities up to national standards. Psychiatrist Dr. M. N. "Mac" Beck pointed out the advantages of having diagnostic services for mental patients near the Hillsborough Hospital. Not all members of the medical profession supported the new hospital, including some of the nurses. Gradually, though, public opinion coalesced behind the project, and, in March 1977, Premier Campbell announced that it could go ahead with provincial backing. The federal Department of Veterans Affairs would contribute $1 million, and $2.8 million for equipment and furniture would have to be raised through public contribution.

Completion of the Queen Elizabeth Hospital triggered changes to other facets of medical services in Charlottetown. Its size permitted residency training in certain specialities. More importantly, the new hospital made possible the rationalization of the city's health care network. The vacated Prince Edward Island Hospital became the Prince Edward Home, replacing the previous PEI Hospital building on Kensington Road which had served as a home for the aged but lacked modern amenities, particularly activity areas. As the chronic care hospital in the old Beach Grove Hotel was a fire hazard with no clinic and a small kitchen, residents from there also moved to the Prince Edward Home.[75] The former Provincial Sanatorium on McGill Avenue housed both a rehabilitation centre and a mental health clinic. The clinic, in particular, had been swamped with patients since 1967. The new hospital provided badly needed space. Some patients from the McGill Avenue building were moved into the Queen Elizabeth Hospital when it opened, while others were transferred to the Prince Edward Home. The sanatorium remained in use, however, serving in part as an addictions centre.[76]

The massive restructuring of Charlottetown's hospital network was part of a trend in the delivery of health care. Highly trained specialists and costly equipment were more effectively utilized in larger institutional settings. There were also changes in the front-line delivery of medical services. Patients were less likely to be treated in their homes, and practitioners were more inclined to work in clusters rather than on their own. The Polyclinic had foreshadowed this development. After the war, new physicians were added to its staff and medical services were provided in a greater variety of

75 The facility was renovated and turned into a long-term care home.

76 The sanatorium was eventually closed and torn down in 2001.

specialties. To house the expanded operation, a bigger clinic opened on Fitzroy Street in June 1949. The following year, the Polyclinic's success prompted four physicians connected with the Charlottetown Hospital to open the Charlottetown Clinic. Their aim was to provide family medical services with as many specialized services as possible. The clinic was originally located in a former livery stable on Queen Street, but, by 1960, the arrival of two additional specialists and more nurses and administrative staff resulted in a new clinic being built at the corner of Rochford and Sydney Streets. By 1975 the building had been expanded twice, in 1968 and 1973, and the number of practitioners had grown to 18. Similar expansion took place at the Polyclinic; it had 22 full-time practitioners by 1981. These clinics, innovative in their time and resented by some members of the medical fraternity, had been instrumental in vastly expanding the range of medical services and technical expertise in the city. The doctors at the Polyclinic were generally connected with the Prince Edward Island Hospital and hence the city's Protestant community, while those at the Charlottetown Clinic had links to the Charlottetown Hospital and the Catholic population. With a single state-of-the-art hospital and declining sectarian allegiances, the *raison d'être* of the two community medical clinics lessened somewhat. The Charlottetown Clinic closed soon after the Queen Elizabeth Hospital opened. Some of its physicians moved to the Riverside Medical Centre, and others opened individual offices.

Water and Sewerage

Until 1945, Charlottetown's water supply was adequate for ordinary demand, but during dry spells or periods of high consumption, shortages could occur. Renewed urban growth in the postwar years made acquiring new water sources an imperative. In 1947 the search began. The water commission's consultant, W. S. Lea, recommended that 10 wells be sunk at the Union Road site that had been briefly considered in 1927. It yielded a very considerable flow of water, second only to the Brackley Point Road wells. By 1949 chlorinated water was being piped from the Union pumping station to the Brackley main line and on to the reservoir. These additional supplies allowed the city to cope with increased usage and a gave a margin of comfort in meeting existing requirements. Besides the new wells, the water commission constructed dams along the steams adjacent to the Brackley and Malpeque Road water stations. By holding back the water, these dams helped to maintain the water table by increasing the moisture content of the surrounding land. Finally, City Council prohibited new connections to the water system by anyone outside city limits, and those already connected saw their rates go up to double the city level.

Although the city was now adequately supplied with water, the same was not true for suburban areas. Requests from Parkdale and Spring Park in 1950 for help in establishing waterworks were rebuffed by Eugene Cullen, then Minister of Industry and Natural Resources, who argued that such aid would set a precedent for other communities and the province could not provide for them all. Although testing indicated in 1952 that the safety of water from wells in suburban areas had improved, several investigations conducted in 1954 found seriously contaminated wells in Spring Park and Parkdale. The provincial department of health and welfare speculated that the threat of an epidemic with loss of life had existed. Fire protection was another major consideration in seeking piped water service. Provincial government studies concluded in 1954 that a waterworks and sewerage system were required for the entire suburban area beyond Charlottetown. Two years later, the city along with Parkdale and Sherwood recognized that a united approach was needed to address their common water and sewerage problems.

For its part, the city was most concerned with its fringes, Park Street, Upper Queen and the area west of North River Road just south of the city limits. As they were not yet densely settled, installing water mains and sewers in these places had financial implications for ratepayers generally. After failing to pressure the province into taking on the task, the city hired W. H. Crandall Engineering Associates of Moncton, New Brunswick, to compare the costs of separate and integrated water and sewerage systems for Charlottetown and the neighbouring communities and propose a design for the preferred system. In their 1957 report, the engineers stated that separate systems were "utterly ridiculous" because "topography, which governs sewer design, seldom recognizes municipal boundaries." Hence, the three separate drainage areas along the city's northern limits could be most cheaply served by integrating them into the existing system. Then, extending services to the neighbouring communities "would involve little additional [water] storage." Crandall believed that water supplies were adequate but likely to be stressed in fire emergencies, and, therefore, he recommended installing meters to curb wastage.[77] No action was taken with respect to the meters, but, armed with this report, the water commission extended water mains in the unserviced areas by 1960.

By this time, problems had been identified with the ability to move water through the system. A New York firm, Pitometer Associates, was hired in 1961 to survey the water lines for leaks. They found losses due to leakage in both the underground pipes and some customers' toilets and taps. More seriously, the overall capacity of the system was less than one-half of that needed for fire purposes. This deficiency had serious implications for fire safety and, hence, insurance rates, and plans were quickly prepared to redress the situation. A new reservoir was built beside the existing one on Mount Edward Road, and a large transmission main was laid from the reservoir to the distribution system on Belvedere Avenue. New distribution mains were then laid southward from Belvedere Avenue. Older pipes were reinforced, and inspections of water fixtures in private buildings were conducted to discover those that were defective and to order their repair. All of this work was completed by 1964. One step recommended by the New York firm was rejected by the water commission: meters were still not put onto private residences because it was cheaper to live with the wastage.

Continued growth in demand for water renewed fears of water shortages by 1967. A new 500-foot-deep well was bored that year at the Brackley site. Tests were

77 One additional pumping station was needed to cover summer demand. The existing system, with the possible exception of some extensions completed during the Second World War, was in excellent repair and was functioning as designed.

subsequently conducted at both the Brackley and Union well fields to see if both shallow and deep wells would provide further reliable supplies. Shallow wells less than 100 feet deep proved the best option. Suburban growth brought ever-increasing demands for more water. Hillsborough Park asked to be connected to the city's system in 1971. Although the provincial government favoured the step, the city was reluctant. Eventually, Hillsborough residents were serviced by Sherwood which, in turn, bought its water from Charlottetown. By 1974 demand throughout the system had increased over 50 per cent in a decade, and further distribution capacity was needed.

Following another study, this time by Canadian-British Consultants Limited, a large main to deliver increased flows of water from the Brackley and Union well sites was laid along Union and St. Peter's Roads to the main on Mount Edward Road. Suburban demand necessitated the construction of a booster station at Sherwood to meet the needs of customers in that community and beyond, as well as at the new airport. Less than 7 per cent of the latter project's costs was borne by Charlottetown. The rest came from Sherwood and the provincial and federal governments. With further requirements in mind, the water commission decided in 1982 to participate in a survey of the Winter River to discover future sources of water and to find the best way to manage supplies. There was clearly going to be an ongoing need to find more water, and this was equally clearly going to have to be done on a regional basis.[78]

As early critics of municipal water service pointed out, piped water inevitably created problems of disposal. In the postwar era, sewerage became entangled with the much larger issue of environmental degradation as pollution became a growing concern. The original sewerage system involved separate lines for storm water and sewage. Sanitary waste was pumped into the harbour through an outfall at the foot of Pownal Street. Although the use of blind wells, or outhouses, was completely banned in 1952, not all areas were connected to the sewers. Those without connections used septic tanks, which sometimes overflowed in wet seasons. Little was done to resolve the situation during the 1950s, although the city allowed Parkdale to build a sewer line along streets in Charlottetown to an outfall into the Hillsborough River. Sewage from the area of Belmont, John, Beech and Park Streets emptied into the Hillsborough at the eastern end of town as well. Sewerage, for the residents of Sherwood, also involved the Hillsborough River. Construction of their system began at the outfall and worked inland until all of the community was serviced. Installation of water lines in Sherwood generally came after the sewers.

After amalgamating with Spring Park in 1958, the city commissioned Crandall Associates to design a sewer network for its unserviced western districts. Unlike the original system, the new one was to combine sanitary sewage and storm water. Work on the first stage of the project proceeded reasonably smoothly. New lines were laid in the area east of North River Road to collect effluent and carry it past Government

78 Between 1964 and 1968, water consumption by water commission customers increased from 1.82 million gallons per day to 2.22 million gallons. Individual usage jumped from 97.4 gallons per day to 116.2 gallons.

Pond to an outfall running 1,200 to 2,500 feet into the mouth of the North River. A cheaper option to pump this sewage into the harbour at the foot of Connolly's Wharf had been opposed by the Health Officer, Dr. W. L. MacDonald. The area west of North River Road was more problematic. A main sewer line, with outfalls at both ends,[79] was to run parallel to the North River shore between Kirkwood Avenue and York Lane. While these plans were being considered, a newspaper report from Summerside alleged that an engineer working for Crandall had completed a survey that showed pollution in the harbour was already bad enough to make a sewage treatment plant necessary. This came as a surprise to both Mayor Edwin C. Johnstone and Chairman of the Water Commission, Roy Bevan. Heretofore a plant had never been seriously suggested. It was not a welcome idea for budget-conscious politicians.

The suburban sewage debate intensified towards the end of 1959. Dr. MacDonald initially opposed plans to discharge waste into the North River off Kirkwood Drive, but he changed his mind on the understanding that solids in the outflow would be ground and chlorinated first.[80] Even so, fears persisted that the North River and Brighton Shore would become polluted. Landowners from York Point and along the North River petitioned City Council to dump the sewage into the harbour instead.[81] Pollution in the North River, they claimed, would block cottage development and force the Red Cross to cancel swimming lessons. Residents of Brighton, Charlottetown's most prestigious district, mobilized to advocate costly changes to the projected plan. They also sought independent expert advice on possible alternatives to the Crandall scheme. Council reviewed the various options at a meeting held on April 11, 1960. Crandall Associates stuck with their proposal for an outfall at the end of York Lane. The water commission, on the other hand, favoured pumping the sewage from York Lane to the existing outfall at Government Pond. In the end, City Council adopted the water commission's plan.

The increasing use of the harbour and adjoining rivers as a sewage lagoon began to take its toll. The Health Officer reported during the summer of 1960 that the water quality at the swimming areas near the western end of town was poor. By June 1962, Dr. MacDonald warned citizens that very high bacteria counts made swimming dangerous in the Hillsborough River, particularly between the bridge and the Riverside Hospital, and in the area in the North River between Kent Street and HMCS Queen Charlotte. In response, officials from the city and province met to discuss the nature of the pollution and investigate solutions. Meanwhile, the water was to be tested daily and the public advised of pollution levels. Cancellation of swimming classes at

79 The Kirkwood Drive outfall would carry mainly excess runoff during severe storms, perhaps once a month according to Crandall.

80 Crandall recommended a Barminutor that would grind and accelerate the effects of oxygen on the bacteria.

81 Interestingly, there was a sewage outfall at York Point and another from Beach Grove which emptied raw sewage into the North River at this time. These concerned Dr. MacDonald but attracted less public attention.

After debating the merits of discharging sewage from the growing western suburbs directly into the North River, the city opted to have it pumped to the existing outfall at Government Pond.

Kirkwood Drive beach sparked an upwelling of protest in Brighton. One complainer blamed the problem on Beach Grove. The provincial government promptly resolved to treat the sewage from Beach Grove and the Riverside Hospital. In addition, a Water Pollution Advisory Committee was established with representatives from Charlottetown, Parkdale, Sherwood, the provincial government and the water commission. The problem was recognized as regional, not local to the city.

A study by J. L. Richards and Associates of Ottawa, completed in December 1963, confirmed that the harbour from Victoria Park to the Riverside Hospital was significantly polluted, though there was no serious pollution of the entire harbour and river estuaries. The principal sources were the Canada Packers plant, the Parkdale outfall and the Dorchester Street pumping station. As a solution, the consultants recommended an interceptor line running from the Parkdale outfall to a large, new outfall at *HMCS Queen Charlotte*.[82] They also suggested that sewage be chlorinated prior to discharge, and that the city tighten its by-laws to control waste from industries and government agencies. The city could also return to separate systems for storm water and sanitary sewage and build a sanitary trunk sewer for its northwestern sector.

82 This would carry sewage from Parkdale, Canada Packers, the Park and Beech Streets area, plus the effluent from the Pownal Street outfall.

Despite a cautiously favourable response from the advisory committee, there was little progress on implementing the report. Over two years later, the complaints that gave rise to the Richards study were still being heard at City Hall. They continued for the rest of the decade as the smell from the harbour and Hillsborough River at low tide became notorious.

One recommendation from Richards was acted upon: in 1965 Prince Edward Island established a water authority similar to those in New Brunswick and Nova Scotia. Under this agency, the advisory committee was expanded to include eight communities in the greater Charlottetown area. A consulting engineer completed a new study of the harbour in 1968 with a view to providing a master sewerage plan for the entire metropolitan area. Part of the Comprehensive Development Plan addressed the need for sewage treatment plants in five designated growth centres. Charlottetown, of course, was one of the centres. Making the capital part of an Island pollution control program may have defused charges of favouritism. Planners also concluded that a single plant should serve Charlottetown, Parkdale and Sherwood; a single facility would require fewer personnel and control the treatment processes better. Besides, there was no suitable location for a city-only plant.

A preliminary study for such a plant was completed in 1970–71 and subsequently approved by the three municipal Councils. Initial cost of the project was expected to be $3 million, of which part was covered by provincial and federal grants. A new regional authority, the Charlottetown Area Pollution Control Commission, was created to manage the facility, and it was granted a federal loan. Twenty-five per cent of the amount was forgivable as was one-quarter of the interest. The objective was to treat all municipal wastes and allow for recreation and further urban development without deterioration of the water quality in the harbour. Construction began on a site on Riverside Drive in Parkdale. Costs rose to $4 million, but with federal grants the municipal share only rose from $1,260,000 (42 per cent of $3 million) to $1,332,000 (33.3 per cent of $4 million).[83] The plant employed a sludge-refining system that produced gas to heat the building and mud to be trucked to a waste disposal site. When it opened officially in October 1975, pollution levels in the water of the harbour showed a "vast improvement." People were again able to swim at various points around the harbour and adjoining river estuaries, including Victoria Park, York Point, Rosebank, West River and Bunbury. Not all problems were resolved, however. Pollution from Canada Packers and oil still found its way into the water, and development at the edge of the metropolitan area meant ongoing expansion of the sewerage system. Once again, experience with pollution control and sewerage demonstrated that thinking regionally was becoming a hallmark of governance in the Charlottetown area. The need for sound planning and efficient, effective public administration was forcing individual communities to look beyond their particular boundaries for solutions to many of their challenges.

83 Funding sources were listed as PEI, one-third; Ottawa, one-third; the federal Department of Regional Economic Expansion, one-sixth; Canada Mortgage and Housing Corporation, one-sixth.

Public Safety

While environmental protection took new forms, public security involved more conventional issues. In February 1946, a total of 97 arrests were made in Charlottetown, most for drunkenness. This came at a time when the Chief of Police had already complained that the force was seriously understaffed. In March 1946, Council passed a resolution to seek permission from the province to have the city policed by the RCMP. Responsibility for public safety stayed, however, with the city, and enforcement of prohibition remained a problem. The police formed a three-man committee in December 1946 to ensure the prohibition act was obeyed. After prohibition was replaced in 1948 by a new temperance act that was effectively a system of liquor control, the revenue from fines imposed under it was directed to the province, which meant that the city now bore the cost of enforcing liquor regulations without the benefit of income for its efforts. This situation was reversed in April 1949, but alcohol remained a burden for law enforcement. Bootleggers thrived, and the occasional merchant sold shaving lotion and other alcohol-based fluids as a beverage.[84] Even after regulations were considerably loosened in the 1960s, enforcement continued to be a challenge.

It was not the peccadilloes of the drinking public that ultimately caused the police force its greatest grief, but its own deficiencies. Some of these, again, had a connection with manpower issues. The complaints of understaffing raised immediately after the Second World War were not adequately addressed for over two decades. Occasionally, an additional officer was added to the force, but the total overall complement remained below the norm for cities of Charlottetown's size. In addition, the force got stuck with tasks that were only marginally within the realm of police work. At various times, these included animal control, when the city found it difficult to retain the services of a dogcatcher, and tax collection. This lack of manpower and its inefficient deployment had implications for crime prevention. The police blamed a spate of burglaries in 1976 on a shortage of personnel.

By 1965 the force comprised 25 officers when, according to the chief, it should have had 33. Understaffing continued into the 1970s, and there were only 29 officers in 1972, at which point in time a study was launched to assess the department's requirements. The Henthorne Report on civic administration, completed in November 1972, recommended the force be given an additional 10 police officers over the next three years, as well as new facilities, and that a Deputy Chief and four of the new officers be hired within the year.[85] There were also operational difficulties within the force. Problems with overcrowding at the Queens County Jail in 1963 resulted in prisoners being released almost as soon as they were incarcerated. Discipline within the police force became a concern. In a serious incident in 1964, a police officer was accused of beating a handcuffed offender to the point that onlookers feared for his life. Matters

---

84 Vanilla and lemon extract are reported to have been popular beverages as well.

85 Charlottetown's ratio of police officers to population in 1972 was 1.3 per 1,000, the same as Summerside. The national average was 1.9 per 1,000 while in New Brunswick it was 2.1 per 1,000.

seemed to deteriorate in the 1970s. In 1974 a policeman was charged with assault after an incident at the county jail. Some officers were accused of napping during the night shift. There were reports of drunkenness, sometimes on liquor filched from the police bond room. One constable reportedly called a bootlegger to restock a party at his home. Most of this was covered up, but one incident dating back to June 1976 prompted an enquiry in February 1977. Two constables had searched a car and found 58 bottles of beer in the trunk. They seized the bottles and took them to the police station. Because the bottles had been legally stored in the trunk, they had to be returned to the owner, but 12 bottles had meanwhile gone missing. The problem was resolved by giving the owner 12 bottles taken from someone else. Unfortunately, the missing 12 bottles, complete with police seals, turned up in Kensington. The public then got wind of the whole affair.

Troubles within the department raised concerns about leadership. In 1963 Sterns Webster was appointed Chief of Police, replacing Charles W. MacArthur who had been chief since 1949. A member of the force since 1939 and deputy chief at the time of his appointment, Webster was not expected to rock the boat. These expectations were in part borne out. During Webster's watch, significant changes were made with respect to equipment. The wider use of patrol cars made the force more mobile, radar was acquired to control speeders in 1964 and side arms were issued as standard equipment in 1973. He failed, however, to invoke substantial organizational change. Relations between the police and the public were also highlighted as problematic. In 1974 City Council decided the time had come to import some Upper Canadian efficiency. This was in keeping with the mood of the times, in bureaucratic circles at least, and as a result a senior member of the Metropolitan Toronto Police, Donald Saunders, was hired as chief. His task was to reorganize the ranks "into a more efficient, effective unit."

Matters did not go well for Chief Saunders. Initially, he had hopes of transforming the force from a paramilitary organization into one in which individual officers would contribute their ideas. The police would be encouraged to treat the public with respect and to undertake further training and education. He introduced other changes as well. A "platoon" system was established wherein police officers were inspected daily and then assigned to specific cars to patrol prescribed areas of the city. He also expected officers to keep notebooks in which details of all activities were entered. Finally, officers were no longer allowed to go home for lunch but were given one hour to take their meals at the station. Hostile reaction was almost immediate, especially among more senior members of the force who objected to Toronto practices in a Charlottetown situation. Two resigned, and others signed a petition asking Council to remove their boss. Mayor Frank Zakem and three aldermen formed a review committee and interviewed various parties. They reaffirmed their confidence in the chief but concluded that additional middle managers were needed.

The review did not end the unrest. More resignations followed. Of the seven who quit by February 1976, all but one were veterans. Despite this unhappiness, city politicians found that the community was being better patrolled and that liaison with the RCMP had improved. Mayor Zakem agreed that the changes were necessary but felt that they could have been implemented less rigorously. Ongoing problems with the force prompted Zakem to ask Stanley Juniper, a consultant and former Mountie, to prepare a confidential report on the operations of the police department. Juniper proposed that the police committee should assume a greater role in developing policies, rules and regulations and that the arbitrary authority of the chief be curbed. The chief should also be given training in labour-management relations, and more effective channels of communications among the management of the force, the political overseers and the media should be established.

By the time the Juniper Report had been received, Premier Alex Campbell had appointed Justice Melvin McQuaid to hold an enquiry into the operations of the police force. By April 1977, McQuaid had learned of a department torn apart by "a lack of policies, rules or regulations, by uncertainty over who had final control and by unsatisfactory pay scales." He recommended the police committee and police commission be amalgamated, and all new policy orders and directives be effectively communicated to all members of the force. The force, in turn, had to build better links with the public. Justice McQuaid pointed his finger at City Council which, he charged, had failed in its duty of managing the police. No by-laws, for instance, concerning its operations had been enacted. He called for a by-law that would officially establish the force, provide rules, regulations and procedures for its operation and enact a code of discipline. Other recommendations addressed the behaviour of individual department members. As a result of these recommendations, some were fired or disciplined, and one accused officer was exonerated. By and large, Mayor Zakem accepted the need for the kinds of changes prescribed by Justice McQuaid. And what happened to Chief Saunders? He was fired in November 1979 after a clash with Mayor Frank Moran and replaced by Charles Ready, a 23-year veteran of the force.

In the Fire Department, most of the drama was operational rather than administrative. The spectacular fire that levelled the Market House on April 29, 1958, was only one of a number of major blazes to occur during the decades following the Second World War. On August 18, 1951, Whelan Memorial Hall and a number of important businesses were lost when a fire tore through the block bounded by University Avenue and Kent, Prince and Grafton Streets. The grandstand at the exhibition grounds suffered two serious fires in 1959, and several families were left homeless when an apartment building at the corner of Pownal and Water Streets was destroyed on the night of January 29, 1979. Despite these major conflagrations and myriad smaller fires, the incidence of such losses diminished, particularly after the early 1960s. The reason, it was claimed, was more efficient firefighting.[86]

The postwar era began with the fire department living with the legacy of the previous half-century. It was largely a volunteer force with three permanent officers who staffed the station round the clock, seven days a week. Some of their equipment was aging or inadequate, and such shortcomings limited their effectiveness. For instance,

86 The number of calls had risen.

The Fire Department continued to modernize after World War II. By 1973 there were four full-time staff and 52 volunteers with two ladder trucks and four pumper trucks.

by 1960, approximately 20 buildings in the city were too tall to be serviced without an aerial ladder truck, which the department lacked. Alerting the firemen when they were needed could also be problematic. After an alarm was telephoned to the fire station, individual firemen were notified by a magneto bell system with signal units in each volunteer's home. The equipment dated from 1889 and was what remained of a set-up that once included 24 alarm boxes installed on utility poles throughout the city. The alarm boxes proved unsatisfactory and were disconnected, and by 1950 the domestic circuits were malfunctioning as well. During one particular storm, the bells in the homes failed to operate, while on another occasion some of them jangled throughout the night. An air horn was acquired in 1951 to alert personnel who were away from their homes, and a new home alarm system was eventually procured.

The department also received more firefighters and new equipment. Pumper trucks were acquired in 1946 and 1947. Auxiliary firemen were added to the force in 1947 and again in 1952. A Fire Marshall, Herbert Jewell, was hired in 1950 with responsibilities for building inspection. He became a full-time Fire Marshall in 1961, and a Deputy Fire Marshall was named in 1959. A Chief Engineer was added to the department in 1966. In 1961 the city purchased an aerial ladder truck. By 1973 there were four full-time staff and 52 volunteers with two ladder trucks and four pumper trucks. Concurrent with these changes, other developments were making Charlottetown a safer place. These included the installation of sprinkler systems and heat detectors with alarm connections to the fire hall in various public buildings and the mandatory installation of smoke detectors in commercial properties and private homes.

Public Morality and Social Welfare

Housing, which had emerged as a problem before the war, continued to trouble the city. Returning veterans, some with war brides, competed for scarce accommodation. Not only was there an absolute shortage of housing, but many older homes were "dirty and dilapidated." Although City Council wanted to ensure repatriated soldiers remained in town to support the postwar economy, many arrivals were from other parts of the Island, and Council wanted the province to help finance their emergency accommodation. To alleviate the housing shortage, the city decided to establish residences in vacant buildings at the airport. Plans were unveiled in November 1945 and, by January 1946, 54 families were living at "Maple Hills," as the estate was named, with another 46 expected. The city anticipated that, in time, rents would recoup some of the cost of converting and refitting the airport buildings. Meanwhile, it pressed the province for financial help.

The shortage surprised some in government. The president of the federal Wartime Housing Limited, B. K. Boulton, claimed in February 1946 that neither had he heard of the problem in Charlottetown nor had his organization been approached about the situation in the city. His successor, Major-General H. A. Young, later stated that he had been told by Mayor Earle MacDonald that there was no emergency. The mayor for his part retorted that he did not know and had never communicated with the general. Eventually, the federal and provincial governments agreed to share the costs of the Maple Hills project on an equal basis, thus relieving the city of its burden. In 1948, however, the province decided to end the arrangement and, in doing so, federal involvement as well. Those living there faced eviction.

Apart from the airport development, hopes for a solution to the housing crisis had initially been pinned on a proposal by Housing Enterprises Limited to build 13 four-unit apartment buildings. A representative of the company came to Charlottetown in May 1945 and surveyed possible sites. Choosing a location east of Orlebar Street, the company asked the city to assist the project by fixing the assessment on the dwellings at $100,000. Then, in 50 years, the property would revert to the city. After winning the construction contract, M. F. Schurman went to Ottawa where he was promised priority with the required building materials. Canada was still subject to diverse controls at the time, and construction supplies were regulated by the Department of Reconstruction and Supply. Unfortunately, projected costs, at $300,000, were unexpectedly high and would result in rents of $50–60 per month. This was well in excess of what the intended market could bear. The scheme fell through. When C. D. Howe, the federal government's overbearing Minister of Reconstruction and Supply, was asked what the federal government was doing about the housing shortage in Charlottetown, he replied that City Council was "unfriendly and unco-operative." Whether that was true or not is hard to ascertain, but the upshot of the situation was that, although Council backed the Housing Enterprises project, the homes failed to materialize. The housing crisis continued.

By this time, a familiar pattern of growth had become apparent in Canadian cities: new residences were primarily constructed in the suburbs. Over time, this left the poorest members of the community living in older, deteriorating housing stock in the city centre. Many of these folk were unable to benefit from programs to assist in the construction of affordable homes, such as that which existed in the 1920s. Certainly, the free market was proving unable to provide them with adequate housing, either to own or to rent. Cities, as the frontline service providers when it came to housing their populations, faced a monumental task in this regard. The situation across the country was mirrored in Charlottetown.

Partial resolution of the problem came in 1946 when the federal government created the Central (now Canada) Mortgage and Housing Corporation to provide readily accessible mortgages to potential home-owners and promote the construction of affordable housing. The activities of the corporation soon expanded into the provision of social and rental housing. By October 1947, City Council was discussing the possibility of having 20 low-cost rental units erected on the Housing Enterprises land under the auspices of CMHC. They reached an agreement by June 1948 to have 29 new units built. The arrangement was to run for 50 years. In the words of Mayor MacDonald, the houses "were expected to greatly eliminate the housing shortage in the city."[87]

Unfortunately, the matter was not so easily resolved. A mere two years later, the city's health officer reported a dearth of new housing for the lower income group. These people were "the larger portion of our population," and unless something were done in the near future, overcrowding would "most certainly" follow. In May 1951, the city moved to prevent predatory rents by creating a rent control board with the power to review proposed increases. Even so, this did not prevent overcrowding and deterioration of the poorer housing stock. By the end of 1951, the health officer noted some people were living in overcrowded conditions "approaching that of the dark ages." Nor was rent control effective. The following year, a newspaper report described slum landlords who were collecting excessive rents for ill-repaired houses that lacked sanitation. The Catholic Welfare Bureau confirmed such circumstances in 1954 when it called upon the city to create a permanent body to study and implement housing policies. Co-operative housing might be the solution, the bureau suggested. Regrettably, not much was done to improve the situation for the rest of the 1950s although the city began a survey of all boarding houses in 1959.

The housing shortage reached crisis proportions in 1960, coinciding with a nationwide economic downturn. Women and children were sitting in the police station for hours because they had no other shelter. A coalition of welfare agencies, churches, service clubs, labour and the Canadian Legion called for a federal housing survey. They cited the example of Halifax where some progress in urban renewal had been achieved. Halifax mayor Charles Vaughan visited Charlottetown and commented on the extent of "blighted or obsolescent" properties that rendered little to the city in taxes but produced "sizeable incomes to their owners," noting that Charlottetown's

87 A federal grant to Toronto led in 1950 to Canada's first urban renewal project, Regent Park, in which slums were cleared to make way for low-rent housing. The next year, the first rent-to-income project built under a federal-provincial agreement began in St. John's, Newfoundland. It provided 140 affordable homes.

low property tax rate already constituted a housing subsidy. He supported the calls for a housing survey as an essential first step, and highlighted a federal-provincial agreement under which the federal government paid three-quarters of the cost of a housing plan, with provinces and municipalities contributing one-eighth each. Halifax had gained $6 million from the federal government in this way. Mayor Walthen Gaudet mused that urban renewal might be a suitable project for the 1964 centennial. The way forward seemed to point to government-assisted co-operative housing initiatives. A survey and plan would mark the path.

The province took an initial step in 1960. It created a commission to enquire into housing conditions and to encourage the formation of co-operatives to build "sufficient and suitable" housing. Providing loans for up to 75 per cent of the costs, the federal government assisted the construction of co-operative housing. Before the end of the year, a 60-home co-op development was slated for North River Road. Under pressure from organizations and individual citizens in Charlottetown, the province hired Walter P. de Silva as its town planner in 1960. One of his first tasks was to commence a housing survey for Charlottetown.

Co-operative housing projects created a ripple effect in the rental market. The city put into place a system by which rental properties, when they were vacated by tenants moving into co-op housing, would be incorporated into the scope of the housing survey and then inspected. If the city found a building to be deficient, it could order the owner to bring it up to standard. If not, the city would have it demolished. This approach produced less-than-dramatic results, so in 1963 the city created the Rented Premises Authority, consisting of the health officer and the building and fire inspectors. They had the power to enter and inspect premises rented for habitation and force the owners to make necessary repairs. In all of this, the absence of a complete inventory of the rental housing stock and a housing plan made substantial progress difficult. Managing the rental market effectively was difficult. As the City Recorder admitted in 1962, the city was not even able to enforce rent control or prevent evictions. High rents and deficient housing continued to plague the poor.

Spurred on by the reports of Councillor Dorothy Corrigan on the conditions of the city's poor, Mayor Gaudet reconvened the housing conference in November 1963 to discuss low-cost housing for the needy. Attending were representatives from the same groups as attended in 1960, plus delegates from the provincial government. The time for city intervention seemed right; the federal government would pay 75 per cent of construction costs and 50 per cent of municipal costs to acquire the land for slum clearance.

Armed with the support of the conference, the city obtained provincial permission in October 1964 to ask CMHC to conduct a feasibility study into low-income housing. Between October and the following March, 200 people spontaneously applied for accommodation if it were to become available. At this time, the city still lacked the authority to expropriate land required for a project. Nevertheless, discussions of a low-income housing project proceeded with the involvement of a representative group of citizens and CMHC. In April a citizens' meeting at City Hall asked the city to construct 100 units. According to the *Patriot*, there was "a feeling of almost joyous anticipation" permeating the room. One commentator boasted that no other city of comparable size in the region had started such a project. The representative from CMHC noted that Charlottetown was the first community in which citizens' groups and the general public had spurred the municipal government into action. By May 1965, the city resolved to build 100 housing units, subject to federal approval.

The citizens' group recommended multi-family buildings — a mix of duplexes, row houses and multiple-unit low rise apartments — as the most cost-effective. Costs were targeted in the range of $10,000–$12,000 per unit to permit a minimum rent of $37.50 per month. Higher rents could be charged, depending upon the ability to pay, but they were to be no more than 25 per cent of a family's income. CMHC rules permitted welfare recipients to occupy up to 20 per cent of the units if welfare agencies paid the normal rents. Though recognizing that a stigma was often attached to low-rent developments, CMHC claimed that projects were generally accepted by the community at large after a year or two. Sometimes, the projects even induced improvements in nearby properties. Nevertheless, the April meeting was urged to keep co-operative housing and CMHC low-income housing separated. Dorothy Corrigan expressed concern about segregating lower-income families and enquired about scattering small developments of four to eight units about the city.

CMHC asked the city to identify prospective building sites in September 1965. Any hopes that construction would follow quickly soon foundered as the project got bogged down in bureaucratic red tape, politics and doubt. Although property-owners were demanding top dollar for their land, CMHC expected to pay a nominal amount.[88] By April 1966, the city found an owner willing to sell at a price it could afford. Then the provincial government stepped in and took control of low-income housing. Civic politicians pressed the provincial government to act, but the province only studied the situation and promised a concrete policy soon. The situation changed once again when the Shaw Conservatives were defeated by the Campbell Liberals in the 1966 provincial election. The new government returned the responsibility for low-cost housing to the city, and the process began once more.

With the city in charge again, low-rent housing moved forward, but on a smaller scale. A vacant lot was acquired on Upper Queen Street, and CMHC was asked to develop plans for 18 row-housing units. The demand for space was overwhelming, with 213 applications for the 18 homes being built. In December 1968, Council reaffirmed its determination to address the housing shortage. Although some Councillors preferred co-operative housing to low-rent public projects, while another thought 500 units were needed immediately, Council agreed that up to 100 homes were to be built. Despite these good intentions, not much progress on additional public housing was made in 1969. The decade ended as it began with consternation at City Hall and many residents still living in slums. This in turn spawned protest. A large meeting

88 A potential site was selected by October 1965, but land was expensive, up to $1,500 per acre, so the scale of the undertaking was reduced to 50 and then 25 homes.

This end of King Street was part of the area selected in 1975 by the Neighbourhood Improvement Program.

held at the Basilica Recreational Centre in November 1969 characterized the landlord as a villain. Poverty Committee leader Alex Burke[89] joined with UPEI students, clergy and politicians as well as large numbers of the poor to denounce dwellings infested with rats, cockroaches and bed bugs and to demand stricter oversight of landlords and a commission of enquiry.

The 1970s was a decade of discord, innovation, progress and disappointment. A Tenants' Union was formed in 1969 to defend the interests of various disadvantaged groups including those consigned to sub-standard housing. This organization delighted in exposing abuse, including the plight of one family living in a slum owned by a woman well-known for her good works with the Red Cross. A Poor People's Parade, organized in January 1971 as part of a national anti-poverty demonstration, demanded the provincial government build adequate housing instead of the Brudenell resort complex. As if to underscore the marginalization of society's poorest, a proposed low-rent housing development on Belmont Street faced cost increases that made a revised rental scale necessary, though some Councillors warned higher prices would defeat the purpose of the project.

89 Burke was quoted as commenting, "To hell with the parking situation, let's get the people out of the slums." This referred to another major current concern: adequate parking downtown.

At the same time, there were experiments with alternate ways of providing decent, affordable housing. One concept was shell housing, or the completion of the major elements of a home with the interior finishing left to the buyer. A new program announced in 1972 involved CMHC and the province and provided for the acquisition of 50 sub-standard homes that would then be upgraded and made available on a rent-to-own basis to low-income families. The federal government created the Neighbourhood Improvement Program to conserve and improve older, rundown residential areas and to encourage better community environments. In Charlottetown, an area bounded by Water, Haviland, Rochford, Richmond and Great George Streets was selected for improvement in May 1975. Although the program had a significant positive impact on housing in the area, by 1980, planners still worried about possible deterioration of the housing stock.

In addition, 30 new public housing units for 177 people were built in the Dresden Court development on Belmont Street. Rent averaged $64 per month, affordable for tenants with incomes of $205 to $380 per month. High land costs in the core persisted, however — a fact that made further intervention by government necessary if a movement of people to the outskirts of the city was to be avoided. The fountain from which the finances for urban renewal flowed, the federal government, proved intermittent. Volumes tended to increase at election times and diminish thereafter. A major breakthrough came in 1976 when the Roman Catholic Episcopal Corporation sold 87 acres adjacent to the University of Prince Edward Island to provide space on the site for 400–450 homes for low- and middle-income families.[90] An agreement was reached in which the public share of the costs was divided on the basis of 25 per cent for the city and 75 per cent for CMHC. While the Marysfield subdivision addressed some of Charlottetown's housing needs, the challenge of renewing much of the downtown housing stock remained. Inner city decay was common in Atlantic Canada, as elsewhere in the country, and Charlottetown was no exception. Yet, halting the decline was possible, if only with great effort.

Inadequate housing was a symptom of a wider problem with poverty. Hardship had not ended with the Depression, and the city maintained an emergency relief program until 1948. At that time, the Catholic Social Welfare Bureau emerged from a reorganization of the social services department of the Sisters of St. Martha, and reliance was placed upon it, along with the Canadian Legion, the Salvation Army, the Benevolent Irish Society and the Free Dispensary, to support the needy. In 1952, recognizing that private charities could not be completely responsible for relief, the city resumed the provision of coal and groceries to those in "extreme hardship." Meanwhile the Catholic Social Welfare Bureau had moved to new quarters in 1951 and had taken on the attributes of a modern aid agency. In the words of one report, it emphasized family life "not through indiscriminate and impersonal benefactions, but by encouraging 'the co-operative wish of the recipients' to help themselves." A trained social worker and a registered nurse formed part of the bureau's front-line

90 This was later raised to 580 housing units.

staff. Creation of the Protestant Family Service Bureau in 1956 allowed the city once more to retreat from welfare work by providing each bureau with subventions.[91] The existence of two welfare bureaus also led to the closure of the Free Dispensary in 1956. Services provided by the Dispensary duplicated the work of the other two agencies, and financial support from the public dwindled.

When the Free Dispensary closed, it reported approximately twice as many families to support as it had in 1944. Descriptions of its clients provide insight into the causes of poverty in Charlottetown. Of the ninety-nine families listed, twelve were headed by widows with children, and another eight involved unmarried mothers. One family included an alcoholic father and two alcoholic daughters. Ten families were headed by an alcoholic father, and three included two alcoholic parents. Three families required support because the breadwinners were incapacitated by tuberculosis, and other forms of health problems afflicted ten additional families. Five elderly couples, an old widower, seven aged women and an epileptic received regular support, as did nine old-age pensioners. Twenty-nine families requiring occasional aid completed this snapshot of the poor in Charlottetown. Alcoholism, infirmity and age were significant factors that could lead to poverty, but the greatest element was the single-female-parent family. Unemployment re-emerged as a threat during the economic downturn of 1960. About that same time, the phenomenon of youth who preferred the dole to a dreary job also appeared.

The welfare bureaus did more than distribute emergency aid. Working closely together, they provided family and marriage counselling, promoted social reform, participated in social housing programs, and for years acted as agents for the province and the city in a range of matters including child welfare. Between 1968 and 1977, they provided a day care service for disadvantaged children, and also ran a camp for them. They in addition established Talbot House, a treatment centre for alcoholics.

In 1958 half their government aid came from Ottawa, with the province and city splitting the balance. This only constituted a third of their revenue. Churches and fund-raising campaigns provided most of the balance. The creation of the United Way campaign in 1962 was intended to obviate the need for separate public solicitations. By 1965 the cost of welfare had increased 500 per cent within six years. The federal government was paying an even more substantial portion of the subvention to the bureaus: three dollars for every dollar sent by the municipality. Despite this help, civic politicians were beginning to chafe at their burden. When the province moved to take over welfare payments the following year, one Councillor remarked, it would be "a big headache off our shoulders." Another groused about people on the welfare lists having jobs and driving cars. If those benefitting from government largesse hoped for a more charitable view from the province, they might not have been encouraged by

---

91 The province provided the city with $5,000 for aid. It was divided equally between the two welfare bureaus and supplemented by the city. The bureau was founded by a coalition of eight churches, St. Paul's Anglican, St. Peter's Anglican, Zion Presbyterian, St. James Presbyterian, Trinity United, First Baptist, Central Christian Church and the Salvation Army.

the distinction made by former mayor David Stewart in the legislature between "social security for the needy and rampant welfare for everyone." The province established a Department of Welfare in 1968, and, beginning in 1972, assumed all responsibility for social assistance, including the provision of welfare and the verification of recipients' eligibility. The two Charlottetown welfare bureaus refocused their efforts on programs for the aged, family counselling and legal aid. As with the two hospitals, the welfare bureaus initiated talks about amalgamation in the mid-1960s, and they increasingly integrated their efforts thereafter.

From the vantage point of the present, the years after the Second World War have taken on the glow of unbounded prosperity and economic expansion. This, however, was far from the case. The postwar decades were, in fact, characterized by a series of cycles of growth followed by recessions of varying severity. Each downturn resulted in unemployment and social disruption. Although unemployment insurance mitigated the ill effects to a degree, such support was neither universal nor of prolonged duration. In times of distress, public works were still seen as a means of supporting the economy. Calls for work to commence on the federal building and naval station in 1952 and 1953 cited the need for employment. Since much of the unemployment problem in Charlottetown was seasonal, the municipality resurrected a winter works program in 1958. It continued until at least 1965, and, as in the Great Depression, Victoria Park was the focus of much of the ensuing activity. The "Do It Now" campaign of 1959 was another attempt to generate work. In this case, a coalition of city politicians, businessmen, service organizations and provincial and federal government departments urged citizens to undertake construction projects in the depths of winter.

The most memorable event involving labour in Charlottetown was a work stoppage of another kind: a strike. On September 11, 1947, the Charlottetown local of the United Packinghouse Workers of America, with 70 employees at the Canada Packers plant, voted to join the estimated 14,000 union members who were walking off the job across the country. At issue were wage increases and a master contract to apply to all Canadian packinghouse workers. The national strike ended with the three large meat processing companies, Burns, Swift and Canada Packers, making important concessions. While the Charlottetown strike was a small part of the nation-wide labour disruption, it gained unexpected notoriety because of the vehement response of the Island government.

No sooner had the workers struck the Charlottetown facility than a reaction set in among politicians and the public alike. The average citizen had some sympathy for the workers, who were seeking a fair wage for difficult, disagreeable work. Politicians and the press had different thoughts. The strike was seen as an unnatural tear in the fabric of Island society. Packinghouse workers and farmers were part of a broader community that did not, or should not, turn on one another. Yet the strike prevented farmers from selling their hogs. In the view of Premier Walter Jones, this was an intolerable situation created in part by federal government regulations that made illegal the private slaughter and sale of meat. The press laid the blame at the feet of foreigners who had corrupted the natural instincts of fair-minded workers.

One letter to the editor condemned "long haired continental agitators" who were likely Communists.

After 10 days with no end of the strike in sight, Premier Jones decided to intervene. He offered the Charlottetown workers a 50¢ bonus for every hog they slaughtered within the next three weeks if they would return to the job. This proposal reportedly elicited some interest among the local leadership, but the union's national headquarters turned it down. Frustrated and goaded on by the press, Jones had the legislature place the Canada Packers plant temporarily under government control. He expected strikers to resume their duties at their previous pay levels now that, as he saw it, they were no longer dominated by forces from outside the province. They then would be working for the government to help the farmers. When the strikers refused to return to their jobs, Jones placed Horace Wright, a Minister without Portfolio, in charge of the plant. He engaged strike-breakers to resume operations. Continued picketing by union members was met with a claim by Wright that it was illegal to picket a government plant and molest government workers.

The government's intervention failed to alleviate fully the backlog of hogs. Partly this was due to the low productivity of the strike-breakers, and partly it reflected the dependence of many Island farmers on the slaughterhouse in Moncton, New Brunswick, which remained shut. When the strike officially ended on October 23, all but two Charlottetown strikers voted to accept a pay increase of around 7¢ an hour. Conditions did not immediately return to normal, though, because the government had promised its strike-breakers permanent employment. The plant was not handed back to Canada Packers, and only 25 of its regular workers were hired back by the government. Eventually, Premier Jones and Minister Wright got out of the hog-processing business after stressing the need for an Island-made mechanism to resolve labour-management disputes.[92] Jones and the Liberal Party were not hurt by this aggressive treatment of labour. To the contrary, although the meat packers' strike played very little part in the ensuing provincial election campaign of 1947, the government was returned to office with an additional four seats.

Although subsequent labour disputes were never as dramatic as the packers' strike, relations in the city between employers and their workers occasionally turned sour. The railway strike in 1950 renewed fears of the danger posed by outside influences. In the late 1950s, LPU wage rates provoked concerns among city businessmen and politicians that the port of Charlottetown was being priced out of business. Then, in April 1966, construction workers protesting low wages walked off the job without calling an official strike. In this dispute, talks among unions, employers and the government eventually led to the certification of 16 separate construction unions by the Department of Labour. Efforts to make arbitration an effective mechanism to resolve labour disputes in the city and the whole province followed. A labour-management

92 With the exception of the International Brotherhood of Railway Workers, the government outlawed unions with non-PEI organizational ties in March 1948. This was to ensure there were no Communist union activities on the Island. The law was repealed in March 1949.

Council was formed, and, in April 1967, a joint labour-management conference was held in Charlottetown to spell out the justifiable expectations of both sides in a labour dispute. Workplace joint Councils were recommended, and an expanded role for the provincial labour relations board received widespread support. These initiatives undoubtedly had a positive effect, but familiar issues still confronted labour in the 1970s. Longshoremen were blamed by business for undercutting the competitiveness of the port, and construction unions were attacked for using outside negotiators who had "little interest in the local economy." Despite gestures by business and community leaders to accommodate labour's agenda, local sentiment largely resented disruptions caused by strikes and remained suspicious of meddling, outside union activists.

Entertainment

The years after the Second World War brought rapid change in the way Canadians went about their lives on a daily basis, particularly during their leisure hours. Technology had brought people into closer contact with influences from elsewhere. Social cohesion and the shape of personal relationships had been altered by the economic reversals of the 1930s and the disruptions of war. The meaning of community shifted from connections based upon family and social and religious affinity to a more abstract sense of group that placed government in a pivotal role. These changes were both liberating in that they removed many traditional constraints, and isolating because they weakened the nurturing assurances of predetermined niches. Such changes were general phenomena in which citizens of Charlottetown shared. They didn't occur evenly or affect everyone in the same way, but, by 1984, life in the city was vastly different to what it had been in 1946.

Migration had long influenced the experiences of Charlottetown families. Movement flowed along a two-way street. People from the rural areas of the province came to the city to work or to bide their time before moving on. Those who stayed reinforced the ties that bound the capital to the surrounding countryside. This influx increased after the Second World War, a development that Charlottetown shared with most other Canadian centres. Over the years, the Island's demographic focal point shifted towards its urban centre, and while the distances involved allowed members of Island families dispersed by moves to remain in reasonably close contact, the chances of encountering strangers in town multiplied.

Out-migration was more disruptive for families. In the 19th century, significant numbers of Charlottetonians relocated to New England or neighbouring provinces, and the harvest excursions of the early 20th century took others temporarily to the Canadian heartland. Emigration after the Second World War assumed a somewhat different tone. The population was becoming better educated, and, by the 1960s, many city youth were attending mainland universities. There they often found employment and spouses and proceeded to settle down. Other Charlottetonians left for better employment opportunities and failed ever to return permanently. Those who did come back carried with them wider personal connections and broader perspectives. The city gradually became less provincial and introverted. Even so, concern about the inability of the city to provide secure futures at home for its youth grew as the talent drain proceeded. A solution for the problem remained elusive.

At the same time, Charlottetown experienced a small influx of people from other parts of Canada. Often they had specialized skills not available in the city. Others came from abroad. The university, hospital and governments provided employment for these new arrivals. While many of the folks from away adapted well to their surroundings, others remained somewhat apart from the wider community. That did nothing to lessen suspicions about outsiders and resentment of the preferred status that they sometimes were perceived to have had. Pockets of isolated newcomers also further eroded the patterns of close associations that had previously characterized city families. Gradually the possibilities grew for anonymity in a city that had always been tightly knit.

Churches remained one of the chief mechanisms by which a sense of community was fostered. The vitality of religious organizations survived the Second World War and even strengthened during the 1950s. Churches were regarded as one of the requisite amenities in new housing developments, along with schools and playgrounds. The arrival of people with different religious traditions prompted further growth. For instance, Dutch immigrants who worshipped at the Heartz Community Hall in East Royalty formally constituted themselves as a congregation of the Christian Reformed Church in 1955. Besides places of worship, new facilities included education centres and church halls to cater to the burgeoning number of young people. The Roman Catholic recreation centre associated with St. Dunstan's Basilica was the most ambitious of such projects. Built at a cost of $700,000,[93] it included a library, reading room, bowling alleys, a gymnasium, lounge and offices. Sportscaster Danny Gallivan officiated at its opening in September 1963 before an audience of 700 people.[94]

There were losses as well as gains. Fire destroyed the venerable Heartz Memorial Hall beside Trinity United Church in October 1969, and in 1975 the Redemptorist Fathers left Holy Redeemer Church when the order decided to retrench in the face of the increasing age and declining numbers of its members. By then, growing secularism was beginning to erode the strength of many religious organizations. Although Charlottetown was far from the forefront in the abandonment of worship for the apparently more enjoyable Sunday morning pursuits of sports, shopping or simply lounging around the house, those trends were apparent among city residents. Imperceptibly at first, and then with greater momentum, the habit of church attendance weakened. With time, this process somewhat undercut the moral authority of church leaders and the effectiveness of congregations to fill their traditional roles as social centres and service providers. An early sign of declining respect for traditional social norms came in 1951 when the province neglected to invite a clergyman from the Church of England to a state dinner in honour of Princess Elizabeth and the Duke of Edinburgh, who were currently visiting the province. When Anglicans protested,

---

93 This was a considerable sum for the time, equivalent to almost $5 million in 2008.

94 Gallivan was the husband of Island-born Mary Eileen MacPhee.

Harness racing has been one of the most popular sports throughout much of Charlottetown's history. Grandstand and Exhibition Building c. 1920.

Premier Jones replied curtly that the Island had no established church, and protocol required only two clerics, the Roman Catholic bishop and the president of the Protestant ministerial association. The skirmish calmed down after the Anglicans observed that the government chose to ask the president of the local association rather than the provincial body.[95]

Organized religion was not the only strand of the social fabric to be tested. Depression and war had undercut many of Charlottetown's athletics activities. Sport in the city in the immediate postwar era had deteriorated to such a state, according to one citizen, that he searched in vain for an athletics field or playground that was properly maintained and provided with essential equipment, or for an active society or citizens' group willing "to spend time and understanding to promote a healthy and workable schedule of athletic activity for the young." This did not remain the case for long. Criticism like this from citizens and organizations, such as Prince of Wales College, prodded the Jones government in 1945 to appoint W. W. Reid of Charlottetown to the post of Director of Physical Fitness for the province. He, together with other sports enthusiasts, worked diligently to revive organized sport in the city and province.

The demise of the Abegweit Amateur Athletic Association made the process of revitalization more challenging than it might otherwise have been. The Abbie sports field was a thing of the past, so the best alternative was Victoria Park. Representatives of Prince of Wales College, the local public schools, as well as groups interested in rugby football, baseball and track and field, worked together to develop Memorial Field, which became the springboard for the revival of sports in the city. A three-team baseball league was formed. The Abegweit AAA was resurrected to sponsor track and field athletes and, after 1949, a rugby team. Interest in lawn tennis spread, and in 1951

95 The basis of the Anglican position was that the King, as Defender of the Faith, was the head of the Church of England, and the presence of a representative of his church at a dinner for his daughter was an appropriate mark of respect.

a new clubhouse and improved courts opened in the park. Golf and sailing experienced similar renewals. Although harness racing had remained popular, it benefited from the general upturn in sports and the introduction of night racing and attracted increasingly large audiences in the late 1940s and early 1950s. The adoption of new technology, such as mobile gates and photo finishes, made the Charlottetown Driving Park a mecca for some of the fastest horses on the east coast. In 1960 a new feature, the Gold Cup and Saucer race, was instituted, and it soon became a classic part of the Charlottetown summer season.

Winter sports also experienced a revival. Over at the Forum, a four-club hockey league drew large crowds and produced teams that went on to interprovincial championships. Formed in 1950, a senior hockey club, the Islanders, competed in the Maritime Big Four (later Five) League. The team was competitive and attracted large crowds to their home games. Curling prospered as well, although it lacked the fan appeal of hockey. In 1958 a new rink was built on Euston Street to replace the facility on Grafton Street. A big boost was given to the sport in 1964 when the national men's curling championships, the Macdonald Brier, were held in the city. A youthful PEI squad, headed by Alan Burke of the Charlottetown Curling Club, finished in the middle of the pack but ahead of all other teams from Atlantic Canada. The Brier was a popular success, drawing large audiences. By the 1970s, Charlottetown teams had won the Canadian senior and the world junior men's curling titles.

With the resurgence of sports generally, it was inevitable that some consolidation would follow. In 1955 the Islanders Hockey Club dropped out of the Maritime Big Five League. The preceding year saw the effective end of the Abegweit AAA, beset by financial challenges and a diminished role in an era when sports were structured within specific associations rather than multi-sport clubs. Nevertheless, sports generally were by then firmly embedded as part of Charlottetown's collective culture. In 1960 Dorothy Corrigan presented a report from the Playground Commission which stated that 42,000 children attended city parks during the summer and that the city had a vigorous winter program, including minor hockey. Throughout the 1970s and 1980s, new facilities and well-developed organizations kept competitive and recreational sports programs in a generally flourishing state.

One of the great diversions of the prewar era, movies, had a greater challenge coping with changes in postwar technology and popular taste. What was made to be shown on the screen was determined elsewhere, but audiences were treated to a wide array of offerings. In 1959, for instance, movie-goers could choose films ranging from *Ben Hur*, an epic with a cast of thousands, to serious art films from Europe or *Gidget*, a banal adolescent titillation. With an ever-wider selection of choices on the screen, patrons began to expect different venues. The options tended to track prevailing trends in consumer culture. In the era of expanding automobile ownership, the drive-in theatre allowed families to pack into their cars for an evening at the movies. A later demand for modern, comfortable surroundings led to the opening of the new Prince Edward Theatre on Grafton Street, while the cinema at the Charlottetown Mall responded to the demand for convenient parking.

The big competitor of films for leisure-time audiences was, of course, television. Beginning in 1954, programs were beamed into the Charlottetown area from Moncton where CKCW carried afternoon favourites such as *Howdy Doody* and prime-time thrillers like *Dragnet*. Much of the content was American in origin although the station itself was affiliated with the Canadian Broadcasting Corporation. Later, on July 1, 1956, radio station CFCY began its television service in Charlottetown. It also was a CBC affiliate, but the schedule incorporated local programs, including *Today at Home* and *Teen Hop*. The station had long been a goal of Keith Rogers, CFCY's founder, but, unfortunately, he was not alive to see the realization of his dream. Speaking to the Rotary Club in early 1953, Rogers described an image he had of a man and his family "sitting around the living room with all eyes focused on a 17" or 21" square piece of glass upon which will be continuously depicted, hour after hour, the headline happenings of the day as they occur, intermingled with beautiful dancing girls and the very best of 'Who Done It?' drama." Rogers complained of the slowness with which this dream was being realized, and once his station was on the air, others protested its forced association with the CBC. Even so, Charlottetonians adopted television with a passion.

Despite the widespread appeal and compelling nature of television, it challenged, but never completely undercut, other forms of entertainment, including live performances. In the immediate postwar era, local performing arts groups enjoyed a revival. The Community Concert Association organized seasons of musical events, often staged at the Prince of Wales College auditorium. One of 18 such bodies in the Maritimes, the association was a "non-profit, non-loss organization" aimed at bringing to the community "the best available artistic talent." After a hiatus of several years, the Little Theatre Guild resumed activity in 1947. With a membership of more than 400, it staged its initial performances at the Empire Theatre. Not all of its offerings were appreciated by every patron. The 1947 production of an obscure mystery-comedy, *Gangway for Ghosts* by Jay Tobias, was panned by a correspondent in the *Patriot*, who viewed it as slapstick humour below the mental age of the audience. The Guild had high hopes, however, to reclaim some of the vitality it had known previously, and to that end planned to stage a Broadway play and even radio plays. Although the fortunes of individual organizations like the Little Theatre waxed and waned, there was ongoing enthusiasm for musical and theatrical performances in the city.

The visual arts also had a long tradition in Charlottetown, stretching back to Fanny Bayfield and Robert Harris. They were largely solitary pursuits, however, and often were not as vigorously promoted as other cultural activities. Like many pastimes, painting and drawing had not received a lot of attention during the war, and in 1946 local proponents of art decided that standards had declined to unacceptable levels. The PEI Arts and Crafts Guild began free public classes in 1946, while a group of interested citizens met in December of that year to discuss the establishment of a Children's Art Centre. In this context, as others, there was some anxiety about possible government involvement in the form of financial aid. A reluctance to increase tax-based spending may have been a factor here, but there was another consideration. For one person, at least, "the danger in subsidizing things like culture — as we ought to know from recent European history — is that it can so easily be turned into bureaucratic propaganda."

Such qualms were overcome by 1948 when the Charlottetown Art Centre began to give art lessons to children from city schools. The next year, the Arts and Craft Guild started a campaign to raise money to open an art centre in the market house. The centre was intended to provide art lessons and arrange exhibitions, as well as promote musical concerts and show films. Two rooms in the market house were made available by the city rent-free. From this base, the guild undertook some significant projects. In 1952, for example, it sponsored an exhibition of diploma works from the Royal Canadian Academy at the Harris Memorial Art and Library Building.

Not everyone was supportive of cultural initiatives. The *Patriot*, in an article entitled "Culture Varnish," derided "highbrows" who were presenting briefs to the Massey Royal Commission on the Arts and Letters. These people, the paper asserted, presumed to be "the sole, self-sacrificing custodians of 'culture'" although they failed to define its meaning. It went on to note that their "serious and solemn mien" at times provoked "critical smiles."

Slights like these failed to dull the ardour of the supporters of cultural activities. Chief among them were proponents of a museum. In 1947 the Women's Institute adopted a resolution calling for its creation. Prince Edward Island was the only province without one, the institute noted. Years previously, there had been an antiquarian society in Charlottetown, but many of the "relics" it had collected were dispersed because of a lack of adequate storage. The Harris Building had been intended to accommodate historical objects, but progress in meeting this goal seems never to have amounted to much. In a bold move intended to rectify this and other housing problems facing the arts, Dr. Frank MacKinnon, Principal of Prince of Wales College, proposed a cultural centre be built in Charlottetown as a memorial to the Fathers of Confederation. His brief to the Massey Commission on this vision was applauded by some, including a number of the commissioners, but the proposal also had detractors. Less ambitious solutions were also proposed. The Conservative opposition leader in the provincial legislature suggested that space for a museum might be found in the Queen Square post office when the proposed new federal building opened. Meanwhile artifacts taken from the courthouse and Province House were stored in the basement of Prince of Wales College. Occasionally the Imperial Order of the Daughters of the Empire (IODE) exhibited some of this historical material.

MacKinnon persisted with his efforts. In an address to the Arts and Crafts Guild in December 1950, he asserted that the happiness and progress of a people depended upon cultural heritage, and the Island could not continue as a distinct and effective political and economic unit if it ignored its heritage and neglected its culture. Days later, the Board of Trade offered its support by sending the provincial government a letter applauding the campaign for an archives and museum. In 1953 the Historical Society of PEI was revived by Walter Shaw, then the provincial deputy minister of education, to press for a provincial museum. Supporters claimed that one of the most frequently heard complaints from tourists was the absence of a provincial museum. As an interim measure, the YMCA volunteered to accommodate exhibits and relics collected by the society.

Efforts to obtain a museum persisted well into the 1950s. The city's centennial in 1956 seemed an opportune time to build public support for the project. The Historical Society published a booklet on the city's "historical highlights" and brought in Austin Squires of the University of New Brunswick to speak on museums. In his address, Squires promoted museums as a bulwark of freedom. The Communists, he asserted, destroyed all museums and historical monuments as a first step after they invaded a country. Despite Squires' comment that most museums started as small rooms, the society had nudged no closer to the realization of its objective when fire swept through the market house in 1958. Among the ashes lay a seed of hope. In a commentary on the disaster, the *Guardian* noted that the city now needed a new auditorium and perhaps it and "the long-talked about Provincial Museum and Art Gallery" could be built on the site.

Certainly Frank MacKinnon thought so. He had been quietly developing plans for an arts centre for years. By 1956 he had pried a reluctant agreement from the sceptical Premier Matheson to promote the concept of such a complex as a memorial to Canada's founding fathers. He had even made "amateurish" drawings of what he thought might be desirable. His appointment to the Canada Council in 1957 provided him with useful contacts. Now the fire had produced the ideal building site. In MacKinnon's opinion, the time for action had come. He set about mustering support and establishing a legal entity that could be entrusted with undertaking the project. At home in Charlottetown, there were public stirrings of support. A letter to the editor of the *Guardian* proposed a new civic centre featuring a museum and art gallery to be opened on Market Square in 1964. A meeting of various cultural and service organizations held at the Clover Club in May 1958 discussed the feasibility of having a civic auditorium and art centre built on the site.[96] A brief was presented to the provincial government, emphasizing the lack of facilities in the city and province. A further meeting was held in June at Prince of Wales College. Again the focus of discussion was on a theatre and art centre for the Little Theatre, the Art Society and a music festival. Interestingly, the museum component of the concept was receding from the forefront of the plans.

In the months and years that followed, the efforts at persuasion of MacKinnon and his wealthy associate, Eric L. Harvie, and the sensitive negotiations with various levels of government eventually resulted in a complex of buildings that exceeded the expectations of most Charlottetonians. A key aspect of the new complex was the establishment of the Charlottetown Festival, a summertime celebration of Canadian musical and theatrical talent. The success of this undertaking was by no means a sure

96 Representatives at the meeting came from the Art Society, the Little Theatre Guild, the Business and Professional Women's Club, the Kinsmen, the Camera Club, the Drama Association and the Canadian Legion. Barry Bugden, who was interested in amateur theatricals, was made chair of the meeting.

thing. Fortunately, the popularity of the musical *Anne of Green Gables* somewhat allayed concerns that the Centre would become an economic white elephant. Nevertheless, fears of failure persisted into the 1970s, and grumbles were heard about the Centre's ongoing requests to the city for financial support. In the early years, Charlottetonians and Islanders generally were ambivalent about the festival. "The Festival and what it is trying to do are not understood or appreciated by Island people," concluded the Toronto *Globe and Mail* in 1972. If this were true, it was less than the whole story. In the opinion of the *Patriot*, published in 1974, "Life in this city and province without the Confederation Centre would be inconceivable."

The construction and operation of the Confederation Centre would not have been possible without government support. This was symptomatic of the increasing significance of state intervention in all aspects of civic life. To a degree, government was supplanting community-based organizations as the engine of social mobilization. Groups that drew upon volunteer service and an awareness of shared values and needs continued to exist in Charlottetown, but in the decades following the Second World War, they generally declined in size and vigour. The advent of state medicine, for instance, reduced the appeal of the mutual benefit programs that formed part of the attraction for some fraternal societies. Even so, organizations such as the Imperial Order of the Daughters of the Empire continued to attract members. One of the more enduring of them, the Benevolent Irish Society, made quite a splash with the celebrations of its 150th anniversary in 1975. A large St. Patrick's Day parade was held, along with a Mass at St. Dunstan's Basilica. Service clubs were some of the more active volunteer groups. The Rotary Club held weekly mid-day luncheons, and in 1979 a second club was set up in the Charlottetown-Hillsborough area. The YMCA, unlike some other civic groups, had actually done well during the war. Its facilities attracted servicemen stationed in Charlottetown, in addition to locals. It began a campaign in 1944 to raise money for a new home, but wartime restrictions on the use of building materials frustrated these ambitions. With peace, the effort was renewed, and on February 23, 1949, a new "Y" with a chlorinated swimming pool, gymnasium, auditorium and bowling alleys was opened. An extension for a new pool was erected in 1960.

One organization that was particularly successful in the years following the Second World War was the scouting movement. Buoyed by the baby boom, the eight existing troops in Charlottetown saw their membership expand significantly. Parallel cub, girl guide and brownie programs also prospered. In addition, new scout troops appeared in the suburban regions. One troop was formed in Parkdale in 1945, but the most rapid expansion took place in the 1950s. Sherwood and Parkdale were home to two troops, and the others were located in Spring Park, Cornwall and Southport. Although all of the older Charlottetown scout troops were connected to churches, the suburban troops were sponsored for the most part by secular groups. Only the 2nd Sherwood and the Park Royal troops were church-based. The total number of scouts, cubs and leaders in Prince Edward Island rose steadily from 1950 until 1962, after which time numbers gradually fell off. This was undoubtedly true for the city and reflected the declining numbers of potential recruits as the baby boom era wound down. It may also have reflected the divergence of contemporary youth culture from the ethos of the scouting movement.[97]

A decline in traditional community organizations in Charlottetown and elsewhere was ironically accompanied by a growing sense of historical occasion. Celebrations of benchmark historical dates became a means of asserting the relevance of the past in a future-oriented age. The two decades following the Second World War were unusually filled with special commemorations. The first, the centenary of Charlottetown's incorporation, came in 1955. City Council was determined to make it a noteworthy and festive occasion. It appointed a centennial committee and provided it with a number of substantial grants to ensure a full program with wide appeal. The schedule included a centennial civic dinner in January, a centennial legislative dinner in March and a centennial ball at the end of June. Charlotte Whitton, mayor of another centennial city, Ottawa, was hosted at a civic dinner in April. In late June, a children's week featured a doll parade, a soap box derby, a bicycle race and a talent show, among other events. A beauty Queen was crowned, and a "giant" chicken barbecue was held. Theatrical performances enjoyed a prominent role in the festivities including a presentation of *Jenny Kissed Me* by the Benevolent Irish Society and the Little Theatre production of *Anne of Green Gables*. The festivities reached a climax in early August with a series of events reminiscent of the Confederation Week celebrations of 1939. A parade on August 7 was followed the next day by a procession of floats and an historical pageant. Throughout the year, conventions, reunions and special visits attracted a steady stream of visitors. The civic centennial proved to be a commercial, as well as a popular, success. In subsequent anniversaries, city officials referred back to the proceedings of 1955 for guidance.

Within nine years, Charlottetown was again the centre of a special commemoration, this time the centenary of the meeting of the Fathers of Confederation in 1864. The celebration took place during a period in which several important historical forces were converging. In English Canada, the old ties with the British Isles were eroding while in French Canada the predominance previously given to the Roman Catholic church in various facets of life was being questioned. Both of Canada's socio-cultural groups were thus looking for new identities. In Prince Edward Island, the priority lay more with finding a means to diversify the economy, while in Charlottetown the civic government had become convinced that the city's future as a tourist mecca lay in the provision of modern cultural institutions. By 1960 these forces had produced certain trends: a determination to create a distinctive sense of Canadianism in English Canada, a willingness to contemplate separation in French-speaking Quebec, a desire to attract tourists by exploiting historical and natural assets in Prince Edward Island and, in Charlottetown, firm backing for Frank MacKinnon's vision of a monument to the founding fathers. This conjuncture affected the 1964 proceedings in

97 A similar problem seemed to afflict the cadet program. When asked their opinion, students at Queen Charlotte High School responded that it was good for one's posture, provided exercise and built school spirit, teamwork and discipline. An expectation of all work and no fun discouraged participants.

a significant way. Planners and politicians in Ottawa felt it was necessary to inspire loyalty in Canadians, including Quebeckers, and to create excitement about Canada. Celebrations surrounding the 100th anniversary of Confederation were seen as such an exercise in nation-building. In Charlottetown, Frank MacKinnon and his associates were already promoting the city as the birthplace of Confederation and arguing that their proposal fitted nicely into the emerging plans to celebrate Canadian nationality. The 1964 centennial became an important part of the run-up to the main event in 1967.

By having the right project at the required moment, the proponents of a Fathers of Confederation Memorial were given the chance to succeed. Completion of the cultural complex, however, was to be only the highlight of a province-wide, year-long party. The Centennial Committee led by MacKinnon encouraged every community to stage centennial days featuring parades, sports competitions and concerts. Regular events such as Charlottetown's Old Home Week were subsumed within the centennial theme. The capital staged a series of special activities, all in the "spirit of '64," and received visitors in a grand style.[98] Among them were the various provincial premiers attending a Dominion-Provincial conference in September. They were treated to historical re-enactments of the conference, including the arrival from Quebec of the supply ship, *Ernest Lapointe*, decked out to look like the *Queen Victoria*. Many of these ceremonies took place in front of television cameras, giving the local tourist industry a massive and free publicity boost. In October Queen Elizabeth officially opened the Confederation Centre. The Centre was already functioning, of course, but the Queen's visit capped the year's proceedings. As a whole, the celebrations were regarded as a highly successful effort to blend history, tourism and targeted government spending to stimulate economic activity. They proved that the "Cradle of Confederation" theme had traction. With it, the city and province could haul the tourism component of the economy forward.

The centennial of Confederation followed in 1967, and the citizens of Charlottetown celebrated along with their fellow Canadians. They were mindful, though, that Prince Edward Island had not been one of the original three colonies to enter the union, and knew that another six years would have to lapse before they could observe their own centenary. When this arrived in 1973, the events were shaped to highlight the province's heritage and to appeal to potential tourists. With the slogan, "The Place to be in '73," the provincial government dressed up automobile licence plates and all sorts of promotional material with little bearded Fathers in an effort to reinforce the "Birthplace of Confederation" theme. While Islanders were urged in the spring to turn out in numbers to collect the winter's supply of trash from the roadsides and to make the province visually attractive for visitors in other ways, the public might have been forgiven if its enthusiasm seemed muted by the prospect of the

98 The author first came to Charlottetown as a UNTD officer cadet aboard HMCS *New Waterford* in the summer of 1964. The ship's visit was in honour of the centennial. The city evoked little interest, but there was a great party at the cottage of another cadet, Wes MacAleer.

Re-enactors scramble up the gangway as part of the 1964 Centennial celebrations.

arrival of yet more hordes of outsiders. Nevertheless, Charlottetown's political and business elites mustered to work on the Centennial Commission. They used the tried-and-true approach established for previous celebrations and laid on an active program of community events. Much of the available funding, however, flowed into heritage projects. New museums were opened at Basin Head, Orwell and Green Park. In Charlottetown, the major undertaking was the renovation of the Cundall Home to serve as an historic site and headquarters of the Prince Edward Island Heritage Foundation. With its name changed back to the original "Beaconsfield," the building was opened by the Queen in July as part of her official visit to the city. A large crowd attended the ceremony. Even if such events had by then become almost routine, Charlottetonians still enjoyed the pageantry surrounding a royal tour.

Visits by members of the royal family and other state occasions, such as the opening of the provincial legislature, provided the local militia with an opportunity to perform in public. After the Second World War, however, the city's tradition of military service began to decline. The PEI Highlanders and the Light Horse were merged into the Prince Edward Island Regiment in 1946. In 1950 other functioning units included the 28th Light Anti-Aircraft Regiment, the 5th Signals Regiment, the 21st Field Ambulance, the 21st Armoured Brigade, plus the naval reserve. This seemed to indicate a robust force even if only part of it was composed of Charlottetonians. Indeed, in August 1955, 450 officers and men mustered in the city for a joint church parade with personnel from

The lasting legacy of efforts to commemorate the 1964 centennial was the Confederation Centre of the Arts. To celebrate its own centennial in 1973, the province directed much of the available funding into heritage projects. In Charlottetown, the major undertaking was the renovation of the Cundall Home as an historic site and headquarters for the recently incorporated Prince Edward Island Heritage Foundation. The Queen officially opened the building on July 3, 1973.

three visiting Canadian and American naval vessels. Throughout the 1950s, Prince Edward Island units distinguished themselves in training exercises, and, in 1956–57, the 5th Signals Regiment was named the best militia unit in Canada. Behind these successes, though, lurked some disturbing circumstances.

Since the end of the war, housing had been a major difficulty. The naval reserve, HMCS *Queen Charlotte*, desperately needed a new barracks. An announcement in 1949 that one might be built in Victoria Park, just west of Government House, sparked opposition in the press. This may have prompted inaction on the part of the federal government despite local pressure to erect a facility to create construction jobs. Eventually a new establishment was built on the site of the old Paoli's Wharf at the foot of Haviland Street. Operations commenced there in 1959. Not long after, officials in Ottawa announced that the militia would no longer operate armoured equipment but would instead be geared to civil defence. This change undercut morale, but training proceeded, with scenarios involving nuclear warfare. In the case of exercise Alpha Omega held in 1959, the militia was deployed to Squaw Point to respond to the hypothetical detonation of a 50-kiloton atomic bomb near Tea Hill. A more serious threat to the military's *esprit de corps* emerged in 1963 when the new Liberal minister of national defence, Paul Hellyer, announced cutbacks in the armed services and identified Charlottetown as one of six reserve establishments facing possible closure. Although units survived, Hellyer's subsequent experiment in unification of the three services led to the conversion of the naval station into an armoury. This threatened the camaraderie associated with the traditional formations and, together with the generally anti-military mood of the era, undercut the appeal of service in the reserves for potential recruits. Since the 1960s, ongoing budget cuts and a lack of appreciation of the militia's value fostered a preference among the public for other ways to invest its spare time.

The period between 1946 and 1984 was one of vast change in the social life of Charlottetown. Sometimes the transformations that so drastically altered life in the city and the province are referred to dramatically as "The Break." They could just as aptly be called "The Connection." One of the recurring themes in the city's history was a desire to keep current. Charlottetonians compared themselves and their city with other places in Canada and judged their success by the degree to which their lives reflected the desirable norm elsewhere. Virtues were proclaimed when the societal shortcomings found away were absent at home. The point is that, for the most part, citizens embraced modernity with enthusiasm. Some may have lamented the decline of traditional social standards, but much of that was based on a nostalgia that wiser minds knew to be romanticism. The progress toward up-to-date standards of education, public health and medicine, community and social services and leisure activities was widely applauded. In part, people were being swept along by national trends. To a degree, they were being led by technocrats who inspired concepts like the Leadership Institute to modify attitudes in business, government and the volunteer sector. Provincial governments that were prepared to commit themselves to social support programs and improvements to infrastructure were critical to the promotion of change. The Comprehensive Development Plan was an indispensable tool to effect it. It was the responsiveness of the typical Charlottetonian to the drumbeat of modernity, however, that mainly led to the revolution in lifestyles in this period.

The rules of the game changed significantly for Charlottetown, and indeed for all of Prince Edward Island, in the years after 1945. Where the prevailing government sentiment in the 1920s and '30s was to intervene as little as possible in the normal workings of the economy and society, the state at all levels of jurisdiction was much more proactive after 1945. The willingness of the federal government, in particular, to try to manage affairs, even at the local level, tended to increase as the postwar period progressed. Charlottetonians and other Islanders were major beneficiaries — or victims, depending upon your point of view — of this process.

The impact of government intervention was felt in all aspects of life from medical care to education and from road construction to the provision of industrial and recreational facilities. Some changes came at the insistence of the federal and provincial authorities; others resulted from badgering by local leaders. A major cultural centre was conjured up by a spectacular exercise of high-stakes wire-pulling by private citizens. The Comprehensive Development Plan had a profound influence on the course of change. Significant steps were taken under the plan's auspices to protect the heritage character of the city's core and to preserve its commercial vitality. The waterfront was rehabilitated, and the tourist infrastructure was developed. In an era of federal decentralization and provincial aggrandizement, Charlottetown's role as an administrative centre benefitted from an enlarged Island bureaucracy and the transplantation of a federal government department. The local economy thus became more resilient, and employment opportunities increased.

All of this took place against a backdrop of mass communications that brought people in distant places closer together, eroded their differences and heightened their sense of community distinctiveness. In this era, Charlottetown saw its reliance upon the bounty of the countryside diminish and its influence over the lives of rural Islanders increase. At the same time, the city was being blended into the wider amalgam of Canadian urban life. In the realm of commerce, everything from building design to retail store ownership was increasingly like that in the rest of the country. Popular culture came to resemble closely what was found in other parts of Canada. Charlottetown had become a larger, wealthier, more complex and up-to-date city between 1946 and 1984. The challenge for the years ahead was to reinforce the benefits of these trends while dealing with remaining problems and preserving a distinct sense of self.

CHAPTER 6

Connected

1985-2005

By the 1980s, Canada's cities were being transformed at a rate rarely, if ever, experienced before. Their populations were swelling as people migrated to the places where economic growth and social effervescence were focused. Baby boomers were coming of age and establishing families, and suburbs to house them were springing up in farmers' fields. Better roads, more automobiles, and relatively cheap energy facilitated the expansion. Populations were becoming more diverse as immigrants from non-European countries arrived to bolster Canada's demographic increase. Some were refugees from world trouble-spots while others possessed skills or wealth and were courted by a country in need of both. Many immigrants settled in specific urban districts inhabited by their countrymen; others integrated into the general population. Unlike previous waves of newcomers, they had a choice — Canadians generally had become more familiar with, and accepting of, visible minorities and the cultural diversity they represented. City streetscapes acquired signage in strange languages, restaurants with exotic aromas and places of worship with unconventional architecture. These changes were most apparent in Toronto, Montreal and Vancouver, but to lesser degrees, in communities across the country.

Not all changes were positive. Suburban development drained the commercial vitality out of many downtowns. Traffic plugged major roadways during rush hours, and increasingly outside of them. Pollution increased. Denser populations exposed some of society's sores. Drug and alcohol abuse and crime associated with them grew. In some cities, whole districts were given over to prostitutes, addicts and the homeless. Tight municipal finances made the maintenance of the physical infrastructure more challenging and threatened the provision of social services. Hyper-inflation followed by recession compounded the problems, and prompted senior levels of government to off-load major responsibilities, making matters worse. Amidst the wealth and glitter, some cities began to falter. Toronto, once proclaimed as "the city that works," began to be known for its foul air, murderous streets and, briefly and tragically, SARS epidemic.

Charlottetown seems to have eluded the worst and some of the best of these transformations, but even there, the tides of change lapped at its shores. That was apparent on the evening of Monday, March 13, 1995. The setting could not have been more appropriate. In the same house that Charlottetown's City Council held its first meeting, the Mayor and his aldermen gathered for its last. Between the two meetings lay almost 140 years of history. In fact, history seemed to be a kind of ghostly presence as the actors assembled that night at 70 Sydney Street.[1] The building was formerly the home of Robert Hutchison, the city's first mayor. It had changed considerably since Council met there in 1855. Asbestos cement siding now covered the building's exterior, and a store nestled in its northeast corner, but the same room was called into service, and the wife of the present owner played the role of Mrs. Hutchison. Other historical personages appeared, including Mrs. Hutchison's maid; John Hatch, the town crier; John Hamilton Gray; George Coles; and, incongruously, John A. Macdonald. The aldermen present assumed the roles of the first Councillors and reported on their areas of responsibility. Alderman Catherine Hennessey, who organized the event, spoke of the importance of Charlottetown's heritage and the need for locals to safeguard its "gentleness and privacy" while "using it in tourism." She, like the others, however, was looking to the future. Charlottetown was about to change profoundly.

POPULATION GROWTH AND ETHNIC RELATIONSHIPS

At first glance, the period between 1985 and 2005 appears to have seen a seismic shift in the population of Charlottetown. The 1986 census reported 15,776 people living within the city limits, while the 2001 census set the population at 32,245. In fact, the difference is due to the amalgamation in 1995 of the city and its suburban municipalities rather than any demographic take-off. An examination of the population of the metropolitan area — Charlottetown and its surrounding communities — tells a different story; 53,868 in 1986 and 58,358 in 2001. This was a gain of 8.3 per cent for the 15-year period. The population in 2006 stood at 32,174 for Charlottetown and 58,625 for the metropolitan area. Thus, the recent trend for the city showed a gentle decline and, for the city and environs, a marginal increase.[2] Amalgamation had an impact on Charlottetown's standing in relation to cities of comparable size in Canada. In 1986 it was ranked 212th, just after King, Ontario, and Cranbrook, B.C., and just ahead of Prince Rupert and Port Moody, B.C. In 2001 Charlottetown had jumped to 130th place, smaller than Woodstock, Ontario, and Cap-de-la Madeleine, Quebec, but larger than Moose Jaw, Saskatchewan, and Brant, Ontario.

Significantly, the centrifugal force of the capital on the population of the Island as a whole diminished between 1985 and 2005. In the 1986 census, Charlottetown contained 12.5 per cent of the province's population and the metropolitan area, 46.5

---

1 The events are recorded in a special transcript of the meeting, part of the City Council records. Hutchison's home was owned by Mr. George Ghiz, and Elizabeth Ghiz played Mrs. Hutchison. The meeting also included an appearance by Harry Holman, the Provincial Archivist, who acknowledged receipt of an additional 70 years of municipal records to be held "in trust for all the people."

2 Problems arise when metropolitan areas (census metropolitan areas or census agglomerations) are compared because the boundaries shift from census to census. For instance, the population for the metropolitan area in 2001, 58,358, was adjusted downward to 57,234 when the boundaries used in the 2006 census were considered. On that basis, there has been a 2.4 per cent increase in the population between 2001 and 2006. The decline within the city was 0.9 per cent between 1996 and 2001 and 0.2 per cent between 2001 and 2006, or 1.1 per cent between 1996 and 2006. The population in 1996 was 32,531.

per cent. By 2001 the amalgamated city represented 23.9 per cent of Islanders, but the metropolitan area had declined to 43.1 per cent. The figures for 2006 were 23.7 per cent and 43.2 per cent respectively. Even so, the proportion of Islanders living within the capital's metropolitan area exceeded the 36 per cent of Newfoundlanders living in St. John's and the 40 per cent of Nova Scotians living in Halifax, as well as the 42 per cent of Ontarians living in Toronto. The central position of Charlottetown within Prince Edward Island was eclipsed, however, by the 46 per cent of Quebeckers living within the Montreal metropolitan area and the 51.5 per cent of British Columbians residing in the Vancouver CMA. Still, the preponderance of Islanders living in, and around, Charlottetown prompted one observer to comment that Prince Edward Island was really a city with extended suburbs. Some credence might have been given to this comment by the considerable number of people who commuted to work from outside the metropolitan area. This practice, made possible by improved roads, could also have explained the slowing pace of population growth within the metropolitan area itself.

Ethnically, Charlottetown remained quite true to its roots, unlike many Canadian centres that were becoming ethnically more diverse in the latter years of the 20th century. In 1986, 43.8 per cent of the population was British in origin, with 5.2 per cent French and 1.2 per cent Lebanese. All other groups, Dutch, German, Aboriginal and South Asian, were less than 1 per cent of the population. Fully 42.9 per cent of the population had multiple origins, again mainly from the British Isles. Two interesting changes occurred in the population as recorded in the census of 2001. In a situation where respondents were encouraged to list all of their ancestral origins, the largest number, 39.22 per cent, identified themselves as Canadian. Another 1.5 per cent chose Acadian. The Scots were the second-largest group at 38.5 per cent, followed by the English and Irish at 28.9 per cent each; the French, 17.6 per cent; Germans, 4.3 per cent; Dutch, 2.8 per cent; First Nations, 1.7; Welsh, 1.6; and Lebanese, 1.3 per cent. People whose origins were American, Polish, Italian, Danish and many others were all fewer than 1 per cent of the population.[3]

There was a minimal shift among Charlottetonians with respect to religious affiliation between 1985 and 2005. At the beginning of the period, the city was divided evenly between Protestants and Roman Catholics with a smattering of Eastern Orthodox, Eastern Non-Christians and Jews. Approximately 4 per cent professed no religious belief. By 2001 the picture was slightly more complex. Roman Catholics constituted 46 per cent of the population while Protestants made up 42.7 per cent. Non-specified Christians comprised 2.7 per cent of the population, and the Eastern Orthodox, 0.4 per cent. Those who were unaffiliated with a religion had grown to 7.3 per cent of the population, while together Muslims, Buddhists, Eastern Non-Christians, Hindus,

3 In the 1996 census, Charlottetonians traced their ancestors to a total of 58 homelands, but 40 of them accounted for less than 0.3 per cent of the population. By 1995, including recently arrived immigrants, the total of nationalities had risen to 75, although the number of people connected to most remained small.

Jews and other religions made up 0.91 per cent. The trends suggest a weakening of the established religions, particularly Protestant, with a concomitant growth of atheists and agnostics and Christians lacking links to any faith community. Growth of various non-Christian faiths, however, has only been, at most, limited.

A reason for this stability is suggested by the size and the homelands of Charlottetown's immigrant population. In 1986, 70.1 per cent of city residents were Island-born and this figure remained virtually unchanged at 70.4 per cent in 2001. People born in the rest of Canada made up 25 per cent of the population in 1986 and 25.1 per cent in 2001. This left foreign-born citizens as only 4.9 and 4.5 per cent of the population respectively in 1986 and 2001.[4] Among the immigrant community, Americans, British and Asians made up the three largest groups in 1986, and Americans, other Europeans and British were the major categories in 2001. Although people born in Africa and Asia increased numerically between 1986 and 2001, they actually declined as percentages of the population. Those born in the western hemisphere outside of Canada and the United States increased marginally from 0.1 per cent to 0.2 per cent. Despite an increased variety of backgrounds for immigrants in Charlottetown during these years, immigration did little to make the city proportionally more diverse.

During the period from 1986 to 2001, the wide gap between the number of males and females in Charlottetown began to diminish. In 1986 there were only 79 males to every 100 females, but, by 2001, this had increased to 84:100. Children under 15 years of age were virtually balanced in numbers, 99 boys to 100 girls in 1986 and 101:100 in 2001. A decline in outmigration among young males is perhaps recorded by the diminished gap between males and females in the 15 to 24 age group. There were 87 males to 100 females in 1986 and 90:100 by 2001. Among those in their most economically productive years, 25 to 55, the balance remained the same at 89 males to 100 females, but for those over 55, the gap narrowed significantly from 58 males per 100 females to 66:100. Overall, the demographic statistics suggest that in the period 1986-2001 there were increased opportunities for young males to stay at home, or perhaps a growing similarity in the patterns of migration among young males and females. Meanwhile, men were living longer.

Age distribution within Charlottetown's population reflected the "baby boom and echo" effect. In 1986, 14 per cent of the population was under 15. That proportion increased to 17 per cent by 2001, but the next older group, 15 to 24, dropped from 18 per cent to 15 per cent between 1986 and 2001. Conversely, people aged 25 to 55 increased from 36 per cent of the population in 1986 to 42 per cent in 2001. Those over 55 dropped from 32 per cent to 26 per cent in the same period. The data point to a generally aging population in the opening years of the new millennium, and this will likely be the case as people in the 25 to 55 age group approach retirement.[5]

---

4 This inability to attract immigrants has not significantly changed since then. They made up 4.7 per cent of the population in 2006.

5 The 2006 census showed this to be the case.

Continuity also characterized the economic profile of Charlottetown's neighbourhoods during this period. Decisions about where to live seem to have been dictated by economic status as much as anything else, although there was considerable intermingling of people of different levels of affluence. Brighton remained a prestigious area, and other districts, such as Lewis Point, as well as the shoreline of Charlottetown harbour in Stratford, have emerged as desirable addresses. Most new suburban areas contained a range of middle-class homes, while the centre of the city held many of the less-well-off, although, even there, pockets of desirable housing remained and new, more expensive housing was built. Even in a city as small as Charlottetown, the early 21st-century appeal of living in the downtown core was being felt. These trends reflect a population in which couples were less likely to have children and more households were occupied by single individuals.[6]

POLITICAL LIFE

If the evolving structure of Charlottetown's population had any impact in the political arena, one might be tempted to think that it was in selection of the mayor as all five who held office between 1985 and 2005 were Roman Catholics. This is in marked contrast to the opening pages of the city's history in which all 12 mayors between 1855 and 1904 were Protestants. Unlike the early days, however, when sectarian issues were a strong motivating factor behind the way people voted, current elections appear to be little influenced by religious affiliation. Other considerations, among them personal popularity and effective campaign organizations, seem to be key. By the 1990s, provincial politics intruded more insistently into the municipal arena than may have formerly been the case. Mayoralty victories indicate the effectiveness of Conservatives in mustering the local vote.[7]

The single most important task facing municipal politicians in the period 1985–2005 was balancing the city's books. Municipal finance was by no means a new difficulty and certainly not one that was unique to Charlottetown, but circumstances became especially challenging, particularly in the early 1990s. The essential problem was paying for new and more costly services with a declining population and a fairly static tax base. Both demographic and economic growth were flowing to the suburban municipalities, taking with them the commercial tax base in the form of industrial parks and shopping malls which permitted low residential tax burdens. The city, on the other hand, was left with old infrastructure to repair and services that were partly necessitated by suburbanites who did not defray the costs.

This was not, however, the situation that prevailed in the mid-1980s. In fact, the transfer of the responsibility for schools from the city to the province in 1978 resulted

6 These trends are established by a comparison of the censuses of 1996, 2001 and 2006.

7 The effects of provincial political organizing could be seen in the municipal elections of 1997 when the sitting mayor, Ian "Tex" MacDonald, a former Conservative turned Liberal, was defeated by Conservative George MacDonald. When George MacDonald stepped aside to run (unsuccessfully) in the provincial election of 2003, he was succeeded by Conservative Clifford Lee.

in large operating surpluses, with the 1985 surplus standing at $196,526.[8] Such a favourable fiscal climate encouraged the city to embark upon a number of ambitious construction projects. Thus, in 1986, besides servicing major developments, such as the Veterans Affairs headquarters and the waterfront, the city was ready to take on extensive renovations to City Hall, hosting the Canada Winter Games in 1991, revitalizing the downtown and improving recreational facilities.

In 1992 fortunes were dramatically reversed. Municipal income, particularly from government properties, dropped precipitously just as increased charges for garbage tippage, labour and employer contributions to Unemployment Insurance and the Canada Pension Plan drove up costs. The result was a projected deficit of $221,242 for 1993. Civic debt had also increased to pay for the City Hall restoration, construction of a new parking garage and holding the Winter Games. Unfortunately, Charlottetown had the highest residential tax burden in the province and the second-lowest median income. This made raising municipal property tax rates to cover costs daunting. Instead, the city attacked expenditures and streamlined operations so that the 1994 budget was balanced without tax increases.

Although opinion among city politicians was not unanimous — Alderman John Squarebriggs argued expenses were deferred for years until they all had to be faced at the same time — most placed the blame for Charlottetown's financial plight on discriminatory provincial policies. One aspect of the problem was the power of the province to set assessments. According to Alderman Sibyl Cutcliffe, valuations on provincial buildings were one-third below their true levels. The size of the revenue stream from the province to the city relative to what other jurisdictions received was another, very important issue. For the city, fairness in the distribution of provincial revenue derived from property taxes was critical. Residential taxes were collected in Charlottetown for the city and for the province.[9] The provincial tax rate in 1993 was 75¢ per $100 of assessment. In 1977 approximately 43 per cent of the income the province received from this source was returned to the city. This dropped to less than 15 per cent in 1993. In this period, the tax dollars collected had increased by 254 per cent while the grants to Charlottetown had gone up by only 23 per cent. If inflation, which increased by 107 per cent during this time, were factored in, the grants to Charlottetown had actually been cut by 84 per cent. Meanwhile, grants to other municipalities had gone up a gross amount of 278 per cent. The flow of property taxes from Charlottetown to other places appeared excessive. This was particularly true for residential property taxes. Charlottetonians recognized that provincial revenues from taxes on commercial properties were justly shared with other Islanders because businesses in the city served the whole province. Residential property taxes were another matter.

8 The surplus in 1985 was higher than in the preceding year but lower than in 1983.

9 The provincial property tax was intended to cover schools, an expense that had been a municipal responsibility before 1978 and had been met through property taxes. In recognition of the varying abilities of municipalities to pay, equalization adjustments were made in school funding. Tax money from wealthier areas flowed to poorer ones in order to standardize the quality of education across the province.

Discrimination against Charlottetown was apparent in various other ways as well. Most Island municipalities had services, such as snow removal, street maintenance, paving and policing, provided by the province.[10] Charlottetown, and a few other communities, did not. Equalization payments failed to bridge the gap. The city was given $35 per capita for policing, but the actual cost was $175. About 15.5 kilometres of city streets formed part of the provincial highway network, but the provincial grant covered only about 65 per cent of the cost of maintaining them, while extensions of the same roads in adjoining municipalities were entirely maintained by the provincial government. The only just resolution to this situation, in the opinion of the city, was to amend the inequitable tax structure. In a heartfelt address to Council, Alderman Richard Brown argued that Charlottetown's deficit was a message to the people of Prince Edward Island that if they wanted "a good and vibrant capital city," they had better help the city "to get an equal share of those revenues from the Province" or they were "going to lose [out]."

Part of the challenge in confronting the provincial government was a lack of political clout in the legislature. Charlottetonians were grossly under-represented compared to the rural areas of the province. City politicians charged that the venerable Canadian principle of representation by population was at stake. To help resolve the inequity, the city appealed to the provincial supreme court which eventually ruled in its favour. In part, the court found that approximate parity of representation from the three counties was not justified, and conditions within the province could not support the handicap given to rural voters over urban ones. The province was instructed to revise the electoral boundaries so that variations of population among the ridings did not exceed a factor of plus or minus 10 per cent.

The province had not been standing idly by while all of this was happening. As part of a process to manage land issues more effectively, it had established the Royal Commission on Land, headed by the Clerk Assistant of the Legislature, Douglas Boylan, to investigate changes in land use, ownership and appearance. Part of Boylan's report, *Everything Before Us*, submitted in 1990, urged amalgamation of the Charlottetown area municipalities. Prompted by this proposal, the province commissioned Smith, Green and Associates to consider municipal reform, and after receiving recommendations in their *Municipal Studies Report* that parallelled the Boylan recommendations, the government prepared a white paper on how such consolidation might be effected. Three options were brought forward for discussion: amalgamation, regionalization and annexation. A consultation process was initiated by the appointment of a commissioner, Lorne R. Moase, to gather reaction to the possible changes. Although the province was prepared to consider creating a regional government for the Charlottetown area (Sherwood and Parkdale had vigorously opposed the Boylan recommendation), the city preferred amalgamation, but only if it were accompanied by tax reform, which, for it, remained the central issue. For his part, Mayor John Ready felt that

10 Of course, residents in these communities paid property taxes as well, and thereby financially contributed for the services provided.

Mayor John Ready felt that amalgamation was inevitable, but it had to be accompanied by provincial electoral reform.

amalgamation was inevitable, but it had to be accompanied by provincial electoral reform. Other city politicians feared amalgamation's possible negative consequences: a loss of volunteerism as the larger city moved to a professional fire department, downloading of provincial responsibilities, job insecurity for city employees and decline of the downtown core.

The various area communities responded to amalgamation differently. While Charlottetown favoured it as long as its tax concerns were rectified, Parkdale preferred the status quo and rejected it outright. Sherwood was less definite in its opposition and suggested a more limited union of suburban communities. Hillsborough Park, on the other hand, supported amalgamation. West Royalty, with its large commercial tax base, was hesitant and resented the government's aggressive approach to the idea, while East Royalty and Winsloe were fatalistic about the situation considering the tone of the government's white paper. The more distant communities of Bunbury, Southport, Cross Roads and Keppoch-Kinlock; and Cornwall, Eliot River and North River, not only opposed amalgamation with Charlottetown but proposed local amalgamations, a step that the government finally accepted.

Following these consultations, the provincial legislature passed the Charlottetown Area Municipalities Act on May 17, 1994. Under it, three new entities were shaped out of the myriad communities within the Charlottetown area: Charlottetown, Charlottetown West and Charlottetown South. The new City of Charlottetown was made up of the old city plus Parkdale, Sherwood, East Royalty, Hillsborough Park, Winsloe, West Royalty and the Queen Elizabeth Hospital grounds. The Town of Charlottetown West, later renamed Cornwall, included Cornwall, Eliot River and North River, and the Town of Charlottetown South, now Stratford, drew together Bunbury, Southport, Cross Roads, Keppoch-Kinlock, Battery Point and part of Alexandra. Although it was widely perceived that Charlottetown was driving the amalgamation process, the city's mayor, Ian "Tex" MacDonald, later pointed to the province's desire to "save a whole lot of dollars in terms of having too many administrations out there" as the main factor.

Under the new act, elections for the expanded municipality were scheduled for October 3, 1994. "Tex" MacDonald was elected the first mayor, handily beating his main opponent, Larry Hughes of Sherwood. Thereafter, the new Council operated under the transitional provisions of the Municipalities Act. Amalgamation officially came into effect on April 1, 1995, and the old Charlottetown passed into history. The former ward structure went with it; new wards had been defined for the

Ian "Tex" MacDonald was elected the first mayor of the expanded municipality on October 3, 1994.

October elections. There were 10 of them, laid out to avoid conforming to previous electoral divisions.[11] Although these divisions undermined local community spirit somewhat, they were intended to promote a feeling of togetherness on the part of citizens within the new, bigger city. To encourage a sense of continuity, many of the new wards used historical names.

Despite the widespread expectation that operational efficiencies could be achieved by merging several, smaller communities into a single, larger one, the practicalities of such consolidations were largely theoretical in 1995. Winnipeg and its neighbouring municipalities had been drawn together into a unicity in 1972, but the Halifax Regional Municipality was not formed until 1996, and amalgamations in Toronto, Ottawa and Montreal followed in 1998, 2001 and 2002 respectively. There was no beaten path for Charlottetown to follow. The city chose an approach to consolidation in which attaining short-term cost savings through staff reductions was not a principal objective. Administrators believed that amalgamation would roll out most smoothly if existing employees felt secure in their jobs. Without the threat of job losses, the work force bought into the process, and the transition took place with less disruption than was subsequently experienced in other jurisdictions. The decision not to force the distant suburban communities into the amalgamated city may also have smoothed the path and avoided a reaction like the de-amalgamation debacle in Quebec following the 2002 municipal "fusions forcées."

Amalgamation did not resolve some important disputes between the city and the province. Finances remained an important bone of contention. Unlike the city, the provincial government anticipated amalgamation would produce savings of $4.1 million, $1.7 in public works alone. In thinking otherwise, the city recognized that additional police officers were needed to assume duties formerly provided by the RCMP at provincial expense. There were also requirements to pay for fire services and street maintenance in the suburbs. These conflicting perspectives came into the open during negotiations over the Comprehensive Urban Service Agreement. This was the basic understanding between the city and the province over which new responsibilities the enlarged city was to assume and what offsetting grants would be available from

11 They are Ward 1, Queens Square; Ward 2, Belvedere; Ward 3, Brighton; Ward 4, St. Avard's; Ward 5, Spring Park; Ward 6, Mount Edward; Ward 7, Beach Grove; Ward 8, Highfield; Ward 9, Stonepark; Ward 10, Falconwood.

the province to pay for them. The pivotal issue was whether the province or the city would be responsible for roads. The decision was not straightforward; it involved details connected with the maintenance of sidewalks and storm sewers as well as renewal of culverts. In the end, it all boiled down to money. The province concluded that $20,000 per kilometre was sufficient to maintain a provincial road while the city calculated that one of its streets needed $31,500. The difference between the two figures was due to the lesser amounts the province paid for cleaning and labour — the province used contract and seasonal labour — and costs connected with storm sewers. As the April 1, 1995, date for inaugurating the new city drew closer, negotiators realized that an agreement on services could not be reached in time. A memorandum of understanding covering street maintenance for April 1995 was the best that could be achieved.

Although an initial agreement was reached by May 1995, under which the city took on additional costs for streets and policing in return for a reduction of the provincial property tax rate, a final understanding of the appropriate level of funding was not. The essential outline of a fair agreement from the city's perspective nevertheless emerged. Charlottetown was to be regarded as a full-service municipality responsible for policing, fire protection, streets, storm sewers and related planning, and it would receive tax credits from the province in compensation for carrying out these

The Charlottetown Area Municipalities Act created three new entities out of the numerous communities within the metropolitan area: Charlottetown, Charlottetown West and Charlottetown South. The new City of Charlottetown was made up of the old city plus Parkdale, Sherwood, East Royalty, Hillsborough Park, Winsloe, West Royalty and the Queen Elizabeth hospital grounds.

duties. What remained unresolved was the level of compensation. The city contended that, if the province ceased collecting taxes on residential properties, the revenues thus made available to the city would cover the cost of these services. The province refused to vacate this tax area or to turn over the money that was raised from it.

Charlottetown West, later renamed Cornwall, included Cornwall, Eliot River and North River. Charlottetown South, now Stratford, drew together Bunbury, Southport, Crossroads, Keppoch-Kinlock, Battery Point and part of Alexandra. By 2001, 43 per cent of the province's population lived in the metropolitan area – almost 24 per cent in the amalgamated city.

In August 1998, a Joint Provincial-Municipal Committee, including Charlottetown's Intergovernmental Affairs Committee and the local MLAs, was created to seek some form of reconciliation. New funding considerations came to light, such as the right-of-way fees collected by the province from Maritime Electric and Island Telephone, none of which were passed on to the city, and the non-payment of municipal taxes by UPEI, Holland College and Queen Elizabeth Hospital. Other considerations that arose included provincial taxes on income, gas, tobacco and alcohol, as well as federal equalization payments generated by Charlottetown's population. "The deeper we got into the issue, the more we realized how complicated it is," commented Jamie Ballem, Conservative MLA and chairman of the committee. The Liberal opposition in the legislature accepted the city's position on residential property taxes in February 1999. An interim agreement, running from March 9, 1999, until March 31, 2001, authorized increased payments to the city. In the meantime, a consulting firm, KPMG, was hired to analyze the tax issues involved.

Although the city had contributed funds to what was intended to be an impartial study, from the city's perspective, the province had co-opted the process and dictated the results. Charlottetown's representations were apparently ignored. The KPMG report, issued in December 2000, was largely unresponsive to the city's arguments. Local streets should be handled by the municipality and provincial roads by the province. On the issue of sharing revenues, the consultants found that it was not unusual for provinces and cities to levy property taxes, but it was for them to share the revenues. They recommended that existing tax credits be replaced by grants. Finally, while recognizing the costs Charlottetown incurred by being the provincial capital, the consultants dismissed suggestions that ongoing financial considerations should be made on those grounds. During subsequent negotiations with the province for a CUSA renewal, the city expressed its unhappiness with the proposed financial arrangements. The province offered a new five-year deal that included a $1 million per annum transfer, but, to get it, the city was obliged to promise not to raise its concerns about CUSA again. Eventually, the city accepted the arrangement, which ran to 2006.

During the ongoing controversy over taxation, the city and province continued their other battle over representation in the legislature. In response to the Supreme Court ruling concerning electoral boundaries, the provincial government appointed an electoral boundaries commission to investigate how to comply. In its report, *Changing the Political Landscape*, presented to the legislature in the spring of 1993, the commission recommended constituencies should vary in population by a factor of no more than plus or minus 14 per cent. The new government, headed by Catherine Callbeck, delayed action on electoral reform and eventually presented a revised Electoral Boundaries Act that would permit a maximum variation among ridings of plus or minus 25 per cent, with an overall difference in population between the largest and smallest of 50 per cent. In practice, the 27 electoral districts had variances of plus or minus 20 per cent with a total variation of about 40 per cent. The city felt the legislation failed to conform to the court ruling and, along with other urban municipalities, decided to challenge the new acts in the Supreme Court.[12] With a hearing set for the last week of March and first week of April 1996, the government opted to delay addressing the issue until after the upcoming provincial election, set for November 18, 1996. That election went ahead using the disputed boundaries and resulted in the replacement of the Liberals[13] with the Progressive Conservatives under Pat Binns. Shortly afterwards, Chief Justice K. R. MacDonald dismissed the city's application.

The failure of the city to prevail in either of the disputes concerning taxation and representation underscores the difficulties of a junior order of government challenging its political master. It also may speak to the complexity and subjectivity of the

12 The other municipalities were Summerside, Sherwood, Parkdale, West and East Royalty, Hillsborough Park and Winsloe.

13 Catherine Callbeck resigned as Liberal leader prior to the 1996 general election and was replaced by Keith Milligan, who was Premier in October and November 1996 before the Liberals were soundly beaten by the Conservatives.

matters being contested. Equally, the unresolved issues demonstrate the imbalance in power between the levels of government and the lack of symmetry between power and equity. Moreover, during the early 1990s, the city also had difficulties getting the federal government to pay adequate grants in lieu of taxes on its extensive property holdings. In this case, the city could only address the shortfall through the province, which was itself suffering the effects of federal cutbacks and downloading of responsibilities. The difference between the city in 1855 and in 1996 in relation to its immediate political masters was the willingness to contest disputes in court and on the political battlefield.

The differences with the province over revenue and representation were not the only political issues animating Charlottetown's politics between 1985 and 2005. Questions involving heritage, development, Sunday store opening[14] and the state of the streets elicited considerable attention and comment. Although significant matters, and, for some, deeply felt, they did not tend to gain tremendous traction during civic election campaigns. The dynamics of municipal politics have also changed, an example being the competition for the mayoralty. Whereas it was once an honour to be conferred for a term on august civic fathers, it became a contested office, and, once elected, incumbents tended to receive a second term. This reflected the pattern at the provincial level. Whether longer terms will encourage municipal leaders to press for more favourable treatment for their citizens and more autonomy in the management of their affairs remains to be seen. With political alliances along provincial party lines influencing Councillors, much may depend upon the alignment of political interests at the cabinet table and council board at any given time.

URBAN LANDSCAPE

Jane Jacobs, the late Toronto-based urban critic and writer, noted in 1986 that planning a city isn't a science, it's an art. According to Jacobs, cities should embrace the concept of mixed land use, jumbling together housing and businesses, the old with the new. Cities should be compact, lively and built to foster a sense of community. At one time, Jacobs' ideas flew in the face of conventional planning wisdom, but they persisted and gradually gained acceptance. One may wonder whether they apply to small cities like Charlottetown; she would probably argue that they did. If this were the case, changes in the built environment of the Island's capital since 1985 would probably have both pleased and vexed her.

The period 1985–2005 began with the news that, in 1984, Charlottetown issued the most building permits ever, 215, with a value exceeding $13 million. The boom was expected to continue. In fact, the next two decades saw extensive changes to the cityscape. Not all construction was new because, by the 1990s, the spread of concepts

14 Prince Edward Island resisted Sunday shopping but eventually ran two pilot projects for a period of six weeks prior to Christmas to gauge public reaction. In 2008 Sunday opening between noon and 5 p.m., June to December, was brought in. It was well-received.

of heritage preservation resulted in considerable renovation of existing buildings, and this had a significant impact on the city's fabric.

In a community in which public administration was so important, the construction by all three levels of government was inevitably significant. New federal offices on Fitzroy Street near Queen were one such example. In design, the complex was intended to blend in with the city's traditional architecture. A second building, the Canadian Food Inspection Agency Laboratories on Mount Edward Road, was a more contemporary design. It opened in 1995. The major federal initiative, however, was a large centre of operations on University Avenue between Fitzroy and Euston Streets. The 17,500-square-metre (188,368-square-foot) undertaking, dubbed "The Jean Canfield Building," was announced with great fanfare in 2003. Designed by Bergmark, Guimond Hammarlund Jones/Urbana to be environmentally friendly, its features included a heat-reflecting roof and mechanisms to capture and use rain water. As initial bids for construction proved to be high, the government put the project on hold in 2004 while it sought ways to trim costs. Eventually, the underground parking was eliminated, and in 2005 Pomerleau Construction was awarded the contract. The old, soon-to-be-redundant Dominion Building on Queen Street was then put up for sale to developers. Two other substantial federal projects were the 3,300-square-metre (35,500-square-foot) airport terminal that went into service in 1986, and the reserve navy establishment, HMCS *Queen Charlotte*, which was built on the waterfront and opened in 1997.

Provincial government projects were not as high-profile and focused on renovations. The 1950 wing of the old Charlottetown Hospital was converted for use as an office building, but was later demolished to make way for a parking lot. Another renovation involved the Sir Louis Davies Law Court building. It reopened in 1999.[15] New construction included the PEI Food Technology Centre, built on the edge of the UPEI campus in 1988 and expanded in 2003–04.

The municipality, more than any other level of government, espoused heritage preservation during this period. At the urgings of Alderman Eddie Rice, City Council opted for a massive overhaul to City Hall rather than build new quarters.[16] Restoration and renovation began in 1988 with the reversal of some unsympathetic modernizations made in the 1960s and the conversion of the area formerly occupied by the fire department to office space and a tourist information bureau. Further changes in 1998 and 1999 converted the space previously used by the police department to administrative purposes. In a less spectacular renovation, in 1999, the former water commission building on Kirkwood Drive was converted to serve as the police headquarters.

There was, of course, new municipal construction, including the Civic Centre erected at the Charlottetown Driving Park to host the 1991 Canada Winter Games. Contentious at the time, the decision to proceed with the project was made in July

15 During this refurbishment, the simple façade was embellished by a chrome strip, a surprisingly effective flourish.

16 The rescued City Hall was declared a National Historic Site in 1988.

In the late 1980s, Council opted to overhaul City Hall instead of building anew. This c. 1970 postcard shows some of the unsympathetic modernizations (note the in-filled window and door openings) that were reversed during the renovation. City Hall was declared a National Historic Site in 1988.

1988. Completed in March 1990, it was a collaborative venture involving the three levels of government and UPEI. The city also built the Farmers' Market on Belvedere Avenue in the early 1990s and two parking facilities, the Pownal Parking Garage, which went into service in July 1988, and the Fitzroy Parkade that opened on the site of the former Eaton's store in December 2003.

Although construction of new churches did not have the same impact on the cityscape as in former times, there was considerable activity in this regard, especially in the suburban areas. Among other developments, the Community Baptist Church on Sherwood Road and Sts. Peter and Paul Antiochian Orthodox Church on St. Peter's Road opened in 1995; the Sherwood Church of Christ completed an addition in 1996, and the St. Mark's Presbyterian congregation moved to a new church on Tamarac Avenue in 2001.[17]

With the declining birth rate, school construction lagged somewhat compared to the postwar period. Renovations were completed at Colonel Gray and Birchwood schools and Charlottetown Rural was enlarged and renovated in 1994. The Francophone community got a facility of its own when École François-Buote and Carrefour de L'Île-Saint-Jean opened in 1991 on Acadian Drive, east of the Queen Elizabeth Hospital. The West Royalty Elementary School moved to a new building on

17 Faith Bible Church erected an addition to its main building in 2006, and Central Christian Church built a new sanctuary and converted the old one into a fellowship hall in 2006-2007. An extensive overhaul of the exterior fabric of St. Dunstan's Basilica was completed in 2008.

Commonwealth Avenue in 2001. In 1995 the Charlottetown Hospital School of Nursing on Haviland Street was vacated and then modified for use by Holland College as the Tourism and Culinary Institute. Holland College opened a new residence, Glendenning Hall, in 2005, at the corner of Edward and Grafton Streets. In May of that year, plans were also announced for the construction of a home for the new Centre for Labour Force Innovation at the college's central campus.[18]

In contrast, construction took place at UPEI throughout the period 1985–2005. The most important addition was the massive Veterinary College that opened in 1985. Its size was disguised by placing much of the building below ground level.[19] Historic Main Building was completely renovated, with great care taken to preserve the best architectural features while providing more functional spaces and correcting faults like steeply sloping floors. It reopened in 1989. The K. C. Irving Chemistry Centre opened in 1996, an innovative pre-fabricated Classroom Centre followed in 2001 and the Duffy Science Centre was extensively renovated in 2005.

Much of the University's construction was for non-academic spaces. The Chi-Wan Young Sports Centre was completed in 1990, as was the Wanda Wyatt Dining Hall. They were followed by the W. A. Murphy Student Centre in 2002. The Capital Area Recreational Inc. (CARI) Aquatics Facility and MacLauchlan Arena were built as a joint venture by Charlottetown, Stratford, Cornwall and the University, with considerable help from senior levels of government. It opened in 2003. The simply, but aptly, named "New Residence" welcomed its first occupants in 2005.[20]

Commercial development also exhibited a combination of new construction and renovation. In the downtown core, an effort was made to update existing buildings. One of the most effective projects involved the railway station. Conversion of it to office space was completed in 1996. The intention was originally for it to house the *Guardian*, but the deal was cancelled after a change in the newspaper's ownership. The Workers' Compensation Board occupied the space instead. Another old structure, the nearby 1874 stone "Copperhouse," was renovated and turned into the Charlottetown Visitor Information Centre in 1997.[21] New centre-town construction included Peake's Wharf, a waterfront project that combined a 150-slip, full-service marina with retail shops, a restaurant and a bar, all designed to fit aesthetically into their heritage surroundings. As for new construction, the BDC tower, always planned as part of the Confederation Court Mall project, was finally built and opened in 1989 along with an elevated pedway connecting the tower with the Queen Street parking garage and the mall. The former Holman's of PEI, which closed finally in

18 The new wing was opened in October 2006.

19 A major addition to AVC was completed in 2006.

20 Soon thereafter, Marian Hall was decommissioned as a residence and work began to convert it to a home for the School of Business. A large wing was added, and the new building, McDougall Hall, opened in 2008.

21 The Visitors' Information Centre has since moved to Founders' Hall, and the Copperhouse was rented to the Mi'kmaq Confederacy.

1989,[22] and the mall itself underwent a total refit. Also in the central business district, the Atlantic Technology Centre at the corner of University Avenue and Fitzroy Street opened in September, 2002. It was a 12,077-square-metre (130,000-square-foot), four-storey complex designed to act as an incubator for information technology, film and new media start-up businesses. Over at the Exhibition Grounds on Kensington Road, the historic stands of the Charlottetown Driving Park were replaced between 2003 and 2005 by a glitzy, modern, $25-million building.

In suburban areas, commercial development followed the trend to big box stores found across North America. The first was a Canadian Tire store that opened in September 1985. Located off University Avenue, close to the junction of highways 1 and 2, the store catered to Charlottetonians, suburbanites and Islanders from further away, all of whom would reach the place, appropriately enough, by car. In the years that followed, other mass retailers, including Sobeys, Wal-Mart and Home Depot, put up cavernous structures and added to the asphalted expanse of parking. Home Hardware was a major retailer that resisted the suburban allure when it placed its new store on St. Peter's Road in Parkdale. In 2005 another big-box "power centre" was launched in West Royalty with the opening of a Sears department store. The 10,034-square-metre (108,000-square-foot) establishment on Highway 2, just north of Highway 1, was the first "off-mall" Sears department store in Canada and was clearly intended to serve the whole province. Whatever reservations the municipal and provincial governments had formerly felt concerning suburban shopping were clearly by then a thing of the past.

Residential housing followed a similar pattern of development. In the historic downtown, the emphasis was on restoring existing buildings. Individual homes were improved, and others, like Fairholm at the corner of Prince and Fitzroy Streets and Hillhurst further down Fitzroy, were renovated and converted into upscale inns. Two old small hotels and a number of houses were restored and updated to form the Great George boutique hotel complex. The Sacred Heart Home was turned into seniors' apartments in 1997. New construction included affordable housing, such as the King Square and the Gateway co-operative housing developments and high-end rental apartments and condominiums.[23] Expensive in fill housing was built along the North River between it and North River Road.

Outside the central core, large, expensive single-family homes on large lots appeared in areas, such as Barbour Circle in Sherwood and Sheffield in Lewis Point.[24] Developments like Sandlewood and Park Meadows in West Royalty, Green Meadow Drive in Winsloe and Horseshoe Hill Estates in East Royalty offered medium-to-large homes on substantial lots. Houses were generally smaller in developments that

22 Holman's in Charlottetown closed in 1985, but with independent businesses operating as a licensed department store, Holman's of PEI, continued until 1989.

23 The luxurious Northumberland on Pownal Street and Paoli's Wharf overlooking the harbour were two landmark condominium developments completed after 2005.

24 Another development in this category, Bridle Path Estates, in East Royalty, was started around 2005.

In 1996 Charlottetown had 83 parks covering 500 acres, ranging in size from community "pocket parks" to the two main ones, Victoria and Confederation Landing Park.

included Royalty Vale in West Royalty, and River Ridge and the Habitat for Humanity project in Hillsborough Park. Some communities, for instance Park West Estates in Winsloe, offered smaller single-family homes and duplexes on standard lots, while others including Elena Court, Love Subdivision and Colonial Creek in the Sherwood-East Royalty area contained a mix of multiple units and singles. Typically, new suburban communities were dispersed across a wide swath of rolling land at the city's periphery. The pastoral setting provided some of them with charming vistas that were used to good advantage.

Charlottetown continued to pay considerable attention to its parks. In the summer of 1985, Victoria Park opened with improvements to the tennis courts, playground, washrooms and parking. In 1990 a plan to improve the park further was undertaken by landscape architects, Morello and Associates, with public input. The perimeter road was retained as a two-way circulation route, but in 1991 the middle roadway was blocked to traffic. There was a great variety of opinion on how the park should be used, proof, if it was needed, of a high level of popular concern about green space.[25]

Victoria Park, however, no longer completely dominated discussions of parkland. Efforts were being made to create a welcoming face to the city on the harbour. An overall plan for a park on the waterfront industrial land was outlined to City Council in September 1993 by Hough, Stansbury and Woodland, Limited. Principal features included scenic pathways, perennial gardens and sitting areas. In 1994, after CADC acquired the old Texaco tank farm, work began with the help of ACOA funding. The resulting Confederation Landing Park, which opened in 1995, reinforced the city's efforts to brand itself as Canada's birthplace and became the setting for the "Festival of Lights" on Canada Day and the "Festival of the Fathers" on Labour Day. CADC developed the park but leased it to the city for $1 for five years. After that time, the city was to buy it for $1 and maintain it. Some Councillors worried about the cost of maintenance, but there was little debate about its value to the city. The setting was enlarged when CADC acquired the old CN car shop in 1998 and created an interpretation centre within it focusing on the Confederation story. This new attraction, Founders' Hall, opened on July 1, 2001.

To unify the whole shoreline, CADC developed an interconnected system of boardwalks, walkways and trails that eventually ran 12 kilometres along the waterfront between Victoria Park in the west to the Queen Elizabeth hospital in the east, including 3.8 kilometres beside the harbour. The Irish Settlers' Memorial, at the point behind Queen Charlotte Armoury, was a significant feature within this right-of-way. Taking the shape of a Celtic Cross, with a terrace composed of 32 flagstones, one from each Irish county, the monument was dedicated on July 1, 2001.

In 1996 Charlottetown had 83 parks covering over 500 acres ranging in size from community "pocket parks" to the two main ones. Even more parkland was contemplated, such as at the former landfill in East Royalty.[26] The federal government's decision to withdraw from the Dominion Experimental Farm opened opportunities to exploit Ravenwood's bucolic setting. Conceptual plans drafted by Daniel K. Glenn Ltd. for the "Friends of the Farm" and CADC envisaged gardens, paths and walkways through landscaped and natural settings, and included ponds, orchards, meadows, an event field and a vineyard. In one of the oldest sections of the city, the Joseph A. Ghiz Memorial Park was opened in 2001 at the corner of Kent and Edward Streets in memory of the popular late premier. A setback was received when Hurricane Juan

---

25 In 2008, for a three-month summer trial period, the inward bound lane of the Park Roadway was kept open as a one-way street and the outbound lane was dedicated to pedestrians, rollerbladers and bicyclists.

26 Efforts to realize this objective have met with practical obstacles, such as bits of debris working themselves to the surface.

swept over the city on September 29, 2004, destroying trees and boardwalks in various locations, including the city squares. Some of the trees lost were planted during the first round of municipal beautification in the late 19th century.

Recent efforts to make Charlottetown more attractive were partly to increase its appeal for tourists. To that end, Richmond Street at Victoria Row was converted to a pedestrian walkway during the summer months, and sidewalks along Queen Street from Richmond to Water Street were widened and made more visually appealing by the use of interlocking brick. Considerable funds were invested in road maintenance. To alleviate traffic congestion downtown, the arterial highway was built in an arc from Highway 2 on the west to Riverside Drive on the east.[27] Traffic through the city was thus able to move quickly between the Hillsborough Bridge and principal routes running north and west. The bridge itself, widened and improved, was reopened by Premier Pat Binns on August 26, 1998. Flow of traffic to the bridge from the city core was facilitated by the Water Street Parkway. Despite plans to widen University Avenue south of Belvedere, by 2005, the streetscape retained the crowded, jumbled appearance of strip development, as did St. Peter's Road in Parkdale.

The implications for the harbour of some of the changes to the face of Charlottetown were profound. From a decaying industrial zone in the early 1980s, it made the transition to an attractive, public space designed to welcome visitors and foster recreation. Abandonment of the PEI Railway by Canadian National in 1989 made the space occupied by waterfront tracks and rail yards available for those purposes. The actual marine installations were also in decline by 1985. Late that year, fire damaged the old, pre-1900 buildings on the Marine Wharf, creating safety hazards. Despite the heritage nature of the structures, they were pulled down in 1986. Later, the wharf was upgraded, and in April 2005 ownership was transferred from Transport Canada to the Charlottetown Harbour Authority Inc. The agreement provided a subvention of $19 million from the federal government to be used over 15 years to maintain the facility. One costly challenge for the future involved the mega-sized cruise ships that the city sought to attract to the port. The marine terminal was too small to accommodate the largest of them and would have to be expanded before Charlottetown was to claim its share of this lucrative business.[28]

Extensive modernization of utilities was similarly undertaken between 1985 and 2005. This included upgrades to the power system,[29] extension of municipal water and

27 The roadway has been extended to the Upton Road and in the future is expected to join Highway 1, beyond Cornwall, via a new bridge over the North River.

28 The marine terminal was upgraded during 2007–08 by extending the pier and building a new welcome centre. The south berth increased to 183 metres (600 feet) with a depth of 13.5 metres (44 feet). The cruise ship operators responded by adding visits and lengthening the stopovers.

29 The Charlottetown generating station of Maritime Electric, along with the Borden generating station, were held in reserve in case power supplies from the mainland were interrupted. The Charlottetown station received a major upgrade in 2005 when a 50-million-watt diesel turbine was installed at a cost of $35 million. It could supply one-quarter of the Island's peak demand for power. With the upgrade, a new stack appeared on the horizon.

The second mayor of the amalgamated city, George MacDonald, convened a "capital symposium" in 2002 to provide a mechanism for envisioning sustained economic growth.

sewerage services, installation of old-fashioned design light fixtures in the historic district and relocation of telephone wires underground. For those who communicated without wires, "Wireless Charlottetown" promised free access to the world wide web. In 1995 three small district heating plants built in the early 1980s were acquired from the province by Trigen Energy Canada Inc. and subsequently linked together. Heat generation was consolidated at the energy-from-waste plant on the waterfront where energy was recovered from municipal garbage, sawmill waste and a small amount of oil.[30] The new facility — one of the most modern district energy systems in Canada — became operational in 1998 and has a 15-kilometre hot-water distribution network that serves 84 buildings including provincial government office buildings, UPEI, Holland College, two malls and apartment and commercial buildings. The same system also air conditions UPEI and the Queen Elizabeth Hospital.

All of the changes in the urban landscape took place within an emerging planning framework. The city's first official plan, made in 1980, was extended by the 1987 development plan and strategy. Besides highlighting the problems posed by suburbanization, the document moved beyond zoning regulations and development controls to address the need to mobilize civic resources to effect positive change. Many of the concepts foreshadowed here were subsequently implemented, including improving the downtown core, revitalizing the waterfront and branding the city as the birthplace of Confederation. Significantly, the planners recognized that Charlottetown was constrained by policies beyond its jurisdiction and demographic shifts beyond any government's control. The Boylan Report offered a solution to some of the former set of problems at least. Following amalgamation, a study by the Department of Community Affairs and the Attorney General examined ways to avoid the same problems of urban sprawl and competition in the future and concluded that development would have to be controlled in the Special Planning Area beyond Charlottetown.

Within the new city, the *Charlottetown Plan* charted a course to cope with an aging population and new information technology while providing a legacy of waterfront

30 Approximately 33,000 tonnes of garbage are consumed annually. The company was purchased by US Energy in 2001 and renamed PEI Energy Systems Inc. Since then, ownership was acquired by two different Canadian income trusts, but these sales did not affect operations.

development, open space corridors and protected rural areas. Its varied, sometimes competing, objectives included encouraging a compact urban form; promoting a vibrant downtown with stable residential neighbourhoods; preserving existing low-density neighbourhoods; strengthening suburban and neighbourhood commercial areas; encouraging diversified development in new sub-divisions; and introducing new classes of industrial development, as well as home-based businesses. In addition, CADC and the Capital Commission of PEI completed a master plan for improving the streetscape on University Avenue from Euston to Grafton, Grafton Street to Queen, Queen to Water, Great George between Water and Richmond and the side streets abutting Queen Street.

Jane Jacobs would have applauded efforts to retain and improve the inner city heritage zone, such as the designation of Great George Street as a National Heritage Street in 1990. Construction of various housing types in proximate areas and acceptance of home-based work sites were progressive steps. CADC's projects demonstrated skill and imagination, and access to federal funding programs provided the means to accomplish much. Expansion of suburban Stratford and Cornwall, however, was ominous. Construction of large and expensive town offices and the discord that preceded the development of the CARI Complex were hints that local ambition and competition might impede effective planning and administration of the Charlottetown area. The extent to which the pre-amalgamation problems return remains to be seen. Among the arts required to plan a city are the art of compromise and the art of the possible.

ECONOMIC GROWTH AND METROPOLITAN DEVELOPMENT

Between 1985 and 2005, Charlottetown enjoyed a buoyant economy, based upon a stable public sector, growth as the province's commercial centre and expanding tourism. Construction of the Confederation Bridge added extra economic bounce. Nevertheless, all of these elements depended in considerable measure upon economic factors beyond municipal control, and their futures were far from certain.

In 2002 Mayor George MacDonald convened a "capital symposium" to provide a mechanism for envisioning sustained economic growth. It was intended to establish planning objectives with respect to physical development, culture, economic stability, retail services, education and other matters. A steering committee would chart a course to reach the desired goals. The committee's chairman, Harry O'Connell, cited Charlottetown's advantages: its history and beauty, a navigable port and modern airport, a first-class hospital, loyal workforce, effective relationships among three levels of government and, significantly, a "vibrancy and political strength in its smallness" that allowed the city to react quickly. The city's lack of size had, in this respect, become advantageous.

Challenges included the need to build consensus among stakeholders and to develop a strategic plan for development. In 2005 a subsequent symposium with selected invitees met to review development concepts and establish a plan with a 15-year horizon. Supporting documents with outcomes and goals were produced, and provision was made for an ongoing process of revision. By then, collaboration among various interests and economic sectors was recognized as one of the outcomes that promised to pay the best dividends. The location of the CARI Complex at UPEI, where it served both the community and the university, was an example of such collaboration.

In any economy, the presence of jobs in public administration provides an element of stability. Secure, reasonably well-paid, and not as subject to fluctuations in demand as in the private sector, government employment offers assured income for individuals and communities. Occasionally, however, governments may go through spasms of downsizing for financial reasons. One such period was in the 1990s when tens of thousands of jobs were abolished in Canada and major responsibilities were downloaded from senior levels of government. Charlottetown, with its many federal and provincial government jobs, seems to have weathered the storm relatively well. In 1991 government service was the largest occupational category by industry employing 12.9 per cent of the city's workers, while the 2001 census, using 1997 data, recorded that 12.1 per cent of the city's labour force worked in public administration.[31]

If the public sector was holding its own, services in the private sector were doing a little better. The decision in 1993 to award the contract for building a fixed link across the Northumberland Strait had important implications for Charlottetown's economic outlook. Although the construction site was well-removed from the city, design and administrative work generated direct employment as well as spin-off jobs. As early as May 1991, City Council appointed a Fixed Link Committee to work at maximizing the local job creation opportunities. It encouraged potential contractors to establish some of their operations in the capital and urged city businesses to become involved in the planning process. The committee also identified measures to minimize possible inconveniences and maximize potential benefits of the mega-project. When Strait Crossing Incorporated of Calgary won the contract, the city extracted a promise from the company to provide employment locally. After this objective was met, the federal department of public works was pressed to put its project offices in the city. Beyond direct employment, the benefits of a buoyant provincial economy, supported by an estimated 2,600 temporary construction related jobs and increased demand for goods and services, led to prosperous times for Charlottetown. In addition, the opening of the Confederation Bridge and the ensuing influx of tourists offered new possibilities for hoteliers and downtown merchants.[32]

Not all the economic news was rosy. A recession from 1990 to 1992 placed a cloud over the retail sector. The economic downturn hurt retail sales nationally and promoted a consumer fixation on low prices. In the vicious competition that ensued, Eaton's

31 These two figures cannot be compared directly since the statistical base was altered by amalgamation, but they suggest overall stability.

32 This brightened the prospects for the Prince Edward Hotel and Convention Centre. After the collapse of the Dale Corporation and the rescue of the complex by the government, the province sold it at a loss to Canadian Pacific Hotels. It was subsequently operated as part of the Delta Hotel chain.

went bankrupt in 1997 and K-Mart was forced to retrench in 1998. Their branches in Charlottetown closed, and their market share was taken up by Zellers[33] and by various big box retailers and super-sized grocery chains, such as Wal-Mart, Home Depot, Future Shop and Atlantic Superstore (Loblaws) and Sobeys. By overshadowing local businesses and driving some, like Henderson and Cudmore, a clothing retailer, from the scene, the big-box goliaths represented the final integration of Charlottetown's marketplace into the orbit of national and North American retail commerce. Survival was possible for local businesses, but it sometimes required an adjustment of their business models to obtain greater wholesale buying power through alignment with national chains. The impact of these processes was readily apparent to anyone passing by the generic, University Avenue streetscape. The labour market, though, may have benefitted from this restructuring as the proportion of the city's work force in the wholesale and retail trade sector rose from under 13 per cent in 1991 to 14.6 per cent in 2001.[34]

While Charlottetown's hopes to develop a robust manufacturing sector were never fully realized, they were likewise never discarded. The city's official plan provided for heavy industrial development in the Sherwood Industrial Park and light industry in parks in West Royalty, Sherwood and Parkdale. Plans also included a business park for offices and research laboratories in the institutional area lying between University Avenue and Mount Edward Road.

Certain segments of Charlottetown's manufacturing sector proved to be quite durable. They included some of the city's earliest kinds of enterprises that processed local natural products: businesses such as Purity Dairy; Atlantic Fish Specialties, a producer of smoked and specialty seafood products; and Garden Province Meats, a pork and beef product maker.[35] COWS ice cream became internationally renowned, and with the introduction of a distinctive line of clothing in 1985, the brand developed a kind of cult status. McAskill Woodworking Limited, a clock and custom furniture maker, was another primary resource-based manufacturer.

Several niche industries did well. Some continued the tradition of metal fabrication begun when local manufacturers served the agricultural and fishing industries. A number of them were survivors from the Development Plan era of wide-ranging experimentation in new product production; others were newer. They included Charlottetown Metal Products; Padinox Inc., maker of Paderno cookware; Weld Tech Industries;

---

33 Zellers occupied the former K-Mart premises briefly, but in 1999 the site was redeveloped and much of the previous big-box building was demolished. A new Atlantic Superstore opened in March 2000. Zellers moved to the Charlottetown Mall.

34 Charlottetown's official plan promised to control and tighten up the commercial strip, but the logic of the motoring consumer and cookie-cutter design and architecture may prevail. The 1991 figure does not differentiate between wholesale and retail trade. In 2001 wholesale trade employed 2.34 per cent of workers and retail, 12.21 per cent. The employment numbers may have been influenced by the recession being experienced in 1991.

35 Garden Province Meats was taken over by the Natural and Organic Food Group in 2006. Later, the company experienced financial difficulties, and the plant was closed on March 29, 2008, when the new Ghiz Liberal government refused to subsidize further operational losses.

Tube-Fab Machined Products; and Diversified Metal Engineering Limited, a company started in 1991 to design and engineer equipment for food, beverage and industrial processing and marine exhaust systems. Island Control Limited produced marine and industrial control systems. All served specific national and international markets.

A newer line of business responded to the Island's rich botanical and marine resources and its traditional primary-resource industries by manufacturing value-added bioresource products. Diagnostic Chemicals Limited made chemicals and bio-chemicals for use in human and veterinary testing laboratories. A spin-off company, BioVectra dcl, was formed in 2000 to make specialized pharmaceuticals and biotechnology products. Aqua Health Limited, founded in 1984, produced veterinary products and vaccines and was acquired by Novartis Animal Health in 2000. It has since expanded. Fortius Canada, which commenced operations in 2001, specialized in nutritional and sports-related supplements for humans and natural products for animals. It came to Charlottetown from Calgary, attracted in part by the opportunity to work with UPEI and the Atlantic Veterinary College in the development of new products. Atlantis Bio-Actives Corporation was established in 2002 to produce biopharmaceutical ingredients extracted from botanical sources. Progressive BioActives Inc. started as a home-based business in 2004 and focused on the production of purified yeast cell wall extracts for livestock applications. It, too, grew and subsequently moved to its own quarters.[36]

Expansion of this economic sector was supported by two important government agencies. The Crops and Livestock Research Centre of Agriculture and Agri-Food Canada developed technologies for crop production, and the PEI Food Technology Centre, established in 1987, offered technical support for the food processing industry. Both organizations developed expertises in bioresource development. An important step was taken in 2001 to exploit the burgeoning world-wide market for nutritional products when the National Research Council spearheaded the formation of the Bioresources Technology Cluster. This consortium of government agencies, private companies and UPEI identified nutritional genomics as an appropriate focus for research and development. This led to the start of construction in 2004 of the NRC Institute for Nutrisciences and Health on the UPEI campus.[37] Not only would NRC-INH spawn technology to support further business growth, it had the potential to become a significant employer itself, with a projected staff of 100 scientists, technicians and researchers.

The PEI BioAlliance Inc. was created in 2005 to foster ongoing growth of the bioscience business sector, in Charlottetown and across the Island. Members claimed 650 full- and part-time employees, 400 in 20 private companies and 250 in 10 public-sector academic, research and government organizations. They invested $40 million

36 The company was acquired by Australian-based Stirling Products in 2007.

37 The building was renamed The Regis and Joan Duffy Research Centre in 2008 to honour Regis Duffy's pioneering role in the development of Charlottetown's bio-technology industry and the family's philanthropy.

a year in research and development and realized $60 million in sales, 90 per cent of which were to export markets. A development strategy released in November 2005 targeted growth that by 2010 would produce 1,000 private-sector employees working for firms realizing $200 million in profits, and investing $60 million in research and development.

A rapidly expanding demand for digital services of all kinds opened other opportunities for economic development in the Charlottetown area. These included various service experts, technical analysts, call centres and consulting firms. Computerized products and digital innovation can be developed in places that lack extensive secondary industry, if the people with the requisite creativity and technical skills are found there. Charlottetown's success in this economic sector depended upon its ability to attract and hold such individuals. The new, state-of-the-art Atlantic Technology Centre was intended to encourage this process by serving as a "business incubator" for entrepreneurs and start-up technology and media businesses. The centre was a collaborative venture involving business, the provincial and federal governments, and academia. DeltaWare Systems, an information technology consulting business, was one of the enterprises to make the new facility its home. The centre was planned to accommodate up to 500 information technology employees, reflecting the optimism with which the future of the IT sector in the city was viewed. Whether this optimism was justified remains to be seen, but the success of companies like iWave Information Systems augured well.

The story involving Seaman's Beverages is less encouraging. The venerable Charlottetown business was bought by Pepsi Bottling Group in 2002. Soon afterwards the product line was halved and sales to the mainland were halted. Continued production of one of Canada's last remaining independent soft drink brands may be in jeopardy.[38] Despite such setbacks, the number of people employed in manufacturing grew between 1991 and 2001 from 4.3 per cent of the labour force to 5.7 per cent.

The links between Charlottetown and its immediate hinterland, as well as points beyond, have been one of the critical factors in shaping the economic and cultural life of the city. For most of its history, the communications routes have inhibited economic development. Since 1985, improvements to provincial highways have made access to the city easier. Much of this work was the consequence of the opening of the Confederation Bridge on July 1, 1997, an event that forever changed both the city and province by integrating them into the national highway network. Beyond general upgrades and widening of the main roads, specific improvements included extensive modifications to the North River Bridge and Causeway, the West River Causeway and the Hillsborough Bridge.[39] Construction of the arterial highway connecting the access points to the city to allow traffic to bypass the downtown was delayed for years

38 On May 8, 2008, the PEI government discontinued its ban on the use of beverage cans. The bottling line at the Seaman's Charlottetown plant was closed, and the building was turned into a distribution centre.

39 The work on the North River Causeway and Bridge was completed around 1998, the year in which modifications to the Hillsborough Bridge were completed.

because of difficult negotiations among five separate municipalities, but it eventually proceeded. These changes cumulatively made the capital readily accessible from all parts of the Island and beyond. The city's role as a service centre and a place for commuters to work was enhanced, and many of the historical impediments to trade and commerce were removed.

The airport was also upgraded. In addition to the new terminal building, the so-called Skyplex Building was erected in 1992 to provide storage for private aircraft. Further changes included runway reconstruction, establishment of a business park in 2000 and construction of a taxiway and parking aprons to service the park. In 2004 the main terminal was extended to accommodate security screening equipment and additional personnel. The value of the airport as an economic engine was demonstrated by the growth of Prince Edward Air, a scheduled courier, air ambulance and charter service, founded by Robert M. Bateman in 1989.

An important administrative step in connection with the management of the airport was unveiled in 1995 by a federal announcement of plans to get out of the airport-management business. The proposal called for a system of 26 national airports under the control of independent non-profit airport authorities, with Transport Canada retaining ownership of the land and fixed assets. City Council was reluctant to become involved, but failure to co-operate would have resulted in the airport's closure and movement of its business to Moncton. With some misgivings, Council provided $5,000 to assist a local planning group to assess the feasibility of establishing an airport authority. Working with the Chamber of Commerce, the province and the city subsequently agreed to the establishment of the Charlottetown Airport Authority Inc. to represent the interests of all stakeholders. In 1999 management of the airport was transferred to the new authority.

Meanwhile at the seaport, the harbour was dredged in 1985, and the Railway Wharf was converted to the Charlottetown Marine Terminal. The port facilities were similarly sold in 1999 to the private sector with no guarantee that they would continue to operate. The new owner, the Charlottetown Harbour Authority Inc. (CHAI), was a not-for-profit entity backed by local stakeholder groups. The CHAI developed the marketing theme of "Historic Charlottetown Seaport" and targeted the cruise line industry as a principal port customer. These efforts were quite successful, with visitorship rising from eight ships carrying 2,115 passengers to 23 vessels and 23,894 visitors between 1998 and 2005.[40] Commodities still passed through the port. Main items consisted of crushed rock aggregate for road and other construction, petroleum products and commercial fertilizers. Exports were mainly potatoes and other cash crops.

Another significant step in communications at the local level came with the introduction of a bus service in 2005. Public transport had always been a hard sell for Charlottetonians, who cherished the convenience of the automobile, and previous attempts to establish a service foundered on widespread apathy. In the new millennium, senior levels of government, prompted by concerns about the environment, became more interested in the issue. This changed the economics of public transport, and

40 The projected visitorship in 2008 after improvements to the port was 40 ships with 69,380 passengers.

the city finally got a service. The mechanism by which this was accomplished was an innovative public-private partnership in which the city received funding from senior levels of government and used it to lease buses and subsidize the fare. The private partner, Trius Tours, acquired the buses and operated the system.[41] Four lines fanned out from Queen Square to provide access to most districts, although travel between outlying areas remained awkward. Furthermore, routes did not extend to Stratford and Cornwall, forcing commuters there to continue to travel by car.[42]

When it came to electronic communications, Charlottetown's role in 2005 was central for the Island, as the home of two of the province's three commercial radio broadcasters and its CBC radio stations, as well as the CBC English-language television station. Locally based Island Cablevision served the entire province and continued to do so as EastLink, after it was purchased by the Halifax-based company in 1998. Prince Edward Island's internet service providers were also congregated in the city.

Tourism was one of the principal factors driving the Charlottetown economy after 1985. It featured in economic planning and in the shaping of the city's physical structure. Considerable effort was expended in branding Charlottetown as the "Birthplace of Confederation." Founders' Hall and the Fathers of Confederation Players Program[43] promoted this concept and supplemented the experience of visiting Province House and seeing the actual venue of the Charlottetown Conference. The Capital Commission of Prince Edward Island was formed in 1995 to take over tourist marketing from the city. As a non-profit organization, it received support from ACOA, Tourism PEI, CADC and the city to develop tourism and organize marketable events.[44]

In 1992 the-then Capital Commission launched a four-day festival around Labour Day dedicated to the Fathers of Confederation. Despite being named one of the 100 top events by the American Bus Association in 1998, the Festival of the Fathers was eventually dropped, although the Festival of Lights, begun in 1996 and associated with Canada Day, proved more durable. Meanwhile, the Charlottetown Festival continued to draw crowds to the Confederation Centre with its varied program of musical theatre and comedy.

---

41 In 2007 Charlottetown Transit received an award from the Canadian Urban Transit Association for increasing ridership. It almost doubled between December 2005 and January 2007. This was recognition of an exemplary public-private partnership in which the public was a funding partner while all the obligation and responsibility lay with the private partner. The four lines were North River Road to West Royalty, University Avenue to Winsloe, St. Peter's Road to Parkdale and Sherwood, and Kensington Road to East Royalty. Additional routes were later added.

42 Cornwall undertook an experiment in public transit in May 2008 to facilitate commuter travel while the North River causeway was being repaired. This service was extended to the end of the year, and subsequently beyond, despite concerns about its viability. Stratford began a new transit service in September 2008 and public reaction there was encouraging.

43 Founders' Hall failed to meet planners' expectations in its first five years. Instead of an anticipated visitorship of 75,000 per year, the average was 45,000.

44 The Capital Commission merged with Meetings PEI in March 2006 to become Tourism Charlottetown and the Prince Edward Island Convention Partnership Inc.

Variety seems to be a key requirement to perpetuate a winning brand, for tourist destinations as much as consumer products. Brands have to be refreshed while remaining faithful to their core concepts. Charlottetown tried to do this and created new attractions to draw visitors in the shoulder and off-seasons. In 2004, 252,350 visitors to Prince Edward Island gave Charlottetown as their principal overnight destination. This represented just over one-third of all visitors to the province. While there was potential for further growth, uncontrollable factors, such as security fears, like those arising from the 9/11 terrorist attacks, or a rise in energy costs that made travel more costly, remained a threat. Some factors, however, were under the control of Charlottetonians battling other tourist destinations for the scarce tourist dollar. They included keeping prices competitive and providing good value.

Despite the diversification of Charlottetown's economy since 1985, almost half of its labour force worked in four industrial categories: government service, retail trade, hospitality and health and social services. Three occupational groups accounted for approximately 60 per cent of workers.[45] New initiatives in informational technology and scientific research promised to pay dividends in the future. The long-term vibrancy of Charlottetown's economy depended upon success in a broad range of economic activities.

SOCIAL LIFE

Between 1985 and 2005, the power of communications technology bore upon individuals and communities as never before. These years saw the rise of the internet and cell phone, *cum* "wireless email devices," and the explosion of the multi-channel television universe. Even without sufficient airline connections and the Confederation Bridge, Charlottetonians were connected with Canada and the world beyond as never before. Communications brought the world to them, and, inevitably, the world changed the city and the people who inhabited it. Cultural tastes and moral values were challenged by broad, outside trends. While this had always been the case, the strength of these influences, their immediacy and appeal were new. The pressure of change was reinforced by personal travel, for work, education or pleasure. As a result, Charlottetonians increasingly resembled other Canadians from Halifax, Ottawa or Calgary. The results were noticeable in a myriad of ways, such as the lingua franca of adolescents and the speed and attitude of rush-hour drivers. Still, a distinctive sense of place survived.

The great expansion of primary and secondary schools that resulted from the postwar baby boom was clearly over by 1985. In its place came retrenchment. Smaller families meant declining enrolments which, in turn, cut into the ranks of teachers

45 These groups were sales and services (30 per cent); business, finance and administration (15 per cent); and trades, transport and equipment operators (15 per cent). These numbers were based upon 2001 census data.

and other staff, such as counsellors. A demographic bounce resulting from the baby-boom "echo" temporarily moderated, but did not fundamentally alter, this trend. In fact, it was augmented somewhat by the wider acceptance of home-schooling. Subsidies for kindergartens, on the other hand, allowed more of the very young to attend than formerly. At the other end of the scale, more youth completed Grade 12 and were undertaking further education. Both Holland College and University of Prince Edward Island expanded as new programs were added to the curricula. UPEI developed postgraduate studies and opened a new School of Nursing in 1992. The Atlantic Veterinary College added a new dimension and scholarly depth to the university. Trades education and life-long learning also grew in response to demand. Thus, while the demographics of education have changed, the overall environment remained vibrant.

Health care, like education, tracked the changes found elsewhere in Canada. Many of the key areas concerning the health and well-being of Charlottetonians were taken over by senior levels of government, and key decisions were made well beyond local control. The power of the purse had led to its inevitable conclusion. Unfortunately, by the 1990s, soaring health care costs in the province prompted cutbacks in the interests of fiscal stability. Fewer public health initiatives and a shortage of physicians stressed the system just as an aging population began to make greater demands upon it. The result was longer waiting times for medical services and procedures and public anxiety about the future.

More recently, some health-care improvements have been realized. The Queen Elizabeth Hospital opened a cancer unit and acquired a magnetic resonance imaging (MRI) scanner and a second mammogram machine. Front-line services gradually shifted to clinics that tended to supplant individual medical practices and had the capacity to replace emergency-room treatments. Various "wellness" campaigns were launched, including those dealing with preventative medicine and women's health issues. In 2003 the province underscored the emphasis on preventative medicine by adopting the Smoke Free Places Act to try to reduce the prevalence of disease resulting from exposure to second-hand smoke. In tone, much has changed from the days when kindly physicians made house calls, but the high demand for medical services and the complexity of treatments have necessitated the transformation of what constitutes best practice.

Of all the measures taken to ensure public health, arguably the provision of high-quality water and sewerage services remains the most important. Despite the investments made in these services, problems with water contamination appeared in both Sherwood and West Royalty. In addition, the primary treatment standards of the 1970s were superseded by new approaches calling for the secondary disinfection of wastewater. Protection of groundwater resources was addressed by the provincial waste watch program, which in 2002 required all homes, institutions and businesses to follow specific management guidelines. Concern about outdated wastewater treatment facilities resulted in the construction of a new treatment plant in 2005. The joint federal-provincial-municipal project was designed to reduce the strength of wastewater pollutants by 90 per cent, using a biological process. A new strategy for the management of sludge from the municipal plant and from septic tanks in the city was also developed.

Fire protection, like safeguarding water supplies, was one of the earliest objectives of municipal government and one that occupied its attention continuously since incorporation. As the city's operations became more complex, this fundamental service may have faded from the public's consciousness, but its importance remained undiminished. A rash of arson incidents in the downtown area in the late 1980s renewed a general awareness of the danger of fire. Generally, however, the number of catastrophic fires declined with the implementation of new building standards and installation of fire suppression systems.

There were still some spectacular conflagrations. For instance, in June 1987, the old Rochford Square School was severely damaged when fire tore through the part that had formerly been St. Andrew's Parish Church. During a ferocious storm in February, 1992, a blaze broke out in a store in the city centre, and, before it was extinguished, five business had been destroyed. Less than a decade later, workers on the roof of the Alumni Gym at UPEI ignited flames that destroyed the building, a portion of which the architects had intended to incorporate into their renovation. Homes did not escape such ravages, although most events were not as evident as the loud explosion that damaged a residence in the city's north end one August evening in 1997 or as deadly as a fire in the east end that claimed the life of an eleven-year old boy in October 2002.

In recent decades, the fire department was better able to deal with emergencies because of improved training and equipment and more personnel. In 2005 the force was composed of 77 volunteer and 10 career firefighters. In 2000 the 911 emergency service was finally launched. It was an important aid to public safety, and, although late in coming — Prince Edward Island was the last province to institute such a service — it saved lives. This was particularly true for responses to automobile accidents. Amalgamation resulted in the merger of the Charlottetown force with the firefighters serving Sherwood and Parkdale. The new department was composed of two districts, one centred in the facility beside City Hall and the other at a building on St. Peter's Road in the eastern part of the city.

In contrast to the fire department, where major events have lessened over time, the police department experienced no let-up in serious incidents. Charlottetonians who generally thought of their community as safe were shocked by the antics of Roger Charles Bell, "Loki 7," who was found guilty in 1997 of committing a series of bombings over an eight-year period. Explosions outside the Law Courts building in 1988 and Province House in 1995 did minimal damage and caused only one injury, but an attempt to blow up a propane terminal in 1996 could have been catastrophic, if it succeeded. Fortunately, the bomb was defused. Police also had to deal with morals cases, such as the arrest and conviction in 2003 of a young baseball player for sexual offences involving underaged girls. It shocked the community and exposed the activities of other high school students who engaged in similar activities. High-profile cases of pedophilia in 1994 and 2006 were even more disconcerting because of the perpetrators' standing in the community and the predatory nature of the crimes. Two murders in the 1990s and another in 2002 eroded any complacency that Charlottetown was immune from even the most violent of crimes. In fact, police had to deal with a wide range of crime, running from illicit drug dealing, smash-and-grab robberies and major fraud to illegal gambling, domestic violence and high-tech crime, including child pornography. Charlottetown was hardly a centre of criminality, but it had a sinister streak that deviated from its *Anne of Green Gables* image.

In an effort to combat crime, the police department responded with a mixture of measures both to enforce and encourage compliance. Specialized units were organized to deal with specific types of crimes, and firearms were increased in size to keep pace with the weaponry of criminals. New traffic radar, breathalyzer equipment and digital record systems improved the efficiency of police operations. Community policing programs among youth groups and in the schools were created to win public support for law enforcement. Substations were opened at the Charlottetown Mall and in Sherwood, and bicycle and foot patrols were established in the downtown core. Police officers were better trained, with graduation from a police academy a requisite for new recruits. The police department grew in response to amalgamation, with a complement reaching 54 officers, including increased numbers of females, and 14 civilian staff.

Bootlegging caught the spotlight after the provincial government modified legislation in 2004 to give police more powers to suppress illegal bars. It was regarded as more of a local tradition than an illegal activity, initially tolerated as a way around antiquated liquor laws and more recently seen as a harmless extension to the drinking day. Fines of up to $20,000 for repeat offenders signalled a new official view of the matter. There was no expectation at the time that all bootleggers would be caught and closed down, but those that remained would "have to operate quietly to avoid the eye of police." Perhaps to everyone's surprise, the heavy penalties had their intended effect, and few took the risk to remain in operation.

By then, alcohol was not the only addictive substance in wide circulation. It had long since been joined by soft recreational drugs, marijuana and hashish, and use of these substances was perceived as increasing since the 1980s. Growth in the use of hard, highly addictive drugs was a more menacing development. Cocaine and crystal meth were considered the most serious, but there was also widespread use of ecstasy, benzedrine (bennies), date rape drugs and home-made concoctions. This form of drug abuse led to criminal activities and contributed to homelessness.

Homelessness itself was not widely acknowledged to exist in Charlottetown, but it was present, if well-hidden. There was less of it, perhaps, than in earlier times, and not all of the homeless were indigent or incapacitated by drugs and alcohol. Those without homes included people with poorly managed mental illnesses. Rather than living on the streets, some homeless people tended to drift from address to address. An attempt between 1992 and 1997 to maintain a homeless shelter, Bedford MacDonald House, ended after it failed to muster sufficient community support and even faced some local opposition. Since 1999, money from the federal government under the National Homelessness Initiative was invested in various projects to address the problem. The Bedford MacDonald House was restarted in a new location in 2004, and the Harvest House Ministries opened two shelters, while the Native Council operated a rooming house. Unfortunately, federal funding was directed towards the purchase of property, leaving ongoing operational costs dependent upon local fund-raising. This placed the long-term survival of the shelters at risk. In 2005 the federal government and the John Howard Society of PEI teamed up to create a support team to assist homeless youth and those at risk of becoming so. This, in addition to the programs of churches, schools and other community agencies, mitigated the situation somewhat.

Most Charlottetonians, of course, had homes, but as the 20th century drew to a close, they tended to spend less time there than in previous eras. Pressures of work and outside attractions drew them away. Smaller families made people more mobile and less likely to pursue quiet domestic activities. Similarly, various religious communities had to compete for time as more people emphasized affiliations with secular organizations and activities. Charlottetonians seem to have spent less time watching television than their counterparts in other cities. Certainly, Islanders as a whole devoted fewer hours to this inactivity than the residents of all provinces but Alberta.[46] Many in the city focused on sports. Minor leagues were active in hockey, soccer, baseball and basketball. Organized programs existed for ringette, tennis, badminton and football, as well as figure skating, speed skating and cross country skiing. The Canada Winter Games, which Charlottetown hosted in February 1991, brought together hundreds of the best athletes from across the country. The facilities created for the games provided a venue for other sporting activities, including the home games of the PEI Senators of the American Hockey League. A farm team of the NHL Ottawa Senators, the local Senators began operations in 1993 and lasted three years before being moved to a larger market. They were replaced by the PEI Rocket, a Quebec Major Junior League franchise that arrived from Montreal in 2003.

The activities and atmosphere at the nearby Charlottetown Driving Park changed substantially when the old stands gave way to the new state-of the art facility. The old building had become so inadequate that the very survival of harness racing in the capital was threatened, but the new one included a casino holding 225 video lottery terminals, earning it the appellation, "Racino." The VLTs raised concerns about encouraging gambling addictions, but in a struggle between the ethics of the situation and the opportunity to save horse racing, social conscience took second place.

In the 1990s, Charlottetown became a major host for sporting championships. The Confederation Bridge may have had a hand in this by making the city more

---

46 This was particularly true for people over 18 years. Younger viewers had habits closer to the national norm.

accessible, but tourist marketing identified such events as a significant source of visitors and worked hard to secure them. Many Charlottetonians, as well, attended as spectators. In 1996 the city hosted the Canadian Mixed Curling Championship, and in 1999 the Scott Tournament of Hearts, Canada's Women's Curling Championship. The Canadian Youth Sailing Championship was held in the city in 2001, and the Senior Women's Canadian Fastpitch Championship took place the following year. The National Junior A Hockey Championship followed in 2003, and the Canadian Senior Men's and Women's Soccer Championships in 2004. The Skate Canada National Championships were a highlight in 2005. Between 1991 and 2005, 32 different national and regional championships were held in Charlottetown in sports as varied as amputee golf, junior racquetball, harness racing and women's team squash.

Other forms of live entertainment did equally well. Visits by Bryan Adams (1998), Ashley MacIsaac (1998), The Guess Who (2000), Nickelback (2003) and Blue Rodeo (2003), among many others, offered visitors and locals a diet of well-known performers. Charlottetown contributed its own share of well-known artists to the music scene, some of the most notable of whom were *The Jive Kings*, a jazz group; the rock groups, *The Rude Mechanicals* and *Haywire;* Celtic-folk musician, Dennis Brunton; and Rik Barron, a children's entertainer originally from Newfoundland. Vocalists Nancy White and Joey Kitson, of the former Celtic rock group, *Rawlins Cross*, and songwriters Urban Carmichael and Paul Broadbent came from, or were based in, Charlottetown. The Charlottetown Festival featured the perennial *Anne of Green Gables*, but regularly hosted other performances, such as Alan Bleasdale's gritty 1987 portrayal of the life of Elvis Presley, *Are You Lonesome Tonight?*, and *Emily*, a musical based on some of Lucy Maud Montgomery's work. Not everything received popular acclaim — the 1996 performance of *Guys and Dolls* was a flop — but overall the festival retained its appeal. In addition to the festival, the East Coast Music Awards, staged in the city in 1996 and 2001, were highlights of the city's musical calendar.

Some pastimes that organized participants more formally, including fraternal societies and youth groups, which had once been important vehicles of sociability, faded in the period 1985–2005. It was not an era in which structure and hierarchy were particularly valued. Opportunities to establish social contacts were as easily realized at the Belvedere Golf Club or the Charlottetown Yacht Club, for instance, as in fraternal orders. Many working families, with both parents in the paid labour force, lacked the time for extensive community involvement. Nevertheless, the Rotary Club, the Lions and, to a lesser degree, the Kinsmen and Kiwanis attracted active members. So, too, did the Masons and organizations based upon special affinities, such as the Canadian Legion, IODE and the Benevolent Irish Society. Newer groups catering to particular interests or causes appeared, Habitat for Humanity being one such example. The establishment of new public recreational facilities provided competition for organizations like the YMCA. In the 1980s, the "Y" tried to broaden its appeal by opening an adult fitness centre, but, burdened with debt and unable to attract a broad clientele, it closed its doors in 1996. Similarly, the Basilica Recreational Centre became less of a focus for Roman Catholics by the end of the century, and the Diocese of

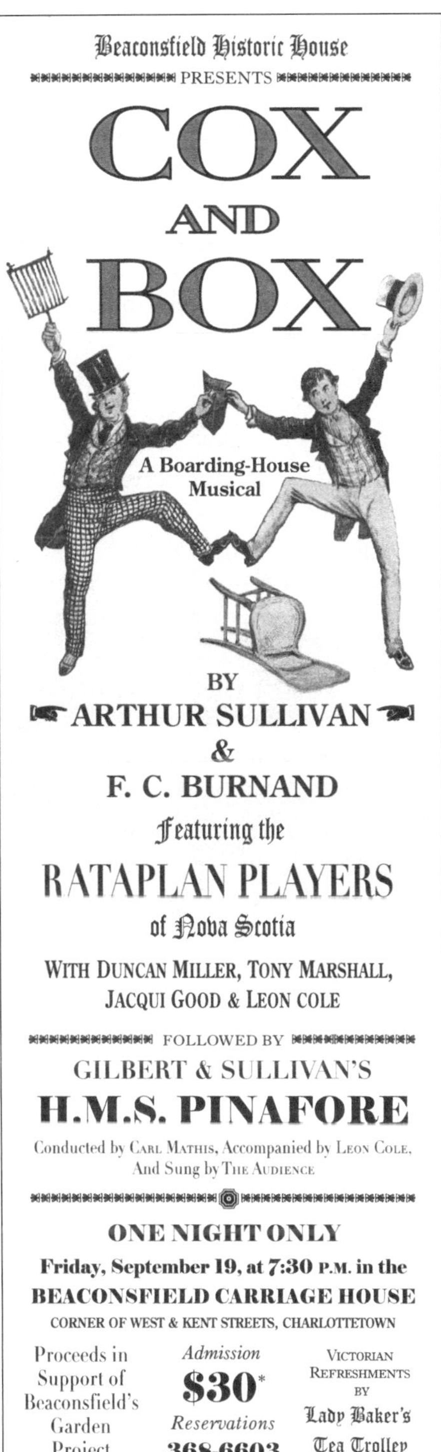

Though attention tends to focus on the Charlottetown Festival, the small-scale and amateur theatre that has been part of Charlottetown's social life since the early 19th-century continues into the 21st.

Charlottetown began to assess its future.[47] As a sign of the times, Charlottetown's Y's Men's After School Club provided day care and child care for preschool and elementary school children at seven centres across the city.

The Boy Scouts and Girl Guides were two other long-standing groups to find themselves somewhat at odds with the mood of the times. Although membership dropped, new programs and appealing internet websites strove to keep pace with current tastes. A high point was reached in July 1989 when the seventh Canadian Scouts Jamboree was held across Charlottetown harbour at Fort Amherst. For the event, an estimated 5,000 tents to accommodate 10,000 scouts filled the fields adjacent to the fort. The Canadian Forces Reserve experienced similar reductions in this period. Budget cutbacks and a general perception that the role of the citizen soldier or sailor was not as appealing as heretofore may explain the decline, but like the scouts and guides, the militia and naval reserve continued to attract a significant and dedicated membership. The opportunity to serve with overseas missions underscored the underlying purpose of the military, and the opening of the new HMCS *Queen Charlotte* heightened the attraction of the senior service.

There was no absence of important public celebrations in the years between 1985 and 2005. In former times, royal visits would have

47 The building was sold to a private operator in 2007 who continued to run it as Murphy's Community Centre.

been particular highlights of the social calendar, and, although they created quite a stir during these years, excitement levels never reached those of 1939 or 1973. This was undoubtedly due to changing patriotic sensibilities, but also the fact that the visitors were the Queen's younger sons, rather than Her Majesty or the Prince of Wales. What was lost in seniority, however, was gained in frequency: Prince Andrew and the Duchess of York visited in July 1989, and Prince Edward came in 1987 and retured with his wife, the Countess of Wessex, in 2000 and 2005.

The bimillennium created a much larger stir. It had everything, including a sense of occasion as the date rolled over to 2000, the frisson of anxiety stemming from potential Y2K disasters, and optimism bred from good times. The latter sentiment was fed by newspaper articles, such as the one entitled, "Boom Times in Province's Capital City," and by statements like "This is going to be Prince Edward Island's century" from Premier Pat Binns. Local golfer, Lorie Kane, had just finished an outstanding season on the LPGA circuit and was named the *Guardian*'s "Newsmaker of the Year." Nearly local hockey sensation Brad Richards was playing for Team Canada in the World Junior Hockey Championships in Sweden. The mood was definitely upbeat, except, perhaps, for those worrying about blackouts and airplane crashes due to malfunctioning computers. These folks may have been reassured by the emergency co-ordination centre set up on the 6th floor of the National Bank Building and by the presence of bio-medical staff at the hospital to cope with a disaster. In any event, no Y2K problems were reported. For the most part, people anticipated the celebrations with relish.

Festivities got off to an early start when the owner of a company celebrating 50 years of business decided to thank his customers by staging a fireworks display for families at 7 p.m. on December 29. The 15–20 minute show, shot from York Point, featured music as well as fireworks and ended with a burst of light accompanied by the strains of the 1812 Overture. The main millennium show centred on Queen Square where the Capital Commission organized a program of 17 musical groups, with performances starting at noon on December 31. The early events were geared for children and were held in the Confederation Court Mall. Seniors were treated to performances of barbershop quartets, swing music and popular entertainers at Memorial Hall. Lennie Gallant staged two free concerts in the theatre of the Confederation Centre. At 4 p.m., the outdoor presentations began, with television coverage hosted by CBC news anchors, Roger Younker and Sheryl MacKay. Native Islander Jonathan Torrens returned to host Charlottetown's feed to the rolling worldwide televising of millennium celebrations. Festivities continued in the bitter cold and attracted a crowd of 10,000 who watched as the show ended at midnight with a huge fireworks display.

The scene was somewhat more subdued five years later as Charlottetown ushered in its 150th anniversary year. Unseasonably warm weather attracted a sizeable crowd of 5,000 to Victoria Park where family entertainment began at 5:30 p.m. with children's activities, live entertainment and treats and refreshments. A prayer for peace was offered at 7:00 p.m., prior to the 7:30 fireworks finale. Later, a New Year's Eve gala and reception was held at the Delta Hotel. Proceedings featured an appearance by Queen Charlotte and an exchange of greetings with the Mayor of Ottawa whose city was also celebrating its sesquicentennial. Observance of the actual anniversary day was low-key. It was marked by a ceremony at the Communities in Bloom meeting on August 10. The *Guardian*, which had previously issued a special publication, "A City's Journey," distributed a historical post card to honour the occasion. At the end of the year, a sealed time capsule containing various commemorative items was locked into an old safe set into the wall of the bell tower of City Hall.[48] This ceremony ended the 150th anniversary celebrations.

The years between 1985 and 2005 were ones of expansion and optimism in Charlottetown. During this period some long-standing challenges related to the governance of the greater municipal area had been resolved. Key adjustments in the economy had been made, and new business frontiers were defined and explored. This transition was aided by the entrepreneurial creativity of people like Regis Duffy, founder of Diagnostic Chemicals Limited, and by the establishment of physical and intellectual connections between the city and the world beyond the Island's shores. At the commercial level, expansion took place at the edge of town, and the challenge of maintaining a vital downtown core persisted.[49] Government continued to provide jobs, and public institutions, particularly UPEI and Holland College, evolved into vehicles for social and economic transformation as well as innovative centres of learning. Tourism was doing well and showed promise of further expansion using a mix of contemporary entertainment, history and the unique claim to be the "Birthplace of Confederation." The city enjoyed a varied cultural life, and if social conditions were not always as idyllic as some would hope, there was a growing tolerance of — even a desire for — diversity. Perhaps most important of all, Charlottetonians had mastered the art of collaboration. CADC, the BioAlliance and the CARI Complex were three examples that demonstrated the benefits of community organizations, business and governments working together to reach agreed-upon goals.

While Charlottetown had its share of dedicated leaders, creative entrepreneurs and inspired visionaries, there was still a lingering conservatism to the place. This quality, mixed with some self-satisfaction, was caught in a comment by Alderman John Squarebriggs who, returning from Moncton where streets had been choked with snow, compared them to the relatively open thoroughfares of Charlottetown and proclaimed, "I am proud, very proud to be a resident of the city of Charlottetown and have been all my life, and we do the best we can with what we have, and I think we do an excellent job." This echoed the view of the *Guardian* almost 70 years

48 The time capsule is to be opened in 2055.

49 It is possible that the earlier moratorium on mall development merely put off the day of reckoning for downtown businesses. With the Bridge in place and shoppers haemorrhaging to stores in Moncton and other mainland locations, the option to postpone construction of new big-box stores could no longer be afforded. At least, by then, economic benefits from suburban retail developments flowed into city coffers.

previously with respect to the cut of the city's cloth.[50] There was in the city's mindset a prevailing sense of caution backed by a realistic calculation of what was possible to achieve. Charlottetown was not a "boom or bust" city; it had neither the resources for explosive growth and great fortune nor the vulnerabilities that made utter disaster possible. Its progress was not that of an ocean liner driven relentlessly forward by a mighty engine and an endless supply of fuel. Instead the city was like a sailing ship, advancing by a series of tacks and turns determined by the elements of nature and executed with the skill and labour of its crew. The history of the Island capital may not impress the beholder with its majesty or threaten him with its backwash, but it has a grace and intricacy that gives it interest and dignity. And like a sailboat tied up at the docks by Charlottetown harbour, it is loved by its owners and is an inheritance for their successors.

50 Squarebriggs' comment was made in 1986. The earlier statement appeared in 1918 and is quoted in Chapter 3.

Bibliography

PRIMARY SOURCES

Manuscripts and Government Records

Baker Library. Harvard University. R. G. Dun and Company Collection, Canada, Vol. 9.

Canada. Department of Regional Economic Expansion (DREE). "Development Plan: Prince Edward Island: A 15-Year Federal-Provincial Program for Economic Expansion and Social Adjustment." 1969.

Canada. DREE. File 10170-10, 1978; File 10170-13, 1978; File 23210/1, Vols. 1–2, 6, 1975–1981; File 23213, Vol. 1, 1975; File 34000, Vol. 1, 1973–1975; File 43106/2, 1971; File 43117, 1970–1971; "Background Spatial Strategy, Prince Edward Island," January 1979.

City of Charlottetown. City Council Minutes and Tapes. 1986–1995.

_____. Comprehensive Urban Service Agreement (CUSA) file. 1995–2000.

_____. Memorandum and Letter from Mayor Ian MacDonald to Premier Pat Binns. March 24, 1997.

_____. Memorandum of Understanding between Prince Edward Island and the City of Charlottetown. Signed by Harry Gaudet, CEO of Charlottetown, and Ginger Breedon, Deputy Minister of Public Works. March 28, 1995.

Glenbow Archives, Calgary. Eric Harvie Fonds. G 1/Series 43. Fathers of Confederation Memorial Citizens Foundation, 1958–1976. Letter from Douglas W. Ambridge to Eric Harvie. September 9, 1963.

Library and Archives Canada (LAC). Jarvis Papers. Microfilm M-1963. E. J. Jarvis to William Jarvis. November 30, 1836.

LAC. MG 30, B4, Vol. 9, File 96. Statement of Orders Placed by the Imperial Munitions Board. January 25, 1919.

_____. Pope, Joseph. "Early Days in Charlottetown, 1854–1872." Ch. 1 of a manuscript of memoirs. Microfilm No. M-586.

_____. Visual Heritage Division. Watercolour painting by Charles Randle. C-277.

Public Archives and Records Office of Prince Edward Island (PARO). "Report on the Provincial Mental Hospital of Prince Edward Island" ("Chambers Report"). Typescript. September 1953.

PARO. Acc. 2353/63. "Report of the Commissioner on Educational Finance and Related Problems in Administration, P.E.I." April 1960.

_____. Acc. 2385. B. F. Tinney. "The Charlottetown Young Men's Christian Association, 1856–1965." Unpublished paper. May 1966.

_____. Acc. 2510/1. P. Pope. *Report on Industry*. 1917.

_____. Acc. 2535/15. Diocesan Church Society. 1956.

_____. Acc. 2594A. Charlottetown YMCA. *Annual Report*. 1903–1904; 1904–1905.

_____. Acc. 2784, Box 25, File 1045. Island Development Plan.

_____. Acc. 2784, Box 25, File 1053. Kates, Peat, Marwick and Co., Concordia Estates Ltd. "Comments on the Potential Development of Charlottetown and Its Impact on the Tourist Industry of P.E.I." September 21, 1970.

_____. Acc. 2784, Box 29, File 1274. Douglas Boylan, Secretary to the Council to Deputy Ministers, Chairmen and General Managers. April 20, 1972.

_____. Acc. 2784, Box 25, File 1051. Comprehensive Island Development Plan. December 1969.

_____. Acc. 2784, File 1045. Comprehensive Island Development Plan. Notes on the P.E.I. Comprehensive Development Plan. March 7, 1969.

_____. Acc. 2784, File 1049. Comprehensive Island Development Plan. December 1970.

_____. Acc.2825, No. 89. Florence Kent. "A History of Charlottetown." n.d.

_____. Acc. 2851. W. B. Wellner Fonds.

_____. Acc. 2881, Vol. 508. Peake, Brecken Fonds.

_____. Acc. 3007/4. Minute Book of the Children's Aid Society.

_____. Acc. 3007/6. Children's Aid Society.

_____. Acc. 3147. Greater Charlottetown Chamber of Commerce fonds. Board of Trade Council Minutes. Vols. 4–9.

_____. Acc. 3147. Greater Charlottetown Chamber of Commerce fonds. Board of Trade General Minutes. Vols. 1–3.

_____. Acc. 3263. Diary of T. W. Carrington. Entry for July 10, 1837.

_____. Acc. 3311/1. Hartwell Daley. *Volunteers in Action: The Prince Edward Island Division Canadian Red Cross Society, 1907–1979*. Summerside: Williams and Crue. 1981.

_____. Acc. 3473, Items 1–3. Cundall Diaries.

_____. Acc. 4158, Vol. 6. Cundall Letter Book. Cundall to Henry R. Lordly. May 17, 1897.

_____. Acc. 4210. T. E. MacNutt. "Charlottetown's Four Market Houses." Unpublished manuscript. n.d.

_____. Acc. 4315. Violet MacEachern and Arlene MacDougall. *Our West River Heritage*. Self-published. 1993.

_____. Acc. 4426, Vol. 1. Letter from Rev. Angus B. MacEachern to Bishop Plessis. November 14, 1823.

_____. Acc. H.F. 78.210.4. Clippings dated March 8, 1916; May 20, 1916; March 8, 1917; n.d.

_____. Colonial Office Records, CO 226/5/56. Despatch from Governor Walter Patterson. June 6, 1773.

_____. Colonial Office Records, CO 226/7/38. Peter Stewart to Lord George Germain. July 10, 1779.

_____. RG 10, Vol. 109. Report of the Library of the Legislative Assembly for 1903. Undated document initialled by W. H. Crosskill.

_____. RG 10, Vol. 65. Administration, Health and Welfare. Journal, 1936–1941.

_____. RG 10, Vols. 109–110. Department of Education.

_____. RG 18. Census of 1848. Comment of C. D. Rankin.

_____. RG 20, Vols. 1–16, 763–827. City Council Minutes, 1855–1985.

_____. RG 20. III Taxation and Licensing, A. Assessments (g) Personal Property.

_____. RG 20. Public School Reports, 1901, 1902, 1915 and 1919.

_____. RG 20, Vol. 225. Real Estate Assessment Book.

_____. RG 20, Vol. 237. Income Tax Assessment Book.

_____. RG 20, Vol. 292. Liquor Stores Inspected, 1892; Saloon and Tavern Layout Book, 1892–1897.

_____. RG 20, Vol. 30. Poll Book.

_____. RG 20, Vol. 36. Letter Book.

_____. RG 20, Vol. 60. Building Permit Request Forms, 1946–1950.

_____. RG 20, Vol. 64. Minutes of the Charlottetown Board of Health.

_____. RG 20, Vol. 75. Ledger.

_____. RG 20, Vols. 39–40. City of Charlottetown Correspondence.

_____. RG 20, Vols. 440–457. Police Magistrates Court Records, 1878–1928.

_____. RG 20, Vols. 576–577. Commissioners of Sewers and Water Supply Minute Books.

_____. RG 20, Vols. 755, 757. Minutes of the Charlottetown Board of School Trustees, 1946–1947, 1958.

_____. RG 34/10. Prince Edward Island. Advisory Reconstruction Committee. *Interim Report of the Prince Edward Island Advisory Reconstruction Committee*. Charlottetown. 1945.

_____. RG 44. Confederation Centre Collection. "Reaction to Development Plan." No author. n.d.

_____. RG 44. Confederation Centre Collection. Administrative correspondence. 1965–1966 and n.d.

_____. Unaccessioned reference material. History of Charlottetown reference cards.

Prince Edward Island Regimental Museum. Scrapbooks. Vols. 1–2.

Reports and Printed Documents

Agnew Peckham and Associates, Ltd. *Review of Hospital and Related Facilities Prince Edward Island*. March 1967.

American Psychiatric Association. "Report on the Provincial Mental Hospital of Prince Edward Island" ("The Chambers Report"). Typescript. September 1953.

Atlantic Development Board. *Annual Report*. 1967

_____. *Report of the Industrial Park*. June 21, 1974.

Australia. Australian War Memorial, Encyclopedia. Prime Minister Robert G. Menzies: wartime broadcast. Edited transcript. http://www.awm.gov.au/encyclopedia/prime_ministers/menzies.thm.

Canada. *Census of Canada*. 1871–2006.

_____. Parliament of Canada. House of Commons. *Debates*. 1924, 1926, 1934, 1938, 1948, 1951–1953, 1955, 1961.

_____. Statistics Canada. CANSIM tables 502-0002 and 502-0003 and Catalogue No. 87F0006XIE.

_____. *Survey of Facilities: A Study of Hospital Physical Plant Facilities in Charlottetown, P.E.I.* Ottawa: Department of National Health and Welfare, Health Facilities Design Division. 1971.

_____. Veterans Affairs Canada. Canadian Forces Advisory Council. "The Origins and Evolution of Veterans Benefits in Canada, 1914–2004." Ottawa: DVA Reference Paper. Section M. March 2004.

Canadian-British Engineering Consulting Ltd. *Charlottetown Pollution Control Study*. February 1970.

Charlottetown Free Dispensary. *Report*. Undated typescript. March 1954–1955.

Charlottetown Metropolitan Committee. *Report*. May 1957.

Charlottetown Parking/Transit Study. March 1977.

Charlottetown Area Industrial Park Study. 1969.

Charlottetown Plan: The Official Plan: strategic directions for Charlottetown in the twenty-first century and beyond. July 1999.

Charlottetown. *Charlottetown Plan* (revised). 1980.

_____. *Planning and Housing Survey of the City of Charlottetown*. 1962.

Crandall, W. H. "Water and Sewer for Metropolitan Charlottetown: A Report on the Comparative Costs of Separate and Integrated Systems." c. January 1957.

de Silva, Walter P. *A Planning and Housing Study of the City of Charlottetown, P.E.I.: A Preliminary Study*. Charlottetown: City of Charlottetown. 1962.

Downtown Business Association. *Study on Mall Impacts*. 1980.

Laventhol, Krekstein, Horwath and Horwath. "Convention Centre Study." 1973.

Maritime Provinces Higher Education Commission. Appendix J. *Second Annual Report, 1975–76*.

Maritime Resource Management Services. *Charlottetown Plan Review*. Vol. 1. 1986.

Matthews, John C. *The Report of the Survey of the Public Schools of Charlottetown, P.E.I.* Charlottetown. 1952.

Operation Design Canada. *Community Profile for Greater Charlottetown*. 1978.

Prince Edward Island. *Acts of the General Assembly*, "An Act for the Introduction of Medical Inspection in the Public Schools in the City of Charlottetown." May 4, 1916.

_____. *Acts of the General Assembly*. "An Act in Amendment of the 'Charlottetown Liquor Regulation Act.' " 1899.

_____. *Acts of the General Assembly*. "An Act prohibiting the sale of Intoxicating Liquor." 1900.

_____. *Acts of the General Assembly*. "An Act respecting Queen's County Jail." April 13, 1907.

_____. *Acts of the General Assembly*. "An Act to amend 'The Charlottetown Sewerage Act.' " April 25, 1901.

_____. *Acts of the General Assembly*. "An Act to amend the 'Public Schools' Act, 1877.' " May 9, 1894.

_____. *Acts of the General Assembly*. "An Act to regulate by Police and Municipal Regulations the Sale of Intoxicating Liquors in the City of Charlottetown, and so to preserve therein Public Decency and repress Drunkenness and Disorderly Conduct," or "Charlottetown Liquor Regulation Act." May 3, 1892.

_____. *Acts of the General Assembly*. 43 Victoria, Cap. XV. 1880.

_____. *Acts of the General Assembly*. 50 Victoria, Cap. 15. 1887.

_____. *Acts of the General Assembly*. 53 Victoria, Cap. 21. 1890.

_____. *Acts of the General Assembly*. 55 Victoria, Cap. 10. 1891.

_____. *Acts of the General Assembly*. 61 Victoria, Cap. 15. 1898.

_____. *Acts of the General Assembly*. Cap. 15. "An Act for the protection of neglected and dependent children." 1910.

_____. *Acts of the General Assembly*. III Edward VII, Cap XVII. 1903.

_____. *Acts of the General Assembly*. V Edward VII, Cap. XXIII. 1905.

_____. Commission of Shopping Centres. *Report*. December 31,1980.

_____. *Debates and Proceedings of the Legislative Council*. 1886.

_____. Department of Development. *Review of the Manufacturing Sector*. April 1977.

_____. Department of Education Reports. "Report of the Superintendent of Charlottetown Schools." 1965.

_____. Department of Health and Welfare. "Report of the Chief Health Officer." 1952.

_____. Department of Health and Welfare. Division of Sanitary Engineering. "Annual Report." 1954.

_____. Department of Health. "Annual Report." 1961.

_____. Department of Health. Water Pollution Advisory Committee. "Report." 1963.

_____. Department of Industry and Commerce. "Decentralization of Federal Government Services to Prince Edward Island." 1975.

_____. Government of P.E.I. *The Case of Prince Edward Island: a submission presented to the Royal Commission on Dominion — Provincial Relations by the Government of Prince Edward Island*. Charlottetown: Irwin Printing. 1938.

_____. House of Assembly. *Debates*. 1966, 1969, 1973.

_____. *Journal of the House of Assembly*. Grand Jury Representation. January 12, 1882.

_____. *Journal of the House of Assembly*. "An Act To Incorporate an Industrial Development Commission for the City of Charlottetown." March 29, April 7 and April 11, 1967.

_____. *Journal of the House of Assembly*. 1920.

_____. *Journal of the House of Assembly*. March 16, 1955.

_____. *Legislative Assembly Journal*. 1855–1893.

_____. P.E.I. Industrial Corporation. *Annual Reports*. 1955, 1957.

_____. *Parliamentary Reporter*. 1881, 1885.

_____. *Parliamentary Reports, 1857*. April 8, 1857.

_____. Prince Edward Island Advisory Reconstruction Committee. *Interim Report*. Charlottetown. 1945.

_____. *Report of the Prince Edward Island Development Commission*. Charlottetown: King's Printer. 1917.

_____. *Report of the Royal Commission on Higher Education for Prince Edward Island*. Charlottetown. 1965.

_____. *Statutes of Prince Edward Island*. "An Act further Amending the City of Charlottetown Incorporation Act." April 11, 1924; April 2, 1932; April 1, 1935; May 2, 1940; April 19, 1945; April 10, 1954; April 12, 1958; April 13, 1960; April 6, 1962; April 25, 1968; April 7, 1971; April 14, 1972.

_____. *Statutes of Prince Edward Island.* "An Act to Empower the City of Charlottetown to Acquire and Operate an Electric Plant and Distribution System." 1936.

_____. *Statutes of Prince Edward Island.* "Housing Commission Act." Cap. XX. 1960.

_____. *Statutes of Prince Edward Island.* "The Public Library Act." April 4, 1935.

_____. *Statutes of Prince Edward Island.* April 4, 1935.

_____. *Parliamentary Reporter.* March 22, 1860.

Prince Edward Island Hospital. *Annual Report.* 1893.

Robertson, Allan J. Development Planning Associates Ltd. "Retail Space Report." Prepared for the Charlottetown Area Regional Planning Board. February 1978.

Stevenson Kellogg Management Consultants. "Report of the Industrial Park." Atlantic Development Board. 1967.

_____. *The Greater Charlottetown Urban Area Opportunities Study* (Stevenson Kellogg Report). Vols. 1–2. 1973.

Touche, Ross, Bailey and Smart. "Province of Prince Edward Island Provincial-Municipal Fiscal Study." August 1969.

West Royalty. "Official Plan for West Royalty." c. 1991.

Winsloe. "Official Plan for Winsloe." c. 1988.

Newspapers

Atlantic Advocate. Vol. 59 (September 1968).

Broad Axe. Vol. 1, No. 7. April and May 1972.

Downtown Pulse. September 2005.

Examiner (Charlottetown).1855–1921.

_____. "Colonial Parliament House of Assembly Summary." April 7, 1862.

_____. "Local Legislature." Transcription of a speech by L. H. Davies. April 17, 1876.

_____. "Society in Charlottetown Forty Years Ago." January 7, 1867.

_____. Transcription of a speech by L. H. Davies to the House of Assembly. April 17, 1876.

_____. Transcription of a speech by the P.E.I. Colonial Secretary to the House of Assembly. May 17, 1858.

Financial Post Business Yearbook. 1925, 1940, 1945, 1950, 1965, 1974.

Globe and Mail. 1974–1977.

Guardian (Charlottetown). 1900–2007.

Guardian — Patriot Centennial Edition. August 9, 1973.

Haszard's Gazette. 1854–1855.

Herald (Charlottetown). 1884–1885.

Palladium. Vol. 1, No. 1. September 4, 1843. p. 3.

Patriot. 1855–1974.

Protestant and Evangelical Witness. 1859.

Royal Gazette. January 10, 1832; July 25, 1843.

Watchman. September 5, 1913.

Weekly Advertiser (Charlottetown). 1856.

Interviews

Michael Arnold, President, Dyne Holdings Limited. August 2006.

Sharon Becker, Payroll Services Officer, City of Charlottetown. July 26, 2005.

Joseph Coady, Director of Public Services, City of Charlottetown. July 25, 2005, and July 16, 2008.

Captain J. J. Connolly (Boyde Beck, Interviewer). Summer 1982.

Nancy Coughlin, Administrative Assistant, City of Charlottetown. July 26, 2005.

Rev. Ian Glass, Charlottetown (by telephone). For information concerning the recreational arrangements in Sherwood and Parkdale. Autumn 2005.

Kathy Hambly, Executive Director, Greater Charlottetown Chamber of Commerce. July 2008.

Joe Kiley, Charlottetown (by telephone). For information concerning the recreational arrangements in Sherwood and Parkdale. Autumn 2005.

Ernie Morello, Landscape Architect, Charlottetown Area Development Corporation. July 2008.

Betty Pryor, Utility Technician, City of Charlottetown. July 28, 2005.

Charles Scott, Sr., Ottawa. Regarding the Confederation Centre. September 27, 2005.

Sterling Squarebriggs (Earle Kennedy, Interviewer). Unpublished transcript. 1980.

SECONDARY SOURCES

Unpublished Theses and Papers

Baldwin, Douglas O. "Volunteers in Action: The Role of Volunteer Associations in Promoting Government Health Care on Prince Edward Island, 1900–1931." Unpublished paper. c. 1981.

Battersby, Kenneth A. "Land Use and Economy of Prince Edward Island." Unpublished MA thesis. Dalhousie University. 1941.

Cusack, Leonard John. "The Prince Edward Island People and the Great Depression." Unpublished MA thesis. University of New Brunswick. 1972.

Druet, Dirk. "Brighton and Victoria Park: The Growing Years, 1918–1945." Unpublished paper written for the Canadian Museum of Civilization. April 2004.

Gordon, Christine. "Charlottetown: 1985–Present Day." Unpublished paper written for the Canadian Museum of Civilization. 2006.

Holman, Harry T. "Great Expectations, or Charlottetown Education, 1900–1980." Unpublished paper written for the National Museum of Man. 1982.

_____. "Urban Conditions in Charlottetown 1900–1980: Public Health, Sanitation, Welfare, Charities, Water and Sewerage and Housing." Unpublished paper written for the National Museum of Man. July 1982.

Keizer, Stirling. "Humanitarians Go On Leave: Poor Relief in Charlottetown." Unpublished paper written for the National Museum of Man. c. 1981.

Lea, R. G. "The Schools of Charlottetown." Unpublished research paper. Confederation Centre Public Library. Prince Edward Island Collection. c. 1990.

MacDonald, G. Edward. "Cradling Confederation: The Origins of the Confederation Centre of the Arts, Charlottetown." Unpublished research paper prepared for the National Vision Task Force for the Confederation Centre of the Arts. Abridged version. January 2005.

MacDonald, Marc. "The History of Planning and Land Use in Charlottetown." Unpublished research report and chronology written for the Canadian Museum of Civilization. 2006.

MacEachern, Alan Andrew. "No island is an island: a history of tourism on Prince Edward Island, 1870–1939." Unpublished MA thesis. Queen's University. 1991.

MacLeod, Evelyn Jean. "Margaret Gray Lord's Charlottetown World." Unpublished Honours BA thesis. Mount Allison University. 1984.

Maynard, Scott. "Town of Parkdale." Unpublished history compiled in 1990.

McKenna, Sister Mary Olga. "Higher Education in P.E.I., 1945–1980." Transcript of proceedings of a special University of Prince Edward Island (UPEI) seminar held December 5, 1980.

_____. "History of Higher Education in the Province of Prince Edward Island." Unpublished paper presented to the Canadian Catholic Historical Association. St. John's, Nlfd.: Memorial University. 1971.

McRae, Matthew John. "Manufacturing Paradise: Tourism, Development and Mythmaking on Prince Edward Island, 1939–1973." Unpublished MA thesis. Carleton University. February 2004.

Michael, Gordon D. "The Administration of Public Schools in Prince Edward Island to 1974." Unpublished MA in Education thesis. Dalhousie University. 1975.

Parry, Ken T. "The City of Charlottetown, 1770–1855: Charlottetown Before Incorporation and the Reasons for Incorporation." Unpublished essay. UPEI. 1985.

Rider, Peter E. "The Imperial Munitions Board and its Relationship to Government, Business and Labour, 1914–1920." Unpublished PhD thesis. University of Toronto. 1974.

_____. "Seizing Opportunities: Charlottetown and the Mentality of Expansion." Unpublished paper presented to the Canadian-American Urban Development Conference, Guelph, Ontario. August 24–28, 1982.

Robertson, Ian Ross. "Religion, Politics and Education in Prince Edward Island, 1856–1877." Unpublished MA thesis. McGill University. 1968.

Thorpe, F. J. "What Was Built." Ch. 2 of "The Politics of French Public Construction in the Islands of the Gulf of St. Lawrence." Unpublished PhD thesis. University of Ottawa. 1974.

University Study Group. "A Single University for Prince Edward Island." Unpublished report. May 28, 1965.

Published Books and Articles

1914 Patrol. *History of Scouting in Prince Edward Island, 1909–1973*. Charlottetown: A New Horizons Historical Project. 1973.

A City's Journey. Charlottetown: *The Guardian*. April 2005.

Anonymous ("By a Late Resident of that Colony"). *Information to Emigrants. An Account of the Island of Prince Edward*. London: James Asperne. c. 1820.

_____. "Our Prominent Men — Hon. A. B. Warburton, D.C.L." *The Prince Edward Island Magazine and Educational Outlook*. Vol. 6, No. 4 (June 1904). pp. 140–45.

_____. *Historical Sketch of Zion Presbyterian Church*. n.p. 1935.

_____. *The Women of the Kirk*. Charlottetown: St. James Presbyterian Church. 1977.

_____. "Are Our City Councillors Hypnotized?" *The Prince Edward Island Magazine*. Vol. 1, No. 3 (May 1899). pp. 87–89.

_____. "Is There Any Practical Way of Dealing with the Liquor Problem in Charlottetown?" *The Prince Edward Island Magazine*. Vol. 1, No. 1 (March 1899). pp. 1–3.

_____. "Our Prominent Men — Horace Haszard, M.P." *The Prince Edward Island Magazine*. Vols. 5–6, Nos. 11–12. n.d. pp. 387–89.

_____. "The Prince Edward Island Militia." *The Prince Edward Island Magazine*. Vol. 4, No.6 (August 1902). pp. 247–51.

Armsworthy, Cassandra. "Offering Opportunity — Sir William C. Macdonald and Prince Edward Island." *The Island Magazine*. No. 57 (Spring/Summer 2005). pp. 34–40.

Arsenault, Georges. *The Island Acadians*. Trans. Sally Ross. Charlottetown: Ragweed Press. 1989.

Atkinson, Ron H., Chris Austin and Ross Howard. *A Legacy of Faith: History of the Charlottetown Baptist Church Since 1836*. Charlottetown: First United Baptist Church. 2006.

Auld, Walter C. *Voices of the Island: History of the Telephone on Prince Edward Island*. Halifax: Nimbus. 1985.

Author unknown. "Advantages of Prince Edward Island." *New Monthly Magazine* (September 1818). pp. 116–17.

_____. *A Short Account of Prince Edward Island*. London: Madden and Company. 1839.

_____. "Varia," *The Prince Edward Island Magazine*. Vol. 3, No. 6. (c. August 1901). pp. 233–35.

Baedeker's Canada tourist guide for 1900. Leipsic: Karl Baedeker. 1900.

Baldwin, Douglas O. " 'But Not a Drop to Drink': The Struggle for Pure Water." In Douglas Baldwin and Thomas Spira, eds. *Gaslights, Epidemics and Vagabond Cows*. Charlottetown: Ragweed Press. 1988a. pp. 103–24.

_____. "Amy MacMahon and the Struggle for Public Health." *The Island Magazine*. No. 34 (Fall/Winter 1993). pp. 20–27.

_____. "Medical Science, Technology, and Politics: The Creation of Charlottetown's Sewerage System." In Douglas Baldwin and Thomas Spira, eds. *Gaslights, Epidemics and Vagabond Cows*. Charlottetown: Ragweed Press. 1988. pp. 125–37.

_____. "Pigs, Epidemics, and Hospitals: The Struggle for Public Health Services." In Douglas Baldwin and Thomas Spira, eds. *Gaslights, Epidemics and Vagabond Cows*. Charlottetown: Ragweed Press. 1988. pp. 51–69.

_____. "The Growth and Decline of the Charlottetown Banks, 1854–1906." *Acadiensis*. Vol. XV, No. 2 (Spring 1986). pp. 28–52.

Baldwin, Douglas O. and Helen Gill. "The Island's First Bank." *The Island Magazine*. No. 14 (Fall–Winter 1983). pp. 8–13.

Baldwin, Douglas O. "Volunteers in Action: The Establishment of Government Health Care on Prince Edward Island, 1900–1931." *Acadiensis*. Vol. XIX, No. 2 (Spring 1990). pp. 121–47.

Ballem, H. Charles. " 'Our Phil': Philip Blake Macdonald and the Road to the Olympics." *The Island Magazine*. No. 28 (Winter 1990). pp. 15–20.

_____. "Bill Halpenny, First Island Olympian." *The Island Magazine*. No. 15 (Spring/Summer 1984). pp. 23–27.

_____. *Abegweit Dynasty, 1899–1954*. Charlottetown: PEI Museum and Heritage Foundation. 1986.

_____. *More Than Just a Game: One Hundred Years of Organized Sport in Prince Edward Island, 1850–1950*. Charlottetown: Acorn Press. 2004.

Beck, Boyde. "Tunnel Vision." *The Island Magazine*. No. 19 (Spring/Summer 1986). pp. 3–8.

_____. *Prince Edward Island: An (Un)Authorized History*. Charlottetown: Acorn Press. 1996.

Beck, Boyde and Edward MacDonald. *Everyday & Extraordinary: Almanac of the History of Prince Edward Island*. Charlottetown: PEI Museum and Heritage Foundation. 1999.

Bell, A. Kenneth. *Getting the Lights: The Coming of Electricity to Prince Edward Island*. Charlottetown: PEI Museum and Heritage Foundation. 1989.

Blanchard, Francis C. "The French and Acadian Period." In Michael F. Hennessey, ed. *The Catholic Church in Prince Edward Island, 1720–1979*. Charlottetown: R.C. Episcopal Corporation. 1979. pp. 1–21.

Bolger, F. W. P. "Nation Building at Charlottetown, 1864." In F. W. P. Bolger, ed. *Canada's Smallest Province*. Charlottetown: Prince Edward Island 1973 Centennial Commission. 1973. pp. 144–50.

Bruce, Marian. *A Century of Excellence: Prince of Wales College, 1860–1969*. Charlottetown: Island Studies Press/PWC Alumni Association. 2005.

Callbeck, Claudette J. ed. *A History of the Prince Edward Island Hospital School of Nursing, 1891–1971*. Charlottetown: n.p. c. 1974.

Callbeck, Lorne C. *The Cradle of Confederation*. Fredericton: Brunswick Press. 1964.

Cameron, James. "The Garden Distressed: Church Union and Dissent on Prince Edward Island, 1925." *Acadiensis*. Vol. XXI, No. 2 (Spring 1992). pp. 108–31.

Campbell, Duncan. *History of Prince Edward Island*. Charlottetown: Bremner Brothers. 1875.

Canada. Government of Canada. *Canada Year Book*. 1945.

Carnegie Corporation of New York. *Carnegie Library Demonstration in Prince Edward Island, 1933–1936*. Charlottetown: P.E.I. Libraries. 1936.

Charlottetown. *Accounts of the City of Charlottetown*. 1921–1961.

_____. *Annual Report of the City of Charlottetown*. 1885–1913.

Charlottetown Centennial Committee. *Charlottetown Centennial Official Souvenir Booklet, 1855–1955*. Charlottetown: The Charlottetown Centennial Committee. 1955.

Charlottetown Water Commission. *History of the Charlottetown Water Commission, 1887–1987*. Charlottetown: Charlottetown Water Commission. c. 1987.

Chiang, Hung-Min. *Chinese Islanders: Making a Home in the New World*. Charlottetown: Island Studies Press. 2006.

Clark, A. H. *Acadia. The Geography of Early Nova Scotia to 1760*. Madison, Wis.: University of Wisconsin. 1968.

_____. *Three Centuries and the Island*. Toronto: University of Toronto Press. 1959.

Community Planning Association of Canada. *Third Regional Conference of the Community Planning Association of Canada*. September 28, 1951.

Cullen, Mary K. "Charlottetown Market Houses: 1813–1958." *The Island Magazine*. No. 6 (Spring/Summer 1979). pp. 27–32.

_____. "The Transportation Issue, 1873–1973." In F. W. P. Bolger, ed. *Canada's Smallest Province*. Charlottetown: Prince Edward Island 1973 Centennial Commission. 1973. pp. 232–63.

Cullen, Sister Ellen Mary. "Growth and Expansion (1891–1929)." Ch. V in Michael F. Hennessey. ed. *The Catholic Church in Prince Edward Island, 1720–1979*. Charlottetown: The Roman Catholic Episcopal Corporation. 1979. pp. 103–18.

Curley, Rosemary. "Expansion of Charlottetown Along the Hillsborough Shore." *The Island Magazine*. No. 58 (Fall/Winter 2005). pp. 28–31.

de Jong, Nicolas J. and Marven E. Moore. *Shipbuilding on Prince Edward Island: Enterprise in a Maritime Setting 1787–1920*. Hull, Que.: Canadian Museum of Civilization. 1994.

Downing, Dorothy. "High-Tech in Small Towns." In George J. DeBenedette and Rodolphe H. Lamarche, eds. *Shock Waves: The Maritime Urban System in the New Economy*. Moncton: Canadian Institute for Research on Regional Development. 1994.

Drake, Carolyn. "Fighting Fires." In *A City's Journey*. Charlottetown: *The Guardian*. 2005. pp. 66–70.

E.L.M. (pseudonym). "Charlottetown Fifty Years Ago." *The Prince Edward Island Magazine*. Vol. 2, No. 8 (October 1900). pp. 249–56.

Falkus, M. E. "The British Gas Industry Before 1850." *Economic History Review*. 2nd series. Vol. 20 (1967).

Ferguson, Dr. Milton J. "Foreword" to Carnegie Corporation of New York. *The Carnegie Library Demonstration in Prince Edward Island, Canada, 1933–1936*. Charlottetown: P.E.I. Libraries. 1936.

Ferguson, Rob. "The Search for Port La Joye." *The Island Magazine*. No. 27 (Spring/Summer 1990). pp. 3–8.

Fingard, Judith, Janet Guildford and David Sutherland. *Halifax: The First 250 Years*. Halifax: Formac. 1999.

Forbes, E.R. "Consolidating Disparity: The Maritimes and the Industrialization of Canada during the Second World War." *Acadiensis*. Vol. 15, No. 2 (Spring 1986). pp. 3–27.

Forsey, Eugene. "Some Notes on the Early History of Unions in P.E.I." *Canadian Historical Review*. Vol. XLVI, No. 4 (December 1965). pp. 346–51.

Grandy, Robert. *Census 2006, Age and Gender, Prince Edward Island*. Ottawa: Service Canada. 2007.

Green, John Eldon. *A Mind of One's Own: Memoirs of an Albany Boy*. Charlottetown: Tangle Lane. 2006.

Harvey, D. C., ed. *Journeys to the Island of St. John or Prince Edward Island, 1775–1832*. Toronto: Macmillan. 1955.

Harvey, D. C. *The French Régime in Prince Edward Island*. New Haven: Yale University Press. 1926.

Haszard, Horace. "Charlottetown's Attractions for Visitors." *The Prince Edward Island Magazine.* Vol. 1, No. 5 (July 1899). pp. 197–99.

Heartz, Frank Richard, and Ruth Heartz-MacKenzie. "The Baron." *The Island Magazine.* No. 48 (Fall/Winter 2000). pp. 15–22.

Hennessey, Catherine and Edward MacDonald. "Arthur Newbury and the Greening of Queen Square." *The Island Magazine.* No. 28 (Fall/Winter 1990). pp. 25–29.

Hennessey, Catherine. "Painting a History: The Story of Holland Grove." *The Island Magazine.* No. 46 (Fall/Winter 1999). pp. 26–29. Quotation from Elizabeth L. MacDonald. p. 27.

Hennessey, Michael F., ed. *The Catholic Church in Prince Edward Island, 1720–1979.* Charlottetown: The Roman Catholic Episcopal Corporation. 1979.

Heron, Craig. *Booze: a distilled history.* Toronto: Between the Lines. 2003.

Hill, S. S. *A Short Account of Prince Edward Island ...* . London. 1839.

Holman, H. T. "Slaves and Servants on Prince Edward Island: The Case of Jupiter Wise." *Acadiensis,* Vol. XII, No. 1 (Autumn 1982). pp. 100–4.

Holman, Harry. " 'A Lamp to Light their Paths': Lighting the Streets of Charlottetown." In Douglas Baldwin and Thomas Spira, eds. *Gaslights, Epidemics and Vagabond Cows.* Charlottetown: Ragweed Press. 1988. pp. 138–52.

Hopkins, J. Castell, ed. *The Canadian Annual Review of Public Affairs for 1922.* Toronto: The Canadian Annual Review Limited. 1923.

_____. *The Canadian Annual Review of Public Affairs for 1917 (War Series).* Toronto: The Canadian Annual Review Limited. 1918.

_____. *The Canadian Annual Review of Public Affairs for 1918.* Toronto: The Canadian Annual Review Limited. 1919.

Hornby, Jim. *Black Islanders.* Charlottetown: Institute of Island Studies. 1991.

_____. *In the Shadow of the Gallows: Criminal Law and Capital Punishment in Prince Edward Island, 1769–1941.* Charlottetown: Island Studies Press. 1998.

Irvin, A. "The Bastille of Charlottetown." *The Prince Edward Island Magazine.* Vol. 1, No. 2 (April 1899). pp. 73–75.

_____. "Charlottetown in 'The Olden Times.' " *The Prince Edward Island Magazine.* Vol. 1, No. 5 (July 1899). pp. 188–92.

Jackson, R. W. *An Economic Profile of Prince Edward Island.* Charlottetown: Department of Labour, Industry and Commerce. 1970.

J.E.W. (pseudonym). "Charlottetown — Past and Present." *The Prince Edward Magazine.* Vol. 3, No. 12 (1901). pp. 444–48.

Johnstone, Edward. "Victoria Park." In *Historical Highlights of Prince Edward Island.* Charlottetown: PEI Museum and Heritage Foundation. 1955.

Johnstone, Walter. "Letters Descriptive of Prince Edward Island." In D. C. Harvey, ed. *Journeys to the Island of St. John or Prince Edward Island, 1775–1832.* Toronto: Macmillan. 1955.

Keeping, B. C. "The Development of Public Health in Prince Edward Island." *Canadian Journal of Public Health.* January 1935.

Kennedy, Earle, and Boyde Beck. " 'An Island Unit': The 2nd Siege Battery in the Great War." *The Island Magazine.* No. 49 (Spring/Summer 2001). pp. 31–41.

Lafferty, Louis W. *The Structure of Opportunity: An analysis of business industry in the economy of Kings County and Charlottetown, Prince Edward Island.* Montague, P.E.I.: Prince Edward Island NewStart. 1969.

Large, Betty Rogers, and Tom Crothers. *Out of Thin Air: The Story of CFCY, "The Friendly Voice of the Maritimes."* Charlottetown: Applecross Press. 1989.

Lawson, John. *Letters on Prince Edward Island.* Charlottetown: Haszard. 1851.

Lea, R. G. *History of the Practice of Medicine in Prince Edward Island.* Charlottetown: PEI Medical Society. 1964.

_____. *The Polyclinic, 1925–1981*, Charlottetown: Dillon Printing. c. 1981.

Lennox, Jeffers. "An Empire on Paper: The Founding of Halifax and Conceptions of Imperial Space, 1844–55." *Canadian Historical Review.* Vol. 88, No. 3 (September 2007). pp. 373–412.

Lockerby, Earle. "The Comte de Saint-Pierre and Île Saint-Jean." *The Island Magazine.* No. 61 (Spring/Summer 2007). pp. 7–14.

Lord, Margaret Gray. *One Woman's Charlottetown: diaries of Margaret Gray Lord, 1863, 1876, 1890.* Edited and annotated by Evelyn J. MacLeod. Hull, Que.: Canadian Museum of Civilization. 1988.

MacAndrew, Barbara. "Prince Edward Island ... One Hundred Years." *Atlantic Advocate.* January 1973. pp. 15–17.

MacDonald, A. A. "No. 5 Co. at Home and in Camp." *The Prince Edward Island Magazine.* Vol. III, No.7 (September 1901). pp. 250–54.

MacDonald, Edward, and Carolyn (Roberts) McQuaid. " 'Spirituous Liquors': Brewing and Distilling in 19th Century Charlottetown." *The Island Magazine.* No. 58 (Fall/Winter 2005a). pp. 32–39.

MacDonald, G. Edward. "The Master of Beaconsfield, Part Two: Henry J. Cundall." *The Island Magazine.* No. 34 (Fall/Winter 1993). pp. 7–14.

_____. *If You're Stronghearted.* Charlottetown: Prince Edward Island Museum and Heritage Foundation. 2000.

_____. *The History of St. Dunstan's University, 1855–1956.* Charlottetown: Board of Governors of St. Dunstan's University and Prince Edward Island Museum and Heritage Foundation. 1989.

MacDonald, Hesta. *History, 1953–1973: The P.E.I. Federation of Home and School Associations.* Charlottetown: Island Offset. 1973.

MacDonald, Sister Carmel. "An Era of Consolidation." In Michael F. Hennessey, ed. *The Catholic Church in Prince Edward Island, 1720–1979.* Charlottetown: Roman Catholic Episcopal Corporation. 1979. pp. 58–70.

MacIntyre, Wendell. "A Long and Winding Thread." *The Atlantic Advocate.* Vol. 79, No. 2 (October 1988). pp. 31–33.

MacIntyre, Wendell P. H. "The Longest Reign." In Michael F. Hennessey, ed. *The Catholic Church in Prince Edward Island, 1720–1979.* Charlottetown: Roman Catholic Episcopal Corporation. 1979. pp. 71–102.

MacKinnon, D. A., and A. B. Warburton, eds. *Past and Present of Prince Edward Island.* Charlottetown: Bowen. c. 1903.

MacKinnon, Darin and Boyde Beck. "Islanders and the Boer War." *The Island Magazine.* No. 26 (Fall/Winter 1989). pp. 3–12.

MacKinnon, Darin. "Colonel Waring's Filthy Business." *The Island Magazine.* No. 55 (Spring/Summer 2004). pp. 22–28.

_____. "Louise and Lorne: The Vice-Regal Visit of 1879." *The Island Magazine*. No. 48 (Fall/Winter 2000). pp. 3–9.

MacKinnon, Frank. "Charlottetown Through the Years … ." In *The Charlottetown Centennial*. Charlottetown: Charlottetown Centennial Committee and the Tribune Press. 1955. pp. 12–41.

_____. "Prince Edward Island." In John Saywell, ed. *Canadian Annual Review of Politics and Public Affairs, 1972*. Toronto: University of Toronto Press. 1973.

_____. "Prince Edward Island." In John Saywell, ed. *Canadian Annual Review of Politics and Public Affairs, 1973*. Toronto: University of Toronto Press. 1974.

_____. "Prince Edward Island." In John Saywell, ed. *Canadian Annual Review for 1965*. Toronto: University of Toronto Press. 1966.

_____. "Prince Edward Island." In John Saywell, ed. *Canadian Annual Review for 1969*. Toronto: University of Toronto Press. 1970.

_____. *Honour the Founders! Enjoy the Arts!* Charlottetown: Fathers of Confederation Buildings Trust. 1990.

_____. *The Government of Prince Edward Island*. Toronto: University of Toronto. 1951.

MacNutt, T. E. "Education in Charlottetown." In *The Charlottetown Centennial*. Charlottetown: Charlottetown Centennial Committee and the Tribune Press. 1955. pp. 92–95.

MacNutt, W. S. "Political Advance and Social Reform, 1842–1861." In F. W. P. Bolger. *Canada's Smallest Province*. Charlottetown: Prince Edward Island 1973 Centennial Commission. 1973. pp. 115–34.

MacPherson, Andy. "Province's Air History Proves Exciting Saga." *Patriot*. August 9, 1973.

Maloney, John H., Nicolas de Jong and Douglas B. Boylan. "The First Centuries." In F. W. P. Bolger. *Canada's Smallest Province*. Charlottetown: Prince Edward Island 1973 Centennial Commission. 1973. pp. 1–36.

Manning, Randolph W. "Cows and Convalescents: Government House as Health and Education Centre, 1917–1924." *The Island Magazine*. No. 24 (Fall/Winter 1988). pp. 19–24.

_____. *Accounting for Progress: A History of the Institute of Chartered Accountants of Prince Edward Island*. Summerside: ICAPEI. 1998.

Marquis, Greg. "Enforcing the Law: The Charlottetown Police Force." In Douglas Baldwin and Thomas Spira, eds. *Gaslights, Epidemics and Vagabond Cows*. Charlottetown: Ragweed Press. 1988. pp. 86–102.

_____. "History of Policing in the Maritime Provinces." *Urban History Review*. Vol. XIX, No. 1 (October 1990). pp. 84–99.

_____. "Murder in the Bog." *The Island Magazine*. No. 14 (Fall/Winter 1983). pp. 29–32.

McAlpine's P.E.I. Directory, 1924–1925. Halifax: Royal Print and Litho Ltd. c. 1924.

McKenna, Sister Mary Olga. "Higher Education in Transition, 1945–1980." In Verner Smitheram, David Milne and Satadal Dasgupta, eds. *The Garden Transformed: Prince Edward Island, 1945–1980*. Charlottetown: Ragweed Press. 1982.

Miller, Zane L. "Scarcity, Abundance, and American Urban History." *Journal of Urban History*. Vol. 4, No. 2 (February 1978). pp. 131–55.

Monro, Alexander. *New Brunswick with outline of Nova Scotia and Prince Edward Island*. Halifax: R. Nugent. 1855.

Moore, F. S. "Our Island Militia." *The Prince Edward Island Magazine*. Vol. II, No.2 (April 1900). pp. 57–62.

Morrison, J. Clinton. "D. R. Morrison: Island Builder." *The Island Magazine*. No. 20 (Fall/Winter 1986). pp. 13–18.

O'Grady, Brendan. *Exiles and Islanders: The Irish Settlers of Prince Edward Island*. Montreal and Kingston: McGill-Queen's University Press. 2004.

O'Meara, B. J. *Report of the Division of Dental Public Health*. Study prepared for the PEI Department of Health. 1960.

O'Neill, Paul. *A Seaport Legacy: The Story of St. John's, Newfoundland*. Erin, Ont.: Press Porcepic. 1976.

Peake, Linda M. "Establishing a Theatrical Tradition: Prince Edward Island, 1800–1900." *Theatre Research in Canada*. Vol. 2, No. 2 (Fall 1981). pp. 117–32.

Pollard, J. B. "The Visit of King Edward VII to P.E. Island." *The Prince Edward Island Magazine*. Vol. 5, No. 11 (c. January/February 1904). pp. 370–76.

Protestant Family Service Bureau. *The Protestant Family Service Bureau, 1956–1979: Twenty-Four Years of Service to Families and the Community*. Charlottetown. 1980.

Rayburn, Alan. *Geographical Names of Prince Edward Island*. Ottawa: Energy, Mines and Resources. 1973.

Rider, Peter E. " 'A Blot Upon the Fair Fame of Our Island': The Scandal at the Charlottetown Lunatic Asylum." *The Island Magazine*. No. 39 (Spring/Summer 1996). pp. 3–9.

_____. "An Introduction" to Douglas L. Durkin, *The Magpie*. Toronto: University of Toronto Press. 1975. pp. VI–XXI.

_____. "Benjamin Charles Prowse." In Ramsay Cook, ed. *Dictionary of Canadian Biography*. Vol. 15. Toronto: University of Toronto Press. 2004.

_____. " 'Stirring and Restless Times': Charlottetown in the Interwar Years." *The Island Magazine*. No. 58 (Fall/Winter 2005). pp. 2–9.

Robertson, Ian Ross. "George Coles." In Marc La Terreur, ed. *Dictionary of Canadian Biography*. Vol. X. Toronto: University of Toronto Press. 1972. pp. 182–88.

_____. "The Posse Comitatus Incident of 1865." *The Island Magazine*. No. 24 (Fall/Winter 1988). pp. 3–10.

Rogers, Flora Smith. *Trinity United Church, Charlottetown, 1809–1964*. Charlottetown. 1964.

Rogers, Irene L. *Charlottetown: The Life in Its Buildings*. Charlottetown: PEI Museum and Heritage Foundation. 1983; revised edition, 1992.

Romkey, B. *The History of Charlottetown Airport*. n.p. 1960.

Saywell, John, ed. *Canadian Annual Review of Politics and Public Affairs, 1974*. Toronto: University of Toronto Press. 1975.

Saywell, John, ed. *Canadian Annual Review of Politics and Public Affairs, 1975*. Toronto: University of Toronto Press. 1976.

Selkirk, Lord. *Lord Selkirk's Diary*. 1803. Reprinted Toronto: Champlain Society. 1958.

Sellick, Lester B. "Keith S. Rogers." In *Some Island Men I Remember*. Hantsport, N.S.: Lancelot Press. 1980.

Sharpe, Errol. "The Politics of Education and Religion." In *A People's History of Prince Edward Island*. Toronto: Steel Rail Publishing. 1976.

Sinnott, J. Cyril. *A History of the Charlottetown Clinic*. Charlottetown: The author. 1975.

Slumkoski, Corey. " 'Animals on the Hoof': The Prince Edward Island — Newfoundland Cattle Trade, 1943–1949." *The Island Magazine*. No. 59 (Spring/Summer 2006). pp. 16–21.

Stelter, Gilbert A. "The Classical Ideal. Culture and Urban Form in Eighteenth-Century Britain and America." *Journal of Urban History*. Vol. 10, No. 4 (August 1984).

Stevens, G. R. *Canadian National Railways*. Vol. 1. Toronto: Clarke, Irwin. 1960.

Stewart, John. *An Account of Prince Edward Island ...* . London, 1806. Reprinted New York: Johnson Reprint Corporation. 1967.

Stewart, W. S. "The Government Guarantee and the Dominion Packing Company." *The Prince Edward Island Magazine*. Vol. 4, No. 8 (October 1902). pp. 295–300.

T (pseudonym). "The City of the Dead." *The Prince Edward Island Magazine*. Vol. 5, No. 7 (September 1903). p. 238.

Trade Directory of P.E.I., 1935. Charlottetown: Thos. R. Tees. c. 1935.

Tuck, Robert C. "The Story Behind All Souls' Chapel." *The Island Magazine*. No. 22 (Fall/Winter 1987). pp. 10–13.

_____. *Gothic Dreams*. Toronto: Dundurn Press. 1978.

Upton, L. T. S. "Indians and Islanders: The Micmacs in Colonial Prince Edward Island." *Acadiensis*. Vol. VI, No. 1 (Autumn 1976). pp. 21–42.

Vail, Delmar J. "Prince Edward Island." In *The Vermonter*. Reprinted in *The Prince Edward Island Magazine*. Vol. 5, No. 7 (September 1903). pp. 225–37.

Walsh, Edward. "An Account of Prince Edward's Island, 1803." Introduced by H. T. Holman. *The Island Magazine*. No. 15 (Spring/Summer 1984). pp. 9–13.

Warburton, A. B. *A History of Prince Edward Island*. Saint John, N.B.: Barnes & Company. 1923.

Ward, Wallace, and William R. Burnett, eds. *History of Scouting in Prince Edward Island, 1909–1973*. Charlottetown: A New Horizons Historical Project. 1973.

Watson, Julie V. "Charlottetown: Affluence Reincarnated." *Atlantic Business*. Vol. 13, No. 3. 2002.

Weale, David. *A Stream out of Lebanon*. Charlottetown: Institute of Island Studies. 1988.

Webber, David. *A Thousand Young Men: The Colonial Volunteer Militia of Prince Edward Island, 1775–1874*. Charlottetown: Prince Edward Island Museum and Heritage Foundation. 1990.

Weeks, W. A. "Military History of Prince Edward Island." In D. A. MacKinnon and A. B. Warburton, eds. *Past and Present of Prince Edward Island*. Charlottetown: Bowen. c. 1903.

X (pseudonym). "The YMCA." In *The Prince Edward Island Magazine*. Vol. 4, No. 4 (1902). pp. 140–43.

Notes on Sources

Although there were a myriad of primary and secondary sources from which the information found in this history of Charlottetown was drawn, RG 20, the records of the City of Charlottetown held at the Public Archives and Records Office of Prince Edward Island, was the single, most important one. This fonds, along with the published *Accounts of the City of Charlottetown*, provided a detailed historical record. Another collection, Accession 3147, the records of the Greater Charlottetown Chamber of Commerce (Board of Trade), complemented the municipal records superbly. Government publications, particularly *Statutes of Prince Edward Island*, were essential to establishing the legal framework of the municipal corporation.

Newspapers are frequently invaluable repositories of historical information. Three were especially significant for this study: *The Examiner*, *The Patriot* and *The Guardian*. On two festive occasions, important histories of the city were published. *The Charlottetown Centennial Official Souvenir Booklet, 1855–1955*, Charlottetown: The Charlottetown Centennial Committee, 1955, was much more substantial than the title suggests and provided a good jumping-off point for many topics. A similar service was performed by *A City's Journey*, largely written by Carolyn Drake and Mary MacKay and published by *The Guardian*, April 2005. It also was a source of contemporary information not found elsewhere.

The contents of two journals were so frequently useful that the journals themselves deserve to be mentioned as single entities. *The Prince Edward Island Magazine*, seven volumes of which appeared between 1899 and 1905, contained many articles, both brief and more extended, on the city and its inhabitants. Since 1976, *The Island Magazine* has published many important carefully researched papers on subjects relating to Charlottetown.

Four publications were frequently of service for a variety of topics. Douglas Baldwin and Thomas Spira, *Gaslights, Epidemics and Vagabond Cows: Charlottetown in the Victorian Era*, Charlottetown: Ragweed Press, 1988, offered detailed studies on a variety of themes that were critical for 19th-century municipal development. Irene Rogers, *Charlottetown: The Life in Its Buildings*, Charlottetown: Prince Edward Island Museum and Heritage Foundation, 1983, 1992, went beyond architectural history into the economic and social aspects of life in the city. Edward MacDonald, *If You're Stronghearted: Prince Edward Island in the Twentieth Century*, Charlottetown: Prince Edward Island Museum and Heritage Foundation, 2000, was a work of solid scholarship written in an unusually engaging style that frequently touched upon matters having a direct impact on Charlottetown. Boyde Beck and Edward MacDonald, *Everyday and Extraordinary: Almanac of the History of Prince Edward Island*, Charlottetown: Prince Edward Island Museum and Heritage Foundation, 1999, offered up numerous informational nuggets on events in the life of the Island capital.

A more detailed statement on sources, organized by chapter, follows. Citations refer to entries in the bibliography.

CHAPTER 1 — *ORIGINS*

An earlier version of this chapter appeared as "The Early Years" in Douglas Baldwin and Thomas Spira, eds., *Gaslights, Epidemics and Vagabond Cows*, Charlottetown: Ragweed Press, 1988. Prince Edward Island has been well-served by a number of key studies of its early history, and each of them contains material on Charlottetown. Clark (1959) set the geographical stage. Information on the Mi'kmaq came from Maloney (1973), with additional details from Upton (1976). The basic sources for the French regime were Harvey (1926), Clark (1959) and Warburton (1923). Lockerby (2007) covered the Compagnie de l'Île Saint-Jean while Thorpe (1974) provided details on the construction of Port LaJoye. Ferguson (1990) and Clark (1968) described the population of Port LaJoye before the conquest.

The English approach to the building of towns in the Georgian era is the subject of two interesting papers by Lennox (2007) and Stelter (1984). Glimpses into everyday life in early Charlottetown were provided by Walsh (1984), Callbeck (1964), Stewart (1967) and Warburton (1923). Colonial Office records (CO 226) provided details that have the immediacy of personal witness. Military matters were touched upon by the foregoing sources and elaborated by Webber (1990). Arsenault (1989) described the Acadian community under English rule, and Holman (1982) documented the circumstances faced by slaves and coloured servants in the city's early years.

Statistics on the growth of Charlottetown in the early 19th century came from the censuses of 1798, 1827, 1833, 1841, 1848 and 1855. O'Grady (2004) developed the Irish contribution to the city's population. Ordinary life was portrayed in Joseph Pope's memoirs (LAC, n.d.) and in the diaries of Margaret Gray Lord (1988). The built environment was described by Irwin (1899), Anonymous (1820), an Unknown Author (1818) and Rogers (1983, 1992). MacDonald (1979) covered the construction activities of the Roman Catholic diocese, while Bruce (2005) dealt with the Central Academy. Hill (1839) and Hennessey (1999) described the housing, and Monro (1855) and Lawson (1851) recorded the overall ambiance of the town.

A chapter in de Jong (1994) delineated the shipbuilding industry in Charlottetown. Details on public administration and commerce came from Campbell (1875), Monro (1855), Author Unknown (1839) and Author Unknown (1818), Lawson (1851) and the Jarvis Papers (LAC, mfm. M-1963). Rogers (1983, 1992) offered important facts about the growth of manufacturing. Johnstone (1955) and Author Unknown (1839) added details on the presence of various occupational groups. Warburton (1923) and Irwin (1899) helped to document Charlottetown's communications links in the pre-incorporation era.

The social life of the city was touched upon in many of the foregoing works, as well as MacKinnon (1955). Lea (1990) traced the history of education, as well as the practice of medicine (Lea 1964). Lord Selkirk (1803) and Lawson (1851) commented about the state of the water supplies, and Campbell (1875), Parry (1985) and *The Palladium* (1843) documented the threat of fire and efforts to contain it. Archival records from Carrington (PARO, Acc. 3263), MacEachern (PARO, Acc. 2825) and Kent (PARO, Acc. 4426), as well as Monro (1855), dealt with the living conditions of many of the town's poor. *The Examiner*, Monro (1855), E.L.M. (1900) covered the more prosperous elements and their activities. Webber (1990) was indispensable for coverage of the later military events. Concluding remarks drew upon Miller (1978) and Fingard (1999), as well as Rider (1982).

Photo Credits: **Page 3**: National Archives and Library (NAL); **Page 6**, top to bottom: NAL, NAL, Prince Edward Island Museum and Heritage Foundation (PEIMHF); **Page 7**: PEIMHF; **Page 9**: Public Archives and Records Office (PARO) O,239 D; **Page 11**: PEIMHF; **Page 13**: from *An Island Sketchbook*, by Benjamin Bremner; **Page 14**, top to bottom: PARO 2331, 2702.31, 2320.55; **Page 16**, PEIMHF (top), NAC (left), PARO 2702.8 (right); **Page 18**: Confederation Centre Art Gallery and Museum (CCAGM), Beazley Sketchbook; **Page 21**: PEIMHF; Page 23: PEIMHF.

CHAPTER 2 — *STRUGGLE*

Key information throughout Chapter 2 came from the municipal records for Charlottetown (PARO, RG 20). City Council Minute Books, supplemented by a letter book, poll book, assessment books and a ledger, were the critical volumes. These sources were supplemented by newspapers, principally *The Examiner*, but also *The Patriot* and to a lesser extent *The Weekly Advertiser*, *The Protestant and Evangelical Witness* and *Haszard's Gazette*. Discussion of Charlottetown's Black community was informed by Hornby (1991). Snippets in the Wellner fonds (PARO, Acc. 2851) added context to early city politics.

Discussion of the built landscape benefitted from an unpublished manuscript of Charlottetown's four market houses by T. E. MacNutt (PARO, Acc. 4210), Atkinson (2006), J.E.W. (1901) and especially Rogers (1983, 1992). Holman (1988) traced the history of street lighting. This was complemented by details from the Parliamentary Reports of the Prince Edward Island Legislature.

The R. G. Dun and Company collection at the Baker Library at Harvard University gave an insider's view of business and the business community in the city's formative years. Baldwin (1983) traced the fortunes of the local banks, while de Jong (1994) did the same for the shipbuilding industry. Stevens (1960) covered the development of the railway from a lofty Central Canadian perspective.

Various secondary sources helped to complete the description of social life in Charlottetown from incorporation to 1879. Although there is ample room for further work on education, Hennessey (1979), MacNutt (1979 and 1973) and MacKinnon (1951) were very useful for its coverage. Sharpe (1979) and Robertson (1968) added the all-important political dimension. Baldwin (1988b) traced efforts to secure adequate public health services for the city. Baldwin (1988a) did the same for the struggles over municipal water services. Fire, which so ravaged the city, had a similar effect on George Coles. Robertson (1972) told the story. Marquis (1988 and 1983) recounted the trials and tribulations of the police force and law enforcement. Robertson (1988) documented the curious *Posse Comitatus* incident. Beck (1996) was the source of information on the Orangemen's Riots. Rider (1996) explored the scandal at the lunatic asylum. Two articles from the *Island Magazine* provided insight into the liquor question: MacDonald (2005a) and, for the story of F. R. Heartz, Heartz (2000). Social life, including royal visits and the entertainment at the time of the Charlottetown Conference, were effectively treated by Lord (1988), Pollard (1904), MacKinnon (2000) and Bolger (1973). Peake's (1981) important, but little known, study of local theatre showed how both local and travelling productions amused Charlottetonians in the early years of the city's history.

Photo Credits: **Page 30**: City of Charlottetown (CC); **Page 31**: CC; **Page 32**: PARO 2702.10; **Page 34**: CC; **Page 35**: PEIMHF; **Page 36**, top to bottom, PARO 2301, 3466.HF.70.2858; Page 39: PARO 2301.213, 2301.112; Page 41, top to bottom: PARO 3218.62, 3466.72.27, 3466.HF.77.52; **Page 44**: PARO 3466.HF.76.124.4; **Page 45**: PEIMHF; **Page 47**: PARO 2301; **Page 48**: CCAGM, Beazley Sketchbook; **Page 51**: PARO 3466.HF.74.27.3.223; **Page 55**: PEIMHF; **Page 56**: Courtesy Catherine Hennessey; **Page 59**: PEIMHF; **Page 60**: PEIMHF; **Page 63**, top to bottom, PARO 2320; PEIMHF; **Page 68**: PARO 2702; **Page 69**: PARO 3466.HF.79.40.1, CC; **Page 71**: PEIMHF; **Page 73**: PARO 3466.HF.74.27.3.117; **Page 79**, top to bottom: PEIMHF, PARO 3109.40, 3466.HF.79.114.335.128; **Page 84**: PARO 2301.22; **Page 85**: PARO 3466.HF.72.27; **Page 87**: PARO.

CHAPTER 3 — *EXPANSION*

Heavy reliance was placed in this chapter on primary sources and newspapers. The records of the City of Charlottetown (PARO, RG 20) were of prime importance. City Council Minutes, supplemented by correspondence and records pertaining to health, sewers and water supply, the police, and courts and licensing provided vistas on all aspects of Charlottetown life. During the period 1880–1920, the Board of Trade had a major impact upon the economic life of the community, and the council and general minutes of the organization, held at PARO (Acc. 3147), documented that role. *The Examiner* and *The Patriot*, and after the turn of the 20th century, *The Guardian* recorded Charlottetown's politics, economy and society. *The Herald* and *The Watchman* also offered up useful tidbits on specific occasions.

In the discussion of the urban population, Weale (1988) and Chiang (2006) were sources of information on the Lebanese and Chinese communities. During a period of legislative change in the city's legal framework, reference was made to various provincial statutes, as recorded in official government publications. The changing face of the built environment was recorded by Haszard (1899), Vail (1903), Author unknown (1901) and T (1903), as well as the indispensable Rogers (1983, 1992). Cullen, M. (1979) made significant contributions to the discussion of market houses, as Tuck (1978, 1987) and Cullen, E. (1979) did for churches, and MacDonald (1989) and Bruce (2005) for the colleges. An anonymous article (1904) on A. B. Warburton, as well as Tuck (1978), Hennessey (1990), Johnstone (1955) and an anonymous article on Horace Haszard (n.d.) documented the efforts to develop and preserve Charlottetown's green spaces. Auld (1985) was an essential source on Charlottetown's telephone service. Holman (1988) and Bell (1989) covered street lighting. The author would like to thank Catherine Hennessey for a personal communication that explained the varying names of what is now University Avenue.

In the section on economic development, de Jong (1994) was again very helpful for shipbuilding. Various previous studies by Rider (2004, 1974, 1975, 1982) contributed to the discussion of the economy, as did Beck (1999). Baldwin (1986) covered banking in the city. Stewart (1902) offered a view on bonusing. Cullen (1973) provided an excellent treatment of the issue of continuous communications. Beck (1986) dealt with early efforts to have a tunnel to the mainland.

In the section of social life, Armsworthy (2005) treated the educational initiatives of Sir William Macdonald, Manning (1988) dealt with the health and education centre at Government House, and MacDonald (1989) and Bruce (2005) covered the colleges. Baldwin (1988b), MacIntyre (1979), Lea (1964), Baldwin (1993) and MacDonald (2000) filled in important parts of the picture on health care. Baldwin (1988a) and Charlottetown Water Commission (1987) traced the efforts to provide ongoing sources of pure water to the city. Baldwin (1988c) and MacKinnon (2004) dealt with the outflow. Marquis (1990) helped to frame the discussion of law enforcement, and Lord (1988) contributed some important gossip. Irvin (1899) described conditions faced by those convicted and sent to jail. MacDonald (2005a) and Heron's encyclopaedic book on booze (2003) were very helpful with the discussion of temperance, while an anonymous article on the liquor problem (1899) provided a contemporary perspective. Keizer (1981) made an important contribution to the discussion of poor relief, supplemented by MacDonald (1993) and Lord (1988). Key aspects of that discussion were drawn from the minute books of the Children's Aid Society (PARO, Acc. 3007/4). Forsey's research note (1965) was helpful in providing details on labour organization. Discussion of sports in the city benefitted greatly from two books by Ballem (1986, 2004), as well as his article on Halpenny (1984). X (1902) provided details on the establishment of the YMCA, and the annual reports of the "Y" tracked its evolution. As in the previous chapter, Peake (1981) was one of the few secondary sources on the theatre. MacKinnon (1903) was very useful with its coverage of fraternal organizations in the city, while Moore (1900), an anonymous author (1901), Weeks (1903) and MacKinnon (1989) dealt with the militia. Kennedy (2001), Hopkins (1918, 1919) and MacDonald (2000) traced the contributions and sacrifices Charlottetonians made in the Great War.

Photo Credits: **Page 97**: CC; **Page 98**: CC, PARO, RG20.719.B5; **Page 99**: PARO 2702.154; **Page 100**: PEIMHF; **Page 102**: PARO 3466.HF.78.72.34; **Page 103**: PARO 3466.HF.72.66; **Page 104**: PEIMHF; **Page 105**: top to bottom, PARO 3218, 3466.HF.78, 3466.HF.72.66; **Page 108**: Diocese of Charlottetown; **Page 110**: top to bottom, PARO 2966, 3466.HF.72.66; **Page 112**: PARO 3218.61; **Page 114**: top to bottom: PARO 3218.15, 3218.18; **Page 116**: PARO 3218.47; **Page 117**: PARO 3909.19; **Page 120**: PEIMHF; **Page 121**: PEIMHF; **Page 122**: PEIMHF; **Page 123**: PEIMHF; **Page 128**: PEIMHF; **Page 137**: PEIMHF; **Page 139**: PEIMHF; **Page 140**: PEIMHF; **Page 141**: PARO 3466.HF.72.66; **Page 145**: top to bottom, PEIMHF; **Page 147**: PARO 3466.HF.70.2873; **Page 149**: PEIMHF; **Page 151**: top to bottom, PARO 4720.4.20, PEIMHF; **Page 157**: PARO 4162.58; **Page 160**: PARO 3218; **Page 170**: PARO 3948.1; **Page 171:** top to bottom, PEIMHF, PARO 2320.77; **Page 174**: PARO 3218, PEIMHF; **Page 178**: PARO 2301.81; **Page 180**: PARO 4240.73.

CHAPTER 4 — *RECESSION*

The information in this chapter was drawn mainly from the Charlottetown municipal records, particularly the City Council minutes (PARO, RG 20) and the annual *Accounts of the City of Charlottetown*; the minutes of the Board of Trade (PARO, Acc. 3147); and the two principal local newspapers, *The Guardian* and *The Patriot*. Provincial records, especially *Statutes of Prince Edward Island*, were important in framing the discussion of politics. MacDonald (2000) was invaluable in providing the broader context of events in the city and in clarifying ambiguities. Cusack (1972) is an important study that was helpful in documenting economic conditions during the Great Depression. Manning (1998) provided information relevant to George P. Nicholson and the management of city finances in the 1930s.

The time period covered by Chapter 4 lies largely after the coverage of Irene Rogers, *Charlottetown: The Life in Its Buildings*, and reliance for changes in the urban landscape fell more heavily upon the primary sources. Specific studies contributed to the discussion of particular topics: Morrison (1986) on the relocation of the old Charlottetown Hospital, Manning (1988) on the Rena McLean Memorial Hospital, Callbeck (1974) on the PEI Hospital School of Nursing and Druet (2004) on Brighton and Victoria Park. Bruce (2005) and MacDonald (1989) again were essential to understanding the physical changes at the colleges. Auld (1985) provided information on the expansion of the telephone company's infrastructure.

In the section on economic development, the primary sources were supplemented by federal census records and data from the *Financial Post Business Yearbooks* for 1925, 1940 and 1945. Bell (1989) recounted the expansion of Maritime Electric across the province, while Battersby (1941) helped with his assessment of manufacturing in the interwar period. Additional information on the economy was gleaned from Prince Edward Island's submission to the Royal Commission on Dominion-Provincial Relations and the *Canada Year Book* (1945). MacIntyre (1988) told the story of the Landrigan woollen mill. Forbes (1986), in a typically insightful and forceful way, established the regional context for the Island economy during the Second World War. Slumkoski (2006) traced the trade in cattle between the Island and Newfoundland in the 1940s. Cullen (1973) provided the wider communications context within which trade took place. The author is indebted to Boyde Beck for his personal communication describing the tactics used by one truck driver to fit his vehicle onto the *Prince Nova*. Large (1989) and Sellick (1980) told the story of early radio on Prince Edward Island; Beck (1996) did the same for Carl Burke. Two MA theses contributed greatly to the treatment of tourism: MacEachern (1991) and McRae (2004).

The discussion of social life benefitted from various background papers prepared for the Canadian Museum of Civilization by student researchers in the summer of 1982. Holman (1982) was particularly important for education. MacDonald (1973) touched upon the early years of the Home and School Association. MacDonald (1989) and Bruce (2005) provided enrolment numbers for the colleges. Manning (1988), Ferguson (1936) and Shaw (1936) contained information on the provision of library services. In the area of health, Callbeck (1974) and Lea (1981) discussed medical institutions, while Baldwin (1981 and 1993), Keeping (1935) and Daley (PARO, Acc. 3311/1, 1981) described the equally important efforts in the area of public health. Important parts of the outline of water and sewerage were drawn from Charlottetown Water Commission (1987). Discussion of crime was made fuller by Hornby (1998). Cusack (1972) was essential to an understanding of the social impact of the Great Depression, as was PARO, RG 10, Vol. 65 for the payments made for direct relief. Various authorities described the activities of the churches in the interwar era: Cameron (1992), Rogers (1964) and two anonymous publications, one on Zion Presbyterian Church (1935) and the other on the Kirk of St. James (1977). Ballem (2004 and 1990) were, of course, key sources for the discussion of sports. Boyde Beck kindly shared the comment of Captain J. J. Connolly (Interview, 1982) concerning importance of sports as a motivator for recruits to the naval reserve in the 1930s. Ward (1973) was a helpful source on the scouting movement, and MacDonald (2000) contained a wealth of information and understanding concerning Islanders in the Second World War. The innocence of some of the Charlottetonians in uniform was underscored by Squarebriggs (Interview, 1980).

Photo Credits: **Page 188**: CC; **Page 189**: CC; **Page 190**: CC; **Page 193**: CC; **Page 194**: PARO 2675.9: **Page 199**: PARO 4352 P-1; **Page 200**: PARO 3466.HF.77.34; **Page 201**: PEIMHF; **Page 202**: PARO 3466.HF.74.225.56; **Page 203**: PEIMHF; **Page 204**: PEIMHF; **Page 107**: PEIMHF; **Page 208**: PEIMHF; **Page 211**: PEIMHF; **Page 212**: CC; **Page 213**: PARO 3218; **Page 215**: PEIMHF; **Page 218**: PEIMHF; **Page 223**: PARO 4652; **Page 224**: PEIMHF; **Page 225**: PEIMHF; **Page 229**: PEIMHF;

Page 235: PEIMHF; **Page 237**: PARO 4541; **Page 238**: PEIMHF; **Page 241**: PARO 4132; **Page 243**: PARO 3281.16; **Page 244**: PARO 3150.124; **Page 246**: PARO 3218.73; **Page 248**: PARO 2320.64; **Page 250**: PEIMHF; **Page 251**: PEIMHF; **Page 255**: PEIMHF; **Page 256**: PEIMHF; **Page 257**: PEIMHF; **Page 258**: PARO 3466.HF.76.217; **Page 259**: PARO 4770 3.7; **Page 261**: PEIMHF; **Page 266**: PARO 4507.6; **Page 268**: PARO 2320.112; **Page 269**: PEIMHF.

CHAPTER 5 – *RECOVERY*

In addition to the original source materials that have been central throughout this study, government documents and oral testimony have been important for this chapter, which deals with more recent times. The author was fortunate to have been allowed access to city records, which had not yet been turned over to the Public Archives and Records Office, and to the records of the Charlottetown Office of the then federal Department of Regional Economic Expansion (DREE). Other government records, including *The Statutes of Prince Edward Island*, have been essential reading at a point in time when the conjoining of municipal and provincial governments had become frequent in the area of public policy formation.

Government planning documents, including de Silva (1962), shed light on the population growth after the Second World War. The Charlottetown Metropolitan Committee, *Report* (1957) helped to set the stage for the drawn-out amalgamation process. Touche, Ross *et al* (1969) contributed to an understanding of civic finances. Michael (1974) explored some of the political ramifications of education. O'Meara (1960) did the same for fluoridation. MacKinnon (1951) was a starting place for consideration of municipal politics.

The quotation of Douglas W. Ambridge that appears in the introduction to the section of the urban landscape was drawn to the author's attention by Dr. Edward MacDonald, and this generosity is gratefully acknowledged (see, Glenbow Archives). Cullen, M. (1979) traced the fate of the market house while MacKinnon (1990), MacDonald (2005b), and an interview with Charles Scott, Sr. documented the creation of the Confederation Centre. Discussion of the challenges facing urban planners can be found in de Silva (1962). Lea (1990) provided information on the public schools, while MacDonald (1989) and Bruce (2005) dealt with the institutions of higher learning. Details reflecting the evolution of Charlottetown and its suburban communities came from planning documents of the various communities and from interviews with Joseph Coady, Nancy Coughlin, Sharon Becker and Betty Pryor, whose personal memories filled blanks left by the written documents. Ballem (2004), Curley (2005) and interviews with Rev. Ian Glass and Joe Kiley outlined the development of recreational facilities. Maynard (1990), Bell (1989) and Auld (1985) dealt with the improvements to the municipal infrastructure.

Discussion of federal involvement in the economy drew heavily from DREE records, supplemented by MacKinnon (1966, 1974), *Financial Post Business Yearbooks*, (1950, 1965 and 1974) and provincial government reports. Lafferty (1969), the same *Financial Post Business Yearbooks*, the Stevenson Kellogg Report (1973) and DREE records furthered the discussion of manufacturing. Cullen (1973), Jackson (1970), Slumkoski (2006), Auld (1985), MacPherson (1973), Romkey (1960) and articles in *The Globe and Mail* contributed important information concerning communications. Matthew McRae's fine thesis (2004) informed the examination of tourism, as did PARO RG 34, RG 44, Acc. 2784, Acc. 4315; DREE records; and Laventhol (1973).

In the section on social life, Matthews (1952) was particularly significant for the examination of education. McKenna (1982) and Bruce (2005) outlined the evolution of higher education. The shortcomings of the mental health hospital were outlined in the Chambers Report (1953). Agnew (1967) provided similar information on the two general hospitals. Lea (1981) and Sinnott (1975) covered the two medical clinics. Treatment of water and sewerage matters benefitted from Charlottetown Water Commission (1987) and also Crandall (1957), Canadian-British Engineering (1970), PARO, Acc. 2784, and Prince Edward Island Department of Health (1963). In addition to local sources, *The Globe and Mail* followed the trials and tribulations of the police force. Social welfare featured in Canada, House of Commons, *Debates*, (1948, 1973), and was the focus of attention in Protestant Family Service Bureau (1980) and Green (2006). Ballem (1986, 2004) was indispensable to an account of sports. Large and Crothers (1989) dealt with broadcasting, and MacKinnon (1990) thoroughly described the creation of the Confederation Centre, while McRae (2004) placed the 1964 celebrations into their wider context. The 1914 Patrol (1973) presented an admirable account of scouting, and the Prince Edward Island Regimental Museum's Scrapbooks contributed to the treatment of changes to the militia.

Photo Credits: **Page 273**: PEIMHF; **Page 279**: CC; **Page 281**: CC; **Page 286**: CC; **Page 288**: CC; **Page 291**: 3026.131; **Page 293**: PEIMHF; **Page 294**: PARO 3466.HF.79.73.15.1; **Page 296-97**: PARO 3680.2.21; **Page 303**: PARO 3680.1.83; **Page 309**: courtesy Peter Rider; **Page 311**: PEIMHF; **Page 312**: PEIMHF; **Page 321**: PEIMHF; **Page 324**: PARO 4352.s2.ss2; **Page 326**: PARO 2320.20; **Page 328**: PARO 2843.D.9; **Page 329**: PARO 2843.27; **Page 335**: PEIMHF; **Page 336**: PARO 2320.64; **Page 338**: PEIMHF; **Page 340**: PARO 3523.92, 3523.62; **Page 344**: PEIMHF; **Page 347**: PEIMHF; **Page 350**: PARO 3466.HF.MP.74.1.9, 17, 6; **Page 366**: PEIMHF; **Page 371**: PARO 2843.c.10; **Page 376**: PEIMHF; **Page 383**: PARO 3218.81; **Page 391**: PEIMHF; **Page 392**: PEIMHF.

CHAPTER 6 — *CONNECTED*

The time period covered by Chapter 6, 1985–2005, was too recent in many respects to be considered history. Many of the sources to which a historian would normally turn were unavailable to the author. Instead, reliance was placed upon oral testimony and what archaeologists call "ground proofing," or making on-site examinations personally. Even so, there were some standard historical sources available, including *The Guardian* and records of the City of Charlottetown still held at City Hall. The author would like especially to thank Pam Leard, Executive Assistant to the Chief Administrative Officer, for facilitating his access to city documents. Various websites proved to be useful in providing information and in the checking of facts. Even the census records, essential for the section on population growth and ethnic relationships, could be found online for this chapter.

In the treatment of political life, Callum Beck provided the religious affiliation of each of the city's mayors. The author would like to acknowledge his generosity for sharing this information. Joe Coady, Director of Public Services, was kindly willing to undergo a second lengthy interview concerning amalgamation and the operation of the expanded city. Much important information on those topics was also derived from the city's CUSA files. MacDonald (2006) presented an interpretative narrative on the politics of amalgamation that proved to be balanced and cogent.

A considerable portion of the section on urban development resulted from first hand examination of city and conversations with people who either influenced the changes or witnessed them. Among them were 25 Charlottetonians who were interviewed by Christine Gordon in order for her to write "Charlottetown: 1985–Present Day," a manuscript report that provided a lot of data for this section and the next two. Websites were helpful in varying degrees, but the CADC site provided considerable information concerning that organization's various ventures. When the site missed a detail, Ernie Morello filled in the blank. *The Downtown Pulse* described "Wireless Charlottetown," and two planning documents, Maritime Resource Management Services (1986) and *Charlottetown Plan* (1999) described the planning environment. This was enhanced by MacDonald (2006).

Watson (2002) contained a good overview of the state of the city's economy at the beginning of the 21st century. Downing (1994) outlined its possible downside. Michael Arnold and Kathy Hambly were very helpful in describing the contemporary economic scene. Much of the extraordinary expansion of Charlottetown's bioscience businesses was documented on the websites of the various companies. Important improvements in the transportation facilities were also to be found on websites for the airport and harbour. PARO, Acc. 4315 was the source for details on the West River Causeway.

The section on social life drew upon many oral statements, although *A City's Journey* (2005), a fine piece of research and writing, was very helpful. Statistics Canada's CANSIM tables helped to document how Charlottetonians spent their leisure time.

Photo Credits: **Page 402**: CC; **Page 403**: CC; **Page 404**, CC; **Page 405**: CC; **Page 409**: PEIMHF; **Page 412**: CC; **Page 425**: CC; **Page 429**: PEIMHF; **Page 432**: PEIMHF.

Colour Section: ***Photo Credits:*** The image of St. Dunstan's Cathedral burning is PARO 3466. HF.103.133.2. The elevation drawing of the Charlottetown Forum is PARO 3680.2.50.9. The proposed bungalow elevation is PARO 3680.1.150.1. The other images are from the PEIMHF collection.

Index

A

B

D

M

R

T

Y

Z